PEARSON   ALWAYS LEARNING

A Brief Guide to Writing from Readings/Selected Readings Included

The University of Alabama

Taken from:
*A Brief Guide to Writing
from Readings,* Sixth Edition
by Stephen Wilhoit

Pearson Learning Solutions, 501 Boylston Street, Suite 900, Boston, MA 02116
A Pearson Education Company
www.pearsoned.com

Printed in the United States of America

1 2 3 4 5 6 7 8 9 10 V354 18 17 16 15 14 13

000200010271756943

JL/OP

ISBN 10: 1-269-19845-9
ISBN 13: 978-1-269-19845-5

COPYRIGHT ACKNOWLEDGMENTS

"Autism and Vaccination - The Current Evidence," by Lisa Miller and Joni Reynolds, reprinted from *Journal for Specialists in Pediatric Nursing* 14, no.3 (2009), by permission of John Wiley & Sons, Inc.

"Vaccinations: Myths and Facts," reprinted by permission from the *University of California Berkeley Wellness Newsletter* (November 2004).

"Law, Privacy, and Information Technology: A Sleepwalk Through the Surveillance Society?" by Mark O'Brien, reprinted from *Information & Communication Technology* 17, no. 1 (2008), Taylor & Francis.

"Playing with Fire: The Civil Liberties Implications of September 11th" by John B. Gould, reprinted from *Public Administration Review* 62 (2002), by permission of John Wiley & Sons, Inc.

"The 'X-Rated X-Ray': Reconciling Fairness, Privacy, and Security," by David A. Mackey, reprinted from *Criminal Justice Studies* 20, no.2 (2007), Taylor & Francis.

CONTENTS

Chapter 3 PARAPHRASE *47*

Chapter 4 SUMMARY *61*

Chapter 7   RHETORICAL ANALYSIS OF WRITTEN TEXTS   *127*

Chapter 12 DOCUMENTATION *275*

Chapter 13 REFERENCE LISTS AND WORKS CITED ENTRIES *287*

Appendix PEER REVIEW GUIDELINES   *307*

Anthology of Readings   *317*

Philosophy/Religious Studies—Vocation
Introduction
Readings

Language—Limiting Free Speech on College Campuses
Introduction
Readings

PREFACE

In the sixth edition of *A Brief Guide to Writing from Readings*, my goal remains unchanged from the earlier editions: to help students master one of the most common academic genres—writing from readings. Toward this end, and based on responses from students and faculty using the book, I have made several significant changes to the sixth edition. The changes include the following:

- twelve new readings: three readings on school dress codes, three readings on the link between television viewing and childhood violence, three readings on animal welfare, and single readings on campus privacy and security and Generation Y
- greater emphasis on readings drawn from academic sources
- six new sample student essays
- new instruction on writing abstracts
- refashioned coverage of working with visual texts, emphasizing their rhetorical analysis to better match the instruction on writing rhetorical analyses of written texts
- documentation samples that incorporate guidelines established by the 2008 *MLA Style Manual and Guide to Scholarly Publishing* and the 2010 *Publication Manual of the American Psychological Association*

To accommodate these changes, I have reduced the number of appendices in this edition, integrating the material into the body of the text, and I have dropped both instruction on CSE documentation and writing timed essays, which reviewers indicated were little used.

Though much has changed in this edition of *A Brief Guide*, much also remains the same. Faculty and students have long noted the collegial tone of the book and the utility of the summary charts located at the end of each chapter in addition to the revision checklists. These features have all been retained. From the first edition, I have tried to maintain a clear, process-oriented approach to writing instruction, laying out for writers a series of steps they can follow or modify as needed when composing source-based essays.

As in previous editions of the textbook, the sample readings are drawn from a range of disciplines; however, this edition places greater emphasis on academic sources. Readings vary in length and in difficulty, but all are intended to pique student interest and serve as prompts for class discussion. Each sample student essay I include in the text can serve as a model for students to follow in terms of its thesis, organization, and use of sources, but none of them is perfect. Students should be encouraged to read the sample essays in this textbook as critically as they read any other material in college. They may identify several ways each essay can be improved. In fact, instructors might consider asking their students to do just that: to use the instruction offered in *A Brief Guide* to critique and revise these sample essays.

In the end, my hope, as always, is that the instruction offered in this textbook will help students develop the skills they need to successfully complete source-based college writing assignments, to read texts honestly and critically, and to explore connections they find between the material they read and their own knowledge, experience, and beliefs.

SUPPLEMENTS

Instructor's Manual

An Instructor's Manual is available for *A Brief Guide to Writing from Readings*. The Instructor's Manual includes a brief introduction to each chapter, an examination of problems students commonly face when writing each type of source-based essay, and a series of exercises and assignments designed to help students improve their writing.

The New MyCompLab Web Site

The new MyCompLab integrates the market-leading instruction, multimedia tutorials, and exercises for writing, grammar, and research that users have come to identify with the program with a new online composing space and new assessment tools. The result is a revolutionary application that offers a seamless and flexible teaching and learning environment built specifically for writers. Created after years of extensive research and in partnership with composition faculty and students across the country, the new MyCompLab provides help for writers in the context of their writing, with instructor and peer commenting functionality; proven tutorials and exercises for writing, grammar, and research; an e-portfolio; an assignment builder; a bibliography tool; tutoring services; and a gradebook and course management organization created specifically for writing classes. Visit www.mycomplab.com or ask your sales representative for more information.

ACKNOWLEDGMENTS

I would like to thank the following reviewers for their helpful suggestions as I prepared each new edition of *A Brief Guide to Writing from Readings:* Curtis R. Burdette, Central Michigan University; Jennifer Campbell, University of Denver; Jacqueline E. Cason, University of Alaska, Anchorage; Tim Catalano, Marietta College; Jane Creighton, University of Houston–Downtown; Sally Ebest, University of Missouri, St. Louis; Daniel P. Galvin,

Clemson University; Karen Gardiner, University of Alabama; Monica E. Hogan, Johnson County Community College; Wesley Jones, University of Mary; Greg Luthi, Johnson County Community College; David D. Knapp, Front Range Community College; Raj Mohan, Cleveland State University; Anne Pici, University of Dayton; Kathy Overhulse Smith, Indiana University–Bloomington; and Mary Trachsel, University of Iowa.

Stephen Wilhoit

Chapter 1

CRITICAL READING

DEFINITION AND PURPOSE

Most successful college writers are also sophisticated, critical readers. They assume a skeptical attitude toward texts: instead of believing whatever they read, they critically examine the author's ideas and their own responses to the reading. They are active, reflective readers who ask questions about the words on the page, mark passages, take notes, and draw connections between the author's ideas and their own experiences and knowledge. They are open to new ideas, but do not accept them without serious, reflective consideration. Unreflective readers, however, tend to accept unquestioningly what they see in print. In their view, if something has been published, it must be accurate. Instead of asking questions about what they read, they tend to accept the author's words at face value.

A major difference, then, between reflective and unreflective readers is the way they try to learn from what they read. Unreflective readers usually believe that the meaning of a text can be found in the words on the page: to understand a text, all a reader has to do is understand the meaning of the author's words. For them, reading is a rather simple, straightforward process: they read through a text, look up any words they do not know, isolate the author's main ideas, perhaps take some notes, then move on to the next reading. They also tend to believe that because the meaning of a text resides in the author's words, students reading the same material ought to come away with the same information; the text should mean roughly the same thing to any competent reader who studies it.

Reflective, critical readers, however, tend to adopt a different view of reading. They believe that the meaning of a text resides in the *interaction* between the reader and the words on the page: to understand a text, readers must be aware of how their own knowledge, feelings, and experience influence their *interpretation* of the words on the page. For them, reading is a rather dynamic, fluid process: they read through a text skeptically, assess the author's words and ideas in light of their own knowledge and experience, jot down some notes that capture their questions and responses, reread the text after they have had some time to consider what the author had to say, and then move on.

Viewing reading as an interactive process can help you better understand the complex nature of writing from sources and the need to be an active, critical reader. For example, it helps you understand why a story you read your first year in high school means something different to you when you read it again your first year in college. The words on the page have not changed, you have, and because you have changed, the "meaning" of the story has changed for you as well. This interactive view of reading also helps explain how twenty students in an introductory philosophy class can read the same meditation by Descartes and come away with twenty slightly different interpretations of the piece. Active, critical readers understand that for any given person the meaning of a text results from the interaction between the words on the page and that reader's knowledge, feelings, and expertise; reading involves more than a simple transfer of information from the words on the page to the mind of the reader.

Does this mean that all interpretations of a reading are equally valid? No. While every person forms his or her own understanding of a reading, people can and often do misread texts: they may not read carefully, they may not understand certain terms or ideas, or they may lack the knowledge and experience they need to form an adequate interpretation of the text. As a safeguard against misinterpretation, critical readers discuss the material with others who have read it. Comparing their own reading of a text with a teacher's or a peer's reading can help clarify the material and prevent misunderstanding.

In addition, the author of the piece plays an important role in reading. Good writers try to influence their readers' understanding of and response to a text. When writing, authors manipulate the language, structure, and content of their prose to achieve a certain effect on their audience. Success is never guaranteed, but good writers know that they can at least influence how readers might respond to their work through the choices they make while composing. Critical readers take this into account when approaching a text—they try to be aware not only of what they bring to the reading, but also of the choices the writer has made to achieve a certain goal.

Learning to read material actively and critically can be difficult. However, critical readers tend to understand course material more fully, prepare for class more efficiently, and write from readings more effectively. Following are a number of suggestions aimed at helping you become a more active, critical reader.

Central to this process is the ability and willingness to ask good questions about your reading of a text and to keep a written record of your responses. Critical readers refuse to sit back passively while they read; they actively question and respond to texts in light of their own knowledge, feelings, and experience.

ASKING QUESTIONS ABOUT WHAT YOU READ

Instead of passively accepting the ideas an author presents, a critical reader attempts to engage in a dialogue with the text, posing and working out answers to tough questions concerning the material's purpose, audience, language, and content.

The most productive critical questions center on the connections that exist between a text's author and his or her audience, subject, and language. Everything you read has been written by someone for someone about something using certain words on a page. Learning how to identify and question the relationship between these various aspects of a reading can help you understand the material more fully and determine its meaning and importance.

Typical questions you should ask of a reading include:

- Who is the author of the piece?
- What is her stand on the issue she's addressing?
- What are her interests, qualifications, or possible biases?
- What was her intent when writing this piece?
- Who is the intended audience?
- How does the author support her contentions?
- What language has she used to convey her ideas on this topic to this audience for this purpose?
- Based on my own knowledge and experience, what do I think about her ideas, intent, language, and support?
- How well does the author achieve her goal?

When you are confronted with conflicting sources of information on a topic (as is frequently the case in college), asking questions such as these is a particularly important way to sort out the authors' different positions, evaluate the worth of each source, and decide who presents the clearer, more convincing case.

Forming a full, critical understanding of a reading requires asking the right kinds of questions about the author, subject, audience, and language of the piece. In the next section you will find a series of questions to ask before, during, and after your reading. However, these questions are merely suggestive, not exhaustive; they indicate only starting points for your critical assessment of a text. Your teacher and peers may suggest other questions to ask as well. Finally, it is a good idea to write out your answers to these questions. Do not rely on your memory alone to keep track of your responses.

QUESTIONS TO ASK BEFORE YOU BEGIN A CLOSE READING OF A TEXT

Whether you are assigned to read material in history or art, biology or sociology, before you begin you need to ask yourself a series of questions concerning the author and publication in which the piece appeared as well as your own knowledge of and attitude toward the topic. Answering these questions may help you determine any biases present in the reading and help ensure that you remain open to any new perspectives or information the author has to offer.

Questions concerning the Author

* Who is the author?
* What are his credentials?
* What else has he written on the topic?
* What possible biases might have influenced his work?

Before you begin to read a text, try to assess the credibility and expertise of the person who wrote the piece. Who is the author, and what are his or her qualifications for writing on this topic? If, for instance, you are writing a paper about global warming for your English class and find an article you want to use in your essay, note whether you are reading a research report produced by a scientist who conducted her own studies on the topic, an informative article composed by a reporter who interviewed that scientist, or an opinion piece written by a television star who has no particular expertise in climatology. The first author is probably well qualified to offer expert opinion; the second author, while less qualified than the first, may still be a legitimate source of information. However, approach the third author skeptically: good actors are rarely good scientists. If you plan to use any of these readings to support a position of your own in an essay, understand that academic readers will tend to believe authors with solid, professional credentials and demonstrated expertise in the topic.

Also determine, as best you can, any biases operating in the authors' work. Note who the writers work for, who supported their research, who publishes their results. No writers are completely objective; all writers bring to their work certain biases or preferences, whether political, religious, or methodological. These biases may influence the type of study authors conduct, the type of evidence they use to support their contentions, the language they employ, and the conclusions they draw. When researching a paper on abortion, for instance, it would be important to note whether the author of a piece is a member of the National Abortion Rights Action League or Operation Life, even if the writer claims to be presenting the results of an objective study. In college you will often read expert testimony that presents conflicting views and interpretations of the same topic, data, or event. Often your job as a *writer* is to examine these different perspectives, compare their quality or worth, and use them to form and defend a position of your own. However, recognizing potential authorial bias in a reading does not disqualify it as a legitimate source of information: it simply puts you in a better position to read the work skeptically and to ask better, more critical questions.

Most academic journals include brief biographical entries on the authors at the beginning or end of each article or in a separate section of the journal typically labeled "Contributor Notes" or "Contributors." Many popular magazines also include some information on the author of each article they publish. (If you cannot find this information, see a reference librarian for help locating biographical dictionaries. Later, including in your essay the credentials of the authors whose work you are quoting or paraphrasing can help increase the credibility of your assertions.)

Questions about the Publication

- In what regard is the publication held by professionals in the field?
- Toward what type of readership is the publication aimed?
- How long ago was the piece published?
- What, generally, is the editorial stance of the publication?

When assessing the quality of a publication, your first questions ought to address its credibility and audience. Do members of the profession or the academy consider this a reputable journal? Does it publish scholarly work or general interest features? What type of reader is this publication trying to reach: scholars or the general public? Answering these questions can help you determine whether work published in this journal or magazine is appropriate for inclusion in an essay of your own.

To answer these questions about the publication, first consult your teacher. He or she can probably tell you in what regard a particular journal is held by professionals in the field. Also, if you want to consult only scholarly sources of information, you may want to limit your research to scholarly indexes and databases—drawing information from *The Applied Science and Technology Index* or ABI/Inform rather than from *The Readers' Guide to Periodical Literature* and InfoTrac. Again, your teacher or a reference librarian can help you identify scholarly reference works.

Just as individual authors have certain biases or preferences that may influence their writing, publications have certain editorial slants that may influence what they print. Some publications will have definite political or ideological agendas. For example, *The New Republic* and *The National Review* are not likely to publish the same article on gun control. Other publications may exhibit certain methodological biases: they prefer to publish only historical studies or empirical studies or Marxist studies of a topic. Determining the editorial or methodological slant of a publication can be difficult: if you have not read widely in a field, you may not know a great deal about its principal publications. Often, your best recourse in gathering this type of information is to scan the titles and abstracts of other articles in the journal to determine its political or methodological preferences or, if you are reading newspaper or magazine articles, to read the editorials.

However, a particular periodical's political or methodological slant does not necessarily make it any more or less valid a source of information. Recognizing these preferences, though, should help you read material more skeptically. A publication's biases may affect the content of the articles it publishes, its authors' interpretations of statistics, even the nature of the graphics and illustrations accompanying the text. When you are thoroughly researching a topic, gathering information from several different sources is one way to guard against one-sided, unbalanced treatments of a topic.

Questions concerning Your Own Views of the Topic

- What are my beliefs about the issue addressed in the reading?
- How open am I to new ideas on this topic?

Just as every author and publication presents material from a particular perspective, readers, too, bring their own prejudices and preferences to a text. Though absolute objectivity may be impossible for readers and writers to attain, knowing your own predispositions toward the topic an author addresses can help you guard against unfairly judging someone else's arguments or shutting yourself off from potentially helpful ideas.

Author Peter Elbow suggests two frames of mind students ought to assume when reading material. First, he advises students to play the "believing game"—that is, to assume that what the writer has to say is correct. If the author of the piece is right in what he says, how do his ideas influence your current views on the topic? What are the implications of the author's ideas? Can you draw any connections between what the author has to say and what you already know? Next, Elbow suggests that students play the "doubting game"—that is, assume a more critical stance toward the author's ideas. What are the weaknesses in the writer's arguments? What are the limitations of his ideas? In what ways are the author's ideas incompatible with what you already know about the topic?

Being aware of your own stance on an issue *before* you begin to read something for the first time can help you play the believing and doubting games more effectively. First, reading with your own beliefs firmly in mind can help you recognize which ideas are hard for you to accept or even to consider fairly. We all resist ideas that run counter to our beliefs: giving them legitimacy forces us to question our own positions. However, being a critical reader means you are willing to do just that, to consider ideas that you might otherwise ignore or reject. When you dismiss an idea in a source text, consider why: if it is only because that idea runs counter to your views, try playing the believing game before moving on.

Second, reading with your beliefs firmly in mind can help you recognize which ideas are hard for you to question and criticize. We all like to read material that confirms our present positions, because such reinforcement is comforting and reassuring. However, as a critical reader you must be willing to question authors who voice opinions you endorse, to criticize fairly and thoroughly ideas you are predisposed to accept unquestioningly. If you accept information without question, consider why: if it is only because you agree with the author, try playing the doubting game before moving on.

QUESTIONS TO ASK WHILE YOU READ AND REREAD MATERIAL

After you have read material with these questions in mind, reread it. If necessary, read it a third or fourth time—very few of us truly understand a text the first time we read it. When rereading material, though, you should consider another set of questions that focus your attention on the audience, purpose, content, and organization of the piece, along with your response to the author's ideas.

Questions concerning the Audience of the Piece

- What audience does the author seem to be trying to reach?
- What type of reader would be attracted to the author's writing, and what type would be alienated by it?
- How does your sense of the text's audience influence your reading of the piece?

Audience is one of the most important concepts in writing: an author's sense of audience will greatly affect, among other things, the language she uses, the material she includes, and the organizational strategy she employs. However, *audience* can be a difficult term to define. In one sense, it refers to actual people a writer may know. When composing a letter to a friend, for instance, a writer can make fairly accurate predictions about the way her reader will react to what she says or the language she uses.

In another sense, though, *audience* can have very little to do with specific people the author has in mind as he writes a text. Much of what you read in college, for example, was written by people who possessed a much more nebulous sense of audience as they wrote. They knew the *type* of reader they were trying to address (for example, a first-year student taking an introductory geology course) or perhaps the *type* of reader they wanted to interest (for example, people curious about feminist interpretations of literature). When writing, they did not have in mind as their audience a specific, individual reader. Instead, they were trying to produce prose that would attract or interest a particular type of reader.

Therefore, as you read and reread material, try to determine the audience the author is trying to address: how is she attempting to interest or appeal to that type of reader? How successful is she in achieving that goal? Pay attention to the language, content, and organization of the piece as you try to answer questions such as these:

- Was the author trying to reach a general reader, an educated reader, or a specialist?
- What language does the author use to try to reach this audience? What examples? What graphics?
- What type of reader would actually find the work helpful, informative, valuable, or difficult?
- Would any readers be alienated by the material in the piece? Why?

Answering these questions will help you better understand how the text you are reading came to assume its present form. When writing, authors choose language, examples, and a structure they believe will help them achieve their desired effect on an audience. Part of reading a text critically is determining in your mind how successful each writer has been in making these choices.

Realize, too, that when you read something, you become a member of that writer's audience. *Your* response to what you read is extremely important to note as you try to understand what the author has to say. Is the writer communicating his ideas effectively to you? Do you find the material in the piece interesting or boring, helpful or irrelevant, engaging or alienating? What choices has the writer made that led to these responses? What knowledge or experience do you bring to the text that contributes to your reaction? Understanding the complex relationship between the audience and the writer of a piece can help you become a more sensitive, critical reader.

Questions about Purpose

- What was the author's purpose in writing the piece?
- What is the author's thesis?
- Does the author successfully achieve his or her goals?

Generally, when writing a text, an author will have one of three aims: to entertain, to inform, or to persuade his readers. Many times a work will serve multiple purposes—it will both entertain and inform, or inform and persuade. However, as a critical reader, you ought to identify the primary purpose of the piece you are reading. To criticize an article for failing to present an effective argument on a topic would be unproductive and unfair if all the author intended was to write an informative essay.

However, determining an author's purpose or goal can be difficult. In social science and natural science journals, look for the author's stated purpose in his abstract or thesis ("The purpose of this article is . . ." and "The authors seek to prove that . . ."). The conventions of most humanities journals, however, require authors to be less straightforward or declaratory in stating their purpose, but again thesis statements and abstracts are good places to start your search. Even if the author states his or her goal somewhere in the paper or abstract, be wary. When you finish rereading the piece, ask yourself, "Given the content, language, and structure of this piece, what do *I* believe to be the writer's primary goal or purpose?"

Questions about Content

- What are the author's major assertions or findings?
- How does the author support these assertions or findings?

When examining the content of any reading, try first to locate the author's thesis and paraphrase it. A thesis statement will be either stated or implied. If it is stated, you will be able to point to a sentence or two in the reading that serves as the thesis. If it is implied, a general idea or argument unites and guides the writing, but the author never explicitly puts it into words. When you paraphrase this general idea or argument, you have identified the thesis. In either case, as a first step in analyzing a reading's content, restate the author's thesis in your own words to form a clear idea of what the author is trying to accomplish in the piece.

Next, note how the author supports her thesis—identify her primary ideas, arguments, or findings and the evidence, reasons, or examples she offers to support them. As you reread the piece, ask yourself what empirical, philosophical, theoretical, or other type of evidence or reasoning the author has provided to support her thesis and achieve her goal.

Finally, be sure to examine what you already know about the topic—what you have learned in the past and what you are learning now by reading *this* piece. Has the author left out any important information or arguments? Has she neglected certain interpretations of evidence others have offered? If so, why do you think that is? How can the reading's content be explained by its author, audience, or purpose?

Questions about Organization

- How is the material organized?
- What headings and subheadings does the author provide?
- What does the organization of the essay tell you about the author's view of the material?
- What gets stressed as a result of the organization?

As a writer composes his piece, he has to make a series of decisions about organization: he needs to determine the order in which he will present his findings, ideas, or arguments. Good writers organize their material purposefully—to make their article clear, to make their book more persuasive, or to make their findings more accessible. Through the order in which they present their material and through their use of paragraph breaks, headings, and subheadings, they try to help the reader understand or accept their views.

As you read a source text, think critically about its organization. First, form at least a rough idea of how the writer has organized his ideas. What are the major sections of the text? In what order are the ideas, arguments, or findings presented? You might want to produce a scratch outline or list that captures the reading's organization. Also, use the headings and subheadings the author provides to get a better understanding of how he views his material and how he sets priorities among his findings. For example, what ideas, arguments, or findings get emphasized through the author's selection of headings? How do the headings and subheadings guide you through the piece? Are there any instances in which you think a heading or subheading is misleading or poorly stated? Why?

Questions about the Author's Sources

- How does the author use other people's ideas or findings?
- How credible are the sources the author uses to support his ideas or findings?

As you analyze the content of a reading, examine the sources the author relied on when writing. What is documented? Flip back to the works cited list or bibliography at the end of the piece. Where does the author's information come from? Is the paper based on library research, primary research, or interviews? If much of the text's material comes from previously published work, how credible are the sources the author used to support her claims? For example, is the author relying on scholarly sources of information? Is there any apparent bias in the author's use of source material: is most of her material taken from journals that share similar editorial stances, or has the writer tried to draw information from sources representing a variety of political, theoretical, or methodological perspectives? Answering questions such as these can help you determine the credibility and utility of the author's ideas, arguments, or findings.

Questions about Graphics

- How clear are the charts, graphs, tables, or illustrations the author provides?
- How well does the author explain the graphics?
- How well do the graphics support or explain what the author has to say?

Graphics include charts, tables, graphs, drawings, and pictures. While authors may add graphics to entertain readers, most include them to support arguments, summarize findings, or illustrate ideas. As you read a text, try to determine how the author is using graphics in her work and how clear, helpful, or informative you find them.

Questions about Your Reactions and Responses

- How do I feel about the topic, issues, or findings addressed in the reading?
- What is convincing? What is unclear?
- What ideas in the piece contradict my understanding of the topic?
- What ideas in the piece are new to me? Which ones do I accept and which ones do I reject?

People's beliefs and knowledge influence how they read material—what they take note of, what they understand the author to be saying, what they remember after they read the piece. Understanding your response to the material you read can help you become a more critical reader and a more effective writer in several ways. First, honestly assessing your response can help you be balanced and fair. As a skeptical reader you need to be both critical of ideas you at first enthusiastically support and open to ideas you at first strongly reject.

Second, examining your response to what you read can help you decide on and develop effective paper topics—your responses may help you identify an interest or question you can later pursue more thoroughly in an essay. Especially consider what you learn from a reading. What information is new? How do the author's ideas or findings confirm or contradict what you have come to think? Examining your answers to questions such as these can result in some interesting essays.

MARKING TEXTS

Look at the books of active, critical readers and you will see pages filled with underlined passages, marginal comments, questions, and reactions. Because they have recognized the close link between reading and writing, they rarely read without a pencil in hand. They underline the reading's thesis statement and any important passages they find. As they question the material they are reading, they annotate the text and write down the answers to the questions they ask so that when they return to the material later they can recall the author's purpose and findings, remember how they responded to the author's ideas, and locate the information they want to use in their papers.

The two most common ways of marking texts are highlighting and annotating. Highlighting typically involves underlining, circling, bracketing, or color coding passages, while annotating involves writing comments or questions in the margin or at the end of the text.

HIGHLIGHTING TEXTS

Highlighting involves underlining, color coding, or in some other way marking important passages in a reading. Most students tend to highlight too little or too much. Some never make a mark in their books. Perhaps they were trained in high school not to mark up readings, or maybe they are concerned about the resale value of their books. Whatever their reason, these students rarely, if ever, highlight material they read. Other students highlight too many passages in a reading—practically every sentence is underlined, and almost every paragraph is shaded yellow or pink. You have to be selective in what you highlight: you mark up a reading in order to understand it more clearly and to identify important passages you may return to later when you write your paper.

In order to highlight a reading effectively, you need to develop your own marking system, a kind of code that helps you locate certain types of information in a text. Good writers usually develop unique ways of highlighting readings: they underline certain kinds of passages, place brackets around specific types of information, and circle other parts of the text. Later, when they return to the reading to write their paper, they can easily find the information they need. Following are some suggestions about what to mark in a text:

1. Mark an author's thesis, primary assertions, and supporting evidence.
2. Mark the names of authors, dates of studies, locations of research projects, and other important facts mentioned in the reading.
3. Mark key passages you might want to reread, quote, or paraphrase later as you write your paper.
4. Mark words or terms you do not know so you can look up their definitions.

Establish your own way of highlighting a text: circle authors' names, bracket dates, use a yellow highlighting pen to mark any passages you may want to quote and blue ink to indicate questionable statements, or whatever variations make sense to you. Once you establish your own highlighting system, writing from readings will become much easier for you.

ANNOTATING TEXTS

While you are highlighting a reading, you should also annotate it—that is, *write out* your responses, questions, observations, or conclusions. Generally, there are two types of annotations you will use: marginal and end comments. Marginal annotations are notes that you make to yourself in the top, bottom, or side margins of the page; end annotations are notes that you make at the end of the text.

Marginal Annotations

Marginal annotations are typically short and in many cases may make sense only to the person who wrote them. Generally, they can be divided into content notes, organization notes, connection notes, questions, and responses.

Content notes typically identify the meaning or purpose of the marked passage. For example, after bracketing an author's first argument—that eliminating a particular government program may have negative consequences on the poor, for instance—you may write in the margin, "Argument 1—consequences for poor." When you review a reading to find material you want to use in your paper, content notes help you easily locate what you need, which is particularly important if you are completing a research project involving multiple readings.

Organization notes identify the major sections of a source text. After underlining an article's thesis, you may write *thesis* in the margin in order to find it more easily later, then bracket the first few paragraphs and write *introduction* in the margin. You might draw a line down the margin beside the next few paragraphs and write *first argument* in the margin, then highlight the next section and write *refutation of first argument*. Organization notes help you understand how the author has structured the piece and may help you locate particular sections of the text you would like to review.

Connection notes identify the links you see between an author's ideas and those offered by other writers or between ideas an author develops in different sections of a reading: "this idea echoes Weber's argument," "illustrates first point," or "contradicts teacher's position." As you read an article, you should note how the author's ideas confirm or refute ideas developed by other writers. Note the connections in the margin of the essay you are reading in case you want to examine the link more closely later: do not rely on your memory. If you are reading multiple sources on the same topic, distinctions between the texts can quickly blur; you may have a difficult time remembering who wrote what if you do not write good connection notes. Also, use connection notes to trace the development of each writer's thesis. Note in the margin of the reading the link between the various ideas, arguments, or findings the writer offers and his or her thesis.

Questions can serve several purposes. First, they can identify passages you find confusing: in a question, try to capture *precisely* what you find confusing in a passage, especially if you will have a chance to discuss the reading in class. Second, questions can help you identify in a reading the material you want to dispute. Try to capture in a critical question or two why you disagree with what the author has written. Finally, questions can identify where the author has failed to consider important information or arguments. These are typically "what about" questions: "What about the theory proposed by Smith?" "What about people who can't afford day care?" Your goal is to indicate with a question possible limitations to an author's ideas or arguments.

Response notes record your reactions to what you read. These notes may indicate which ideas you accept, which ones you reject, and which ones you doubt. They can range from a simple "yes!" or "huh?" to more elaborate and detailed reactions that allow you to explore your response in some detail.

Remember to keep your marginal notes brief. Their purpose is to help you read the text more critically and recall your responses and questions when you reread the material.

End Annotations

End annotations typically make some type of comment on the source as a whole and can assume different forms, including summaries, responses, and questions.

Summaries offer brief, objective overviews of a reading. You may want to write a one- or two-sentence summary at the end of a reading, especially if you are reading several source texts for your paper. The purpose of these summaries is to jog your memory about the reading's content or thesis so you don't have to reread the entire text. These summaries are especially helpful if you have to read several texts with similar titles: it is easy to confuse these readings, and the summaries can often help you find the particular text you need.

Responses capture your reaction to the work as a whole. Try to capture in your note your response to the author's ideas, argument, writing style, or any other aspect of the reading that strikes you as important. These responses can help you form comments to offer in class when you discuss the piece, and often they serve as a good starting point for developing a topic for a paper: you may want to investigate and develop your response more thoroughly and formally in an essay.

Questions written at the end of a reading typically address the source's clarity, purpose, or effectiveness. Your questions might address the reading's claims, evidence, or reasoning; its syntax, tone, or structure. Other questions might address the reading's relationship to what you already know about the topic or what you have already read. These questions help you draw connections between the readings and your own knowledge and experience. Still other questions might indicate specific aspects of a topic you still need to investigate ("I wonder how his ideas might have an impact on part two of my paper—need to reconsider?") or links between two or more authors' claims that need further consideration ("Do her arguments refute the textbook's claims?").

You will usually jot down several different types of endnotes when you finish reading a text. You may write out a brief one- or two-sentence summary, a few questions, and a response. These endnotes can prove very helpful when you return to the material later: they indicate your assessment of the source text's content, strengths, weaknesses, and worth.

Together, highlighting and annotating can help you fully understand a reading and determine the best way to use it in your own writing. A word of warning, though: do not be blinded by your own annotations and highlights. When you review a source text you have already marked and annotated and are now planning to use in your paper, be critical of your *own* highlighting and annotations. Be sure to question whether your highlighting and annotations *really* capture the source's key points. As you review your comments and marked passages, ask yourself whether you feel the same way now about the reading. If you have been engaged in researching a topic, are you now in a better position to assess the value and meaning of the reading before you? Have your views changed? Also, try to answer the questions you asked in the margins or at the end of the article. Reassess your original reactions.

SAMPLE ANNOTATED READING

Review the following sample annotated reading. Your system for marking a reading will likely be different from the system used here. Note, though, how the reader used highlighting and annotations to gain a better understanding of the author's content, structure, language, and purpose.

Hard Choices

Check bio. notes — who is this person?

Patrick Moore, Ph.D.

founded Greenpeace

More than 20 years ago, I was one of a dozen or so activists who founded Greenpeace in the basement of the Unitarian Church in Vancouver, British Columbia. The Vietnam War was raging and nuclear holocaust seemed closer every day. We linked peace, ecology and a talent for media communications and went on to build the world's largest environmental activist organization. By 1986, Greenpeace was established in 26 countries and had an annual income of more than $100 million.

open w/ personal information

In its early years, the environmental movement specialized in confronting polluters and others who were damaging public lands and resources. Groups such as Greenpeace played a valuable role by ringing an ecological fire alarm, wakening mass consciousness to the true dimensions of our global predicament.

Brief history of environ movement

ecological movement wins?

By the 1980s, the battle for public opinion had been won. Virtually everyone inside and outside politics and industry expressed a commitment to environmental protection and good stewardship. Environmentalists were invited to the table in boardrooms and caucuses around the world to help design solutions to pressing ecological problems.

Are companies environ friendly now?

Rather than accept this invitation to be part of the solution, many environmentalists chose instead to radicalize their message. They demanded restrictions on human activity and the uses of natural resources that

Thesis?

too "radical"

anti-science ?

not build on earlier successes

far exceed any scientific justification. That tactical decision created an atmosphere in which many environmentalists today must rely on sensational rhetoric and misinformation rather than good science. Programs have gone forward without input from more knowledgeable environmentalists and other experts; the public debate has been needlessly polarized as a result of the movement's unwillingness to collaborate with others less radical.

environ. not work w/others ?

In addition to choosing a dubious tactic, the environmental movement also changed its philosophy along the way. It once prided itself on subscribing to a philosophy that was "transpolitical, transideological, and transnational" in character. Non-violent direct action and peaceful disobedience were the hallmarks of the movement. Truth mattered and science was respected for the knowledge it brought to the debate.

says current movement rejects truth & science

Thesis

That tradition was abandoned by many environmental groups during the 1990s. A new brand of environmental extremism has emerged that rejects science, diversity of opinion, and even democracy. These eco-extremists tend to be:

note headings

*Anti-technology and anti-science. Eco-extremists entirely reject machinery and industry; they invoke science as a means of justifying the adoption of beliefs that have no basis in science to begin with.

anti-science

*Anti-free enterprise. Although communism and state socialism have failed to protect the environment, eco-extremists are basically anti-business. They have not put forward an alternative system of organization that would meet the material needs of society.

anti-business

point not developed well

*Anti-democratic. Eco-extremists do not tolerate dissent and do not respect the opinions and beliefs of the general public. In the name of "speaking for the trees and other species," we are faced with a movement that would usher in an era of eco-fascism.

anti-democratic

The international debate over clearcutting offers a case study of eco-extremism in action. Groups such as Greenpeace and the Sierra Club have mounted major

example of clearcutting

need clearcutting

campaigns against clearcutting, claiming that it is responsible for "deforestation" on a massive scale in Canada and elsewhere. In fact, no such deforestation is taking place in Canada or the United States, and a ban on clearcutting could do more harm than good.

It is an (ecological fact) that many types of forest ecosystems thrive most successfully when they are periodically cleared and allowed to regenerate. Fire, volcanic eruptions, windstorms, insect attacks, disease and climate change (ice ages) destroy massive areas of forests, part of a natural cycle of forest destruction and renewal that has existed since long before modern humans arrived on the scene.

[margin note:] ignores diversity— usually replanted w/only one type of tree

The use of (hype and myths) by Greenpeace and the Sierra Club is symptomatic of the larger problems facing the modern environmental movement. Confrontation too often is preferred over collaboration, and (eco-extremism) has shoved aside the earlier spirit of tolerance and concern for the fate of humanity. The results have been harmful to the movement as well as to the environment we seek to protect.

[margin note:] hype and myths of Green & Sierra

As an environmentalist in the political center, I now find myself branded a traitor and a sellout by this new breed of saviors. My name appears in Greenpeace's "Guide to Anti-Environmental Organizations." But surely the shoe belongs on the other foot: The eco-extremists who have taken control of the nation's leading environmental organizations must shoulder the blame for the anti-environmental backlash now taking place in the United States and elsewhere. Unless they change their philosophy and tactics, the prospects for a protected environment will remain dim.

[margin notes:] he is in political center— how defined? / founder now an enemy? / why a backlash?

Patrick Moore earned a Ph.D. in ecology from the University of British Columbia in 1972. He was a founding member of Greenpeace and for seven years served as director of Greenpeace International.

[margin note:] credentials— but who does he work for?

[margin note:] Summary— "Eco-extremists" reject science, truth, alternative views →why lose pop. support?

NOTE TAKING

Especially when working on an extended writing project, you may want to take notes on a source text after carefully reading and annotating it. If you are working on a research paper for a class, check with your instructor about any requirements he or she might have concerning your notes. Some teachers, for example, require their students to take notes on index cards following rather specific guidelines. Other teachers set no guidelines concerning notes. It is always a good idea to check with your instructor concerning his or her requirements.

If you take notes on index cards, be sure you indicate somewhere on each card the title and/or author of the work you are reading. If your cards get out of order, you need some way of identifying the source of the information on each card. If you are more comfortable taking notes on paper, try to use only one side of each sheet. Using your notes to write your essay is easier if you are not constantly flipping over sheets of paper to find the information you need.

Some writers like their notes to consist only of quotes; others mix quoted, paraphrased, and summarized material. Some write notes in complete sentences; some use a combination of sentences, sentence fragments, and even single words or diagrams. As with annotations, you will need to work out your own system for taking notes, one that helps you sort out and organize the useful material you find in the sources you read.

The next sections provide some guidelines to keep in mind as you take your notes. Following them can help you avoid problems later as you use your notes to write your paper.

Before Jotting Down Any Notes, Always Write Down the Source Text's Full Bibliographic Information

Whenever you take notes on a reading, be sure to write down the author's full name, the exact title of the piece, the full title of the publication, all the publication information, and the inclusive page numbers. Often students will be completing a paper the night before it is due and realize they used material that needs to be documented. Without having the full bibliographic information with their notes, they have to make a frantic last-minute dash back to the library. If you are careful to write down this information before you take your notes, you can avoid some problems later.

In Your Notes, Carefully Distinguish between Material You Quote and Material You Paraphrase

One of the major sources of unintentional plagiarism is faulty note taking. This problem occurs when, in taking your notes, you copy down a passage word-for-word from a source text but fail to enclose that passage in quotation marks. If you then copy that material directly from your notes into your paper—thinking you originally paraphrased the passage—and fail to quote it in your essay, you will be guilty of plagiarism. You can avoid this problem if you carefully indicate with quotation marks which passages in your notes are exact quotations and which are paraphrases of an author's ideas.

Carefully List Page Numbers

In your notes, be sure to indicate the exact page number of the source text that contains the material you are quoting, paraphrasing, or summarizing. You will need this information later for proper documentation.

Pay Attention to the Punctuation in the Source Text

If you are quoting material in your notes, reproduce the original punctuation exactly as it appears on the page. Many times students misquote material because they incorrectly copied the original punctuation into their notes.

In Your Notes, Clearly Differentiate between the Author's Ideas and Your Own

Again, failing to differentiate between what an author says about a topic and what you have to say is a major source of unintentional plagiarism. As you take your notes, you may want to jot down some observations or ideas of your own—reading other people's ideas will often lead you to new insights of your own. However, if you do not make the distinction clear in your notes—if, when reviewing your notes, you cannot tell which ideas were yours and which were the other writer's—you might attribute ideas to authors who never suggested them or take credit for ideas that were originally developed by someone else. To make this distinction clear in your notes, perhaps you could place your ideas and reflections in brackets.

Be Consistent with Your Note-Taking System

Whether you use a notebook, looseleaf paper, index cards, or a personal computer for taking notes, be consistent in how and where you note bibliographic information, page numbers, and your responses to the material. Adhering to a system will make it easier for you to find material in your notes and will help you avoid making mistakes.

Additional Reading

Getting Serious about Eradicating Binge Drinking

Henry Wechsler

Henry Wechsler *directs the College Alcohol Studies program at Harvard's School of Public Health.*

Most of us are aware that binge drinking is a major problem on many college campuses. Since the Harvard School of Public Health's first College Alcohol Study used that term, in 1994, to describe the drinking pattern of significant numbers of American college students, the problem has drawn media attention across the nation. Despite this, the problem has not declined over the past four years. In fact, our latest research findings, released in September, showed little change in the proportion of college students who binge. Among more than 14,500 students surveyed at 116 institutions, 43 percent reported that they had binged at least once in the preceding two weeks, compared with 44 percent in the earlier study.

Although the number of students who abstain from alcohol grew to 19 percent this year from 15.6 percent in the first study, among students who drink we found an increase in drunkenness, in drinking deliberately to get drunk, and in alcohol-related problems—including injuries, drunk driving, violence, and academic difficulties. For example, among students who drink, 52 percent said a major motivation was "to get drunk," compared with 39 percent in the first study. Thus, despite a spate of widely publicized student deaths in alcohol-related incidents, the binge goes on.

Why isn't this behavior decreasing? For one thing, binge drinking has been so deeply entrenched for so long at colleges that it can't be expected to disappear overnight. However, the more important reason that change eludes us is that some colleges have relied too much on one approach to solve the problem—trying to get the binge drinkers themselves to stop, rather than focusing equal attention on factors that make it easy for students to drink too much.

Of course, some campuses use multiple approaches to attack the problem, but many focus most of their energies on educational efforts directed at drinkers, particularly during events such as the recent Alcohol Awareness Week. Such educational efforts are an important way to teach some students the facts about alcohol abuse. But those efforts overlook the environment around binge drinkers that condones and supports and often even encourages their behavior.

So what are the factors that promote binge drinking at colleges? One is that students who binge tend to think they represent the norm; they argue that they're just doing what most of their peers do. Most binge drinkers don't think they have a problem. They think they are only having fun, and most consider themselves to be moderate drinkers. Doing research into actual behavior and then informing students about how many students actually binge—generally fewer than binge drinkers believe—can help to reduce the behavior.

Another approach to changing student norms is to focus on the disruptive behavior of binge drinkers. Colleges are civic communities, and all too frequently they are disrupted by the behavior of students who drink excessively. Rather than search for contraband alcohol, a college would be wise to engage student leaders in helping administrators work out a clearly worded code of conduct that penalizes drunken behavior—and then to enforce it consistently.

Students who become drunk and disorderly should be made to take responsibility for the messes that they have created: They should have to clean up vomit in the bathrooms made unusable on weekends, help care for drunken students at the college health center, repair damage from vandalism, and pick up litter. The punishment should fit the crime.

But with repeat offenders, colleges need to consider enforcing a "three strikes and you're out" policy for alcohol-related violations of the student conduct code.

At the center of binge drinking on many campuses are fraternities and sororities. While they attract only a small percentage of students nationally, they continue to play a prominent role in campus life at many institutions. Our data shows that in fraternity houses, four of five residents binge, and more than half are frequent binge drinkers. And fraternity parties are attended by many more students than just members. They attract even some high-school seniors—future college students who are introduced to binge drinking as a social norm. Not surprisingly, most of the alcohol-related deaths of college students recently reported in the media involved fraternity parties.

While some colleges have begun to address the drinking culture created by fraternities, many administrators are still hesitant to move strongly against fraternities, for fear of angering alumni donors who fondly remember their own college years of partying. But administrators have a responsibility to protect all of their students against alcohol-related disruptions and injuries, and should not wait for tragedy to strike before they revoke official recognition of fraternities that consistently cause problems. Colleges also can require all first-year students who live on campus to reside in dormitories, and not in fraternity or sorority houses. Of course, then those colleges must work to create interesting alcohol-free activities centered in the residence halls, to show students that out-of-control drinking need not be the focus of social life.

A third impetus for binge drinking on college campuses—one rarely mentioned publicly—involves alumni at tailgate parties during homecoming activities and sporting events. Any alcohol-control measures adopted for students must also apply to visiting alumni. Banning alcohol at home sporting events for everyone except alumni who contribute more than $50, as one college did recently, is not a good way to win students' support for new alcohol-control policies. I would hope that most alumni, if informed that an institution is trying to cope with a serious problem, would cooperate. Colleges that base their decision making on fund-raising concerns must ask themselves: What will cost the college more money—alumni who might decrease their contributions if they're cut off from alcohol at sporting events, or a few large jury awards of damages to families of injured or deceased students?

Another center of college binge drinking is found in athletics programs. Athletes binge more than other students, according to our data. In fact, involvement in athletics—compared with time spent in other activities—increases rather than decreases a student's propensity for binge drinking. Students involved in athletics are one and a half times as likely to be binge drinkers as are other students. This tradition is kept alive through the beer-advertising blitz that surrounds sports. After all, Mark McGwire's 70th home run was hit at Busch Stadium.

As a first step, college athletics officials should stay clear of alcohol-industry promotions and advertising. Further, although coaches at some colleges require team members to abstain from alcohol during the competitive season, relatively few coaches are involved in campus-wide programs to reduce alcohol abuse. Colleges should make it a priority to enlist their coaches and athletics directors in programs designed to reach all students with the message that binge drinking interferes with performance in every area of their lives. The National Collegiate Athletic Association should encourage this. Colleges also should press coaches to stress the institution's commitment to preventing alcohol abuse when they recruit high-school athletes.

Another important point of intervention is at the high-school level. Half of college binge drinkers start in high school. Colleges should begin to address this problem at high schools that send a large number of freshmen to their campuses, by sending college students from those high schools back to talk to the younger students about alcohol and other substance abuse. The volunteers should stress that one in five college students nationally abstains from alcohol, and that another two in five drink, but not to excess.

High-school students are more likely to believe the messages of college students than those of teachers and other adults. Let future freshmen get their first view of college life from these volunteers, rather than from attending fraternity parties or tailgate events. Once freshmen have unpacked and settled in, it may be too late to tell them about college rules on alcohol use. That message should be sent before they even apply.

Colleges also need to focus more attention a block or two away from the campus—on the ring of bars and liquor stores that encircles many institutions. Colleges need to map the density of those establishments; many institutions have more than 50 such alcohol outlets surrounding them. These are formidable competitors for students' attention, and cannot be coped with by the college alone; community leaders must be enlisted to help, particularly in barring the low-price specials that the outlets use to compete with each other: two-for-one offers, cut-rate drinks and free food during happy hours, and free drinks for women on certain nights. Some states and communities already have laws that ban those types of sales. Remember, the problem is not alcohol itself; it is the availability of a large volume of alcohol at a low price, usually to be consumed in a short period of time.

All of the problem areas that I've cited cannot be attacked by every college at once. Some issues may be more pressing than others on particular campuses, and the solutions must be fashioned to fit local circumstances.

Some important actions are being taken by colleges and universities across the country. Many are trying to sever the connection between alcohol and sports by banning advertising in the programs for sporting events and prohibiting alcohol at college stadiums. Some colleges are discontinuing the practice of not holding classes or exams on Fridays, and are no longer allowing local bars to advertise drink specials in campus publications. And some colleges are experimenting with new student-housing arrangements, such as living–learning centers that take faculty members and classes into the dorms, to try to completely change the environments there.

Institutions also are trying to give students more alcohol-free entertainment options. Some are working with neighborhood groups, as well as community and state officials, to find legal and other means of controlling students' behavior off campus. Other colleges are imposing stricter sanctions on students who break the rules—notifying parents after a certain number of infractions, and suspending or expelling repeat offenders.

What institutions need to avoid are one-dimensional programs that focus on particular students but ignore the ways in which colleges help enable some students to continue binging for four years. Not holding classes or exams on Fridays, for example, enables students to binge from Thursday to Sunday without interruption. Making new rules, but not enforcing even the old ones—for example, banning alcohol in the dormitories, but allowing it to be carried in unmarked cups—tells students that the college is not serious about eradicating the problem.

To anyone who thinks that binge drinking is behavior that cannot be changed, I offer the following challenge. At the next meeting you attend, look around and count how many people are smoking. Not many years ago, the room would have been filled with smoke. Today, because of the wide recognition that smoking hurts both the smoker and people nearby, through secondhand effects, the air is clear. Binge drinking can become equally unacceptable on college campuses.

Summary Chart

CRITICAL READING: ASKING QUESTIONS

1. **Questions to Ask before You Begin a Close Reading of a Text**

   Questions concerning the author
   - *Who is the author?*
   - *What are her credentials?*
   - *What else has she written on the topic?*
   - *What possible biases might have influenced her work?*

   Questions concerning the publication
   - *In what regard is the publication held by professionals in the field?*
   - *Toward what type of readership is the publication aimed?*
   - *How long ago was the piece published?*
   - *What, generally, is the editorial stance of the publication?*

   Questions concerning your own views of the topic
   - *What are my beliefs about the issue addressed in the reading?*
   - *How open am I to new ideas on this topic?*

2. **Questions to Ask while You Read and Reread Material**

   Questions concerning the audience of the piece
   - *What audience does the author seem to be trying to reach?*
   - *What type of reader would be attracted to the author's writing, and what type would be alienated by it?*
   - *How does your sense of the text's audience influence your reading of the piece?*

   Questions concerning the purpose of the piece
   - *What was the author's purpose in writing the piece?*
   - *What is the author's thesis?*
   - *Does the author successfully achieve his or her goals?*

   Questions concerning the content of the piece
   - *What are the author's major assertions or findings?*
   - *How does the author support these assertions or findings?*

   Questions concerning the organization of the piece
   - *How is the material organized?*
   - *What headings and subheadings does the author provide?*

- *What does the organization of the essay tell you about the author's view of the material?*
- *What gets stressed as a result of the organization?*

Questions concerning the author's sources
- *How does the author use other people's ideas or findings?*
- *How credible are the sources the author uses to support his ideas or findings?*

Questions concerning graphics in the piece
- *How clear are the charts, graphs, tables, or illustrations the author provides?*
- *How well does the author explain the graphics?*
- *How well do the graphics support or explain what the author has to say?*

Questions concerning your reactions and responses to the piece
- *How do I feel about the topic, issues, or findings addressed in the reading?*
- *What is convincing? What is unclear?*
- *What ideas in the piece contradict my understanding of the topic?*
- *What ideas in the piece are new to me? Which ones do I accept and which ones do I reject?*

Summary Chart

CRITICAL READING: MARKING TEXTS

1. **Highlighting Texts**

   Highlight the text's thesis, primary assertions, and supporting evidence.

   Highlight the names of authors, specific dates mentioned, and principal sources cited.

   Highlight key passages you may want to reread, quote, or paraphrase later.

   Highlight terms you do not understand or want to discuss in class.

2. **Annotating Texts**

   Marginal annotations
   - *Content notes: identify the meaning or purpose of the marked passages.*
   - *Organization notes: identify the major sections of the text.*
   - *Connection notes: identify links between readings and within a reading.*
   - *Questions: identify confusing, controversial, or questionable passages.*
   - *Response notes: identify your reactions to the reading.*

   End annotations
   - *Summaries: convey a brief overview of the reading.*
   - *Responses: convey your overall reaction to the piece.*
   - *Questions: convey your assessment of the reading's clarity, purpose, or effectiveness.*

Summary Chart

CRITICAL READING: NOTE TAKING

1. Before jotting down any notes, always write down the source text's full bibliographic information.
2. In your notes, carefully distinguish between material you quote and material you paraphrase.
3. Carefully list page numbers in your notes.
4. Pay attention to the punctuation in the source text.
5. In your notes, clearly differentiate between the author's ideas and your own.
6. Be consistent with your note-taking system.

Chapter 2

QUOTATION

DEFINITION AND PURPOSE

When you use someone else's words in your paper, you have to place them in quotation marks and supply proper documentation. Quoting and documenting material tells your readers where they can find that *exact* language in the source text. If you make any significant changes in a passage you are quoting, you need to indicate the alterations in your text with ellipses, brackets, or an explanation.

Generally, if you take more than three words in a row from a source text and incorporate them word-for-word in your essay, you need to place quotation marks around the passage. However, there are several exceptions to this general guideline. For example, if you repeat in your paper someone's official title as it appears in the source text (e.g., president of the school board), you do not need to quote the title, even if it is longer than three words. Also, if you use in your paper a *single* word or term from a source text that is significant or unusual, you *may* need to quote it. Learning what to quote and when to quote takes some time, practice, and thought. Making good decisions about quoting can be easier, though, if you keep in mind one of the main reasons for quoting material: you want to acknowledge an author's distinctive language.

When employed properly and judiciously, quotations can add color and credibility to your writing; they can help make your papers clearer, more entertaining, and more persuasive. If used improperly, quotations can give the impression that you cannot think through a topic for yourself or cannot articulate ideas in your own words. Therefore, knowing how to quote material properly is an extremely important part of writing from readings.

GUIDELINES ON WHEN TO QUOTE MATERIAL

You ought to have a good reason for quoting material in your paper. Do not quote material just to fill up space or to avoid thinking about your topic. Instead, you ought to consider how quoting material will help you support your thesis or explain important ideas to your reader. The next sections list some guidelines to help you decide when to quote a word or passage and suggestions on how to use that material in your paper. As you plan and draft a source-based paper, consider ways to integrate *a few* carefully selected quotations with your own writing to present your ideas as clearly and effectively as possible.

QUOTE PASSAGES WHEN THE AUTHOR HAS WRITTEN SOMETHING IN A DISTINCTIVE OR ESPECIALLY INSIGHTFUL OR INTERESTING WAY

Often an author will express an idea so well it is difficult or impossible for you to express it better by paraphrasing it. The author may have expressed the idea succinctly, employed especially effective adjectives or metaphors, or supplied an especially interesting example. In such cases, quote the word or passage—it may help make your paper more entertaining or persuasive.

QUOTE MATERIAL THAT LENDS SUPPORT TO A POSITION YOU ARE TRYING TO MAKE IN YOUR PAPER

Letting your readers see for themselves that an expert agrees with a position you are advocating can help persuade them to accept your argument or can help them better understand your position. You must be sure, though, that in your effort to find support for your position, you do not misrepresent an author's thoughts or findings. By leaving words out of a quotation or by adding language to it, you should not misrepresent what the author actually had to say. For example, several years ago a student of mine quoted an editorial writer as saying, "President Reagan's proposed budget cuts will . . . double the number of people living in poverty." I checked the original editorial; the actual sentence read, "President Reagan's proposed budget cuts will not double the number of people living in poverty." By leaving out the word *not*, this student clearly misrepresented the author's intended meaning. Such changes to a quotation are unethical.

Also, in an effort to find support for your thesis, do not limit your research to those authors who agree with the position you are advancing. For several reasons, this strategy is a mistake. First, in doing research, you should learn about a topic by studying many different views. Quite often writers change their position as they write and rewrite their papers; sifting through the material they have read frequently leads them to rethink and restate their thesis. Second, you may want to quote authors who present ideas that challenge your thesis: doing so can increase your credibility in the eyes of many readers. Finally, by seeking out alternative perspectives and learning more about the topic, you place yourself in a better position to defend your assertions, improving the likelihood that your readers will value what you have to say on the topic because of your expertise. Therefore, do not neglect opposing viewpoints when searching for material to quote in your paper.

When you use expert testimony to support a position in your paper, it is a good idea to mention the person's credentials in your paper:

> According to Helen Carter, former president of the First National Bank, ". . ."
> Milton Friedman, noted economist and winner of the Nobel Prize, contends that ". . ."

Citing the credentials of the experts you quote may help convince your readers to accept or at least seriously consider what they have to say. Again, you do not need to cite the credentials of every author every time you quote from his or her work. You also do not want to cite so many credentials that the sentence is hard to read. Variety is the key to using quotations well—cite the credentials when you think they are significant, and do so in a way that fits the overall tone of your paper.

QUOTE AUTHORITIES WHO DISAGREE WITH A POSITION YOU ARE ADVOCATING OR WHO OFFER ALTERNATIVE EXPLANATIONS OR CONTRADICTORY DATA

Often it is a good idea to quote authors who offer views or data that call into question the position you are advocating in your paper. Many beginning authors balk at this idea. They believe that introducing opposing views will only weaken the impact of their thesis. However, when you include in your paper a variety of perspectives, your readers are more likely to perceive you to be fair and thorough in your treatment of the subject: these quotations demonstrate that you recognize and understand alternative points of view. Second, such quotations allow you the opportunity to examine critically the other person's position, acknowledging its worth or value when needed and criticizing it when appropriate.

If you decide to quote authors who challenge your thesis, you must somehow address their ideas or findings, usually in one of four ways. You need to explain in your own words:

a. how that author's ideas do not seriously damage your thesis,
b. how that author's ideas or findings may actually support your contentions,

c. how your thesis may be altered slightly to accommodate the author's ideas, or

d. how that author's ideas are incorrect or at least questionable.

If you do not somehow address the opposing ideas you quote in your paper, your reader will likely be confused, wondering how that material fits your paper's thesis.

GUIDELINES ON WHEN NOT TO QUOTE MATERIAL

When writing from sources, students often rely too heavily on quoted material: their essays are a string of quotations. These papers more accurately represent the ideas and language of the source texts than they do the ideas and language of the student. To avoid producing a paper like this, consider these guidelines outlining when you should *not* quote material. Use quotations *selectively*; they should never make up the bulk of your paper.

DO NOT QUOTE PASSAGES MERELY TO FILL SPACE

Too often when writing from sources, students try to pad their essays with extensive quotations, and their final papers end up being a patchwork of quoted material. This is especially true when students are writing to meet a length requirement. If a teacher wants a paper eight to ten pages long, some students think the easiest way to reach that length is to keep piling on quotations. However, in college your readers will usually want to know what *you* think about your subject, what conclusions *you* have reached through your research, how *you* understand material. Do not substitute other people's views and voices for your own; use theirs to *support* your own.

DO NOT QUOTE PASSAGES AS A SUBSTITUTE FOR THINKING

In addition to using quotations to fill space, too often students rely on quotations alone to clarify, defend, or substantiate a finding or position. They may introduce an idea in a topic sentence, then string together two or three quotations to substantiate the point they want to make. Instead of presenting their own ideas in their own language, they rely on quoted material to present and defend their case.

The better course to follow is to integrate selected quotations into your essay carefully: their purpose is to advance your argument or support your conclusions or findings. Do not expect a quotation alone to convince your readers to accept some contention you want to make. As you work through a writing assignment, find language that reflects and communicates the conclusions you have drawn and the assertions you want to make. When appropriate, support or illustrate your position with quoted material. Also remember that when you do quote material, in most cases you will need to comment on it, explaining in your own words the quotation's meaning, relevance, or importance.

DO NOT QUOTE PASSAGES BECAUSE YOU DO NOT UNDERSTAND THE AUTHOR'S IDEAS WELL ENOUGH TO PARAPHRASE THEM

As you read material in college, you will often run into words you do not know, ideas that seem strange, arguments that are hard to follow, research methodologies and discussions of findings that seem to be written in a language of their own. If you have to write papers based on these readings, do not rely on quotations as a way to avoid thought. You need to understand the material you quote. As a general guideline, if you cannot paraphrase the material, do not quote it. That is, if you cannot convey that information in your own words, quoting it is probably a bad idea.

INTEGRATING QUOTATIONS INTO YOUR WRITING

There are several ways to place quoted material in your papers. You should study and practice several of these techniques because varying the way you integrate quotations into your writing can make your papers more interesting.

One of the real difficulties in learning to write from readings in college is the fact that different disciplines follow different rules concerning the proper way to document and punctuate quotations. Two primary style manuals used in your college courses are those published by the Modern Language Association (MLA), primarily used in humanities classes such as English and history, and by the American Psychological Association (APA), primarily used in social science classes such as psychology and sociology. Because each of these manuals offers its own set of rules concerning the proper punctuation and documentation of quotations, when you receive an assignment, always ask your instructor which style manual he or she expects you to follow. (See Chapters 12 and 13 for a complete discussion of the documentation guidelines suggested by each.)

TWO BASIC TYPES OF QUOTATIONS

When you quote material, you will either set it off in a block quotation or integrate it into the body of your essay. Your choice depends on length: longer passages must be block quoted, while shorter quotations should be integrated.

Properly punctuating quotations can be tricky: again, the rules you follow depend on the academic stylebook your teacher wants you to follow. Although the two major style manuals generally agree on how to punctuate integrated quotations, they offer different guidelines for formatting, punctuating, and documenting block quotations. Pay close attention to how the following sample quotations are punctuated. All of the sample quotations will draw on passages from the following essay published in *America*.

Generation Text

The Dark Digital Age: 13 to 17

Mark Bauerlein

Mark Bauerlein *is a professor of English at Emory University and author of* The Dumbest Generation: How the Digital Age Stupefies Young Americans and Jeopardizes Our Future.

Children between the ages of 13 and 17 who have a mobile phone average 1,742 text messages each month, according to a report by the Nielsen Company in September 2008. That comes to nearly 60 per day. They also make 231 voice calls each month, close to eight per day. They play games on the device as well, and browse the Web, take pictures and log hours of social networking.

No wonder so many of them consider the cellphone (for some it is a BlackBerry or an iPhone) an essential part of their lives. Half of all young people between the ages of 8 and 12 own one such device, according to a Harris Interactive poll conducted in July 2008. The rate rises to around four out of five for teenagers; that's a 36 percent increase over the previous three years, which means that these tools have swept into young people's lives with the dispatch and coerciveness of a youth fad (like Pokemon and Harry Potter). The devices are more than just consumer goods. They are signs and instruments of status.

The age-old force of peer pressure bears down hard. Indeed, 45 percent of the teens that sport one agree that "Having a cellphone is the key to my social life"—not just helpful or useful, but "the key." If you don't own a cellphone, if you can't text, game, network and chat, then you are out of the loop. It is like not being picked to play kickball back in the primitive days of neighborhood sandlot gatherings. If a 16-year-old runs up 3,000 text messages in one month (and does not have a flat payment plan), mom and dad take the phone away. It's just a silly, expensive toy, they think.

But the 16-year-old thinks, "You have destroyed my life!" And for them, this seems true. Digital tools are the primary means of social contact. When they lose them, kids feel excluded and unpopular, and nothing hits a 16-year-old harder than the disregard of other 16-year-olds. They do not care what 40-year-olds think, and they do not worry about what happened at Thermopylae or what Pope John Paul II said about the "splendor of truth." They care about what other students in biology class think, what happened last week at the party and what so-and-so said about them.

It is an impulse long preceding the advent of the microchip, but digital devices have empowered that impulse as never before. Think about the life stage of adolescence. Teenagers stand at a precarious threshold, no longer children and not yet adults, eager to be independent but lacking the equipment and composure. They have begun to leave the home and shed the influence of parents, but they don't know where they are headed, and most of them find meager materials beyond the home out of which to build their characters. So they look to one another, emulating dress and speech, forming groups of insiders and outsiders, finding comfort in boyfriends and girlfriends, and deflecting more or less tenuously the ever-present risk of embarrassment.

Everyone passes through this phase, but this generation's experience marks a crucial change in the process. In the past, social life proceeded intermittently, all day at school and for a few hours after school. Kids hung out for an afternoon over the weekend and enjoyed a movie or party on Friday or Saturday night. Other than that, social life pretty much ended. They went home for dinner and entered a private space with only a "landline" as a means of contact (which appears to young people today a restricted connection—show them a rotary phone and watch them scowl). Teenage social life and peer-to-peer contact had a limit.

Teenagers did not like it. I certainly didn't want to listen to my parents when I turned 16. But the limit was healthy and effectual. Adolescents needed then and need now a reprieve from the tribal customs and peer fixations of middle school and high school. Wounds from lunchroom gossip and bullying, as well as the blandishments of popularity and various niche-crowd memberships, disable the maturing process. These form a horizon of adolescent triumphs and set the knowledge of history, civics, religion, fine art and foreign affairs beyond the pale of useful and relevant acquisitions. If a sophomore sat down on a bus with the gang and said, "Hey, did you see the editorial on school funding in *The Times* this morning?" the rest would scrunch up their faces as if an alien being sat among them.

Youthful mores screen out such things, which is all the more reason for parents to offer an alternative. A home and leisure life separate from teen stuff exposes youths to heroes and villains that surpass the idols of the senior class, to places beyond the food court and Apple Store, to times well before the glorious day they got their driver's license. It acquaints them with adult duties, distant facts and values and truths they will not fully comprehend until much later. They don't like them and rarely find them meaningful, but in pre-digital times teens had nowhere else to go after they entered the front door. They had to sit at the dining table and listen to parents talk about grocery shopping, vacation plans, Nixon, gas prices and the news.

No longer. In 1980, when an angry parent commanded, "Go to your room—you're grounded!" the next few hours meant isolation for the teen. Today, the bedroom is not a private space. It's a social hub. For many kids, the bedroom at midnight provides a rich social life that makes daytime face-to-face conversations seem tame and slow. Amid the pillows with laptop or BlackBerry, they chat with buddies in 11th grade and in another state. Photos fly back and forth while classmates sleep, revelations spill forth in tweets ("OMG, Billy just called Betty his ——"), and Facebook pages gain flashier graphics.

In this dynamic 24/7 network, teen activity accrues more and more significance. The events of the day carry greater weight as they are recorded and circulated. The temptation for teens to be self-absorbed and self-project, to consider the details of their lives eminently memorable and share-able, grows and grows. As they give in online, teenagers' peer consciousness expands while their historical understanding, civic awareness and taste go dormant before they have even had much chance to develop. This is the hallmark of what I have called the Dumbest Generation. These kids have just as much intelligence and ambition as any previous cohort, but they exercise them too much on one another. They are building youth culture into a ubiquitous universe, and as ever, youth culture is a drag on maturity. This time it has a whole new arsenal.

THE BLOCK QUOTATION

The APA and MLA style manuals both agree that longer quotations must be set off from the rest of the text, but they differ in how they define "longer":

- APA states that quotations of 40 words or more must be block quoted.
- MLA says to block quote passages that would be more than four typed lines in your paper.

Regardless of the style manual you follow, you should introduce a block quotation with a colon. You do not add quotation marks at the beginning or end of the passage, and all the punctuation in the source text stays the same in the block quotation.

APA Guidelines

According to the APA style manual, you should start a block quotation on a new line in your paper, setting the left margin of the quotation one-half inch in from the original left margin. Subsequent lines of the quotation align on that indent. (If you are quoting additional paragraphs in the source text, indent the first line of each an additional half inch.) The right margin stays the same, and the whole passage is double-spaced.

Example 1

In "Generation Text," Mark Bauerlein (2009) describes how the nature of "being grounded" has changed due to advances in technology:

> In 1980, when an angry parent commanded, "Go to your room—you're grounded!" the next few hours meant isolation for the teen. Today, the bedroom is not a private space. It's a social hub. For many kids, the bedroom at midnight provides a rich social life that makes daytime face-to-face conversations seem tame and slow. Amid the pillows with laptop or BlackBerry, they chat with buddies in 11th grade and in another state. Photos fly back and forth while classmates sleep, revelations spill forth in tweets ("OMG, Billy just called Betty his ——"), and Facebook pages gain flashier graphics. (p. 36)

Kids sent to their bedroom today do not face isolation. Thanks to modern technology, they can stay in constant contact with their friends.

Analysis

Notice that the period at the end of the quotation precedes the parenthetical citation. (If the quotation runs longer than one page in the source text, use "pp." to introduce the inclusive page numbers.) There are no quotation marks added at the beginning or end of the block quote. The words "Go to your room—you're grounded!" are quoted because they have quotation marks around them in the source text. If any words are italicized in the source text, they remain italicized in your block quote. Note also that the left-hand margin of the block quotation is indented a half inch.

MLA Guidelines

MLA says to begin a block quotation on a new line, indent the left margin one inch (and a quarter inch more for new paragraphs within the block quote), leave the right margin unchanged, and double-space the block quotation.

Example 2

In "Generation Text," Mark Bauerlein describes how the nature of "being grounded" has changed due to advances in technology:

> In 1980, when an angry parent commanded, "Go to your room—you're grounded!" the next few hours meant isolation for the teen. Today, the bedroom is not a private space. It's a social hub. For many kids, the bedroom at midnight provides a rich social life that makes daytime face-to-face conversations seem tame and slow. Amid the pillows with laptop or BlackBerry, they chat with buddies in 11th grade and in another state. Photos fly back and forth while classmates sleep, revelations spill forth in tweets ("OMG, Billy just called Betty his ——"), and Facebook pages gain flashier graphics. (36)

> Kids sent to their bedroom today do not face isolation. Thanks to modern technology, they can stay in constant contacts with their friends.

Analysis

Note how the parenthetical documentation follows the period at the end of the quotation. No quotation marks are added to the block quote. The words quoted from the original passage retain their punctuation. There is a new left margin, but the right margin remains unchanged.

Example 3

Bauerlein introduces "Generation Text" by citing some interesting, and perhaps startling, statistics concerning children's use of technology:

> Children between the ages of 13 and 17 who have a mobile phone average 1,742 text messages each month, according to a report by the Nielsen Company in September 2008. That comes to nearly 60 per day. They also make 231 voice calls each month, close to eight per day. They play games on the device as well, and browse the Web, take pictures and log hours of social networking.
>
> No wonder so many of them consider the cellphone (for some it is a Black-Berry or an iPhone) an essential part of their lives. Half of all young people between the ages of 8 and 12 own one such device, according to a Harris Interactive poll conducted in July 2008. The rate rises to around four out of five for teenagers; that's a 36 percent increase over the previous three years, which means that these tools have swept into young people's lives with the dispatch and coerciveness of a youth fad (like Pokemon and Harry Potter). (34)

According to Bauerlein, this technology has spread quickly in the culture like so many other fads.

Analysis

Since this block quotation runs longer than one paragraph, note how the first line of the second paragraph is indented an additional quarter inch.

THE INTEGRATED QUOTATION

Short quotations should be integrated in the body of your essay rather than set off in a block quotation. As you will see, you have several ways to integrate quoted material into your paper. Try to use several of these techniques when writing an essay—such variety can help make your paper more interesting to read.

The APA and MLA style manuals generally agree on where to place quotation marks, how to use single and double quotation marks, and how to otherwise punctuate integrated quotations. Remember that all quotations must be documented. Again, see Chapter 12 for a detailed discussion on how to document quotations. In the following samples, I alternate between APA and MLA documentation conventions.

Introduce a Quotation with a Verb

Probably the most common way of introducing a quotation is to give the author's name, perhaps his or her credentials, maybe even the title of the work, followed by an appropriate verb—*says, notes, comments, contends, asserts*, and so on. Place a comma after the verb of saying.

Example 4 (MLA Documentation)

> Bauerlein, believing that owning a cell phone is a sign of social status and inclusion, writes, "Indeed, 45 percent of the teens that sport one agree that 'Having a cellphone is the key to my social life'—not just helpful or useful, but 'the key'" (34).

When you integrate material from a source text that already contains quotation marks, the regular quotation marks in the original (" ") are changed to single quotation marks (' ') in your paper.

Note the punctuation at the end of the sentence; the final period follows the parenthetical citation. If the last sentence of the quotation ends with an exclamation point or a question mark, include it before the closing quotation mark and place a period after the parenthetical citation. This punctuation guideline holds true for the APA and MLA style manuals.

Example 5 (APA Documentation)

> Bauerlein (2009) states that this generation of students, unlike others, expect to use only modern technology to communicate. In the past, he writes, children ". . . went home for dinner and entered a private space with only a 'landline' as a means of contact (which appears to young people today a restricted connection—show them a rotary phone and watch them scowl) (p. 35).

Again, note how a comma follows the verb (in this case, "writes"), how the material quoted in the source text is placed in single quotation marks, how the ellipsis indicates part of the passage was left out of the quote, and how the final period follows the documentation.

Example 6 (MLA Documentation)

> Bauerlein claims, "Children between the ages of 13 and 17 who have a mobile phone average 1,742 text messages each month . . ." (34).

Introduce a Quotation without a Verb

A more formal way of integrating a quotation into your paper is to introduce it with a colon. Commonly, quotations used as illustrations or elaborations of a point you have just made are introduced this way. Make sure that the colon comes at the end of a complete sentence; leave one space between the colon and the opening quotation mark.

Example 7 (APA Documentation)

> Toward the end of his essay, Bauerlein (2009) assumes a darker tone: "This is the hallmark of what I have called the Dumbest Generation. These kids have just as much intelligence and ambition as any previous cohort, but they exercise them too much on one another" (p. 36).

Example 8 (MLA Documentation)

> In generations past, teens needed a place to escape their peers: "Adolescents needed then and need now a reprieve from the tribal customs and peer fixations of middle school and high school" (Bauerlein 35).

Note that in this last example, because I did not use Baurerlein's name in the passage, I had to include it in the citation.

Run Your Sentence and the Quotation Together

This particular technique can be hard to master. Instead of separating your words from the quoted passage with a comma or colon, you run the two together seamlessly, relying on the quotation marks to let your reader know when you begin using someone else's language. Integrating quotations in this way, while sophisticated stylistically, can also lead you to misquote material if you are not careful. As students first learn to run their sentence and the quotation together, they tend to alter the quotation to fit the sentence they are writing rather than to alter their sentence so it fits the quotation. As you practice this method of quoting material, try to craft your sentence so it runs smoothly into the quotation. If you have to change the quoted passage in any substantive way, you must indicate the changes (see the section on "Altering Quoted Material and Avoiding Misquotations," which follows).

When you employ this technique properly and read your essay aloud, a listener would not be able to tell where the quotation started and ended. Note that you do not need to place a comma before the quoted material or insert an ellipsis if you are picking up the quotation in midsentence.

Example 9 (APA Documentation)

> Baurerlein (2009) believes that "the age-old force of peer pressure bears down hard" (p. 34).

In this example, note that the capital *T* in *The* can be changed to lowercase without the addition of brackets. Also, when using this approach, you do not need to include an ellipsis if you begin a quotation in midsentence.

Example 10 (MLA Documentation)

> Changes in education and technology have "set the knowledge of history, civics, religion, fine art and foreign affairs beyond the pale of useful and relevant acquisitions" (Baurerlein 35).

Pick Out Only Certain Words to Quote in Your Sentence

You do not always have to quote entire passages or sentences in your paper. Often you want to quote only a few key words or phrases. Be sure, though, to include proper documentation even if you quote only one word.

Example 11 (MLA Documentation)

> Bauerlein believes teens "stand at a precarious threshold" and that they are "eager to be independent" (35).

This particular example needs only one parenthetical citation because all the quoted material comes from the same page in the source text. If it came from different pages in the source text, parenthetical citations would follow each quoted word or phrase.

Example 12 (APA Documentation)

> According to Bauerlein (2009), because "peer pressure bears down hard" (p. 34), the children's use of social technologies "accrues more and more significance" (p. 36).

ALTERING QUOTED MATERIAL AND AVOIDING MISQUOTATIONS

When you place quotation marks around material in your essay and document that passage, you are telling your readers that if they turn to that page of that source text they will find that passage as it appears in your paper: the words and punctuation have not been changed. If that is not the case—if you have made any substantive changes to material you are quoting—then you need to acknowledge those alterations. Especially important is learning how to indicate that you left words out of a quotation, added words to a quotation, or changed the emphasis given words in a quotation.

Leaving Words Out of a Quotation

Use an ellipsis (. . .) to indicate that you left material out of a quotation. Add a fourth dot to act as a period if you omit the end of a sentence or leave out an entire sentence when block quoting. When you introduce a quotation with a colon, include an ellipsis if you pick up a quotation in the middle of a sentence in the source text.

Example 13 (MLA Documentation)

> Bauerlein observes, "No wonder so many of them consider the cellphone . . . an essential part of their lives" (34).

Example 14 (APA Documentation)

Escaping the detrimental effects of social technologies, students will better learn adult behaviors: ". . . adult duties, distant facts and values and truths they will not fully comprehend until much later" (Bauerlein, 2009, p. 35–36).

Adding Words to a Quotation

When you add words to a quotation, use square brackets, not parentheses, around the words. Add material to quotations sparingly. Do it only when absolutely necessary to avoid confusing your readers.

Example 15 (MLA Documentation)

Home life is devalued, "So they [teenagers] look to one another, emulating dress and speech . . ." (Bauerlein 35).

Noting Emphasis Added to a Quotation

If you want to emphasize a word or passage in a quotation, put it in italics. The stylebooks offer different guidelines on how to indicate the addition of emphasis to a quotation:

* APA style: immediately after the emphasized words, place in square brackets the words "emphasis added."
* MLA style: after the quotation itself, place in parentheses the words "emphasis added," after the page number (if any). Or place "emphasis added" in square brackets immediately after the emphasized words.

If you do not indicate otherwise, readers will assume any words italicized in a quotation appear in italics in the source text.

Example 16 (APA Documentation)

Bauerlein (2009) notes that "everyone passes through this phase, but this generation's experience marks a *crucial change* [emphasis added] in the process" (p. 35)

Example 17 (MLA Documentation)

English Professor Mark Bauerlein observes that "everyone passes through this phase, but this generation's experience marks a *crucial change* in the process" (35, emphasis added).

Summary Chart

GUIDELINES ON QUOTATIONS

1. **When to Quote Material**

   Quote passages when the author has said something in a distinctive or especially insightful or interesting way.

   Quote material that supports the assertions you make in your paper.

   Quote authorities who disagree with a position you are advocating or who offer alternative explanations or contradictory data.

2. **When Not to Quote Material**

   Do not quote passages merely to fill in space.

   Do not quote passages as a substitute for thinking.

   Do not quote passages because you do not understand the author's ideas well enough to paraphrase them.

Summary Chart

INTEGRATING QUOTATIONS INTO YOUR WRITING

1. **Block Quotations**

   Employ this method with longer quotations.

   Follow guidelines established by the style manual your instructor requires.

2. **Integrated Quotations**

   Introduce the quotation with an appropriate verb.
   - *precede with a comma*
   - *employ a verb of saying that fits the overall tone of your essay, such as:*

says	holds
states	maintains
asserts	contends
claims	explains

   Introduce the quotation without a verb.
   - *a more formal way of introducing the quotation*
   - *precede with a colon*

   Run your sentence and the quotation together.
   - *edit your sentence so it fits the tone and syntax of the quoted passage*

   Pick out only certain words to quote.
   - *quote interesting uses of language such as coined or controversial terms*
   - *quote terms to draw attention to them*

QUOTATION REVISION CHECKLIST

	Yes	No
1. Did you check your quoted passages against the original to make sure the wording is accurate?	____	____
2. Is the capitalization of words in the quotation proper and accurate?	____	____
3. Is the punctuation in the quotation proper and accurate?	____	____
4. Do you need to add italics, underline certain words, or use single quotation marks in the quotation?	____	____
5. Did you check the punctuation you employed to introduce the quotation?	____	____
6. Did you check the format of your block quotations?	____	____
7. If you added words to or deleted words from the source passage, did you confirm that you have not misrepresented the author?	____	____
8. Is the format of your documentation at the end of the quotation in the correct style?	____	____
9. Did you list the right page number or numbers in your documentation?	____	____

Chapter 3

PARAPHRASE

DEFINITION AND PURPOSE

When you paraphrase a passage, you express an author's arguments, findings, or ideas in your own words. Much of the writing you do in college will require you to paraphrase material. Some of these assignments will simply ask you to gather and convey information. To write this type of paper, you study the work of various authors, then paraphrase what they have written, trying to convey to your readers as clearly and accurately as possible what each has to say about the topic.

In other assignments you will rely on paraphrased material to help you develop and defend an argument. Paraphrasing the work of experts who agree with your position in a paper can be quite persuasive. Even paraphrasing the work of authors who *disagree* with a position you have assumed in your essay can be helpful: after you objectively present that opposing view, you can examine its strengths and weaknesses and adjust your position to accommodate ideas you can neither discredit nor dismiss. However, when paraphrasing information as a part of an argument you are advancing, you must fairly represent an author's views. It is always tempting to misrepresent what people say, especially when you disagree with them, either by oversimplifying their position or by employing misleading language. Try to resist these temptations; always try to be fair to an author when you paraphrase his or her work.

Finally, paraphrasing allows you to convey your unique understanding of a reading. Paraphrases of the same material written by different students are not likely to be exactly the same because writing a paraphrase involves a series of choices: each writer decides what information to include, what language to use, and what organization to employ. Though you should attempt to be objective in your paraphrase of a reading, the details you choose to include and the language you choose to substitute for the author's will be communicating your unique view of the passage.

QUALITIES OF A GOOD PARAPHRASE

Generally, a good paraphrase of a passage exhibits four characteristics. It is thorough, accurate, fair, and objective:

- *Thorough*—it will include all of the author's primary ideas or findings.
- *Accurate*—it will reflect what the author actually wrote.
- *Fair*—your choice of language will be as evenhanded as possible.
- *Objective*—you will avoid voicing your own opinion on the topic or on the quality of the source text.

THOROUGH

A paraphrase of a passage differs from a summary of a passage in its comprehensiveness. In a summary, you try to reduce the source material to its most essential message; in a paraphrase, you try to capture the entire content of the passage. Because you change words and sentence structure when paraphrasing material, your paraphrase of a passage may actually be longer than the original text. Summaries, however, will always be shorter than the original passage. Even though your goal is to be thorough, writing a paraphrase involves making some choices concerning content: you may leave out what you believe to be insignificant details, examples, or explanations found in the source text. Guiding these decisions, though, should be your desire to produce as complete a paraphrase as possible.

ACCURATE

Because you are not quoting authors when you paraphrase their work—because you are substituting your words for theirs—you must take care to be accurate in what you write. Your paraphrase should offer your reader a precise restatement of what the author wrote: though the language is different, your paraphrase should convey the same information or arguments found in the source text. However, accuracy can be hard to achieve. Even slight changes in language can drastically alter the meaning of a passage. Therefore, when writing and revising a paraphrase, check your work against your understanding of the source text. Have you at all misrepresented the *content* of the other writer's piece? Would the author read your paraphrase and agree that you have, indeed, captured what he or she wrote?

FAIR

Being fair in your paraphrase is related to being accurate. Writing a paraphrase involves putting into your own words someone else's ideas, arguments, or findings. When doing so, first you want to be fair to the author whose work you are paraphrasing. In exchanging your words for his or hers, you want to be as evenhanded as possible. Avoid language, for example, that implies a judgment on your part or makes an author's work appear more sophisticated or more simplistic than it actually is. Second, you want to be fair to your readers. When people read your paraphrase of an author's work, they expect you to give them a fair and accurate understanding of that material. They do not expect you to censure or praise the source text—that's the function of a critique, not a paraphrase.

For a number of reasons, paraphrases are often inaccurate or unfair. First, students often *misread source texts* and make flatly incorrect assertions about the author's work. This type of problem can be avoided through a careful, critical reading of the source text before you try to paraphrase it and by discussing the reading with others. Second, students often *paraphrase material out of context.* Their paraphrase of a passage is misleading because in the larger context of the work the passage has an entirely different meaning from the one reflected in the student's essay. This type of error frequently occurs if the author of the source text is summarizing opposing views in his work. Students who paraphrase this material out of context will frequently misrepresent the author's views, making it appear the author actually agrees with his critics. When you paraphrase someone else's ideas, be sensitive to the relationship between the passage you are working with and the meaning of source text as a whole. Finally, students often produce unfair paraphrases of a source text by *relying on emotionally charged or heavily connotative language.* If an article talks about "presidential aides" and you substitute "presidential cronies," "presidential lackeys," or "presidential co-conspirators," you probably are not being entirely fair in your paraphrase.

OBJECTIVE

A good paraphrase does not take sides. Students often fail to be objective in one of three ways. First, as discussed above, they may employ language that clearly editorializes. In writing a paraphrase, try to use language that fairly and accurately captures the meaning and intent of the source text, not language that reflects your views of the topic or the quality of the source text itself. Second, in writing a paraphrase, sometimes students want to comment directly on the topic the author is addressing. When paraphrasing an author's views on abortion rights, for instance, they may want to articulate their stand on the issue. That material does not belong in a paraphrase, where your goal is to communicate someone else's views. Finally, students sometimes want to include in their paraphrase comments on the quality of the author's work—that they found the argument convincing or faulty, that the author's style was cumbersome or flowing, that the article was "good" or "bad." These types of comments are appropriate for a critique, not for a paraphrase. Your goal in a paraphrase is to be as objective in your content and language as possible.

Before you try to paraphrase someone else's ideas, though, be sure you understand what he or she has written. Again, one of the most common causes of inadequate paraphrasing is failing to grasp the meaning of the source text. Therefore, whether you are paraphrasing a sentence, paragraph, chapter, or essay, you need to understand fully what the author has written before you attempt to put that person's ideas into your own words. Your paraphrase of that person's ideas or findings must be complete, accurate, fair, and objective. It cannot meet these standards if you are confused or at all uncertain about what the author has written.

However, paraphrasing a passage can also be an effective way of determining its meaning. If you are not sure what a passage means, try paraphrasing it. Putting someone else's ideas into your own words is often the best way for you to understand what the author has written. Always reread your paraphrase and the source text to be sure you have been thorough and fair, especially if the paraphrased material is going to be a part of a paper you are turning in.

HOW TO PARAPHRASE MATERIAL

Generally, you paraphrase material by changing words, changing sentence structures, or changing the order of ideas in a passage. More often than not, you will make all three types of changes each time you paraphrase someone's ideas.

CHANGING WORDS

One way to paraphrase a passage is to substitute your words for the author's. However, finding appropriate synonyms for words in the source text can often be challenging. Many students are tempted to turn immediately to a thesaurus for a list of possible replacement words. However, it is usually better to try to come up with appropriate synonyms on your own. Remember, writing a paraphrase involves putting someone else's ideas into *your* own words. If you can come up with replacement words that are fair, accurate, and appropriate for the tone of your paper, use them. If you cannot come up with a new word on your own, then turn to a thesaurus. However, after you look up a possible substitute word in the thesaurus, check its definition in a dictionary to see if the word accurately reflects the meaning you want to convey. The words you find in a thesaurus are not always interchangeable; there are often subtle differences in meaning you can determine by checking the definition of each term in a good dictionary.

Whether you rely on your own resources or on a thesaurus, using synonyms in a paraphrase raises similar concerns:

a. Does the new word convey the author's original idea accurately and objectively?
b. Does the new word fit the overall tone of the rest of your essay? Is it too formal or informal? Too technical or too general?

Often, it may be impossible to find an adequate substitute for a word or phrase in a passage: perhaps the author coined a phrase or used an unusual or shocking term. In such cases, it is appropriate for you to quote the language found in the source text (see Chapter 2 for guidelines on quoting material). When paraphrasing material, though, try to keep the number of quotations to a minimum. Also, remember that *all* paraphrased passages you include in your papers must be documented—even though you change the language of the source text when you paraphrase, you need to acknowledge through your documentation the source of the *ideas* you are discussing.

Below are examples of passages paraphrased primarily through word substitution. You will find the original passage, a rough-draft paraphrase, and a final paraphrase. The original passages in all of the following examples are drawn from the readings included in Chapters 1 and 2.

Example 1

A. Original

"Teenagers stand at a precarious threshold, no longer children and not yet adults, eager to be independent but lacking the equipment and composure."

B. Rough-Draft Paraphrase

Teenagers stand at a dangerous moment in their lives, between childhood and adulthood, wanting to be independent but not possessing the ability and maturity to do so.

C. Final Paraphrase (APA Documentation)

Teens face a dangerous time in their lives, between childhood and adulthood, wanting desperately to live on their own but not possessing the skills and maturity they need to enter the next phase of their lives (Bauerlein).

Discussion: In my rough draft, I changed a few words: "precarious threshold" became "dangerous moment in their lives," "no longer children and not yet adults" became "between childhood and adulthood," and "lacking the equipment and composure" became "not possessing the ability and maturity to do so." In places, my first attempt was still too close to the wording in the original passage, and I wasn't sure I captured the connotative meaning of several words. I liked "between childhood and adulthood," but I retained the word "independent" (which I thought I needed to change), "ability" did not seem like the right word to replace "equipment," "moment" wasn't the right word to replace "threshold," and I did not think the end of my paraphrase captured what the author meant in the context of the original. So in my next draft, I changed "moment in their lives" to "time in their lives," changed "ability" to "skills" (which I think comes closer to the author's word—"equipment"), and added the last part of the sentence to clarify what I think the author meant in the original. The basic sentence structure has remained the same; I've only tried to change some of the words.

Example 2

A. Original

"For many kids, the bedroom at midnight provides a rich social life that makes daytime face-to-face conversations seem tame and slow."

B. Rough-Draft Paraphrase

Many kids, even in their bedrooms in the middle of the night, have a richer social life electronically than they do talking one-on-one to their friends during the day.

C. Final Paraphrase (MLA Documentation)

Thanks to technology, many kids have a more exciting life electronically with friends overnight in their bedrooms than they have talking with them one-on-one during the day (Baurerlein 36).

Discussion: This was a difficult text to paraphrase out of context. In the original work, the author is clearly discussing the impact of technology on teenagers' social lives, but that word, "technology," does not appear in the passage. In my rough draft, I added the word "electronically" after "social life" to capture this meaning. The word "midnight" became "middle of the night," and "daytime face-to-face conversations" became "talking one-on-one to their friends during the day." I switched "rich social life" for "richer social life," which clearly needed to be changed or quoted. In my final draft, I opened the sentence with "Thanks to technology" to place the passage in context, changed "richer social life" to "more exciting life electronically." Again, I'm still not entirely happy with this paraphrase because I've only substituted words—it would be a better paraphrase if I also employed the techniques described below.

CHANGING SENTENCE STRUCTURE

Besides changing words, when composing a good paraphrase of material, you may also need to alter the sentence structure employed in the source text. Often such changes involve rearranging the order of ideas in a sentence or altering the order of dependent and independent clauses.

Example 3

A. *Original*

"Although communism and state socialism have failed to protect the environment, eco-extremists are basically anti-business."

B. *Rough-Draft Paraphrase*

"Eco-extremists" oppose business interests even though communism and state socialism have failed to protect the environment.

C. *Final Paraphrase (MLA Documentation)*

"Eco-extremists" oppose business even though communist and socialist governments have permitted environmental degradation (Moore 16).

Discussion: In my rough draft, I first changed the order of the ideas in the sentence. I could not think of an appropriate substitution for "eco-extremist" so I quoted it and changed "anti-business" to "oppose business." In my final draft, I had to find a better way of addressing the second half of my paraphrase. I started by changing "communism and state socialism" to "communist and socialist governments" and reworded the idea about failing to protect the environment to "have permitted environmental degradation." Looking at it now, I think "degradation" may not be the best word—some additional changes might be needed.

COMBINING SENTENCES

When you paraphrase longer passages, you will often have to "combine" sentences in the source text to paraphrase the material adequately. After you read the entire passage, you may feel that you can condense the information into fewer sentences while still being thorough and fair in your paraphrase. By changing words, altering sentence structures, and combining in one of your sentences information found in two or more source sentences, you can often achieve a smooth, effective paraphrase of material.

Example 4

A. *Original*

"In addition to choosing a dubious tactic, the environmental movement also changed its philosophy along the way. It once prided itself on subscribing to a philosophy that was 'transpolitical, transideological, and transnational' in character. Non-violent direct action and peaceful disobedience were the hallmarks of the movement. Truth mattered and science was respected for the knowledge it brought to the debate."

B. Rough-Draft Paraphrase

In recent years the environmental movement has adopted a new philosophy. It once believed its philosophy cut across political, ideological, and national lines. While its adherents believed in direct action and peaceful disobedience, truth also mattered, as did science, which brought knowledge to the debate.

C. Final Paraphrase (APA Documentation)

According to Patrick Moore (1995), the environmental movement has changed its guiding philosophy. They used to believe their ideas cut across political, ideological, and national lines. They also believed in peaceful protests, respected the truth, and valued science for the information it brought them.

Discussion: In my rough draft, I condensed the four sentences found in the source text into three sentences in my paraphrase. I was especially interested in combining the last two sentences. At the same time, I was trying to change some of the words. For example, I altered "transpolitical, transideological, and transnational" but let stand much of the language in those last two sentences. To begin my final draft, I added the author's name and dropped "in recent years," which I had added in the rough draft. In the next two sentences I tried to echo the term "philosophy" with the word "believed" and achieve parallel structure by using "They" twice. I continued to change some of the terms, substituting "peaceful" for "non-violent" and again tried to achieve some sense of parallel structure in my last sentence (which combines two sentences in the source text).

"UNPACKING" SENTENCES

Sometimes a sentence in a reading may be so densely written, so full of ideas, that in your paraphrase you may need two or three sentences to convey the same information. When "unpacking" a sentence like this, your goal remains to convey the author's ideas fairly and thoroughly in your own language. Be sure first, though, that you fully understand the source passage—densely written material is often hard to read.

Example 5

A. Original

"So they look to one another, emulating dress and speech, forming groups of insiders and outsiders, finding comfort in boyfriends and girlfriends, and deflecting more or less tenuously the ever-present risk of embarrassment."

B. Rough-Draft Paraphrase

Because many teenagers are still trying to define themselves, they look to each other for support. They end up dressing alike. They define who their friends are. They look to boyfriends or girlfriends. All the time, though, they are trying not to embarrass themselves.

C. *Final Paraphrase (MLA Documentation)*

Many teenagers look beyond their home and parents to define themselves. Instead, they look to each other for support. Ironically, in an effort to define their individuality, they end up dressing like their peers, forming cliques, and devoting themselves to girlfriends or boyfriends. All the time, though, they try, more or less successfully, to keep from embarrassing themselves (Bauerlein 35).

Discussion: This was a difficult passage to paraphrase. First, the original sentence makes little sense out of context, so in my rough draft, I paraphrased the sentence that leads up to this one in the source text: "Because many teenagers are still trying to define themselves." I then broke up the original sentence into five sentences, each covering one of the main ideas in the source text. This passage, though, was choppy and repetitive; I needed to combine them for better coherence. The final version has four sentences, and in the third sentence I added "ironically" to capture the tone and intent of the original sentence as I interpreted it. Even at this stage, though, I think the first two sentences could be combined to make the paraphrase even more concise—perhaps going back to the syntax I used in the rough draft.

COMBINING STRATEGIES: PARAPHRASING LONGER PASSAGES IN SOURCE TEXTS

There may be times when you have to paraphrase passages from a source text that are several sentences or even several paragraphs long. When this is the case, you will likely need to employ all of the strategies discussed in this chapter.

Example 6

A. *Original*

At the center of binge drinking on many campuses are fraternities and sororities. While they attract only a small percentage of students nationally, they continue to play a prominent role in campus life at many institutions. Our data shows that in fraternity houses, four of five residents binge, and more than half are frequent binge drinkers. And, fraternity parties are attended by many more students than just members. They attract even some high-school seniors—future college students who are introduced to binge drinking as a social norm. Not surprisingly, most of the alcohol-related deaths of college students recently reported in the media involved fraternity parties.

While some colleges have begun to address the drinking culture created by fraternities, many administrators are still hesitant to move strongly against fraternities, for fear of angering alumni donors who fondly remember their own college years of partying. But administrators have a responsibility to protect all of their students against alcohol-related disruptions and injuries, and should not wait for tragedy to strike before they revoke official recognition of fraternities that consistently cause problems. Colleges also can require all first-year students who live on campus to reside in dormitories, and not in fraternity or sorority houses. Of course, then those colleges must work to create interesting alcohol-free activities centered in the residence halls, to show students that out-of-control drinking need not be the focus of social life.

B. *Rough-Draft Paraphrase*

Even though only a small number of students join fraternities and sororities in college, they are responsible for much of the binge drinking on U.S. campuses. In fact, one study showed that four or five fraternity and sorority members binge drink, more than half, frequently. In addition, high-school students sometimes attend Greek parties, introducing them to binge drinking even before they enroll in college. Recently, several students have even died after becoming drunk at fraternity parties.

Although they know fraternities are often the site of binge drinking, college administrators are often reluctant to crack down on them because they are afraid of angering alumni donors who themselves were Greeks. However, in doing so, administrators fail to uphold their responsibility to protect all students. One way to attack the problem would be to require all freshmen to live in dorms, but schools would then also have to provide alcohol-free recreational opportunities to demonstrate that students do not have to get drunk to have fun.

C. *Final Paraphrase (MLA Documentation)*

In the United States, while only a small number of students join fraternities and sororities in college, they are responsible for much of the binge drinking. One study showed that four out of five fraternity and sorority members binge drink (over fifty percent, frequently) and often introduce binge drinking to high-school students who attend their parties. Although administrators know that fraternities are often the site of binge drinking (and that some students have died after getting drunk at fraternity parties), they are reluctant to crack down on them—many potential alumni donors were Greeks and may object to such action. To address the problem, administrators could prohibit freshmen from living in Greek housing, but they would also have to provide alcohol-free recreational opportunities to demonstrate that students do not have to get drunk to have fun (Wechsler 21).

Discussion: As I moved through the rough draft into the final paraphrase, I tried to condense and simplify the sentences in the source text while remaining comprehensive. I ended up with one paragraph instead of two, although the order of the ideas in my paraphrase still follows the order of ideas presented in the original. I'm still not sure that I like substituting "Greek" for "fraternities and sororities" in the paraphrase of the expression "crack down on them" (it may be too informal). To condense the material, I used parentheses twice to enclose material I thought was of secondary importance. Also note that I need to provide documentation only once, at the end of the paraphrased passage.

BLENDING YOUR WRITING WITH PARAPHRASED MATERIAL

Often in academic writing you will be blending your writing with material you're paraphrasing from source texts. Through documentation and attribution, you will guide your readers through the passage, clarifying which prose is yours and which is paraphrased. I have numbered the sentences in Example 7 below to make it easier to discuss the passage.

Example 7 (Using APA Documentation)

> [1]Clearly, binge drinking is a problem on many college campuses, but who is to blame? [2]Author Henry Wechsler (1998) lays part of the responsibility at the feet of fraternities and sororities. [3]According to Wechsler, although only a small number of college students actually "go Greek," fraternity and sorority members account for a disproportionate number of binge drinkers. [4]Fraternities, in particular, seem to promote binge drinking, since four out of five students living in a fraternity house report that they binge drink. [5]If college administrators know that fraternities and sororities are a major site of binge drinking on their campuses, why don't they act to stop that behavior? [6]Wechsler believes it comes down to money. [7]They are afraid to offend alumni donors who were themselves Greeks by cracking down on fraternities and sororities. [8]If these alumni feel that the administration is unfairly targeting Greeks, they will be less likely to donate money to the school.

Discussion: In this example, sentences 3, 4, and 7 are paraphrased from the source text and are therefore documented. Sentences 1, 2, 5, 6, and 8 are ones I wrote and therefore do not need to be documented. Note how citing the source text at the end of sentence 4 provides sufficient documentation for sentences 3 and 4.

DOCUMENTATION

Remember that any material you paraphrase from a source must be properly documented. Failing to document paraphrased material is a form of plagiarism. While the various forms of documentation you will encounter in college are discussed in Chapter 12, remember that every discipline expects writers to document all paraphrased material properly.

Summary Chart

HOW TO PARAPHRASE MATERIAL

1. **Read, reread, and annotate the material.**
   - *Use a dictionary to find the meaning of any words you do not know.*
   - *Form your own opinion about the meaning of the passage.*

2. **Change words in the passage.**
   - *Substitute synonyms for key terms in the passage.*
   - *Substitute pronouns for nouns when appropriate.*
   - *Change the verbs.*

3. **Change the sentence structure in the passage.**
   - *Rearrange the order of ideas presented in the source text.*

4. **Combine sentences found in the source text.**
   - *Combine into single sentences ideas presented in two or more sentences in the source text.*

5. **Unpack sentences found in the source text.**
   - *Convey in two or more sentences ideas presented in one sentence in the source text.*

Paraphrase Revision Checklist

	Yes	No
1. Have you provided the full title of the source and identified its author?	_____	_____
2. Have you employed a variety of methods to paraphrase the material?	_____	_____
3. Have you checked to be sure your paraphrase accurately captures the author's ideas?	_____	_____
4. Have you remained as objective as possible in choosing language for your paraphrase?	_____	_____
5. Have you avoided offering your opinions on the topic of the reading or on the writer's style?	_____	_____
6. Have you checked your language to make sure each word you have chosen means what you think it means, has the connotation you want it to have, and fits the general tone of your paraphrase?	_____	_____
7. Have you reviewed your sentence structure for clarity and variety?	_____	_____
8. Have you provided appropriate transitions between the ideas you paraphrase?	_____	_____
9. Have you provided proper and accurate documentation?	_____	_____
10. Have you properly punctuated your documentation?	_____	_____

Chapter 4

SUMMARY

DEFINITION AND PURPOSE

Summarizing a reading involves two separate processes: (1) identifying the important material in the text and (2) restating the material in your own words. Because part of your job when writing a summary is deciding what to include from the reading and what to leave out, summaries are always shorter than the source text. Like paraphrases, summaries are always written in your own words (you can use quotations in a summary, but only sparingly), and they should be as objective as possible (you do not include in a summary your own opinions, beliefs, or judgments, and you try to use neutral language).

The ability to summarize readings is fundamental to academic, source-based writing. You will likely be summarizing information when you prepare a lab report, review a movie, write a research paper, or take an essay test. Instructors will often ask you to summarize articles or book chapters to be sure you can read carefully and critically, identify key ideas and important supporting evidence or arguments, and express that information clearly in your own words.

Sometimes summaries are part of a longer work. In a history research paper, for example, you may summarize the work of several different theorists while presenting an argument of your own. Other times, though, summaries will be "freestanding"—graded as independent formal essays. Your goal in writing them is to convey in your own words only the most important ideas, arguments, or findings in a reading. To write these types of assignments, you need to form a clear understanding of the source text, decide what to include in your summary and what to leave out, and choose language that clearly and objectively conveys the author's ideas.

Other times, though, you will use summaries to support a larger argument you are advancing in an essay. First, you may summarize the arguments or findings of experts who agree with the position you have assumed in your thesis; readers may accept your position if they see that other authorities support it as well. Second, you may summarize the work of experts who call into question your thesis. Doing so will help your work appear informed and balanced, again improving your credibility in the eyes of many academic readers. Be sure, though, that if you do summarize opposing views in your essay you then somehow address them. For example, following your summary, you can critique that information—pointing out its strengths and weaknesses—and explain how the opposing ideas affect the validity of your thesis.

Whether your summary is part of a longer work or stands on its own, it must make sense to someone who has not read the source text. If, for example, you are working as a loan officer in a bank and your boss hands you a financial report to summarize, she wants to be able to understand your summary without having to read the report herself. She wants *you* to read the report carefully and distill from it the information she needs to know.

TYPES OF SUMMARIES

In college you will probably write two different types of summaries: informative and explanatory. An informative summary simply conveys the author's main ideas, data, arguments, and supporting material; an explanatory summary conveys this information as well, but also indicates the overall structure of the source text, explaining how the author develops his or her assertions. Informative summaries are shorter than explanatory summaries and are usually incorporated into longer works or take the form of an **abstract**. Explanatory summaries are longer than informative summaries, follow the organizational scheme of the source text, frequently refer to the name of the source text's author, and usually serve as independent, freestanding essays.

Below are two different summaries of the opening lines of the Gettysburg Address, one informative and one explanatory. As you read them, note the differences in content, structure, and word choice.

Example 1

Source Text

> Four score and seven years ago our fathers brought forth on this continent, a new nation, conceived in Liberty and dedicated to the proposition that all men are created equal. Now we are engaged in a great civil war, testing whether that nation, or any nation so conceived and so dedicated, can long endure.

We are met on a great battlefield of that war. We have come to dedicate a portion of that field, as a final resting place for those who here gave their lives that that nation might live.

Informative Summary

Eighty-seven years ago the United States was founded on the idea that all people are created equal. Currently a civil war is testing whether such a nation can survive. A portion of this battlefield is to be designated as a cemetery for those who fought in the war.

Explanatory Summary

Lincoln opens the Gettysburg Address by remarking that eighty-seven years ago the United States was founded on the idea that all people are created equal. He next points out how the country is engaged in a civil war that will determine whether such a nation can survive, then acknowledges the occasion of the speech: to dedicate part of a great battlefield as a cemetery for the combatants.

Notice that the point of the informative summary is simply to capture in your own words the important ideas found in the source text. In an explanatory summary, though, you repeatedly refer to the author of the work and indicate how the piece was organized through your choice of verbs ("opens," "points out") and transition words ("next," "then").

QUALITIES OF A GOOD SUMMARY

Informative and explanatory summaries need to be comprehensive, brief, accurate, neutral, and independent.

- *Comprehensive*—it conveys all the important information in the reading.
- *Brief*—it conveys this information concisely.
- *Accurate*—it correctly conveys the author's ideas, findings, or arguments.
- *Neutral*—it avoids judgments concerning the reading's topic or style.
- *Independent*—it makes sense to someone who has not read the source text.

COMPREHENSIVE

Your summary needs to include all of the important ideas, assertions, or findings contained in the source text as well as the most significant information or arguments the author provides to support them. When you paraphrase a passage, you try to capture in your own language everything the author has written. However, when you summarize that same passage, you have to be more selective in choosing material to include. You need to identify what you believe to be the most important material in the passage and include only that in your summary. In this way your summary is comprehensive—you have not left out any important information.

Does that mean that if a number of people were summarizing the same article, all of their essays would be identical, at least in content? No. Determining what to include in a summary requires judgment. Each individual writer must decide what is most important in the source text. Some writers will make good choices; some will make poor choices. Even those making good choices may decide to include different information. Consequently, students assigned to summarize the same reading will likely produce slightly different essays. If you carefully and critically read the source text before you begin to write your summary, and if you check your work against the source text before you turn it in to be sure you have included all of the important information, you will probably produce a comprehensive summary.

BRIEF

In writing a summary, you have to balance two concerns: you want your summary to be comprehensive, but you also want it to be brief. The point of writing a summary is to *reduce* a text to its most essential information. In a summary, brevity is usually achieved through carefully selecting your content and words. First you need to include (1) the reading's primary ideas, arguments, or findings, and (2) the primary means of support the author offers for his or her contentions. Second, you must always be concerned about word count: if you can say something gracefully in four words rather than five, say it in four; if you can condense material by cutting unnecessary prepositions or adjectives, cut them. Composing a good summary requires disciplined writing.

ACCURATE

Your readers depend on you to be accurate in your summary. You have to be careful not to misrepresent—purposefully or accidentally—what the author wrote. Instead of reading the source text, your readers are depending on you to provide them a thorough, accurate, and fair overview of the piece. Misrepresenting an author in your summary is unfair to both your reader and the original author. However, accuracy can be hard to maintain. Because in a summary you are substituting your language for the author's, even slight changes in words can drastically alter the meaning of a passage. Therefore, when you review your summary, check it against the source to be sure you have accurately represented what the author wrote. Make sure you have not misrepresented the author's ideas or findings either by omitting some important information or by using inaccurate, slanted, or vague language.

NEUTRAL

Summaries should be objective. No matter how much you would like to praise or criticize an author's argument, interpretation of data, or style of writing, such comments do not belong in a summary. In a summary you do not present your views on the topic the author is addressing, you do not comment on the quality of the author's argument or writing, and you do not voice any of your opinions at all. Instead, you try to present what the author has written accurately and objectively. When reviewing your summary, make sure you have not included your own opinions and that you have used objective language. By avoiding highly charged or judgmental terms, you can help ensure that your summary is neutral, balanced, and fair.

When there are problems with objectivity in a summary, more often than not they appear in one of three places: at the beginnings of paragraphs, in the middle of long paragraphs, and at the very end of the piece. At the beginnings of paragraphs, students sometimes react to the material contained in the previous paragraph; instead of moving on to summarize the author's next point, they respond to the previous one. In the middle of paragraphs, students sometimes begin to debate the author. They may notice that the author has presented a weak argument, for example, and feel compelled to point that out. Such criticisms are appropriate for a critique, not for a summary. Finally, at the ends of summaries, students sometimes add the kind of concluding line commonly found in high school book reports, "Overall, I really liked this book because. . . ." or "Though I found the author convincing, sometimes I had a hard time. . . ." Such statements do not belong in an objective, neutral summary.

INDEPENDENT

Your summary ought to make sense to someone who has not read the source text. Keep in mind the purpose of a summary. If, for instance, your employer asks you to summarize a report, she wants to learn from your summary the main points of the report without having to read the original text. Your summary must be able to stand on its own—read independently, it has to make sense. To achieve this goal, you need to pay special attention to word choice when drafting your summary. For example, are there any terms that, taken from the context of the source text, will need to be defined in your summary? Have you included in your summary any pronouns that refer to an antecedent in the source, not to an antecedent in your summary? Have you referred to people who were identified in the source but are not identified in your summary?

To make sure your summary is independent, let someone read it who has not read the source text before you turn it in for a grade. Ask that person to mark any words or passages he or she finds confusing.

HOW TO SUMMARIZE A TEXT

READ, REREAD, AND ANNOTATE THE SOURCE TEXT

Obviously, the first step in writing a summary is to read the material you are summarizing. As you read through it for the first time, try to get a sense of the passage's main ideas and structure—a sense of what the author covers and the order in which the ideas are presented. Next, read the material again, only more slowly this time. As you reread, carefully mark the passage, highlighting important material and taking notes in the margin that identify the main points, key supporting information, and the structure of the piece.

If you are summarizing a paragraph, locate and mark the topic sentence. If there is no topic sentence, paraphrase the main point of the paragraph in the margin. If you are summarizing an entire essay or article, locate the thesis. If the author states the thesis, underline it and make a note in the margin. If the thesis is implied rather than stated, paraphrase the main point of the piece at the end of the passage. If the source text has headings and subheadings, note how they help structure the piece.

SUMMARIZE EACH SECTION OF THE SOURCE TEXT

Identify the major sections of the piece—where the author discusses one idea or develops one argument or explores one finding. These sections may consist of a single paragraph or a group of paragraphs. In the margin of the passage or on a separate sheet of paper, briefly summarize each section of the text. Using your own words, note the primary idea, assertion, or finding being developed in each section along with the primary supporting material the author provides—the most effective example, the most telling statistic, the most important authority cited.

CHECK THE SECTION SUMMARIES AGAINST THE SOURCE TEXT

The brief summaries you produce of each section of the source text will help you incorporate the material into a longer essay you are writing, compose an abstract of the source text, or produce an explanatory summary of the reading. Now is a good time to check these brief summaries against the source text to ensure they are accurate, neutral, comprehensive, and clear.

HOW TO WRITE AN ABSTRACT

As stated earlier, the goal of an informative summary is to convey as briefly and accurately as possible the primary content of a source text or perhaps just a certain section of that text. When you incorporate summarized material into a longer essay you are writing—a report or research paper, for example—you may introduce the material by referring to the author's name and/or the title of the piece before you add it to your essay. A special form of an informative summary in academic writing is an abstract. Abstracts are usually paragraph-long informative summaries of a reading and frequently accompany scholarly texts. Most often located under the title of the text, an abstract provides a succinct overview of the reading, informing readers of the text's primary assertions, findings, or arguments. When you are engaged in a research project, abstracts can be invaluable: when you locate a source text that looks interesting, by reading the abstract alone you can decide whether to read the entire piece or move on to the next one.

After you draft your abstract, be sure to check it against the original to ensure that the abstract is comprehensive and independent—it ought to make the main points of the reading clear to someone who has not read the text. Also be sure that you are paraphrasing the source text throughout your abstract: the language you use should be yours. Sometimes you might have to quote specific terms the author has used if they are particularly important or novel.

HOW TO WRITE AN INFORMATIVE SUMMARY ESSAY

An informative summary is longer and more detailed than an abstract, covering the author's primary assertions, findings, and arguments, as well as how they are supported. Informative summaries frequently follow the source text's organization—summarizing the text's first main point first, the second main point next, and so on. This is not necessary, however, if using a different organizational strategy would make your summary stronger. In the end, your informative summary should be comprehensive, brief, accurate, neutral, and independent.

In the *opening section* of your essay, introduce the topic or context of the reading, provide the source text's full title and the full names of its authors, and state your thesis. You might also want to provide the author's credentials or the publication information of the source text (where and when it was originally published). Your thesis will be a paraphrase of the source text's thesis.

In the *body* of your informative summary, paraphrase the primary content of the source text. You may want to use the one-sentence summaries of each section you composed earlier as a guide. Just paraphrase the content of the readings—do not embellish or editorialize. Your goal is to write a thorough summary of the source text that is both clear and neutral. Do not comment on the text's content, style, or structure. Plagiarism can be a problem with summarizing a text: be sure you paraphrase the material properly. You may quote material in an informative summary, but you should use quotations sparingly.

Informative summaries do not have conclusions like other forms of source-based essays. Instead, you close your paper by summarizing the source text's last key assertion, finding, or argument. Do not editorialize at the end of your summary—do not include any judgmental statements like "Overall, the author did a good job of presenting her ideas" or "The piece was extremely interesting and easy to read." Your summary should be neutral and objective.

As always, review your rough draft against the source text as you revise to ensure that your summary is comprehensive and that you have adequately covered the source text's primary content.

HOW TO WRITE AN EXPLANATORY SUMMARY ESSAY

As with an informative summary, an explanatory summary conveys the primary content of a text. However, it describes not only what the reading says but also how it is put together through frequent references to the author's organizational strategy. When a teacher asks you to write a summary of a text, this is the type of document he or she usually has in mind: an explanatory summary of the reading that is comprehensive, brief, accurate, neutral, and independent.

In the *opening section* of your summary—usually the first paragraph or two—introduce the topic of the source text, give the title of the piece you are summarizing, mention the name and credentials of the person who wrote the piece, and include your thesis. In a summary, your thesis will likely be a paraphrase of the source text's thesis.

In the *body* of your summary, present in your own words the author's primary assertions, conclusions, or findings, as well as the supporting examples or statistics you believe your readers will need to know to understand and appreciate the author's contentions. Use as a guide the brief summaries of each section of the text you wrote earlier. An explanatory summary is different from an informative summary because in the body of your essay you will make frequent references to the author of the piece and explain how the source text is structured through your use of transitions. Assume you are working with an article by Alice Smith. Your explanatory summary will include many passages such as these: "Smith opens her essay by . . . ," "Next, Smith discusses . . . ," "Smith's third main argument is . . . ," and "Smith concludes her essay with. . . ." All of these example passages include the author's name and some listing or transition word (e.g., "first," "next," "then"). You do not have to use the author's name in every sentence, just when you are moving from your summary of one section of the source text to another section so your reader has a clear sense of the source text's structure.

Generally, summaries do not need a *conclusion*; simply end your essay with a summary of the author's last point. If you want or need a formal conclusion, make it a brief restatement of the author's thesis.

Once you have finished the rough draft of your explanatory summary essay, reread the source text to ensure that you have captured all of the important content of the reading. To be sure that your summary is clear, ask someone who has not read the source text to read your summary and identify any passages he or she finds confusing. Remember: unless you are told otherwise by your teacher, assume your audience has not read the source text. Also check the tone of your summary. It ought to be objective and neutral.

DOCUMENTATION

Summarized material should be documented. Many students do not feel they need to document summaries because they are using their own language to convey the author's ideas. However, when you write a summary, you still need to give the author credit for those ideas, arguments, or findings. Documentation also tells your readers where they can locate the source text if they want to read the whole piece themselves.

Reading

Following are three summaries—an abstract, an informative summary, and an explanatory summary—of the following article, "From *Animal House* to *Big Brother*: Student Privacy and Campus Security in an Age of Accountability" by Ron Chesbrough. It originally appeared in *Student Affairs Leader*.

From *Animal House* to *Big Brother*: Student Privacy and Campus Safety in an Age of Accountability

Ron Chesbrough

Ron Chesbrough is the vice president of student affairs at Hastings College in Nebraska. He is also a member of Student Affairs Leader's editorial board.

Two Scenarios: A student at a large university spots a gun on the desk of a fellow student during class. Frightened, the student sends a text message to someone outside of the classroom, who in turn contacts the University Police Department. Members of the University Police respond immediately, going to the classroom and removing the student and the gun. In the process, they learn that the gun is a toy gun used in the popular game "Assassin." They seek out the other students engaged in the game and confiscate their toy guns. A notice is sent to the university community describing the incident in detail and announcing the prohibition of this game on university property.

A student at a small private college reports to the dean of students that she has read disturbing poems on the Facebook page of another student. The dean reviews the postings, which contain references to being unhappy and questioning the purpose of life. The dean calls the student in and requires that he undergo a full psychiatric evaluation based on the poems.

Background

We have learned recently many times over, and with crushing severity, what we have long known—that college campuses are risk-inherent environments. We have also been tragically reminded of a corollary fact—that one of our greatest challenges in creating and preserving safe environments on our campuses is the ability to find and strike a proper balance between our students' rights to privacy and their rights to a safe and healthy living and learning community. This is not a new imperative for us; it is simply one that has gained importance in recent years and with recent events on our campuses.

In the wake of the tragedy of the Virginia Tech shootings of nearly a year ago and those that have followed, the intersection of student privacy rights and community safety is, now more than ever, one where the traffic light is changing erratically. With the lights blinking red, green, and yellow on all sides, institutions and professionals are left largely to their own interpretations and intuitions about when to go, stop, or proceed with caution when it comes to student privacy rights.

From emergency alert text messaging systems to patrols of Facebook and MySpace and all things in between, colleges and universities are searching for the new right relationship with students in the interest of campus safety.

Take, for example, a recent article in the *Wall Street Journal*, featured in the February 1 issue of *Student Affairs Leader*, [that] described Cornell University's new "alert team" and related university-wide training to recognize and report signs of student emotional distress and behavioral concerns ("Bucking Privacy Concerns, Cornell Acts as Watchdog," *WSJ*, December 28, 2007). These practices place Cornell "squarely in the center of a debate over the rights of American college students," according to the article. Just what is the debate, we should ask, and how have we arrived here?

FERPA in Transition

The Family Education Rights and Privacy Act (FERPA) has long governed the treatment of student privacy rights in higher education. Its protections and allowances are familiar enough by now to not bear detailed repeating here, although a refresher on the various amendments to FERPA, particularly over the past decade, is not a bad idea.

It is also useful to gain some familiarity with the shifting ground of case law in matters concerning student privacy rights and our duty to protect students from harm—whether from themselves or others.

Two recent cases worth reading again in this regard are *Shin v. Massachusetts Institute of Technology* and *Schieszler v. Ferrum College*. In both cases the courts found a special duty to care (in these cases to prevent self-harm) based on the unique relationship between students and their academic institutions.

If we set aside the legitimate and compelling question of an institution's ability to "prevent" harm to all students at all times, we can see that the real central issue here is one of discernment and disclosure.

In other words, how do we maximize our ability to detect or discern threats to safety on our campuses? And once a possible or plausible threat is discerned, to what end and to whom do we disclose this information? And finally, what are the implications of this discernment/disclosure puzzle for our relationships with students?

Disclosure

To begin, we might begin to rethink our definition of "privacy" in this scenario. We might also question the original intent of FERPA—asking who and what it was originally intended to protect, and from whom. Here it seems clear that the original and ongoing intent of FERPA is to provide reasonable protections against undue intrusions into the education records of students by those not determined under law to have legal rights to such access, and to provide students with their own due process rights to the same information pertaining to them and being held by the institution.

Where institutions keep information of a disciplinary nature, and where such records do not constitute criminal records, the same protections and rights have applied, with notable recent amendments allowing disclosure of information to certain others (e.g., parents, victims) when in relation to certain types of potentially noncriminal records (e.g., campus drug/alcohol violations, sexual violence).

Similarly, allowances exist for disclosure of certain medical or treatment records held by the college to both parents and others as directed by FERPA. Finally, the Jeanne Clery Act not only allows but also requires both annual reporting and timely warning (in cases of an ongoing threat) of criminal activity on our campuses.

Given these provisions for disclosures under FERPA and what some would argue is a gross historic misunderstanding of more general parental disclosure rights of the institution under FERPA, it is fair to say that we have often overstated protections afforded to students under this law.

It is safe to say, historically speaking, that we have often erred on the side of overprotecting these rights, especially in the grey areas of FERPA, that many would argue still exist after more than four decades and numerous amendments to the legislation. But are we moving too far, too fast into this new intersection of student privacy rights and campus safety?

Who Bears Responsibility—and to Whom

In their recent look at critical issues for student affairs professionals, Arthur Sandeen and Margaret J. Barr had this to say about the rising complexity of the question of student safety on our campuses: "Legal requirements, institutional missions, parental expectations, chronic psychological problems of students, and student behaviors require both the profession and institutions to answer this fundamental question" (Sandeen & Barr, 2006, p. xii). Their chapter entitled "Who Has the Responsibility for the Lives of Students?" is an attempt to answer this question.

I would argue, as perhaps they would, that this is not a new question, but an old one posed in a new context, with new and literal meaning imbued by recent events on our campuses nationwide. It is not the "who" in this question that has changed, but the "how."

How are we differently responsible for the lives of our students in the current era, and as importantly, how do we best fulfill that responsibility when faced with the kinds of scenarios posed at the outset? Put differently, how do we begin to rebalance the right of all students to a safe learning environment with the rights of those whom Sandeen and Barr refer to as our "disturbed" students, students whom they suggest are coming to us in increasing numbers (Sandeen & Barr, pp. 155–180)?

A Beginning Attempt

To begin, we need to revisit this concept of the disturbed student, first coined by Ursula Delworth, two decades ago in a definition that has almost eerie accuracy in today's environment of high-stakes disturbance on campus. These students, according to Delworth, can demonstrate an outward (anger and lashing out) or inward (depression and withdrawal) focus, and hold the potential to harm themselves or others (Delworth, 1989). Of particular importance, according to Delworth, is our recognition and response to those students who are both disturbed and disturbing of the campus environment.

We should refresh ourselves in the clear communication roles and responsibilities among campus administrators and health professionals established by Hollingsworth and Dunkle (2005) in our coordinated response to these students. And in this we should heed Arthur Sandeen's (1989) reminder that "an institution that decides it can not afford the resources required to address the problems of the disturbed and disturbing student may discover the costs of ignoring them are too great" (p. 61).

We should set clear behavioral expectations of our students in the classroom, in residence halls, and in the campus community at large. These are simply those norms that we insist should exist for the emotional and physical comfort of all members of the learning community, and they should be indexed to those instances where a certain behavior might reasonably be seen as imposing on or limiting the rights of other members of the community to a safe, healthy, and positive living and learning environment.

We should anticipate both the reasonable accommodations that might be made to students unable to meet certain behavioral requirements consistently or in all settings, and the absolute limits of behaviors that fall outside of the pale of the learning community. And we should clearly state what our responses would be in either case.

If we intend to not allow play guns on campus, or if concerning posts to a Facebook page are cause for college response, then students should be aware of this and the consequences of behaving in these ways. This takes hard and deliberate thought and imagination, and ought to involve a hearty dose of student and faculty input. It will lead to debate, discussion, and disagreement—but it is precisely this debate that needs to occur, in anticipation of difficult campus events rather than in response to them.

Students, and their parents, should be made to understand that college officials will exercise their full rights under FERPA to share information deemed necessary between college health officials and administrators; between administrators and parents or appropriate outside officials; and between members of the faculty, staff, and administration of the college or university as allowed by law—to ensure the safety of all members of the community to the best of their ability. And the mechanisms for said sharing should be transparent and readily understood by all members of the learning community and its constituents.

Implications

Some will point to a chilling effect of a learning environment so characterized. I would argue the opposite. What is chilling in the present environment is the relative lack of these types of safeguards in the face of clear and repeated evidence of our need for them. What is discomforting is the unease we feel at the intersection of student privacy rights and community safety—and it is discomforting not just for student affairs practitioners, but also for students, staff, faculty, and parents alike.

In this environment, it falls most logically to student affairs professionals to take the steps necessary to police this intersection and to work with others to develop the proper new traffic signals for this new environment.

It can also be said that this new posture poses new legal liability threats to institutions that may be claiming, by making such clear statements of intent, to be able to prevent bad things from happening on their campuses. Arguably, due diligence does in fact take on a new meaning in light of commitments like those described to attempt to discern and report potential threats to safety.

At the same time, we enter an environment wherein the lack of such stepped-up attempts may soon be discerned as a failure of due diligence, particularly as institutions move individually in these directions and as findings from various reports raise the question for legislators, parents, and others as to what our due diligence ought to, in fact, entail.

Still others may find such measures to have a discriminatory or dampening effect on admission for those students disclosing in that process a pre-existing diagnosis that may make them more prone to "concerning" exhibitions of behavior. All the better that college officials have more knowledge about the support needs of incoming students from the outset in order to put in place appropriate accommodations and to take the "handoff" from those who have provided supports and accommodations up to that point.

We might ask ourselves which student with special needs has the better chance of success in a college environment: the student who has disclosed what has helped him or her to succeed, or the student with special needs who is silent?

Finally, to those who herald this as a return to an even more extreme version of *in loco parentis* in our relationships with our students than we have so recently congratulated ourselves on shedding, I would say not quite, and perhaps the opposite. If we look closely at the legal doctrine of *in loco parentis,* we find that it describes a circumstance in which one assumes responsibility for a child without formally adopting the child. Applied to schools and colleges, this has typically meant that, by our actions, policies, and formal statements we agree to accept responsibility for our students "in the place of" their parents. Here I am arguing for something different.

I am arguing that we find new ways to hold our students accountable for their own actions, and that we involve parents as active partners and appropriate outside professionals whenever the need is evident. Staying with the Latin, we might call this the doctrine of *modestus pateo,* or, loosely translated, orderly openness. More simply, we might think of where we have arrived in higher education in this and many other regards as the *age of accountability*—to our students, their parents, our colleagues, and our many constituencies—in all that we do.

If campus safety at your institution is still something that the student affairs professionals are left to figure out and stew over, then it is time for change. The issues raised here about student privacy, campus safety, and our right relationship with our students in this age are not student affairs issues; they are issues of concern and importance to every member of the college community. Everyone must join the conversation. We are all standing at the same intersection, and the lights are still flashing red, green, and yellow.

References

Delworth, D., (1989). Dealing with the Behavioral and Psychological Problems of Students. New Directions for Student Services, no. 45. San Francisco: Jossey-Bass.

Hollingsworth, K. and Dunkle, J. "Dealing with Disturbed and Disturbing Students: Best Practices and Their Implications." Paper presented at the National Association of Student Affairs Personnel Administrators Annual Conference, Tampa, FL, 2005.

Sandeen, A., (1989). "A Chief Student Affairs Officer's Perspective on the AISP Model," in U. Oelworth (Ed.), Dealing with the Behavioral and Psychological Problems of Students. New Directions for Student Services, no. 45. San Francisco: Jossey-Bass.

Sandeen, A. and Barr, M. J., (2006). Critical Issues for Student Affairs: Challenges and Opportunities. San Francisco: Jossey-Bass.

Wall Street Journal, Bucking Privacy Concerns: Cornell Acts as "Watchdog," 12/28/2007.

Schieszler v. Ferrum College, 233 ESupp.2d 796 (W.D.Va. 2002).
Shin v. MIT, 2005 Mass. Super. LEXIS 333, *32.

SAMPLE ABSTRACT

The author discusses a dilemma facing campus administrators: keeping students safe while protecting their privacy rights. The author argues that administrators may be reading FERPA restrictions too narrowly, failing to collect and share information that might protect students. He states that student safety is the responsibility of the entire campus community and that students' parents may play a more expanded role in forming a viable solution to the problem.

SAMPLE INFORMATIVE SUMMARY ESSAY

Ron Chesbrough's "From *Animal House* to *Big Brother*: Student Privacy and Campus Safety in an Age of Accountability" examines the tension that exists between college administrators' desire to keep students safe while at the same time protecting their privacy rights. After the fatal shootings at Virginia Tech, administrators have had to reconsider their existing policies.

Difficulties arise due to the Family Education Rights and Privacy Act (FERPA), legislation that has long served to protect student privacy. FERPA may prevent college authorities from addressing potential threats because doing so might violate a student's right to privacy. On the other hand, courts have held that colleges have a special obligation to protect the safety of students.

To address this dilemma, school administrators need to revisit the intention of the FERPA act, which was to ensure the privacy of student academic records and provide students due process rights. Allowances in the law enable schools to contact parents and other appropriate authorities about student health or disciplinary problems. In the past, schools have erred on the side of caution and have generally not communicated their concerns about particular students to off-campus authorities.

Particular attention needs to be paid to how schools address "disturbed" students who for medical or non-medical reasons pose a possible threat to other students. Schools must employ health care professionals who can help these students, convey to all students the school's standards of behavior, develop plans for accommodating students who need extra help coping with school, ban firearms from campus, and inform parents and students that school administrators will use all the powers FERPA provides to protect the safety of everyone on campus.

Some may find these actions too severe or opening colleges up to litigation should a tragedy occur. However, proper due diligence on the school's part is required to ensure student safety and privacy. Central to this effort is holding students accountable for their actions and enlisting the help of students and parents when formulating new school policies.

SAMPLE EXPLANATORY SUMMARY ESSAY

In "From *Animal House* to *Big Brother*: Student Privacy and Campus Safety in an Age of Accountability," author Ron Chesbrough explores how to make college campuses safer. Reacting to recent tragedies such as the killings at Virginia Tech, Chesbrough questions how best to balance the needs for student safety and student privacy, especially in light of safeguards guaranteed by the Family Education Rights and Privacy Act (FERPA). He argues that college administrators may need to operate out of a more liberal reading of FERPA regulations and enlist the aid of parents to meet the needs of students who may pose safety issues for a school.

Chesbrough opens his essay by defining a problem all college administrators face: how to ensure student safety while maintaining the privacy rights of students who may exhibit threatening or concerning behavior or actions. Central to the debate is how administrators interpret the restrictions placed on colleges through FERPA. While agreeing that FERPA has many benefits, Chesbrough notes how two recent court cases have redefined schools' responsibilities to protect students from themselves and their peers. He then poses an additional question to consider: under these new interpretations of FERPA, how do college administrators know when to release information about students who might pose a risk to the school and when to keep such information confidential?

To answer this question, Chesbrough examines the original intent of FERPA: who was it intended to protect and from what? He concludes that the act was passed primarily to protect student academic records and to ensure students due process rights concerning the release of those records. However, Chesbrough notes, FERPA allows for the release of some student medical information to parents while the Clery Act compels college administrators to act in a timely manner and with due diligence to address campus threats.

Chesbrough then offers a number of initial steps that might be taken to improve campus safety within FERPA restrictions: better define what a school means by a "disturbed" student, establish a clear communication protocol across campus to respond to any dangerous situations, share with students what constitutes acceptable and unacceptable behavior, and clarify university policy regarding firearms and Facebook postings.

Closing his essay, Chesbrough contends that taking these steps will make campuses safer while still maintaining student privacy rights. While there is a threat to privacy in identifying students who have potentially harmful mental or emotional conditions, administrators can enlist the aid of parents to help ensure that these students receive the assistance they need and that the safety of other students is protected.

Summary Chart

HOW TO SUMMARIZE TEXTS

---

1. **Read, reread, and annotate the material.**

   Carefully read the material, paying particular attention to the content and structure of the piece.

   Reread and annotate the material, being sure to note:
   - *the thesis;*
   - *the primary assertions, arguments, or findings; and*
   - *the primary means of support for each point.*

2. **Write one-sentence summaries of each section of the text.**

   Identify the major sections of the reading, in which the writer develops one idea before moving on to the next.

   In your own words, restate the main point developed in each section of the text and primary means of support the author provides.

3. **Write the first draft of your summary.**

   Introduce the topic of the reading.

   Include, early in your essay, the author's full name and the full title of the piece.

   In the body of your summary, elaborate on the one-sentence summaries, clearly explaining the important content of the reading.

4. **Check the rough draft of your summary against the source text. As you review your work, make sure your summary is:**

   Comprehensive—you have included in your summary all of the author's important ideas, assertions, or findings.

   Accurate—in choosing words and selecting material for your summary, you have not misrepresented the author's positions or findings.

   Neutral—in choosing words and selecting material for your summary, you have attempted to be objective and fair.

   Independent—your summary will make sense to someone who has not read the source text.

5. **Rewrite your summary.**

   Based on your evaluation of your rough draft, make any needed changes in the content, organization, or language of your summary.

   If you are writing an explanatory summary, include any transition words you need to guide your reader through your work.

Summary Revision Checklist

	Yes	No
1. In the opening section of your summary have you:		
• introduced the topic of the essay?	_____	_____
• given the full title of the source text?	_____	_____
• given the full name of the author?	_____	_____
• included *your* thesis?	_____	_____
2. In the body of your essay do you summarize only one point at a time?	_____	_____
3. Have you accurately and fairly put into your own words all of the author's important findings, arguments, or ideas?	_____	_____
4. Have you identified the primary means of support the author provides for each finding, argument, or idea?	_____	_____
5. By cutting material or words, have you tried to make your summary as brief as possible while still being comprehensive?	_____	_____
6. To be neutral, have you avoided comments on the:		
• topic of the piece?	_____	_____
• author's ideas?	_____	_____
• author's style?	_____	_____
7. To help ensure that your summary will make sense to someone who has not read the original work, have you:		
• defined any unusual or technical terms?	_____	_____
• identified any people you refer to in your work?	_____	_____
• provided a sufficient context for understanding the author's assertions or findings?	_____	_____
8. Do you have adequate paragraph breaks and transitions?	_____	_____
9. Have you supplied proper documentation?	_____	_____

Chapter 5

RESPONSE ESSAYS

DEFINITION AND PURPOSE

Response essays ask you to examine, explain, and often defend your personal reaction to a reading. In this type of essay you explore why you liked the reading, agreed with the author, found the piece informative or confusing—whatever your response might be. There are no necessarily "right" or "wrong" reactions to material; instead, response essays are usually evaluated on the basis of how well you demonstrate an understanding of the reading and how clearly you explain your reactions.

Sometimes teachers grade response essays the same way they grade any other assignment. Other times they assign ungraded response essays—usually as a way to help students develop material for graded essays. Still other teachers combine response essays with other types of papers; for example, they might ask students to summarize and then respond to a reading, or to respond to a reading and then critique it. Sometimes teachers will specify which aspects of the text they would like you respond to in your essay (for example, the author's thesis or use of figurative language); other times they will leave the choice of content up to you. In short, the response essay is a very flexible assignment employed widely by teachers in college. Writing this type of paper helps you understand your personal reaction to what you read: what you think about the topic, how you judge the author's ideas, and how the words on the page affect you as a reader.

Effective response essays demonstrate a strong connection between the source text and your reaction. Your responses are triggered by what you read, by certain words on the page. It is important to keep that connection strongly in mind as you compose your response essay. First, you need to put into words your responses to the source text. Second, you need to identify which words on the page triggered those responses. Third, you need to determine, then explain for your reader, why and how those words triggered those responses.

In writing this type of essay, you cannot simply state your response and move on: "I liked this. I didn't like that." "This interested me; that puzzled me." Instead, you must develop and explain your response: what, *exactly*, is your response; what part of the text triggered it; what, *exactly*, is the relationship between the words on the page and your reactions to them? While the idea of "developing" your response may seem odd, remember that you are writing for a reader, not just for yourself. You want your reader to be able to understand and appreciate both your response and what led you to have it. Clearly, writing a response essay is more difficult than it might first appear.

QUALITIES OF A GOOD RESPONSE ESSAY

Part of what makes a good response essay difficult to write is that it must be honest, informed, clear, and well supported.

- *Honest*—it reflects your true responses.
- *Informed*—it reflects an accurate and thorough understanding of the source text.
- *Clear*—it makes sense to your readers.
- *Well supported*—it demonstrates a close link between your responses and the source text itself.

HONEST

A response essay should focus on your sincere, thoughtful reactions to what you read. You want to identify your responses to the material and explore their relationship to the text itself: What gives rise to your reactions? How do they affect your reading of the author's work? These essays are highly subjective— you focus on *your* reactions to the text. Consequently, you should not pretend your responses are other than what they truly are. If you found a work boring, for example, do not claim that you found it intriguing simply because you think that is the way you are *supposed* to respond.

INFORMED

Can your responses, then, ever be "wrong"? In one sense, they cannot—your responses are your responses. That does not mean, though, that all responses to a reading are equally informed. If, for example, your response is based on a misunderstanding of the source text—if you criticize an author for saying something she never said—then your response is misguided. Responses can also be naive, shortsighted, or biased. These responses are not, in a sense, "wrong," but neither are they very insightful. Informed response essays are based on a clear understanding of the source text: the more you know about a topic, author, or reading, the more likely your response will be informed.

Take, for example, an experience I had a few years ago. I asked a group of students to respond to a satirical political essay before we discussed the piece in class. The students who recognized the satire produced fine response essays. However, the students who did not understand that the author was being satirical terribly misread the piece and produced misguided essays. Their responses were honest—the responses accurately reflected their reading of the text—but they were not informed.

CLEAR

When your readers finish your response essay, they should understand (1) how you reacted to the reading and (2) how your reactions are tied to the source text. Problems with clarity often arise from weak content, weak organization, or poor word choice.

Problems with clarity involving **content** occur when the person writing the response essay fails to state clearly the nature of his or her response, fails to identify which aspect of the source text gave rise to that response, or fails to explain the relationship between his or her response and those aspects of the text. Unless all three are clearly stated and explored, readers can be left confused about the nature of your response to the reading.

Other problems with clarity involve **organization**. Be sure that your essay has a fully developed opening and closing section and a clearly stated thesis. A good response essay also explores only one reaction at a time and provides clear transitions between the various sections of the paper. Problems with clarity can occur when you shift too quickly from discussing one response to discussing another—without a good transition, the change of focus might not be clear to your reader.

Finally, problems with clarity often involve the **language** used in response essays. Too often students use vague language to explore their reactions—words that mean something to them but nothing to their readers. Though response essays are highly subjective, when you turn them in for a grade, they must be addressed to a more public audience. Good response essays can be difficult to write for just this reason: you have to find language that clearly and efficiently communicates to others your subjective responses to a reading.

WELL SUPPORTED

In good response essays, students support and explain their reactions to the text with specific, elaborated examples. If, for example, a student claims that she was offended by an author's illogical assertions, she should quote some of those passages and explain why she finds them illogical. If another student reads the same work and finds the same passages convincing because they match his experiences, he should also quote some examples and explain why he finds them convincing. In either case, the student supports her or his responses by citing from the source text examples that gave rise to them and then clearly explaining the relationship between those examples and their responses.

WRITING THE RESPONSE ESSAY

CAREFULLY READ THE MATERIAL

The problem with many response essays is that the students have not *fully* understood the source text before they begin to write. Some students respond to only part of the reading, without indicating they understand how the material fits into the author's overall thesis. As a result, their responses often seem limited or even biased; their work tends to ignore important issues raised in the source text. Other students simply misread the source text—basing their response on something the author neither wrote nor intended.

Therefore, when you are assigned to respond to a reading, read it several times and briefly summarize it before you write your essay (see Chapter 4 for advice on writing summaries). Summarizing the piece first can help ensure that your response will be based on a full and accurate understanding of the text's content, structure, tone, and thesis.

Explore Your Responses to the Reading as You Annotate the Text

To develop material for your response essay, as you read and annotate the text, note your responses briefly in the margin of the piece. Sometimes just jotting down a key word or two will do; other times you may need to write out a question you have. Even punctuation marks, such as exclamation points or question marks, can help you keep track of your reactions. When you are finished, expand on these notes at the end of the reading or on a separate sheet of paper. Your goal is to capture in a few sentences your overall response to what you have just read. These notes will form the basis of your response essay. In deciding what to mark and what kinds of comments to write as you read the source text, try answering the following questions.

How Do You React Emotionally to What the Author Has Written?

Your subjective, emotional reaction to a reading is a good place to start generating material for a response essay. Does the text make you angry? Excited? Bored? To explore these reactions, ask yourself several questions:

1. What, exactly, has the author written that makes you feel this way?
2. At what point in your reading did you have these reactions?

3. Which words on the page or ideas caused this response?

4. In short, what has the author done to make you respond this way? Examine the choices the writer made concerning content, organization, and style. What aspects of the text contribute to your response?

As you try to capture your responses in writing, carefully examine your reactions and, when possible, tie them to specific words, passages, or graphics in the text.

How Do the Ideas Offered in the Reading Compare with Your Experience or Your Sense of Reality?

We have all had the experience of hearing or reading something that has a ring of truth or falsehood. Something in a reading makes sense to us because it squares with our experience; it sits right with what we have come to understand about the world. As you reread and annotate a reading, note which of the author's ideas you tend to agree with or question based on their match to your own experience.

There is a real danger, though, in judging what others say by the standards of our experience alone. All of us bring to a reading important but limited experiences. When an author's statements do not match our sense of reality, we should not act defensively and immediately dismiss her ideas. Likewise, simply because we tend to agree with an author does not mean we ought to accept her ideas uncritically. Writing a response essay will give you the chance to question what you believe in light of what the author writes and to understand how your experiences influence the way you react to new ideas.

How Do the Ideas Offered in the Source Match What Others Have Had to Say on the Topic?

When you read a source, you bring with you not only what you think and feel based on your own experience, but also what you know, what you have already learned from your reading and education. There is no reason to ignore this knowledge when you write your response essay. In fact, whether the source text confirms or contradicts what you already know about the topic may be one of the reasons for your reaction to the piece. Be sure to note any reactions you have based on the match between the author's ideas and those proposed by other authors you have read.

COMPOSE YOUR ROUGH DRAFT

When you write your response essay, you will need to introduce the source text, provide your reader with a brief summary of its content, and then develop and clarify your reactions.

Introduce Your Topic, Source Text, and Thesis

When composing the opening of your response essay, you have four goals: introduce the topic of your essay, introduce your source text, state your thesis, and capture reader interest. Once you introduce the source text's topic, provide its title and its author's full name. Your thesis for this type of essay will be a statement of your overall response to the reading and, if you like, an indication of how you will develop or explore that response in the body of your paper. If you employ an "open" thesis statement for your essay, you will indicate your overall response to the piece:

- I found parts of the essay confusing.
- Reading this essay proved to be an emotional challenge.

If you employ a "closed" thesis statement for your essay, you will indicate your overall response to the source text and also indicate how you will develop that response in the body of your paper:

- I found parts of the essay confusing, especially its structure and many of its allusions.
- Because members of my family have been touched by the issues the author discusses, reading this essay proved to be an emotional challenge.

Either type of thesis can work equally well.

Finally, to capture reader interest you may want to use one of the following strategies:

- Open your essay with a provocative or interesting question raised by the reading or your response to it.
- Open your essay with an interesting quotation from the reading.
- Open your essay with a personal anecdote or hypothetical story related to the topic of the reading.
- Open your essay with a reference to a current controversy or public issue related to the topic of the reading.

Summarize the Source Text

After introducing the source and stating your thesis, give a brief summary of the reading. Generally, this summary will be only a paragraph or two long, highlighting the reading's most important findings, conclusions, or arguments. In the summary, anticipate what you will address in the body of your response. For example, if you know you will be questioning the validity of some of the author's claims, summarize his claims in this part of your essay. When they come up again in the body of your response, your reader will remember them and will be able to follow your assertions more easily.

State and Explain Your Responses Clearly and Concisely

In the body of your essay, you explore your responses, clearly and thoroughly, one at a time. This process might sound simple, but clearly and thoroughly stating and explaining your response to a reading can be difficult primarily because it is *your* response. The language you use when describing your reaction may make perfect sense to you but might well be unclear to your reader. For instance, if you were reading someone else's response essay and the writer complained that the source text made her feel "wheezy," would you really know what the person meant? Perhaps her explanation would make it clear, but the language she uses to characterize her response may hinder her readers' ability to understand her reaction. Therefore, a first step in clarifying your response for a reader is to choose language that others can understand. Likewise, explain the terms you use. For example, if you contend that a source is "confusing," explain whether you had difficulty understanding the writer's language, findings, structure, or some other aspect of the text.

Next, be sure to provide specific examples from the source text to help your reader understand each response. When you have a particular response to a reading, something on the page triggered it. In your essay, identify those "triggering" passages before you explain the dynamics of your response. For example, if you contend that a source text is confusing, identify and perhaps quote a passage you cannot understand, then explain what it is about the writing you find difficult to follow (the logic of the passage? the wording? the structure?).

WRITE YOUR CONCLUSION

With a response essay, your conclusion should restate your overall response to the source text, echoing your thesis. To give a sense of closure to your essay, you should also try to mirror the strategy you employed to capture reader interest in the opening of your essay. For example, if you opened your essay with a question, return to that question in your conclusion and provide an answer. If you opened with an anecdote or story, refer back to it in your conclusion, perhaps indicating how that anecdote or story turned out. If you opened with a quotation from the source text, consider closing with a quotation as well.

REVISE YOUR ROUGH DRAFT

As you revise the rough draft of your response, pay particular attention to your assertions, organization, language, and support.

Review Your Assertions

When you review the assertions you make in your response essay, your primary concern is accuracy:

- Have you truly captured your reactions to the reading?
- Have you openly, honestly, and thoroughly explored your response to the material?
- Does your essay offer an accurate representation of your reaction?
- When other people read your essay, will they be able to understand and appreciate your reaction?

To check your assertions, first reread the source text and see whether you still feel the same way about it. Even a short time away from a reading may enable you to reconsider your reactions—maybe your views have changed. If they have changed, revise your essay. Also, in reviewing the source text, be sure you reread the annotations you originally made. Have you addressed the concerns, questions, and reactions you noted as you earlier annotated the piece?

Review Your Support and Explanations

As you revise your response, examine the way you illustrate and explain each of your responses. Remember that your responses should be tied to specific aspects of the source text, such as words, images, and graphics. When you compose your response, you need to explain for your reader the link between the source text and your reaction. In the body of your essay, you should state a response, point out what aspect of the reading led to that reaction (perhaps quoting the passage), and then explain clearly and thoroughly how that material led you to that response. As you revise your draft, make sure you accomplish all three goals in each section of your essay.

Review Your Organization

Next, when you review the organization of your rough draft, check to be sure you have fully developed opening and closing sections and have a clearly stated thesis. In the body of your essay, be sure that you are developing only one response at a time. Often when you write your rough draft, examining one reaction will lead you to a new response, one you have not previously considered. That is one of the real powers of writing: it not only helps you capture ideas in words but often will help you generate new ideas as well. When this happens, some writers will follow that new idea even if it does not belong in that part of the essay, knowing that in the next draft they can place it elsewhere. Other writers prefer to write a note to themselves to explore that new idea later, not wanting to lose track of the idea they are currently exploring. When you review your rough draft, check to see that you are developing only one response at a time in your essay.

Finally, be sure you indicate to your reader—through paragraph breaks and transition words—when you shift focus from one response to the next. Adding these signals to your paper makes it easier for your reader to follow your line of thought. Since you are writing about *your* responses, you know when you have changed focus; your readers, though, may have a harder time recognizing the structure of your essay. Adding appropriate paragraph breaks and transitions can help.

Review Your Language

As indicated earlier, word choice—finding and choosing appropriate terms to express your reactions—can be truly problematic when you are writing response essays. First, your initial reactions to what you read may be so

emotional or so abstract that you cannot put them into words. You may struggle to find appropriate language. Second, your first efforts at finding words
may result in highly "private" writing; since they arise from your own knowledge and experience, the terms you use may make sense only to you. In this
case, you need to find terms that can communicate your responses to others.
Before you turn in the final draft of your response essay, be sure to have someone else read your work, someone you trust to give you an honest appraisal of
your language. Ask that person to indicate any part of the response he or she
does not understand because of the words you are using.

SAMPLE RESPONSE ESSAY

This sample essay is responding to "From *Animal House* to *Big Brother*:
Student Privacy and Campus Safety in an Age of Accountability" by Ron
Chesbrough, found in Chapter 4 of this book. If you are unfamiliar with the
article, read it before you read the following response essay.

A Response to "From *Animal House* to *Big Brother*: Student Privacy and Campus Safety in an Age of Accountability"

As Ron Chesbrough notes in his essay "From *Animal House* to *Big
Brother*: Student Privacy and Campus Safety in an Age of Accountability," violent episodes, like the shootings at Virginia Tech a few
years ago, have raised serious concerns about campus safety. Though
my roommates and I have discussed this issue a few times and we
had a floor meeting to talk about emergency evacuation plans at the
beginning of the term, Chesbrough's essay offers a perspective on
the problem I hadn't considered: what policies can the administration
at a school adopt to keep students safe? As a first-year college student, I found Chesbrough's essay informative but not very helpful. In
the end, he fails to offer very satisfying answers to the problems he
raises.

Campus safety happens to be an issue I deeply care about. When
the shootings took place at Virginia Tech, my sister was attending
Redford College, which is not far from Blacksburg. When I saw the
news coverage on television, I started texting my sister immediately
to be sure she was safe. She told me the students at her school were
also keeping up with the story and were a little nervous, but that
I shouldn't worry because nothing like that had ever happened at
her school. I felt better, but when I thought about it, what happened
at Virginia Tech could happen at any college in the country.

In his article, Chesbrough explores why the violence erupted at
Tech and offers a few explanations I had not considered. For example,
I had not realized the kinds of restrictions administrators face due
to FERPA (the Family Education Rights and Privacy Act). From
orientation, I knew that my school could not release my grades to
anyone without my permission, even to my parents. I was surprised

to learn that FERPA regulations might have kept the administrators at Virginia Tech from acting to prevent the attack. According to news reports, the shooter, Seung-Hui Cho, had a history of mental illness and had received treatment while a high school student. Virginia Tech officials were not informed of Cho's past problems, and when they started to emerge on campus, FERPA regulations kept administrators from telling his teachers or others because Cho did not authorize the release of that information.

This whole scenario is just frustrating, especially for college students like me who could be facing similar dangers and not know it. Respecting a student's privacy is important, but should privacy concerns override safety concerns? I think they should not, but Chesbrough explains why Tech officials did not act. "Due diligence" requirements would seem to mandate that school officials step in to restrain students whose behavior is dangerous. Not acting could open them to lawsuits should something terrible happen. However, if the officials act and nothing happens, they can be sued for violating the student's privacy. I agree with Chesbrough that parents should inform the administration of any pre-existing emotional problems a student has when he or she enters school. Instead of using this information to keep these students from enrolling at the school, administrators can use it to provide the students the help and support they need.

Chesbrough's ideas all seem reasonable, but I do not think they offer a satisfying response to the problem. When balancing the privacy needs of potentially dangerous students against the safety of the entire student body, schools should take greater action to protect the campus. Simply knowing up front which entering students have emotional and psychological problems does not guarantee that the students will seek appropriate treatment on campus. Instead, schools should consider provisional admission for these students— they can stay enrolled on campus as long as they verify that they are getting appropriate treatment. The treatment can remain private, but the administration has to make sure it is taking place. The campus health center could be charged with monitoring the students' treatment, ensuring that they are taking the medicines or receiving the counseling they need. If these students do not keep up with the treatments prescribed by their physician or therapist, they are expelled from school. This solution is not perfect because treatments are not perfect, but it would help ensure that troubled students are receiving help while maintaining their privacy.

Most of the time I do not worry about campus safety. If students take the right precautions on our campus (like never going out alone at night, staying with groups of people, locking doors and windows at night), they can avoid problems. After reading this article though, I am more concerned. How many students on campus have severe emotional or psychological problems? How many of them are getting help so that our school does not become another Virginia Tech?

Summary Chart

HOW TO WRITE A RESPONSE ESSAY

1. **Carefully read the material.**

   Your goal is to form a clear understanding of what the writer has to say.

   Identify and be able to paraphrase the writer's thesis and main assertions or findings.

2. **Reread and annotate the text.**

   As you reread the material, begin to examine your responses by asking yourself the following questions:
   - *How do I react emotionally to what the author has written?*
   - *How do the ideas offered in the source text match my experience and my sense of reality?*
   - *How do the ideas offered in the text match what others have had to say about the topic?*

   Note in the margin your responses to these questions using some combination of the following:
   - *key words*
   - *questions*
   - *statements*
   - *punctuation marks*

   When you are finished, write out in a few sentences your response to the material.

3. **Compose your rough draft.**

   Introduce the topic, your source text, and the full name of the author or authors.

   Summarize the source text.

   State and explain your responses clearly and concisely one at a time.
   - *State your response. (For example, the material made you angry.)*
   - *Explain the terms you are using. (What do you mean by "angry"?)*

Summary Chart: How to Write a Response Essay *(continued)*

- *Tie that response to some aspect of the source text.*
  What material in the reading made you feel that way?
- *Explain how that material gave rise to that response.*
  Why or how did that material make you feel angry?
- *Write your conclusion.*
  What was your overall response to the material?

4. **Revise your rough draft.**

Review your assertions about your reactions.
- *Are they honest?*
- *Are they informed?*
- *Are they clear?*
- *Are they well supported?*

Review your organization.
- *Are your opening and closing sections constructed well?*
- *Are you addressing one response at a time?*
- *Are there clear transitions between the responses you explore?*
- *Are your responses tied to some guiding thesis?*

Review your language.
- *Are you using terms your readers are likely to understand?*
- *Are you invoking a consistent tone, not becoming too informal, too angry, or too satiric when that does not match the tone of your response as a whole?*

Review your support.
- *Have you tied each response to some aspect of the text?*
- *Have you added enough textual references to make clear the connections between the reading and your response?*
- *Have you attempted to explain those connections?*

RESPONSE ESSAY REVISION CHECKLIST

	Yes	No
1. In the introductory section of your essay, have you:		
• introduced the topic of the reading?	_____	_____
• included the full and exact title of the reading?	_____	_____
• included the full name of the author?	_____	_____
2. Have you included a thesis statement that captures your overall response to the reading, a response you develop in the body of your essay?	_____	_____
3. Have you considered the accuracy and honesty of the responses you include in your essay?	_____	_____
4. Have you clearly stated each of these responses?	_____	_____
5. Have you explained the terms you used to characterize each of your responses?	_____	_____
6. Have you tied each of your responses to some aspect of the source that gave rise to it?	_____	_____
7. Have you explained how the material in the source text gave rise to your response?	_____	_____
8. Have you developed only one response at a time in each section of your essay?	_____	_____
9. Have you used language that helps your reader understand when you are moving from your discussion of one response to the next?	_____	_____
10. Have you explained the connection between each response you explore and your overall thesis?	_____	_____
11. Have you reviewed the language you use to make sure your word choice is clear and accurate?	_____	_____

Chapter 6

CRITIQUE

DEFINITION AND PURPOSE

While response essays focus on your personal reactions to a reading, critiques offer a more formal evaluation. Instead of responding to a reading in light of your experience and feelings, in a critique you evaluate a source text's quality or worth according to a set of established criteria. Based on your evaluation, you then assert some judgment concerning the text—whether the reading was effective, ineffective, valuable, or trivial. Critiques, then, are usually argumentative. Your goal is to convince your readers to accept your judgments concerning the quality of the reading.

These judgments will be based on certain criteria and standards. **Criteria** are certain aspects of a reading that serve as the basis of your assessment—for example, the text's style or use of evidence. **Standards** serve as the basis for evaluating a criterion—what makes a certain "style" good or bad, acceptable or unacceptable? What counts as "valid" evidence in a reading? When you critique a reading, you will employ either **general** academic criteria and standards (those used to evaluate source material in many fields) or **discipline-specific** criteria and standards (those used by scholars in a particular field of study and generally not applicable to material studied in other disciplines).

In college composition courses you may learn how to critique a source text using general evaluative criteria—for example, how to assess the quality of a reading based on its structure, style, or evidence. These criteria can help you evaluate source material in a variety of classes. In your other college courses you may learn discipline-specific evaluative criteria typically used to assess source material in that field of study. For example, in an English literature course you may learn the criteria used by scholars to critique a poem or a play; in an accounting class, you may learn to employ the criteria and standards experts in that discipline use to critique a financial report or prospectus.

Students often find the idea of writing a critique intimidating: they are not sure what the assignment is asking them to do, how to generate material for their paper, what to include in their essay, how to support their assertions, or what tone to assume. However, you are probably more familiar with this type of writing than you realize since you are often exposed to one special form of critique: the movie review. If you ever listened to movie critics argue over a film, you are familiar with the basic structure of a critique. If you ever discussed the strengths and weaknesses of a movie and tried to get a friend to go see it (or to avoid it), then you have already engaged in critique. Examining how a film critic writes a review of a movie can help you understand how to write a critique of a reading.

THE FILM REVIEW AS CRITIQUE

First, consider the nature of a movie critic's job: he watches a film, analyzes and evaluates what he sees, forms some judgment based on that analysis and evaluation, then writes his review, trying to clarify and defend his judgments with specific references to the film and clear explanations of his assertions. In writing his review, the critic does not address every aspect of the film; he addresses only those aspects of the movie that best support his judgment of it. If, for instance, he thought a film was wonderful, he would address in his review only the aspects of the film that, in his opinion, made it exceptional— for example, the direction, the photography, and the acting. If he thought the film was uneven—some parts good, other parts weak—he would offer in his review examples of what made the film effective (maybe the plot or the lighting) and examples of what made it ineffective (maybe the musical score and the special effects).

Think about the way you discuss a film with someone. Maybe the conversation runs something like this:

"So, did you like the movie?"

"Yeah, pretty much. I wasn't too sure about some of the dialogue—sounded pretty lame sometimes—but the special effects were good and the acting was ok."

"The acting was just 'ok'? What didn't you like? I thought the acting was great."

"Well, there was that scene early in the film, right before he shot the guy; I just didn't buy it when he . . ."

In this conversation, one friend asserts a position about the film, is challenged, then begins to defend or explain her view. To convince her friend to accept her judgment, she will likely discuss specific aspects of the film she believes best illustrate her views.

Most of us are accustomed to talking about movies, television shows, or CDs this way—we form and defend judgments about what we see, hear, and read all the time. However, we are usually more comfortable evaluating movies than we are critiquing arguments, book chapters, or lab reports. First, when it comes to movies, we are probably familiar with many of the source texts—we have seen lots of films—and most of us feel we can knowledgeably discuss what we have seen. We can generate, fairly easily, lots of examples from a movie to support our views. Second, we know *how* to talk about films: we know how to identify and discuss particular aspects of a movie—certain criteria—that influence our judgment. We know that when we analyze a movie we can address the dialogue, the acting, the special effects, and so forth. Finally, we know the standards usually applied to evaluate various aspects of a film; we know what passes for good dialogue, good acting, good special effects, and so on. In short, when we discuss a movie, we know how to *analyze* it (what parts to focus on for review), *evaluate* it (what kinds of questions to ask of each part when assessing its quality), and *defend* our assertions (how to examine specific scenes from the film that support our judgments).

These are the same basic skills you employ to critique readings in college. To critique readings, you need to engage in:

- *Analysis*—break readings down into their essential parts.
- *Evaluation*—assess the quality of those various parts.
- *Explanation*—link your judgments to specific aspects of the readings and make those connections clear and convincing to your reader.

Even though you have probably engaged in this process quite often when discussing movies or television shows, you may have a hard time using these skills to critique readings. First, you are probably less familiar with how critiques look and sound than you are with how movie reviews look and sound. When you are assigned to write a critique, no model may come to mind. Second, the readings you are asked to critique in college can be hard to understand. You cannot critique a reading until you are certain you know what it has to say. Finally, you are probably less familiar with the criteria and standards used in college to analyze and critique readings than you are with the criteria and standards used to review films. When you are asked to critique a philosophical essay on the nature of knowledge, do you know how to break that reading down into its key parts and what kinds of questions to ask of each part to determine its quality? When asked to critique a chapter of your history book, do you know what to look for, what questions to ask? Learning how to critique readings such as these is a central goal of your college education, a skill you will obtain through practice in many different disciplines.

Examining how a movie critic organizes a review can also help you understand how to structure a critique. For example, a critic typically opens her review with a "thesis" that captures her overall assessment of the film. This thesis may take the form of a statement early in the review, a graphic placed beside the review—for example, five stars or two stars—or frequently a comment at the end of the review. Sometimes the critic will love the film; she will give it five stars and a rave review. Sometimes she will hate the movie; she will give it one star and a terrible review. Still other times she will have a split decision; she will give it two and a half stars and in her review acknowledge the strengths and weaknesses of the movie. Next, the critic will typically offer a brief summary of the film so her readers can follow what she has to say in the review. Then, in the body of the review, she will address only the aspects of the film that best illustrate or defend her thesis: she will introduce a particular element of the film (for example, the special effects), comment on its quality (claim they were especially effective), describe a specific example or two from the film (perhaps the climactic battle scene), and explain how that specific example illustrates or supports her judgment (what made the special effects in that battle scene especially good).

Writing a critique involves much the same process. After reading the text, you'll form a judgment of its quality or worth based on some set of criteria and standards. This judgment will form the thesis of your critique, which you will explain or defend in the body of your essay, with specific references to the reading. As you draft your thesis, keep in mind the range of judgments open to the film critic. To critique a reading does not necessarily mean only to criticize it. If you honestly think a reading is weak, based on your evaluation of its various parts, then say so in your thesis. If, however, you think the writing is quite strong, say that. If your judgments fall somewhere in the middle—some parts are strong while others are weak—reflect *that* in your thesis. Your thesis should reflect your carefully considered opinion of the reading's overall quality or worth, whatever that judgment may be.

Next, you will offer a brief summary of the text so your reader can follow what you later have to say about the piece. In the body of your critique, you will choose for examination only the parts of the reading that best illustrate or defend your thesis: you will introduce a particular aspect of the reading (for example, its use of statistical evidence), describe a specific example or two from the reading (perhaps the way statistics are used to support the author's second argument), and explain how that specific example illustrates or supports your judgment (what makes the statistical evidence especially compelling in this section of the text).

Your goal, then, in writing a critique mirrors in many ways the goal you would have in writing a movie review. Your task is to analyze and evaluate a reading according to a set of established criteria and standards, pass judgment on the reading's quality or worth, then assert, explain, and defend that judgment with specific references to the reading.

WRITING A CRITIQUE

Writing a critique typically involves five steps:

1. Read and annotate the text.
2. Analyze and evaluate the piece: break it down into its primary parts and judge the quality of each part.
3. Write your thesis and decide which aspects of the reading you will focus on in your essay.
4. Compose your rough draft.
5. Rewrite your critique.

This is only a general guide. Throughout college you will learn much more specific, specialized ways to critique readings.

STEP 1—CAREFULLY READ AND ANNOTATE THE SOURCE TEXT

Before you start to write a critique, you first need to develop a clear understanding of the reading you are about to analyze and evaluate. The material you read in college is often challenging; you have to work hard to understand exactly what the author is asserting. However, this work is unavoidable; it makes little sense to evaluate a piece of writing when you are not completely sure what point the author is attempting to make. As you annotate a reading for a critique, keep in mind the following suggestions.

Note the Author's Thesis, Primary Assertions, and Primary Means of Support

Be sure that you mark the author's thesis, highlight and summarize each major point the author makes, and highlight and summarize how the author supports each idea, argument, or finding. Are the thesis and primary assertions clearly stated? Does the thesis direct the development of the paper? Are the assertions supported?

Note the Author's Use of Graphics, Headings, and Subheadings

What graphics does the author provide? What is their function? How do the headings and subheadings organize the piece? Are the headings and graphics effective? How so?

Note the Author's Diction and Word Choice

Consider the kind of language the writer is employing. Is it formal or informal? Is it overly technical? Is it appropriate? Do you notice any shifts in diction? Are some sections of the text more complicated or jargon laden than others? Note any strengths or weaknesses you see in the author's language.

Note the Author's Tone

What seems to be the author's attitude toward the topic? Is he being serious, comical, or satiric? Does the tone seem appropriate, given the writer's topic and thesis? Are there any places in the text where the tone shifts? Is the shift effective?

Note the Author's Audience

When you finish the piece, determine what the writer seemed to assume about his readers. For example, is the writer addressing someone who knows something about the topic or someone likely reading about it for the first time? Is the author assuming readers agree or disagree with the position being forwarded in the piece? Judging from the content, organization, diction, and tone of the piece, which type of reader would tend to accept the author's position and which would tend to reject it?

Note the Author's Purpose

Decide, in your own mind, the primary aim of the piece. Is the author attempting to entertain, inform, or persuade readers? Where in the text has the author attempted to achieve this aim? How successful are those attempts? Note at the beginning or end of the reading your comments concerning the author's purpose.

Summarize the Piece

After you have read and studied the text, write a brief summary of the piece, either at the end of the reading or on a separate sheet of paper (see Chapter 5 for tips on summarizing a reading).

When you have finished reading, rereading, and annotating the source text, you should have a clear understanding of its content, organization, purpose, and audience. Try to clear up any questions you have about the reading before you attempt to critique it. You want your critique to be based on a thorough and clear understanding of the source text.

STEP 2—ANALYZE AND EVALUATE THE READING

Think back to the process of putting together a movie review. When a movie critic watches a film, she forms a judgment of its quality based on certain things she sees or hears. As she watches the movie, she will examine and judge certain aspects of the film, including its

acting	scenery	lighting
direction	costuming	plot
special effects	dialogue	action
theme	pacing	makeup
cinematography	stunts	music

Her evaluation of these various elements of the film, either positive or negative, will form her overall judgment of the movie—her thesis.

What, then, should you look for when analyzing a reading? What parts of a text should you be isolating for evaluation as you read and reread the piece? In part, the answer depends on the course you are taking: each discipline has generally agreed-on ways of analyzing a reading. As you take courses in anthropology or physical education, you will learn how experts in those fields analyze readings. However, analyzing certain general aspects of a reading can help you better understand material in a wide variety of classes. Regardless of the course you are taking, you might start to analyze a reading by identifying its:

- thesis and primary assertions or findings,
- evidence and reasoning,
- organization, and
- style.

Once you have analyzed a reading, isolating for consideration its essential elements, your next task in writing a critique is to evaluate the quality of each element. Here, writing a critique differs from writing a response essay. In a response essay, your goal is to articulate your personal, subjective reaction to what you have read. In a critique, though, you are expected to evaluate the reading according to an established set of standards. Think about the movie critic's job again. Most reviewers employ similar criteria and standards when evaluating a film. If a reviewer decides to critique the musical score of a film, she knows the types of evaluative questions one usually asks about this aspect of a movie: How did the music contribute to the overall mood of the film? Was it too intrusive? Did it add humor or depth to the scenes? Did it heighten drama? Was it noteworthy because of the performers who recorded it? Her answers to these questions will lead to her final assessment of this particular aspect of the film. (Of course, another reviewer employing the same criteria and applying the same standards could come to a different judgment concerning the quality of the music in the film; for example, one reviewer might think it heightened the drama in a particular scene while another might think that it did not.)

In college, you will quickly discover that the criteria and standards used to evaluate readings vary from discipline to discipline. Teachers often employ evaluative criteria unique to their field of study, especially in upper-level courses in which the professor is preparing students to enter a profession. In lower-level courses designed to introduce you to a field of study, you may encounter a different sort of problem. Teachers in different fields may be asking you to employ the same or similar criteria, but their standards are very different. Suppose, for example, you are asked to evaluate the style of a particular reading in both an education and an English course. Your job is the same—determine, stylistically, whether this is a well-written essay. Your answer might be different in each class. According to the stylistic standards advocated by the school of education, you might have before you a well-written essay. According to the standards advocated by the English department, however, the same piece of writing might not fare so well. As always, work closely with your teacher when evaluating a reading to be sure you are applying an appropriate set of criteria and standards.

Below is a series of questions you can ask to begin your analysis and evaluation of a reading's thesis, assertions, evidence, reasoning, organization, and style. The questions are meant to serve only as general guidelines. Your teacher may have much more specific questions he would like you to ask of a reading or evaluative criteria he would like you to employ. Together, analysis and evaluation enable you to critique a reading. After breaking a reading into its essential parts and judging their effectiveness, you will form the thesis of your critique—a judgment of the reading's quality or worth—which you will develop and defend in your essay.

Analyzing and Evaluating a Reading's Thesis and Primary Assertions or Findings

Sometimes identifying an author's thesis can be relatively easy—you can point to a specific sentence or two in the text. Other times, though, an author will not state his thesis. Instead, the thesis is implied: some controlling idea is directing the development of the piece even though the author never puts it into words. If this is the case, you will need to identify and paraphrase this controlling idea yourself and evaluate it as if it were the thesis.

Many times, identifying the author's primary assertions or findings can be easy, too. For example, if the author has made effective use of paragraph breaks, topic sentences, headings, or graphics, you can usually locate his primary assertions fairly easily. However, do not rely on these means alone to identify the author's main ideas. Not every source text is well written. Often, important assertions get buried in an article; key findings may be glossed over. As you analyze a reading, make up your mind about its primary assertions or findings independently of what the author may indicate. Also, be sure to distinguish between primary assertions and their evidence or support. Very often a student will identify as a primary argument of a reading some statistic or quotation that the author is using only as a piece of evidence, something to support the actual assertion he is trying to make. In short, to analyze a reading's thesis and primary assertions, consider the following questions:

- What is the author's thesis? Is it stated or unstated? If stated, highlight it; if unstated, paraphrase it.
- What are the primary assertions in the reading? Highlight each one and paraphrase it in the margin of the text.
- What is the primary means of support offered to illustrate or defend each assertion? Again, highlight this material.

In determining the quality of a reading's thesis and primary assertions or findings, you can begin by questioning their clarity, effectiveness, and organization. The thesis, whether stated or implied, should direct the development of the piece. Each major finding or assertion should be clearly stated and linked to that thesis through the effective use of transitions, repetition of key terms, or headings. To evaluate an author's thesis and findings, you might begin by asking the following questions. If your answers are positive, you can likely claim that the author has effectively presented and developed his thesis; if your answers are negative, be sure to articulate exactly where the problems exist.

- Is the thesis clearly stated? Does it control the organization of the piece? Is it consistently held or does the author shift positions in the essay?
- If the thesis is implied rather than stated, does it still serve to direct the organization of the piece? Are you able to paraphrase a comprehensive thesis on your own, or does the material included in the piece preclude that?
- Are the author's assertions or findings clearly stated?
- Are the author's assertions or findings somehow tied to the thesis?

Analyzing and Evaluating a Reading's Evidence and Reasoning

Here you identify two separate, but related, aspects of a reading: (1) the evidence an author provides to support or illustrate her assertions and (2) the author's reasoning process or line of argument.

First, try to identify the types of **evidence** the author uses to support her thesis. (At this point do not try to evaluate the effectiveness of the evidence—that comes later.) The types of evidence used to support a thesis vary greatly in academic writing, so again be cautious when using these guidelines to analyze the readings in any particular course. However, to begin your analysis of the evidence an author employs, you might try asking yourself this series of questions:

- In supporting her assertions or findings, what kinds of evidence has the author employed? Has the author used any of these forms of evidence:

statistics	empirical data	precedent
expert testimony	emotional appeals	case histories
personal experience	historical analysis	analogies

- Where in the article is each type of evidence employed?
- Is there a pattern? Are certain types of evidence used to support certain types of claims?
- Where has the author combined forms of evidence as a means of support?

Analyzing an author's **reasoning process** is more difficult because it is more abstract. First, you identify how the author uses evidence to support her thesis and how she develops and explains her ideas, her line of reasoning. Second, you examine the assumptions an author makes concerning her topic and readers. As she wrote the piece, which aspects of the text did she decide needed more development than others? Which terms needed clarification? Which argument or explanation needed the most support? In analyzing the author's reasoning process, these are the kinds of questions you might ask:

- In what order are the ideas, arguments, or findings presented?
- What are the logical connections between the major assertions being made in the piece? How does one idea lead to the next?
- What passages in the text explain these connections?
- What assumptions about the topic or the reader is the author making?
- Where in the text are these assumptions articulated, explained, or defended?

Standards used to assess the quality of an author's evidence and reasoning will vary greatly across the disciplines. For example, you might want to determine whether an author offers "adequate" support for his or her thesis. However, what passes for adequate support of a claim will be quite different in an English class from what it will be in a physics course or a statistics course: these fields of study each look at "evidence" and the notion of "adequacy" very differently. In other words, a good general strategy to employ when critiquing a reading is to determine the adequacy of its evidence; however, how that strategy is implemented and what conclusions you reach employing it can vary depending on the course you are taking. Part of learning any subject matter is coming to understand how scholars in that field evaluate evidence; therefore, answer the following questions thoughtfully:

- Does the author support her contentions or findings?
- Is this support adequate? Does the author offer enough evidence to support her contentions?
- Is the evidence authoritative? Does it come from legitimate sources? Is it current?
- Does the author explain *how* the evidence supports or illustrates her assertions?
- Has the author ignored evidence, alternative hypotheses, or alternative explanations for the evidence she offers?
- In developing her position, are there any problems with unstated assumptions? Does the author assume something to be the case that she needs to clarify or defend?
- Are there problems with logical fallacies such as hasty generalizations, false dilemmas, or appeals to false authorities?
- Has the author addressed the ethical implications of her position?
- Is the author's reasoning a notable strength in the piece? Is it clear and convincing?

Your answers to these questions will help you determine whether there are serious problems with the evidence and reasoning employed in the reading.

Analyzing and Evaluating a Reading's Organization

Here you want to identify how the author orders the material contained in the reading. As the author develops a set of findings or ideas, lays out his reasoning for the reader, and offers examples and explanations, what comes first? Second? Third? How has the author attempted to mold these parts into a coherent whole? When analyzing the organization of a reading, you might begin by considering the following questions:

- In what order are the ideas or findings presented?
- How has the author indicated that he is moving from a discussion of one point to the discussion of another point?
- What is the relationship between the thesis of the piece (stated or unstated) and the order in which the assertions or findings are presented?
- How has the author tried to help the reader understand the organization of the reading? Identify where in the text the author has used any of the following to help guide his readers through the text:

headings and subheadings	repetition of key terms
transition words or phrases	repetition of language from the thesis
transition paragraphs	repetition of names or titles

If any aspect of a reading's organization makes it difficult for you to understand the author's message, you may want to examine it in your critique. Clearly explain the nature of the problem and how it damages the reading's effectiveness. Likewise, if the organization is especially strong, if it significantly enhances the reading's clarity or effectiveness, you can point that out in your critique and explain how it helps the text. Here are some questions to consider when evaluating the source text's organization:

- Is there a clear connection between the major assertions of the essay? Does there seem to be some reason why one idea precedes or follows another?
- Are all the assertions clearly related to the overall thesis of the piece?
- Has the author provided headings or subheadings to help readers follow his line of thought? How effective are they?
- Has the author provided adequate transitions to help readers move through the writing and see the logical connection between the assertions he is making? How effective are they?

Analyzing and Evaluating a Reading's Style

Stylistic analysis is a complicated process—an academic specialty in and of itself within the field of English studies. In most of your college courses, though, when analyzing style you will likely focus on issues of clarity and convention. First, when you critique a reading, you might comment on its clarity. You will want to identify which aspects of the writer's word choice and sentence structure help you understand what she has to say or which serve to complicate your reading of the text. Other times, you may ask a different set of questions concerning style, especially in upper-division courses. Your assignment will be to assess how well an author adheres to the stylistic conventions of a discipline. For example, you might explore whether the author's language, tone, and syntax are appropriate for a particular type of writing or field of study. To begin your analysis of style, here are some questions you might ask about a reading:

- What level of diction is the writer employing (how formal is the prose)?

    formal   conversational
    informal   a mixture

    Identify which words or passages lead you to this conclusion.
- What is the tone of the piece (what is the author's apparent attitude toward the topic)?

    serious   satiric   involved
    humorous   angry   detached

    Identify which words or passages lead you to this conclusion.
- What kind of language is used in the piece? Identify any passages using specialized language, emotional language, or jargon.
- What types of sentences are used in the reading?

    simple, compound, complex, complex-compound
    long or short
    active or passive
    a mixture of types

When critiquing a reading's style, you evaluate elements of the author's prose such as diction, tone, word choice, and syntax. Again, stylistic standards vary greatly across the disciplines. While teachers in various disciplines may use similar terms when describing "good" style in writing—that it should be clear and concise, for example—how they define their criteria is likely to vary. Clear and concise writing in a chemistry lab report may have little in common, stylistically, with clear and concise writing in a philosophy research report. Below are some questions that might help you begin to evaluate certain aspects of an author's style. Remember, though, that your answers may well depend on the stylistic standards accepted by a particular discipline:

- How would you characterize the diction of the piece: formal, informal, or somewhere in the middle? Is it consistently maintained? Is it appropriate? Does it contribute to the effectiveness of the piece?
- How would you characterize the tone of the piece? Is it inviting, satiric, or humorous? Is it appropriate, given the topic and intent of the piece? Does the tone enhance or damage the effect of the writing?

- Is the author's word choice clear and effective? Or does the writer rely too heavily on jargon, abstractions, or highly technical terms?
- Is the author's word choice needlessly inflammatory or emotional? Or do the words convey appropriate connotations?
- Are the sentences clearly written? Are any of the sentences so poorly structured that the source is difficult to read and understand?
- Are the sentence types varied? Is the syntax appropriate given the audience and intent of the piece?

STEP 3—WRITE YOUR THESIS AND DECIDE WHICH ASPECTS OF THE READING WILL BE THE FOCUS OF YOUR ESSAY

At this point you need to develop your thesis and decide which aspects of the reading you will use to develop your critique. To formulate your thesis, you need to decide which elements of the source text best illustrate or defend your judgment. You want your reader to understand and accept your thesis, but this acceptance can come about only if you clearly explain each claim you make about the reading and offer convincing examples from the text to illustrate and defend your contentions.

In your critique, you do not need to address every aspect of the source text. Remember how the movie critic supports her assertions about a film. No review addresses every aspect of a movie. Instead, the critic chooses to discuss in her review only those elements of the movie she thinks most clearly and effectively illustrate her judgment. Maybe she will address only the acting and direction, perhaps only the dialogue, plot, and special effects. Perhaps she will choose to mention, only briefly, the costuming and musical score, then concentrate more attention on the film's cinematography.

Follow the same line of thinking when you decide which aspects of the reading to address in your critique. To illustrate and defend your thesis, you may choose to look only at the logic of the piece and its structure. However, you may choose to ignore both of these and concentrate, instead, on the writer's style. Maybe you will decide to look briefly at the evidence the author offers, then concentrate most of your attention on the organization of the piece. Your decisions should be based on two fairly simple questions: (1) Which aspects of the reading most influenced your judgment of its quality and worth? (2) Which aspects will best illustrate and support your thesis? Choose only those aspects of the reading for examination in your critique.

Your thesis in a critique is a brief statement of what you believe to be the overall value or worth of the source text based on your analysis and evaluation of its parts. In stating your thesis, you have several options. You can say only positive things about the reading, only negative things, or some mixture of the two. Your main concern at this point is that your thesis honestly and accurately reflects your judgment.

Also, your thesis statement can be either open or closed. In an open thesis statement, you offer your overall judgment of the piece and nothing else. In a closed thesis statement you offer your judgment and indicate which aspects of the reading you will examine when developing your essay. Below are some sample open and closed thesis statements for a critique—positive, negative, and mixed.

Positive Thesis Statement

Open

Jones presents a clear, convincing argument in favor of increased funding for the school district.

Closed

Through his use of precise examples and his accessible style, Jones presents a clear and convincing argument in favor of increased funding for the school district.

Negative Thesis Statement

Open

Jones's argument in favor of increased funding is not convincing.

Closed

Due to numerous lapses in reasoning and problems with the organization, Jones's argument in favor of increased funding is not convincing.

Mixed Thesis Statement

Open

Although uneven in its presentation, Jones's argument in favor of increased funding for the school district is, ultimately, convincing.

Closed

Even though there are some problems with the organization Jones employs in his report, his use of expert testimony makes his argument for increased funding for the schools convincing.

STEP 4—WRITE YOUR ROUGH DRAFT

While there are many ways to structure a critique, the suggestions that follow can serve as a general guide.

Introductory Section

- Introduce the topic of the reading.
- Give the title of the piece and the name of its author.
- Give your thesis.
- Summarize the source text.

In the opening section of your critique you should introduce the topic of the reading and give your reader its exact title and the full name of its author. You will also include here your thesis and a brief summary of the reading (one or two paragraphs long). The exact order you choose to follow when covering this material is up to you. Some writers like to begin with the summary of the source text before giving their thesis; some prefer to give their thesis first. Overall, though, your introductory section should only be two or three paragraphs long.

Body

- Examine one element of the reading at a time.
- Cite specific examples of this element from the reading.
- Explain your evaluation of each example you offer.

State the Criteria and Your Judgments

In the body of your critique you will explain and defend the judgment you made in your thesis, focusing on one aspect of the reading at a time. Topic sentences in a critique usually indicate the element of the reading you will be examining in that part of the essay and whether you found it to be a strength or liability—for example, "One of the real strengths of the essay is the author's use of emotional language."

Offer Examples

Whatever aspect of the reading you are examining—logic, word choice, structure—give your readers specific examples from the source text to clarify your terms and demonstrate that your judgment is sound. For example, the student who hopes to prove that the author's use of emotional language is one of the reading's strengths will need to quote several examples of language from the text he believes are emotional. Offering only one example might not be convincing; readers might question whether the student isolated for praise or criticism the single occurrence of that element in the text.

Explain Your Judgments

After you have specified the aspect of the reading you are examining in that part of your critique and have offered your readers examples from the text, you will need to explain and defend your judgment. After the student mentioned above cites a few specific examples of the author's emotional language, he will need to explain clearly and convincingly *how* that language strengthens the author's writing. Simply saying it does is not good enough. The student will have to explain how this type of language helps make the author's article clearer or more convincing.

In this section of the critique you will likely develop and explain your unique perspective on the reading. Suppose you and your friend are critiquing the same reading. You could both agree that it is effective and could even choose to focus on the same elements of the reading to defend and illustrate this judgment; for example, you could both choose to focus on the author's use of evidence. The two of you will probably differ, though, in your explanation of how and why the author's use of evidence is strong. You will offer your individual assessments of how the writer effectively employed evidence to support his thesis.

Conclusion

- Wrap up the paper.
- Reassert the thesis.

In your concluding section, try to give your reader a sense of closure. Consider mirroring in your conclusion the strategy you used to open your critique. For example, if you opened your essay with a question, consider closing it by answering that question; if you began with a quotation, end with a quotation; if you opened with a story, finish the story. You might also consider restating your thesis—your overall assessment of the piece—to remind your readers of the judgments you developed in the body of your essay.

STEP 5—REWRITE YOUR CRITIQUE

In rewriting your critique, check to make sure your work is accurate, thorough, organized, and clear.

- *Accurate*—it reflects your true assessment of the source text.
- *Thorough*—you completely explain your assertions.
- *Organized*—readers can easily follow the development of your critique.
- *Clear*—you have explained all the terms you need to explain and supported any assumptions that might reasonably be questioned.

Check for Accuracy

When reviewing your work, first check for accuracy. You want to be sure that your essay reflects your honest assessment of the source text. Starting with your thesis, look through your essay to make sure the assertions you make, the supporting material you employ, and the explanations you offer accurately reflect your point of view.

Check the Development of Your Assertions

Next, make sure you have been thorough in developing your critique. Check to be sure you have offered examples from the source text to support and illustrate your claims and that you have explained your reasoning clearly and completely. Add material—quotations, examples, and explanations—where you think it is needed.

Check the Organization

As you review the organization of your critique, make sure your thesis guides the development of your essay. Are you examining only one aspect of the reading at a time? If not, move material around to improve the organization in your essay. Have you provided adequate transitions to help your reader move through the piece? Do you repeat key terms or provide transition words that remind your reader of your thesis or signal the relationship between the various assertions you make?

Check for Clarity

Check your critique for clarity. Have you used any terms that need to be defined? Have you made any assertions that readers would find unclear? Have you made any assumptions that need to be explained or defended? When necessary, change the content, word choice, or sentence structure of your essay to make your ideas more accessible to your readers.

READINGS

The essay "Zero Tolerance and Student Dress Codes" by Nathan Essex was published in *Principal*. "A Uniform Look," by Yasmine L. Konheim-Kalkstein, appeared in the *American School Board Journal*. Following the readings is a sample critique essay.

Zero Tolerance and Student Dress Codes

Nathan L. Essex

Nathan L. Essex *is a professor of law and president of Southwest Tennessee Community College.*

In recent years, zero-tolerance policies have emerged in public schools as a means of reducing and preventing violence. From their inception, most of these policies were aimed at deterring serious student offenses involving possession of firearms and other weapons, drugs, tobacco, and alcohol.

However, zero-tolerance is taking a different twist in a small Texas school district where over 700 students were suspended in a single month last year for violating a zero-tolerance dress code policy. Under its policy involving student dress, the suburban Duncanville Independent School District in Texas penalizes students in grades 7–12 with a one-day suspension for the first violation, two days for a second violation, and two days plus loss of school privileges for a third violation.

These suspensions, which attracted national attention and threats of lawsuits by parents, raise four fundamental questions:

- How far should school officials go in enforcing zero-tolerance policy relating to student dress?
- Does the student dress in question pose a health or safety hazard?
- Does student dress create material or substantial disruption?
- Is there an educational justification for zero-tolerance dress code restrictions?

There is little debate that school officials are vested with broad and implied powers designed to protect the health and safety of students and maintain a peaceful school environment. Consequently, school officials may promulgate *reasonable* rules and regulations necessary to address health and safety concerns and orderly conduct among students (Essex 2002). A central issue involving zero-tolerance in the Texas district is whether the dress code policy is reasonable. Emphasis on reasonableness centers around the well-established fact that students have protected constitutional rights and that those rights must be weighed against a compelling need to restrict them.

Courts have generally supported the view that school boards have the authority to regulate student dress and appearance if they become so extreme as to interfere with the school's favorable learning atmosphere (Alexander and Alexander 2001). Challenges to dress code enforcement have relied on a number of legal issues, including First Amendment freedom of speech and Fourteenth Amendment rights to due process and liberty. However, the courts have not consistently agreed upon application of these rules regarding dress code enforcement. For example, they have upheld regulations prohibiting excessively tight skirts or pants and skirts more than six inches above the knee, while disallowing regulations prohibiting Freda trousers, tie-dyed clothing, and long skirts.

Justifying Dress Codes

Codes that place restrictions on student dress are not unusual in public schools. However, they must be justified by demonstrating that the students' attire materially or substantially disrupts school operations, infringes on the rights of others, creates health and safety concerns, or focuses too much attention to students' anatomy. According to the *Tinker* ruling, disruption must be viewed as more than a mere desire to avoid the discomfort and unpleasantness that always accompanies an unpopular view or an unidentified fear or apprehension (*Tinker v. Des Moines Independent Community School District*, 393 US 503 at 511.89 S. Ct. 733, 21 L. Ed. 2nd, 731 1969).

However the courts provide broad latitude to school officials on matters involving dress so long as they provide a justification for invoking restrictions. Dress is generally viewed as a form of self-expression reflecting a student's values, background, culture, and personality. Thus, students must be provided opportunities for self-expression within reasonable limits. Student rights regarding dress must be balanced with school officials' responsibility to provide a safe, secure, and orderly educational environment for all students.

Therefore, while students have a responsibility to conform to reasonable dress standards, school officials have a responsibility to ensure that rules do not unduly restrict the personal rights of students. As school officials implement zero-tolerance policies, they are expected to do so in a thoughtful and deliberate fashion, ensuring that their approach is fundamentally fair and legally defensible. Dress codes that do not weigh the severity of the infraction, the student's history of past behavior, the process, and First Amendment rights are at best highly risky.

A Drastic Dress Code

In the Duncanville District, the dress code forbids Capri pants, overalls, sweat pants, athletic jerseys, tank tops, and tube tops. Students are not permitted to wear low-riding, hip-hugging pants or display body piercing. No hats or hooded sweatshirts may be worn. Belts are required unless pants or skirts lack belt loops. Shirts and blouses must be tucked in at all times and should be long enough to stay in. No dress or grooming is permitted that, in the principal's judgment, is "startling, unusual, immodest, disruptive, or brings undue attention to the student's anatomy."

As can be seen, many of these requirements are highly subjective and may create confusion for students. For example, what constitutes unusual or startling dress? School rules should not be so broad and nebulous as to allow for arbitrary and inconsistent interpretation. Fundamental fairness requires that students know precisely what behaviors are required of them by school officials.

It is important to remember that schools must exercise fair and reasonable administrative authority that will withstand court scrutiny. For example, there is a question as to whether the suspension of a 13-year-old honor student for having her shirt untucked was reasonable, even though she immediately tucked it in after she was pulled aside by an administrator. Another student was suspended when her shirt had come untucked when she sat down, and she was not allowed to tuck it back. All students were asked to stand up in their classrooms so that an administrator could determine whether shirts were tucked in and belts worn. If these practices were challenged in court, there would likely be a question of fairness, particularly if no disruption occurred, the student had no history of misbehavior and, did in fact, attempt to conform to the school's policy.

The Key Element: Fairness

School officials should proceed with caution as they develop dress codes, especially those that involve zero-tolerance. Student dress may be restricted if school officials can provide concrete evidence that it communicates a message that appears to invite disruption. However, if student dress does not communicate such a message, school officials must demonstrate a reasonable justification for restrictions. The burden of proof rests with them, although community representatives—parents, community leaders, and citizens—should be involved in the policy development to ensure that it reflects community values and sentiments.

Policies that do not take into account the seriousness of the infraction, the student's record of behavior in school, and the immediate need to act are very risky, as are dress codes that provide no flexibility in enforcement and result in suspension for very minor infractions. When challenged in these cases, the burden will fall on school officials to justify the rules on the basis of past disruption or a legitimately based expectation of disruption.

School officials should always be guided by fundamental fairness and a regard for the individual rights of all students. The Supreme Court's *Tinker v. Des Moines* case reminded all of us that students do not shed their constitutional rights at the schoolhouse door. In formulating dress codes, school officials should demonstrate fairness not because the court requires it, but because it is the right thing to do.

References

Alexander, Kern and David Alexander. *American Public School Law*, 5th ed. Belmont, Calif.: West/Thomson Learning. 2001.

Essex, Nathan. *School Law and Public School: A Practical Guide for School Leaders*, 2nd ed. Boston: Allyn and Bacon. 2002.

A Uniform Look

Yasmine L. Konheim-Kalkstein

Yasmine Konheim-Kalkstein *is a doctoral student in educational psychology at the University of Minnesota.*

Since the 1990s, the practice of having public school students wear uniforms—like their private school peers—has been credited with some amazing results. School uniforms, proponents have said, can lead to improved discipline and classroom behavior, increased school attendance, respect for teachers, better school performance, higher student self-esteem and confidence, lower clothing costs, promotion of group spirit, reduction in social stratification, and lower rates of violence and crime. Uniforms, in short, seem like the solution to all of education's problems.

Of course, there have also been naysayers. They argue that requiring school uniforms violates students' rights, that uniforms are not responsible for decreased violence, that students will find other ways to compete, and that uniforms have no direct bearing on academic achievement.

Which side is correct? Like so many other educational issues, the truth probably lies somewhere between the two extremes. For answers, we can look to the research on and articles about school uniforms, particularly in the areas of violence prevention, school climate, and finances.

Early Signs of Success

Schools have always had dress codes, of course. But in 1986, Baltimore's Cherry Hill Elementary School became the first U.S. public school to adopt a school uniform policy. The policy was an attempt to reduce clothing costs for parents and to help curb social pressures. According to a 1996 issue of *Communicator,* a newsletter published by the National Association of Elementary School Principals, Cherry Hill Principal Geraldine Smallwood reported increased attendance, reduced suspensions, less frequent fighting, increased test scores, and improved school performance after students began wearing uniforms.

A similar success story was reported when, in 1995, Long Beach, Calif., became the first large urban school district to require uniforms for all students in kindergarten through eighth grade. Five years later, overall crime in the school district had dropped by 91 percent. Suspensions were down 90 percent, sex offenses had been reduced by 96 percent, and vandalism had gone down 69 percent.

New York City adopted a policy in 1999 that allowed schools to vote on whether to opt out of a new school uniform policy. About 70 percent of the city's elementary schools adopted school uniforms. In 2000, the Philadelphia School Board unanimously adopted a district-wide policy requiring some type of uniform. That same year, 60 percent of Miami public schools required uniforms, as did 80 percent of public schools in Chicago. Also, 37 state legislatures enacted legislation empowering local districts to determine their own uniform policies.

With so many school districts adopting such policies, it seemed as though uniforms were doing something to prevent violence, improve school climate, or help parents out financially. A look at the research and literature on the effect of school uniforms on these areas is revealing and can help you decide if such a policy would be useful in your district.

Reducing Violence

Proponents suggest that school uniforms can reduce violence in schools by diminishing gang influence and easing competition over clothing as a source of conflict.

In fact, gang violence is one of the most influential reasons for adopting uniform policies. In urban schools, fashion trends are often characterized by gang-related clothing. In theory, then, school uniforms would prevent gang activity by not allowing students to wear gang colors or gang insignia. And in practice, there is some evidence that this is true.

For example, a 1999 *Education World* article by Glori Chaika reported a significant drop in gang violence in Chicago schools that adopted school uniforms. Similarly, in a 2003 *Education and Urban Society* article, Kathleen Wade and Mary Stafford reported that teachers at schools with uniforms perceived lower levels of gang presence than teachers at schools with no uniforms. This difference was significant, despite the fact that the uniform schools were in areas with slightly higher numbers of gang-related crimes. However, students in both types of schools perceived gang presence at the same level. Students may see other signs besides clothing that hint of gang activity.

Clothing has caused other school conflicts as well. After introducing uniforms, the Birmingham, Ala., schools reported a drop in weapon and drug incidents, and Houston schools noted a decrease in violent crime. Interestingly, however, Miami-Dade counties report that fights nearly doubled at their middle schools after schools adopted a uniform policy.

How valid are the findings linking school uniforms to decreased violence? There is substantial criticism on that point. In many of these school districts, other changes in policy were being promoted at the same time—such as having more teachers patrolling the hallways. These additional variables confuse the issue and must be controlled for statistically in the research before drawing conclusions.

Improving School Climate

Obviously, less violence in schools translates to a better school climate, another area that is said to be affected by school uniforms. And indeed, there is some evidence that school uniforms may improve a school's environment by reducing competition, improving student self-esteem, and improving academic achievement.

Writing in the *NASSP Bulletin* in 1997, Richard Murray reported on the results of a survey of 306 middle school students in Charleston, S.C. Murray found that students in a middle school with a uniform policy had a significantly better perception of their school's climate than did students in a school without a uniform policy. Similarly, in Charleston secondary schools, a South Carolina State University doctoral student found in 1996 that a school with a uniform policy reported higher attendance, self-esteem, and academic scores.

Winston Tucker, a University of Minnesota researcher, investigated the perceptions of St. Paul teachers in 1999. He found that in schools where uniforms were worn, teachers perceived more positive behavior and peer interactions. They also reported fewer cliques, less teasing, and better self-esteem. On the other hand, Wade and Stafford's survey of teachers and students revealed no difference between perceptions of school climate in schools with and without uniforms.

Research on school uniforms and test scores is equally mixed. For example, a 1998 study by David Brunsma and Kerry Rockquemore, published in *The Journal of Educational Research,* refuted the belief that uniforms will result in higher test scores. Using data from the National Educational Longitudinal Study of 1988, they found that in Catholic schools, school uniforms had no direct effect on substance abuse, behavioral problems, or attendance. More recently, however, researcher Ann Bodine criticized the inferences drawn from this study. In a 2003 article in the same journal, she contended that examination of public schools shows a positive correlation between uniforms and achievement.

Like the research on a possible relation between school uniforms and reduced violence, findings on uniforms and school climate have yielded no clear conclusion.

Saving Money

Advocates of school uniform policies argue that uniforms will save families money. But Pamela Norum, Robert Weagley, and Marjorie Norton, writing in the *Family and Consumer Sciences Research Journal* in 1998, concluded that families who buy school uniforms spend more on clothing than families who are not required to do so. However, a subsequent paper, presented by Michael Firmin, Suzanne Smith, and Lynsey Perry at the 16th Annual Ethnographic and Qualitative Research in Education Conference, points out that many parents believe a policy requiring school uniforms lowers clothing costs, and others believe it would do so in the long run.

It seems clear that introducing a uniform policy results in more expense in the beginning, but more research is needed to determine whether school uniforms save families money. The experience of families at different socioeconomic levels should be compared, rather than averaging across socioeconomic levels. It is possible that families who struggle financially might depend on hand-me-downs or thrift stores to begin with, and the cost of a new uniform substantially increases their clothing costs.

If a uniform policy is adopted, it will be important to take into account how to provide uniforms for students whose families can't afford them. Some school districts collect outgrown uniforms to distribute to needy families. Some give out donated money so parents themselves can select their children's uniforms. California requires school districts to subsidize the cost of uniforms for low-income students, and the U.S. Department of Education's "Manual on School Uniforms" suggests that some type of assistance should be given to needy families.

In some cases, school uniforms could save money, but it's clear that uniforms could be a financial burden for many families.

Legal Considerations

Legal issues have surrounded the school uniform debate for two primary reasons: claims that the school has infringed on the student's First Amendment right to free expression and claims under the 14th Amendment that the school has violated the student's liberty to control his or her opinion.

The 1998 case of *Canady v. Bossier Parish School Board* addressed the constitutionality of student uniforms. In this landmark case, the Supreme Court upheld a school's right to implement a school uniform policy, given four conditions:

- First, that the school board has the power to make such a policy;
- Second, that the policy promotes a substantial interest of the board;
- Third, that the board does not adopt the policy to censor student expression; and
- Fourth, that the policy's "incidental" restrictions on student expression are not greater than necessary to promote the board's interest.

The American Civil Liberties Union has taken a stance against school uniform policies and cautions schools against omitting an opt-out provision from such policies. "For a public school uniform policy to be legal, it has to have an opt-out provision," wrote the ACLU's Loren Siegel on the organization's website in 1996. "Every child in this country has the right to a public school education, and that right cannot be conditioned upon compliance with a uniform policy. Some parents and children will have religious objections to uniforms. Others won't want to participate for aesthetic reasons."

As we can see, powerful quantitative evidence suggests that uniforms can reduce school violence, but these studies have not accounted for confounding variables. Perceptions of teachers, parents, and administrators seem to strongly support the idea that school climate is affected positively by school uniforms. They have reported more positive learning environments and peer interactions after the introduction of uniform policies. There remains, however, a lack of research on student's perspectives on school uniforms.

The research is not conclusive, but the testimonials from teachers, parents, and administrators alike are hard to ignore. Whether to require school uniforms should be a school or district decision, and guidelines should be followed to make sure students' rights are not violated. That is particularly important in cases where religious practice calls for clothing or head covering that is not consistent with the accepted school uniform. Provision should also be made for those families who can't afford to purchase uniforms.

When these concerns are addressed—and when the idea is supported by the community—school uniforms can be successful.

SAMPLE CRITIQUE

An Unconvincing Argument concerning School Uniforms

As author Yasmine Konheim-Kalkstein notes in the opening line of her essay, "A Uniform Look," over the past few decades schools across the country have debated whether to require high school students to wear uniforms. However, are school uniform requirements effective in meeting their goals: reducing school violence, raising school attendance, bolstering student grades, and reducing the cost of school for parents, just to name a few? On a first reading of the essay, it may appear that Konheim-Kalkstein's goal is to answer these questions impartially by surveying the research published on the topic. However, she withholds her thesis until the last sentence of the piece, revealing her true intention: "When these concerns are addressed—and when the idea is supported by the community—school uniforms can be successful" (119). A close reading of her essay, though, shows that Konheim-Kalkstein fails to support even this assertion.

In the opening section of her essay, Konheim-Kalkstein acknowledges two sides in the debate over the effectiveness of school uniforms, yet she consistently emphasizes arguments and research findings that favor the pro-uniform position. For example, she cites statistics from schools in New Jersey, Long Beach, California, New York City, and Chicago that all demonstrated positive results from requiring elementary school students to wear uniforms and concludes, "With so many school districts adopting such policies, it seemed as though uniforms were doing something to prevent violence, improve school climate, or help parents out financially" (116). Konheim-Kalkstein terms the research on school uniforms "revealing" (116) and states that they can "help you decide if such a policy would be useful in your district" (116). Since this article was published in *American School Board Journal*, one can assume that "you" in the previous sentence refers to school board members.

Indeed, at first glance, the figures Konheim-Kalkstein presents concerning the link between uniform requirements and school violence are impressive. She cites an *Education World* article that reported a drastic drop in gang violence at schools that required uniforms and another article from *Education and Urban Society* that says these results were replicated at other high schools as well. Yet, Konheim-Kalkstein must admit that these statistics may reveal only a correlation between uniform requirements and drops in school violence. She offers no proof that requiring students to wear uniforms actually caused a drop in violence or gang activity; in fact, she states that "other changes in policy were being promoted at the same time—such as having more teachers patrolling the hallways" (117). Any one factor, or any combination of factors, could be responsible for the drop in violence, yet Konheim-Kalkstein wants to attribute it to school uniforms. In fact, from the students' perspective, the uniforms had no effect on violence-related gang activity (117). In the end, Konheim-Kalkstein states that these "additional variables confuse the issue and must be controlled for statistically in the research before drawing conclusions" (117). On this first point—that uniform requirements help reduce gang activity and violence—Konheim-Kalkstein actually offers only testimonial evidence in support of her thesis that "school uniforms can be successful," evidence countered by the experiences of students at those schools.

Konheim-Kalkstein next examines the relationship between uniform requirements and "school climate" (117), indicating some evidence exists that schools requiring student uniforms benefit from reduced competition, higher self-esteem, and higher grades and test scores (117). After citing several studies that reported a link between uniform requirements and better school climates, Konheim-Kalkstein cites only one that showed no such relationship. Moving on to focus on the relationship between uniforms and higher academic achievement, she cites several studies which showed no link between the two, but ends that section of her essay by referring to more recent research that demonstrates "a positive correlation between uniforms and achievement" (118). In the end, though, Konheim-Kalkstein must concede: "Like the research on a possible relation between school uniforms and reduced violence, findings on uniforms and school climate have yielded no clear conclusion" (118). This concession again calls into question Konheim-Kalkstein's thesis, that school uniform policies can be successful.

Konheim-Kalkstein next turns her attention to arguments that requiring school uniforms saves families money by reducing clothing costs for the children. She cites a conference paper in which the authors found that parents "believe" (118) requiring uniforms will save them money in the long run, but again the evidence she examines leads to a different conclusion. A study published in *Family and Consumer Sciences Research Journal* "concluded that families who buy school uniforms spend more on clothing than families who are not required to do so" (118). In fact, Konheim-Kalkstein concludes that school uniform requirements may prove too expensive for students in lower socioeconomic classes. After reviewing all the evidence, Konheim-Kalkstein is forced to admit that "it's clear that uniforms could be a financial burden for many families" (118).

Konheim-Kalkstein closes her essay by examining primarily legal issues involved in requiring students to wear uniforms in school, starting with the Supreme Court case (*Canady v. Bossier Parish School Board*) that affirmed the constitutionality of such programs so long as they met four criteria:

- first, that the school board has the power to make such a policy;
- second, that the policy promotes a substantial interest of the board;
- third, that the board does not adopt the policy to censor student expression; and
- fourth, that the policy's "incidental" restrictions on student expression are not greater than necessary to promote the board's interest. (119)

However, school uniform laws have been opposed by the American Civil Liberties Union (ACLU), which asserts that any school uniform policy must have an "opt out" provision for children and families who believe the requirements inhibit their freedom of religion or free speech, objections that Konheim-Kalkstein does not address (119). American courts have long held that freedom of expression extends to people's clothing, including that of students. Konheim-Kalkstein does not offer a clear position on this question. Instead, she implies that if a school uniform policy meets the four criteria outlined above, it would be legal.

Despite all of the contradictory research and gaps in her argument, Konheim-Kalkstein still wants to maintain that requiring school uniforms "can be successful" (119). To do so, she puts the best possible spin on the evidence she presents in her essay:

> As we can see, powerful quantitative evidence suggests that uniforms can reduce school violence, but these studies have not accounted for confounding variables. Perceptions of teachers, parents, and administrators seem to strongly support the idea that school climate is affected positively by school uniforms. They have reported more positive learning environments and peer interactions after the introduction of uniform policies. (119)

However, these positive assertions can be seriously questioned by the information and arguments Konheim-Kalkstein presents. For example, she provides ample reason to question each of the positive claims she makes for school uniforms, admittedly basing her claim for their efficacy on teacher or parent testimonials (119). Read as a whole, the article actually offers a strong argument against the institution of school uniform policies because there simply is no preponderance of evidence to support any of the benefits such a move is supposed to bring about. Konheim-Kalkstein's "A Uniform Look" casts great doubts on whether school uniform policies can successfully achieve the benefits supporters ascribe to them.

Summary Chart

HOW TO WRITE A CRITIQUE

1. Carefully read and annotate the source text.
- *Read and reread the text.*
- *Identify the author's intent, thesis, and primary assertions or findings.*
- *Write an informal summary of the piece.*

2. Analyze and evaluate the reading, breaking it down into its parts and judging the quality of each element.

Identify and evaluate the author's logic and reasoning.
- *Is the thesis clearly stated, and does it direct the development of the text?*
- *Are the author's primary assertions reasonable and clearly tied to the thesis?*
- *Are there problems with logical fallacies?*
- *Are the author's positions or findings logically presented?*

Identify and evaluate the text's evidence.
- *Does the author support his or her assertions or findings?*
- *Is the support offered adequate to convince readers?*
- *Is the evidence authoritative?*
- *Is the evidence current?*
- *Does the author explain how the evidence supports his or her assertions or findings?*
- *Has the author ignored evidence or alternative hypotheses?*

Identify and evaluate the text's organization.
- *Is there a clear connection between the assertions developed in the essay?*
- *Are the assertions or findings tied to a guiding thesis?*
- *Does there seem to be a reason for one assertion following another, or do they seem randomly organized?*

Identify and evaluate the text's style.
- *Is the author's diction consistently maintained?*
- *Is the author's word choice clear and effective?*
- *Is the author's tone consistent and effective?*
- *Are the author's sentences clear?*

Summary Chart: How to Write a Critique (continued)

3. **Formulate your thesis and choose the criteria you will include in your essay.**
   - *Draft a thesis, a brief statement concerning the overall value or worth of the source text.*
   - *Choose which elements of the reading you will focus on in your critique.*

4. **Write your rough draft.**
   - *Introduce the topic, source text, and your thesis.*
   - *Establish your evaluative criteria and your judgments of them.*
   - *Offer examples to substantiate each of your criteria and judgments.*
   - *Explain your judgments, clarifying how the examples you provide support your assertions.*

5. **Rewrite your critique.**

   Check to make sure your writing is accurate.
   - *Does your writing honestly reflect your judgment?*
   - *Does your writing misrepresent the author?*

   Check to make sure your writing is thorough.
   - *Do you cover all the aspects of the source text you need to cover?*
   - *Do you clearly and thoroughly explain and support your assertions?*

   Check to make sure your writing is organized.
   - *Does your thesis statement guide the development of your essay?*
   - *Have you provided transitional devices to help lead your reader through your work?*

   Check to make sure your writing is clear.
   - *Is your terminology clear?*
   - *Are your sentences clear?*
   - *Are your examples and explanations clear?*

CRITIQUE REVISION CHECKLIST

	Yes	No
1. Have you included the title of the reading and the author's name in your introduction?	_____	_____
2. Does your thesis make clear your overall assessment of the reading?	_____	_____
3. Toward the beginning of your critique, have you provided a brief summary of the reading?	_____	_____
4. In the body of your critique, do you examine only one element of the reading at a time?	_____	_____
5. Do you clearly state a judgment concerning each element of the reading you explore?	_____	_____
6. Do you provide examples from the reading to support and illustrate your judgment of each element you examine?	_____	_____
7. Do you clearly and thoroughly explain your judgments concerning each example you provide from the reading?	_____	_____
8. Have you employed proper evaluative criteria and standards?	_____	_____
9. Have you provided clear transitions between the major sections of your paper?	_____	_____
10. Is there a clear relationship between each section of your paper and your thesis?	_____	_____
11. Have you provided proper documentation for all quoted, paraphrased, and summarized material?	_____	_____
12. Have you revised your paper for accuracy? In other words, does the final draft reflect your honest appraisal of the reading?	_____	_____
13. Have you reviewed the language in your paper to make sure your words adequately capture and communicate your judgments?	_____	_____
14. As you review your work, do your judgments still stand? Do you need to change your thesis or any part of your paper?	_____	_____

Chapter 7

RHETORICAL ANALYSIS OF WRITTEN TEXTS

DEFINITION AND PURPOSE

A rhetorical analysis essay is a special form of critique (see Chapter 6). In a critique essay, you determine a source text's overall value or worth by critically examining a set of relevant criteria; in a rhetorical analysis essay, you determine a source text's rhetorical effectiveness by examining how the author employs language and/or visual images to achieve a particular effect on an audience. This chapter addresses how to compose a rhetorical analysis of a written text; the following chapter offers instruction on how to compose a rhetorical analysis of a visual text.

Writing a rhetorical analysis of a reading requires you to answer three related questions:

- What response is the author of the reading trying to elicit from his or her readers?
- How does the author employ language to elicit that response?
- How well does the author succeed in achieving this response?

Composing a rhetorical analysis requires you to examine a source text from the perspective of both a reader and a writer, assessing how well an author achieves certain rhetorical goals in a text.

Rhetorical analysis of print texts is based on certain assumptions about how writers write and the way writing works. First is the assumption that writing is purposeful, that every text is written by someone who directs it toward some audience to achieve some purpose. To accomplish their ends, writers make a series of strategic choices—they choose this approach to the topic instead of that approach, this set of arguments rather than that set of arguments, this evidence instead of that evidence, this thesis rather than that one, this organizational plan in place of another, this word rather than that word. In a rhetorical analysis essay, you critically examine this series of choices, identifying and critiquing the strategies a writer employs to achieve his or her rhetorical goals.

A second assumption is that text and context are intimately connected, that text is fundamentally influenced by the context in which it is written. Writers work within a set of givens, a rhetorical context or situation that includes their reasons for writing the text, their purpose or aim, their audience's needs or interests, and their knowledge of the topic they are addressing. To be effective, writers must adapt their writing to meet the needs of the given rhetorical situation. If they ignore or misconstrue any element of the rhetorical situation, their writing will be less effective than it might otherwise be. Because writers typically want to produce the most effective text possible, they take particular efforts to ensure that their language suits the text's audience, purpose, message, and occasion. Therefore, to evaluate a text's rhetorical effectiveness, you must understand the context in which it was written.

A final assumption is that no rhetorical analysis is definitive. Readers often disagree about a text's purpose, intended audience, rhetorical strategies, and effectiveness. Because readers always bring their own knowledge, experiences, sensitivities, and biases to a text, they will form unique, individualized responses to even the most fundamental questions concerning how a reading communicates its meaning. Consequently, when you write a rhetorical analysis essay, you must explain your conclusions as clearly as you can, supporting them with thorough explanations and specific references to the source text.

THE RHETORICAL SITUATION

When you compose a rhetorical analysis essay of a written text, you must examine how an author uses language to achieve a particular response from readers. However, your task is a little more complicated than it might appear at first. You will actually be examining how an author uses language to achieve a particular response from readers *given the specific context in which the writer produced the text*. This "specific context" is called the text's **rhetorical situation**, which includes the author's audience, subject matter, purpose, and occasion for writing. In your paper, you will assess how the writer manipulates language to meet the needs of the rhetorical situation and achieve his or her goals for the text.

A brief example may help explain why understanding the rhetorical situation of a source text is essential to composing an effective rhetorical analysis essay. Suppose your source text is a set of instructions for installing a new hard drive on a computer. Your task is to evaluate how well the instructions achieve their intended purpose. The first thing you notice is that the instructions are full of undefined technical terms—IDE cables, jumper selectors, drive rails, boot drives. Are the instructions effective? Upon consideration, you would have to conclude that the answer is, "It depends." If the instructions are written for someone who is already well versed in computer technology, they may be fine; if they are written for a novice computer owner, they may not be so effective. Composing an effective rhetorical analysis of the instructions requires that you evaluate the writing in light of its purpose and intended audience, two crucial elements of the text's rhetorical situation.

Because understanding a text's rhetorical situation is so fundamental to writing this type of essay, it is worthwhile to examine each element in isolation. The next section contains definitions of various elements of a text's rhetorical situation and a series of questions writers frequently ask of each element as they prepare to write a rhetorical analysis essay.

ELEMENTS OF THE RHETORICAL SITUATION

Author—the person or people who wrote the text

- Who wrote the piece?
- What is the author's background in terms of race, sex, education, political affiliation, economic status, or religion?
- What are the author's possible or likely biases?
- What perspective does the author bring to the topic?
- How does the author "sound" on the page—angry, detached, confused, funny?
- What has the author written about the topic in the past?

Topic—what the text is about

- What is the person writing about?
- Is the author addressing a particular aspect of the topic or the topic as a whole?
- Which aspects of the topic receive the most attention and which receive the least?
- What, exactly, is the author stating about the topic?
- What have others said about this subject matter?
- What is the relationship between what others have written about the topic and what the author is writing about it?

Audience—who the writer is addressing

- To whom is the text addressed?
- If the text is not written to a specific person or group of people, what kind of reader did the author seem to have in mind when writing the piece?

For example, does the author seem to be assuming he or she is addressing a friendly audience or a hostile audience? An expert audience or a novice audience? An academic audience or a popular audience?

- What is the audience's likely knowledge of or attitude toward the author and/or subject matter?
- What assumptions does the author make about the audience? Are these assumptions accurate?

Purpose or Aim—what the author is trying to accomplish in writing the text

- If the author states a purpose or aim for the piece, what is it? To inform, persuade, entertain, educate, provoke to action, draw attention, ridicule, shock?
- If it is not stated, what is the author's implied purpose or aim for the text?
- Is there more than one purpose or aim for the text? If so, what are they? Does one purpose seem more dominant than the others? Which one?
- How does the author's purpose influence the text's content, structure, or language?

Occasion—what prompted the writer to write the piece

- Why did the author feel compelled to write this text?
- What is the historical context of the piece?
- Is the author adding to a debate over a particular political issue or social question? Is the author responding to another writer or text? Is the author responding to a particular historical event or cultural phenomenon?

Writing a rhetorical analysis essay usually requires you to examine the complex interrelationships that exist among these elements. For example, how does the author's audience influence what she writes about the topic or the language she employs? What is the relationship between a text's purpose and the time or place it was written? How effective is the author in producing a text that is appropriate for both the audience and the occasion?

RHETORICAL STRATEGIES

Once you understand the text's rhetorical situation, you are ready to turn your analysis to the author's rhetorical strategies—the way the author manipulates the text's content, structure, or style to achieve his or her aim. **Content** concerns the material an author includes in the text, **structure** concerns the order in which the author presents that material, and **style** concerns the language and sentence structure an author uses to convey that material. A rhetorical analysis essay is unlikely to address every aspect of a text's content, structure, or style. In fact, it may address just one or two of the author's rhetorical strategies. As the person writing the analysis, you will determine which strategies you wish to examine. They will likely be the ones you think are most essential to the author achieving his or her aim.

CONTENT

When composing a rhetorical analysis essay, most writers analyze a text's content in one or two related ways: by examining its arguments, evidence, and reasoning or by examining its persuasive appeals. Because both approaches are closely related, writers will often examine aspects of each in their essays. Both are discussed below.

Arguments, Evidence, and Reasoning

When analyzing a text's rhetorical strategies in terms of its arguments, evidence, and reasoning, you are primarily concerned with examining the claims or assertions a writer makes, the way that writer supports those claims, and the way he or she explains them. You need to ask yourself, given the text's rhetorical situation, why the writer would choose those particular arguments. Are they the best arguments for the writer to make? Why did the writer choose to support those claims the way he or she did? Again, was this the best choice of evidence? How effective were the writer's decisions? Does the writer explain his or her reasoning in the piece, exploring or defending the link between his or her claims and supporting evidence? Are there certain assumptions or leaps of reasoning the writer leaves unstated? Why might the writer have made that choice? Was it a good decision? Below are some questions that can help you analyze and evaluate a text's rhetorical strategies in terms of its arguments, evidence, and reasoning.

Arguments or Assertions

- What arguments or assertions does the author make and how are they related to the rhetorical situation?
- How does the audience, purpose, and occasion of the text influence the author's arguments or assertions?
- Given the audience and purpose of the text, are these the most effective arguments? If so, what makes them effective? If not, why not? What arguments might be more effective?
- What arguments or assertions are emphasized the most? Why did the author decide to emphasize those assertions instead of others?
- What relevant arguments or assertions are ignored or slighted? Why do you think the author chose not to address them?
- How might the intended audience respond to the arguments offered? How well does the author seem to anticipate and perhaps address these likely responses?

Evidence or Examples

- How does the author support his or her assertions? Are they supported by primary or secondary research? By personal experience? By statistics or expert testimony?

- What is the source of the author's evidence for each assertion or argument? Are they particularly effective sources, given the text's rhetorical situation?
- Is the evidence offered appropriate, given the text's rhetorical situation? Does the evidence offered effectively support each claim?
- How might the intended audience respond to the evidence or examples offered? How well does the author seem to anticipate and perhaps address these likely responses?
- Is the presentation balanced or one-sided? In either case, is that choice appropriate given the rhetorical situation?
- How does the author address possible counterarguments or evidence that does not support his or her assertions?
- Are there obvious arguments the author chooses to ignore or gloss over? What are the effects of these omissions? How might they be explained, given the text's rhetorical situation?

Reasoning

- Does the author present a clear and cogent line of reasoning in the text?
- How well does the author move from one assertion to the next?
- How compelling is the connection the author makes among assertions? Between assertions and their supporting evidence?
- Does the text lead logically and convincingly to its conclusion?
- Are there clear connections between the text's thesis and its primary assertions?
- Are there any important assumptions the author leaves unstated? Does leaving them unstated and undefended make the text any less successful?
- Is the reasoning fair and balanced? Should it be, given the text's rhetorical situation?
- Are there any logical fallacies or flaws in reasoning that might hinder the text's effectiveness, given its audience, purpose, and occasion?

Persuasive Appeals

Another set of strategies authors often employ to achieve their rhetorical goals involves appealing to their readers' rationality (logos) or emotions (pathos) or establishing their own credibility as an authority on the topic (ethos). Though one of the three appeals may dominate a particular reading, most effective persuasive texts use elements of all three. In brief, when authors try to persuade readers by presenting a reasonable series of arguments supported by evidence and examples, they are relying on **logos** to achieve their goal; when they try to persuade readers through emotional language or examples or by appealing to the reader's needs or interests, they are relying on **pathos**; when they try to persuade readers by appearing fair, balanced, and informed or by establishing their own credibility and authority on the subject, they are relying on **ethos**. Below are some questions you can ask about a text's persuasive appeals if you are analyzing its rhetorical effectiveness.

Logos

- How reasonable and appropriate are the author's claims, given the rhetorical situation?
- How clear are the author's claims?
- Are the author's claims broad and sweeping or does the author limit or qualify them?
- How well does the author use facts, statistics, and expert testimony to support his or her claims?
- Are the author's claims adequately explained?
- Does the author avoid lapses in reasoning or logical fallacies?
- Does the author address opposing or alternative viewpoints?
- Are there relevant claims the author fails to address?
- Are the author's claims convincing?

Pathos

- Does the author attempt to convince his or her readers through appeals to their emotions?
- To which emotions is the author appealing? To the readers' personal fears or concerns? To the readers' economic or social self-interests? To the readers' desires for acceptance, love, or beauty? To the readers' sense of justice or social responsibility?
- Does the author appeal to his readers' emotions through his choice of arguments, evidence, language, or some combination of the three?
- How are appeals to emotion balanced with other appeals in the text?
- Does the author try too hard to appeal to readers' emotions? Are the appeals to emotion too clumsy or awkward to be effective?
- Is an appeal to the readers' emotions an effective strategy to employ given the rhetorical situation?

Ethos

- How does the author attempt to establish her credibility or authority?
- What level of expertise does the author demonstrate when writing about the topic of her text?
- Does the author's own experience or expertise lend credibility to the text?
- Does the author demonstrate or document the validity of the source texts used to support her assertions?
- Does the author present a balanced or a one-sided argument? Is that approach appropriate, given the rhetorical situation?
- Does the author demonstrate a sufficient understanding of the topic's complex or controversial nature?
- Does the text's tone or the author's voice contribute to or detract from her credibility?

STRUCTURE

While many rhetorical strategies are related to a text's content, others involve its structure. Once writers decide what information or arguments they will include in their essays, they need to decide the order in which to present them. Structure also involves the way a writer introduces and concludes a text and draws connections among parts of the text. Following are some questions you can ask about a text's structure as you evaluate its rhetorical effectiveness.

- In what order does the author present information or claims?
- What purpose might lie behind this order?
- How might the text's structure influence an audience's response to the author's ideas, findings, or assertions?
- Does the text present a clear and consistent line of reasoning?
- Are there clear connections between the text's stated or implied thesis and its topic sentences?
- Does the text's structure enhance its appeal to logic? Does the author draw clear, logical connections among the text's ideas, findings, or assertions?
- Does the structure of the piece enhance its appeal to emotion, particularly in its introduction or conclusion?
- Does the structure of the piece enhance its appeal to credibility? Does the author seem in control of the writing? Does the text hold together as a whole? Are there any obvious flaws in structure that might damage the author's credibility?

STYLE

Finally, when analyzing an author's rhetorical strategies, consider his or her style. Among other elements of writing, style concerns the text's sentence structure, word choice, punctuation, voice, tone, and diction. Here are some questions that can help you assess how style contributes to a text's rhetorical effectiveness:

- What type of syntax does the author employ? How does the author vary sentence length (long or short) and sentence type (simple, compound, complex, and compound-complex; cumulative, periodic, and balanced)? How is syntax related to the audience, purpose, or occasion of the text?
- What types of figurative language does the author employ (for example, metaphors, similes, or analogies)? Are the choices of figurative language appropriate and effective given the text's rhetorical situation?
- What types of allusions does the author employ? Are they appropriate and effective?
- How appropriate and effective is the author's voice, given the text's rhetorical situation?
- How appropriate and effective is the author's tone, given the text's rhetorical situation?
- How appropriate and effective is the author's diction, given the text's rhetorical situation?

ANALYZING A TEXT'S RHETORICAL STRATEGIES—AN EXAMPLE

To better understand how to analyze a text's rhetorical strategies in terms of its content, structure, and style, carefully read the following speech, Abraham Lincoln's Second Inaugural Address. Lincoln delivered this speech on March 4, 1865, in Washington, D.C. Though the Civil War was not yet over, the struggle had turned in the Union's favor, and the end of the conflict was in sight. In this address, Lincoln acknowledges the price the nation has paid for the war and argues that lasting peace and reconciliation will come only through mercy and forgiveness. Many historians and rhetoricians consider this Lincoln's greatest speech.

Lincoln's Second Inaugural Address

Fellow-Countrymen:

At this second appearing to take the oath of the Presidential office there is less occasion for an extended address than there was at the first. Then a statement somewhat in detail of a course to be pursued seemed fitting and proper. Now, at the expiration of four years, during which public declarations have been constantly called forth on every point and phase of the great contest which still absorbs the attention and engrosses the energies of the nation, little that is new could be presented. The progress of our arms, upon which all else chiefly depends, is as well known to the public as to myself, and it is, I trust, reasonably satisfactory and encouraging to all. With high hope for the future, no prediction in regard to it is ventured.

On the occasion corresponding to this four years ago all thoughts were anxiously directed to an impending civil war. All dreaded it, all sought to avert it. While the inaugural address was being delivered from this place, devoted altogether to *saving* the Union without war, urgent agents were in the city seeking to *destroy* it without war; seeking to dissolve the Union and divide effects by negotiation. Both parties deprecated war, but one of them would *make* war rather than let the nation survive, and the other would *accept* war rather than let it perish, and the war came.

One-eighth of the whole population were colored slaves, not distributed generally over the Union, but localized in the southern part of it. These slaves constituted a peculiar and powerful interest. All knew that this interest was somehow the cause of the war. To strengthen, perpetuate, and extend this interest was the object for which the insurgents would rend the Union even by war, while the Government claimed no right to do more than to restrict the territorial enlargement of it. Neither party expected for the war the magnitude or the duration which it has already attained. Neither anticipated that the *cause* of the conflict might cease with or even before the conflict itself should cease. Each looked for an easier triumph, and a result less fundamental and astounding. Both read the same Bible and pray to the same God, and each invokes His aid against the other. It may seem strange that any men should dare to ask a just God's assistance in wringing their bread from the sweat of other men's faces, but let us judge not, that we be not judged. The prayers of both could not be answered. That of neither has been answered fully. The Almighty has His own purposes. "Woe unto the world because of offenses; for it must needs be that offenses come, but woe to that man by whom the offense cometh." If we shall suppose that American slavery is one of those offenses which, in the providence of God, must needs come, but which, having continued through His appointed time, He now wills to remove, and that He gives to both North and South this terrible war as the woe due to those by whom the offense came, shall we discern therein any departure from those divine attributes which the believers in a living God always ascribe to Him? Fondly do we hope, fervently do we pray, that this mighty scourge of war may speedily pass away. Yet, if God wills that it continue until all the wealth piled by the bondsman's two hundred and fifty years of unrequited toil shall be sunk, and until every drop of blood drawn with the lash shall be paid by another drawn with the sword, as was said three thousand years ago, so still it must be said "the judgments of the Lord are true and righteous altogether."

With malice toward none, with charity for all, with firmness in the right as God gives us to see the right, let us strive on to finish the work we are in, to bind up the nation's wounds, to care for him who shall have borne the battle and for his widow and his orphan, to do all which may achieve and cherish a just and lasting peace among ourselves and with all nations.

A Rhetorical Analysis of Lincoln's Speech

In terms of the speech's content, notice how Lincoln makes several related arguments designed to persuade his audience that after the Civil War ends, the North must treat the South with charity and compassion. He opens his address by asserting that he will not detail a course of action for the country's future—clearly everyone in the nation has been and continues to be consumed by the war. Next, Lincoln asserts that the primary cause of the war was slavery. Four years earlier, the Union sought to halt the spread of slavery peacefully. However, the Confederacy, he asserts, would not accept this position and turned to armed conflict instead. Neither side, though, anticipated the duration and ferocity of the war. While both sides in the conflict call on God for victory, Lincoln questions whether any divine power would support the perpetuation of slavery. Interestingly, he sees *both* sides in the war being chastised for their involvement with slavery and hopes that the suffering all are undergoing can purge their collective guilt and set the stage for a more just nation. Lincoln closes his speech by asserting that reconciliation will only succeed if it is based on mercy, forgiveness, and justice, not revenge and recrimination.

Both Lincoln's position as president and the occasion of the speech lend credibility to his address. However, Lincoln enhances his credibility by articulating the North's perspective on the war's causes, a position most of his audience would presumably endorse. Making numerous references to God and God's will also serves to enhance his ethos but serves as an emotional appeal as well: Lincoln hopes the citizens of the North will be swayed to extend mercy to the South after the war by ascribing such a position to divine will. By speaking mercifully and understandingly about the suffering of the South during the war, Lincoln models the behavior and attitudes he hopes the members of his audience will adopt themselves.

Structurally, Lincoln opens his address by commenting on the previous four years of his presidency and acknowledging the country's current struggle before laying out the North's view of the war's cause. Having articulated a position his audience would accept, Lincoln then changes the direction of the speech. Instead of attacking the Confederacy for its secession from the Union, he speaks about the suffering the war has brought to *all* Americans, how neither side in the conflict accurately anticipated the terrible nature of the war, and how the South has already suffered severely for its actions. Audience members might expect Lincoln to call for revenge against the South; instead, he argues that both sides have suffered enough. At the end of his speech, he urges his audience to treat the South with charity.

Stylistically, the speech is remarkable for its somber tone. Though this is an inaugural speech, Lincoln is not celebrating. Instead, his tone reflects the suffering the nation has endured over the previous four years and the hard work that lies ahead of it. Syntactically, he employs balanced sentences to create memorable phrases—"All dreaded it, all sought to avert it," "Fondly do we hope, fervently do we pray," "With malice toward none, with charity for all"—and to emphasize the balanced view he takes concerning the war's consequences. The North and South have both suffered and reconstruction must be based on an understanding of their shared humanity. Lincoln repeatedly employs language from the Old Testament to emphasize his view of the war as a form of divine judgment against the nation for its past offenses. Underlying this argument is the notion that justice lies in the hands of God: if God has scourged the nation for its transgressions, there is no need for humans to further the South's punishment following the war.

This brief rhetorical analysis of Lincoln's speech gives you some idea of how an author can manipulate a text's content, structure, and style to achieve a particular aim.

WRITING A RHETORICAL ANALYSIS ESSAY

STEP 1—CAREFULLY READ THE ASSIGNMENT

As you read the assignment, be sure you understand who *your* audience is for your essay. What can you assume your reader knows about the source text, its author, or the context in which it was written? How much information do you need to provide so your reader will understand your analysis of the text? Also, what can you assume your reader knows about rhetoric? What terms, if any, will you need to define in your essay?

STEP 2—ESTABLISH THE SOURCE TEXT'S RHETORICAL SITUATION

First, establish the rhetorical situation of the source text (see "The Rhetorical Situation" previously). Following are some of the questions you should answer either before or as you carefully read the source text:

- Who is the author?
- What is the writer's message?
- Who is the writer addressing?
- What is the writer's purpose or goal?
- Why is the writer composing this text?
- When was the text produced?
- Where was the text published?

To establish the text's rhetorical situation you might need to do a little research, but writing a rhetorical analysis essay requires that you understand the context in which the text was produced.

STEP 3—DETERMINE THE AUTHOR'S GOAL

In a sentence or two, paraphrase what you think the author is trying to accomplish in the text. What effect does she want to have on the audience? Is the author trying to persuade her readers to adopt a particular position? Does the author want to influence what her readers believe? Is the author trying to elicit a particular emotional response from people who read the text? State the author's purpose or goal, as you understand it, as clearly and specifically as you can.

STEP 4—IDENTIFY AND EVALUATE THE TEXT'S RHETORICAL STRATEGIES

Once you have a clear sense of the text's rhetorical situation, read through it again to identify the strategies the author employed to achieve his goal. Examine the text's content, structure, and style in relation to its rhetorical situation. How has the author manipulated various elements of the text to achieve a particular response from his readers? Spend as much time on this step in the process as you need—the ideas and insights you develop now will help you form a thesis for your essay. Remember that in your essay, you will not address every rhetorical strategy the writer employed. Instead, you will focus on the strategies you think most significantly contribute to the text's ability or inability to achieve its rhetorical goal. As you reread the text, make a list of the ways the author employs content, structure, and style to achieve his purpose, noting specific examples of each from the reading. Based on this list, decide which strategies help the writer achieve his goals and which do not, given the text's audience, topic, purpose, and occasion. State in one or two sentences what makes each strategy successful or unsuccessful.

STEP 5—DETERMINE YOUR THESIS

In your thesis, you will state how successful you think the author is in achieving his or her rhetorical goal and indicate which of the author's rhetorical strategies you will examine in your essay. Your thesis may indicate that the author succeeds in achieving his or her rhetorical goals, fails to achieve them, or succeeds in some ways but fails in others. Whatever your assessment, state it clearly in your thesis, along with the rhetorical strategies you will examine to explain and defend your judgment.

Sample Thesis Statement 1: Author succeeds in achieving his or her rhetorical purpose

> Lincoln's Second Inaugural Address effectively establishes the North's moral imperative for successful Reconstruction by making repeated appeals to authority and emotion.

Sample Thesis Statement 2: Author fails to achieve his or her rhetorical purpose

> Lincoln's Second Inaugural Address fails to establish the North's moral imperative for successful Reconstruction because he relies too heavily on religious allusions and does not adequately address the North's desire for revenge after the war.

Sample Thesis Statement 3: Author has mixed success in achieving his or her rhetorical purpose

> Lincoln's attempts to establish the North's moral imperative for successful Reconstruction in his Second Inaugural Address are aided by his repeated appeals to authority, but they are hindered by his overreliance on religious allusions.

Whatever stand you assume, your thesis statement should establish the purpose and focus of your essay.

STEP 6—WRITE YOUR ROUGH DRAFT

While every rhetorical analysis essay will be structured a little differently, the following outline may help you determine how to organize your paper.

Introductory Section

- Indicate the topic of the source text.
- Introduce the text you are analyzing or evaluating.
- State your thesis.
- Capture reader interest.

In this part of your paper, you need to indicate the topic of your essay, introduce the source text (provide the author's full name and the title of the reading), and state your thesis. One of the real challenges in writing the introductory section of a rhetorical analysis essay is to capture reader interest as well. You may be able to develop reader interest in your essay by opening with a question raised by the source text, starting with an exciting quotation from the reading or providing some interesting information about the reading's author or historical significance.

Summary of Source Text and Overview of the Rhetorical Situation

- Briefly summarize the source text.
- Explain the source text's rhetorical situation.

In one or two paragraphs, summarize the reading and its rhetorical situation. In addition to stating what the author wrote, explain the audience, purpose, and occasion of the piece. Your analysis will depend on readers understanding the source text's rhetorical situation, so explain it carefully in this part of the paper. You will be making frequent reference back to this information in the body of your essay.

Body Paragraphs

- Examine the text one rhetorical strategy at a time (content, structure, or style).
- Cite specific examples from the source text to support any assertion you make.
- Explain the link between the examples you provide and the assertions you make.

As you draft the body of your rhetorical analysis essay, carefully critique the text one rhetorical strategy at a time, explaining whether employing that strategy helps the author achieve his or her rhetorical goal. You will need to illustrate and support your assertions with specific examples from the source text. Generally, each of your body paragraphs will contain (1) an assertion regarding whether a particular rhetorical strategy helps the author achieve his or her rhetorical goal, (2) examples from the source text that illustrate that particular rhetorical strategy, and (3) an explanation of how each example you cite supports your assertion.

Do not make the mistake of thinking that the examples you cite will "speak for themselves," that you do not need to explain how the examples support your assertion because the link will be obvious to anyone who has read the text. Instead, always explain the link between your evidence and your assertion. In fact, the success of your rhetorical analysis essay often depends on the clarity and logic of this explanation: your readers need to understand how the examples you cite support your assertion.

Conclusion

- Wrap up the essay.
- Remind readers of your thesis.
- Maintain reader interest.

In the conclusion of your rhetorical analysis essay, provide your readers with a sense of closure and remind them of your thesis. The conclusion should flow naturally from the body of your essay and recapture your readers' interest. One strategy you might employ is to echo your paper's introduction. For example, if you open your essay with a question, you might want to come back to it in your conclusion; if you open with a quotation, consider concluding your essay with one. This repetition will help give your essay a sense of balance and closure.

STEP 7—REVISE YOUR ESSAY

When revising your rhetorical analysis essay, make sure your work is accurate, developed, organized, clear, and documented.

- *Accurate*—your essay accurately captures your analysis and accurately represents the source text.
- *Developed*—you thoroughly develop and explain your assertions.
- *Organized*—the assertions in your essay are easy to follow and are interconnected.
- *Clear*—you have provided your readers with the information they need to understand your essay and have presented your ideas using clear, accessible language and sentences.
- *Documented*—all quoted and paraphrased material is documented as needed and your readers can easily discern which information comes from the source texts and which information you provide.

Check the Accuracy of Your Assertions and Examples

As you revise, start by checking your essay's content. First, make sure you have covered everything you intended to cover in your paper and that your essay accurately reflects your views. Second, be sure you have not misrepresented the author of the source text—any material you quote or paraphrase from the source text must accurately capture what the author actually wrote. Finally, be sure you fairly and accurately represent the text's rhetorical situation.

Check the Development of Your Essay

All of your assertions need to be fully explained and supported. Because your rhetorical analysis essay will reflect your individual response to and evaluation of the source text, you have to explain all of your assertions thoroughly. Readers need to know not only what you think but also why you think it. Do not expect readers to draw connections between your assertions and evidence on their own.

Check the Organization

First, be sure your thesis statement offers an accurate overview of your essay. The thesis statement should help guide your reader through your rhetorical analysis, previewing assertions you will develop in the body of your essay. Next, check the topic sentences in the body of your essay. Each topic sentence should relate back to the thesis statement, introduce a new idea, and provide a transition from the previous section of your essay. Be sure that you employ effective transitions within your body paragraphs as well, highlighting the logical relationship of one sentence to the next. Finally, check the opening and closing sections of your essay to be sure each accomplishes what it is supposed to accomplish.

Check for Clarity

Are there any terms that need to be defined? Any references drawn from the source text that need to be explained? Any sentences that could be more clear? Check to see that all quoted and paraphrased material will make sense to someone who has not read the source text and that any technical terms that need to be defined are defined.

Check Your Documentation

Because you are working with a source text, be sure that all quoted and paraphrased material is properly documented.

SAMPLE RHETORICAL ANALYSIS ESSAY

The following is a rhetorical analysis of Lincoln's Second Inaugural Address.

RHETORICAL ANALYSIS OF LINCOLN'S SECOND INAUGURAL ADDRESS

When President Lincoln stepped up to the podium to deliver his second inaugural address, he knew the Civil War was reaching its end. Though victory was not certain, events on the battlefield suggested that Union forces would soon put down the Southern rebellion and reunite the country. Lincoln knew he would soon be presiding over a deeply divided country, with many in the North demanding revenge against the southern states, including the arrest and execution of the Confederacy's leaders. A close analysis of Lincoln's address makes clear, however, that he envisioned a reconstruction based on mercy and forgiveness rather than vengeance, a message he forcefully conveys though the somber tone of the speech and its many religious allusions.

Since the Union forces were nearing victory after four years of brutal warfare, one might assume that Lincoln would deliver a joyful second inaugural address. Instead, the speech's tone is somber and reserved. While he states that the war's progress has been "reasonably satisfactory and encouraging to all" (135), Lincoln makes no prediction about its final outcome. He asserts that both sides in the conflict "deprecated" (135) war and that neither "expected for the war the magnitude or duration which it has already obtained" (135). Lincoln claims that "American slavery" (136) was the primary cause of the war, and though he states that the South was at fault for maintaining and spreading the practice, Lincoln claims that God "gives to both North and South this terrible war as the woe due to those by whom the offense came ..." (136). Instead of celebrating the North's impending victory in the war, Lincoln claims that both the North and the South are paying a terrible price for their moral transgressions.

In his speech, Lincoln soberly assesses the causes and consequences of the war and indicates how the nation should proceed once peace comes. The final paragraph of his speech begins with the famous phrase "With malice toward none, with charity for all" (136), summing up Lincoln's message of mercy and forgiveness. The needed course of action now, Lincoln contends, is "to bind up the nation's wounds, to care for him who shall have borne the battle and for his widow and orphan" (136). This statement embraces both sides in the conflict: the nation's obligation is to care for both Yankee and Rebel soldiers, for all widows and orphans. Such mercy is the only way to obtain "a just and lasting peace among ourselves and with all nations" (136). Again, "ourselves" is inclusive: Lincoln is including the people of both the North and South in this statement, pointing the way to a reunited country. Lincoln's reflective, restrained tone in this speech indicates how he would like every citizen of the United States to respond to war's conclusion: with forgiveness, introspection, and understanding.

Lincoln's message of mercy and forgiveness is also furthered by his many religious allusions. Rather than claiming that the North's coming victory in the war has been ordained by God, Lincoln believes that God is neutral in the conflict, that the North and South are united by a common religious heritage: "Both read the same Bible and pray to the same God ..." (136). Though Lincoln doubts that any deity would support human slavery, he warns his listeners, "judge not, that we be not judged" (136). Lincoln's repeated invocations of God strike a note of humility, reminding his audience that their fate is not in their own hands, that Providence dictates the course of history. The North has no reason to gloat in its victory or to judge the South severely after the war. Both sides have suffered judgment already; now is the time to act "with firmness in the right as God gives us to see the right ..." (136).

Lincoln's Second Inaugural Address establishes a somber, reflective tone and employs numerous religious allusions to convey successfully his central message that, in victory, the North must act with mercy, forgiveness, and humility during reconstruction. Revenge and retaliation is not the path to reestablishing a peaceful, united, just nation. "With malice toward none, with charity for all," the nation could be reunited. Unfortunately, one of those attending the speech that day was John Wilkes Booth, who would soon assassinate the president at Ford's Theater. Lincoln never had the chance to put his philosophy of merciful reconstruction to the test.

Summary Chart

HOW TO WRITE A RHETORICAL ANALYSIS ESSAY

1. **Carefully read the assignment.**
   - *Who is your audience?*
   - *What can you assume your audience knows about the source text and rhetoric?*

2. **Establish the source text's rhetorical situation.**
   - *Who is the source text's author?*
   - *What is the source text's topic?*
   - *Who is the source text's audience?*
   - *What is the source text's purpose?*
   - *What was the occasion for writing the source text?*

3. **Determine the author's goal.**
   - *In a sentence or two, state clearly and specifically what you think the author is trying to accomplish in the source text.*

4. **Identify and evaluate the source text's rhetorical strategies.**
   - *strategies involving the text's content*
   - *use of arguments, evidence, and reasoning*
   - *use of logos, pathos, and ethos*
   - *strategies involving the text's structure*
   - *strategies involving the text's style*

5. **Determine your thesis.**
   - *State how successful the author is in achieving his or her rhetorical goal.*
   - *State which rhetorical strategies you will examine in your essay.*

SUMMARY CHART: HOW TO WRITE A RHETORICAL ANALYSIS ESSAY (*CONTINUED*)

6. **Write your rough draft.**
   - *Write the introductory section of your essay, indicating the topic of the source text, its title and author, and your thesis. Capture reader interest as well.*
   - *Summarize the source text and its rhetorical situation.*
   - *Draft the body of your essay, examining one rhetorical strategy at a time and supporting your judgment with specific examples from the source text. Explain how each example you cite supports your claim.*
   - *Write the concluding section of your essay, reminding readers of your thesis and maintaining reader interest.*

7. **Revise your essay.**
   - *Make sure your writing is developed.*
   - *Make sure your essay thoroughly develops and explains your assertions.*
   - *Make sure your writing is organized.*
   - *Make sure the assertions in your essay are easy to follow.*
   - *Make sure the assertions in your essay are connected logically.*
   - *Make sure your essay accurately reflects your thesis.*
   - *Make sure your writing is clear.*
   - *Make sure you have provided your readers with the information they need to understand your essay.*
   - *Make sure you have checked to be sure all of your sentences are clear.*
   - *Make sure your essay accurately represents the source text.*
   - *Make sure all of the material in your essay that needs to be documented is documented.*
   - *Make sure readers can tell which information in your essay came from your source text and which information comes from you.*

Rhetorical Analysis of Written Texts Revision Checklist

	Yes	No
1. Have you analyzed the assignment to determine who *your* audience is?	_____	_____
2. Have you established the source text's rhetorical situation?	_____	_____
3. Have you paraphrased the author's goal?	_____	_____
4. Have you evaluated the author's rhetorical strategies in light of his or her goal?	_____	_____
5. Have you determined which of the author's rhetorical strategies you will evaluate in your essay?	_____	_____
6. Check the introductory section of your essay. Do you:		
• introduce the topic of your source text?	_____	_____
• introduce your source text?	_____	_____
• capture reader interest?	_____	_____
7. Examine the wording of your thesis. Do you:		
• state whether the author successfully achieves his or her goal?	_____	_____
• indicate which rhetorical strategies you will examine in your essay?	_____	_____
8. Do you summarize the source text and describe its rhetorical situation?	_____	_____
9. Check each section in the body of your essay. Do you:		
• examine one rhetorical strategy at a time?	_____	_____
• support your judgments with specific examples from the source text?	_____	_____
• explain the link between your assertions and their supporting evidence?	_____	_____
10. Have your revised your essay for:		
• accuracy?	_____	_____
• development?	_____	_____
• organization?	_____	_____
• clarity?	_____	_____
• documentation?	_____	_____

Chapter 8

RHETORICAL ANALYSIS OF VISUAL TEXTS

DEFINITION AND PURPOSE

Consider for a moment the power of images—how photographs, drawings, or graphics affect the way you experience texts. Images can add emotional punch to a reading, illustrate an assertion, or make a text more entertaining. Images can even make an argument, either alone or in combination with written text. In our daily lives, we are constantly surrounded by visual images. Which ones grab your attention? How do writers manipulate the visual aspects of a text to achieve their desired effects? By analyzing these images, what lessons can you learn about effectively using visual images in your own texts?

The ability to critically read and rhetorically analyze visual texts is becoming an increasingly important skill. Although visual texts have long been a part of human communication (think about the prehistoric cave drawings found throughout the world), they have become more central to communication over the last century. Since the advent of television, our culture has become more centered on visual images, and advances in computer technology have made it increasingly possible for students to incorporate visual images in their own texts. In fact, at some schools, visual presentations—films, streaming video, PowerPoint presentations, and posters—have replaced traditional print-based assignments like term papers and reports. In many majors, students are expected to develop the same kind of fluency in manipulating visual images as they are in manipulating the written word.

This chapter offers advice and instruction on how to read, interpret, and rhetorically analyze the types of visual texts. While you may not have much experience thinking about visual texts the way you will be instructed to do in this chapter, remember that the processes you will employ and the types of questions you will ask closely resemble those you commonly use to read, analyze, and interpret written texts.

READING VISUAL TEXTS CRITICALLY

You might find it odd to consider how you "read" visual texts like photographs, drawings, cartoons, or advertisements. People often draw a distinction between written and visual texts: they "read" words, not pictures. However, as discussed in Chapter 1, reading a text—any text—involves understanding, analyzing, and interpreting it. Similar processes apply to both written and visual texts.

Following are a series of questions you can consider to help you read visual texts critically. Answering them will give you a clearer sense of a visual text's content, creator, purpose, and audience as well as your response to the image.

QUESTIONS CONCERNING THE VISUAL TEXT ITSELF

- What image does the visual represent?
- What are the various parts of the visual?
- What written text, if any, accompanies the visual?

As with written texts, start your reading of a visual text by forming a clear understanding of its literal meaning—what is it in and of itself, what are its parts, and what is its relationship to any accompanying written text? Although this first step may sound easy, it can actually be difficult to examine a visual text objectively, to identify its constituent parts, and to find language that accurately describes what you see. Your first step is to summarize and paraphrase the visual text: state in your own words what you think the visual is depicting. At this point, you are not concerned with the visual's intention or purpose, only with its literal meaning. Pay particular attention to the details of the image. Your eye may immediately be drawn to only one or two aspects of the visual text, but don't stop your analysis there. Examine every aspect of the image—note what's in the background and in the foreground, in light and in shadow, in color and in black and white.

Next, identify the various parts of the visual text. When analyzing a written text, you may discuss its thesis, claims, examples, explanations, structure, and so forth. When analyzing a visual text, you will focus your attention on elements such as these:

Images: What images are contained in the visual? How many are there in the text? Which ones seem to command the most attention? Are there images of people in the text?

If so, who? What are they doing? Are particular objects included in the text? Which ones? What type of setting is depicted in the text: interior or exterior, urban or natural, realistic or fantastic?

Layout: How are the images arranged in the visual? How are they grouped? What aspects of the images are emphasized due to the layout? Which aspects are deemphasized? If there are people in the image, where do they appear in relation to the other images in the text? What appears in the foreground, and what appears in the background? What appears in light and what appears in shadows?

Color: How is color used in the visual text? What colors are used? What is highlighted by the text's use of color, and what is not? If you are examining a black-and-white image, how is shading used to highlight or emphasize particular elements? If there is written text, what color is it? How does color influence the way you respond to the writing?

Appeals: What elements of the visual text are intended to appeal to the reader's emotions, values, or needs? How does the author of the text manipulate its content and/or layout to elicit a particular emotional response from readers? What elements of the text are included to appeal to the reader's intellect or reason? Which elements, if any, are intended to establish the author's credibility or authority?

Note: Carefully examine any written text included in the visual. What does the text say? What is the relationship between the written and visual elements of the text? For example, does the text comment on the images or draw the reader's attention to particular visual elements of the text? How is the writing placed in the text, and where does it appear? Is the placement of the written text significant? Does it impact how you read the visual text?

QUESTIONS CONCERNING THE VISUAL TEXT'S CREATOR OR SOURCE

- Who created the visual text?
- What is the source of the visual text?
- In what publication or website does the visual appear?
- Toward what readership is the publication or website aimed?
- What, generally, is the editorial stance of that publication or website?

Although finding answers to these questions might prove difficult, you should try. As with written texts, identifying the authorship of a visual text is central to understanding and evaluating it. Authorial bias can affect visual texts just as it can written texts. If possible, identify who created the visual text. Who was the artist or photographer? What can you learn about that person's previous work and his or her credentials or affiliations? Approach visual texts as skeptically as you would written texts. We tend to trust visual texts more readily than we do written texts. After all, who hasn't heard the saying, "Pictures don't lie"? Of course, we know that pictures can lie—visual texts can be manipulated as easily as written texts. Visual texts can communicate truths, untruths, or half-truths. Understanding who created a visual text can help you establish its credibility.

Also consider the visual text's source. In what periodical did it appear? On what website? On what television show? In what film? In what advertisement? You need to understand the agenda of the visual text's source. What is the publication or website attempting to accomplish through its use of this particular visual text? Is its intention to inform, persuade, or entertain readers? What biases or agendas might influence the types of visuals a source employs or how it uses those sources? As noted in the chapter on critical reading (Chapter 1), if you are investigating the topic of abortion rights, it would be important to note whether a visual text you are examining was published by the National Abortion Rights Action League or by Operation Life. Each group has its own agenda on this issue, which may well influence how each designs and employs visual texts in its publications or on its website. Again, the possible bias does not disqualify or discredit a visual text. You simply need to take that bias into account when you read, analyze, or evaluate the text.

To better understand a publication's or website's general editorial stance, read some of the articles it publishes or posts and examine other visual texts it provides. While you may not be able to conclude definitively that the particular visual text you are examining reflects the publication's or website's general editorial stance, you will be in a better position to read that material in context. You will be able to conclude whether the particular visual text you are examining is typical of that publication or website.

QUESTIONS CONCERNING THE VISUAL TEXT'S PURPOSE

- What is the intended purpose of the visual?
- How does the creator attempt to achieve that purpose?

Purpose can be difficult to determine when analyzing a text—visual or written— because any text may be serving multiple purposes. Broadly speaking, a visual text may be attempting to inform, persuade, or entertain readers. Although it may be difficult to determine a visual text's exact intent, making an effort to do so is important. You can misread a visual text if you fail to understand its intended purpose.

For example, imagine an advertisement placed in a news magazine by the Sierra Club, one of the nation's largest environmental groups. The full-page ad consists of a black-and-white picture of a mountainside recently cleared of trees by a logging company. All that's left is a seemingly endless string of stumps, charred tree limbs, and muddy pits. In the lower left-hand corner of the page is a single message, printed in white type against the gray background: "The Sierra Club: *www.sierraclub.org.*" What is the purpose of this advertisement? Is it informative, persuasive, or both? Is it trying to inform readers about the Sierra Club's work, encourage them to find out more about the organization, or persuade them to join? While the picture itself may be striking, is the intention of the advertisement to entertain? How do you know? What if the text were different, that is, what if it read: "Help Us Fight Homelessness, *www. sierraclub.org*"? How would this new text change your interpretation of the advertisement's purpose?

Students sometimes run into problems when they read persuasive visual texts as if the texts were merely informative. We tend to read informative texts as if they were objective and factual; after all, that's what makes them different from persuasive texts. From experience, we know we need to read persuasive texts more skeptically than we do informative texts, because the author is actively attempting to sway our opinion about something or move us to act in a particular way. Our defenses are up when we read texts that we believe are persuasive in ways they are not when we read texts we think are primarily informative. In other words, our interpretation of a text's purpose influences how we read that text, how open we are to its message, and how critical we are as readers. Clarifying the purpose of the visual texts you read can help you read them more effectively and accurately.

QUESTIONS CONCERNING THE VISUAL TEXT'S AUDIENCE

- What audience is the visual text's creator trying to reach?
- How has the creator manipulated the visual text to successfully reach that audience?
- How does your understanding of the visual text's intended audience influence the way you read that text?

When you read a visual text, consider the type of reader its author or creator is attempting to reach. Sometimes you can base your conclusion on the publication in which the visual text appears: certain publications cater to certain types of readers. The general readership of *Inside Wrestling* magazine is likely different from the general readership of *Opera Aficionado* (although there may well be people who subscribe to both). Consider the interests and backgrounds of the people who would likely read the periodical or visit the website in which the visual text appeared. How might the author's interest in appealing to that type of reader influence the visual text he or she creates?

Another approach to analyzing audience is to consider the elements of the visual text itself: how did the author's view of his or her audience influence the way he or she constructed the visual text? Put another way, if you did not know the publication or website in which the visual text appeared, how could you determine the writer's or creator's sense of audience by carefully analyzing various elements of the text itself? Consider these questions:

- What types of images are included in the text? Would they appeal to a wide range of readers or to just certain types of readers?
- What examples are included in the text? Would they appeal to a popular or to a specialized audience?
- If there are human models in the text, who are they? What types of people are they? Who might identify with these models? Who might not?
- If there is written text, how formal is it? What cultural references does the written text include? What types of figurative language does it employ? Which readers would likely understand and appreciate this use of language?

Forming an understanding of the visual text's intended audience is important because it will guide the way you analyze that text. Central to analysis is a deceivingly simple question: Why did the author/creator construct the text this way? Assuming a rhetorical intent for all texts—that they are produced to have a particular effect on a particular audience—identifying the intended audience can guide the way you analyze the text itself. In other words, your analysis of the text will be based on your understanding of its intended audience.

QUESTIONS CONCERNING YOUR RESPONSE TO THE VISUAL TEXT

- What is my response to the visual text?
- Which aspects of the visual text elicit that response?
- What are the sources of my response?
- How does my response influence my understanding of the text?

Authors often incorporate visuals into their texts because they know readers are likely to respond to them in ways they will not respond to words alone. Visuals can stir our imagination, move us to anger or sympathy, attract us or alienate us, and cause us to laugh or to cringe. However, we often don't stop to consider our responses to visual texts: we are so wrapped up in responding to them that we don't consider the nature or cause of the response itself. The first step, then, is to recognize and articulate your reaction to a visual text. How does it make you feel? What is your response? Although it might prove difficult, find language that captures your reaction.

Next, identify which elements of the text evoke those responses. People looking at the same visual text may have very different emotional reactions to it, even if they are focusing on the exact same elements. Likewise, two people may have the same emotional response to a text even if they are focusing on different elements: one may be responding to a particular image included in the text and another to the text's layout. As you consider your response to a visual text, try to identify the specific elements that give rise to it. Encountering that text, you felt a particular way—what was in the text, exactly, that gave rise to your response?

Finally, consider why you respond to particular elements of the text the way you do. What knowledge, experience, or values do you have that cause you to react that way? Examining this link can be difficult, but doing so is extremely important, especially if you are going to discuss your response with someone else. For example, you and a classmate may have similar reactions to the same elements of a visual, but why you respond to those elements in a certain way may be very different. Articulating the link between the elements of the text and your responses can help you more fully understand your reactions and how they differ from others'.

READING A VISUAL TEXT—AN EXAMPLE

The following example of a visual text (see the next page) is an advertisement produced by the National Center for Family Literacy and published in the April 2008 edition of *Black Enterprise* magazine. Take a few minutes to carefully study the advertisement, then answer the following questions to get a better sense of how you are reading the visuals and text.

QUESTIONS CONCERNING THE VISUAL TEXT

- What images does the advertisement contain? How would you describe them?
- What do you assume is the relationship between the two people photographed in the advertisement? Why do you assume that? How does the photograph lead you to that conclusion?
- What else does the advertisement contain besides a photograph of the two people? For example, there's copy, but what else is there?
- What does the copy say? What words or ideas stand out in the copy? Why?
- Notice the National Center for Family Literacy name and logo at the bottom of the advertisement. Why are they included? What copy appears below the logo?
- Examine how the images and words on the page are arranged. What purpose might their arrangement serve?
- Notice how the copy employs two shades of gray. What purpose does that alternation serve?
- Which words stand out because they are flush with the margin? Which stand out because they are in dark type?
- What emotional appeals is the advertisement making? Examine how the people are posed for the picture. What appeal is the photographer making? Read the copy carefully. Point out instances in which particular words or phases are included to appeal to readers in specific ways.

Because I can read,
    I can understand. I can write a letter.
    I can fill out a job application.
    I can finally get off welfare.

Because I can read,
    I can learn. I can help my daughter
    with her homework.
    I can inspire her to be better.
    I can be a role model.

Because I can read,
    I can succeed, I can
    contribute. I can live
    my life without fear,
    without shame.
    I can be whatever
    I want to be.

Because I can read.

 National Center for Family Literacy

Literacy can make the difference between poverty and progress.
Visit **www.famlit.org** to help us write more success stories.

©2005 Photographer: Marvin Young

Source: National Center for Family Literacy

QUESTIONS CONCERNING THE VISUAL TEXT'S CREATOR OR SOURCE

- This advertisement appeared in *Black Enterprise* magazine. What do you assume or know about this publication?
- The advertisement was placed by the National Center for Family Literacy. What do you assume or know about this organization?
- Which types of people are likely to read *Black Enterprise*? What can you assume about their backgrounds and interests?
- How has the National Center for Family Literacy used images and copy to appeal to this type of reader?
- Why does the advertisement include copy like the following:
  - "Because I can read, I can understand. I can write a letter. I can fill out a job application. I can finally get off welfare."
  - "Because I can read, I can succeed, I can contribute."
  - "Literacy can make the difference between poverty and progress."

QUESTIONS CONCERNING THE VISUAL TEXT'S PURPOSE

- What is the advertisement's intended purpose? How do you know?
- Is the advertisement primarily a call to action ("Visit *www.famlit.org* to help us write more success stories."), or does it serve other purposes as well? If it serves other purposes, what are they?
- How has the National Center for Family Literacy attempted to achieve their purpose with this advertisement? How are their efforts related to the publication in which the advertisement appears?
- If the goal of the advertisement is primarily to inform readers, what do its creators intend for them to learn? How does the advertisement attempt to do this?
- If the advertisement is primarily a call to action, what is the action its creators want readers to take? How do they attempt to convince or move readers to act in this way?

QUESTIONS CONCERNING THE VISUAL TEXT'S AUDIENCE

- What audience is this advertisement attempting to reach?
- If the advertisement is a call to action, who is supposed to act? How do you know?
- How has the National Center for Family Literacy attempted to reach its intended audience? How has it manipulated the elements of the advertisement—for example, images, copy, layout, color—to reach its audience?

- Who do you assume is the speaker in the advertisement? Who is the first-person narrator? How do you know this? Why might the advertisement be written this way?
- What are the race, gender, and age of the people shown in the advertisement? Why do you think they were chosen as models for this advertisement? How might that choice be related to the intended audience?

QUESTIONS CONCERNING YOUR RESPONSE TO THE VISUAL TEXT

- How do you respond to the advertisement?
- Do you find it interesting? If so, why? If not, why not?
- Are you moved to take any action as a result of reading the advertisement? If so, what action and why? If not, why not?
- Do you respond one way to the photograph of the people and another way to the copy? Why?
- What personal experience or knowledge might influence the way you respond to this advertisement? What is the link between that experience or knowledge and your response?

WRITING A RHETORICAL ANALYSIS OF A VISUAL TEXT

Although on occasion you may be asked to write essays in which you just describe visual texts, you will more commonly be required to analyze and evaluate them rhetorically as well. When you write this type of essay, you will identify how the text's author attempts to achieve a particular rhetorical goal and assess his or her success.

STEP 1—CAREFULLY READ THE ASSIGNMENT

As always, be sure you understand the assignment's intent and requirements. The words *analysis* or *evaluation* may never appear in the assignment. Instead, you might be asked to "assess" or "critique" the text, to decide "how effective" it is, or to argue "how well" it achieves its goal. If you have any questions regarding the goals of the essay you are being asked to write, talk to your teacher.

Also be sure you understand whether you will be evaluating a visual text you locate on your own or if you will be working with an assigned text. If you are free to choose your own visual text for rhetorical analysis, clarify whether there are any restrictions on your choice. For example, does your teacher want you to work with a particular type of visual text (i.e., an advertisement, a political cartoon, a photograph, a sign, or a painting)? Are particular types of visual texts excluded from the analysis? Finally, if the choice of source texts is up to you, have your teacher approve your selection before you begin to write your essay.

STEP 2—ANALYZE AND DESCRIBE THE TEXT

Although this step sounds simple, in some ways it is the most difficult. You need to carefully and objectively examine the text, finding language to describe exactly what you see and read. In several chapters, this textbook discusses the issue of bias when it comes to writing and reading texts—readers need to understand and take into account possible authorial bias when they read texts and acknowledge the biases they themselves bring to the texts they read and write. The same concerns hold true for visual texts as well.

While you need to consider the biases that may have influenced the visual text's creation, you also need to be aware of any biases that could cloud or color your reading of it. Bias can lead you to misinterpret a visual image or actually fail to "see" what is on the page or computer screen because you are not looking for it. Therefore, when you analyze and describe a visual text, try to put aside as best you can any prejudices or assumptions you have concerning the text's content, message, creator, or source. Just as when you write a summary of a print text, your goal here is to be as objective as possible. Try to describe the visual text as objectively and accurately as you can, using language that is neutral and clear.

STEP 3—ESTABLISH THE TEXT'S RHETORICAL SITUATION

To establish the visual text's rhetorical situation, consider your answers to the following questions. Be sure to draw on the insights you gained through your earlier critical reading of the text:

* Who is the text's author or creator?
* Where was the text published, or where does it appear?
* What is the text's message? If there is more than one message, what are they? Does one message dominate?
* Who is the text's intended audience?
* How does the text want to affect that audience? What is the text's purpose?

If you have a hard time answering any of these questions, consider asking someone else—a classmate, roommate, parent, or friend—to examine the text and discuss it with them. Sometimes talking about a visual text with someone is the best way of determining its rhetorical situation.

STEP 4—DETERMINE HOW THE TEXT ATTEMPTS TO ACHIEVE ITS RHETORICAL GOALS

Once you have determined the text's rhetorical goals, identify how its creator manipulates its images and/or text to achieve those ends. Here you would examine how the various elements of the text you identified earlier work separately and together to achieve the text's purpose. Your goal is to find language to describe how the visual text "works," how it communicates its message, and how it accomplishes its goals. The various elements of the text you focus on at this stage in the writing process are the ones you will likely write about in your essay.

STEP 5—DETERMINE YOUR THESIS

Your thesis statement can be either open or closed. An open thesis statement would indicate how successfully you believe the visual text achieved its rhetorical goal. Using the National Center for Family Literacy ad found on page 156, an open thesis statement may read something like this:

> The National Center for Family Literacy produced an advertisement that successfully encourages readers to support their organization.

This thesis identifies what the writer believes to be the advertisement's goal or purpose (to encourage readers to support the sponsoring organization) and asserts a judgment concerning its success.

A closed thesis statement would indicate both your judgment of how well the visual text achieved its goals and the elements of the text you will examine to support your conclusion. Again, using the ad presented on page 156, a closed thesis statement could resemble this:

> Through its copy and its depiction of a mother and her daughter, the National Center for Family Literacy advertisement successfully encourages readers to support their organization.

This thesis still indicates the writer's judgment concerning how successfully the advertisement achieves its goal but also indicates how she will support her claim (by examining the advertisement's use of copy and its portrayal of a mother and her daughter).

STEP 6—WRITE A ROUGH DRAFT

Although the content and structure of the essays you write will vary by the type of visual text you are analyzing and evaluating, the following guidelines will help you write an effective rough draft.

Introductory Section

- Introduce the topic of your essay.
- Introduce the source text you will be working with.
- State your thesis.
- Capture reader interest.

You might consider opening your essay by introducing the topic the visual text addresses, discussing the specific genre of visual text you will be working with (for example, an advertisement or a web page), or paraphrasing the assignment you've been given. Next, introduce the specific visual text you will be working with in your essay, indicating its authorship, source, and perhaps its date of publication. You should also include your thesis statement, typically placed toward the end of your introduction.

Description of the Visual Text and Overview of the Rhetorical Situation

- Describe the visual text.
- Explain the text's rhetorical situation.

In this section of your essay, describe and summarize the visual text you will be working with. Students sometimes understandably question why this section of the paper is needed, especially if the visual text is going to accompany the essay they write: Why describe the text when readers will have access to it? Keep in mind that your description is preparing your readers for the argument you are going to make concerning the text's effectiveness. Through your description, you will bring to your readers' attention the aspects and elements of the text you will discuss in the body of your essay. You will introduce those aspects and elements in this section of your essay and evaluate them later.

The same advice holds true for explaining the visual text's rhetorical situation. You need to tell your reader where and in what context the visual text appeared, who created it, when it was created, and why it was produced. Identify what you believe to be the text's intended audience and purpose. If you believe your readers might interpret the text's purpose differently than you do in your essay, address those concerns here, acknowledging them and defending your own interpretation. The more clearly you explain the text's rhetorical situation in this part of your essay, the easier it will be to write a convincing argument in the body of your paper.

Body Paragraphs

- Develop your thesis one criterion or one example at a time.
- Cite specific examples from the visual text to support your assertions.
- Explain how those examples support the assertions you are making.
- Address possible objections or alternatives to your interpretations, as needed.

As you explain and develop the assertion(s) you put forward in your thesis, examine one evaluative criterion or example from the visual text at a time. For example, if you are basing your evaluation of a text on its use of color, examine one use of color in the text at a time, explaining how it supports the assertion you are making. Afterward, move on to your next example. If you are basing your evaluation on the text's use of color and layout, don't jump back and forth between the two—develop one criterion at a time.

Also, do not assume that the examples you cite speak for themselves or that your readers will understand on their own how the examples you draw from the visual text support the assertion you are making. Instead, carefully explain the link as you see it, and explain how each example lends credibility to your assertion.

Finally, be aware that any conclusions you have reached regarding the visual text are based on your interpretation of that text. Your judgments reflect the way you have interpreted and responded to the images and/or writing. Other readers could legitimately interpret the text differently. As you develop and explain your particular interpretation, note likely objections to your assertions or viable alternative interpretations, when necessary. Acknowledging and addressing these objections or alternatives increases your credibility as a writer and strengthens your assertions.

Conclusion

- Wrap up your essay in an interesting way.
- Remind readers of your thesis.

As with other types of source-based essays, you want to wrap up your analysis/evaluation of a visual text in a way that reminds readers of the primary assertions you've made and that maintains interest. One way to reassert your primary claims is to simply restate your thesis; however, this approach does little to sustain reader interest. Instead, consider closing your essay with an interesting question or provocative assertion, to either challenge other readers' interpretations of the visual text or to predict the future, perhaps speculating on how successful the visual text will be in achieving its desired goals.

STEP 7—REVISE YOUR ESSAY

When revising your analysis/evaluation of a visual text, make sure your writing is clear, developed, and well organized.

- *Clear*—your readers understand the assertions you are making and the link between your evaluations and the source text.
- *Developed*—you have thoroughly explained your assertions and have examined alternative interpretations when needed.
- *Organized*—your assertions are logically connected, and your evaluation is guided by an overarching thesis.

Check for Clarity

When you revise your essay, at some point try to switch roles: you are no longer the author of your paper but someone reading it for the first time. Are there any assertions a reader might have a difficult time understanding? Are there any terms that need to be more clearly defined? Is the connection between your analysis/evaluation and the source text itself always clear?

In other words, would readers understand exactly what aspects or elements of the source text you are analyzing, evaluating, or responding to? Have you explained your assertions thoroughly? Revise your essay as necessary to improve clarity.

Check the Development of Your Essay

Have you supported each of your assertions with references to the source text? Have you explained the connection between your assertions and the source text? The examples you cite from the source text cannot speak for themselves; do not expect your readers to understand the link between your assertions and the evidence you cite. Instead, clearly explain your reasoning.

Check the Organization

First, check your thesis statement. Does it accurately reflect and predict your essay's content and structure? If not, revise it. Second, check your topic sentences. Does each one introduce a new idea, provide a transition from the previous section of your essay, and, in some way, echo your thesis statement? Check the quality of the opening and closing sections of your essay—do they accomplish their intended goals? Finally, add transitions within paragraphs where needed to help guide your readers through your essay.

SAMPLE RHETORICAL ANALYSIS OF A VISUAL TEXT

The following sample essay analyzes and evaluates the National Center for Family Literacy advertisement found on page 156.

AN EFFECTIVE ADVERTISEMENT FOR LITERACY SUPPORT

The idea of an organization devoted to the promotion of literacy paying for a magazine advertisement may seem odd. After all, if people can read the ad, they are already literate and have no need of the organization's services. If they are illiterate, they cannot read the ad at all. So what would be the purpose of such an advertisement? Judging by the ad placed by the National Center for Family Literacy in the April 2008 edition of *Black Enterprise* magazine, the purpose would be to garner support for the organization's programs and services. Through its use of copy, layout, and models, the National Center for Family Literacy demonstrates just how effective such an ad can be.

Unlike many other advertisements in *Black Enterprise*, the one sponsored by the National Center for Family Literacy is simple—using shades of black and white rather than color. Most of the ad consists of copy printed on a white background with two models—seemingly a mother and her daughter—appearing in the bottom right-hand corner. The bottom left-hand corner contains the National Center for Family Literacy name and logo, the message "Literacy can make the difference between poverty and progress," and an appeal to "Visit *www.famlit.org* to help us write more success stories."

The copy consists of the phrase "Because I can read" repeated four times in boldface print. Below three of these phrases—which serve as headings—are first-person statements (presumably from the mother in the ad) printed in a lighter typeface to finish the sentence. Under the first heading, the copy explains how becoming literate helped her find a job and get off welfare. Under the second heading, the copy focuses on how becoming literate helped her become a better mother and role model for her daughter. Under the third, the copy explains how being able to read has enabled the mother to live without fear and shame, allowing her to achieve economic success.

One reason this advertisement works well is that its copy appeals to the type of person likely to read *Black Enterprise* magazine. *Black Enterprise* is aimed primarily at African-American businesspeople, entrepreneurs, and philanthropists, people who have established or work for successful companies, who are looking for business opportunities, or who seek charitable opportunities. Those who read this magazine are aware of how important it is to have a trained, literate workforce and may have a greater understanding of and sympathy for people who must overcome obstacles to succeed.

Consequently, the copy under the first heading reads, "Because I can read, I can understand. I can write a letter. I can fill out a job application. I can finally get off welfare." Many readers of *Black Enterprise* would want to support an organization that helps potential workers learn how to fill out a job application, join the workforce, and move off of welfare. The copy under the second heading appeals to the readers' emotions. Supporting the work of the National Center for Family Literacy will improve the life of the family pictured in the ad—thanks to the organization, the mother can now "help my daughter with her homework," "inspire her to be better," and be a better "role model." Supporting the National Center for Family Literacy is not just in the economic interest of those who read *Black Enterprise*, it is also a humanitarian act.

The copy under the third heading combines elements of the first two. It opens with an echo of the first: "Because I can read, I can succeed. I can contribute." The copy indicates that the National Center for Family Literacy can help women like the one in the advertisement enter the workforce and achieve economic success. The next two statements, however, return to emotional appeals: "I can live my life without fear, without shame. I can be whatever I want to be." The copy is designed to build a bridge between the readers' experiences and the National Center's mission by stressing the need to help people overcome fears and obstacles and by working hard, to succeed.

Also making the National Center for Family Literacy's ad effective is its use of layout—how the copy and visuals are arranged on the page. The phrase "Because I can read," is repeated four times, printed in boldface along the left-hand margin of the page. Due to their placement and appearance, these words catch the reader's eye first. This repeated phrase dominates the ad, leading the reader's eye down the page to the National Center for Family Literacy's logo. The lighter-colored text underneath each heading catches the reader's eye because of its appearance and the repetition of "I": nine of the thirteen lines under the headings begin with "I." The use of first person in these lines makes the advertisement's copy personal, encouraging readers to identify with the mother and daughter pictured in the lower right-hand corner. People are more likely to support a charitable organization if they can identify and empathize with those who will be receiving the aid.

In fact, the depiction of the people in the advertisement also makes it effective. The copy surrounds and frames the two people, a mother and her child. Reading the headings left to right leads the reader's eye directly toward them. The mother is squatting down and her daughter is standing behind her, leaning in, a hand on each of her mother's shoulders. The mother's right hand is on her knee; her left hand rests on top of her daughter's right hand. The mother has a slight, proud grin on her face, while the daughter shows a full-toothed smile. These are average people— the mother appears to be wearing a sweatsuit of some sort and the daughter a polo shirt. The mother and her daughter are quite ordinary people, people whom the readers of *Black Enterprise* might know or see every day on the street. The message of the ad is clear: the National Center for Family Literacy helps average families like this one.

Finally, the facial expressions and race of the mother and daughter are crucial elements of the advertisement. The daughter seems overjoyed with the fact that her mother can now read, while the mother is brimming with confidence. Who wouldn't want to support an organization that would improve the life of such a cute little girl? Significant, too, is the fact that the mother is white while her daughter is biracial. While *Black Enterprise* magazine primarily attracts African-American readers, the advertisement makes clear that the National Center for Family Literacy works to improve the lives of all people, regardless of race.

The National Center for Family Literacy advertisement that appeared in *Black Enterprise* magazine is not aimed at recruiting people who need the center's services. Instead, it is intended to attract possible donors and supporters. Beneath the center's logo at the bottom of the ad is copy that reads, "Literacy can make the difference between poverty and progress," and an appeal to "Visit *www.famlit.org* to help us write more success stories." Readers with a charitable heart may well consider supporting the organization after reading this successful ad.

Summary Chart

HOW TO WRITE A RHETORICAL ANALYSIS OF A VISUAL TEXT

1. **Carefully read the assignment.**
   - *Clarify your purpose.*
   - *Clarify the degree of freedom you have to select a visual text to evaluate.*

2. **Analyze and describe the text.**
   - *Examine every aspect of the text.*
   - *Attempt to put aside any biases you bring to the text.*

3. **Establish the text's rhetorical situation.**
   - *Who is the text's author or creator?*
   - *Where was the text published or where does it appear?*
   - *What is the text's message?*
   - *Who is the text's intended audience?*
   - *What is the text's purpose?*

4. **Determine how the text attempts to achieve its rhetorical goals.**
   - *How do the various elements of the text work separately and together to achieve the text's purpose or goal?*

5. **Determine your thesis.**
   - *Identify what you think the text's goal is and assert a judgment concerning how well it succeeds in achieving that goal.*
   - *Decide if you will use an open or closed thesis.*
   - *If you use a closed thesis, indicate which elements of the text you will examine in your essay.*

SUMMARY CHART: HOW TO WRITE A RHETORICAL ANALYSIS
OF A VISUAL TEXT *(CONTINUED)*

6. **Write a rough draft.**
   - *Write the introductory section of your essay, indicating the topic of your essay, identifying the source text you will be working with, stating your thesis, and capturing reader interest.*
   - *Provide a brief but thorough description of the text and explain its rhetorical situation.*
   - *Draft the body of your evaluation in a manner that is consistent with your thesis, examining one element at a time of the visual text, citing specific examples from the text to support any assertions you make, explaining how those examples support your claims, and addressing possible objections to or questions concerning your interpretation.*
   - *Write the concluding section of your essay, writing up your evaluation, reminding readers of your thesis, and maintaining reader interest.*

7. **Revise your essay.**
   - *Make sure your writing is clear.*
   - *Make sure your writing is well developed.*
   - *Make sure your writing is organized.*

RHETORICAL ANALYSIS OF A VISUAL TEXT REVISION CHECKLIST

	Yes	No
1. Have you carefully analyzed the assignment to determine whether you are supposed to describe, analyze, and/or evaluate the text?	_____	_____
2. Have you carefully examined every aspect of the source text?	_____	_____
3. Have you established the visual text's rhetorical situation?	_____	_____
4. Have you established how the creators of the visual text attempt to achieve their rhetorical goal?	_____	_____
5. Have you determined how well they achieve their goal?	_____	_____
6. Have you expressed your findings in a clear thesis statement that can guide the development of your essay?	_____	_____
7. In the introductory section of your essay, do you:		
• introduce the topic?	_____	_____
• introduce the source text?	_____	_____
• state your thesis?	_____	_____
• attempt to capture reader interest?	_____	_____
8. In the body of your essay, do you:		
• provide an overview or description of the visual text?	_____	_____
• develop your essay one criterion at a time?	_____	_____
• cite specific examples from the text to support your claims?	_____	_____
• explain how those examples support your assertions?	_____	_____
• address possible objections to your interpretation?	_____	_____
9. In the concluding section of your essay, do you:		
• wrap up your essay in an interesting way?	_____	_____
• remind readers of your thesis?	_____	_____
10. Have you revised your essay for:		
• clarity?	_____	_____
• development?	_____	_____
• organization?	_____	_____
11. Have you proofread your essay?	_____	_____

Chapter 9

....

INFORMATIVE SYNTHESIS

DEFINITION AND PURPOSE

In a synthesis, you combine information from two or more readings to support a position of your own. Your aim in the paper can be expository (to convey information) or argumentative (to convince readers that your thesis concerning the readings is correct). In either case, when writing a synthesis, you combine material from two or more readings with your own knowledge and reasoning to explain or support your thesis.

College writing assignments often require you to synthesize material. In some courses the assignment will be direct and clear: "Compare what Author A and Author B have to say about topic X. How are their views alike and how are they different?" Other times the assignment might be more subtle: "Authors A, B, and C all address topic X. Which do you find most convincing?" Completing either assignment would require you to form and defend a thesis by drawing information from two or more readings.

To write a synthesis, you first need to sort through the readings to find information you can use in your paper. Being able to annotate readings thoroughly is essential. Second, you need to find the best way to organize this material around your own thesis and the demands of the assignment. Third, you need to find a place in the essay for your own ideas, findings, or arguments. Composing a synthesis usually involves more than just stringing together quoted and paraphrased material from other writers. Fourth, as you write your paper, you need to keep straight who receives credit for which ideas. Through proper documentation, you need to clarify for your readers when you are drawing on the work of a particular author and when you are developing material yourself. Finally, as you revise your work, you need to keep clearly in mind the rhetorical situation of the assignment. In your efforts to work with other people's ideas, you cannot afford to lose sight of your readers' needs and the purpose of the assignment.

TYPES OF SYNTHESIS ESSAYS

Synthesis essays can assume many different forms in college, some rather specialized and sophisticated. One way to begin sorting through all this variety is to recognize that for the most part the assignments you receive will ask you to compose either an **informative** or an **argumentative** synthesis (see Chapter 10).

The goal of an informative synthesis is to clearly and efficiently communicate the information you have gathered from two or more readings. You do not defend a position of your own or critique the source texts in this type of paper. Your primary aim is to summarize the material in the readings and convey the information to your readers in a clear, concise, organized fashion, often comparing and contrasting the texts. In contrast, the goal of an argumentative synthesis is to convince your reader to accept an argument you are presenting on either the quality of the readings or the topic they address. You use the material in the source texts to support your thesis, sometimes summarizing the readings and sometimes critiquing them.

Either type of synthesis can be organized in a variety of ways. Often writers will choose to employ either a **block** or an **alternating** format. When you use a block format to structure your synthesis, you discuss only one source text at a time. With an alternating format, you switch back and forth between readings as you develop your thesis point by point.

Before examining each type of synthesis in more detail, read the following arguments concerning the relationship between television viewing and childhood violence. What is each author's stance on the topic? What aspects of the topic most capture the author's interest? How convincing is each author's argument?

Media Violence and Children's Emotions: Beyond the "Smoking Gun"

Joanne Cantor

Dr. Joanne Cantor is Director of the Center for Communication Research at the University of Wisconsin—Madison.

Research on media violence is often misunderstood by the general public. There are two important reasons why. One is a methodological issue: It is impossible to do the type of "smoking gun" research that would please the ardent skeptics. The other is that most public discussions of media violence don't adequately address the emotional consequences of viewing. I will briefly discuss the methodological issues and then focus on the important role of emotional reactions both in the risks of media violence and in potential remedies.

As for the methodological problems: We can't randomly assign children early in their lives to watch different doses of violence on television and then 20 years later see which children committed violent crimes. But the same type of limitation also exists for medical research: We can't randomly assign groups of people to smoke differing amounts of cigarettes for 20 years, and then count the number of people who developed cancer.

Tobacco researchers conduct correlational studies in which they look at the amount people smoked during their lives and then see the rate at which they have succumbed to cancer. They control statistically for other factors, of course—other healthy and unhealthy behaviors that either reduce or promote the tendency to develop cancer. Then they can find out whether smoking contributed to cancer, over and above these other influences. And since they can't do cancer experiments on people, they use animal studies. These are artificial, but they tell us something about the short-term effects of tobacco that can't be found from correlational studies. Putting the two types of research together, we now have powerful data about the effects of smoking on the development of cancer.

Similarly, media violence researchers do longitudinal studies of children's media exposure and look at the types of behaviors they engage in over time. We also control for other factors, such as previous aggressiveness, family problems, and the like. We don't look at media violence in a vacuum; we examine whether there is a correlation between television viewing and violent behavior, even controlling for other influences. We also do experiments. Like the animal experiments for cancer, these are not natural situations, but such experiments fill the gaps we cannot fill otherwise. They are meant to show short-term effects, like increases in hostility or more accepting attitudes toward violence—changes that we know increase the likelihood of violent actions, both in the short term and in the long run.

As with tobacco, the two types of media research form a powerful picture. Even though there are many studies that can be criticized, there are many more others that are valid. A recent meta-analysis[1] putting all the studies together, makes a compelling case that media violence does contribute to anti-social behaviors, including violence. It's also misguided to say the effects of media violence on violent behavior are trivial. To give an example, a recent national survey of Israeli middle-schools[2] showed that when World Wrestling Federation was introduced to Israeli TV in 1994, the widespread imitation of the wrestlers' behavior produced an epidemic of serious playground injuries. The mayhem continued until the frequency with which the program aired was reduced and educators offered extensive counseling to counteract the show's impact.

The second reason for misunderstanding media violence—the failure to address emotional consequences—is an area I have been investigating for more than 25 years. Two important areas of emotional effects are hostility and desensitization on the one hand, and fears and anxieties on the other.

Desensitization and Hostility

Desensitization is a psychological process by which an emotional response is repeatedly evoked in situations in which the action tendency that arises out of the emotion proves irrelevant. Desensitization is sometimes used to treat phobias, by gradually and repeatedly presenting a frightening stimulus under nonthreatening conditions. Over time, when desensitization works, the phobic response becomes less and less intense. In a somewhat analogous fashion, exposure to media violence, particularly that which entails bitter hostilities or the graphic display of injuries, initially induces an intense emotional reaction in viewers. Over time and with repeated exposure, however, many viewers exhibit decreasing emotional responses to the depiction of violence and injury. Desensitization to violence has been documented in a variety of outcomes. For example, it has been observed as reduced arousal and emotional disturbance while witnessing violence;[3] as greater hesitancy to call an adult to intervene in a witnessed physical altercation;[4] and as less sympathy for the victims of domestic abuse.[5] Few people would argue that any of these are healthy outcomes.

There is also ample evidence that viewing violence increases viewers' hostile feelings. Some people argue that the well-substantiated correlation between chronic hostility and violence viewing simply shows that people who are already hostile are more likely to choose violence. Well, it's true that violent, hostile people are more attracted to media violence,[6] but research shows that the relationship is bi-directional. A 1992 field investigation[7] is a good illustration of this fact. Researchers went to a theater and asked moviegoers to fill out the Buss-Durkee hostility inventory either before or after they viewed a film that they themselves had selected. The findings showed that both the male and female viewers who had chosen a violent movie were initially more hostile than the viewers who had selected a nonviolent movie. Moreover, viewers' levels of hostility became even higher after viewing the violent movie, but remained at the same low level after viewing the nonviolent movie.

This study once again disproves the sometimes-popular notion of "catharsis," that violence viewing helps purge people of their hostile inclinations. To the contrary. And this increase in hostility is not necessarily short-lived. A 1999 experiment[8] looked at the emotional and interpersonal consequences of repeated exposure to gratuitous violence. Researchers randomly assigned both male and female college students to view either intensely violent or nonviolent feature films for four days in a row. On the fifth day, in a purportedly unrelated study, the participants were put in a position to help or hinder another person's chances of future employment. The surprising results indicated that both the men and the women who had received the recent daily dose of film violence were more harmful to that person's job prospects, whether she had treated them well or had behaved in an insulting fashion. The repeated violence viewing apparently provided an enduring hostile mental framework that damaged interactions that were affectively neutral as well as those that involved provocation.

The research I've presented on the impact of media violence on desensitization and hostility demonstrates that we should not limit ourselves to considering the most obvious, final outcomes of viewing violence, that is, behaving violently, when attempting to understand its harmful consequences.

Fear and Anxieties

There is growing evidence that violence viewing also induces intense fears and anxieties in child viewers. A 1998 survey[9] of more than 2,000 third through eighth graders in Ohio revealed that as the number of hours of television viewing per day increased, so did the prevalence of symptoms of psychological trauma, such as anxiety, depression, and posttraumatic stress. Similarly, a 1999 survey[10] of the parents of almost 500 children in kindergarten through fourth grade in Rhode Island revealed that the amount of children's television viewing (especially television viewing at bedtime) and having a television in their own bedroom, were significantly related to the frequency of sleep disturbances. Indeed, 9% of the parents surveyed reported that their child experienced TV-induced nightmares *at least once a week*.

Finally a random national survey[11] conducted in 1999 reported that 62% of parents with children between the ages of two and seventeen said that their child had been frightened by something they saw in a TV program or movie.

Two recent studies of adults' retrospective reports[12,13] of memories of having been frightened by a television show or movie demonstrate that the presence of vivid, detailed memories of enduring media-induced fear is nearly universal. Of the students reporting fright reactions in the study we conducted at the Universities of Wisconsin and Michigan, 52% reported disturbances in eating or sleeping, 22% reported mental preoccupation with the disturbing material, and 35% reported subsequently avoiding or dreading the situation depicted in the program or movie. Moreover, more than one-fourth of the respondents said that the emotional impact of the program or movie (viewed an average of six years earlier) was still with them at the time of reporting!

Studies like these and many anecdotal reports reveal that it is not at all unusual to give up swimming in the ocean after seeing *Jaws*—in fact, a surprising number of people report giving up swimming altogether after seeing that movie. Many other people trace their long-term fears of specific animals, such as dogs, cats, or insects to childhood exposure to cartoon features like *Alice in Wonderland* or *Beauty and the Beast* or to horror movies.[14] I would like to note here that the impact of frightening media depictions are not *just* "psychological." As disturbing as unnecessary anxieties are by themselves, they can readily lead to physical ailments (especially when they disrupt sleep for long periods of time).

For the most part, what frightens children in the media involves violence or the perceived threat of violence or harm. It is important to note, however, that parents often find it hard to predict children's fright reactions to television and films because a child's level of cognitive development influences how he or she perceives and responds to media stimuli. My associates and I have conducted a program of research to explore developmental differences in media-induced fright reactions based on theories and findings in cognitive development. I have summarized this research and its implications for parents and others interested in children's mental health in my book *"Mommy, I'm Scared": How TV and Movies Frighten Children and What We Can Do to Protect Them*. This research shows that as children mature cognitively, some things become less likely to disturb them, whereas other things become potentially more upsetting.

As a first generalization, the importance of how things look decreases as a child's age increases. This finding is consistent with research showing that preschool children tend to sort and match stimuli based on perceptible characteristics, but as they mature through the elementary school years, this tendency becomes supplanted by the tendency to attend increasingly to the more conceptual aspects of stimuli. Both our experimental[15] and our survey[16] research supports the generalization that preschool children (approximately 3 to 5 years old) are more likely to be frightened by something that looks scary but is actually harmless than by something that looks attractive but is actually harmful; for older elementary school children (approximately 9 to 11 years), appearance carries much less weight, relative to the behavior or destructive potential of a character, animal, or object.

A second generalization from research is that as children mature, they become more responsive to realistic, and less responsive to fantastic dangers depicted in the media. This prediction is based on developmental trends in children's understanding of the fantasy-reality distinction. Our 1984 survey of parents[17] supported this trend. In general, parents' tendency to mention fantasy offerings, depicting events that could not possibly occur in the real world, as sources of their child's fear, decreased as the child's age increased, and the tendency to mention fictional offerings, depicting events that could possibly occur, increased. Further support for this generalization comes from our 1996 survey[18] of children's fright responses to television news. A random survey of parents of children in kindergarten through sixth grades showed that fear produced by fantasy programs decreased as the child's grade increased, while fear induced by news stories increased with age.

A third generalization is that as children mature, they become frightened by media depictions involving increasingly abstract concepts. Again, research in cognitive development shows that the ability to think abstractly increases throughout elementary school and continues to mature during the teenage years. Data supporting this generalization come from our 1986 survey[19] of children's responses to the made-for-television movie *The Day After*. Although many people were concerned about young children's reactions to this movie, which depicted the devastation of a Kansas community by a nuclear attack, the survey showed that the emotional impact of this movie increased as the viewer's age increased. Similarly, our survey[20] of children's reactions to television coverage of the war in the Persian Gulf showed that preschool and elementary school children were more likely to be frightened by the concrete, visual aspects of the coverage (such as the missiles exploding), whereas teenagers were more disturbed by the abstract components of the story (such as the possibility of the conflict spreading).

Coping with Media Violence Effects

An understanding of emotional reactions to media is also important in developing ways to prevent or reduce the harm produced by media violence. Research in cognitive development has helped us discover effective ways to reassure children who have been frightened by media threats. These are explained in *"Mommy, I'm Scared."* Strategies for coping with media-induced fears need to be tailored to the age of the child.[21] Up to the age of about seven, nonverbal coping strategies work the best.[22] These include removing children from the scary situation, distracting them, giving them attention and warmth, and desensitization.[23] Eight-year-olds and older can benefit from hearing logical explanations about why they are safe. If what they saw is fantasy, it helps children in this age group to be reminded that what they have seen could never happen.[24] If the program depicts frightening events that can possibly occur, however, it may help to give older children information about why what they have seen cannot happen to them[25] or to give them empowering instructions on how to prevent it from occurring.[26]

As for reducing the aggression-promoting effect of media violence, an understanding of emotional responses can be helpful in developing mediation strategies that can be used by parents or teachers. For example, as viewers become increasingly desensitized and more hostile, they become less and less likely to empathize with the victims of violence. One criticism of the way violence is usually portrayed on television is that it minimizes the apparent harmful consequences to the victim,[27] both promoting desensitization and increasing the likelihood of the adoption of aggressive attitudes and behaviors.

A genre of media violence that typically trivializes the consequences to the victim is the classic cartoon, Woody Woodpecker, for example. In a study just published[28] we showed not only that watching Woody could increase boys' endorsement of aggressive solutions to problems, but that empathy instructions could intervene in this effect. Second- through sixth-grade boys were randomly assigned one of three groups: (1) a no-mediation group, who watched the cartoon without instructions; (2) a mediation group who were asked, before viewing, to keep in mind the feelings of the man in the cartoon (this was the tree-medic who was the target of Woody's attacks); and (3) a control group, who didn't see a cartoon. As is frequently found in such studies, the kids who had just seen the violent cartoon without instructions scored higher on pro-violence attitudes than the kids in the control condition (showing stronger agreement with statements like, "sometimes fighting is a good way to get what you want"). However, the kids who were asked to think about the victim's feelings showed no such increase in pro-violence attitudes. As a side-effect, this empathy-promoting intervention reduced the degree to which the children found the cartoon funny. An empathy-promoting intervention may have a dual benefit therefore: intervening in the direct effect of viewing and perhaps reducing future choices of similar fare.

More research is needed to explore other ways to intervene in the negative effects of media violence. Given the fact that media violence is such a profitable business, it is not likely to go away in the near future. However, a greater understanding of the emotional consequences of viewing violence will help policymakers, teachers, parents, and children deal with the problem. To my mind, we need better public education for parents and teachers, including better information about media effects, more useful content labels, and additional mediation strategies based on research findings. We also need media literacy education for children, including helping them place what they see in perspective, and encouraging a critical analysis of their own media choices.

Endnotes

1. Paik, H., & Comstock, O. (1994). The effects of television violence on anti-social behavior: A meta-analysis. *Communication Research, 21*, 516–546.

2. Lemish, D. (1997). The school as a wrestling arena: The modeling of a television series. *Communication, 22*(4), 395–418.

3. Cline, V. B., Croft, R. O., & Courrier, S. (1973). Desensitization of children to television violence. *Journal of Personality and Social Psychology, 27*, 360–365.

4. Molitor, F., & Hirsch, K. W. (1994). Children's toleration of real-life aggression after exposure to media violence: A replication of the Drabman and Thomas studies. *Child Study Journal, 24*, 191–207.

5. Mullin, C. R., & Linz, D. (1995). Desensitization and resensitization to violence against women: Effects of exposure to sexually violent films on judgments of domestic violence victims. *Journal of Personality and Social Psychology, 69*, 449–459.

6. Goldstein, J., Ed. (1998). *Why we watch: The attractions of violent entertainment.* New York: Oxford University Press.

7. Black, S. L., & Bevan, S. (1992). At the movies with Buss and Durkee: A natural experiment on film violence. *Aggressive Behavior, 18*, 37–45.

8. Zillmann, D., & Weaver, J. B., III. (1999). Effects of prolonged exposure to gratuitous media violence on provoked and unprovoked hostile behavior. *Journal of Applied Social Psychology, 29*, 145–165.

9. Singer, M. I., Slovak, K., Frierson, T., & York, P. (1998). Viewing preferences, symptoms of psychological trauma and violent behaviors among children who watch television. *Journal of the American Academy of Child and Adolescent Psychiatry, 37*, 1041–1048.

10. Owens, J., Maxim, R., McGuinn, M., Nobile, C., Msall, M., & Alario, A. (1999). Television-viewing habits and sleep disturbance in school children. *Pediatrics, 104*(3), 552 (Abstract). Available at http://www.pediatrics.org/cgilcontent/ful/104/3/c27.

11. Gentile, D. A., & Walsh, D. A. (1999). MediaQuotient(TM): National survey of family media habits, knowledge, and attitudes. Minneapolis, MN: National Institute on Media and the Family.

12. Harrison, K., & Cantor, J. (1999). Tales from the screen: Enduring fright reactions to scary media. *Media Psychology, 1*, 97–116.

13. Hoekstra, S. J., Harris, R. J., & Helmick, A. L. (1999). Autobiographical memories about the experience of seeing frightening movies in childhood. *Media Psychology, 1*, 117–140.

14. Cantor, J. (1998). *"Mommy, I'm scared": How TV and movies frighten children and what we can do to protect them.* San Diego, CA: Harcourt Brace.

15. Hoffner, C ., & Cantor, J. (1985). Developmental differences in responses to a television character's appearance and behavior. *Developmental Psychology, 2*, 1065–1074.

16. Cantor, J., & Sparks, G. G. (1984). Children's fear responses to mass media: Testing some Piagetian predictions. *Journal of Communication, 34*(2), 90–103.

17. Cantor, J., & Sparks, G. G. (1984). Children's fear responses to mass media: Testing some Piagetian predictions. *Journal of Communication, 34*(2), 90–103.

18. Cantor, J., & Nathanson, A. (1996). Children's fright reactions to television news. *Journal of Communication, 46*(4), 139–152.

19. Cantor, J., Wilson, B. J., & Hoffner, C. (1986). Emotional responses to a televised nuclear holocaust film. *Communication Research, 13*, 257–277.

20. Cantor, J., Mares, M. L., & Oliver, M. B. (1993). Parents' and children's emotional reactions to televised coverage of the Gulf War. In B. Greenberg & W. Gantz (Eds.), *Desert Storm and the mass media* (pp. 325–340). Cresskill, NJ: Hampton Press.

21. Cantor, J. (1998). *"Mommy, I'm scared": How TV and movies frighten children and what we can do to protect them.* San Diego, CA: Harcourt Brace.

22. Wilson, B. J., Hoffner, C., & Cantor, J. (1987). Children's perceptions of the effectiveness of techniques to reduce fear from mass media. *Journal of Applied Developmental Psychology, 8*, 39–52.

23. Wilson, B. J. (1989). Desensitizing children's emotional reactions to the mass media. *Communication Research, 16*, 723–745.

24. Cantor, J., & Wilson, B. J. (1984). Modifying fear responses to mass media in preschool and elementary school children. *Journal of Broadcasting, 28*, 431–443.

25. Cantor, J., & Hoffner, C. (1990). Children's fear reactions to a televised film as a function of perceived immediacy of depicted threat. *Journal of Broadcasting & Electronic Media, 34*, 421–442.

26. Cantor, J., & Omdahl, B. (1999). Children's acceptance of safety guidelines after exposure to televised dramas depicting accidents. *Western Journal of Communication, 63*(1), 1–15.

27. *National Television Violence Study*, Volumes 1–3. (1996–1998). Thousand Oaks, CA: Sage Publications.

28. Nathanson, A. I., & Cantor, J. (2000). Reducing the aggression-promoting effect of violent cartoons by increasing children's fictional involvement with the victim. *Journal of Broadcasting & Electronic Media, 44*, 125–142.

Television Violence and Its Effects on Young Children

Betty Jo Simmons, Kelly Stalsworth, and Heather Wentzell

Betty Jo Simmons, Kelly Stalsworth, and **Heather Wentzell** are faculty at Longwood College, Virginia.

Introduction

After the introduction of television in 1939, E. B. White said it was "going to be the test of the modern world. We shall stand or fall by the television—of that I am quite sure" (Asamen & Berry, 1993, p. 10). These prophetic words are proving to be more accurate on a daily basis. With its ability to inform, entertain, teach, and persuade, television unquestionably has tremendous effects upon its viewers. Indeed, television has become the central activity in most homes today. Currently, in the United States, 98% of all households have at least one set. Even more astounding is the fact that it is watched an average of 7.5 hours per day (Asamen & Berry, 1993). Beckman (1997) concurs, saying that children watch more than 28 hours of television each week and in the process the average child, before the age of 12, has viewed over 8,000 murders.

Research on Television Violence

In order to clean up the airways for young audiences, the Federal Communications Commission (FCC) enacted The Children's Television Act in 1990. Many television stations show strictly positive programs, but the negative ones are also still being aired. This point is important because preschool children are curious and easily influenced. They tend to mimic and repeat what they hear and see on television without knowledge of right and wrong.

One of the main concerns with television programming is the violence viewed by children. Berk (1993) says that because young folks cannot fully understand what they see on television, they are very much under its influence. Davidson (1996) agrees that children are extremely vulnerable to television between the ages of 2 to 8 years because of their maturational inability to separate what they view from reality. Attention to violence on television became a matter of serious consideration in the 1950s, with the first congressional hearing taking place in 1952. From 1952 to 1967, many analyses were done of the content of television programs. In the late 1960s and early 1970s, the scrutiny shifted from content alone to specifically discerning the effects of violence on viewers. The resulting findings supported the idea that a causal relationship existed between television violence and aggressive behavior (National Institutes of Mental Health, 1983).

Imitating Violence

Levin and Carlsson-Paige (1996) lament the 1984 deregulation of broadcasting, noting that subsequently teachers began to observe an escalation of violence in their classrooms. They state that "Today, U.S. crime rates are increasing most rapidly among youth who were in their formative early years when children's TV was deregulated and violent programs and toys successfully deluged childhood culture" (p. 17). Governmental investigation led to several studies about the effects of violence. Two of the most well known were done by Bandura and Berkowitz. Bandura (1973), a social learning theorist, purported that children learn primarily through social modeling. From his studies, he concluded that children went through three stages—exposure, acquisition, and acceptance (Moody, 1980). He maintained that increased exposure to aggressive models led to reduced inhibitions toward violence. For example, when a television character acts violently and the consequences are positive, then the viewer is more likely to assume this behavior. Today, unfortunately even the "good" guys feel obligated to blow away their opponents (Munson, 1996).

Berkowitz (1962) examined the effects of television on aggressive drives. He concluded that exposure to televised violence does arouse aggressive behaviors, especially if viewers believe that aggression is justified. Noble (1975) maintains that aggressive behavior is harder to inhibit if viewers have a target which is associated with a television victim. Similarly, a study involving five different countries in which children were subjected to violence through television found evidence that even brief exposures caused them to be more accepting of other aggressive behavior. This research also concluded that the more children watched television, the more accepting they became of aggressive actions (Huesmann & Eron, 1986). Davidson (1996) reports that research done by Leonard Eron of the University of Michigan shows that violence children watched as eight-year-olds became a better predictor of adult aggression than socioeconomic and childrearing factors.

Cullingford (1984) reports on a study done by Shaw and Newell in which they interviewed families about their concerns over television. One of the major findings was that violence went almost unnoticed. Even when people were shown killings and then heavily prompted, most did not think of it as violent. The frightening truth was that "objectionable content" had become so acceptable that it was invisible. Later investigations by Drabman and Thomas (Geen, 1981) used observation to determine the effects of violent films on the way children resolved conflict. They, like Geen, who used blood pressure as the indicator, concluded that violence leads to desensitization (Molitor, 1994; Voojis & Voort, 1993). Thus, it is not hard to understand what Minnow, former chair of the Federal Communications Commission, meant when he said that in the 1960s, he worried that his children would not greatly benefit from television, but in the 1990s, he worries that his grandchildren may be harmed by it (Minnow, 1995).

Violence and Fear

In addition to theories that television can cause children to be more aggressive and less sensitive to the results of violence, there is also the theory that televised violence causes viewers to be afraid. According to this theory, the misconstrued world presented on television is seen as a mirror of reality and viewers become convinced they will fall victim to violence. It is reasoned that viewers absorb information without analyzing it and subsequently develop false beliefs about law enforcement and crime. Chen (1994), who found that crime during prime time is depicted 10 times greater than in reality, gives credence to the notion that television is distorted in its portrayal and resolution of crime and violence.

Levine (1996) says 3- to 5-year-old children live in a magical world that often leaves them terrified of things which completely surprise adults. On the other hand, there are those who disagree that television makes them afraid. According to Hamilton (1993), today's children are much more preoccupied with violence. Therefore, according to Dr. Daniel Koenigsberg, chief of child psychiatry at Saint Raphael Hospital, it is not so much that children are scared by it, as it is that they accept it and are intrigued by it. Thus, it is easy to see that not everyone agrees about the effects that violence has; however, it is generally agreed that it does play a significant role in the children's construction of social reality (Voojis & Voort, 1993).

Children's Programs Featuring Violence

According to Kaplan (1998), the National Coalition on Television Violence has classified the Mighty Morphin Power Rangers as the most violent program "ever studied, averaging more than 200 violent acts per hour" (p. 16). Furthermore, in an experimental study involving 5- to 11-year-olds (26 boys and 26 girls with ethnically diverse backgrounds), Kaplan (1998) reports that children who watched Power Rangers committed 7 times more aggressive acts than those who did not. Recognizing that children imitate what they see, several day care centers, nursery schools, and elementary schools have outlawed Power Rangers in play.

According to Evra and Kline (1990), "One of the dangers for preschoolers or early school-age children is their lack of ability to relate actions, motives, and consequences, and they may simply imitate the action they see" (p. 83). Levin and Carlsson-Paige (1996) purport that children cannot assimilate the Power Rangers into their own naturally limited experiences. Thus, unable to devise meaningful play from what they have seen, they act out "what they are unable to understand, primarily the kicking, fighting, and shooting" (p. 18). Teachers, according to Levin and Carlsson-Paige (1996), have observed that children become so fascinated by the Power Rangers that they excuse their own aggressiveness by saying they must do as the Power Rangers do.

Another show, similar in content, is the Teenage Mutant Ninja Turtles. Violence is also the main attraction in this program. The four heroes are pumped-up turtles named after four famous artists: Michelangelo, Donatello, Leonardo, and Raphael. Their mentor is a skilled ninja rat. Each has a distinctive personality and each fights best with specific weapons. The main "bad guy," Shredder, is so named because he has blades protruding from his clothes, which he does not hesitate to use when fighting. In one episode on the Cartoon Network, Shredder tried to use a robot to take over the world and the Turtles stopped him by fighting. At the end of the show, the characters discuss what is supposed to have been learned by the viewers. However, young children watching these shows would not necessarily learn from these messages because they can take in only so much information at a time. According to Evra and Kline (1990), the lack of understanding and well-developed behavioral control causes the main attraction to be primarily the action.

In what may be called the "Dynamic Duos" are found Bugs Bunny and Elmer Fudd, Tweety and Sylvester, the Road Runner and Wile E. Coyote, and Tom and Jerry. Each pair takes turns trying to outsmart and pummel one another. The goofy and colorful characters attract children and the only message that might be sent to children is how to solve problems through fighting.

Similarly, a new wave of cartoons, such as Beavis and Butthead, The Simpsons, King of the Hill, and Daria, are aimed at an adult audience; yet many children are intrigued by these animated cartoons. Most of the themes in these shows focus on adult life, things that young children would not understand. For example, those that focus on teenage life, such as Beavis and Butthead and Daria, show lazy characters concerned only with materialistic and selfish things. These programs also use adult language that is not appropriate for small children to hear. However, since children do watch these shows, they tend to repeat certain things that they see and hear.

For example, at the beginning to Beavis and Butthead, words come across the screen saying that the cartoon is not realistic and the acts in the show should not be repeated. However, such disclaimers do not register in the minds of children who are more intrigued by action than consequences.

For example, in the early 1960s, Schramm, Lyle, and Parker (1961) were pointing out the inherent danger involved in televised violence. They noted that a 6-year-old told his father he wanted real bullets because toy ones did not kill like Hopalong Cassidy's bullets. It appears that when children watch shows, they often do not remember the plot, but they do remember the actions of their favorite characters. Evra and Kline (1990) found that even 14-month-old children have a tendency toward some type of imitation of television.

Public Reaction

Even though there are shows on television that are designed for preschoolers, many American adults feel that there are still not enough programs for young children. In a press release on October 5, 1995, the Center for Media Education (CME) published the results of a national poll which showed strong public support of more educational programs. To quote from the poll:

> More than four in five American adults (82%) believe there is not enough educational children's programming on commercial broadcast television. Three in five adults surveyed (60%) support specific requirements that broadcasters air an hour of educational programming or more for children each day. More than a third of all parents (35%) would require two hours daily. 80% of Americans believe there are good reasons to regulate children's TV more strictly than programming intended for general or adult audiences. The two most frequently cited reasons for the lack of quality in children's broadcast programming are violent (43%) and insufficient educational programming (25%) (Poll on Children's Television, 1995, Center for Media Education).

These complaints are slowly being attended to with new educational programs and the revival of old ones, such as Schoolhouse Rock and Sesame Street. A rating system has recently been enacted. At the beginning of each show, letters and numbers, ranging from "G" to "Adult" appear at the top left-hand corner of the television screen, stating the appropriateness of the television show.

In 1997, in response to the public's demand for improvement in the quality of children's television, the Federal Communications Commission (FCC) issued stronger rules to regulate the Children's Television Act of 1990. According to the new expectations, broadcasters must produce 3 hours weekly of educational programming. These programs must make education the major focus with clearly articulated objectives, and a designated target age group. Fortunately, more stations are appearing and many of them do show programs that are, for the most part, appropriate for all audiences. Channels such as PBS, Animal Planet, The Family Channel, and the Disney channel are examples. However, there is still the question of violence on television. Especially so, since the Children's Television Act is not definitive about the meaning of educational programming. The act simply says that programs must contribute to the well-being of children "in any respect." The "in any respect" seems to be a loophole that dilutes the original intent (*U.S. News and World Report*, 1997).

Even when educational programs are produced, problems remain. One of them lies with the competition. With the availability of cable, violence continues to be prevalent. Children can and do quickly switch the channel to the Cartoon Network (*New York Times*, 1997). Furthermore, since educational programs are not big moneymakers, producers tend to schedule many of them early in the morning or in spots which are not the most normal viewing times. Another major consideration is what Zoglin contended in 1993, namely, that children are not much attracted to educational shows. He says, "The very notion of educational TV often seems to reflect narrow, schoolmarmish notions" (p. 64). Five years later, Mifflin (1997) pointed out that broadcasters agree because they have a hard time finding educational programs that children will watch (*New York Times*, 1997).

Recommendations

Naturally, children are easily confused when they watch the superhero beat up other characters. Therefore, recognizing and taking a proactive position against televised violence becomes a prime responsibility for all those involved in the care and nurturance of young children. With this premise in mind, the following recommendations are offered:

1. Parents, teachers, and communities must work together to combat the violence that is permeating society. They must work to build community programs to prevent violence and diffuse aggressive behavior. They must work on an individual level to teach acceptable and unacceptable standards.
2. Children must have their television viewing supervised and regulated which means that adults have to show responsible behavior themselves by refusing to watch programs that are violent in nature. If they are unwilling to abolish violent programs in their homes, they must take the time to ask questions of their children, explain the seriousness of violence to them, and help them to evaluate what they witness.
3. Parents must not let television become the dominant part of their family's life. It is imperative that drastic steps be taken to curtail the kind of socially unacceptable behavior, which is routinely and daily invited into the average home.
4. Parents and teachers must help young children develop appropriate behavior for social interactions. Children need guidance in learning to settle disagreements with verbal rather than physical skill.

5. Schools need to take television violence seriously, especially so, since it transfers to inappropriate behavior in the classroom. Thus, school personnel should take immediate steps to involve parents and the community in open dialog through newspaper articles, PTA meetings, and public forums.

6. The curriculum must be based upon the developmental needs of young children. Consideration must be given to fantasy, animism, and the inability of children to separate real from the pretend. Young children should be taught how to make decisions and how to work through problems by finding acceptable alternatives to violent acts.

References

Asamen, J., & Berry, G. (1993). *Children and television: Images in a changing sociocultural world.* London: Sage Publications.

Bandura, A. (1973). *Aggression: A social learning analysis.* Englewood Cliffs, NJ: Prentice Hall.

Beckman, J. (1997). *Television violence: What the research says about its effect on young children.* Winnetka, IL: Winnetka Alliance for Early Childhood.

Berk, L. (1993). *Infants, children, and adolescents.* Boston: Allyn and Bacon.

Berkowitz, L. (1962). *Aggression: A social psychological analysis.* New York: McGraw-Hill.

Center for Media Education (1995). Poll on children's television. Press release, October 1995 (also available online).

Chen, M. (1994). *The smart parent's guide to kid's TV.* San Francisco, CA: KQED Books.

Cullingford, C. (1984). *Children and television.* New York: St. Martin's Press.

Davidson, J. (February 2, 1996). *Menace to society.* Rolling Stone, pp. 38–39.

Defining the "educational" in educational TV for children (September 12, 1994) *U.S. News and World Report,* p. 90.

Evra, J., & Kline, W. (1990). *Television and child development.* Hillsdale, NJ: Lawrence Erlbaum Associates.

Geen, R. (1981). Behavioral and physiological reactions to observed violence: Effects of prior exposure to aggressive stimuli. *Journal of Personality and Social Psychology, 40,* 868–875.

Hamilton, R. (May/June, 1993). TV violence—What influence on young minds? *St. Raphael's Better Health*, 7–11.

Huesmann, R., & Eron, L. (1986). *Television and the aggressive child: A cross national comparison*. Hillsdale, NJ: Lawrence Erlbaum Associates.

Kaplan, P. (1998). *The human odyssey*. Pacific Grove, CA: Brooks and Cole.

Levin, D., & Carlsson-Paige, N. (1996). Disempowering the "Power Rangers." *The Education Digest, 61*, 17–21.

Levine, M. (1996). Handling the "boob tube." *Parents Magazine, 71*, 55–57.

Mifflin, L. (September 11, 1997). Can you spell "compliance," boys and girls? *New York Times*, p. C13.

Minnow, N., & LaMay, C. (August 6, 1995). Abandoned in the wasteland. *Detroit Free Press*, Magazine Section, pp. 12–16.

Molitor, F., & Hirsch, K. (1994). Children's toleration of real life aggression after exposure to media violence: A replication of the Drabman and Thomas studies. *Child Study Journal, 24*, 191–203.

Moody, K. (1980). *Growing up on television*. New York: Times Books.

Munson, M. (1995). Media mayhem. *Prevention, 47*, 86–89.

Noble, G. (1975). *Children in front of the small screen*. Thousand Oaks, CA: Sage Publications.

Schramn, W., Lyle, J., & Parker, E. (1961). *Television in the lives of our children*. Stanford, CA: Stanford University Press.

Television and behavior: Ten years of scientific progress and implications for the eighties (1983). Washington, DC: National Institutes of Mental Health.

Voojis, M., & Voort, T. (1993). Learning about television violence: The impact of critical viewing curriculum on children's attitudinal judgment of crime series. *Journal of Research and Development in Education, 26*, 133–141.

Zoglin, R. (1993). If not the Jetsons, what? *Time*, March 22, p. 64.

Does Cartoon Violence Beget Aggressive Behavior in Real Life? An Opposing View

Fran C. Blumberg, Kristen P. Bierwirth, and Allison J. Schwartz

Fran C. Blumberg is professor at Fordham University's Graduate School of Education; Kristen P. Bierwirth teaches in Linden Public Schools, Linden, New Jersey; and Allison J. Schwartz is a professor at Georgia State University's College of Education.

Nate and Amanda are in the family room playing *Diner Dash*, a computer game in which the goal is to quickly serve restaurant patrons their food before they become angry. Like many of their elementary school-age peers who involve themselves with multiple forms of media simultaneously, they are also watching the Cartoon Network television show *Squirrel Boy* that chronicles the adventures of a young boy whose best friend is a gangly talking squirrel. Their younger sibling, 2-year-old Kenny, also is multi-tasking as he looks up at the television screen to see Rodney J. Squirrel being forced into a catapult by a bully. Nate and Amanda agree that being launched to the moon in a catapult is not as funny as when Rodney was burned in his go-cart while racing down a steep slope. Meanwhile, toddler Kenny's attention becomes diverted to Amanda's stuffed animals when he experiences difficulty following the cartoon story line.

Squirrel Boy, like many cartoons on the popular Cartoon Network, includes comical acts of aggression and violence. This program is not dissimilar to cartoons that younger generations enjoyed, such as *Bugs Bunny* or *Road Runner*, who found the seemingly belligerent antics of cartoon protagonists as comical. Currently, the common wisdom is that cartoon violence is "bad" even when tinged with humor or at least difficult to understand for younger children, as shown in Kenny's experience. As researchers, educators, and practitioners, we know better than to accept common wisdom. We know to look to science for answers, even if some of those answers are ones we do not like nor agree with.

Why Is Cartoon Violence Considered to Be "Bad"?

Violence can be generally defined as any intentional or accidental action that causes physical or psychological harm (as in the case of verbal abuse) to oneself, another person, animal, or at times, an inanimate object (see National Television Violence Study (NTVS) 1997). Cartoon violence is similar in that harm may be inflicted upon characters. However, the nature of cartoon harm may be fairly minor. For example, Potter and Warren's (1998) content analysis of prime time programming indicated that in comedy shows, violence was more likely to be verbal than physical. According to Kirsch (2006), cartoons show less serious acts of violence than adult-oriented dramas. Kirsch also noted that the comedic element of cartoons also may affect young viewers' beliefs about the applicability of violent acts they see in programs to real-world situations.

Among child and adult viewers, longstanding negative effects of exposure to media violence have included decreases in prosocial behaviors, increases in physiological arousal and enhanced aggressive thoughts, behaviors, and feelings (Ostrov et al. 2006). For example, Kremar and Hight (2007) found that preschoolers who watched an action cartoon or super-hero image, as opposed to young children who watched neutral video clips or animated characters, were more likely to create aggressive story endings. These findings supported the contention that a schema for aggression may be activated as a result of having viewed aggressive acts (Anderson and Carnagey 2004). Further, The Kaiser Family Foundation's 2006 report examining children and the electronic media indicated that 68% of parents of children 6 years of age and younger reported having seen their children imitate behaviors shown on television with 24% of these behaviors identified as aggressive (Rideout and Hamel 2006).

Children's understandings of what they view on television may affect how they are impacted by cartoon violence. According to Kendeou and colleagues (2005), the early comprehension skills of young children transfer across different media such as narratives and television. These skills enable them to make causal inferences and establish connections between events (van den Broek et al. 2005). Thus, because they understand the narrative, they should understand the context in which cartoon violence is shown.

However, while aspects of young children's comprehension of narratives may be relatively sophisticated, their understanding of narratives is best when the content is concrete, familiar, and provides structure allowing them to readily make inferences (Kendeou et al. 2007). Thus, young children tend to focus much of their attention on observable actions instead of internal causes such as characters' intentions (Kendeou et al. 2005). Van den Broek et al. (1996) found that 4-year-olds showed difficulty distinguishing central program content from peripheral or incidental content. This failure to selectively attend to relevant story or non-structural properties of events may, in turn, compromise their ability to incorporate the violent behaviors of cartoon characters into their behavioral repertoire (Kendeou et al. 2005).

Children's understandings of what they view on television also may be influenced by their ability to transfer knowledge from what they see in the media to what they do in daily life which, in turn, depends to some extent on their ability to differentiate between fantasy and reality. One cue that they use to make this distinction is animation (Condry 1989). Despite increased realism in animation over time (Fyfe 2006; Rutenberg 2001), most preschoolers still recognize cartoon programs as "make-believe" (e.g., McKenna and Ossoff 1998), and can differentiate cartoon characters engaged in life-like activities from those engaged in pretend activities (Rosen et al. 1997). Skolnick and Bloom (2006) reported that young children recognized that different fictional characters such as SpongeBob and Batman inhabited distinct fictional worlds. This ability has ramifications for their views of what actions are possible in these worlds as opposed to real life.

The character's motives and the consequences of violent actions also may help children interpret events shown on television. Adult intervention also may help children understand relationships between social acts portrayed on television and cues such as motives and consequences (Collins et al. 1981). For example, Pohan and Mathison (2007) note that teachers should recognize the general cultural messages imparted to children via television. These messages pertain to societal depictions of cultural diversity and appropriate modes of social interaction.

What Do Children Think When They See Cartoon Violence?

The impact of exposure to violence may remain regardless of whether children choose to imitate it. For example, Mathews et al. (2005) found neurological evidence of a link between exposure to violence on television and brain functioning. Specifically, non-aggressive children who had been exposed to high levels of media violence showed less activity in the frontal cortex, that area of the brain linked to attention and self-control. This pattern of neural activity was comparable to that of children diagnosed with disruptive behavior disorder (Mathews et al. 2005). Bear in mind that these measurements are made very shortly after exposure to the media violence. However, the crucial question concerns the duration of the impact of exposure to violence over time, particularly if children are able to perceive cartoon violence as fantastic and as immoral.

We do know that children view violent acts as moral transgressions: behaviors that infringe upon the rights and welfare of others (Wainryb and Turiel 1993). According to the domain-specific theory of moral development (see Smetana 2006; Turiel 1998), moral beliefs are influenced by the context in which an action is presented. For example, young children evaluate real life and hypothetical moral transgressions negatively and can provide rudimentary justifications as to why transgressions are impermissible and should receive punishment (Smetana et al. 1999; Smetana 2006).

Young children also differentiate between different types of transgressions, including realistic versus cartoon portrayals (Peters and Blumberg 2004; Smetana et al. 1993; Tisak and Turiel 1988; Turiel 1998) and can consider the degree of harm incurred when assessing the extent to which a transgression warrants punishment. Presumably, children's ability to make differentiated judgments about immoral acts may transfer to their ability to distinguish between the effects of cartoon and television violence and that found in real life situations.

We (Peters and Blumberg 2004) examined this issue in a study in which we showed 3- and 4-year-old children pictures of both realistic and cartoon-like moral transgressions (e.g., hitting, pushing, stealing, and failing to share). The children then were asked to indicate the extent to which the transgressions merited punishment and if so, how severe. They also were asked to justify this assessment. We found that preschoolers negatively evaluated all moral transgressions, both realistic and cartoon. When perceiving the magnitude of the transgression, children viewed physical harm as more egregious than that of psychological harm. Specifically, hitting was seen as more harmful to others and as deserving of greater punishment than failing to share. Additionally, preschoolers judged cartoon transgressions as more harmful than realistic transgressions. Because cartoons are characterized by exaggerated facial expressions and body actions, these characteristics may have influenced the children's perceptions of the cartoon transgressions as "bad."

Conclusion

Television continues to be the "most dominant medium even in those cultures where computers have reached a high diffusion rate" (Lemish 2007, p. 5) and the most significant source of leisure activity among children worldwide. Accordingly, questions concerning the impact of violent television content on vulnerable audiences, such as young children, will remain. We have directed our attention here to children's cartoons which are notably violent. Clearly, definitive conclusions about the potential ill effects of exposure to cartoon violence on young viewers are not easily made. However, scientific support can be found that the frequent comic contextualization of violence coupled with the young children's cognitive repertoire, notably, their abilities to distinguish right from wrong and fantasy from reality, may mitigate the likelihood that young viewers will perpetrate the violent acts shown in cartoons on others in real life. We suspect that this view is consistent most with the perspective of many children who are entertained by Saturday morning cartoons such as Amanda, who emphatically observed, "Everyone knows that cartoons aren't real!"

References

Anderson, C. A., & Carnagey, N. L. (2004). Violent evil and the general aggression model. In A. Miller (Ed.), *The social psychology of good and evil* (pp. 168–192). New York: Guilford Press.

Collins, W. A., Sobol, B. L., & Westby, S. (1981). Effects of adult commentary on children's comprehension and inferences about a televised aggressive portrayal. *Child Development, 52*, 158–163. doi: 10.2307/1129225.

Condry, J. (1989). *The psychology of television.* Hillsdale, NJ: Lawrence Erlbaum Associates.

Fyfe, K. (2006). Wolves in sheep's clothing: A content analysis of children's television. Parents Television Council. http://www.parentstv.org/PTC/publications/reports/childrensstudy/childrensstudy.pdf. Retrieved 20 July 2007.

Kendeou, P., Lynch, J. S., van den Broek, P., Espin, C. A., White, M. J., & Kremer, K. E. (2005). Developing successful readers: Building on early comprehension skills through television viewing and listening. *Early Childhood Education Journal, 33*, 91–98. doi: 10.1007/s10643-005-0030-6.

Kendeou, P., van den Broek, P., White, M. J., & Lynch, J. (2007). Comprehension in preschool and early elementary children: Skill development and strategy interventions. In D. S. McNamara (Ed.), *Reading comprehension strategies: Theories, interventions, and technologies.* Mahwah, NJ: Lawrence Erlbaum.

Kirsch, S. (2006). Cartoon violence and aggression in youth. *Aggression and Violent Behavior, 11*, 547–557. doi: 10.1016/j.avb.2005.10.002.

Kremar, M., & Hight, A. (2007). The development of aggressive mental models in young children. *Media Psychology, 10*, 250–269.

Lemish, D. (2007). *Children and television.* Malden, MA: Blackwell Publishing.

Mathews, V. P., Kronenberger, W. G., Wang, Y., Lurito, J. T., Lowe, M. J., & Dunn, D. W. (2005). Media violence linked to concentration, self-control. *Journal of Computer Assisted Tomography, 29*, 287–292. doi: 10.1097/01.rct.0000162822.46958.33.

McKenna, M. W., & Ossoff, E. P. (1998). Age differences in children's comprehension of a popular television program. *Child Study Journal, 28*, 53–68.

National Television Violence Study (NTVS). (1997). *Technical report* 2. Thousand Oaks, CA: Sage Publications Inc.

Ostrov, J. M., Gentile, D. A., & Crick, N. R. (2006). Media exposure, aggression and prosocial behavior during early childhood: A longitudinal study. *Social Development, 15*, 612–627.

Peters, K. M., & Blumberg, F. C. (2004). Preschoolers' moral judgments: Distinctions between realistic and cartoon-fantasy transgressions. *Proceedings of the 2004 Conference on Interaction Design and Children: Building a Community* (pp. 131–132). New York: ACM.

Pohan, C. A., & Mathison, C. (2007). Television: Providing powerful multicultural lessons inside and outside of school. *Multicultural Perspectives, 9*, 19–25.

Potter, W. J., & Warren, R. (1998). Humor as camouflage of televised violence. *Journal of Communication, 48*, 40–57. doi: 10.1111/j.1460-2466.1998. tb02747.x.

Rideout, V., & Hamel, E. (2006). *The media family: Electronic media in the lives of infants, toddlers, preschoolers and their parents.* http://www.kff.org/entmedia/upload/7500.pdf. Retrieved 20 July 2007 from The Henry J. Kaiser Family Foundation.

Rosen, C. S., Schwebel, D. C., & Singer, J. L. (1997). Preschoolers' attributions of mental states in pretense. *Child Development, 68*, 1133–1142. doi: 10.2307/1132296.

Rutenberg, J. (2001). Violence finds a niche in children's cartoons. *New York Times* (January 28), A1, A19.

Skolnick, D., & Bloom, P. (2006). What does Batman think about SpongeBob? Children's understanding of the fantasy/fantasy distinction. *Cognition, 101*, B9–B18. doi: 10.1016/j.cognition.2005.10.001.

Smetana, J. G. (2006). Social-cognitive domain theory: Consistencies and variations in children's moral and social judgments. In M. Killen & J. Smetana (Eds.), *Handbook of moral development* (pp. 119–153). Mahwah, NJ: Lawrence Erlbaum Associates.

Smetana, J. G., Schlagman, N., & Adams, P. W. (1993). Preschool children's judgments about hypothetical and actual transgressions. *Child Development, 64*, 202–214. doi: 10.2307/1131446.

Smetana, J. G., Toth, S. L., Cicchetti, D., Bruce, J., Kane, P., & Daddis, C. (1999). Maltreated and non-maltreated preschoolers' conceptions of hypothetical and actual moral transgressions. *Developmental Psychology, 35*, 269–281. doi: 10.1037/0012-1649.35.1.269.

Tisak, M. S., & Turiel, E. (1988). Variation in seriousness of transgressions and children's moral and conventional concepts. *Developmental Psychology, 24,* 352–357. doi: 10.1037/0012-1649.24.3.352.

Turiel, E. (1998). The development of morality. In W. Damon (Series Ed.) & N. Eisenberg (Vol. Ed.), *Handbook of child psychology: Vol. 3. Social, emotional, and personality development* (5th ed., pp. 863–932). New York: Wiley.

van den Broek, P., Kremer, K., Lynch, J., Butler, J., White, M. J., & Lorch, E. P. (2005). Assessment of comprehension abilities in young children. In S. G. Paris & S. A. Stahl (Eds.), *Children's reading comprehension and assessment.* Mahwah, NJ: Lawrence Erlbaum.

van den Broek, P., Lorch, E. P., & Thurlow, R. (1996). Children's and adults' memory for television stories: The role of causal factors, story-grammar categories, and hierarchical level. *Child Development, 67,* 3010–3028.

Wainryb, C., & Turiel, E. (1993). Conceptual and informational features in moral decision making. *Educational Psychologist, 28*(3), 205–218. doi: 10.1207/s15326985ep2803_2.

INFORMATIVE SYNTHESIS

DEFINITION

Your goal in writing an informative synthesis is to combine material on some topic you have gathered from two or more readings into a clear, organized essay. After finishing your essay, a reader should have a better understanding of the topic and should know the position of the various authors whose work you include. You are not trying to show how one author is correct in what she says and another is wrong. Neither are you trying to advocate a position of your own on the topic. Instead, you are trying to present other people's ideas or findings as clearly and concisely as you can, highlighting key similarities and differences. Teachers also commonly refer to these papers as "reports" or "comparison-contrast essays."

For example, if you were writing an informative synthesis of the essays included in this chapter, you would want to summarize what each writer had to say about the link between television viewing and childhood violence or at least certain aspects of the subject. In fact, a good way to write this paper would be to isolate for examination certain aspects of the topic that all of the writers address—that way you could draw direct comparisons among the pieces. As you point out for your reader important similarities or differences you see in the various essays, you would not argue that one author is correct in his or her position on the topic and that the others are misguided, nor would you comment on the quality of the writing or argument in any particular essay

To compose an informative synthesis, you employ many of the same skills needed to write summaries. As with writing summaries, you may encounter a number of problems when composing an informative synthesis:

1. Because of their content, language, or structure, the source texts themselves might be hard for you to understand. Because you need to form a clear understanding of the readings before you write about them, you need strong critical reading skills to write a successful synthesis.

2. You will often be looking for subtle differences among readings—not just different arguments or findings authors put forward, but slightly different interpretations of data, slightly different uses of terminology, slightly different emphases. Because a synthesis involves multiple source texts, when you examine a reading you plan to use in your paper, you also have to keep in mind the material contained in the readings you have already read. The more readings you are working with, the harder it is to keep track of the material contained in each and the easier it is to overlook the subtle differences between them.

3. You need to stay as objective as possible when examining the source texts and writing your essay. You do not editorialize in an informative synthesis: your goal is *not* to comment on the topic of the readings or on the quality of their writing. Instead, you need to be open-minded when reading them, to pull out from them material relevant to your thesis, and to present that material as clearly, concisely, and fairly as possible. As when you are writing a summary, remaining neutral can be difficult, especially when you feel strongly about a topic and must include in your informative synthesis ideas that disturb or anger you.

4. Organizing an informative synthesis can also be challenging. You need to decide how to construct your thesis so it adequately guides your reader through your work, how to order the information you include in your paper, and how to employ transitions within the body of your essay.

5. Supplying proper documentation in an informative synthesis can be problematic. One paragraph of your paper may contain information you have drawn from several different authors. Learning how to document such passages properly can be trying; remembering to do it is crucial. Improper documentation can lead to problems with clarity and plagiarism.

WRITING AN INFORMATIVE SYNTHESIS

Because writing an informative synthesis can be challenging, it is best to break the process down into a series of more manageable steps:

1. Analyze the assignment.
2. Review and annotate the readings.
3. Formulate a thesis and organizational plan.
4. Write your rough draft.
5. Revise your draft.

Remember that this method of writing a synthesis will not work for everybody. We all have our preferred way of writing papers, which can vary according to the type of essay we are composing and the time we have to complete the assignment. For example, some writers like to complete a rough draft before they write their thesis, while others must have a thesis in hand before they begin to write; some will rewrite a paper several times before they turn it in for a grade, while others revise very little. Use these directions as a rough guide for writing an informative synthesis. The important principle to keep in mind is to complete your paper in a series of steps, no matter the nature or order of those steps.

Step 1—Analyze the Assignment

Read the assignment carefully to make sure your instructor is asking you to write an informative rather than an argumentative synthesis. If you have any doubt, ask your teacher to clarify the assignment. Make sure you understand how many sources you are required to consult when researching the topic or to include when writing your paper. Also, check on the type of source texts your teacher expects you to use if you are required to collect the readings yourself. Some instructors will want you to use only "academic" sources— material written by experts in the field.

Step 2—Review and Annotate the Readings

Once you have assembled the readings that will serve as the basis of your synthesis, read through them several times with your assignment in mind. In most cases, you will look for specific information in each reading, passages that address the topic of your paper. Thoroughly annotate the reading and then summarize it. As you work with the material, remember to be fair and open-minded. Consider how the author's perspective on the topic is similar to or different from what other authors have written and decide whether you think it should be included in your essay.

Step 3—Formulate a Thesis and an Organizational Plan

Your thesis in an informative synthesis serves an important function. More likely than not, it will indicate the topic of your essay and indicate how you will structure your synthesis: what you will discuss and in what order you will discuss it. Always keep in mind the rhetorical function of your thesis statement. When people read your paper, they need to know early on what you will be discussing and will look to your thesis as a guide.

Your thesis for an informative synthesis can be either open or closed. In an open thesis you indicate the topic and general structure of your paper:

> Cantor; Simmons, Stalsworth, and Wentzell; and Blumberg, Bierwirth, and Schwartz offer a range of appraisals concerning the effect of violent television on young viewers.

or

> While both Cantor and Simmons, Stalsworth, and Wentzell assert that violent television shows negatively impact children, Blumberg, Bierwirth, and Schwartz disagree.

With a closed thesis you list the specific issues you will address in your essay. However, you have to be careful not to put too much information in your thesis—doing so will only lead to cluttered prose. A possible closed thesis statement for the paper described above might read something like this:

> Cantor; Simmons, Stalsworth, and Wentzell; and Blumberg, Bierwirth, and Schwartz offer a range of appraisals concerning the effect of violent television on young viewers based on their examination of children's ability to differentiate reality from fantasy and draw distinctions among different genres of television shows.

Either type of thesis can be effective, but in general, the longer your paper will be, the more likely you are to use an open thesis.

When writing an informative synthesis, you can employ either a block or alternating format to organize your essay. With a **block format**, you discuss what one source says about the topic in relation to your thesis before moving on to what the next source says. However, instead of just summarizing each source text, you also compare and contrast them, pointing out their key similarities and differences. Suppose, for example, that you are writing an essay with the thesis, "Cantor; Simmons, Stalsworth, and Wentzell; and Blumberg, Bierwirth, and Schwartz offer a range of appraisals concerning the effect of violent television on young viewers." In outline form, your paper might look something like this:

Opening Section

Introduce the topic of your essay

Give your thesis

Section on Cantor Essay

Summarize Cantor's position on the topic

Discuss its relationship to the other two readings

Section on Simmons, Stalsworth, and Wentzell Essay

Summarize Simmons, Stalsworth, and Wentzell's position on the topic

Discuss its relationship to the other two readings

Section on Blumberg, Bierwirth, and Schwartz Essay

Summarize Blumberg, Bierwirth, and Schwartz's position on the topic

Discuss its relationship to the other two readings

Conclusion

You might, though, choose to use an **alternating format** to organize your essay, especially if you use a closed thesis. Remember that with a closed thesis, you list the specific issues you will address in your essay. Using an alternating format allows you to discuss what each source says about these specific issues in order. For example, suppose you are writing an essay with this thesis: "Cantor; Simmons, Stalsworth, and Wentzell; and Blumberg, Bierwirth, and Schwartz offer a range of appraisals concerning the effect of violent television on young viewers based on their examination of children's ability to differentiate reality from fantasy and draw distinctions among different genres of television shows." Using an alternating format, your paper might be organized like this:

Opening Section

Introduce the topic of your essay

Give your thesis

Effect of Violent Television and Children's Ability to Differentiate Reality from Fantasy

Cantor's views and their relation to the other authors' views

Simmons, Stalsworth, and Wentzell's views and their relation to the other authors' views

Blumberg, Bierwirth, and Schwartz's views and their relation to the other authors' views

Effect of Violent Television and Children's Ability to Draw Distinctions among Different Genres of Television Shows

Cantor's views and their relation to the other authors' views

Simmons, Stalsworth, and Wentzell's views and their relation to the other authors' views

Blumberg, Bierwirth, and Schwartz's views and their relation to the other authors' views

Conclusion

Of course, you could write the same paper using a block format. If you did, it might be organized like this:

Opening Section

Introduce the topic of your essay

Give your thesis

Cantor Essay

Her views on the relationship between violent television shows and children's ability to differentiate reality from fantasy and how they are similar to and/or different from the views of the other authors on the topic

Her views on the relationship between violent television shows and children's ability to draw distinctions among different genres of television shows and how they are similar to and/or different from the views of the other authors

Simmons, Stalsworth, and Wentzell Essay

Their views on the relationship between violent television shows and children's ability to differentiate reality from fantasy and how they are similar to and/or different from the views of the other authors on the topic

Their views on the relationship between violent television shows and children's ability to draw distinctions among different genres of television shows and how they are similar to and/or different from the views of the other authors

Blumberg, Bierwirth, and Schwartz Essay

Their views on the relationship between violent television shows and children's ability to differentiate reality from fantasy and how they are similar to and/or different from the views of the other authors on the topic

Their views on the relationship between violent television shows and children's ability to draw distinctions among different genres of television shows and how they are similar to and/or different from the views of the other authors

Conclusion

Alternating and block formats have their particular strengths and weaknesses. The alternating format allows you to compare and contrast the views of different writers fairly easily. In this paper, for example, you would be able to present each author's position on the relationship between television violence and children's conceptions of reality and fantasy in its own section of your own essay before moving on to discuss television violence and children's ability to recognize various genres of TV shows. If you were using a block format, you might discuss Cantor's views on page one of your paper and might not get to Blumberg, Bierwirth, and Schwartz's views until page six or seven. Your reader might have a hard time remembering Cantor's views by the time you reached Blumberg and her co-authors. Using a block format, however, allows you to give your readers a good sense of the general argument presented by each author in sequential order. Yet the block format often results in repetitive prose and frequently discourages students from discussing similarities and differences among the readings, simply summarizing each author's views instead.

Regardless of the structure you employ, your job in writing an informative synthesis involves more than summarizing what each critic has to say. In writing this paper, you would not be arguing a position of your own concerning the effect of television violence on children. Instead, you would point out for your readers important similarities and differences among the views advanced by the source texts' authors.

Once you have designed your thesis, you need to go back through the readings, consult your annotations, and locate material you want to include in your essay. Preparing an informal outline can be quite helpful at this point. In your outline, indicate the focus for each part of your paper, the material you will draw from the readings to develop that section of the essay, and the ideas you will contribute.

Step 4—Write Your Rough Draft

The introductory section of an informative thesis should, first, capture your readers' interest. You might consider opening your paper with an interesting anecdote, a case history, an important statistic, or a telling quotation from one of the readings. Writing an effective opening gives you the chance to be imaginative and creative. A second goal of the opening section of your synthesis is to introduce the topic of your essay. The title of the synthesis should give your readers some indication of your essay's topic, but you want to be sure to clarify the topic in your opening section. Finally, the introduction to your essay should contain your thesis statement. Whether your thesis is open or closed, you need to include it in your introduction to serve as a guide to the rest of your synthesis.

In the body of your essay, you will follow the structure supplied by your thesis, explaining ideas one author or issue at a time. If you were writing an informative synthesis using the three articles on television violence as your source texts, in the body of your paper you would summarize, paraphrase, and quote what each author has to say about the topic, including in your essay material that best captures each writer's views and illustrates your thesis. However, not all the material in your informative synthesis will come from the readings. You have significant contributions to make, too. Besides quoting, paraphrasing, and summarizing what various authors have to say, you will contribute transitions, elaborations, clarifications, and connections.

For example, in one paragraph of your essay, you may introduce the issue to be discussed, introduce a reading by giving the author's name and qualifications as well as the title of the article, quote a relevant passage from the piece, restate the author's ideas in your own words to clarify them, point out how the author's stance differs from the author you discussed in the previous paragraph, and provide a transition to your next paragraph. If you devote a sentence to each of these tasks, your paragraph will be six sentences long, with only one sentence coming directly from the reading. The rest of the material in the paragraph comes from you.

When concluding your informative synthesis, you want to reiterate the main issues or findings you have covered in the body of your essay and give your work a sense of closure. You might want to look back at your opening strategy and reemploy it in your conclusion, if possible. For example, if you opened your paper with a quotation, consider ending it with a quotation. If you began with a question, conclude with the same question, perhaps answering it this time. If you began with a story, come back to the story in your conclusion.

Step 5—Revise Your Draft

Revising a synthesis takes time. In fact, it is probably best to revise your paper in several stages. Initially, you might check the **content** of your essay. Here you have two concerns. First, reread what you have written to make sure you are being true to your own intentions. You might ask the following questions of your manuscript:

- Does my thesis accurately reflect my understanding of the readings?
- Have I said in my paper what I wanted to say?
- Have I covered all of the material I hoped to cover when annotating the readings?
- Have I covered the ideas I discovered as I wrote the essay, ideas I did not plan on addressing but developed as I wrote?

A related goal is to review the content of your essay in light of the assignment. Here the questions you ask might include:

- Have I met the demands of the assignment?
- Have I adequately covered the ideas contained in the reading?

- Have I avoided editorializing or arguing a particular position?
- Have I kept my reader in mind? Would this essay make sense to someone who knows little or nothing about the readings? Do any ideas need more development or explanation?

Next, you might review the **organization** of your essay. Here you are concerned with the quality of your thesis statement, topic sentences, and transitions. These are some of the questions you should be asking:

- Does my thesis guide the development of the essay? Put another way, does my essay follow the format suggested or outlined by my thesis?
- Do I have clearly stated topic sentences introducing the major sections of my essay? Are these topic sentences tied to the thesis?
- Have I supplied enough transitional devices to guide my reader through my synthesis, especially when I move from discussing one author to discussing another?

Finally, revise with an eye toward **accuracy** and **clarity**. Here your concerns are word choice, sentence structure, and documentation. Again, you need to ask yourself a series of questions as you review your work, making needed changes when any of your answers are no:

- In choosing words, have I remained as fair and objective as possible?
- Have I successfully avoided jargon and highly technical terms when such language would not be appropriate for my audience?
- Are my sentences easy to read?
- Have I varied the type and length of my sentences?
- Have I quoted material accurately and properly?
- Have I paraphrased material accurately, properly, and fairly?
- Have I documented material thoroughly and properly?

You may need to revise your informative synthesis several times to address all of these concerns adequately.

Check Quotations and Documentation

Before you turn in your final draft for a grade, be sure to check the accuracy of your quotations and documentation. Take the time to check any material you quoted against the source text to be sure you have accurately transcribed the information. Pay special attention to any passages where you have added language to or taken language out of a quotation: these changes should not alter the meaning of the source text. Also, check to be sure that you have documented all of the material in your paper that needs to be documented and that you have employed the proper form of documentation in each instance. Remember that all paraphrased and quoted material in your paper should be documented. Because you are combining information from two or more sources in your synthesis, be sure it is always clear to your reader which source text you are referring to in your documentation.

SAMPLE INFORMATIVE SYNTHESIS

Following is a sample informative synthesis of the three articles on television violence provided earlier in this chapter. Notice how the writer structures the essay and employs material from the readings.

Does Television Violence Pose a Danger to Young Viewers?

Research shows that at least one television set can be found in 98% of American homes and that the people living there watch TV around 7.5 hours a day. Children in those homes watch television about 28 hours a week, and before they are 12 years old have watched more than 8,000 murders on the screen (Simmons, Stalsworth, and Wentzell 181). Does television violence pose a danger to young viewers? Does it make them more violent and promote other anti-social behavior? Though many researchers believe watching violent television has a detrimental effect on children, not everyone agrees. Key differences of opinion center around children's ability to distinguish fantasy from reality and the long-term impact of watching violent cartoons.

In their article "Television Violence and Its Effects on Young Children," Simmons, Stalsworth, and Wentzell argue that children's lives are negatively impacted by television viewing. Their research focuses on two issues: (1) the ability of children to differentiate reality from fantasy when watching TV and (2) the short- and long-term effects of viewing violent shows. Simmons, Stalsworth, and Wentzell maintain "that children are extremely vulnerable to television between the ages of 2 to 8 years because of their maturational inability to separate what they view from reality" (182). They base this assertion on studies by the National Institutes of Mental Health that suggest "a causal relationship existed between television violence and aggressive behavior" (182).

According to the authors, in 1984, the United States government deregulated television which resulted in a greater number of violent television shows being aired. As children watched these shows, they began to imitate what they saw and became more violent, not drawing a distinction between reality and the fantasy world of television. Over time, these violence-prone children have grown up and contributed to today's crime rates. Simmons, Stalsworth, and Wentzell cite the results of a government study which suggests a three-stage process linking television viewing and violence: exposure, acquisition, and acceptance. As children are exposed to increasing amounts of violence on television, they begin to acquire anti-social beliefs and to accept violence as a norm in their lives (182). In fact, the amount of violent television that eight-year-olds watched is a better "predictor of adult aggression than socioeconomic and childrearing factors" (182).

Simmons, Stalsworth, and Wentzell believe that watching violent cartoons is especially damaging to children. They maintain that shows like "Mighty Morphin Power Rangers" are among the most violent on television. In fact, children who watched this particular show were 7 times more aggressive afterwards than children who did not watch the show (183). Watching the confrontations between Bugs Bunny and Elmer Fudd or Tweety and Sylvester teach children that violence is an acceptable way to solve problems. Studies show that "when children watch these shows, they often do not remember the plot, but they do remember the actions of their favorite characters" (185) and imitate them.

Joanne Cantor, Director of the Center for Communication Research at the University of Wisconsin, largely agrees with Simmons, Stalsworth, and Wentzell. In her article, "Media Violence and Children's Emotions: Beyond the 'Smoking Gun,'" Cantor cites a meta-analysis of studies that make a "compelling case" for the argument that watching violent television as children leads to more anti-social, violent behavior as adults (174). However, Cantor offers a more detailed analysis of this link than Simmons, Stalsworth, and Wentzell provide. For example, Cantor also maintains that children's inability to distinguish between reality and fantasy contributes to the negative impact of watching television, but she explains how this phenomenon changes as children mature. Younger children (ages 3–5) are more strongly impacted by fantasy violence; older children (ages 9–11) are more strongly impacted by realistic violence (176–7). In a study of children's reactions to television news, Cantor found that "children in kindergarten through sixth grades showed that fear produced by fantasy programs decreased as the child's age increased, while fear induced by news stories increased with age" (177).

According to Cantor, one reason young children are so influenced by television violence is that it often minimizes how that violence harms the victim. As a result, children become desensitized to the effects of violence on others and are then more likely to act violently themselves—a finding which matches the "exposure, acquisition, and acceptance" process cited by Simmons, Stalsworth, and Wentzell. Cantor mentions cartoons as especially being responsible for children's desensitization to violence. As evidence, Cantor cites a study she conducted in which one group of children watched violent cartoons after they were asked to consider how the victims in those shows might be harmed by the actions inflicted on them, another group watched the cartoons without these instructions, and a third group did not watch any cartoons. She found that "the kids who had just seen the violent cartoon without instructions scored higher on pro-violence attitudes than the kids in the control condition (showing stronger agreement with statements like, 'sometimes fighting is a good way to get what you want')" (178). Cantor warns that these violent attitudes formed in childhood can have long-term consequences, including increased violence in adulthood (174).

An opposing view on the relationship between television viewing and violence among children is offered in "Does Cartoon Violence Beget Aggressive Behavior in Real Life? An Opposing View" by Fran Blumberg, Kristen Bierwirth, and Allison Schwartz. In this article, the authors focus exclusively on the impact that violent cartoons have on children, an issue discussed by both Cantor and Simmons, Stalsworth, and Wentzell. When comparing the nature of violence in prime-time shows and cartoons, Blumberg, Bierwirth, and Schwartz cite studies which demonstrate that "cartoons show less serious acts of violence than adult-oriented dramas" and that the comic nature of cartoons reduces the likelihood that children will believe that the violent acts they see on TV can be applied in real-world situations (190).

Blumberg, Bierwith, and Schwartz agree that children may exhibit negative, aggressive behavior after watching violent TV shows, acknowledging that "a schema for aggression may be activated as a result of having viewed aggressive acts" (190). However, they believe that effects of watching violent cartoons is mitigated by the children's ability to draw a distinction between fantasy and reality: the authors cite several studies which show that when viewing animation, "most preschoolers still recognize cartoon programs as 'make-believe'" and "can differentiate cartoon characters engaged in life-like activities from those engaged in pretend activities" (191).

In addition, Blumberg, Bierwith, and Schwartz contend that most researchers who link cartoon viewing and childhood violence study children shortly after they have watched the violent shows. They question the long-term impact of watching violent cartoons. According to Blumberg, Bierwirth, and Schwartz, children do see violent acts in cartoons as wrong and "immoral," believe the violent acts deserve punishment, believe that perpetuators of cartoon violence are "bad," and can differentiate between realistic and cartoon depictions of violence (192). In short, the authors argue that children's abilities to draw distinctions between reality and fantasy and to apply moral judgments to what they watch on TV make it less likely that they will repeat the aggressive acts they see on television in their daily lives.

The authors of all three articles agree that children are exposed to more violent television shows than ever before and all agree that viewing these shows impacts them in some way. Both Simmons, Stalsworth, and Wentzell and Cantor believe watching these shows has an extremely detrimental effect on children, leading them to commit more violent acts in real life and perhaps increasing the chances that they will grow up to a life of crime. Blumberg, Bierwith, and Schwartz question the connections between television and childhood violence, arguing that children are able to distinguish between fantasy and reality well enough to avoid any long-term consequences associated with viewing violent shows. One point all the authors agree on, though, is that children are best served by watching television shows with their parents who can explain the programs and answer their children's questions.

Summary Chart

HOW TO WRITE AN INFORMATIVE SYNTHESIS

1. **Analyze the assignment.**
   - *Determine whether you are being asked to write an informative or argumentative synthesis.*
   - *Determine the number and types of readings you are expected to use in your paper.*

2. **Review and annotate the readings.**
   - *Review the readings with your assignment in mind, looking for and marking information related to the topic of your paper.*
   - *Briefly summarize each reading.*

3. **Formulate a thesis.**
   - *Determine what stance you will assume in your essay.*
   - *Determine whether you will use an open or closed thesis statement.*

4. **Choose an organizational plan.**
   - *Decide how you will order the ideas you will develop in your essay.*
   - *Decide whether you will present your ideas using a block or alternating format.*

5. **Write your rough draft.**
   - *Follow the organization plan implied or stated by your thesis.*
   - *Summarize and combine (synthesize) material from the source texts to support your thesis.*
   - *Both paraphrase and quote material as necessary.*
   - *Add transitions, elaborations, clarifications, and connections where needed.*
   - *Include a concluding paragraph.*

6. Revise your draft.

Revise to improve the content of your essay.

- *Does your thesis accurately reflect your position and intention?*
- *Have you communicated in your paper what you want to communicate?*
- *Will your paper give your reader a thorough understanding of the source texts and your thesis?*
- *Have you avoided editorializing in your paper?*
- *Would your essay make sense to someone who has not read the source texts?*

Revise to improve the organization of your essay.

- *Does your thesis guide the development of your essay?*
- *Do you provide topic sentences to introduce major sections of your essay?*
- *Have you provided transitions that help lead your reader through your paper?*

Revise to improve the accuracy and clarity of your essay.

- *Have you used language that is as fair and impartial as possible?*
- *Have you avoided jargon and overly technical language when they would not be appropriate?*
- *Have you checked for sentence variety and clarity?*
- *Have you proofread for spelling, punctuation, and usage errors?*

7. Check your quotations and documentation.

- *Have you quoted and paraphrased material properly, accurately, and fairly?*
- *Have you documented all the material that needs to be documented?*
- *Have you documented material employing the proper format?*

INFORMATIVE SYNTHESIS REVISION CHECKLIST

	Yes	No
1. Have you checked your assignment to be sure you have written the proper kind of synthesis essay: informative or argumentative?	____	____
2. In your introduction do you:		
• introduce the topic of the paper?	____	____
• offer your thesis?	____	____
• capture your readers' interest?	____	____
3. Examine the wording of your thesis. Does it clearly indicate what stance you will assume in your essay?	____	____
4. Examine the structure of your essay. Does it follow the organizational plan indicated by your thesis?	____	____
5. Check each section in the body of your essay. Do you:		
• examine just one issue at a time?	____	____
• combine information from your source texts?	____	____
• explain the link between the examples you cite and the assertion you are making?	____	____
• make clear the relationship you see among your source texts?	____	____
6. Examine your transitions. Have you provided adequate signals to help guide your readers through your work?	____	____
7. The first time you introduce a source text, do you give the full title of the piece and the author's full name?	____	____
8. Have you properly documented all quoted, summarized, and paraphrased material?	____	____
9. Have you reviewed your quotations for accuracy and variety?	____	____
10. Is your works cited or reference list correct?	____	____

	Yes	No
11. Have you reviewed your essay to be sure the content accurately communicates your position and intention?	_____	_____
12. Have you reviewed your word choice for clarity and accuracy?	_____	_____

Chapter 10

ARGUMENTATIVE SYNTHESIS

DEFINITION AND PURPOSE

In an argumentative synthesis, you use material from various readings to support and illustrate an argument of your own, usually concerning the quality of writing in the source texts or an issue they address. If your argument centers on the quality of the readings, you might argue that one text is better written or more convincing than the others. If, however, your teacher asks you to present an argument on the issue the readings address, you will draw on the material in the readings to support your thesis.

For a number of reasons, writing an argumentative synthesis can be challenging:

1. As with the informative synthesis, the sources you consult when gathering information for this type of essay can be difficult to read. They will often present complex arguments themselves or employ terminology or research methodologies new to you. Being able to read this material critically is essential if you hope to write a successful argumentative synthesis.
2. As you read these source texts, you will need to critique them. For example, if you are arguing that one is better written than another, you will have to critique both to determine the relative strengths and weaknesses of each. If you are using the readings to develop an argument of your own

on the topic they address, again you will have to critique the source texts to determine the quality of the arguments and information in each. You want to base your argument on the best available material.

3. When you compose your argumentative synthesis, you have to be concerned, first, with the content and quality of *your* argument. You need to decide if the material you are including in your paper will achieve the desired effect on your reader—will your audience be convinced by your argument? At the same time, since you are working with source texts, you have to pay close attention to the way you are using other people's findings or arguments to be sure you are fairly representing their work.

4. Part of composing an argumentative synthesis is deciding how best to order the claims, evidence, findings, or arguments you present. You need to decide which ideas or arguments you will present in which order and to provide effective transitions between and within the major sections of your argument.

5. In supporting your argument with source material, you will need to be quoting, summarizing, and paraphrasing other people's ideas, arguments, and findings. As a result, documentation becomes a challenge. You will need to be explicit and clear in acknowledging the source of the information you use to support your assertions.

THE ELEMENTS OF ARGUMENT

As you develop, draft, and revise your argumentative synthesis, pay particular attention to the three basic elements of any argument: **claims**, **grounds**, and **warrants**. According to British philosopher Stephen Toulmin in *The Uses of Argument* (Cambridge University Press, 1958), every argument involves an assertion (claim) that is supported by evidence (grounds) and rests upon a particular set of assumptions or line of reasoning (warrant). Effective arguments employ clear, limited claims; reliable, appropriate grounds; and fully developed, explicit warrants. Understanding each of these elements can help you compose more effective argumentative synthesis essays.

CLAIMS

A **claim** is an assertion you want your readers to accept. In an argumentative synthesis essay, your thesis statement is a claim, one you will develop and support with other claims in the body of your essay. Suppose, for example, you are writing an argumentative synthesis using the articles on television violence found in Chapter 9 and decide on the following thesis: "Due to her use of statistics, examples, and reasoning, Cantor's argument that viewing violent television shows harms young children is more persuasive than Blumberg, Bierwirth, and Schwartz's argument that children are not harmed by what they watch on TV." Your thesis is a claim: Cantor's argument is stronger than

Blumberg, Bierwirth, and Schwartz's argument. You will support this assertion with three other claims or "because" statements: Cantor's argument is stronger because she employs more effective statistics, better examples, and a clear line of reasoning. In the body of your essay you will develop these three claims with valid grounds and warrants if you want readers to accept your thesis.

When you compose an essay from source texts, most of your claims will be based on what you read and can include:

- claims concerning the source text's topic;
- claims concerning the source text's content, organization, or style;
- claims concerning the quality of the source text's writing; and
- claims concerning your response or reaction to the source texts.

Your teacher may give you several readings to study or require you to collect material on your own outside of class. In either case, you will be expected to critique the readings, form an argumentative thesis or claim, and explain or defend that assertion in your essay.

Well-written claims are **accurate**, **clear**, and **limited**. Any claim you make about a reading should be accurate: you should not misrepresent what an author writes. Claims should also be clear and unambiguous. "There are several good things about Cantor's argument" is not a clear claim. What does the writer mean by "good" or by "things"? When forming claims, be as specific as you can, using language that precisely captures the assertion you want to make. Also, avoid broad, unlimited claims because such assertions are usually inaccurate and difficult to support. Claims like "Cantor's essay is the best piece of writing ever produced" or "There is absolutely no value at all to Cantor's argument" are not sufficiently limited. In writing limited claims, you may find yourself using words like "most" instead of "all," "often" instead of "always," or "likely" instead of "certainly." Limited claims (including limited thesis statements) are easier to explain and defend than unlimited, sweeping claims.

GROUNDS

Grounds is another name for the evidence you use to support a claim. As with claims, when you compose a source-based argumentative synthesis essay, you will draw most of your grounds from readings, though many teachers will allow you to use relevant personal experience to support a claim as well. Source-based grounds can include facts, statistics, testimony, and opinions. Each type of evidence has its own strengths and limitations. When deciding how to employ each in support of a claim, consider the questions that follow. Remember: the quality of your essay often depends on the quality of the grounds you employ to support your claims. If you rely on weak, questionable, or irrelevant grounds to support your claims, your writing is unlikely to convince thoughtful readers.

Facts: information the author of the source text presents as verifiably true

- Is the information up to date?
- Does the information come from a reliable source?
- Is the information documented?
- Is the information clear and unambiguous in its meaning?
- Is the information relevant to the claim you are making?
- Is the information consistent with your understanding, knowledge, or experience?
- Is the information consistent with what other source texts contend?

Examples: illustrations drawn from the source text to support your claim

- Are the examples relevant to the claim you are making?
- How much background information do you need to provide so that your reader will understand the examples you incorporate from the source text?
- Are the examples true or fictional? Is either acceptable given your assignment?
- Do the examples come from a reliable source?
- Are the examples timely?
- Are the examples representative and typical or limited and unique?

Statistics: data the author of the source text employs to support his or her claims

- Do you understand the statistics, what they mean, and their limitations?
- Do the statistics come from a reliable, trustworthy source?
- What are the possible biases of the source text? How might those biases affect the statistics offered in the piece?
- How do the statistics compare with evidence found in other source texts?
- Does the author of the source text acknowledge the limitations of the statistics?
- Are the statistics relevant to the claim you are trying to support in your essay?
- Can you adequately explain the link between the statistics you cite and the claim you are supporting?

Testimony: personal experiences offered by the author of the source text in support of his or her claims

- Does the testimony come from a reliable, qualified source?
- Is the testimony firsthand or secondhand?
- How is the testimony relevant to the claim you are trying to support?
- What background information from the source text will you need to provide so that your reader will understand the meaning and nature of the testimony?
- Does the author of the source text acknowledge the limitations of the testimony?
- How does the testimony complement (or contradict) other grounds provided in the essay?

Opinions: what the author of a source text believes to be true

- Is this the opinion of the source text's author or is the author offering someone else's opinion?
- Is the person sufficiently qualified to offer an opinion worth citing in your essay?
- How will you make clear in the body of your essay that this opinion comes from a reliable source?
- Does the author sufficiently explain and clarify his or her opinion?
- Does the author support that opinion with evidence?
- Is the opinion sufficiently qualified?
- Is the opinion supported by other types of evidence in the source text or by evidence you have gathered from other sources?

Whatever grounds you employ in your essay, be sure they are **relevant**, **reliable**, and **appropriate**. As you defend or illustrate a claim, first be sure the evidence you use is relevant to the assertion you are making. Writing an argumentative synthesis can be confusing because you are working with multiple texts and multiple claims. As you select the grounds you will use to support a particular claim, be sure they clearly relate to that claim and not to some other assertion you are making in your essay. Also, be sure the grounds are reliable—examine the credentials and possible biases of the source text's author, the publication's or Web site's credibility, and the date of publication. Finally, be sure your grounds are appropriate for the assignment and audience. As you write papers in classes across the curriculum, you will discover that what counts as valid grounds in one class may not count as valid grounds in another. Learning what grounds are appropriate for arguments in a field of study is part of learning how to reason like a member of that discipline. Analyze the texts you read in class to determine the kinds of evidence successful authors in that field of study utilize in their arguments and ask your instructor for help if you have doubts about the appropriateness of evidence you plan to use in any essay.

One final note about grounds: Most writers know that they can support a claim in an argumentative synthesis essay by quoting, paraphrasing, or otherwise alluding to the work of authors who agree with the position they are advancing. Citing authorities who support the claims you make improves your work's credibility. However, there are other ways to use source material to support an argument. For example, consider citing authorities who *disagree* with the claim you are making. Incorporating counterexamples into your argumentative synthesis can be effective if you employ them correctly. First, acknowledging alternative positions increases your credibility as a writer. It demonstrates your knowledge of the subject matter, your fairness, and the confidence you have in your own position. However, citing counterexamples alone will not help you achieve these benefits; instead, you must integrate them into your essay by refuting them, conceding to them, or accommodating them.

When you **refute** counterexamples, you offer a fair summary of the opposing view, then demonstrate how that position is wrong, problematic, or otherwise flawed. You can then explain how your position is better. When you **concede** to an opposing view, you acknowledge how and when the opposition might be right in its assertions. However, you then demonstrate how that fact does not seriously damage your own position or thesis. Finally, when you **accommodate** an opposing view, you explain how that position and your own may be equally correct and how, by combining them, one might gain a better, more comprehensive understanding of the issue. In short, be imaginative in your use of source material as grounds in an argumentative synthesis. Just be sure the grounds you use are linked to your claims with strong warrants.

WARRANTS

Warrants are a little harder to understand than claims or grounds because they tend to be more abstract. Simply stated, though, a warrant is a line of reasoning, set of assumptions, or explanation that links a claim to its grounds. When writing an argumentative synthesis, remember that in most cases the grounds will not speak for themselves: you need to explain how they support the claim you are making. For instance, suppose you wrote the following passage, a claim supported by an example:

> Cantor's argument is stronger than Blumberg, Bierwirth, and Schwartz's, in part, due to her use of statistics to support and illustrate many of her claims. For example, she notes that in one study, even as adults, 52% of respondents who had been frightened by a television show when a child still had occasional problems sleeping and 35% reported "avoiding or dreading the situation depicted in the program or movie" (00).

Are you ready to move on to your next claim now? Have you sufficiently supported your claim by citing an example or two from the text? No. What's missing here is your warrant—before you move on to your next claim, you have to *explain how* the use of statistics you cite makes Cantor's argument more convincing than Blumberg, Bierwirth, and Schwartz's. What is it about citing statistics or citing *these* statistics that makes Cantor's argument more convincing? Why might readers be more convinced by Cantor's argument than by Blumberg, Bierwirth, and Schwartz's because Cantor includes these statistics in her essay? As you explain the link between your assertion and the evidence you provide for it, you are articulating your warrant.

As you draft and revise your argumentative synthesis, you need to ask yourself a series of questions concerning the nature and effectiveness of your warrants.

1. *Is my warrant stated or unstated? If unstated, will the link between my claims and my grounds be sufficiently clear for my readers?*
   In everyday conversation, many warrants go unstated: the link between a claim and its grounds is so clear or so readily accepted that no warrant is

needed. In academic writing, however, warrants usually need to be stated and explained. The aim of an academic argument is to let your reader know where you stand on an issue (your claim), to convince your reader to accept this position as reasonable or correct by supporting it with evidence (your grounds), and to explain how this evidence makes the case for the claim (your warrant). Two writers may make the same assertion in their papers and may even support those assertions with similar evidence, but how they explain the link they see between the evidence and the claim will likely differ. In academic writing, warrants can help make your essay distinctive. Therefore, examine your essay for any unstated warrants and decide whether they need to be made explicit. If you think there is any chance your readers may question the link between a claim and its grounds, state your warrant.

2. *Is my warrant logical and reasonable?*

How *do* the grounds you employ actually support your claim? What assumptions are you making about the link between your grounds and claims? Are you assuming that your readers will recognize and accept the connection you see between your claims and grounds? Is the connection you see between them logical and reasonable? Will your readers see the connection as logical and reasonable?

3. *Is my warrant clear, fully explained, and supported?*

Underdeveloped warrants are a common problem with argumentative synthesis essays: writers, understanding that they need to state their warrants, simply fail to explain them adequately. Clear, well-developed warrants are crucial to successful arguments, especially if you believe your audience will question the validity of your claim or grounds. In these cases, you may need to explain your warrant at length, perhaps even acknowledging alternative readings of your grounds as you clarify your own interpretation. Determining whether your warrants are sufficiently explained and supported can be difficult, which is why you should have other people read and critique drafts of your writing. Specifically ask them to read your essay skeptically; to question the validity of your claims, grounds, and warrants; and to indicate any weaknesses they note or questions they have. Sometimes the warrants themselves rest upon unstated assumptions that need to be explained and defended.

ARGUMENT AND PERSUASION

Rhetoricians often draw a distinction between argument and persuasion. Argument, they maintain, involves demonstrating the credibility of a position; persuasion involves moving readers to accept or act on that position. The most commonly acknowledged agents of persuasion are logos (logic), pathos (emotion), and ethos (character): writers can often persuade readers to accept or act on an argument by appealing to the readers' logic or emotions or by sufficiently establishing their own credibility or character (see Chapter 7 for a further discussion of logos, pathos, and ethos).

APPEALS BASED ON REASON

In an argumentative synthesis, successful appeals to **logos** largely depend on the quality of your claims, grounds, and warrants. Clear, qualified claims supported by valid grounds and clear, reasonable warrants will go a long way toward persuading a reader that your position is reasonable enough to accept and act on. Such writing, however, rarely happens by accident. It results from careful, critical drafting and revision. Here are a few steps you can take to improve the logical appeal of your argumentative synthesis essay:

1. **Make clear, limited claims.**
   Be sure all of your claims are clear, reasonable, and limited. Vague claims will not be convincing and neither will unreasonable assertions or sweeping generalizations. The claims you make—including your thesis—form the framework around which you will build your argumentative synthesis. If your claims are unclear, unreasonable, or unconnected to one another, the logical appeal of your essay will be diminished.
2. **Employ grounds that are relevant, credible, and timely.**
   As you decide what evidence or examples to offer in support of a claim, choose the material that is most relevant to your assertion. First, avoid using grounds that are only tangentially related to your claim. Second, be sure the grounds you employ come from credible sources. If you use reliable sources in your essay, readers are more likely to see your assertions as reasonable. Basing your paper on material drawn from questionable sources will bring into question the legitimacy of your own assertions. Finally, be sure the material you use in your paper is timely. As a rule, draw on the most recent research you can find when writing your paper—employing out-of-date source texts may hamper your efforts to sway readers' opinions.
3. **Explain your reasoning process.**
   One of the best ways to improve the logical appeal of your essay is to explain your reasoning process on the page. Lay bare for your readers the reasoning process that led you to your conclusions: elaborate on the meaning of your claims, explain connections among your assertions, explore alternative arguments, and discuss the links you see between your claims and their grounds. Most academic audiences will expect to find this type of discussion and explanation in your essay.

APPEALS BASED ON EMOTION

Successful persuasive appeals to **pathos** can be difficult to achieve but can also be very effective. Employing pathos to persuade readers is tricky because it can have the opposite effect if used incorrectly or clumsily. Pathos can quickly turn into bathos, or unintentionally comic appeals to emotion. However, when used sparingly and appropriately, emotionally charged grounds or language can prove very persuasive. Here are a few suggestions on how to employ pathos effectively in an argumentative synthesis essay.

1. **Include in your essay material that might appeal to your readers' interests.**

   While it is often difficult to know with any degree of certainty what material might appeal to your readers' interests, it may be possible to make some educated guesses. For example, what might interest them given their economic, political, educational, or religious backgrounds? What can you assume they know or may want to know about the topic of your essay? What aspects of the topic interest you? How similar are you to your audience—can you assume they might have similar interests? Though it is very difficult to make completely accurate assessments of what material might interest your readers, the closer you come to hitting the mark, the more likely you are to obtain a positive emotional response to your writing.

2. **Include in your essay material that might appeal to your readers' needs or fears.**

   As you consider what material to include in your argumentative synthesis, can you identify examples, arguments, testimonials, statistics, or other material that might appeal to your readers' needs or address their concerns? Your goal is not to play on your readers' emotions. Instead, you want to connect emotionally with readers, to construct a bridge between your essay and reader needs or concerns, thus helping them see the relevancy of your essay to their lives. Is there material, for example, that might appeal to your readers' concerns about their physical, psychological, or financial safety; need for self-affirmation; or desires for joy or happiness? Successfully employing this type of material in your argumentative synthesis greatly increases the chances that readers will find your essay persuasive.

3. **Employ language that is evocative or captivating.**

   Another way to improve the emotional appeal of your argumentative synthesis is to use especially evocative or captivating language. Words have both denotative (literal) and connotative (emotional) meanings. You will often face instances when you can choose among words that have roughly the same denotative meaning but vary widely in their connotative implications. In these cases, consider using language that more effectively appeals to your reader's emotions. Also consider your use of figurative language. While most academic writers employ extended metaphors sparingly, the use of analogies, allusions, and other figurative language is more common. Your goal is not to produce flowery prose. Instead, your aim is to employ language that persuades readers to accept or act on your arguments by developing in them an emotional understanding of your topic.

APPEALS BASED ON CHARACTER AND CREDIBILITY

In one sense, **ethos** is closely linked to logos because it has to do with the credibility of the claims, grounds, and warrants you employ in your essay. Ethos involves trust and character: do you demonstrate through the quality of the claims, grounds, and warrants you employ in your writing that you are a trustworthy, knowledgeable, fair-minded individual? If you do, then you may persuade some readers to accept your position through your own ethos as a writer. Ethos, though, also has to do with the quality of your own prose. Even if you compose a synthesis with strong claims, grounds, and warrants, you will lose credibility if your prose is marred by misspellings, grammatical problems, typos, or other surface errors. Readers may feel that they cannot trust authors who are careless with their writing; if an author is so sloppy with word choice, syntax, spelling, or punctuation, how sloppy has the author been with his or her research, reasoning, and documentation? Persuasion depends on trust, and you may lose the trust of your readers—and your credibility as a writer—if your writing is full of easily correctable errors. Here are a few steps you can take to improve ethos in your argumentative synthesis:

1. **Present informed, balanced arguments.**
   You will enhance your credibility as a writer if you present a balanced argument in your essay, examining the strengths and weaknesses of your assertions and exploring alternative points of view. Presenting a balanced argument requires you to research and consider a range of perspectives on your essay's topic. Examining this range of perspectives in your essay increases the likelihood of readers seeing you as a knowledgeable, fair-minded writer, and readers are more likely to consider and perhaps adopt arguments presented by writers they perceive as informed and fair.

2. **Demonstrate the credibility of your source texts.**
   Another way to enhance your ethos is by demonstrating the credibility of the source texts you use in your essay. Readers are more likely to accept or act on your arguments if they perceive that your claims are supported by authoritative sources. In-text documentation is one way to demonstrate that your arguments are supported by credible sources. You can also establish the authority of your source texts by including in your essay the full name of the person who wrote the text and a summary of his or her credentials when you first quote or paraphrase material from him or her.

3. **Employ fair, balanced language.**
   Just as you want the content of your argumentative synthesis to be fair and balanced, you also want to avoid language that might make you appear narrow-minded or uninformed. While on occasion you will want to employ emotionally evocative language (see discussion of pathos above), consistently employing words that make you sound shrill, sarcastic, or hostile will usually hinder your efforts to persuade readers to consider or accept your arguments, especially if you are addressing a neutral or possibly antagonistic audience. In these cases, you might be better served using language that is more judicious and fair.

4. **Proofread your work carefully.**
Finally, remember that the quality of your own prose influences whether your readers perceive you as a credible authority. Argumentative synthesis essays that are full of surface-level errors are unlikely to persuade many readers. Rightly or wrongly, most readers will judge the quality of your argument by the quality of your prose: in their minds, error-laden writing is likely to reflect error-laden thinking. You can help ensure that your writing is persuasive simply by proofreading your essay thoroughly before you submit your final draft for review.

WRITING AN ARGUMENTATIVE SYNTHESIS

Because argumentative syntheses are so complex, writing them in a number of steps or stages is often helpful. Here are some of the steps you might consider following when writing an argumentative synthesis:

1. Analyze the assignment.
2. Annotate and critique the readings.
3. Formulate a thesis.
4. Choose an organizational plan.
5. Write your rough draft.
6. Revise your draft.
7. Check quotations and documentation.

STEP 1—ANALYZE THE ASSIGNMENT

Some teachers will not specify the type of argument they want you to present in your synthesis. If this is the case, you will need to decide for yourself whether you want to focus on the quality of the writing in the readings or on the issue they address. However, if a teacher specifically asks you to focus your argument on the quality of the source texts, his assignment might include directions such as these:

> Review the readings in Chapter 6 of the textbook. Which author do you believe presents the most convincing case? Why?

> * * * * *

> Review the readings in Chapter 6 of the textbook. Which piece is better written? How so?

In the first assignment, the teacher wants you to analyze, evaluate, then compare the **arguments** presented by the various writers, arguing that one presents the best case. In the second assignment, the teacher wants you to analyze, evaluate, then compare the **styles** of the various writers, arguing that one produces the best-written text.

However, when a teacher wants you to take a stand on the topic the readings address, her directions may read something like this:

> Review the readings in Chapter 6 of the textbook. Where do you stand on the issue? Present an argument in favor of your position using the readings for support.

Here the teacher wants you to read the articles, think about the arguments presented by each author, reflect on your own knowledge and feelings concerning the topic, then present an argument in which you assume and defend a position of your own on the issue.

Once you have determined the type of argument the teacher wants you to write, check the assignment to determine the number and types of sources the teacher wants you to use in your paper. Sometimes instructors specify a certain number of readings you must use in your paper, asking you, for example, to base your paper on four to six sources. Other times teachers specify the types of readings you have to use: those provided in class, those you find on your own in the library, academic sources only, and so on. If you have any questions about the number or type of readings you need to use in your synthesis, be sure to check with your instructor.

STEP 2—ANNOTATE AND CRITIQUE THE READINGS

As you begin to collect the readings you plan to use when writing your argumentative synthesis, you need to annotate and critique them (see Chapter 6 for advice on critiquing readings). First, annotate each reading, identifying its thesis, primary assertions, and evidence. Next, analyze and critique the content and structure of each reading. If you base your argument on other authors' faulty writing or reasoning, your essay will likely reflect their weaknesses; likewise, if you base your argument on solid, well-written sources, your argument will likely be stronger. The questions you want to ask of a reading include:

- What, exactly, is the main point of this reading?
- How has the author supported his ideas, arguments, or findings?
- How well has the author explained or supported his ideas, arguments, or findings?
- Do I find the reading convincing? Why or why not?
- How have the structure and tone of the piece influenced my reaction?
- What is the quality of the writing?
- How do the author's ideas, arguments, or findings compare with those found in the other sources I have read?

Place your annotations in the margins of the reading, on sheets of paper, or on index cards. If you use paper or index cards, be sure you copy all the bibliographic information you will need to complete a reference list entry on the source, in case you use any of that material in your paper. In an argumentative synthesis, all quoted, paraphrased, or summarized material needs to be documented.

STEP 3—FORMULATE A THESIS

Formulating a clear thesis statement is an essential step in writing a successful argumentative synthesis. Your thesis statement tells your readers the position you plan on advancing in your paper and will likely indicate the structure of your essay. Put another way, your thesis statement establishes in your readers' minds certain expectations concerning the content and form of your paper. When you satisfy those expectations, your readers will have an easier time following your argument; if you do not, however, readers may feel your work is confusing and disorganized. So you need to spend some time forming and refining your thesis statement.

In an argumentative synthesis you advance a position of your own concerning the quality and/or topic of the readings. If you are focusing on the quality of the readings themselves, you can assume a number of different positions. For example, suppose you are writing an argumentative synthesis using the readings on television violence found in Chapter 9. You may argue that one essay is more convincing than another:

> While both Cantor and Simmons, Stalsworth, and Wentzell argue that watching violent television shows harms children, Cantor offers the more persuasive argument.

Or you may argue that one work is better written than another:

> While both Cantor and Simmons, Stalsworth, and Wentzell argue that watching violent television shows harms children, Cantor's essay is more clearly written.

In either case, the thesis sets out the position you will be developing in your paper.

As with other types of essays, thesis statements for argumentative syntheses can be either open or closed. While both of the examples above are open thesis statements, they could easily be modified to give the reader a better indication of what exactly will be covered in the paper:

> While both Cantor and Simmons, Stalsworth, and Wentzell argue that watching violent television shows harms children, Cantor offers the more persuasive argument through her use of statistics and compelling examples.

> * * * * *

> While both Cantor and Simmons, Stalsworth, and Wentzell argue that watching violent television shows harms children, Cantor's essay is more clearly written because she avoids unnecessary jargon and employs a more casual style of writing.

If, however, your goal in composing an argumentative synthesis is to assert a position of your own on the topic of the readings, your thesis will read a little differently, something like this (employing an open thesis):

> Although researchers offer varying assessments and positions, watching violent television shows is harmful to children.

Or perhaps this (employing a closed thesis):

> Although researchers offer varying assessments and positions, watching violent television shows is harmful to children because they often imitate the violent acts they see, come to see violence as normative, and carry with them the effects long after they have grown up.

STEP 4—CHOOSE AN ORGANIZATIONAL PLAN

If you use a **block format** to organize your essay, you would critique in turn what each author has to say about the topic, then advance your own position. Suppose you were working with this thesis: "Although researchers offer varying assessments and positions, watching violent television shows is harmful to children because they often imitate the violent acts they see, come to see violence as normative, and carry with them the effects long after they have grown up." In outline form, your paper might look like this:

Argumentative Synthesis—Block Format

Opening Section

Capture reader interest

Introduce the topic

Give your thesis

Discussion of Blumberg, Bierwirth, and Schwartz Article

Introduce the article—title, author, publication information

Summarize the article—Blumberg, Bierwirth, and Schwartz's argument

Critique the article—strengths and weaknesses of their argument

Tie criticisms to specific passages in the article

Fully explain or defend your criticism

Draw links with other source texts

Discussion of Simmons, Stalsworth, and Wentzell Article

Introduce the article—title, author, publication information

Summarize the article—Simmons, Stalsworth, and Wentzell's argument

Critique the article—strengths and weaknesses of their argument

Tie criticisms to specific passages in the article

Fully explain or defend your criticism

Draw links with other source texts

Discussion of Cantor Article

Introduce the article—title, author, publication information

Summarize the article—Cantor's argument

Critique the article—strengths and weaknesses of her argument

Tie criticisms to specific passages in the article

Fully explain or defend your criticism

Draw links with other source texts

Your Argument Concerning Harmful Effects of Violent Television Shows on Children

How watching violent television shows harms children because children imitate the violence they see

Tie arguments to specific examples from the articles

Fully explain and defend your assertions

Refer back to other authors' opinions to bolster your position

How watching violent television shows harms children because children come to see violence as normal or acceptable behavior

Tie arguments to specific examples from the articles

Fully explain and defend your assertions

Refer back to other authors' opinions to bolster your position

How watching violent television shows harms children because the effects the shows have on them stay with children for years

Tie arguments to specific examples from the articles

Fully explain and defend your assertions

Refer back to other authors' opinions to bolster your position

Conclusion

In the opening section of your paper, you would introduce the topic of your essay, capture reader interest, and offer your thesis. In the body of your paper, you would critique the arguments offered by each of your source texts, focusing your attention on what they have to say about why or how watching violent television shows harms children. Finally, you would present your own argument, supporting your position with specific references to the source texts to help support or explain your thesis.

If you prefer, you could organize the paper using an **alternating format**, structuring your essay around the aspects of the topic you have chosen as your focus rather than each source text. In this case, your paper might be organized like this:

Argumentative Synthesis—Alternating Format

Opening Section

>   Capture reader interest

>   Introduce the topic

>   Give your thesis

Discuss how watching violent television shows harms children because children imitate the violence they see

>   Explain your assertion

>   Support your argument with convincing grounds, including material from the source texts

>   Explain how your position differs from the positions presented in the source texts

Discuss how watching violent television shows harms children because children come to see violence as normal or acceptable behavior

>   Explain your assertion

>   Support your argument with convincing grounds, including material from the source texts

>   Explain how your position differs from the positions presented in the source texts

Discuss how watching violent television shows harms children because the effects the shows have on them stay with children for years

>   Explain your assertion

>   Support your argument with convincing grounds, including material from the source texts

>   Explain how your position differs from the positions presented in the source texts

Conclusion

In the opening of your paper, you would again introduce the topic of your essay, capture reader interest, and state your thesis. In the body of your essay, you would argue, in order, that watching violent television shows harms children because they imitate the acts they see, because they come to believe that violence is a normal, acceptable way to act, and because the effects remain for years. In developing your argument, you would explain your claims or assertions, support them with grounds (e.g., evidence, examples, reasons) and include material from the source texts when appropriate, and discuss how your position differs from the ones presented in those texts.

Once you have drafted at least a preliminary thesis for your paper and have some sense of the assertions that will serve as the focus of your synthesis, you will need to return to the readings to locate material to include in your essay. Remember that the focus of an argumentative synthesis should be the argument you are advancing, not the material from the readings. In other words, your first responsibility is to develop a sound argument; the source material serves to illustrate or support *your* assertions.

STEP 5—WRITE YOUR ROUGH DRAFT

When you feel you are ready to begin writing your rough draft, be sure you have in front of you all of your source texts and notes. Some students like to begin writing immediately—they need to see some of their ideas in writing before they can decide on a final thesis or organize their paper. Other students have to begin with a clear thesis and outline in hand. Follow the method of composing that is most comfortable and successful for you.

When writing your essay, you will support your argument with material from the readings. You can use source material to give your readers background information on the topic (quote or paraphrase material you think your reader needs to know to understand your argument), to support your assertions (quote or paraphrase material that substantiates or illustrates your claims), or to acknowledge opposing views (quote or paraphrase material that calls into question your assertions; you then must decide whether to refute, accommodate, or concede to these different perspectives).

STEP 6—REVISE YOUR DRAFT

Revising your argumentative synthesis to make it ready for others to read is a time-consuming process again best approached in a series of steps. First, revise to improve the **content** of your paper, focusing on the quality and clarity of the argument you are advancing. Here are some questions you might ask about your draft as you revise to improve its content:

- Have I clearly indicated the point I want to prove?
- Have I clearly indicated the reasons I believe others should accept my position?
- Have I supported each of those reasons with expert testimony, statistics, or some other means of support as well as with clear explanations?
- Have I acknowledged opposing views in my paper when necessary? Have I found ways of refuting, accommodating, or conceding to them?

Next, review the **organization** of your essay, asking these questions:

- Is the thesis statement clearly worded, and does it control the structure of the essay?

- Have I provided clear transitions between the major sections of my essay?
- Are there clear connections between the material I draw from the readings and my own elaborations and explanations?

Finally, when checking the **accuracy** and **clarity** of your work, ask yourself:

- Have I chosen words that are clear yet contribute to the effect I wanted to elicit from my readers?
- Are my sentences clearly structured with adequate variety?
- Have I quoted and paraphrased material accurately and properly?
- When incorporating quoted or paraphrased material in my synthesis, have I supplied enough background information on the source text so the material makes sense to my readers?
- Have I defined all the terms I need to define?
- Have I documented all the material that needs to be documented?

STEP 7—CHECK QUOTATIONS AND DOCUMENTATION

Before you turn in your final draft for a grade, set aside time to check the accuracy of your quotations and documentation. First, make sure that you have quoted material accurately by comparing your text against the source text. Second, be sure that you have documented all of the material in your paper that needs to be documented, including all paraphrased information. Because you are combining information from several source texts in your synthesis and presenting your own argument as well, be sure your readers can always tell through your documentation the source of the material you include in your paper.

SAMPLE ARGUMENTATIVE SYNTHESIS

Following is an argumentative synthesis essay drawing on the readings found in Chapter 9. As you read the essay, consider how it is structured, how it uses material from the source texts, and how the writer develops the paper's argument.

Lost Innocence: The Dangers of Television Violence for Young Viewers

Most American children have grown up watching violent television shows. Whether prime-time drama or Saturday morning cartoons, children are exposed to a wide range of violent television programs. In fact, according to researchers Betty Simmons, Kelly Stalsworth, and Heather Wentzell, before children are 12 years old they have witnessed over 8,000 murders on television. They also found that only 2% of American homes do not have a television (181). In effect, then, almost all American children are exposed to television violence, a fact that warrants concern. Television violence harms children because it causes them to confuse fantasy and reality, encourages them to imitate the violent acts they see, and results in psychological damage that may last a lifetime.

Cognitively, young children have a difficult time separating the fantasy of the television world from the reality of their lives. Whether they are watching cartoons or newscasts, movies or commercials, children often believe what they see on the set is real. Simmons, Stalsworth, and Wentzell cite one of many studies which show "that children are extremely vulnerable to television between the ages of 2 to 8 years because of their maturational inability to separate what they view from reality" (182). As a result, what children watch on television shapes their view of the world, a world which is a frightening place full of potential threats and violence. Almost all parents have had to comfort a frightened child at bedtime because something on television frightened him or her, whether it was a monster destroying a city, a maniac stealing a child, or images of soldiers being killed on the nightly news. At young ages, everything children see on television is equally real. According to Joanne Cantor, Director of the Center for Communication Research at the University of Wisconsin, "There is growing evidence that violence viewing . . . induces intense fears and anxieties in child viewers" (175):

> A 1998 survey of more than 2,000 third through eighth graders in Ohio revealed that as the number of hours of television viewing per day increased, so did the prevalence of symptoms of psychological trauma, such as anxiety, depression, and posttraumatic stress. . . . Indeed, 9% of parents surveyed reported that their child experienced TV-induced nightmares *at least once a week.* (175)

The children in these studies were frightened because they believed that the violence they saw on television was all real and posed a potential threat to their safety and security. As Simmons, Stalsworth, and Wentzell claim, young children "live in a magical world that often leaves them terrified of things which completely surprise adults" (183).

Educators Fran Blumberg, Kristen Bierwirth, and Allison Schwartz, however, believe that watching violent television shows, especially cartoons, is not detrimental to children's well-being. These researchers support their assertions by citing the results of several studies, but their own prose casts doubts on the validity of their claims. For example, they cite a 2006 study by Kirsch which asserts that cartoon violence is different than violence portrayed on other types of shows—it is more verbal than physical and therefore less harmful. However, they paraphrase Kirsch as concluding that "the comedic element of cartoons *also may* affect young viewers' beliefs about the applicability of violent acts they see in programs to real-world situations" (190, emphasis added).

Blumberg, Bierwirth, and Schwartz end up conceding that children may have a difficult time differentiating television, even cartoons, from real life, as other researchers have concluded. In fact, they even cite studies of brain activity which demonstrate "neurological evidence of a link between exposure to violence on television and brain functioning," activating the area of the brain associated with self-control and "disruptive behavior disorder" (192). Blumberg, Bierwirth, and Schwartz downplay these results by pointing out that the studies have nothing to say about the long-term effects of childhood exposure to violent television. Presumably, any neurological changes that result from children watching violent television shows are short-lived and therefore not harmful. Finally, Blumberg, Bierwirth, and Schwartz argue that children who view violent cartoons make moral judgments about what they see, agreeing that violent characters should be punished. However, they then leap to an unconvincing conclusion: "*Presumably*, children's ability to make differentiated judgments about immoral acts *may* transfer to their ability to distinguish between the effects of cartoon and television violence and that found in real life" (192, emphasis added). Blumberg, Bierwirth, and Schwartz's arguments do not adequately call into question the many other studies that demonstrate children's inability to differentiate between reality and fantasy on television.

This inability to distinguish between what is make-believe and what is real on television holds real consequences for children. Besides increasing children's fears, this confusion contributes to the fact that children often imitate what they see on TV. Simmons, Stalsworth, and Wentzell note that because children are "curious and easily influenced," they often "mimic and repeat what they hear and see on television" (181). Most everyone can testify to the truth of this statement. Most people have seen young children engage in light-saber fights after watching *Star Wars* or bop some kid on the head after watching some cartoon on Nickelodeon. Children may mean no harm by imitating what they see on television, but the consequences can be tragic, as when they imitate what they see the Rock, Randy Horton, or the Undertaker do on Worldwide Wrestling or play with firearms they find in the home because they have seen characters use guns on TV. The National Institutes of Mental Health affirms a causal link between "television violence and aggressive behavior" in children (Simmons, Stalsworth, and Wentzell 182). Researchers Evra and Kline agree, asserting that "One of the dangers for preschoolers or early school-age children is their lack of ability to relate actions, motives, and consequences, and they may simply imitate the action they see" (quoted in Simmons, Stalsworth, and Wentzell 184). In other words, young children likely do not understand the real-life consequences of imitating the violence they see on TV.

While asserting that "definitive conclusions about the potential ill effects of exposure to cartoon violence on young viewers are not easily made," Blumberg, Bierwirth, and Schwartz conclude that several factors reduce the chances that children will imitate the violence they see on television:

> ... scientific support can be found that the frequent comic contextualization of violence coupled with young children's cognitive repertoire, notably, their abilities to distinguish right from wrong and fantasy from reality, may mitigate the likelihood that young viewers will perpetrate the violent acts shown in cartoons on others in real life. (193)

These researchers seem to believe that children possess the cognitive and moral maturity required to keep them from imitating violent acts they see on TV. Again, though, they hedge their conclusion with "may"; in the end, they have to acknowledge that children may, in fact, imitate the violence they see on television, as numerous other studies have found. According to Cantor, children lack the ability to understand the impact of their violent acts: "One criticism of the way violence is usually portrayed on television is that it minimizes the apparent harmful consequences to the victim, both promoting desensitization and increasing the likelihood of the adoption of aggressive attitudes and behaviors" (178). On many television shows, especially cartoons, violence is depicted as normal, harmless, and even funny. The more frequently children see violence depicted this way, the less likely they are to understand the harm violent acts can have on others:

> ... a study involving five different countries in which children were subjected to violence through television found evidence that even brief exposures caused them to be more accepting of other aggressive behavior. This research also concluded that the more children watched television, the more accepting they became of aggressive actions. (Simmons, Stalsworth, and Wentzell 182)

Given that every week children watch over 28 hours of TV (181), they may come to see violence and aggression as normal and acceptable aspects of life.

Finally, the life-long impact of watching violent television shows as a child may warrant the most concern. Perhaps young children confuse reality and fantasy when they watch TV and maybe they do imitate some of the violent acts they see; however when they grow up, one would assume that children grow out of these beliefs. At a certain point in their lives, children do come to realize that TV is not "real" and that hurting others has real consequences. Unfortunately, however, watching violent television shows as children may have lasting effects. Many of the claimed links between watching violent television shows as children and later anti-social behavior are startling. For example, some researchers assert that current high crime rates may be attributed to what today's criminals watched on television: "U.S.

crime rates are increasing most rapidly among youth who were in their formative early years when children's TV was deregulated and violent programs and toys successfully deluged childhood culture" (Simmons, Stalsworth, and Wentzell 182). Other studies have shown that the amount of violent television shows criminals watched when they were eight years old is a better predictor of their adult aggression than other socioeconomic factors (182). Cantor cites a study conducted at the Universities of Wisconsin and Michigan which asked adults to reflect back on frightening television shows they watched as children:

> . . . 52% reported disturbances in eating or sleeping, 22% reported mental preoccupation with the disturbing material, and 35% reported subsequently avoiding or dreading the situation depicted in the program or movie. Moreover, more than one-fourth of the respondents said that the emotional impact of the program or movie (viewed an average of six years earlier) was still with them at the time of the reporting. (176)

These studies do not claim that watching violent television shows as children causes adults to be fearful or turn to a life of crime. Instead, they point out a correlation between exposure to television violence as a child and anti-social behavior among some adults. At a minimum, research shows that what people watch on television as children contributes to who they become as adults.

Given the overwhelming evidence that watching violent television can have both short- and long-term negative consequences for children, what action is needed to address the problem? It seems unlikely that violence will be eradicated from television shows any time soon; even trying to take such actions raises serious freedom of speech issues. Instead, the best course of action is for parents to monitor what their children watch, limit their exposure to violence on TV, and explain to them the harmful effects violence has on others. Joanne Cantor explains how such acts can mitigate the ill effects of television violence on children and concludes her article with one last suggestion: "We also need media literacy education for children, including helping them place what they see in perspective, and encouraging a critical analysis of their own media choices" (178).

Additional Readings

Four Legs Good, Two Legs Bad: The Anti-human Values of "Animal Rights"

Wesley J. Smith

Wesley J. Smith *is a senior fellow at the Discovery Institute and consultant to the Center for Bioethics and Culture.*

If you are reading these words, you are a human being. That used to matter morally. Indeed, it was once deemed a self-evident truth that being a *Homo sapien* created intrinsic moral value based simply and merely on being human—a principle sometimes called "human exceptionalism."

No more. Human exceptionalism is under unprecedented assault across a broad array of societal and intellectual fronts. Bioethics, as this journal has often described, is a primary example. The predominating view among mainstream bioethicists is that human life per se does not matter morally. Rather, to be considered a full member of the moral community, one must achieve the status of being a "person" by possessing sufficient cognitive attributes such as being self-aware over time or being able to value one's life.[1]

This approach creates a potentially disposable caste consisting of hundreds of millions of humans: all unborn life—early embryos may not have a brain, and fetuses are generally considered unconscious; infants—they have not yet developed sufficient capacities; and people like the late Terri Schiavo—who have lost requisite capacities through illness or injury. The point of personhood theory is insidious: It grants permission to kill human non-persons or use them as mere natural resources ripe for the harvest.

Bioethics is by no means the only existent threat to human exceptionalism and to its corollary, the sanctity/equality-of-human-life ethic. Materialistic Darwinism also denigrates the unique moral value of human life based on the philosophical belief that because human beings evolved out of the same primordial mud as the rest of earth's flora and fauna, we are consequently not special or unique. The fervent embrace of human unexceptionalism led one Darwinian materialist to assert, "We are all of us, dogs and barnacles, pigeons and crabgrass, the same in the eyes of nature, equally remarkable and equally dispensable."[2]

John Derbyshire, of *National Review* fame, has similarly written that a Darwinian understanding of biology leads to the conclusion that human beings are only "special in the way that an elephant is special by virtue of having that long trunk....We are part of nature—an exceptionally advanced and interesting part, but ...not *special*."[3] (Emphasis within the text.)

A third equally dangerous threat to the equality/sanctity-of-human-life ethic—the subject of the balance of this article—comes from the animal-rights/liberation movement. Indeed, animal liberation is particularly subversive to our perceived status as a unique and special species because it advocates the creation of an explicit human/animal equality. Moreover, of the three threats to human exceptionalism I have mentioned (and there are others), only animal-rights activists engage in significant violence and lawlessness to coerce society into accepting their values. Thus, not only is animal-rights/liberation a unique danger to human exceptionalism (particularly among the young), but it also presents a potent threat to the rule of law.

The Ideology of Animal Rights

Defenders of the sanctity/equality-of-human-life ethic need to combat animal rights as forcefully as they do personhood theory. To understand why, we need to look past the public image of animal-rights/liberation groups, such as the People for the Ethical Treatment of Animals (PETA), as committed animal lovers who engage in wacky advocacy tactics such as posing nude to protest fur. For beneath this relatively benign facade lurks an ideologically absolutist movement that explicitly espouses equal moral worth between humans and animals.

What's wrong with wanting to protect animals? Absolutely nothing. Indeed, advocating for animal welfare can be a noble cause. But this isn't the ultimate agenda of animal rights/liberation. Thus, to understand the profound threat the movement poses to human exceptionalism, it must be distinguished from the animal-welfare movement.

The first distinguishing factor between animal rights and animal welfare is that, unlike the former ideology, the latter approach accepts human exceptionalism. As a consequence, animal welfarists argue that while human beings may have a right to use animals for our betterment and enjoyment, we also have a fundamental duty to do so in a proper and humane manner. Welfarists also believe we have a human duty to prevent unnecessary animal suffering. Thus, they engage in activities such as neutering feral cats and campaigning on behalf of more humane methods of slaughtering food animals.

In contrast, animal rights/liberation—while often engaging in welfare-type actions—is actually a radical departure from animal welfare. Whereas welfarists urge steady improvement of our treatment of animals and take actions to reduce animal suffering, the goal of the liberationists is to completely end every human use of animals. Thus, Gary L. Francione, director of the Rutgers University Animal Rights Law Center, seeks the eradication "of the property status of animals."[4] In his view there should ultimately be no domesticated animals. Similarly, PETA asserts that "animals are not ours to use—for food, clothing, entertainment, experimentation, or any other reason."[5]

To truly understand the subversive nature of the animal-rights philosophy, we have to look deeply into the movement's ultimate beliefs. For example, is the life of a monkey as precious as that of a human being? Animal-rights believers say yes. Is butchering a cow morally equivalent to lynching a black man during the Jim Crow era? PETA's "Animal Liberation Project" explicitly stated that it is.[6] Is artificially inseminating turkeys the moral equivalent of rape? Yes, according to Gary Francione, who criticized Peter Singer (and a colleague) for participating in a turkey-insemination demonstration. "I suggest that there is no non-speciesist way to justify what Singer and Mason claim to have done," Francione raged, "without also justifying the rape of a woman, or the molestation of a child, in order to see what those acts of violence 'really involved.'"[7] Many animal-rights activists and academics assert that animals should be considered "persons" with legal rights including full standing in the courts. Legislation will soon be introduced in Spain to grant full personhood rights to great apes.[8]

We cannot fully comprehend why animal liberationists believe these things—and why the most radical among them act violently against those they consider animal abusers—without understanding that liberationists *fervently* reject any hierarchy of moral worth between humans and animals. And this raises an important question: If being human does not convey moral worth to the liberationist, what does?

Space doesn't permit a complete exposition of all aspects and every nuance of animal-rights ideology. For our purposes, it is sufficient to explore the two primary ideological approaches: one that focuses on sentience as the source of moral value, and another that focuses on what has been called "painience," that is, the ability to feel pain.

Rutgers's Gary Francione is the best-known animal-liberation theorist advocating sentience as the primary measurement of moral value. "I argue that all sentient beings should have one right: the right not to be treated as our property—the right not to be valued exclusively as means to human ends," Francione stated in an interview.[9] (For these purposes, sentience can be defined as "a state of elementary or undifferentiated consciousness.")[10] In this view, since animals are not unconscious, they have a "right" not to be used instrumentally. Hence, each and every human use of animals—no matter how seemingly benign—is as wrong as if the same use were made of a non-consenting human being. Thus, to the true liberationist, cattle ranching is as odious as slavery because cows and humans are both sentient beings.

The second primary approach to crafting moral equality between humans and animals takes a slightly different trail to arrive at the same anti-human destination. In this view, if a being is capable of feeling pain, that attribute alone creates "equality of the species." Richard Ryder, a former professor at Tulane University, has written that the ability to feel pain—a capacity he calls "painience"—is what confers moral worth. Since animals can feel pain, he writes, the goal should be to "gradually bring non-humans into the same moral and legal circle as ourselves," toward the end that we "will not be able to exploit them as our slaves."[11]

PETA adopts the same concept in a slightly broader fashion. The issue for PETA is not just pain per se, but existential as well as physical suffering. Since PETA asserts that any use of animals by humans causes suffering, the group opposes sheep raising and wool shearing, eating dairy products, zoos, medical research using animals—even seeing-eye dogs. Or as Ingrid Newkirk, the head of PETA, once infamously stated, "There is no rational basis for saying that a human being has special rights. A rat is a pig is a dog is a boy."[12] Illustrating the profound harm to human welfare that would result from society's acceptance of animal-rights/liberation ideology, when Newkirk was asked if she would sacrifice five thousand rats or chimpanzees if it would result in a cure for AIDS, she retorted, "Would you be opposed to experiments on your daughter if you knew it would save fifty million people?"[13]

At this point, we need to consider the beliefs of Peter Singer, who is often called the godfather of animal rights because his 1975 book *Animal Liberation* is widely seen as having jump-started the modern movement. But unlike the true animal liberationist, Singer is not explicitly opposed to all animal research, or even, necessarily, to the eating of meat. (For example, he recently approved of using monkeys in Parkinson's disease research.[14]) Instead, Singer is an "interest utilitarian," that is, he believes that actions are not right or wrong per se, but must be judged upon their anticipated or actual consequences. Under this view, those actions which best serve the interests of most (not necessarily human) beings are those that should be pursued.

Utilitarianism isn't new, of course. But Singer became notable by asserting in *Animal Liberation* that the interests of animals should be given "equal consideration" to the interests of people in making utilitarian analyses. To do otherwise, he declared, is "speciesism"—that is, discrimination against animals—a wrong as odious in his view as racism and sexism.[15] Thus, when Singer was told recently that experiments on 100 monkeys benefited 40,000 people, he decreed that the experiment was "justifiable."[16] But he would almost surely have said the same thing if the experiment had been with cognitively disabled human beings, since the interests of the many were served by using those with lesser capacities. Indeed Singer once suggested that cognitively disabled people, rather than chimps, should have been used in hepatitis-vaccine experiments—because the human beings have lower capacities than normal chimpanzees.[17]

A Campaign to Diminish the Intrinsic Value of Human Life

It is tempting to dismiss such assertions and beliefs as being so far into fringe territory that they are not worthy of serious concern. I believe the contrary is true. For many years the argument over animal rights has been generally one-sided: Supporters are vocal and energized, while those who oppose according animals "rights" are generally subdued. As a consequence, animal-rights values are seeping into public consciousness. For example, a 1995 Associated Press poll found that 67 percent of respondents agreed with the statement "an animal's right to live free of suffering is just as important as a person's right to live free of suffering."

More worrisome, animal-rights/liberation ideology seriously threatens to undermine human exceptionalism—especially with the young, among whom liberationists make their most intense conversion efforts. PETA is particularly active in this regard. As the largest international animal-rights advocacy group, with hundreds of thousands of dues-paying members and a big following among the Hollywood set, in 2004, PETA received contributions of $27.8 million. More than 30 million people viewed its websites and the organization sent out monthly e-news action alerts to more than 200,000 subscribers. Its media department booked more than 2,700 interviews for its representatives. And PETA is targeting the young: Its education department reached 235,000 teachers and *11 million* students with educational materials, also sending out 332,000 copies of *Grr!* magazine to kids and teens.[18]

PETA's advocacy can only be described as profoundly misanthropic in that it literally equates the worst evils perpetrated by the most notorious governments with normal practices of animal husbandry. PETA's infamous "Holocaust on Your Plate" pro-vegetarian campaign is a case in point. For more than two years, PETA representatives literally toured the world—focusing most heavily on college campuses and places where young people gather in large numbers—arguing that eating meat and wearing leather were morally akin to horrors of the Holocaust.

This reprehensible message wasn't presented between the lines or done subtly in the hope that the reader would infer the comparison. Rather, eating-meat-equals-killing-Jews was the explicit and unequivocal theme of the entire national campaign. First, there were the pictures. PETA juxtaposed pictures of emaciated concentration-camp inmates in their tight-packed wooden bunks with pictures of chickens being kept in cages. In another truly despicable comparison (on several levels), a picture of piled bodies of Jewish Holocaust victims was juxtaposed with images of the bodies of dead pigs. (If the KKK did that, it would be called hate speech.)

The text of the campaign was just as offensive. In a section titled "The Final Solution," PETA made this astonishing comparison: "Like the Jews murdered in concentration camps, animals are terrorized when they are housed in huge filthy warehouses and rounded up for shipment to slaughter. The leather sofa and handbag are the moral equivalent of the lampshades made from the skins of people killed in the death camps."

Forget for the moment that Hitler was sometimes a vegetarian and that the Nazi government passed some of the most far-reaching animal-protection laws of the era. That PETA can't distinguish between the unspeakable evil of the Shoah and animal husbandry reveals a perverted sense of moral values that is almost beyond comprehension. (PETA eventually apologized for "Holocaust on Your Plate," but not because they realized they were wrong factually and morally for making the odious comparison. Rather, in a typical non-apology apology—entitled "An Apology for a tasteless comparison," PETA's executive director Ingrid Newkirk sought to justify the entire approach: "The 'Holocaust on Your Plate' Campaign was designed to sensitize people to different forms of systematic degradation and exploitation, and the logic and methods employed in factory farms and slaughterhouses are analogous to those used in concentration camps. We understand both systems to be based on a moral equation indicating that 'might makes right' and premised on a concept of other cultures or other species as deficient and thus disposable.")[19]

A Movement Growing More Violent

The animal-rights/liberation threat goes far beyond the philosophical. Because animal rights/liberationists believe that slaughtering animals for food is akin to murder, and that medical research using them is morally equivalent to Mengele's experiments in the death camps, violence in the name of saving animals is a growing threat. Indeed, according to John E. Lewis, deputy assistant director of the FBI's Counterterrorism Division, animal-rights terrorism has become one of the FBI's most urgent concerns: "One of today's most serious domestic terrorism threats comes from special interest extremist movements such as the Animal Liberation Front (ALF), the Earth Liberation Front (ELF), and Stop Huntingdon Animal Cruelty (SHAC) campaign. Adherents to these movements aim to resolve specific issues by using criminal 'direct action' against individuals or companies believed to be abusing or exploiting animals or the environment."[20]

While no one has yet been murdered (with perhaps the exception of Dutch politician Pim Fortuyn, who was shot to death by an animal-rights fanatic), harassment, intimidation, vandalism, and threats of violence and death have become routine tactics employed by the most radical activists against those they deem abusers of animals. For example, in the United Kingdom, a farm family that raised guinea pigs for medical testing was subjected to years of personal threats and property vandalism by animal liberationists who demanded they get out of the guinea-pig-raising business. The family had courageously refused to be intimidated, but when the liberationists *robbed the grave* of a beloved relative and refused to give the body back, they had finally had enough. Seeing no relief in sight, and desperately wanting to be left alone, the family gave in.[21]

In the U.S., the often-criminal activities of Stop Huntingdon Animal Cruelty (SHAC) epitomize the lengths to which some liberationists will go to impose their will on society. SHAC was formed to literally put Huntingdon Life Sciences, a medical-testing laboratory, out of business. Toward this end, SHAC pioneered a particularly insidious terrorist tactic called "tertiary targeting." Here's how it works: SHAC militants seek to completely isolate Huntingdon from the wider business community and thereby drive it out of business. To accomplish their mission, SHAC not only targets executives and employees of Huntingdon, but the company's product and service providers, such as banks, insurance companies, auditors, etc. To force these companies to cease doing business with Huntingdon, SHAC websites identify targets, providing home addresses, phone numbers, and the names and ages of children and even where they attend school. Targeted people may receive anonymous death threats or mailed videotapes of family members taken by SHAC activists. Companies have been bombed. Homes have been invaded and vandalized.

The tactic is insidiously effective. SHAC and their allies have intimidated scores of businesses, including the auditing firm Deloitte & Touche, into cutting ties with Huntingdon Life Sciences. In the United Kingdom, so many banks have been intimidated from doing business with Huntingdon that the company has had to turn to the Bank of England for a commercial account. Even the New York Stock Exchange backed off on listing Huntingdon's parent company in October, 2005—on the very day it was to be placed on the Big Board—after Exchange executives' personal information was published on SHAC websites.[22] (The company was finally listed in December, 2006, a never-explained delay of more than a year.)

With the notable exception of Francione—who laudably and unequivocally condemns threats and violence in the name of animal rights—the silence from most mainstream leaders of the movement in the face of such tactics has been deafening. PETA, for example, refuses to condemn SHAC and a similar outfit called the Animal Liberation Front (ALF), and has even compared lawlessness in the name of animal rights to the Underground Railroad and the French Resistance.[23] Worse, Jerry Vlasak, an especially notorious animal-rights leader, told a U.S. Senate subcommittee hearing that the "murder" of those "who hurt animals and will not stop after being told to stop" is "morally justified."[24]

Conclusion

Most people, particularly those in the pro-life movement, take human exceptionalism for granted. They can no longer afford to do so. The great philosophical question of the 21st century is whether we will knock ourselves off of the pedestal of moral distinctiveness. The stakes of this debate over human exceptionalism, which includes but is not limited to the animal-rights issue, could not be more important. After all, it is our exalted moral status that both bestows special rights upon us and imposes unique and solemn moral responsibilities—including the human duty not to abuse animals.

Unfortunately, the liberationists are oblivious to this point. By denying our unique status as human beings they dilute the very concept of evil and reduce it to the banal. Slavery is evil: Raising sheep is not even wrong. The Rwandan and Cambodian genocides were evil: Humanely slaughtering millions of animals to provide the multitudes with nourishing food is not even wrong. Rape is evil: Inseminating mares and milk cows is not even wrong. Mengele's human experiments were pure evil: Testing new drugs or surgical procedures on animals to save children's lives is not even wrong.

Even more fundamentally, the way we act toward one another and the world is based substantially on the nature of the beings we perceive ourselves to be. In this sense, the entire planet will rue the day that liberationists succeed in convincing society that there is no justification for the reigning hierarchy of moral worth. After all, if we ever came to consider ourselves as just another animal in the forest, that would be precisely how we would act.

Notes

1. For example, see John Harris, "The Concept of the Person and the Value of Life," *Kennedy Institute of Ethics Journal,* December 1999, pp. 293–308, and Tom Beauchamp, "The Failure of Theories of Personhood," Ibid., pp. 309–323.
2. John Darnton, "Darwin Paid for the Fury He Unleashed: How a Believer Became an Iconoclast," *San Francisco Chronicle,* September 25, 2005.
3. John Derbyshire, "God and Me," *National Review Online,* October 30, 2006.
4. Gary L. Francione, "Animals as Property," 2 *Animal Law* i, 1996.
5. See PETA website, *www.peta.org.*
6. Maria Garriga, "Outrage on the Green," *New Haven Register,* August 9, 2005. See also, Wesley J. Smith, "Liberation Theology," *National Review Online,* August 4, 2005.
7. Gary L. Francione, "Abolition of Animal Exploitation," *The Abolitionist,* September 2006.
8. See Wesley J. Smith, "Let Great Apes Be Apes," *San Francisco Chronicle,* June 18, 2006.
9. "The Animal Spirit" website, "An Interview with Professor Gary L. Francione on the State of the U.S. Animal Rights Movement," found at: http://www.theanimalspirit.com/garyfrancione.html.
10. See Answers.com, http://www.answers.com/topic/sentience.
11. Richard Ryder, "All Beings That Feel Pain Deserve Human Rights," *Guardian,* August 6, 2005.
12. Interview in *Washingtonian,* August 1986.
13. Michael Specter, "The Extremist," *New Yorker,* April 14, 2003, p. 57.
14. Wesley J. Smith, "The Animal House Falls Apart," *National Review Online,* November 30, 2006.

15. Singer writes about speciesism ubiquitously. See, for example, the revised and updated Peter Singer, *Animal Liberation* (New York, Avon Books, 1990), Chapter 1, "All Animals Are Equal," pp. 1–23.
16. Gareth Walsh, "Father of Animal Rights Activism Backs Monkey Testing," *Sunday Times* (London), November 26, 2006.
17. Jill Neimark, "Living and Dying with Peter Singer," *Psychology Today*, January-February 1999, p. 58.
18. Source: "PETA Annual Review, 2004."
19. See, for example, Joseph J. Sabia, "PETA Cheapens the Holocaust," *Front-Page Magazine.com*, October 16, 2003. See also, Wesley J. Smith, "PETA to Cannibals: Don't Let Them Eat Steak," *San Francisco Chronicle*, December 21, 2003.
20. Statement of John E. Lewis before the Senate Committee on Environment and Public Works, May 18, 2005. See also, Catherine E. Smith, "Threats. com," *Intelligence Report*, Southern Poverty Law Center, Summer 2005.
21. Peter Richards, "Animal Rights Militants Admit Grave Robbing," *Guardian*, April 11, 2006.
22. See Wesley J. Smith, "Wall Street Goes Wobbly," *Weekly Standard*, October 17, 2005.
23. Source: PETA Website, "Ask Carla."
24. Transcript: United States Senate Committee on the Environment and Public Works hearing, October 26, 2005.

Building a Culture of Animal Welfare: Past, Present and Future

Leticia V. Medina

Leticia V. Medina *serves as the Manager of Animal Welfare & Compliance at Abbott Laboratories and is a council member of the Institute for Laboratory Animal Research.*

1. Introduction

In the past century, and especially over the past 50 years, a growing emphasis has been placed on animal welfare around the world. In the United States a very significant reason for this growing interest is a dramatic change in how individuals perceive animals. This shift is largely due to a change in demography. Much of the population has moved from rural environments where they would have been exposed to agricultural animals to more urban environments where their exposure is often limited to pet animals (G. Golab, AVMA, personal communication). The United States Department of Agriculture (USDA) commissioned the philosopher, Bernard Rollin, to expound the reasons why U.S. society's view of anticruelty had changed so drastically in the last half of the 20th century. He listed five social and conceptual reasons but then stated "they are not nearly as important as the precipitous and dramatic changes in animal use that occurred after World War II. These changes include huge conceptual changes in the nature of agriculture and a significant increase in animal research and testing (Rollin, 1995, 2004)."

Concurrently, there has been a significant increase in the number of animal welfare and animal rights organizations. Animal welfare organizations promote responsible, humane care for all animals and recognize that people have moral responsibilities to ensure animal welfare for animals that are used for human purposes (Blackwell & Rollin, 2008). Animal rights extremist organizations promote a philosophy that animals should be given equal rights to humans and they strongly oppose what they consider to be the exploitation of animals for human purposes, such as biomedical research. "Between 1960 and today, the number of active animal rights groups has grown from about 15 to more than 250 in the U.S. alone. The Foundation for Biomedical Research (FBR) estimates there are about 20 major national animal rights groups that focus exclusively or primarily on animal research (M. Stebbins, FBR, personal communication)." Globally, there are over 900 independent animal welfare and/or animal rights organizations in over 150 countries (WSPA-USA, 2008).

The past 50 years have also seen significant advances in science and medicine. Examples include the development of lifesaving vaccines (polio, rubella), cardiovascular bypass surgical procedures and treatments for many ailments such as diabetes and cancer. Many of the advances have been based on data from animal research. Although a majority of the public may not understand how research with mice can benefit humans and other animal species, there is plenty of scientific data to prove the importance and validity of animal research. FBR reports that "seven of the last ten Nobel Prizes in medicine have relied at least in part on animal research (FBR, 2008)." A majority of human medical advances are eventually adopted for veterinary use and thus result in enhanced animal welfare practices. For example, scientists have learned more about recognizing and responding to pain and distress in a wide variety of animal species.

Throughout this period of advancing scientific and medical knowledge, there has been a parallel increase in animal welfare regulatory oversight, development of training programs for laboratory animal care specialists and development of alternative research and testing methods (Quimby, 1994). These changes have all played a role in the biomedical research community's growing interest and commitment to enhanced laboratory animal welfare.

This paper provides a brief overview of how society has been moving towards adopting a stronger culture of animal welfare. Primary emphasis will be on the culture of animal welfare within biomedical research programs with a brief review of the past, where we are at present, and where we might be headed in the future.

2. Past

A review of animal protection history shows that a majority of cultures adhere to a code of ethical conduct with regards to animals. Even one of the earliest recorded laws, the Code of Hammurabi, 1780 BC, includes mention of animal protection: "not even a dog that entered the city could be put to death untried (Johns, 1910)." The rise of organized animal protection agencies in the U.S. began in the last half of the 19th century (Wolfle, 2003). It is clear that the vast majority of animal welfare laws exist in response to public concerns and perceptions about the care and treatment of animals. A review of the Animal Welfare Act (AWA) shows that the original law was passed in 1966 in direct response to public concerns about animals used in research (Schwindaman, 1999). Since then, public interest in animal welfare has continued to grow as evidenced by the following statement: "By the early 1990s, the U.S. Congress had been consistently receiving more letters, phone calls, faxes, e-mails, and personal contacts on animal-related issues than on any other topic (Rollin, 2004)."

Animal welfare concerns were also being recognized and addressed from within the biomedical research community. The Animal Care Panel (ACP) was founded in 1950 by five research veterinarians that recognized the need to develop expertise with laboratory animals to ensure optimal animal welfare and good science (Brewer, 1999). In 1967, the ACP was changed to the American Association for Laboratory Animal Science (AALAS) (Wolfle, 2003). AALAS members are dedicated to the humane care of laboratory animals and to quality research that benefit people and animals. Likewise, the American Board of Laboratory Animal Medicine (ABLAM) was founded in 1957 and renamed in 1961 to the American College of Laboratory Animal Medicine (ACLAM) to encourage education and research in laboratory animal medicine and to establish standards for laboratory animal veterinarians (Wolfle, 2003). In 1965, the American Association for Accreditation of Laboratory Animal Care (AAALAC) was founded by leading veterinarians and researchers to raise the standards for laboratory animal care through a voluntary assessment and accreditation program based on the Guide for the Care and Use of Laboratory Animals (NRC, 1996) or current revision. In 1996, AAALAC changed their name to the Association for the Assessment and Accreditation of Laboratory Animal Care, International to reflect their commitment to improve life sciences and animal care and use practices around the world (Wolfle, 2003). Currently, there are more than 770 animal care and use programs in 29 countries that have earned AAALAC International accreditation (AAALAC, 2008).

In 1985, the Improved Standards for Laboratory Animals amendment to the AWA was passed and established new concepts in the regulation of research facilities. This amendment mandated the formation of an Institutional Animal Care and Use Committee (IACUC), relief of pain and distress, limits on survival surgeries, exercise for dogs, psychological well being for nonhuman primates and the creation of the Animal Welfare Information Center (Kulpa-Eddy et al., 2005). These changes were promulgated to ensure more rigorous oversight of laboratory animal care and use practices and higher standards for animal welfare.

Animal welfare within biomedical research programs continues to improve. Although analgesics are given more consistently to larger species than to small rodents undergoing surgery, recent studies report behavioral changes indicative of pain in rats undergoing laparotomies without analgesics (Roughan & Flecknell, 2001). As scientific studies elucidate these pain reactions and the biomedical research community becomes more adept at recognizing subtle behavioral changes in rodents, analgesia practices will continue to improve.

Rollin defends the biomedical research community when he states, "Now it is clear that researchers are not intentionally cruel. Rather, they are motivated by plausible and decent intentions: to cure disease, advance knowledge, ensure product safety, develop advanced surgical techniques for use in human health (Rollin, 2004)." He acknowledges that despite this lack of intention they may still inflict suffering on the animals they use (Rollin, 2004). The biomedical research community must acknowledge that at times laboratory animals feel pain or distress. In fact, a majority of animal research is quite innocuous but some research does cause animal pain or distress because of the diseases or biological processes that are studied. In those instances, the ethical obligation is to use nonanimal alternatives if available, but if not available, ensure the fewest animals are used and minimize animal pain and distress by using supportive care and the rigorous application of humane endpoints.

3. Present

The current generation of animal care, veterinary and research staff has never worked in a program where laboratory animal welfare wasn't emphasized. Individuals in the animal research field understand that animal welfare is a priority not only because ethical science demands it but also because loss of public support could be devastating to future scientific and medical progress. As science has taught us more about how to improve animal welfare, public concern has brought a greater focus to animal welfare issues globally. A 2007 opinion survey in Britain revealed that 76% of the general public accepts animal experimentation as long as there is no unnecessary suffering caused to the animals (MORI, 2007).

In research programs across the world, minimum animal welfare standards are no longer viewed as best practices. Rather, programs are going above and beyond these minimum legal requirements and guidelines to establish unique ways to enhance animal welfare. One way they accomplish this is by adopting alternatives, also known as the 3Rs of refinement, reduction and replacement, as first described by Russell and Burch (1992). Many institutions have created special positions or committees to focus on environmental enrichment, alternatives and animal welfare initiatives that go above and beyond the mandatory IACUC oversight. Examples of the "above and beyond" approach include Merck's Animal Alternatives Committee (James et al., 1995), and Abbott's Caring for Animals in the Research Environment (CARE) Committee (L. Medina, unpublished data). These institutions and many more have recognized that it is no longer good enough to adhere to the laws and guidelines; instead they are contributing to furthering animal protection practices in biomedical research. Thus, many institutions are funding alternatives research and developing animal welfare award programs to reward staff that initiate and promote alternatives.

There are more organizations globally that focus on promoting alternatives such as the Center for Alternatives to Animal Testing (CAAT), the National Centre for the Replacement, Refinement and Reduction of Animals in Research (NC3Rs) and the United Federation of Animal Welfare (UFAW). These organizations vary in their missions, but most fund research projects to advance the knowledge or application of one or more of the 3Rs. Other organizations have been created as part of a government's commitment to examining how to validate alternative methods for drug safety testing (Laroche et al., 2007).

An important area of progress today is pain management for laboratory animals. The increase in biomedical research has contributed to veterinary and human medical knowledge and enabled significant enhancements to animal welfare. For example, as recently as the early 1990's, veterinarians did not routinely provide analgesia for cats undergoing spays. Less than 20 years later, it would be unacceptable to forgo analgesics.

A growing number of scientists agree that unrelieved pain induces secondary negative affects, such as fear and anxiety in animals (Phillips, 2007). Research investigators hesitate to adopt alternative practices without scientific evidence to prove that these changes will not negatively impact their study data. The Australian Code states, "The underlying presumption in the selection and use of a pain management protocol is that, while pain and distress cannot easily be evaluated in animals, investigators and teachers must assume that animals experience these in a manner similar to humans unless there is evidence to the contrary (see section 1.20 of the Code) (NHMRC, 2008)." The question about whether analgesics add an unacceptable variable to certain types of animal research is systematically being answered by scientists who run side-by-side studies to show if analgesics affect animal study data. ACLAM's position statement on pain and distress in laboratory animals clarifies, "Pain is an undesirable variable in most research projects and, if not relieved, can lead to unacceptable levels of stress and distress in animals (ACLAM, 2008)." Each scientific scenario must be carefully analyzed as some animal models could be invalidated by analgesics that induce changes in pain receptors. Whereas analgesic use for laboratory rodents was rare in the late 1990s, it is a much more common practice today, but it's not as widespread as it should be. A recent report indicates that, "although the use of analgesics has increased over the past ten years, the overall level of post-operative pain relief for laboratory rodents is still low (Richardson & Flecknell, 2005)." This is an animal welfare issue that needs more attention. IACUC and animal welfare committees must not continue to accept the response, "we think that analgesics might affect our data." The animal research community must take responsibility to ensure the most current knowledge about rodent pain control is used and studies must be performed to validate rodent analgesic use in research to promote animal welfare.

The creation of advanced technologies such as automatic blood sampling has led to less pain and distress in laboratory animals and thus more consistent data. Instead of restraining animals for each blood sample collection, the animals are surgically implanted with vascular catheters, provided analgesics and allowed time for recovery. Then the vascular catheter from the animal is attached to tubing which runs through a computer-run blood-sampling machine. Animals may move in their home cages and often sleep through the majority of the blood samples, thus avoiding the acute stress from restraint. Studies with rats have shown that automated blood sampling plus oral analgesics results in reduced corticosterone, which is often elevated with acute pain or distress (Goldkuhl et al., 2008). These refined methods may also reduce animal use because crossover pharmacokinetic studies can be conducted in rats that previously would have required separate sets of animals.

Replacement methods are also being embraced as they become available and are validated to provide data that was formerly produced in animal studies. There are a growing number of examples of alternatives such as the in vitro Limulus Amoebocyte Lysate (LAL) assay as an alternative for the rabbit pyrogen test (Ding & Ho, 2001). There are a growing number of high-throughput in vitro assays used to screen compounds for cardiovascular safety, such as the hERG assay. This assay replaces some, although not all, animal studies required by the Food and Drug Administration as part of an integrated cardiovascular risk assessment for new compounds (Porsolt et al., 2005).

Each year, more animal research programs are going above and beyond the minimum standards to seek voluntary accreditation by AAALAC. In addition, companies that use contract laboratories for animal studies are routinely performing audits to ensure that these suppliers are adhering to animal care laws and guidelines. All of these measures have contributed to building a culture of animal welfare in animal research programs internationally.

4. Future

As the world becomes smaller and smaller through increased technology and travel, globalized standards for animal welfare will become more prevalent. One of the more significant indications of global concern about animal welfare was the 2005 addition of animal welfare guidelines to the international Animal Health Code (Kahn, 2007) by the World Organization for Animal Health (OIE). OIE is comprised of more than 170 member countries and its primary focus is to prevent the spread of epizootic animal diseases through increased transparency and collaboration among members. There are eight guiding principles for animal welfare outlined in the Animal Health Code with a majority of these principles being applicable to laboratory animal research programs worldwide. The OIE animal welfare principles include the internationally recognized "five freedoms" and "3Rs" as well as the statement "that the use of animals carries with it an ethical responsibility to ensure their welfare to the greatest extent practicable (OIE, 2008)."

Advances in laboratory animal welfare will continue with increased resources and attention being devoted to this important issue. Alternatives that have been developed will continue to gain widespread acceptance by countries that are in close communication and collaboration to ensure harmonization of scientific and regulatory practices. For example, the European, U.S. and Japanese centers for the validation of alternative methods have worked together to accept alternative skin irritation/corrosion toxicity tests through rigorous review and scientific validation (ICCVAM, 2008). Future enhancements of high throughput screening will allow even greater screening of compounds without animals to select a few for further development in animal studies. Potentially, bioreactors, bacteria, insects and worms will play larger roles in early drug discovery work as we learn how to gain the most knowledge out of simple living systems and extrapolate them to data that is applicable to human and nonhuman mammals.

Additionally, non-animal surgical or technical training tools will become more common in veterinary, medical and undergraduate coursework. Highly complex, anatomically similar models of human and animal body parts are being created and used for various types of training ranging from endotracheal intubation to cardiovascular stent placement. Teachers should embrace these changes as long as they meet the needs of students but insist on retaining certain animal training practices if there is evidence to show that some training is optimized when performed with animals. One compromise is when animal shelters invite veterinary students to perform spay and neuter surgeries. Student surgical training is achieved while animal welfare is advanced.

Computers will play an increasing role as our advances in intelligent design allow us to build increasingly complex systems. To date, there is no computer that mimics the enormously complex and numerous cell-cell interactions and biochemical communications that exist within a living person or animal. However, there has been great progress in our understanding of molecular biology, genetics and in developing human subsystems for use in research. These advances provide powerful tools for research that avoids unnecessary use of animals. It cannot be emphasized enough that despite this progress animal research will remain a vital part of an integrated research program to help further clarify the complex scientific and medical questions that remain to be answered (Williams, 2006). Thus, the research community must remain ever vigilant and committed to making science more humane and less dependent on animals, whose involvement in this noble endeavor is nonetheless not voluntary.

5. Concluding Remarks

Innovation in research methods will result in refined techniques that reduce animal use, reduce pain and distress and replace animal models. Humane science is the goal. Establishing clear lines of responsibility, humane endpoints, and a thorough plan for monitoring and intervention strategies helps to prevent, minimize and alleviate pain and distress in laboratory animals (NIH, 2008). There are still opportunities to improve but overall the international biomedical research community has made tremendous strides in adopting practices that promote a culture of animal welfare. Animal welfare is not only an ethical imperative but also important for good science and for the continued support of the public. Biomedical research continues to unravel many of life's mysteries and assist with the discovery and development of lifesaving healthcare products for both people and animals. The challenge remains for individuals and institutions involved with animal research to invest more into animal welfare research so that additional alternatives can be discovered and humane science will continuously advance.

References

AAALAC, 2008. Data for this paper were retrieved from the Association for Assessment and Accreditation of Laboratory Animal Care International, Frederick, Maryland. 2008. World Wide Web (URL: http://www.aaalac.org). (September, 2008).

ACLAM, 2008. Data for this paper were retrieved from the Guidelines—Position Statements, Pain and Distress in Laboratory Animals, American College of Laboratory Animal Medicine (ACLAM), Chester, New Hampshire, 2008. World Wide Web (URL: http://www.aclam.org/education/guidelines/position_pain-distress.html). (September, 2008).

Blackwell TE, Rollin BE. Leading discussions on animal rights. J Am Vet Med Assoc 2008;233(6):868–71.

Brewer NR. The Architectonics of Laboratory Animal Science. In: Mcpherson C, Mattingly S (editors). 50 Years of Laboratory Animal Science. Memphis: American Association for Laboratory Animal Science; 1999.

Ding JL, Ho B. A New Era in Pyrogen Testing. Trends in Biotech 2001;19(8):277–81.

FBR, 2008. Data for this paper were retrieved from Education, Nobel Prizes, Foundation for Biomedical Research (FBR), Washington, DC. World Wide Web (URL: http://www.fbresearch.org/Education/NobelPrizes/tabid/427/Default.aspx). (October, 2008).

Goldkuhl R, Carlsson HE, Hau J, Abelson KSP. Effect of subcutaneous injection and oral voluntary ingestion of buprenorphine on post-operative serum corticosterone levels in male rats. Eur Surg Res 2008;41:272–78.

ICCVAM, 2008. Data for this paper were retrieved from the ICCVAM Evaluation of EPISKIN^{TM}, EpiDerm^{TM} (EPI-200), and the Rat Skin Transcutaneous Electrical Resistance (TER) Assay: In Vitro Test Methods for Assessing Dermal Corrosivity Potential of Chemicals. Interagency Coordinating Committee on the Validation of Alternative Methods (ICCVAM), Research Triangle Park, NC, 2008. World Wide Web (URL: http://iccvam.niehs.nih.gov/). (October, 2008).

James ML, Mininni LA, Anderson LC. Establishment of an animal alternatives committee. Contemp Topics in Lab Anim Sci 1995;34(3):61–4.

Johns CHW. Babylonian Law—The Code of Hammurabi, the 11th Edition of the Encyclopedia Britannica, Cambridge: Cambridge University Press; 1910.

Kahn S. The role of the World Organisation for Animal Health (OIE) in the development of international standards for laboratory animal welfare. Proc. of 6th World Congress on Alternatives & Animal Use in the Life Sciences, Alt Anim Test and Exper 2007 (Special issue);14:727–30. Available on Center for Alternatives to Animal Testing (CAAT), 2008. World Wide Web (URL: http://altweb.jhsph.edu/wc6/paper727.pdf). (November, 2008).

Kulpa-Eddy JA, Taylor S, Adams KM. USDA perspective on environmental enrichment for animals. ILAR Jour 2005;46(2):83-94.

Laroche C, Lalis G, Brekelmans C. The European partnership for alternative approaches to animal testing. Proc. of 6th World Congress on Alternatives & Animal Use in the Life Sciences, Alt Anim Testing and Exper 2007 (Special issue);14:769-73. Available on Center for Alternatives to Animal Testing (CAAT), 2008. World Wide Web (URL: http://altweb.jhsph.edu/wc6/paper769.pdf). (November, 2008).

MORI, 2007. Data for this paper were retrieved from Views on Animal Experimentation, a research study conducted by the Ipsos MORI research group: World Wide Web. (URL: http://www.ipsosmori.com/_assets/publications/pdf/views-on-animal-experimentation-report.pdf) (September, 2008).

NHMRC, 2008. Data for this publication were retrieved from The Assessment and Alleviation of Pain and Distress in Research Animals, Guidelines to promote the wellbeing of animals used for scientific purposes, National Health and Medical Research Council (NHMRC), Australian Government. 2008. World Wide Web (URL: http://www.nhmrc.gov.au/ PUBLICATIONS/synopses/_files/ea18.pdf) (November, 2008).

NIH, 2008. Data for this publication were retrieved from the Guidelines for Pain and Distress in Laboratory Animals: Responsibilities, Recognition and Alleviation, Office of Animal Care and Use, Animal Research Advisory Committee (ARAC) Guidelines, National Institutes of Health (NIH) 2008. World Wide Web (URL: http://oacu.od.nih.gov/ARAC/Pain_Distress.pdf) (September, 2008).

NRC (National Research Council). Guide for the Care and Use of Laboratory Animals. Washington: National Academy Press, 1996.

OIE, 2008. Data for this paper were retrieved from the Introduction to the Recommendations for Animal Welfare, World Organization for Animal Health (OIE), Paris, France, 2008. World Wide Web (URL: http://www.oie.int/eng/normes/mcode/en_chapitre_1.7.1.htm). (September, 2008).

Phillips P, 2007. How does pain rank as an animal welfare issue? Australian Animal Welfare Strategy Science Summit on Pain and Pain Management Proceedings. World Wide Web (URL: http://www.daff.gov.au/__data/assets/pdf_file/0003/299082/clive-phillips.pdf). (September, 2008).

Porsolt RD, Picard S, Lacroix P. International Safety Pharmacology Guidelines (ICH S7A and S7B): Where Do We Go from Here? Drug Dev Res 2005;64:83–9.

Quimby FW. Twenty-five years of progress in laboratory animal science. Lab Anim 994;28:158–71.

Richardson CA, Flecknell P. Anesthesia and post-operative analgesia following experimental surgery in laboratory rodents: are we making progress? Altern Lab Anim 2005;33(2): 119–27.

Rollin BE. Farm Animal Welfare: Social, bioethical and research issues. Ames: Iowa State University Press, 1995.

Rollin BE. Annual Meeting Keynote Address: Animal agriculture and emerging social ethics for animals. J Anim Sci 2004;82:955–64.

Roughan JV, Flecknell PA. Behavioural effects of laparotomy and analgesic effects of ketoprofen and carprofen in rats. Pain 2001;90:65–74

Russell WM, Burch RL. The Principles of Humane Experimental Technique (Reprinted by Universities Federation for Animal Welfare 1992). Available at Center for Alternatives to Animal Testing (CAAT), Baltimore, Maryland. 2008. World Wide Web (URL: http://altweb.jhsph.edu/publications/humane_exp/het-toc.htm). (September, 1998).

Schwindaman DF. The History of the Animal Welfare Act. In: Mcpherson C, Mattingly S (editors). 50 Years of Laboratory Animal Science. Memphis: American Association for Laboratory Animal Science; 1999.

Williams RW. Animal Models in Biomedical Research: ethics, challenges and opportunities. In: Runge MS, Patterson C (editors). Principles of Molecular Medicine, Second edition. Totowa: Humana Press; 2006.

Wolfle T. 50 Years of the Institute for Laboratory Animal Research (ILAR): 1953-2003. ILAR Journal 2003; 44(4):324–37.

WSPA-USA, 2008. Data for this paper were retrieved from the About Us, World Society for the Protection of Animals (WSPA), Boston, Massachusetts. 2008. World Wide Web. (URL: http://www.wspa-usa.org/pages/12_about_us.cfm). (September, 2008).

Animal Suffering: Learning Not to Care and Not to Know

William Crain

William Crain *edits the publication* ENCOUNTER Education for Meaning and Social Justice.

At a recent New Jersey public hearing, the topic was a proposed black bear hunt. A small boy walked up to the microphone, said his name was Bobby, and told the officials that shooting bears was terrible. "How would you like it if someone shot at you? You wouldn't like it, would you?" Then Bobby threw up his arms and said, "But you won't care what I say because I'm only 7 years old," and walked back to his seat in a dejected manner.

Many parents and teachers have observed that young children have a strong affinity to animals. Preschool teachers often keep gerbils, hamsters, and other small animals in their classrooms to make the settings attractive to the children. Cartoons and children's books also appeal to children by featuring animals as their central characters. Donald Duck, Mickey Mouse, and the Three Little Pigs are children's staples.

In fact, animals are so important to young children that they routinely dream about them. Psychologist David Foulkes (1999) found that 3- to 5-year-olds dream about animals more than about people or any other topic, and animal dreams are nearly as common among 5- to 7-year-olds. Other researchers also have found that animals take center stage in children's dreams (Crain 2003, 50).

But as children grow up in the Western world, they find that their deep feelings for animals aren't shared by their dominant culture. Like Bobby, they are often dismayed by adult indifference to our fellow creatures.

The Rude Awakening

For most children, the first and most upsetting confrontation with adult views seems to occur when children discover the source of the meat they eat. In a preliminary study of 28 urban, middle class children, one of my undergraduate students, Alina Pavlakos, found that most 5-year-olds didn't know where meat comes from. They all knew they ate meat, but when asked, "Do you eat animals?," most said, "Nooo!," as if the idea were outrageous.

Pavlakos found that children soon learn otherwise, most by the age of six or so. As several writers (Goodall 2005, 142; Singer 2002, 215) have informally observed, some children become so distraught when they learn the facts that they want to become vegetarians, but their parents rarely permit it. Even the developmental psychologist Lawrence Kohlberg (1981, 15), who usually championed children's independent thinking, spent six months persuading his young son to abandon vegetarianism.

From Caring Child to Detached Adult

We need much more research on how children respond to adult practices and views with respect to animals and food. It seems that in the process of socialization children undergo a considerable transformation—from a caring child to a detached adult. Most U.S. adults eat meat, tolerate hunting, and don't lose sleep over the treatment of animals in zoos, rodeos, circuses, or research labs. In fact, when it comes to today's most widespread and horrible animal suffering—that on factory farms—most adults know little about it. This, at least, is what another undergraduate student, Srushti Vanjari, and I have found.

From December, 2005, to the present, Vanjari and I have distributed brief questionnaires in two colleges (The City College of New York and the

University of Miami), in two hotel lobbies, and at a senior citizen center in the New York metropolitan area. Our sample totals 213 respondents. We selected one hotel that was expensive and another that was inexpensive to tap into different social classes. In these samples, 73 to 90% of the respondents rated their knowledge of factory farms as either slight or nonexistent (with a large majority of these respondents rating their knowledge as nonexistent).

Admittedly, our surveys are informal, and several of my colleagues have questioned our results. They believe that the current decade has witnessed a dramatic rise in vegetarianism as people have become aware of the mistreatment of animals. This also is the impression of some major writers. For example, Michael Pollan wrote in 2006 that "vegetarianism is more popular than it has ever been, and animal rights, the fringiest of fringe movements until just a few years ago, is rapidly finding its way into the cultural mainstream" (p. 305). Actually, a 2008 Harris poll found that only 3.2% of U.S. adults followed a vegetarian diet, and only half of these did so out of a concern for animal welfare (Vegetarianism in America 2008).

It is possible of course that a dramatic rise in animal consciousness is now beginning for real. But we need data—not impressions—to know. It's quite possible that a large majority of adult Americans continue to view animal suffering with detachment, if they know about it at all.

How, then, might our society produce this detachment? The following are some mechanisms at work (see also Joy 2006).

Detachment Mechanisms

Media Screening

Factory farms and slaughter houses are usually in relatively isolated, rural parts of the country, so most people aren't exposed to them. Still, the media might bring the factory farms into our homes, but it does not. Except for an occasional late-night cable documentary, it's rare to see footage of animals on factory farms on television or in motion pictures (Singer 2002, 216).

Language

Sometimes our language hides the identity of animals as food. We eat pork, not pigs; veal, not calves; meat, not flesh. The killing of wildlife, too, is disguised. Wildlife managers and hunters say a person "takes" or "harvests" deer. They almost never say a person actually "kills" an animal.

The 19th century philosopher Arthur Schopenhauer (1995, 177) pointed out that the English language more subtly distances us from animals by referring to them with the impersonal pronoun it, as if animals were mere objects. The personal pronoun who is incorrect. Our language also replaces who with the impersonal pronouns that and which. So just as it's ungrammatical to speak of "the shovel who is by the door," it's also improper to speak of "the bird who is by the door." Our language requires us to use the words that or which, as if the bird were a thing—not a living being.

Denial

It's not just the media and our language that hide the suffering of animals from us; we also hide it from ourselves. Many of us would rather not learn about the treatment of animals, especially when it might spoil our meals (Robbins 1987, 143; Singer 2002, 217).

John Robbins refers to our wish to look away as "repression" (1987, 143–144) and "denial" (1987, 144–145). These are defense mechanisms in psychoanalytic theory, and of the two, denial more accurately describes what occurs in the case of animal suffering. Most of the time, people try to keep from looking at the facts. However, in psychoanalytic theory, defense mechanisms work unconsciously, beneath awareness. When people consciously defend themselves against knowledge, then, it's not pure denial, but a kind of "conscious denial."

Statistics and Abstractions

As Jonathan Balcombe (2006) points out, our society also distances us from animals by considering them as population statistics rather than individuals. Population statistics are more general and abstract, and it's easier to think about reducing the size of a population than to imagine a particular animal being killed.

Thus documents such as New Jersey's *Comprehensive Black Bear Management Policy* talk about "population control" and "desired densities" (New Jersey Fish and Game Council 2007, 36). Even some defenders of animals focus on populations. The Blue Ocean Institute (2009) asks us to avoid eating fish such as groupers and Atlantic bluefin tuna because their numbers are in peril. The Institute recommends that we eat fish such as Atlantic herring and chub mackerel because these fish stocks are at healthy levels.

But what about the individual fish? Each fish pulled from the sea writhes and gasps for oxygen. Each wants to live.

Humans can think of animals as population statistics because of our mental capacity for abstraction and generalization. The developmental psychologist Heinz Werner (1948, 271–272) described how this capacity develops as the child grows. Children under the age of 10 years or so tend to think in specific pictorial images. For example, young children don't consider "space" in general but think of particular spaces, such as their bedroom, the pond down the street, or the space under the stairs where they like to hide. Only later, as children move toward adolescence, can they think about space more abstractly and generally, as when they understand that the rule "area = height × width" applies to *any* area.

Western scientific culture places a high value on such equations because they use quantitative measurement. As a measurable quantity, space doesn't depend on personal preferences, opinions, or emotions. It is purely objective. Using the same abstract approach, wildlife managers speak of target deer densities such as 20 deer per square mile. Phrasing the goal in this way has considerable appeal in our science-admiring society. The danger is that it distances us from what we are actually doing—killing individual deer.

It is especially easy to think of herd animals as population statistics, rather than individuals, because they strike us as so similar. But the more researchers learn about a species, the more they discover that each animal has an individual personality. This is true with respect to deer, black bears, wolves, and many mammals (Inglis 2005; Balcombe 2006). Even fish, including sharks and octopuses, have individual temperaments (Balcombe 2006, 54-57, 210). It seems that whenever scientists look beyond statistics and get to know the members of a species, individuality comes to the fore.

Abstract reasoning detaches us from animals in many ways. Sometimes we keep discussions on a theoretical plane. A case in point is Richard Louv's immensely popular book, *Last Child in the Woods* (2005). This book has done more than any other to raise public awareness about children's alienation from nature. Louv wants children to have direct experience with nature and develop reverence for it. But Louv defends hunting and fishing, and it's difficult to see how killing an animal for sport shows reverence for the animal. To defend his position, Louv moves to the abstract intellectual level. When it comes to fishing, Louv says the central question is whether fish feel pain, and the answer "depends on your definition of pain and suffering" (pp. 192–193). Louv chooses not to delve into the matter, but says that the answer "is not so clear as it may seem. Certainly, the definition is not settled" (pp. 192–193). So what appears straightforward to us when we watch a fish gasping for oxygen becomes a matter of abstract definition—and therefore removed from our emotional responsiveness (Crain 2006).

Motives for Maintaining Detachment

Will people become more sensitive to animal suffering? Perhaps, but it won't happen automatically. Detachment serves emotional purposes, making life more comfortable for us.

Avoiding Empathic Pain

As Robbins suggests, if we open ourselves to animal suffering, we cannot help from sharing some of their pain. Because of our natural empathy, we hurt too. Robbins (1987, 145) adds that we suffer because we are not apart from animals; "our pain arises from our kinship with life." To avoid the pain, we look the other way.

The Need for Cultural Belonging

If we do open ourselves to animal suffering, we are likely to want to do something about it. In particular, we are likely to try a vegetarian diet. But this opens us to another kind of distress—that which comes from being separate from our culture.

In his book, *The Omnivore's Dilemma* (2006), Michael Pollan discovered how a vegetarian diet can frustrate the need for cultural belonging. As part of his investigation of meat-eating in our society, Pollan decided to try out vegetarianism himself. During this time, Pollan wrote, "Healthy and virtuous as I may feel these days, I also feel alienated from traditions I value: cultural traditions like the Thanksgiving turkey, or even franks at the ballpark, and family traditions like my mother's beef brisket at Passover. These ritual meals link us to our history along multiple lines: family, religion, landscape, [and] nation" (Pollan 2006, 315).

As students of anthropology know, Pollan has a point. In every society one might consider, food is central to the social fabric. Food is tied to rituals, taboos, gender roles, forms of indebtedness, land rights, and feasts of social solidarity (Haviland 1990, 396–397).

Thus, to deviate from a society's customary way of eating is to alienate oneself from the dominant culture. Since humans have a strong need to belong, departure from social norms is emotionally difficult. In fact, the child psychologist Susan Isaacs implied that a young child's wish to adopt a vegetarian diet can cause mental disturbances. A vegetarian diet, she said, would cut the child off "in the most unhealthy way from the common ethos of his time" (1966, 164). When I have asked my vegetarian students about Isaacs's statement, they generally have said it's an exaggeration, but they do acknowledge that their vegetarianism has caused tensions within their families and has made them feel isolated, odd, or different.

Conclusion

Opening ourselves to animal suffering, then, isn't easy. Applying "detachment mechanisms" blocks us from emotional pain and satisfies the strong need to belong to the mainstream culture. However, personal growth sometimes means confronting negative feelings and departing from the mainstream. We develop strength and maturity by attending to our own sense of what is right.

References

Balcombe, J. 2006. Pleasurable kingdom. London: Macmillan.

Blue Ocean Institute. 2009. Seafood. Full list. Available online at <www.blueocean.org/seafood/seafood-search-result?type=all>

Crain, W. 2003. Reclaiming childhood: Letting children be children in our achievement-oriented society. New York: Holt.

Crain, W. 2006, Spring. Review of Last Child in the Woods by Richard Louv. Encounter: Education for Meaning and Social Justice 19 (1): 47–48.

Foulkes, D. 1999. Children's dreaming and the development of consciousness. Cambridge, MA: Harvard University Press.

Goodall, J., with G. McAvoy and G. Hudson. 2005. Harvest of hope. New York: Warner Books.

Haviland, W. A. 1990. Anthropology (6th ed.). Fort Worth, TX: Holt, Rinehart and Winston.

Inglis, J. 2005. The science behind Algonquin's animals-Researchers-Jeremy Inglis. Available online at <www.sbaa.ca/researchers.asp?cn=289>.

Isaacs, S. 1966. Intellectual growth in young children. New York: Shocken Books. (Originally published in 1930).

Joy, M. 2006. Food for thought. Carnism and the psychology of eating meat. VegFamily. Available online at <www.vegfamily.com/articles/carnism.htm>.

Kohlberg, L. 1981. The philosophy of moral development: Essays on moral development, Vol. 1. New York: Harper & Row.

Louv, R. 2005. Last child in the woods: Saving our children from nature-deficit disorder. Chapel Hill, NC: Algonquin Books.

New Jersey Fish and Game Council. 2007, July 24. Draft Comprehensive Black Bear (Ursus americanus) Management Policy, Part I. Available online at <www.state.nj.us/dep/ fgw/pdf/2007/CouncilDraftBearPolicy.pdf>.

Pollan, M. 2006. The omnivore's dilemma. New York: Penguin.

Robbins, J. 1987. Diet for a new America. Novato, CA: Kramer.

Schopenhauer, A. 1995. On the basis of morality. Translated by E. F. J. Payne. Providence, RI: Berghahn. (Originally published in 1839.)

Singer, P. *Animal liberation*. 2002. New York: HarperCollins.

Vegetarianism in America. 2008. *Vegetarian Times*. Available online at <www.vegetariantimes.com/features/archive_of_editorial/667>.

Werner, H. 1948. Comparative psychology of mental development. New York: Science Editions.

Summary Chart

HOW TO WRITE AN ARGUMENTATIVE SYNTHESIS

---

1. **Analyze the assignment.**
   - *Determine whether you are being asked to write an informative or argumentative synthesis.*
   - *Determine the number and types of readings you are expected to use in your paper.*

2. **Review and annotate the readings.**
   - *Review the readings with your assignment in mind, looking for and marking information related to the topic of your paper.*
   - *Briefly summarize and critique each reading.*

3. **Formulate a thesis.**
   - *Determine what stance you will assume in your essay.*
   - *Determine whether you will use an open or closed thesis statement.*

4. **Choose an organizational plan.**
   - *Decide how you will order the ideas you will develop in your essay.*
   - *Decide whether you will present your ideas using a block or alternating format.*

5. **Write your rough draft.**
   - *Follow the organization plan implied or stated by your thesis.*
   - *Combine your insights, ideas, arguments, and findings with material in the source texts to develop and support your thesis.*
   - *Both paraphrase and quote material as necessary.*
   - *Add transitions, elaborations, clarifications, and connections where needed.*
   - *Include a concluding paragraph.*

6. **Revise your draft.**

    Revise to improve the content of your essay.
    - *Have you clearly indicated the point you want to prove?*
    - *Have you clearly indicated the reasons you believe others should accept your position?*
    - *Have you supported each of those reasons with expert testimony, statistics, or some other means of support as well as with clear explanations?*
    - *Have you acknowledged opposing views in your paper when necessary? Have you found ways of refuting, accommodating, or conceding to them?*

    Revise to improve the organization of your essay.
    - *Is the thesis statement clearly worded, and does it control the structure of the essay?*
    - *Have you provided clear transitions between the major sections of your essay?*
    - *Are there clear connections between the material drawn from the readings and your own elaborations and explanations?*

    Revise to improve the accuracy and clarity of your essay.
    - *Have you chosen words that are clear and contribute to the effect you want to elicit from your readers?*
    - *Are your sentences clearly structured with adequate variety?*
    - *Have you defined all the terms you need to define?*
    - *Have you proofread for spelling, punctuation, or usage errors?*

7. **Check your quotations and documentation.**
    - *Have you quoted and paraphrased material properly, accurately, and fairly?*
    - *When incorporating quoted or paraphrased material in your synthesis, have you supplied enough background information on the source text so that the material makes sense to your readers?*
    - *Have you documented all the material that needs to be documented?*
    - *Have you documented material employing the proper format?*

ARGUMENTATIVE SYNTHESIS REVISION CHECKLIST

	Yes	No
1. Have you checked your assignment to be sure you have written the proper kind of synthesis essay: informative or argumentative?	_____	_____
2. Have you carefully read, annotated, and critiqued all of the source texts you will use in your essay?	_____	_____
3. Examine the wording of your thesis statement. Does it clearly state the stance you will assume in your essay?	_____	_____
4. Check the opening section of your essay. Does it:		
• introduce the topic of your paper?	_____	_____
• capture reader interest?	_____	_____
• include your thesis statement?	_____	_____
5. Examine each section in the body of your essay. Do you:		
• focus on just one issue at a time?	_____	_____
• make clear assertions?	_____	_____
• support your assertions with evidence?	_____	_____
• explain the link between each assertion and its supporting evidence?	_____	_____
6. Check the organization of your essay. Do you:		
• follow the organizational plan indicated by your thesis?	_____	_____
• provide transitions to help guide your reader through your essay?	_____	_____
7. Have you supported your assertions with some combination of quoted, summarized, and paraphrased source material?	_____	_____
8. Have you documented all the material that needs to be documented?	_____	_____

	Yes	No
9. Have you checked the content of your essay to be sure it accurately communicates your position and intention?	_____	_____
10. Have you reviewed your sentences for accuracy and variety?	_____	_____
11. Have you reviewed your word choice for clarity and accuracy?	_____	_____
12. Is your works cited or reference list correct?	_____	_____

Chapter 11

PLAGIARISM

DEFINITION

Plagiarism occurs when writers take credit for work that is not really theirs. Because it encompasses a wide range of errors in academic writing, from improper citation to calculated fraud, plagiarism is an especially common problem for writers unfamiliar with the conventions of source-based writing. These writers often do not realize that any material they quote or paraphrase from a reading must be documented to avoid plagiarism.

Penalties for plagiarism vary from school to school, department to department, even instructor to instructor. They can range from a warning, to a failing grade on a paper, to a failing grade for a course, to expulsion from school. The academic community takes plagiarism seriously, but with care and honesty you can avoid problems and give the authors of the readings you use the credit they deserve for their work.

FORMS OF PLAGIARISM

Plagiarism is a difficult problem to address because it can assume so many different forms and involves so many different types of errors, some more serious than others. Understanding the various forms that plagiarism can assume will help you avoid problems.

PURCHASING A PAPER

Sometimes students will decide to purchase a paper rather than write one themselves. Whether you buy one from a fellow student or from a commercial vendor, purchasing a paper and turning it in as if it were your own is clearly a form of plagiarism. You are purposely taking credit for work that is not truly yours. Your teachers expect you to do your own work. Sometimes they may ask you to work with other students to write an essay, but even then you will be expected to do your own work in the group. Purchasing a paper—or even part of a paper—from someone and turning it in as if were your own is never acceptable.

TURNING IN A PAPER SOMEONE ELSE HAS WRITTEN FOR YOU

This form of plagiarism, related to the first, occurs when two students decide to let one take credit for work the other has actually completed—a student may ask his roommate to write a paper for him then turn it in for a grade. If caught, both students may face some sort of penalty for plagiarism. In other cases, roommates taking different sections of the same class may hand in the same paper to their instructors without permission. In this case, both students have committed plagiarism. Finally there are instances where a student retrieves a paper from the "fraternity" or "sorority" file, collections of papers written for various courses kept for students to copy and turn in (high tech versions of this file are the collections of student papers kept on university computer systems). These papers may have been written by people the student has never known; however, if the student represents it as her own work, that student is guilty of plagiarism.

TURNING IN ANOTHER STUDENT'S WORK WITHOUT THAT STUDENT'S KNOWLEDGE

This form of plagiarism has increased over the past few years as more and more students write their papers on computers. Here a student searches another student's computer files for a paper, copies the paper, then turns it in as if it were his own work. This is clearly a form of plagiarism.

IMPROPER COLLABORATION

More and more teachers are asking students to work together on class projects. If a teacher asks you to collaborate with others on a project, be sure to clarify exactly what she expects you to do individually when preparing the final essay. Sometimes a teacher will want a group of students to produce a single paper. The members of the group decide among themselves how they will divide the labor, and all group members get equal credit for the final essay. Though the group members should help each other complete the essay, if you are asked to complete a certain task as part of the larger project, make sure you give credit to others, when appropriate, for any material that was not originally your own. Other times a teacher will want the members of the group to work individually on their own papers; the other group members serve as each other's consultants and peer editors rather than as coauthors. In this case, you should acknowledge at the beginning of your essay or through documentation in the body of your paper any ideas or material you did not develop yourself.

COPYING A PAPER FROM A SOURCE TEXT WITHOUT PROPER ACKNOWLEDGMENT

This form of plagiarism occurs when a student consults a website, an encyclopedia, book, or journal article, copies the information directly from the reading into his paper, puts his name on the essay, and turns it in for a grade. Sometimes a student will compose an entire essay this way; sometimes he will copy only part of his paper directly from a source. In either case, copying from a reading without proper quotation and documentation is a form of plagiarism. So is copying material directly from a computerized encyclopedia. Even though your computer may come with an encyclopedia on CD, you cannot copy material from it and turn it in as your own work without proper documentation and acknowledgment.

CUTTING AND PASTING MATERIAL FROM SOURCES

Instead of copying all of the material for a paper from a single source text and passing the work off as their own, students increasingly lift material from several source texts and weave it together to construct a paper. This form of plagiarism is especially common when students gather information from the Web. Copying chunks of text from several Web sites into an essay and passing it off as your own work is unacceptable. All of the material drawn from Web sites must be properly documented.

LIFTING IMAGES FROM THE WEB OR OTHER SOURCES

If you copy photographs, pictures, charts, artwork, cartoons, or any other type of visual image from the Web or any other source, you need to document its source and give proper credit to its creator. Normally you would cite its source in a caption below the image or include the information as a way of introducing the image in your essay. Include a works cited or reference list entry for it at the end of your essay.

COPYING STATISTICS

Properly cite and document any statistics you use in your paper. If they come from a source text, including a Web site, they need to be documented. The same holds true if you include statistics from your own research in an essay you write. Indicate in your essay the source of these statistics and include a proper works cited or reference entry for them.

COPYING MATERIAL FROM A SOURCE TEXT, SUPPLYING PROPER DOCUMENTATION, BUT LEAVING OUT QUOTATION MARKS

Many students have a hard time understanding this form of plagiarism. The student has copied material directly from a source and has supplied proper documentation. However, if the student does not properly quote the passage, the student is guilty of plagiarism. The documentation a student provides acknowledges the writer's debt to another for the ideas she has used in the paper, but by failing to supply quotation marks, the writer is claiming credit for the language of the passage, language originally employed by the author of the source text. To properly credit the author for both the ideas and the language of the source text, the student needs to supply both proper quotation marks and proper documentation.

PARAPHRASING MATERIAL FROM A READING WITHOUT PROPER DOCUMENTATION

Suppose a student takes material from a source, paraphrases it, and includes it in his paper. Has this student committed an act of plagiarism? The student has if he fails to document the passage properly. The language is the student's own, but the original ideas were not. Adding proper documentation ensures that the author of the source text will receive proper credit for his ideas.

SELF-PLAGIARISM

The concept of self-plagiarism is difficult for many students to grasp: How is it possible to plagiarize or "copy" my own work? Self-plagiarism is considered an act of academic dishonesty for one primary reason: When teachers give students a writing assignment, they expect the student will turn in original work. If a student simply "recycles" an earlier paper—turns in a paper she or he had written in the past or for another class—the teacher is not receiving original work. Plagiarism also occurs if a student uses parts of an earlier paper in a current assignment without acknowledging their source. Keep in mind that unless otherwise indicated, teachers expect original work in the papers they assign—properly acknowledge and document material that comes from any outside source, including your own prior writing.

HOW TO AVOID PLAGIARISM

DO YOUR OWN WORK

Obviously, the first way to avoid plagiarism is to do your own work when composing papers—do your own research and write your own essay. This suggestion does not mean, however, that collaborating with others when you write or getting needed help from your teacher, tutor, or classmates is wrong. Many instructors will suggest or even require you to work with others on some writing projects—classmates, writing center tutors, friends. Just be sure the paper you turn in fairly and accurately represents, acknowledges, and documents the efforts you and others have put into the essay. If you get help on a paper you are writing, make sure that you can honestly take credit for the unacknowledged ideas and language it contains. If important or substantial ideas or words in the paper came from someone else, be sure to document those contributions properly. When you turn in a paper with your name on the title page, you are taking credit for the material in the essay. You are also, though, taking responsibility for that material—you are, in effect, telling your reader that you compiled this information, developed these arguments, or produced these findings and will stand behind what you have written. Taking that responsibility seriously, doing the hard work of writing yourself and composing papers that represent your best efforts, can help you avoid problems with plagiarism.

TAKE GOOD NOTES

One common source of unintentional plagiarism is poor note taking. Here is what can happen: a student goes to the library and looks up an article she thinks will help her write her paper. She reads the piece and, taking notes, copies down information and passages she thinks she might use in her essay. However, if she is not careful to put quotation marks around passages she takes word-for-word from the source, she can be in trouble when she writes her essay. If she later consults her notes when drafting her paper, she may not remember that the passage in her notes should be quoted in her paper—she may believe she paraphrased the material when taking notes. If she copies the passage exactly as she has it written in her notes and fails to place it in quotation marks in her paper, she has plagiarized the material, even if she documents it. Remember, to avoid plagiarism, passages taken word-for-word from a source must be quoted *and* documented. Therefore, be very careful when taking notes to place quotation marks around material you are copying directly from a reading. If you later incorporate that material in your essay, you will know to place the passage in quotation marks and document it.

To avoid problems, consider developing a consistent system for taking notes. In many high schools, students are required to write their notes on index cards with the source text's full bibliographic information on each card. If you find this system of note taking helpful, you can continue it in college. If you found this method too repetitive and time-consuming, you can make a few alterations. For example, you can take notes on lined paper, citing the bibliographic information at the top and the source text's page numbers along the left margin. Consider writing on only one side of the paper, though, so you're not flipping sheets around when you write your essay. You might consider using a research journal as a place to keep all of your notes for an assignment. One common practice among academics is to keep content notes from source texts on the left hand side of the journal and their own responses, insights, and questions on the right hand side so as not to confuse the two (these are frequently referred to as "dual entry" journals). Whatever system you use, employ it consistently and be sure to indicate in your notes what material is copied verbatim from a source and which is paraphrased.

PARAPHRASE PROPERLY

Another source of unintentional plagiarism is improper paraphrasing. When you paraphrase material, you have to be sure to change substantially the language of the source passage (see Chapter 3 for guidelines on paraphrasing material). If you do not do a good job paraphrasing a passage, you can be guilty of plagiarism even if you document the material. If in your paraphrase there are phrases or clauses that should be quoted (because they appear in your paper exactly as they appear in the source), you will be guilty of plagiarism if you do not place quotation marks around them, even if the whole passage is properly documented.

SUPPLY PROPER DOCUMENTATION

When you proofread a source-based essay, set aside time to look for problems involving documentation before you turn it in. Problems like these can be hard to detect; you need to pay close attention to finding them as you review your work. Make sure everything that should be documented is properly cited. If you ever have any questions about whether to document a particular passage or word, see your instructor. Because instructors know the documentation conventions of their particular fields of study, they can often give you the best advice. If you have a question about whether to document a passage and you cannot reach your teacher for advice, you should probably err on the side of documentation. When responding to your work, your teacher can indicate whether the documentation was absolutely necessary.

Remember, whenever you quote *or* paraphrase material, you need to supply proper documentation, indicating the source of those words or ideas. Most students remember to document quotations. Remembering to document paraphrased material can be more problematic, especially if you have been told *not* to document "common knowledge." Though this may appear to be a fairly simple guideline, in practice it can be confusing and vague. What is **common knowledge?** What qualifies as common knowledge varies from discipline to discipline in college and from audience to audience. Information that does not need to be documented in a history research paper may need to be documented in a philosophy research paper—the information is common knowledge for readers in history but not for readers in philosophy. Among one group of readers, certain facts, references, statistics, claims, or interpretations may be well known and generally accepted; among other readers, the same material may be new or controversial. For the first group of readers, documentation may not be necessary; for the second, it probably is. Again, if you ever have a question concerning whether something should or should not be documented, ask your instructor, who has expert knowledge about the discipline.

Many students express dismay over this guideline because it means that if they are writing a paper on a topic relatively new to them, they will have to document almost everything. When you are writing certain kinds of papers in certain classes, there may be no way to avoid having documented material in almost every paragraph. However, this situation is not "bad"; in fact, it is to be expected when you are writing on a subject new to you. There are ways to consolidate your documentation so the citations do not take up too much space in your essay (see the two "Consolidating References" sections in Chapter 12).

ONLINE PLAGIARISM CHECK

Many professors employ online plagiarism detection services like TurnItIn. com. These services search electronic versions of your paper to detect strings of words that match strings in the vast collection of source texts and prior student papers the company maintains on its server. At many schools, professors ask students to turn in the final drafts of their papers electronically so they can use a service like this. Other professors ask students to run rough drafts of their papers through the service in order to detect and fix passages that might be plagiarized. Check with your instructor or school librarian to see if you can take advantage of a service like this as you draft your essay.

CLARIFY COLLABORATION GUIDELINES

If you are asked to collaborate with others on a project, be sure to clarify the guidelines your teacher wants you to follow. You want to be sure you know what your teacher expects of each student in the group. Are the individual members of the group supposed to work together to produce a single essay? Are the group members supposed to help each individual member of the group write his or her own paper? How much help is acceptable? Can another student supply you with the material or arguments you will use in your essay? Can others help you with the organization, perhaps suggesting how you should structure your work? Can other students write part of your paper for you? Can others revise your paper for you, changing the language when needed? Be sure you know what your teacher expects before you begin work on a collaborative project, and be sure to ask your teacher to clarify how she expects you to acknowledge and document the help you receive from others.

Summary Chart

PLAGIARISM

---

1. Forms of Plagiarism

Purchasing a paper

Turning in a paper someone else has written for you

Turning in another student's work without that student's knowledge

Improper collaboration

Copying a paper from a source text without proper acknowledgment

Cutting and pasting material from multiple sources

Lifting images from the Web or other sources

Copying statistics

Copying material from a source text and supplying proper documentation, but leaving out quotation marks

Paraphrasing material from a reading without proper documentation

Self-plagiarism

2. How to Avoid Plagiarism

Do your own work.

Take good notes.

Paraphrase properly.

Supply proper documentation.

Use an online plagiarism check.

Clarify collaboration guidelines.

PLAGIARISM CHECKLIST

	Yes	No
1. Are all of your quotations properly documented?	_____	_____
2. Is all paraphrased material properly documented?	_____	_____
3. Have you acknowledged or documented the help you have received in writing your paper?	_____	_____
4. If this is a group project, have you checked the original assignment to be sure your work conforms to the teacher's guidelines?	_____	_____
5. Does the paper truly represent your own original work and effort?	_____	_____

Chapter 12

....

DOCUMENTATION

DEFINITION AND PURPOSE

Proper documentation for your papers serves several functions. First, it allows your readers to know exactly where to find specific information if they want to check the accuracy of what you have written or if they want to learn more about the subject. When combined with a reference list or bibliography, proper documentation enables readers to locate information easily and efficiently. Second, documentation gives credit to others for their ideas, arguments, findings, or language. When you write from readings, you are joining an ongoing conversation—people have likely written on the topic before you began your research and will likely write on it after you have finished your essay. With documentation, you acknowledge the work of those previous authors and locate your work clearly in that conversation. Finally, as a practical matter, proper documentation helps you avoid plagiarism. Many instances of unintentional plagiarism result from improper documentation. You can avoid these problems if you take a few minutes to check the accuracy of your documentation before you turn your papers in for a grade.

TYPES OF DOCUMENTATION

In college, you will encounter two primary methods of documentation: (1) in-text parenthetical documentation and (2) footnotes or endnotes. When you use in-text parenthetical documentation, you indicate where that information can be found in the original source by placing a citation in parentheses right after the quoted or paraphrased material. With footnotes or endnotes, you place a raised (superscript) number after the quoted or paraphrased material, and then indicate where in the source text that information can be found. Your citation will be placed either at the bottom of your page (in a footnote) or at the end of your paper (in an endnote). Over the past few years, parenthetical methods of documentation have largely replaced footnotes and endnotes. You may still find professors, though, who prefer those older forms of documentation. Always check with your teacher if you have any questions about the type of documentation you should be using in a class.

PRIMARY ACADEMIC STYLE MANUALS

The biggest problem you will face when documenting papers in college is lack of uniform practice, as styles of documentation will vary from class to class. When you write papers in college, your teacher will expect you to follow the guidelines set out in the style manual commonly used in that field of study, a set of directions writers in that discipline follow when composing and documenting papers.

Teachers in humanities classes (English, history, philosophy, art) often follow the guidelines established by the Modern Language Association (MLA), as published in the *MLA Handbook for Writers of Research Papers* (7th ed., New York: Modern Language Association, 2009). Teachers in the social sciences (sociology, anthropology, psychology, criminal justice) tend to follow the rules set by the American Psychological Association (APA), which appear in *Publication Manual of the American Psychological Association* (6th ed., Washington, DC: American Psychological Association, 2010). However, you may have a class with a sociology teacher who prefers that you follow MLA rules or a philosophy teacher who wants you to use APA style. Also, teachers within a given field may want their students to follow different style manuals. During the same term, for example, you may be taking two communication courses, with one teacher asking you to use MLA documentation and the other wanting you to follow APA guidelines. If teachers do not specify the format they want you to follow, always ask them which style manual they want you to use when writing your paper. If a teacher voices no preference, then choose one format and follow it consistently.

The APA and MLA style manuals agree that writers should employ in-text parenthetical documentation and explanatory footnotes; however, they disagree over the exact form this documentation should assume. Though differences between the formats dictated by these style manuals may seem minor, knowing how to properly document your work helps mark you as a member of a particular academic or research community. Not knowing how may mark you as a novice or outsider.

The following are guidelines for using APA and MLA styles of documentation. The examples offered are not comprehensive. They may be sufficient for some of the papers you write, but you may have to use types of source texts not covered below. If you do, you can find each of the major style manuals in your college library; consult them if the following examples do not answer your questions.

APA GUIDELINES

IN-TEXT DOCUMENTATION

The APA recommends an author-date-page method of in-text documentation. When you quote material, note parenthetically the last name of the author whose work you are using, the year that work was published, and the page number in the reading where that material can be found. When you paraphrase material, you need to note the last name of the author whose work you are using and the year that work was published, but you do not need to include a specific page number in the documentation. What you include in a parenthetical citation can change, though, depending on the information you have already included in the body of your paper. For example, if the author's name has already been used to introduce the material, you do not repeat the name in the parenthetical citation.

Source with One Author

When you quote a passage from a source that has only one author, place the author's last name in parentheses, followed by the year the work was published and the page number where the passage can be found in the source text, all separated by commas. Precede the page reference with "p." if the passage is located on one page in the source text ("p. 12") and with "pp." if the passage runs on more than one page ("pp. 12–13"):

Example 1

> "Drug-using women may be in a position to capitalize most on the advantages of women-inspired prevention methods, and be hindered the least by the disadvantages, as compared with other groups of at-risk women" (Gollub, 2008, p. 108).

If you were to paraphrase that passage, following APA guidelines, you would not include in the documentation a specific page number, only the author and year of publication:

Example 2: Paraphrase

> Prevention methods designed and inspired by women may offer more help to drug-using women than to other similar at-risk groups (Gollub, 2008).

Note the space between the end of the paraphrased passage and the parenthetical citation. Also, the period for the sentence follows the documentation (which is not the case with block quotations). Remember not to repeat information in your parenthetical citation that is included in the body of your essay. For example, if you mention the author's name to introduce a quotation or paraphrase, that information does not need to be repeated in the parenthetical citation. The year of publication should be in parentheses (preferably right after the author's name), and the page number, also in parentheses, should be after any quoted source material:

Example 3

> According to Erica L. Gollub (2008), "Drug-using women may be in a position to capitalize most on the advantages of women-inspired prevention methods, and be hindered the least by the disadvantages, as compared with other groups of at-risk women" (p. 108).

Source with Two Authors

If a work has two authors, cite the last names of both authors when you refer to their work. Separate the names with an ampersand (&) if you are citing them parenthetically, but use "and" if they appear in the body of your text:

Example 4

> "At the beginning of the AIDS epidemic, the large size of high-risk groups, and their lack of organization around public health issues virtually guaranteed that high levels of collective action to combat AIDS would be extremely low" (Broadhead & Heckathorn, 1994, p. 475).

Example 5: Paraphrase

> According to Broadhead and Heckathorn (1994), because the group of people most likely to be affected by AIDS was so large and tended not to focus on health issues, a poor response to the epidemic was almost certain.

Source with Three to Five Authors

The first time you refer to work from a source with three to five authors, list the last names of all the authors in the order in which they appear in the source. Again, use an ampersand before the last name when citing the authors parenthetically. In subsequent references to the work, cite the last name of the first author followed by "et al." (which means "and others"):

Example 6

> A recent study has shown that people who are infected with the HIV virus live longer and healthier lives when they receive various combinations of antiretroviral treatments (Kalichman, Eaton, Cain, Cherry, & Pope, 2006).

Example 7

A recent study by Kalichman, Eaton, Cain, Cherry, Pope, and Kalichman (2006) has shown that people who are infected with the HIV virus live longer and healthier lives when they receive various combinations of antiretroviral treatments.

Example 8

Kalichman et al. (2006) found that . . .

If shortening a citation through the use of "et al." will cause any confusion (that is, if two or more citations become identical when shortened), include as many names as necessary to distinguish the works.

Source with Six or More Authors

If a work has six or more authors, cite only the last name of the first author followed by "et al." and the year of publication:

Example 9

A recent study in Africa confirms that among sexually active people, regular condom use helps prevent the spread of HIV and AIDS (Laga et al., 1994).

Example 10

A recent study in Africa by Laga et al. (1994) confirms that among sexually active people, regular condom use helps prevent the spread of HIV and AIDS.

As in the previous examples, if shortening a citation through the use of "et al." will cause any confusion, list as many authors' last names as needed to differentiate the works, and then replace the remaining names with "et al."

Source with No Author

When a work has no author, cite the first word or two of the title and the year of publication. If the source text is a journal article or book chapter, the shortened title will appear in quotation marks; if the work is a pamphlet or a book, the shortened title should be italicized:

Example 11

"The world has recognized that an adult with AIDS in Zambia has as much right to treatment as one in Norway. Children should not be left to die simply because they cannot pay" ("Children," 2005, p. 16).

Example 12

In "Children and AIDS" (2005), the editors of the *New York Times* argue, "The world has recognized that an adult with AIDS in Zambia has as much right to treatment as one in Norway. Children should not be left to die simply because they cannot pay" (p. 16).

Because the title of the article is used to introduce the quotation in Example 12, it is not repeated in the parenthetical citation.

Sources Whose Authors Have the Same Last Name

If two authors have the same last name, differentiate them by their first initials:

Example 13

> Surveys have found that many people avoid discussing AIDS because they feel they know too little about the topic (J. Brown, 1991); consequently, a number of companies are beginning to develop programs to educate their workers (L. Brown, 1991).

Two or More Sources by the Same Author

If you are referring to two or more works by the same author, differentiate them by date of publication separated by commas. If both are included in the same parenthetical citation, order them by year of publication:

Example 14

> Because AZT has proved to be ineffective in controlling the effects of AIDS (Brown, 1993), scientists have been working hard to develop a vaccine against the virus, especially in Third World countries where the epidemic is spreading quickly (Brown, 1994).

Example 15

> A series of articles in *New Scientist* by Phillida Brown (1993, 1994) traces efforts to develop adequate treatments to combat AIDS.

Two or More Sources by the Same Author Published the Same Year

If you are referring to two or more works by the same author published in the same year, differentiate them by adding lowercase letters after the dates:

Example 16

> Two recent articles (Brown, 1994a, 1994b) trace the efforts to improve AIDS treatment in Third World countries.

The "a" article is the reference that appears first in the reference list, the "b" second, and so on.

Electronic Sources of Information

If you refer to the work as a whole, include the author's last name and the year of publication. If, instead, you are citing specific information in the source text, include the author's last name, the year of publication, and the page number.

If the pages are not numbered, include the paragraph or section number in the source text where the material can be found preceded by "para.":

Example 17

> According to one expert, AIDS has killed 14 million people over the past 20 years (Underwood, 1999, para. 1).

As always, do not repeat information in the citation that is already present in your essay.

Consolidating APA-Style References

If you want to include references to two or more sources in one parenthetical citation, arrange them alphabetically by the last name of the authors and separate them with semicolons:

Example 18

> Many recent studies have examined the best treatment options for women who suffer from HIV infection (Gollub, 2008; Kalichman et al., 2006; Wanjama, Kimani, & Lodiaga, 2007).

FOOTNOTES AND ENDNOTES

Some style manuals still advocate using footnotes or endnotes as the primary means of documenting source-based essays, but the APA suggests they be used sparingly, only to supply commentary or information you do not want to include in the body of your paper. These notes are numbered consecutively in the text with superscript numerals.

Example 19

> A survey of recent articles published on AIDS shows a growing interest in developing reliable research methods to test high-risk groups, such as drug abusers and prostitutes.[1]

The notes may be placed at the bottom of the page on which they appear or on a separate page at the end of the paper with the word "Footnotes" centered at the top. The footnotes are double spaced in numerical order, preceded by superscript numerals. The first line of every note is indented five to seven spaces.

MLA GUIDELINES

IN-TEXT DOCUMENTATION

MLA style uses an author-page system of in-text documentation. When you quote or paraphrase material, you tell your reader parenthetically the name of the author whose work you are using and where in that reading the passage or information can be found. If your reader wants more information on this source text (for instance, whether it is a book or an article, when it was published, or what journal it appeared in), she will refer to the works cited list at the end of your paper, where you provide this information.

The exact form of the parenthetical documentation—what information goes into the parentheses and in what order—varies depending on the type of source you are referring to and what you have already mentioned about the source in the body of your essay.

Source with One Author

When you quote or paraphrase information from a reading that has just one author, place the author's last name in parentheses, leave a space, and then indicate the page number or numbers in the source where the passage or information can be found. Whether you are quoting or paraphrasing material, the period follows the parentheses. In the following examples, pay particular attention to spacing and the proper placement of quotation marks:

Example 20

> "Drug-using women may be in a position to capitalize most on the advantages of women-inspired prevention methods, and be hindered the least by the disadvantages, as compared with other groups of at-risk women" (Gollub 108).

Example 21: Paraphrase

> Prevention methods designed and inspired by women may offer more help to drug-using women than to other similar at-risk groups (Gollub 108).

When using the MLA format, do *not* include "p." or "pp." before the page number or numbers. Again, notice that the final period is placed *after* the documentation. The only exception to this punctuation rule occurs when you block quote information, in which case the period comes before the parenthetical documentation.

Do not repeat in the parentheses information that is already included in the text itself. For example, if you mention the author's name leading up to the quotation or believe your reader will know who the author is from the context of the quotation, you do not need to repeat the author's name in parentheses:

Example 22

> According to Erica L. Gollub, "Drug-using women may be in a position to capitalize most on the advantages of women-inspired prevention methods, and be hindered the least by the disadvantages, as compared with other groups of at-risk women" (108).

MLA style requires you to record specific page references for material directly quoted or paraphrased. If you are quoting or paraphrasing a passage that runs longer than one page in a reading, indicate all the page numbers where that information can be found:

Example 23

> According to Gollub, many recent studies have investigated the sexual practices of drug users who are infected with the HIV virus (107–8).

Source with Two Authors

If a work has two authors, list the last names of the authors in the order they appear in the source, joined by "and." If you mention the authors in the body of your essay, include only the page number or numbers in parentheses:

Example 24

> "At the beginning of the AIDS epidemic, the large size of high-risk groups, and their lack of organization around public health issues virtually guaranteed that high levels of collective action to combat AIDS would be extremely low" (Broadhead and Heckathorn 475).

Example 25: Paraphrase

> According to Broadhead and Heckathorn, because the group of people most likely to be affected by AIDS was so large and tended not to focus on health issues, a poor response to the epidemic was almost certain (475).

Source with Three Authors

If a work has three authors, list the last names of the authors in the order they appear in the source, separated by commas, with "and" before the last name:

Example 26

> Recently, researchers have begun to examine the AIDS epidemic by combining a wide range of scientific and social perspectives and methodologies (Fan, Conner, and Villarreal).

Since this citation refers to the entire work, no specific page reference is provided.

Source with More Than Three Authors

If a source has more than three authors, include the last name of the first author followed by "et al.":

Example 27

> A recent study has shown that people who are infected with the HIV virus live longer and healthier lives when they receive various combinations of antiretroviral treatments (Kalichman et al. 401).

Source with No Author

If a work has no author, parenthetically cite the first word or two of the title. If the work is a journal article or book chapter, the shortened title will appear in quotation marks. If the work is longer, the shortened title should be italicized. If you mention the title of the work in the body of your essay, you will need to include only the page number or numbers in parentheses:

Example 28

> "The world has recognized that an adult with AIDS in Zambia has as much right to treatment as one in Norway. Children should not be left to die simply because they cannot pay" ("Children" 16).

Example 29

> In "Children and AIDS," the editors of the *New York Times* argue, "The world has recognized that an adult with AIDS in Zambia has as much right to treatment as one in Norway. Children should not be left to die simply because they cannot pay" (16).

Sources Whose Authors Have the Same Last Name

If two different authors have the same last name, differentiate them in your documentation by including their first initials:

Example 30

> Surveys have found that many people avoid discussing AIDS because they feel they know too little about the topic (J. Brown 675); consequently, a number of companies are beginning to develop programs to educate their workers (L. Brown 64).

Two or More Sources by the Same Author

If you are referring to two or more works by the same author, differentiate them in your documentation by putting a comma after the last name of the author and adding a shortened version of the title before citing the specific page reference:

Example 31

> Because AZT has proved to be ineffective in controlling the effects of AIDS (Brown, "Drug" 4), scientists have been working hard to develop a vaccine

against the virus, especially in Third World countries where the epidemic is spreading quickly (Brown, "AIDS" 10).

Again, the shortened title of an article or chapter is placed in quotation marks; the shortened title of a longer work would be italicized.

Electronic Sources of Information

If the pages in the electronic source text are numbered, include the author's last name and the page number. If, instead, the paragraphs or sections in the source text are numbered, include the author's last name and the paragraph or section number or numbers (use "par." for one paragraph, "pars." for more than one paragraph). *Separate the author's last name and the paragraph numbers with a comma.* If the source text does not number pages, paragraphs, or sections, include only the author's last name.

Consolidating MLA-Style References

Many times in papers, you will include in one paragraph information you gathered from several different sources. When you document this passage, arrange the references alphabetically by the last names of the authors and separate them with semicolons:

Example 32

Many recent studies have examined the best treatment options for women who suffer from HIV infection (Gollub; Kalichman et al.; Wanjama, Kimani, and Lodiaga).

No page numbers are included here because the passage refers to the general topic of the articles, not to specific information in them.

FOOTNOTES AND ENDNOTES

The MLA suggests that footnotes or endnotes be used only to supply commentary or information you do not want to include in the body of your paper. Whether you are adding content notes (explanations of or elaborations on ideas you have discussed in the body of your paper) or bibliographic notes (a list of sources your readers might want to consult if they are interested in learning more about the topic you are discussing), try to keep them to a minimum because they can be distracting.

Number footnotes and endnotes consecutively in the body of your essay with superscript numerals:

Example 33

A survey of recent articles published on AIDS shows a growing interest in developing reliable research methods to test high-risk groups, such as drug abusers and prostitutes.[1]

If you are using footnotes, the citation appears at the bottom of the page on which the corresponding number appears. If you are using endnotes, all the citations appear in numerical order at the end of your paper on a separate page with the heading "Notes" centered one inch from the top margin. Double-space after typing this heading; then begin the citations. All the citations are double-spaced and begin with the corresponding superscript number followed by a space. Indent the first line of each note five spaces or one-half inch from the left margin.

Chapter 13

REFERENCE LISTS AND WORKS CITED ENTRIES

DEFINITION AND PURPOSE

A reference or works cited list comes at the end of your paper. In it you provide all of the bibliographic information for the sources you used when writing your essay. You have one entry for every source you refer to in the body of your paper, an entry that lists for your readers the information they would need to locate the source and read it themselves.

With in-text documentation you indicate where you found the specific information or language you used in your paper, usually including only the last name of the author and the page number on which the material is located. In your reference list you will give your reader much more information concerning this reading: the author's full name, the full title of the piece, and the place and year of publication. Also, while in-text documentation indicates a specific page where the material can be found, a reference list citation indicates all the page numbers of the source.

A works cited or reference list is sometimes also called a *bibliography*, but the two may not be the same, depending on the style you are following. While the entry format for each is the same, in a bibliography you might include an entry for every source you *consulted* when researching your paper; in a works cited list you include an entry only for the sources you actually *included* in your paper. Suppose you consulted ten books or articles when researching a topic for a paper but used only seven of them in your final draft. If your teacher asked you to put together an APA bibliography for your essay, you would have ten entries. If she asked you for a works cited or reference list, you would have only seven entries. If you are unsure what to include in your list of references, consult with your teacher.

Putting together a works cited or reference list can be tedious and time-consuming because there are specific forms you have to follow. These forms are dictated by the type of source you are using and the style manual you are following. Your job is to follow these forms exactly. There is an important reason for this uniformity. When you put together a works cited list in the proper form, you are providing a valuable service for your readers: when writers in a discipline agree to follow the same format for reference lists, readers can easily determine where to locate the sources that interest them because they know how to read the entries.

Complicating your efforts to put together a proper reference list is the fact that each field of study has its preferred ways of structuring entries. While the information in the entries generally stays the same across the disciplines, the order in which you present that information varies widely. As described in the previous chapter, teachers in the humanities tend to follow the guidelines established by the Modern Language Association (MLA) and those in the social sciences typically employ the guidelines established by the American Psychological Association (APA). When putting together a works cited or reference list, your best approach is to follow the guidelines and sample entries as closely as you can, placing the information from your source exactly where it appears in the model. Pay very close attention to capitalization, spacing, and punctuation.

The samples provided in this chapter follow the guidelines of the major style manuals, but they are not comprehensive. As you write a paper, you may use types of readings not covered in these examples. If this occurs, you can obtain a copy of each style manual at your library and follow the sample entry it contains for the type of text you are employing.

APA FORMAT

SAMPLE REFERENCE LIST ENTRIES

In an APA reference list, you include the name of the author, the title, and the publishing information for all of the readings you use in the body of your essay. You include the authors' last names, followed by a comma and the initials of their first and middle names. If a source has more than one author, list their last names first followed by their initials and a comma, then use an ampersand (&) to introduce the final name. Book and journal titles are italicized; article titles are not (neither are they placed in quotation marks). In the titles of books and articles, you capitalize only the first word of the title and subtitle (if any) and any proper nouns and proper adjectives. The format for listing the publishing information varies by the type of source, so pay close attention to the accompanying sample entries and follow them precisely. The first line of every entry is flush with the left margin; all other lines are indented, and all entries end with a period.

Journal Article, One Author

Gollub, E. L. (2008). A neglected population: Drug-using women and women's methods of HIV/STI prevention. *AIDS Education & Prevention, 20*(2), 107–120.

- Note how the author's first and middle initials are used.
- Note where the year of publication is listed.
- Note how the title of the article is not placed in quotation marks.
- Note which words are capitalized and which are not in the title of the article.
- Note how the journal title and volume numbers are italicized.

Journal Article, Two Authors

Broadhead, R. S., & Heckathorn, D. D. (1994). AIDS prevention outreach among injection drug users: Agency problems and new approaches. *Social Problems, 41*(3), 473–495.

- Note the order of the names: last name first followed by initials. The names are separated by a comma and the second name is introduced by an ampersand.
- The year of publication comes next, noted parenthetically.
- Note that the "A" in "Agency" is capitalized because it is the first word in the subtitle.
- Note that the volume number follows the title of the journal; it is also italicized.

Journal Article, Three to Seven Authors

Kalichman, S., Eaton, L., Cain, D., Cherry, C., Pope, H., & Kalichman, M. (2006). HIV treatment beliefs and sexual transmission risk behaviors among HIV positive men and women. *Journal of Behavioral Medicine, 29*(5), 401–410.

- When there are three to seven authors, list all of their names.

Journal Article, More Than Seven Authors

Laga, M., Alary, M., Nzila, N., Manoka, A. T., Tuliza, M., Behets, F., . . . Pilot, P. (1994). Condom promotion, sexually transmitted diseases treatment, and declining incidence of HIV-1 infection in female Zairian sex workers. *The Lancet, 344,* 246–248.

- When there are eight or more authors, list the first six, then include an ellipsis and the last author's name.
- When you cite an article like this in the body of your essay, you will use the first author's surname followed by "et al." (Laga et al., 1994).

Article from a Monthly Periodical

Minkel, J. R. (2006, July). Dangling a carrot for vaccines. *Scientific American*, *295*, 39–40.

- For a monthly periodical, indicate the month of publication after the year, separating the two with a comma.
- Be sure to include the volume number as well, after the journal title.

Article from a Weekly Periodical

Clinton, B. (2006, May 15). My quest to improve care. *Newsweek*, *147*, 50–52.

- Indicate the month and day of publication after the year, separating the year and month with a comma.
- Include the volume number after the journal title.

Newspaper Article

Dugger, C. W. (2008, March 9). Rift over AIDS treatment lingers in South Africa. *New York Times*, p. 8.

Chase, M. (2005, April 20). Panel suggests a 'Peace Corps' to fight AIDS. *Wall Street Journal*, pp. B1, B5.

- Note the placement of the date: year followed by month and day, with a comma separating the year and month.
- The title of the newspaper is capitalized and italicized.
- Precede the page number with "p." if the article is on one page and with "pp." if it runs longer than one page.
- If the newspaper is divided into sections, indicate the section along with the page number.

Newspaper Article, No Author

Children and AIDS. (2005, February 16). *New York Times*, p. 16.

- When there is no author, begin the citation with the title.

Book with One Author

Hinds, M. J. (2008). *Fighting the AIDS and HIV epidemic: A global battle.* Berkeley Heights, NJ: Enslow.

- Note that the order of information for citing a book parallels the order of information for citing an article.
- Book titles are italicized. The first word in the title is capitalized and so are all proper nouns and proper adjectives and the first word in the subtitle.
- Following the title, indicate the city of publication and the publisher.

Books with Multiple Authors

Douglas, P. H., & Pinsky, L. (1991). *The essential AIDS fact book*. New York: Pocket Books.

Wanjama, L. N., Kimani, E. N., & Lodiaga, M. L. (2007). *HIV and AIDS: The pandemic*. Nairobi: Jomo Kenyatta Foundation.

- List multiple authors by their last names and initials, separating them with commas, and using an ampersand to introduce the final author.
- If a book has up to seven authors, list all of their names in your reference citation. For more than seven authors, see the previous guideline for periodicals. In the body of your paper, when you parenthetically cite a source with six or more authors, use only the first author's name followed by "et al." and the year of publication.

Two or More Works by the Same Person

Squire, C. (1997). *AIDS panic*. New York: Routledge.

Squire, C. (2007). *HIV in South Africa: Talking about the big thing*. London: Routledge.

- Arrange the citations in chronological order, the earliest first.

Book, Corporate Author

National Gay and Lesbian Task Force. (1987). *Anti-gay violence: Victimization and defamation in 1986*. New York: Author.

- If the publisher is the same as the corporate author, simply write "Author" after the city where the work was published.

Book, Later Edition

Fan, H. Y., Conner, R. F., & Villarreal, L. (2007). *AIDS: Science and society* (5th ed.). Sudbury, MA: Jones and Bartlett.

- If you are using a later edition of a book, list the edition number parenthetically after the title.

Edited Book

Cohen, A., & Gorman, J. M. (Eds.). (2008). *Comprehensive textbook of AIDS psychiatry*. New York: Oxford University Press.

- If one person edited the book, place "(Ed.)" after his name. If more than one person edited the work, place "(Eds.)" after their names.
- Pay particular attention to the periods in this citation. It is easy to leave some of them out.

Book, No Author or Editor

Corporate responses to HIV/AIDS: Case studies from India. (2007). Washington, DC: World Bank.

- When the title page of a book lists no author, begin your citation with the title.
- Note that in this type of entry, the edition number will precede the year of publication.

Multivolume Book

Daintith, J., Mitchell, S., & Tootill, E. (Eds.). (1981). *A biographical encyclopedia of scientists* (Vols. 1–2). New York: Facts on File.

- Indicate for your reader how many volumes comprise the work. This information follows the title.

One Volume of a Multivolume Book

Daintith, J., Mitchell, S., & Tootill, E. (Eds.). (1981). *A biographical encyclopedia of scientists* (Vol. 1). New York: Facts on File.

- When you use just one volume of a multivolume work, indicate the volume number parenthetically after the title.

English Translation of a Book

Jager, H. (Ed.). (1988). *AIDS phobia: Disease pattern and possibilities of treatment* (J. Welch, Trans.). New York: Halsted Press.

- Open the citation with the name of the author or editor.
- Following the title, give the translator's name followed by a comma and "Trans."
- Note that in giving the translator's name, you begin with her initials, followed by the last name.
- Again, pay attention to all the periods included in this citation.

Article or Chapter from an Anthology

Many times in writing a source-based paper you will use a work contained in an anthology of readings. When this is the case, follow this format in your reference list:

Bethell, T. (2006). The African AIDS epidemic is exaggerated. In D. A. Leone. (Ed.), *Responding to the AIDS epidemic* (pp. 18–22). Detroit: Greenhaven Press.

Patton, C. (1993). "With champagne and roses": Women at risk from/in AIDS discourse. In C. Squire (Ed.), *Women and AIDS* (pp. 165–187). London: Sage.

- Open your citation with the name of the author whose ideas or language you included in your paper.
- Next, give the title of the specific reading you referred to in the body of your essay.
- Next, give the name of the author or editor of the anthology and the larger work's title (the title of the book is italicized). Precede this information with the word "In" (note capitalization).
- Follow the title with the specific page numbers on which the article can be found. In this case, Patton's article can be found on pages 165–187 of Squire's book; Bethell's article can be found on pages 18–22 of Leone's book.
- Close the entry with the publishing information.

Article in a Reference Work

Acquired immune deficiency syndrome. (1990). In *The new encyclopaedia Britannica* (Vol. 1, p. 67). Chicago: Encyclopaedia Britannica.

Haseltine, W. A. (1992). AIDS. In *Encyclopedia Americana* (Vol. 1, pp. 365–366). Danbury, CT: Grolier.

- When the entry in the reference work is signed, begin the citation with the author's name; when it is not signed, begin the citation with the title of the entry.
- Include the year the reference work was published, the title of the work (italicized), the volume number and inclusive page numbers of the entry (noted parenthetically), followed by the publishing information.

Personal Interview

Under APA guidelines, all personal communications are to be cited in the text only. Include the name of the person you interviewed (first and middle initials, full last name), the words "personal communication," and the date of the interview (month, day, year), all separated by commas:

(F. Smith, personal communication, June 24, 1995)

Electronic Sources of Information

The standards for citing electronic sources of information are still in flux. You can find the most current version of the APA's standards online at www.apa. style.org/elecref.html.

In 2007, APA updated its guidelines for including electronic sources of information in reference lists. The major changes include these:

- When possible, include the Digital Object Indicator (DOI) number rather than the URL for online articles.
- Still include the URL for online reference sources, such as dictionaries and encyclopedias.
- Including the name of the database used to locate online articles is no longer required.
- Include the retrieval date only if the material is likely to be changed or updated.

Information on CD-ROM

AIDS. (1995). *The 1995 Grolier multimedia encyclopedia.* [CD]. Danbury, CT: Grolier.

- List the name of the author or authors (if known), last name first followed by first and middle initials. Because this source text has no author, the entry begins with the title.
- List the date of publication in parentheses.
- Give the title of the chapter or entry you consulted for your paper.
- Give the title of the publication that contained the chapter or entry.
- Indicate the electronic medium (i.e., CD) in square brackets.
- List the publication information.

Online Information Database

AIDS. (2008). In *Encyclopaedia Brittannica online.* Retrieved July 1, 2008, from http://www.britannica.com

- Give the author's name. If the entry is unsigned, begin with the entry's title.
- Give the date of publication.
- Give the title of the database (preceded by "In").
- Give the retrieval date.
- Give the database's URL.
- DO NOT end the entry with a period (someone might think the period is part of the URL).

Article from an Online Publication

This is the format to use if your source text exists only electronically. If the article does not also appear in print somewhere, use this form for your reference list entry:

Ambinder, M. (2007, December 8). Huck and AIDS. Retrieved from http://
  theatlantic.com

- Give the name of the author followed by the date of publication.
- Give the title of the article.
- Give the URL where the article can be retrieved.
- You do not need to give the date of retrieval.

Previously Published Article Found Online

Underwood, A. (1999, February 8). How the plague began. *Newsweek, 133*,
  59. Retrieved from http://www.newsweek.com

Kalichman, S. C., Eaton, L., Cain, D., Cherry, C., Pope, H., & Kalichman,
  M. (2006). HIV treatment beliefs and sexual transmission risk behaviors
  among HIV positive men and women. *Journal of Behavioral Medicine,
  29*(5), 401–410. doi: 10.1007/s10865-006-9066-3

- Give the name of the author(s).
- Give the date of publication.
- Give the title of the article.
- Give the journal's title and volume number (along with the issue number
  when relevant).
- Give the inclusive page numbers of the article.
- If the article has a DOI indicator, give it.
- If the article does not have a DOI indicator, give the retrieval URL.
- If the entry ends with an URL or DOI number, do not place a period at
  the end.

E-Mail

The sixth edition of APA's *Publication Manual* considers e-mail messages to
be "personal communication," which should be cited in text only. In parentheses, include the name of the person who sent you the e-mail message (first
and middle initials followed by the full last name), the words "personal communication," and the date of the communication (month, day, year):

(F. Smith, personal communication, December 1, 1998)

SAMPLE APA-STYLE REFERENCE LIST

List all of your references at the end of your paper, beginning the list on a
new page. At the top of the page, center the word "References." After the
heading, double-space and list your citations in alphabetical order according to the last name of the author or first key word in the title if there is
no author. The first line of every citation should be set flush left. Indent
subsequent lines.

References

AIDS. (2008). In *Encyclopaedia Brittannica online*. Retrieved July 1, 2008, from http://www.brittannica.com

Ambinder, M. (2007, December 8). Huck and AIDS. Retrieved from http://www.theatlantic.com

Bethell, T. (2006). The African AIDS epidemic is exaggerated. In D. A. Leone (Ed.), *Responding to the AIDS epidemic* (pp. 18–22). Detroit: Greenhaven Press.

Chase, M. (2005, April 20). Panel suggests a 'Peace Corps' to fight AIDS. *Wall Street Journal*, pp. B1, B5.

Children and AIDS. (2005, February 16). *New York Times*, p. 16.

Clinton, B. (2006, May 15). My quest to improve care. *Newsweek, 147*, 50–52.

Cohen, A., & Gorman, J. M. (Eds.). (2008). *Comprehensive textbook of AIDS psychiatry*. New York: Oxford University Press.

Corporate responses to HIV/AIDS: Case studies from India. (2007). Washington, DC: World Bank.

Douglas, P. H., & Pinsky, L. (1991). *The essential AIDS fact book*. New York: Pocket Books.

Dugger, C. W. (2008, March 9). Rift over AIDS treatment lingers in South Africa. *New York Times*, p. 8.

Fan, H. Y., Conner, R. F., & Villarreal, L. (2007). *AIDS: Science and society* (5th ed.). Sudbury, MA: Jones and Bartlett.

Gollub, E. L. (2008). A neglected population: Drug-using women and women's methods of HIV/STI prevention. *AIDS Education & Prevention, 20*(2), 107–120.

Hinds, M. J. (2008). *Fighting the AIDS and HIV epidemic: A global battle*. Berkeley Heights, NJ: Enslow.

Kalichman, S. C., Eaton, L., Cain, D., Cherry, C., Pope, H., & Kalichman, M. (2006). HIV treatment beliefs and sexual transmission risk behaviors among HIV positive men and women. *Journal of Behavioral Medicine, 29*(5), 401–410. doi: 10.1007/s10865-006-9066-3

Laga, M., Alary, M., Nzila, N., Manoka, A. T., Tuliza, M., Behets, F., . . . Pilot P. (1994). Condom promotion, sexually transmitted diseases treatment, and declining incidence of HIV-1 infection in female Zairian sex workers. *The Lancet, 344*, 246–248.

Minkel, J. R. (2006, July). Dangling a carrot for vaccines. *Scientific American, 295*, 39–40.

Squire, C. (1997). *AIDS panic*. New York: Routledge.

Squire, C. (2007). *HIV in South Africa: Talking about the big thing*. London: Routledge.

Underwood, A. (1999, February 8). How the plague began. *Newsweek, 133*, 59. Retrieved from http://www.newsweek.com

Wanjama, L. N., Kimani, E. N., & Lodiaga, M. L. (2007). *HIV and AIDS: The pandemic*. Nairobi: Jomo Kenyatta Foundation.

MLA FORMAT

SAMPLE WORKS CITED ENTRIES

In a works cited list following MLA style, include the name of the author and full title of the works you cited in the body of your essay, along with relevant publication information. When listing the authors, include their full names, last name first. Titles of articles are placed in quotation marks; titles of books are italicized. In titles, the first and last words are capitalized along with any key words, proper nouns, and proper adjectives in between. Journal titles are italicized, and you should list all the pages you read in the source text. Do not precede page numbers with "p." or "pg."; simply list inclusive page numbers. Finally, MLA style employs hanging indentation: begin the first line of each entry at the left margin and indent all subsequent lines one-half inch.

Note: 2008 saw the publication of the third edition of the *MLA Style Manual and Guide to Scholarly Publishing*. In this edition of its style manual, MLA substantially revised its guidelines for works cited entries. Over the next few years, as teachers and scholars become more familiar with these new guidelines, expect to see articles in print that use both old and new versions. The sample works cited entries below follow the new, third edition guidelines.

Major changes made in the third edition of the *MLA Style Manual and Guide to Scholarly Publishing* include the following:

* Add the medium of publication to each entry (e.g., "Print," "Web," or "CD").
* Place book, journal, or Web titles in italics; do not underline them.
* Include the volume and issue number for every journal citation.
* When working with online sources, only include the URL when your reader would not otherwise be able to find your source.

Journal Article, One Author

Gollub, Erica L. "A Neglected Population: Drug-Using Women and Women's Methods of HIV/STI Prevention." *AIDS Education & Prevention* 20.2 (2008): 107–20. Print.

* Give the full name of the author as it is printed with the article, last name first. Place a period after the name.
* The title of the article is placed in quotation marks. Note how the first and last word of the title are capitalized as are all key words in between. Also note that the period at the end of the article title goes inside the closing quotation mark.
* The title of the journal is italicized.
* Indicate the inclusive page numbers of the article.
* Indicate the medium of publication.

Journal Article, Two or Three Authors

Broadhead, Robert S., and Douglas D. Heckathorn. "AIDS Prevention Outreach among Injection Drug Users: Agency Problems and New Approaches." *Social Problems* 41.3 (1994): 473–95. Print.

Mitchell, Roger E., Paul Florin, and John F. Stevenson. "Supporting Community-based Prevention and Health Promotion Initiatives: Developing Effective Technical Assistance Systems." *Health Education & Behavior* 29.5 (2002): 620–39. Print.

- When there are two or three authors, list all of them in the order they appear in the article. Give the first author's last name, then his first name. Give the other authors' names first name first. Separate the names with commas and introduce the last name with "and."

Journal Article, More Than Three Authors

Kalichman, Seth, et al. "HIV Treatment Beliefs and Sexual Transmission Risk Behaviors among HIV Positive Men and Women." *Journal of Behavioral Medicine* 29.5 (2006): 401–410. Print.

- When there are more than three authors, list only the first author, last name first. Follow that name with the expression "et al." (which means "and others").

Article from a Monthly Periodical

Minkel, J. R. "Dangling a Carrot for Vaccines." *Scientific American* July 2006: 39–40. Print.

- Note the month of publication after the title. Months can be abbreviated, except for May, June, and July.
- Note that there is *no* comma between the month and year.
- Note that you do *not* include the volume number of the work, only the month and year.

Article from a Weekly Periodical

Clinton, Bill. "My Quest to Improve Care." *Newsweek* 15 May 2006: 50–52. Print.

- After giving the title of the piece, list the day, month, and year of its publication in that order, without any punctuation between them.

Newspaper Article

Chase, Marilyn. "Panel Suggests a 'Peace Corps' to Fight AIDS." *Wall Street Journal* 20 Apr. 2005: B1+. Print.

Dugger, Celia W. "Rift over AIDS Treatment Lingers in South Africa." *New York Times* 9 Mar. 2008: 8. Print.

- If the newspaper article is signed, give the writer's name, last name first.
- After the title of the piece, give the name of the newspaper, italicized.
- Next, give the date of publication: day, month, then year without any intervening punctuation.
- Give the page number, indicating the section number or letter when applicable.
- Use a plus sign (+) to indicate interrupted pagination.

Newspaper Article, No Author

"Children and AIDS." *New York Times* 22 Feb. 2005: 16. Print.

- If the article is unsigned, begin the entry with the title.

Book with One Author

Hinds, Maurene J. *Fighting the AIDS and HIV Epidemic: A Global Battle.* Berkeley Heights: Enslow, 2008. Print.

- Again, note how the entry begins with the author's last name.
- Note how the title is italicized and how the first, last, and key words are capitalized.

Book with Multiple Authors

Douglas, Paul Harding, and Laura Pinsky. *The Essential AIDS Fact Book.* New York: Pocket Books, 1991. Print.

Wanjama, Leah Niambi, et al. *HIV and AIDS: The Pandemic.* Nairobi: Jomo Kenyatta Foundation, 2007. Print.

- When a book has two or three authors, list all their names. Begin with the last name of the first author; the names of the other authors are listed first name first. Separate the names with commas and use "and" before the last name.
- If there are more than three authors, list only the first author and follow it with "et al."

Two or More Books by the Same Person

Squire, Corinne. *AIDS Panic.* New York: Routledge, 1997. Print.

—. *HIV in South Africa: Talking about the Big Thing.* London: Routledge, 2007. Print.

- When you have two or more books by the same author or authors, list them on your works cited list in alphabetical order by the first key word in the title.
- For the first work by the author, give his or her full name, last name first. For subsequent entries by the author, instead of repeating the name, type three hyphens followed by a period. Then list the title of the work and the relevant publishing information.

Book, Corporate Author

National Gay and Lesbian Task Force. *Anti-gay Violence: Victimization and Defamation in 1986*. New York: National Gay and Lesbian Task Force, 1987. Print.

- Treat a corporate author just as you would an individual author.

Book, Later Edition

Fan, Hung Y., Ross F. Conner, and Luis Villarreal. *AIDS: Science and Society*. 5th ed. Sudbury: Jones and Bartlett, 2007. Print.

- Indicate the edition number after the title.

Edited Book

Squire, Corinne, ed. *Women and AIDS: Psychological Perspectives*. London: Sage, 1993. Print.

Cohen, Ann, and Jack M. Gorman, eds. *Comprehensive Textbook of AIDS Psychiatry*. New York: Oxford UP, 2008. Print.

- If one person edited the work, place "ed." after his name. If there is more than one editor, use "eds."

Book, No Author or Editor

Corporate Responses to HIV/AIDS: Case Studies from India. Washington, DC: World Bank, 2007. Print.

- When there is no author, begin the entry with the title.

Multivolume Book

Daintith, John, Sarah Mitchell, and Elizabeth Tootill, eds. *A Biographical Encyclopedia of Scientists*. 2 vols. New York: Facts on File, 1981. Print.

- Indicate the number of volumes in a multivolume work after the title.

One Volume of a Multivolume Book

Daintith, John, Sarah Mitchell, and Elizabeth Tootill, eds. *A Biographical Encyclopedia of Scientists*. Vol. 1. New York: Facts on File, 1981. Print.

- If you use only one volume of a multivolume work, indicate the volume number after the title.

English Translation of a Book

Jager, Hans, ed. *AIDS Phobia: Disease Pattern and Possibilities of Treatment*. Trans. Jacquie Welch. New York: Halsted, 1988. Print.

- Begin the entry with the name of the author or editor whose work has been translated, followed by the title of the work.
- Next, write "Trans." followed by the name of the translator, first name first.

Article or Chapter from an Anthology

Bethell, Tom. "The African AIDS Epidemic Is Exaggerated." *Responding to the AIDS Epidemic.* Ed. Daniel A. Leone. Detroit: Greenhaven, 2006. 18–22. Print.

Patton, Cindy. "'With Champagne and Roses': Women at Risk from/in AIDS Discourse." *Women and AIDS.* Ed. Corinne Squire. London: Sage, 1993. 165–87. Print.

- First, list the name of the author whose article or chapter you are using.
- Next, give the title, in quotation marks. If the title of an entry already contains quotation marks, the original quotation marks are shifted to single quotation marks in the citation.
- Next, give the title of the work that contained the article and the name of the editor or editors, preceded by either "Ed." if one person edited the work or "Eds." if more than one editor was involved.
- Finally, list the publication information and the page numbers in the larger work where the article or chapter can be found.

Article in a Reference Work

"Acquired Immune Deficiency Syndrome." *Encyclopaedia Britannica: Micropaedia.* 1990 ed. Print.

- If the author of the entry in the reference work is listed, begin with that. If it is not, begin with the heading of the entry, in quotation marks.
- After indicating the heading of the entry, list the name of the reference work and the edition.

Personal Interview

Alexander, Jane. Telephone interview. 16 June 2008.

Smith, John. Personal interview. 16 June 2008.

- List the name of the person interviewed, the nature of the interview (whether done in person, over the telephone, etc.), and the date of the interview: day, month, and year.

Electronic Sources of Information

The most up-to-date information on MLA formats for citing electronic sources of information is available at www.mla.org.

Information on CD-ROM or Diskette

"AIDS." *The 1995 Grolier Multimedia Encyclopedia*. Danbury: Grolier, 1995. CD-ROM.

- Give the name of the author (if known), last name first.
- Give the title of the chapter or entry from which you drew the information (in quotation marks).
- Give the title of the CD.
- Indicate the place of publication, the publisher, and the date of publication.
- Indicate the medium of publication (in this case, CD-ROM).

Online Information Databank

"AIDS." *Encyclopaedia Brittannica Online*. Encyclopaedia Britannica, 2008. Web. 1 July 2008.

- Give the author's name (if known), last name first.
- Give the title of the article or entry. This particular source text is unsigned, so the entry begins with the title.
- Give the title of the online database, in italics.
- Give the name of the databank's sponsoring institution or organization and the date of publication.
- Indicate the medium of publication (in this case, "Web").
- List the date of access. Note how it is listed and punctuated.

Article from an Online Publication

This is the format to use if your source text exists only electronically. If the article does not also appear in print somewhere, use this form for your works cited entry:

Ambinder, Marc. "Huck and AIDS." *TheAtlantic.com*. Atlantic Monthly, 8 Dec. 2007. Web. 2 July 2008.

Underwood, Anne. "How the Plague Began." *Newsweek.com*. Newsweek, 8 Feb. 1999. Web. 3 July 2008.

- Give the author's name, last name first.
- Indicate the title of the work, in quotation marks.
- Give the title of the online database, in italics.
- Give the name of the databank's sponsoring institution or organization.
- Give the date of publication or posting.
- Indicate the medium of publication.
- Indicate the date of access.

Work from an Online Service

"AIDS: Education Cuts the Toll." *Business Week* 5 Dec. 2005: 112. *Academic Search Premier*. Web. 1 July 2008.

Parkhurst, Justin O. "'What Worked?': The Evidence Challenges in Determining the Causes of HIV Prevalence Decline." *AIDS Education & Prevention* June 2008: 275–83. *Academic Search Premier.* Web. 1 July 2008.

Shadlen, Kenneth C. "The Political Economy of AIDS Treatment: Intellectual Property and the Transformation of Generic Supply." *International Studies Quarterly* 51.3 (2007): 559–81. *Academic Search Complete.* Web. 5 July 2008.

- Give the name of the author, last name first.
- Give the title of the article in quotation marks.
- Give the title of the publication (in italics) and the relevant dates of publication and volume/issue numbers (the first sample is from a weekly publication, the second from a monthly publication, and the third from a quarterly publication).
- Give the inclusive page numbers of the article.
- Give the name of the database, in italics.
- Give the medium of publication.
- Give the date of access.

E-Mail

Give the name of the writer (last name first), the title of the message (taken from the "subject" line), an indication of who received the message, and the date of the message.

Edwards, John. "Re: AIDS Sources." Message to author. 31 July 2008. E-mail.

Francis, Heather. Message to Karen Wilhoit. 24 June 2007. E-mail.

- If the subject line of the message is blank, leave out that part of the entry.
- Note how the date of the message is listed: day, month, year.
- Note the medium of publication (in this case, "E-mail").

SAMPLE MLA-STYLE WORKS CITED LIST

Begin the works cited list on a separate sheet of paper at the end of your essay. Centered at the top, write "Works Cited" and then double-space before you begin listing your entries. Entries are alphabetized by the author's last name or by the first key word in the title if there is no author. The first line of each entry begins on the left margin, and all subsequent lines of each entry are indented one-half inch. The entire list is double-spaced.

Works Cited

"AIDS." *Encyclopaedia Brittannica Online.* Encyclopaedia Britannica,

2008. Web. 1 July 2008.

"AIDS: Education Cuts the Toll." *Business Week* 5 Dec. 2005: 112.

Academic Search Premier. Web. 1 July 2008.

Alexander, Jane. Telephone interview. 16 June 2008.

Ambinder, Marc. "Huck and AIDS." *TheAtlantic.com.* Atlantic Monthly,

8 Dec. 2007. Web. 2 July 2008.

Bethell, Tom. "The African AIDS Epidemic Is Exaggerated." *Responding

to the AIDS Epidemic.* Ed. Daniel A. Leone. Detroit: Greenhaven P.,

2006. 18–22. Print.

Broadhead, Robert S., and Douglas D. Heckathorn. "AIDS Prevention

Outreach among Injection Drug Users: Agency Problems and New

Approaches." *Social Problems* 41.3 (1994): 473–95. Print.

Chase, Marilyn. "Panel Suggests a 'Peace Corps' to Fight AIDS." *Wall

Street Journal* 20 Apr. 2005: B1+. Print.

"Children and AIDS." *New York Times* 22 Feb. 2005: 16. Print.

Clinton, Bill. "My Quest to Improve Care." *Newsweek* 15 May 2006:

50–2. Print.

Cohen, Ann, and Jack M. Gorman, eds. *Comprehensive Textbook of

AIDS Psychiatry.* New York: Oxford UP, 2008. Print.

Corporate Responses to HIV/AIDS: Case Studies from India.

Washington, DC: World Bank, 2007. Print.

Douglas, Paul Harding, and Laura Pinsky. *The Essential AIDS Fact Book*. New York: Pocket Books, 1991. Print.

Dugger, Celia W. "Rift over AIDS Treatment Lingers in South Africa." *New York Times* 9 Mar. 2008: 8. Print.

Edwards, John. "Re: AIDS Sources." Message to author. 31 July 2008. E-mail.

Fan, Hung Y., Ross F. Conner, and Luis Villarreal. *AIDS: Science and Society*. 5th ed. Sudbury, MA: Jones and Bartlett, 2007. Print.

Francis, Heather. Message to Karen Wilhoit. 24 June 2007. E-mail.

Gollub, Erica L. "A Neglected Population: Drug-Using Women and Women's Methods of HIV/STI Prevention." *AIDS Education & Prevention* 20.2 (2008): 107–20. Print.

Hinds, Maurene J. *Fighting the AIDS and HIV Epidemic: A Global Battle*. Berkeley Heights: Enslow, 2008. Print.

Kalichman, Seth, et al. "HIV Treatment Beliefs and Sexual Transmission Risk Behaviors among HIV Positive Men and Women." *Journal of Behavioral Medicine* 29.5 (2006): 401–10. Print.

Minkel, J. R. "Dangling a Carrot for Vaccines." *Scientific American* July 2006: 39–40. Print.

Mitchell, Roger E., Paul Florin, and John F. Stevenson. "Supporting Community-based Prevention and Health Promotion Initiatives: Developing Effective Technical Assistance Systems." *Health Education & Behavior* 29.5 (2002): 620–39. Print.

National Gay and Lesbian Task Force. *Anti-gay Violence: Victimization and Defamation in 1986.* New York: National Gay and Lesbian Task Force, 1987. Print.

Parkhurst, Justin O. "'What Worked?': The Evidence Challenges in Determining the Causes of HIV Prevalence Decline." *AIDS Education & Prevention* June 2008: 275–83. *Academic Search Premier.* Web. 1 July 2008.

Patton, Cindy. "'With Champagne and Roses': Women at Risk from/in AIDS Discourse." *Women and AIDS.* Ed. Corinne Squire. London: Sage, 1993. 165–87. Print.

Shadlen, Kenneth C. "The Political Economy of AIDS Treatment: Intellectual Property and the Transformation of Generic Supply." *International Studies Quarterly* 51.3 (2007): 559–81. *Academic Search Complete.* Web. 5 July 2008.

Smith, John. Personal interview. 16 June 2008.

Squire, Corinne. *AIDS Panic.* New York: Routledge, 1997. Print.

—. *HIV in South Africa: Talking about the Big Thing.* London: Routledge, 2007. Print.

Underwood, Anne. "How the Plague Began." *Newsweek.com.* Newsweek, 8 Feb. 1999. Web. 3 July 2008.

Wanjama, Leah Niambi, et al. *HIV and AIDS: The Pandemic.* Nairobi: Jomo Kenyatta Foundation, 2007. Print.

Appendix

PEER REVIEW GUIDELINES

In most cases, your instructor will provide you with a set of guidelines to follow when you review a peer's writing. If your teacher does not give you a set of guidelines to follow, you may want to employ the peer review procedures outlined below. To apply any set of guidelines effectively, though, you need to understand the purpose of peer review and commit yourself to improving your peer's writing. When peers review your work, remember that they are merely suggesting ways you might improve your writing. As the author of the piece, you are responsible for all final editing decisions.

PURPOSE

When you review a peer's writing, you can play three related roles, each serving a unique purpose: average reader, adviser, and editor. As an **average reader**, you offer your genuine response to the manuscript. You should let your peers know which aspects of their writing you find interesting, which parts you find boring, what is clear, what is confusing, what you would like to know more about, and what questions you have. As an **adviser**, along with offering your response to the manuscript, you also make specific suggestions to improve the piece. You can suggest changes in content, organization, format, or style. Finally, as an **editor**, you make specific suggestions for improving the piece and correct any problems you find in the writing.

Whatever role you play, your goal remains the same: to help your peer produce the most effective piece of writing possible. Peer review works best when it is truly reciprocal in nature: you do your best to improve your peer's writing because you know your peer is doing his or her best to improve your writing.

PROCEDURES TO FOLLOW

If you are asked to review a peer's writing, follow the guidelines your instructor distributes. If your teacher does not provide you specific guidelines to follow, employ the following procedures.

Step 1: **Read through the entire paper** carefully without marking anything.

Step 2: Consider whether the paper (or any part of it you are reviewing) **meets the needs of the assignment**. If it does not, tell your peer why you think it does not answer the assignment.

Step 3: Examine the paper's **content**. Point out which sections of the essay are clear, which need further development, which specifically address the assignment, and which seem to stray from it. Offer any suggestions you have for improving the paper's content.

Step 4: Examine the paper's **structure**. Note any problems with the paper's thesis statement or topic sentences. Comment on whether the writer provides clear and effective transitions between paragraphs or among sentences within the paragraphs. Note any passage where you lose track of the writer's train of thought. Finally, comment on the effectiveness of the opening and closing sections of the essay.

Step 5: Examine the paper's **style**. Note any awkward or confusing sentences (if you have a suggestion about how to improve the sentence, offer it). Look for consistency in voice, diction, and point of view, commenting on any problems you find. If you think that any passage is stylistically inappropriate given the assigned audience, let the writer know.

Step 6: **Proofread** for errors in spelling, punctuation, or typing. You can either circle errors you find and leave them for the author to correct or offer corrections of your own.

Step 7: Examine the paper's **documentation**. First, check to see that the author has documented every passage that needs to be documented, noting any questions you have. Second, note any errors you find in the documentation the author provides, such as problems with the documentation's placement, formatting, or punctuation. Finally, proofread the paper's works cited or reference list if there is one.

ACTING ON PEER REVIEWS

As an author, you have the final say concerning the changes you make to your essay. You can accept or reject your peer's suggestions, but whatever decision you make, base it on a careful consideration of your peer's comments.

Accepting every suggestion a peer reviewer offers is usually a bad idea, as is summarily rejecting every suggestion a reviewer makes. Consider each comment individually. Decide whether the peer reviewer's suggestion will improve your manuscript. If it will, make the change. If you think it will not, do not act on the suggestion. If you are unsure about making any change, talk it over with your instructor before you decide.

CREDITS

Bauerlein, Mark. "Generation Text," from *America*, November 2009, Edition 12, pp. 20–22. Copyright © 2009 by America Press Inc. Reprinted with permission. All rights reserved. For subscription information call 1.800.627.9533 or visit www.americamagazine.org.

Blumberg, Fran C., Kristen P. Bierwirth, and Allison J. Schwartz. "Does Cartoon Violence Beget Aggressive Behavior in Real Life? An Opposing View," from *Early Childhood Education Journal*, 36, 2008. Copyright © 2008 by Fran C. Blumberg, Kristen P. Bierwirth, Allison J. Schwartz. Reprinted with permission of Springer.

Cantor, Joanne. "Media Violence and Children's Emotions: Beyond the 'Smoking Gun'," from a paper presented at the Annual Conference of the American Psychological Association, Washington, DC, August 2000. Copyright © 2000 by Joanne Cantor. Reprinted with permission of the author.

Crain, Michael. "Animal Suffering: Learning to Care and Not to Know," from *Encounter*, 22.2, 2009. Copyright © 2009 by Michael Crain. Reprinted with permission of the publisher. All rights reserved.

Essex, Nathan L. "Zero Tolerance and Student Dress Codes," from *Principal*, September/October 2004. Copyright © 2004 by National Association of Elementary School Principals. Reprinted with permission. All rights reserved.

"From *Animal House* to *Big Brother*: Student Privacy and Campus Safety in an Age of Accountability," from *Student Affairs Leader*, Edition 36(7), pp. 1–5. Copyright © 2008 by Magna Publications. Reprinted with permission.

Konheim-Kalkstein, Yasmine L. "A Uniform Look," from *American School Board Journal*, 2006. Copyright © 2006 by National School Boards Association. Reprinted with permission. All rights reserved.

Medina, Leticia V. "Building a Culture of Animal Welfare: Past, Present, and Future," from *Annual Review of Biomedical Sciences*, Edition 10, pp.104–111. Copyright © 2008 by Annual Review of Biomedical Sciences. Reprinted with permission.

INDEX

NOTES

NOTES

NOTES

NOTES

Anthology of Readings

VOCATION: HOW DO YOU KNOW WHAT TO DO WITH YOUR LIFE?

INTRODUCTION

What do you want to do with your life? What can you do to fill your life with meaning and significance? If you are like most students today, you are attending college primarily to prepare yourself for your future occupation, even if you are not sure, right now, what that occupation might be. The authors of readings in this chapter raise a number of important questions that will challenge you to consider the direction your life will take.

All of the authors discuss what it means to have a vocation or a calling in life and explore how we discover or discern what it will be. They believe that at some point in our lives, we all wrestle with the question of how we can lead a more fulfilling life by employing our talents, gifts, and time in the service of others. Some people may say that they have known their calling from childhood, that for as long as they can remember they have felt compelled to teach or practice medicine for example. For others, though, identifying and understanding their vocation comes later in life and attending college often plays a crucial role for them. College affords them the opportunity to identify their talents and interests and the time for introspection and exploration. As several of the authors point out, however, because vocational discernment is so highly personal and so frequently a spiritual quest, faculty are reluctant to discuss it in class or help their students in their journeys. In fact, the role faculty should play in helping students discover their vocations is a central question several of the authors explore.

As you read the essays in this chapter, consider how they speak to your own experiences and questions. What are you being called to do with *your* life?

"The Interdependency of Vocational and Liberal Aims in Higher Education"

Kathleen Knight Abowitz

Kathleen Knight Abowitz *is an associate professor in the Department of Educational Leadership at Miami University.*

"What do I want to be when I grow up?" My four-year-old regularly asks himself this question, and at this point in life, he entertains an astonishing array of possibilities: pizza maker, soccer player, and Jedi Knight currently are top choices. The question of their future life work is also a focus for many college students. But unlike my four-year-old, many college and university students are zeroed in on their vocational pursuits. Often very narrowly focused, many college students simplistically equate a college education with a vocational education. In situations of advising, teaching, or life coaching, we often encounter students who believe that college is largely preparation for a job. Such a view diminishes the importance of the humanistic and intellectual inquiry that is so important to college life. Rather than asking themselves, "How do I wish to live?" many students ask, "How can I learn how to make my living?" This essay explores how faculty and student affairs educators can help students better integrate these two questions.

Erin, an eighteen-year-old woman from rural Ohio, has enrolled in my seminar Sociocultural Foundations of Education, one of the first undergraduate courses in the teacher education program. On the first day of class, we are discussing our expectations of the course and of one another. Erin says, "I want to learn how to be a good teacher." This is a simple and profound wish, one shared by many of her classmates. How do I become a partner in this goal while simultaneously enlarging, expanding, and deepening what Erin means by "being a good teacher"? How do we as classroom faculty and student affairs educators help Erin make personal, intellectual, and holistic meaning of her own vocational aspirations?

Like many of us who advise, teach, or counsel college students, I regularly encounter students who are seeking a particular degree for vocational purposes. Most U.S. students seek degrees because they want to secure what they consider to be a good (that is, white-collar) job. The Higher Education Research Institute's annual survey asked students to rate the reasons they chose to pursue a college degree, and more than 70 percent of all respondents from public universities in 2004 cited the following reasons as very important in deciding to go to college: "to get training for a specific career," "to get a better job," and "to be able to make more money." Contemporary college students overwhelmingly view higher education as the means to the tangible end of employment.

While a student may have a general interest in a wide array of ideas, an emphasis on vocationally oriented learning can edge out wider interests and pursuits. Typical requirements of accrediting agencies have not helped. The liberal aims of education, especially as taught through the humanities fields of philosophy, literature, and the arts, are thus increasingly subjugated to the overwhelming power of courses and learning objectives that are practical, applied, and serve as a direct means to the desired end of employment. A college student completing a licensure program in elementary education in the state of Ohio, for example, must complete only one three-credit course on the historical, philosophical, and cultural foundations of education and schooling as part of a 128-credit-hour program. This signals a way of thinking about work that is segregated from a broader and more holistic view of education itself. This conception of education is not a radical new shift in thinking, nor a way of thinking about professional education unique to the field of education, nor unique to the state of Ohio. It reflects larger culture shifts in the way education and its purposes are viewed.

This segregation of liberal and vocational aims defies the holistic nature of what it means to live a fulfilled human life in which paid work occupies a central but not exclusively defining role. (When I use the term *work* in this essay, I will be referring to paid work, although I recognize that as a member of a family and as a citizen, I do much meaningful work that is unpaid.) While vocational studies focus on the world of work, liberal studies focus on the problems, experiences, and questions of being human. And surely inquiry into the human condition, including questions of purpose, value, and meaning, is not less important than questions of vocation. Indeed, one's work and professional identity formation are infused and shaped by the broader, exciting questions of meaning and existence. Students like Erin want to become good professionals, but preprofessional programs for educators and other vocations must be cognizant that becoming a good teacher is a human, not merely technical, enterprise. Our teaching and curricula need to reflect the connected nature of the vocational and the liberal, two differing but interrelated aims in higher education. Most students see their academic lives—their liberal arts classes and the courses in their academic major—as segregated domains. In the same way that many student affairs educators seek to purposefully stitch together the seams of the curricular and cocurricular domains, so should all educators aim to help our students more purposefully bind together the falsely separated spheres of liberal education and vocational education. An example from my own teaching demonstrates how powerful it can be when we help students to connect questions of professional preparation (vocational aims) with questions of existential meaning (liberal aims).

WHAT SORT OF LIFE DO I WISH TO LIVE? EXPLORATIONS THROUGH ART

As a faculty member in the School of Education and Allied Professions, I regularly teach an applied ethics seminar for graduate students who aspire to work in K–16 educational settings. For most students in a school of education, studying a field like philosophy of education is a one-shot deal. Most vocational programs have no more than a smattering of such offerings, and the program in which I teach is no different. Courses in ethics and philosophy of education usually are outliers within their program. The disadvantage of this position is that it is difficult to teach against the grain of the technical, instrumentalist bent of many vocationally oriented programs. The advantage of this position in both the undergraduate and graduate classes I teach is that the terrain of pedagogical possibilities is wider, and students know that this terrain will likely overlap with personal concerns and questions. Above all, students expect the unexpected in an ethics course. As an explicit study of value and moral meaning, it cannot help but become personal in the sense of intersecting with one's own moral commitments, questions, and strivings. That such personal forms of learning are rare in most college classrooms speaks, perhaps, to why higher education has become meaningful to many students only for instrumental purposes—to get the job.

My goals for this seminar in ethics—to teach moral concepts, to develop moral reasoning skills, to explore moral dilemmas—are, in many senses, typical of other such courses. These are important learning goals, but too often ethics courses can become forums for students to more clearly articulate and justify what they believed when they came in the door on the first day of class rather than inquire into their beliefs, their habits, and their own moral thinking. As I read Martha Nussbaum's *Cultivating Humanity* over several semesters of this course, her notion of the "moral imagination" inspired me as a way to have students see outside their own perspectives. Nussbaum uses this term to refer to the ability to see, perceive, and feel moral situations through "habits of empathy and conjecture" developed particularly through experiences with literature and the arts (p. 90). Nussbaum argues that a college education must include the cultivation of our moral imagination; through our liberal studies, we must develop capacities for what Steven Fesmire calls "empathetic projection," or taking the attitudes of others into account when approaching social issues, and "creative tapping [of] a situation's possibilities" to find innovative and effective solutions to moral problems (p. 65). Because educators must constantly engage with diverse others in morally complex situations, cultivating the powers of moral imagination can be critical to their attaining a successful professional life. I asked myself, "How is my applied ethics curriculum helping students to cultivate the important quality of moral imagination so necessary for an ethical professional and personal life?" The question motivated me to construct an aesthetic experience in some of my undergraduate and graduate courses, including my seminar on applied ethics for educators.

I choose the term *aesthetic experience* consciously. An encounter with works of art is not inherently valuable or important. The value of the aesthetic in teaching for humanistic inquiry is in the kinds of experiences that an encounter with an art object or performance can provoke. To experience art is to experiment, to undergo an encounter that breaks the routine of habit and mundane ways of seeing and living every day. Experiences with art heighten our perceptions and sharpen our imagination. Maxine Greene argues, "Imagination is not only the power to form mental images, although it is partly that. It is also the power to mold experience into something new, to create fictive situations. It is, as well, the power—by means of sympathetic feeling—to put oneself in another's place" (p. 30).

Aiming to expand imaginations and more creatively explore the ethical concepts of compassion and justice, I collaboratively constructed an aesthetic experience for the students in the ethics class with Cynthia Collins, an educator in my university's art museum. I discussed my learning goals with her and shared the text that provided the conceptual underpinning of the class's continued discussions of compassion and justice, Nussbaum's *Cultivating Humanity*. During one fall semester, we constructed an experience for the students that centered on a compelling photography installation entitled "Faces of Freedom Summer" by Herbert Randall.

In 1964, Randall, a young African American and Native American photographer, won a fellowship to spend a year documenting contemporary Negro life. Randall used his fellowship to document the activities of Freedom Summer, a wide-scale volunteer voter registration and educational effort that civil rights activists organized and college students implemented. Because Miami University was one of the training sites for Freedom Summer volunteers, the topic has special significance at our institution.

Beyond the historical connection was the meaning that this particular collection of artworks could hold for a class of future educators. All the students in this particular semester's class aspired to become educators, and many intended to pursue work as student affairs professionals. An exhibit of portraits of activism by college students was ripe with potential connections. For teaching purposes, a meaningful aesthetic experience is one that identifies such potential connections and can be set up through museum exhibits, art studios, and a variety of other venues.

A successful aesthetic experience is one that helps students take in, and go out to, the work of art. "Perceiving is an active probing of wholes as they become visible," according to Maxine Greene (p. 13). To help students take in and reach out to "Faces of Freedom Summer," we assigned reading from the

Nussbaum text before class, focusing on chapters on the moral imagination and the cultivation of compassion. We began the class session, held at the Miami Art Museum, with a brief test. The test was an abbreviated version of the voter registration tests black voters in many Southern states had to pass before being allowed to register to vote during the Jim Crow era. The test's difficulty astounded seminar participants: not a single student passed the test. At this point, we discussed the purpose of the test and how it functioned to keep blacks away from the voting booth. The museum educator then discussed the exhibit in very general terms and introduced a short film that provided a historical context for Freedom Summer. The film gave students a sense of the importance and impact of these activities, lending a greater understanding of the content of the photographs they were about to view.

We then invited students to immerse themselves in the exhibit and provided them ample time to explore each photograph. Each student was asked to select one photograph on which to focus sustained attention. They were then to write about that piece: its composition, visual features, effects, and emotional impact. Following this reflection on a single photograph, we asked students to write responses to a series of questions that explored connections between the photographs and the concepts introduced in the Nussbaum text, such as compassion and justice. The class discussion that immediately followed was a forum for seminar participants to share their perceptions of the art and to enlarge those perceptions by listening to how peers made sense of them.

Students first shared their emotional responses to the photographs, which included portraits of important activists in the movement and of real people suffering through extreme injustice and physical torment, as well as moving representations of courage and dignity exhibited by both the Freedom Summer volunteers and the black activists and voters. The photographs are emotionally stirring, and students took a great deal of time detailing their emotions, how the photographs connected with their personal life, and what bearing they had on their moral choices and professional future.

A question emerged from the discussion that disturbed many seminar participants: "Would I have been one of the people participating in Freedom Summer, or would I have been one of the members of the KKK?" In other words, this white student was asking herself and others, "Which side of this moral question would I have stood on?" One student's self-reflective question became the focus of conversation and evoked an honest, risky, and soul-searching discussion about moral commitments and the boundaries of our social and historical contexts. Where would we have stood in this fight? Where do we stand now on current questions of right and wrong, good and bad, just and unjust? And where did the Freedom Summer volunteers and civil rights activists summon the courage to take the stand they did?

Several days later, I asked students to post their reflections on our Freedom Summer experience on our Web-based discussion board. Several days after the experience, some students indicated that they had begun to integrate their reactions to the photographs with their identities as humans and future educators. For example, the student who posed the question, "Which side would I have stood on in this battle?" contributed this statement:

> In viewing the images . . . I began to see the world in a new way. Of course I felt compassion for the people in the prints and rightfully so. I felt their fight, and was engaged in their struggle. However, through my moral perception and the judgment of similar possibilities, I came to the realization that I may NOT be the one in the photos, but that, due to the place and the time, I may actually be the one causing the oppression of the people that we saw. This is not an easy idea to deal with—but it helped me replace old feelings of hatred and contempt for the oppressors with feelings of compassion and understanding— because I see now that many times we eliminate our opportunity to become world citizens by ignorantly engaging in the perpetuation of cultural norms. They were only hurting themselves in the end—the oppressors—but they could not see that. I could have been one of them, and how truly sad that would have been. [European American female second-year graduate student]

This student articulated the uncomfortable truth that this aesthetic experience exposed: we are moral actors in historical moments, and our own commitments fall short of our idealized version of our best self. Knowledge of self and expansion of moral viewpoints are essential to the work of education and are central to unlocking full knowledge of one's personal power and agency as an educator. Moreover, knowing the privilege and limitations of one's particular cultural identity is an essential step toward serving others and engaging in equitable, transformative educational experiences.

Another student explored the notion of compassion in her reflection on the aesthetic experience:

> Viewing "Faces of Freedom Summer" proved to be one of the most emotional, moving, and thought changing experiences I have ever had. After visiting a concentration camp in Germany during my junior year at [college], I did not believe I would ever experience such intense emotions, namely compassion, for individuals I did not know. However, this exhibit did awaken many emotions inside me. It did so because of Nussbaum's third judgment, the "judgment of similar possibilities." In viewing this exhibit, I experienced it very differently because I am dating an African American. Previously, I could view this exhibit from the White perspective, hoping that I would be a participant in Freedom Summer. However, now I view this exhibit from the lenses of someone who cares about an individual who could have been the victim of such oppression. . . . Viewing this exhibit from this new vantage point severely changed the way I viewed this exhibit and my relation to it. Now, my position is no longer abstract but a real possibility for those I care deeply about. This experience has prompted me to consider how we as educators can facilitate the "judgment of similar possibilities" for our students because of the powerful effects it can have on students

and individuals in general. [European American female second-year master's student]

When I asked students to post their reflections on the online discussion board, I requested that they comment on their own reactions and interpretations of the art and on their views on the role of the arts in educating students in general. In this way, students reflected on their own questions, commitments, and purposes and extended these questions into their future interactions with the students with whom they will be working. Who will we be, as educators? The exhibit and their reflections allowed students to place their own life and their profession into a historical context and imagine what the future might hold. One student expressed the humility and hope that she felt in comparing her own life with the lives depicted in the photographs:

> In regards to the "Freedom Summer" exhibit, viewing those photos reminded me of the struggles individuals have persevered through. Those photos spoke to me about the resiliency of the human spirit and the leaps and bounds a society can make when we work together. It makes me recognize the impact one person or a group of people can have on society. In addition, it also reminds me that while it seems like change rarely occurs, we truly can make dramatic changes in just a short period of time. More than anything, the photos made me stop and think about how trivial many of my concerns are. I often find myself stressed over the amount of reading I have or an inconvenience I experience during my day at the dining hall or trying to find a parking spot. However, when viewing those photos and recognizing the true struggles these individuals endured and their abilities to push through and never give up, it encourages me to really step back and recognize what matters in life. Are my daily 'irks' really worth getting upset about? Or can I use that energy on something more important and meaningful? [European American female second-year graduate student]

"What sort of life am I creating?" is a much larger question than "What kind of paid work do I want to learn how to do?" It is a question of great interest to adults of all ages and in particular to young adults just starting out. "How do I make a meaningful life, both through my professional work and in my own everyday moral actions?" is a question at the heart of a vocational education. Work must be part of a larger existence that is purposefully lived. An experience with art can motivate this questioning because the arts can stir us, trouble us, and transport us in ways that few other teaching media can. However, the arts do not simply or inherently contain pedagogical moments or miracles. The role of the educator is to carefully construct experiences with art to involve a range of reflective and dialogical activities that will promote imagining, integrating, and consolidating meaning.

Because experiences with the arts have the potential to bring vivid personal and social meaning to questions that include "Who am I?" and "Who do I wish to become?" students can place their vocational goals within larger questions of purpose. By reframing assumptions that attending college is preparation for the world of work, experiences with art help place the more technical, instrumental thinking about work aside for more holistic and moral thinking about what kind of professional and personal life one wishes to lead. Such retooling of educational aims brings us to new notions of vocational education.

WORK AND PURPOSE

It is a particularly American assumption that we are our work. Americans work more and vacation less than most comparable Western societies; Americans seem to live for the job. Such cultural constructions belie the complexity and reality of what it means to live a life, in the United States or anywhere else. Ask any college student or recent college graduate what it means to live a rich, ful- filling life, and you'll receive a suitably wide range of responses. A happy fam- ily life. Joyful and nurturing relationships. Fulfilling and fairly compensated work. A sense of peace and spiritual well-being. Meaningful commitments to important organizations, causes, or institutions. And of course, a steady supply of fun, pleasure, color, and excitement. No doubt, work is an important part of life but by no means the sole component. Our students know this, and we know this, too.

Because higher education has become so obsessed with fulfilling vocational aims, our larger and collective sense of education is faltering. Students who enroll in college with the focused aim of being an accountant, teacher, or speech pathologist seek knowledge to build a meaningful life, but if we teach subjects like business, education, or speech pathology as skills, techniques, or mere methods to professional ends, we fail to provide a meaningful education. John Dewey wrote in *Democracy and Education* that there is "a tendency for every distinctive vocation to become too dominant, too exclusive and absorbing in its specialized aspect. This means emphasis upon skill or technical method at the expense of meaning" (p. 308). Dewey called such an emphasis "trade education," or "vocational training," something that has its place in specialized trade schools but is not the exclusive role of colleges and universities. What conditions can make higher education distinct from a trade school?

The answer lies in the definition of *vocation* offered by Dewey: "A vocation signifies any form of continuous activity which renders service to others and engages personal powers in behalf of the accomplishment of results" (p. 319). A vocational education realizes that being an accountant or an educator is not a job but a continual and changing set of activities, involving forms of specialized and general thinking that must adapt over time. A vocational education is one that fully inquires into what it means to serve others, investigating historical, philosophical, and anthropological questions about human relations. A vocational education releases and develops students' abilities, what Dewey called "personal powers," toward the ends of work. Such powers would include many capacities beyond the ability to balance the books or the ability to fairly discipline a student.

Vocational education is more than trade education if we teach a sense of historical, political, cultural, and ethical context for the occupation. Engaging in, for example, accountancy as a "continuous activity over time" means that we understand the historical underpinnings of the occupation, the cultural conditions in which the occupation is set, and the current pressures (political, economic, social, and so on) that affect its current practice. Vocational education is more than trade education if we fully explore the questions surrounding what it means to serve others, whether through studies of cultures, literature, philosophy, poetry, the arts, or similar humanistic inquiry. Finally, vocational education is more than trade education if we focus on developing students' personal powers in holistic ways, engaging their full energies and unique capacities toward their chosen occupation. The result of such education is transformative. Dewey argued that teachers who bring their full personal powers to education will not simply teach within the confines of the occupation as it is now structured but will bring human creativity and agency to making the profession distinctive and renewing it with each generation.

Vocational education cannot ignore larger questions of context, culture, ethics, and politics, nor should it evade students' existential questions. Indeed, questions of purpose, meaning, and identity are central to what it means to occupy a vocation. The journey to becoming a professional is the journey of building one's life, with particular but by no means exclusive focus on one part of that life (the paid work). Making sense of one's life through the learning of a vocation is the educational journey that many of our students should be taking. It is not as if a student decides to become an accountant and explores questions of meaning, value, and purpose outside of those occupational parameters. One's values and sense of purpose shape occupational choice, and one's occupational directions in turn shape interest and values. Vocational education is a transactive experience. To ignore this is to strip higher education of its liberal, and liberating, potential.

Dewey's definition of *vocational education* implies not a continued segregation of liberal education from vocational education but a recognition of their interdependency. The students who experienced the Freedom Summer exhibit were engaged in learning about both how to become an educator and how to become a compassionate and fair person. Their struggles over meanings of compassion and justice were emotional and personal and simultaneously detached and reflectively professional in some ways. The arts facilitate the connections between liberal and vocational, personal and professional, because they cross multiple disciplines, domains, and histories.

Dewey's view of vocational education calls us to soften the hardened categories of liberal education and vocational or professional education in higher education. Liberal education should become more vocationalized in the sense that liberal education should have social relevance and purposes in mind. Vocational education should be liberalized in that any vocational course of study should have larger, holistic humanist aims and purposes in mind. I do not believe that only philosophers, poets, or religious studies professors can help students explore questions of meaning and purpose; neither do I believe that only accountants can help students learn about how best to fairly and competently work with financial clients. We need specialists, but our pedagogical purposes intertwine and expand beyond our specialties.

CAVEATS, IMPLICATIONS, AND CONCLUSIONS

Questions of meaning, purpose, and values do not belong to any one discipline; while these questions should be the focus of certain specialized courses in philosophy, ethics, or similar disciplines, they are questions embedded in the educational journey of all college students. They are questions that cross the vocational-liberal divide that currently exists in our educational thinking. They are questions that, if understood and pedagogically addressed, can make all education, especially vocational education, much more meaningful and transformative.

Liberalizing the current technical, instrumental forms of vocational education requires a great deal from faculty. Many students enrolled in my class were members of an academic program that places a high value on building community, risk taking, dialogical learning, and incorporating students' whole selves into the learning process.

Thus, many students in the class were adept and ready to address questions of meaning and purpose through reflection and dialogue with their peers. Certainly, not all students have had experiences with such environments, and constructing these environments across our campuses will require time, commitment, and resources. But we can all start somewhere, and many campuses and programs are exemplars in this work. Finally, restructuring programs to balance technical, specialized vocational education with the broader, more liberal aims in vocational education may require relinquishing cherished courses or content in favor of different courses and content of a less specialized and technical nature.

Higher education is, among many other things, a preparation ground for the world of paid work. To prepare our students for that world, we must not handicap them with a technical and narrow sense of their future vocation. Rather, in helping them to explore connections between their work and the larger questions of life involving meaning, purpose, and values, we can educate rather than train—and thus enhance their entire growth and development rather than simply the aspects directly related to a specific vocation. The effects will likely result in a greater commitment to and understanding of one's vocation, as one student's remarks following a visit to the art museum suggest:

> By placing art—both the creation of and appreciation of—into the curriculum and co-curriculum of higher education, we can engage with students about the humanity that connects us all. What do students

feel from the art? What is being communicated about being human? How do we communicate those same sentiments now? What do we do with our lives today that is for a higher purpose, that is done because we cannot not do it by the dictates of our convictions? What great questions to pose to students!

NOTES

Dewey, J. *Democracy and Education*. New York: Free Press, 1916. Fesmire, S. *John Dewey and Moral Imagination*. Bloomington, Ind.: Indiana University Press, 2003.

Greene, M. V*ariations on a Blue Guitar: The Lincoln Center Institute Lectures on Aesthetic Education*. New York: Teachers College Press, 2001.

Higher Education Research Institute. *2004 Cooperative Institutional Research Program Institutional Summary*. Los Angeles: Higher Education Research Institute, University of California, 2004.

Nussbaum, M. C. *Cultivating Humanity: A Classical Defense of Reform in Liberal Education*. Cambridge, Mass.: Harvard University Press, 1997.

REFLECTIVE WRITING QUESTIONS

1. In her essay, Abowitz summarizes the results of a study conducted by The Higher Education Research Institute to determine why students choose to pursue a college degree. What would your answer be? Why?
2. As Abowitz sees it, what are the differences between "vocational" and "liberal" education? Do those distinctions make sense to you? Do you see them in your own conception of what it means to get a college education?
3. Abowitz contends that aesthetic experiences can be central to cultivating our humanity. Identify an aesthetic experience from your past. What was it and how did it affect you?
4. As clearly as possible, answer the following questions: "What kind of person do I want to become?" and "How can I best answer the moral challenge to serve others?"
5. What career are you currently pursuing or considering? What draws you to that career? Besides yourself, who else will benefit from the work you do in this career? How might you use your skills, education, and gifts to better serve these people, perhaps in ways that extend beyond the normal demands of the job?

DISCUSSION QUESTIONS

1. Presumably, every student has his or her own reasons for attending college. How are yours similar to or different from the reasons your classmates say they are attending college?
2. How are imagination and empathy important in our lives? What roles can they play in helping us discern and/or pursue our vocations?
3. What specifically are the differences between these two questions: "What sort of life am I creating?" and "What kind of paid work do I want to learn how to do?"
4. Do you agree or disagree with John Dewey's argument that "trade education" or "vocational training" ought not be the sole focus of colleges and universities?
5. What does Abowitz mean when, late in the essay, she claims that vocational education ought to be a "transactive experience?" How might that claim apply to the occupation you are currently pursuing or considering?

The Challenge of Liberal Education: Past, Present, and Future

Ellen Condliffe Lagemann

Ellen Condliffe Langemann, Charles Warren Professor of History of American Education, serves as Dean of the Harvard Graduate School of Education.

We live in a world that is fundamentally new—new in the often fearful interconnectedness of regions, states, and people; new in both the scope of the challenges we face in finding and sustaining peace and in the consequences we face if we fail to achieve peace; and new, too, in the heterogeneity of the peoples with whom we live, work, and communicate. As globalization has changed the world we know, it has brought great opportunity and challenge and it has added renewed vigor to old, familiar questions. One such question is the one I would like to take up: What can we learn from the past to enliven our thinking about liberal education in the present and future?

Let me begin with two comments on the current situation of American higher education. The first is simple. According to a recent report of the Carnegie Corporation of New York, higher education today is significantly more professional and technical in orientation than it was thirty years ago. In 1970, 50 percent of all bachelor's degrees were awarded in a liberal arts subject. In 2000, nearly 60 percent of the degrees were awarded in a pre-professional or technical field. I could multiply the statistics, but I do not think that is necessary to make the point. Today's college students do not have time or money to waste. They are careful consumers. And they are voting with their feet for more vocationally oriented programs of study.

My second observation derives from an essay by the journalist Nicholas Lemann, called "The Kids in the Conference Room." It is about recent college graduates, mostly from highly selective institutions, who are recruited to work at consulting firms for at least a few years after graduation. As Lemann put it, working for McKinsey & Co., or some close approximate, is "the present-day equivalent of working for the C.I.A. in the nineteen-fifties, or the Peace Corps in the sixties, or Ralph Nader in the seventies, or First Boston in the eighties—it is the job that encapsulates the Zeitgeist of the moment." Lemann goes on to point out that working for McKinsey for a few years is "an ideal placeholder" for bright young people, who leave college with heavy debt and no certain idea of where they want to end up vocationally.

To me, there is a disturbing paradox evident in the data presented in the Carnegie Corporation's report and the observation made by Lemann. On the one hand, student course selection indicates that they want their college education to prepare them for careers. On the other hand, by contrast, those students who attend our most selective institutions—all of which, I might add, consider themselves liberal arts colleges and universities—graduate without a clear sense of vocational direction. At a time of extreme social challenge, we seem to have few alternatives between clear and, inevitably, rather narrow vocational preparation and seemingly directionless programs of liberal study. This makes me wonder whether in the challenge of our moment in history there is not a way to enliven the liberal arts by organizing them around deliberate consideration of what it means to have a vocation.

HAVING A CALLING

The word *vocation* implies more than earning a living or having a career. The word vocation implies having a calling: knowing who one is, what one believes, what one values, and where one stands in the world. A sense of vocation is not something fully achieved early in life. For those of us who are lucky, it grows over time, becomes more articulate, and deepens. Granting, then, that a sense of vocation develops over time, it is still not unreasonable to suggest that one purpose of a college education, and a central purpose of liberal education, should be to nurture an initial sense of vocation. This might encompass personal dispositions such as awareness of the importance of deliberate choices, individual agency, and social connection as well as recognition, albeit initial, of the ways of thinking and acting that seem most personally congenial. It should also include a capacity for civic intelligence. This requires that one recognize one's personal stake in public problems, global as well as domestic. It also necessitates respect for tolerance, the rights of others, evidence-based decision making, and deliberative judgment—in a word, respect for the values of due process that are essential to a democratic way of life. Vocation is not simply about an individual calling. It is about one's calling within one's society and, increasingly, across different societies around the world.

Historically, it is quite easy to see the power of vocation as a driving force in the education of individual people. One might even venture that vocation, broadly defined, in the terms I have just described, tends usually to be the theme that links the different experiences that define an individual's education. Bearing in mind that I am trying to draw from history to help us think well about the liberal arts today and tomorrow, let me illustrate the importance of vocation by saying a few words about the education of some very well-known people.

BENJAMIN FRANKLIN

The first person is Benjamin Franklin, who left us a wonderful record of his life in his *Autobiography*. Franklin was born in Puritan Boston in 1706, the tenth son and fifteenth child of Josiah Franklin and his second wife, Abiah. Intended for the ministry by his father, Ben was sent to what is now called the Boston Latin School at the age of eight. He survived only a year. The tuition at Boston Latin was high, and Ben was not sufficiently pious to make a promising candidate for the ministry. His penchant for practical efficiency led him to suggest to his father that he say grace over the family's food once for the entire year rather than before every meal. A struggling candle maker, Josiah quickly realized that Ben was not suited for the church.

At that point, a search for vocation began. Nothing appealed to young Ben, so, in desperation, Josiah apprenticed Ben to his older brother James, who was a printer.

It was as a printer's apprentice that Ben Franklin began quite self-consciously to find ways to understand who he was as a person. He did this initially by taking on the roles of people he was not. While working for his brother James, Ben wrote fourteen essays describing the complaints of a poor rural widow, whom he named Silence Dogood. In so doing, he initiated a process of self-definition that one can also see in *Poor Richard's Almanac*, which Franklin wrote as a prosperous printer in Philadelphia, or in reports and portraits of Franklin as a seasoned diplomat, parading around Paris dressed as a rural hick in a coonskin cap. Repeatedly throughout his life, Ben Franklin sought, defined, and clarified who he was in relation to others, by juxtaposing his own persona with those of others different from him.

KNOWING ONESELF

If what might be described as role playing was an important part of Franklin's search for vocation, so were his various deliberate attempts at self-improvement. As a young man, for example, Ben created a chart to measure his progress toward moral perfection. It began with fairly obvious virtues such as "Temperance—Eat not to dullness. Drink not to elevation." And it ended with more adventuresome ones like "Humility—Imitate Jesus and Socrates."

As a Philadelphia merchant, Franklin organized the Junto, a discussion group that considered ways to better the city and then sponsored projects to carry out specific reforms and improvements. Whether charting his own progress toward perfection or examining his city's adequacy as a growing urban center, Franklin was studying who he was, what his responsibilities were as a virtuous person or a civic leader, and, especially in the case of the Junto, how actions taken for the public good advanced not only the well-being of his fellow citizens of Philadelphia, but also his own stature as a first citizen and, increasingly, as a very wealthy printer and statesman.

If Franklin's own education was energized by an extraordinarily self-conscious effort constantly to find a congenial, public role for himself—a vocation—so, too, were his writings about education predicated on the importance of vocation. Consider as an example, the "Proposals Relating to the Education of Youth in Pennsylvania," which was a plan for what became the University of Pennsylvania. In this document, Franklin admitted, "It would be well if [the youth of Pennsylvania] could be taught *every Thing* that is useful and *every Thing* that is ornamental." But Franklin observed: "Art is long, and [the students'] Time is short. It is therefore propos'd that they learn those Things that are likely to be most useful and most ornamental, regard being had to the Professions for which they are intended," Here, subsequent occupation became an explicit guide in the selection of the subjects to be studied.

In line with his emphasis on vocation, Franklin insisted that the curriculum for the new university be modern. It was to be free of medieval anachronism. Thus, it should include contemporary writers along with the classics. Although all students should study English grammar, instruction in foreign languages should vary by future profession. Franklin did not dispense with all traditional learning, but the curriculum he generated reflected his insistent belief that, by preparing young men for a useful role in the world, advanced learning could have greater meaning for both the individual and the society of which that individual was a part (women, it was then, of course, presumed, did not need advanced education). Having been essential to his own education, vocation became a foundation for the education Franklin recommended for others.

JANE ADDAMS

Jane Addams's life was also inspired by a search for vocation. Growing up in central Illinois, Addams greatly admired her father, a prominent local lawyer and first citizen of Cedarville, Illinois, with whom she had an especially close relationship since her mother died when she was two. She recalled in her autobiography that, as a child, she had spent many hours trying to imitate her father. But, of course, Addams could not imitate her father exactly since as a woman her occupational choices were restricted.

Rather than retreat to a traditional role, Addams instead embraced the fact of gender limitation and defined herself and her generation in opposition to traditional expectations. Speaking of changes in the education offered to women, as a student at Rockford Seminary in 1881, Addams said: "[Women's education] has passed from accomplishments and the arts of pleasing, to the development of her intellectual force, and capability for direct labor. She wishes not to be a man, nor like a man, but she claims the same right to independent thought and action....As young women of the 19th century, we gladly claim these privileges, and proudly assert our independence....So we have planned to be 'Breadgivers' throughout our lives; believing....that the only true and honorable life is now filled with good works and honest toil....[we will] thus happily fulfill Woman's Noblest Mission."

The articulate and self-conscious search for vocation that Jane Addams was able to describe in this statement had been shaped by the formal study in which she engaged at Rockford. The curriculum, while Addams was a student there, included Latin, Greek, German, geology, astronomy, botany, medieval history, civil government, music, American literature, and evidence of Christianity. But, as her peers recalled, "the intellectual ozone" that exuded from "her vicinity" came from her unusual determination and purpose. Jane Addams's insistent wish to find a way to express her ideals and talents, despite the limitations imposed on her as a woman, was clearly an extended and successful search for vocation.

That search, of course, eventually led her to the West Side of Chicago, where, with Ellen Gates Starr, she founded Hull House, a world-famous social settlement that provided social, educational, and cultural services to the diverse immigrant population of that neighborhood. Hull House's fame came, in part, from the fact that Jane Addams helped to support it by writing constantly for magazines and by lecturing. But it is important to realize that it was not merely economics that drove Jane Addams's public expressions. It was both a desire to educate the educated middle-class public about how their neighbors lived and also to continue to work out for herself what she was doing and why it mattered. Questions of vocation continued to drive Jane Addams's education even after she founded Hull House.

W. E. B. Du Bois

As an educated woman, Addams was constrained by the fact of her sex, and yet eager to be effective in the world. One could say that she bore the burden of what her contemporary W. E. B. Du Bois called a "double con-sciousness." Perhaps a sense of social marginality is always at the root of soul-searching concerning who one is and where one can contribute to the common good. Certainly that was the case for Du Bois, who, throughout his long life struggled to understand whether and how he, as a black man, could be an American. Like Addams, Du Bois turned his personal anguish about vocation into sometimes stinging, always acute social criticism. His keenest insight was probably the line that introduced the second chapter of

Souls of Black Folk: "The problem of the twentieth century is the problem of the color line." However that may be, having learned as a young schoolboy in Great Barrington, Massachusetts, that he was seen as different and "a problem" by his classmates, Du Bois spent most of his ninety-five years writing about what he could and could not do as a Black American. Even at the very end of his life, when he left the United States for Ghana, Du Bois was still figuring out his place in the world.

Searching for vocation is a deep human need that different cultures and different historical eras have treated differently. My suggestion here is that colleges and universities today need to acknowledge the educative drive one can see in the lives of people like W. E. B. Du Bois, Jane Addams, and Benjamin Franklin, and, recognizing the essentially vocational character of that drive, find ways to make vocational exploration central to liberal education.

VOCATIONAL EXPLORATION AND FACULTY ROLES

I trust that the difference I assume between vocational and occupational exploration is clear already. Vocational exploration is about identity formation within the context of a particular society and a particular time. Occupational exploration, by contrast, is considering one's job alternatives. Vocational exploration is, in my view, the job of the faculty; occupational exploration is a matter for the office of career services.

To make vocational exploration a more important aspect of liberal education, faculty will need to re-think their roles. They will need to take seriously John Dewey's admonition that if one teaches math, history, or science in school, one must remember that it is people that one is really teaching, and not the subject matter. The subject matter is the medium through which one seeks to nurture habits of deliberation and orientations toward inquiry. It is the medium through which one helps people to learn to learn. Hopefully, the subject matter of the school curriculum is also important knowledge that is worth mastering. Still, it is worth acknowledging that teaching is not merely about furnishing the mind. It is equally, if not more importantly, about shaping, energizing, and refining the mind.

This is difficult for teachers in K-12 schools to keep in mind, and it is even more difficult for professors. Virtually all professors are trained as scholars. A number are now also being trained as teachers. Even when teaching is presented to graduate students as an art to be valued and mastered, it is still one's scholarly credentials that tend to get one a job, and it is certainly one's scholarly credentials that determine whether one wins tenure. Hence, it will take determined, steady work to convince faculty members that they are, first, teaching young people, and secondly, teaching some aspect of the field they profess.

More important, giving increased primacy to overall student development will also necessitate institutional reform. As we all know, colleges and universities, especially the most selective, are reluctant to modify the model that has helped them to thrive for more than fifty years. As Louis Menand recently observed in the *New York Review of Books,* from the end of World War II until quite recently, universities flourished if they gave priority to research and publication and increasingly specialized knowledge. This enabled the faculty to view their teaching and advisement responsibilities as less important than their "own work," which was fairly transparent code for going to the library or laboratory to develop new ideas.

Giving teaching and advisement equal priority among faculty activities will be necessary to engage faculty more centrally in the lives and vocational concerns of their students. And that is not all that will need to be altered to give more emphasis to matters of vocation.

HUMANISTIC VALUES

Generally, today, core liberal arts subjects are taught in ways that are intended to give students an introduction to characteristic ways of thinking in a discipline, to the essential elements of an area, and, more generally, to what I would call the map of knowledge in some particular domain. All that is important. But the purposes currently most commonly associated with liberal arts study represent an unnecessarily narrow conception of why one should read Shakespeare or consider the ideas of French philosophers.

In addition to their canonical value, subjects like these have humanistic value. They can and should encourage thought about oneself and others and about virtue and vice—the good, the bad, and the ugly. They can and should encourage thought about vocation, in the broad sense in which I am using this word. As the philosopher William James once asserted, a liberal education should "help you...know a good man when you see him." That is because a liberal education, at least according to James, is not a matter of taking certain specific courses, but rather of viewing any subject in terms of its "humanistic value," its value to illuminate the human condition.

Of course, in many liberal arts classes there is discussion of the humanistic side of things. But without neglecting canonical perspectives, which are important for helping students locate knowledge in historical or cultural perspective, the humanistic side of things could be given greater emphasis if faculty members spent more time talking with students about what they could learn and what they are learning about their own interests, values, and sense of person and place as well as what they are learning about the subject matter in question.

Going "meta" with students, by which I mean helping them realize that they should be learning about themselves while reading *The Tempest* or debating Camus and not merely becoming culturally literate, is not something, at least in my experience, that faculty members tend to do systematically and on a regular basis. They tend not to do this because they tend not to have learned about meta-cognition. They tend not to know that it is pedagogically powerful to help students understand how and why they can learn what they are learning. Being subject-matter specialists as opposed to teachers, they tend not to touch upon the personal because they are instead inclined to focus on insuring an understanding of, say, the play's structure or meaning. Taking this one step further to capture in addition how and why the play connects to particular students is to take a step beyond a faculty member's role at least as traditionally configured. It would require pedagogical knowledge that many professors lack. But doing this would likely enhance a student's interest. It would offer a vital, personal reason for studying Shakespeare beyond knowing that somehow it is good to be "cultured."

Vocational interests can make the liberal arts more compelling to students, and so can tying programs of liberal education quite directly to the world and its problems. This is happening increasingly on college campuses today as more and more institutions offer programs of service learning. More often than not, however, such programs are special courses often linked to community service of one kind or another. What I have in mind is broader.

Emerson observed that without action "thought can never ripen into truth." If that is, indeed, the case, as I believe it is, then, virtually all college classes should have some kind of practicum attached to them. There is a lot of this already going on, but there needs to be more translation of classroom abstractions into action. This would enhance learning because the test of knowledge is in its application and also because constantly having opportunities to act in the world will help students develop a sense of vocation.

Having to help their students apply the models and theories they were presenting in their classes would also present faculty with a salutary challenge. After all, the efficacy of a professor's ideas would be evident in his or her students' worldly competence. That is a high threshold for faculty accountability, but one that is not out of line in our times. The challenges we face domestically and globally are vast. With poverty, disease, and inequity fueling attacks on secular democracies around the world, we cannot allow colleges and universities to be home to what Alfred North Whitehead called "inert ideas." Instead, we need to encourage faculty to become engaged with the problems around us in ways that will at once contribute to our society as well as to their students and their own competence and even wisdom as scholars.

RECALLING OUR MISSION

None of what I have said is very new or original. But I believe that the problems facing all of us require recalling what our collective mission is. Colleges and universities grew up across the United States for all sorts of reasons. Many were founded to ensure the continuance of a particular religious group. Some were established to increase the land values in a small town. All were intended to educate people who could provide the leadership necessary to improve society. That's why the capstone experience for nineteenth century college students at liberal arts colleges was a course in moral philosophy usually taught by the college's president. The course was intended to ensure that graduates would know their responsibilities as college-educated people (actually, with few exceptions, college-educated men). It provided a last chance to inculcate values and a sense of one's self as an educated citizen. It offered a final window on the opportunities and challenges then current in the locality and the region and across the United States.

I do not entirely live in the past and I do not think we can revive moral philosophy classes. But I do think we need to re-embrace the logic behind them. Liberal education should establish one's sense of direction, one's knowledge of one's self as an active, effective person and citizen. Liberal education should ready one to participate in the defining issues of our times. Whether it's the AIDS epidemic in southern Africa, the chaos of states like Afghanistan that lack basic civil infrastructures, or the social anomalies we observe in our own country where there are, for example, racial achievement gaps among high school students in both wealthy, racially integrated suburbs and blighted urban areas, social challenges like these should be familiar to graduates of liberal arts colleges. They should have helped to define how graduates see themselves making a difference in the world.

By giving renewed emphasis to their vocational purposes, liberal arts colleges and universities can help people live productively, responsibly, and well, amidst all the confusions of the present times. By making matters of vocation central to all they do, liberal arts colleges and universities can play a more direct role in improving the world. This is not to say that detached, seemingly idle speculation and abstract knowledge do not have value—great value—in institutions of liberal learning. They do. My concern is balance and underscoring the educative power of vocational interests. The famed social psychologist Kurt Lewin once said, "There is nothing so useful as a good theory," and following his logic, I would like to close by saying: There is nothing more liberal or liberating than education approached with matters of vocation foremost in mind. Our students seem to know that. We should give them the kind of education they want and deserve.

REFLECTIVE WRITING QUESTIONS

1. Why does Lagemann include the stories of Franklin, Addams, and Du Bois in her essay? How does each of their stories support or extend her thesis?
2. Lagemann states that faculty should play a central role in the vocational exploration of their students. Talk to several of your teachers and ask them whether they agree. If they disagree, what are their reasons? If they agree, how do they believe faculty ought to accomplish this goal?
3. Have any teachers influenced your sense of vocation or helped you identify your calling in life? If so, how did that occur?

4. How can your college courses help you learn more about your interests, values, responsibilities, sense of place, and sense of self? Which ones have or are affecting your education this way?

DISCUSSION QUESTIONS

1. What do you make of the contradiction Lagemann notes in her essay: college students today are increasingly focused on career preparation but graduate without a clear sense of vocation?
2. Lagemann stresses the social aspects of vocation, stating that "Vocation exploration is about identity formation within the context of a particular society. . . ." Why is the social aspect of vocation so important?
3. According to Lagemann, in what ways can a liberal arts education help students discern their vocations?
4. Lagemann argues that teaching is not just about "furnishing the mind" of students. What else is it? Do you agree with her?
5. What does Lagemann mean by liberal arts subjects having "humanistic value?"

"Listening to Life"

Parker Palmer

Parker Palmer has written widely on the nature and purpose of education. He currently serves as a Senior Partner of the Center for Courage & Renewal, an organization he founded. "Listening to Life" is the first chapter in Palmer's book Let Your Life Speak.

> Some time when the river is ice ask me
> mistakes I have made. Ask me whether
> what I have done is my life. Others
> have come in their slow way into
> my thought, and some have tried to help
> or to hurt ask me what difference
> their strongest love or hate has made.
>
> I will listen to what you say.
> you and I can turn and look
> at the silent river and wait. We know
> the current is there, hidden; and there
> are comings and goings from miles away
> that hold the stillness exactly before us.
> What the river says, that is what I say.
>
> —William Stafford, "ASK ME"

"Ask me whether what I have done is my life?' For some, those words will be nonsense, nothing more than a poet's loose way with language and logic. Of course what I have done is my life! To what am I supposed to compare it?

But for others, and I am one, the poet's words will be precise, piercing, and disquieting. They remind me of moments when it is clear–if I have eyes to see—that the life that I am living is not the life that wants to live in me. In those moments I sometimes catch a glimpse of my true life, a life hidden like the river beneath the ice. And in the spirit of the poet, I wonder: What am I meant to do? Who am I meant to be?

I was in my early thirties when I began, literally, to wake up to questions about my vocation. By all appearances, things were going well, but the soul does not put much stock in appearances. Seeking a path more purposeful than accumulating wealth, holding power, winning at competition, or securing a career, I had started to understand that it is indeed possible to live a life other than one's own. Fearful that I was doing just that—but uncertain about the deeper, truer life I sensed hidden inside me, uncertain whether it was real or trustworthy or within reach—I would snap awake in the middle of the night and stare for long hours at the ceiling.

Then I ran across the old Quaker saying, "Let your life speak." I found those words encouraging, and I thought understood what they meant: "Let the highest truths and values guide you. Live up to those demanding standards in everything you do." Because I had heroes at the time who seemed to be doing exactly that, this exhortation had incarnate meaning for me—it meant living a life like that of Martin Luther King Jr. or Rosa Parks or Mahatma Gandhi or Dorothy Day, a life of high purpose.

So I lined up the loftiest ideals I could find and set out to achieve them. The results were rarely admirable, often laughable, and sometimes grotesque. But always they were unreal, a distortion of my true self—as must be the case when one lives from the outside in, not the inside out. I had simply found a "noble" way to live a life that was not my own, a life spent imitating heroes instead of listening to my heart.

Today, some thirty years later, "Let your life speak" means something else to me, a meaning faithful both to the ambiguity of those words and to the complexity of my own experience: "Before you tell your life what you intend to do with it, listen for what it intends to do with you. Before you tell your life what truths and values you have decided to live up to, let you life tell you what truths you embody, what values you represent."

My youthful understanding of "Let your life speak" led me to conjure up the highest values I could imagine and then try to conform my life to them whether they were mine or not. If that sounds like what we are *supposed* to do with values, it is because that is what we are too often taught. There is a simplistic brand of moralism among us that wants to reduce the ethical life to making a list, checking it twice—against the index in some best-selling book of virtues, perhaps—and then trying very hard to be not naughty but nice.

There may be moments in life when we are so unformed that we need to use values like an exoskeleton to keep us from collapsing. But something is very wrong if such moments recur often in adulthood. Trying to live someone else's life, or to live by an abstract norm, will invariably fail—and may even do great damage.

Vocation, the way I was seeking it, becomes an act of will, a grim determination that one's life will go this way or that whether it wants to or not. If the self is sin-ridden and will bow to truth and goodness only under duress, that approach to vocation makes sense. But if the self seeks not pathology but wholeness, as I believe it does, then the willful pursuit of vocation is an act of violence toward ourselves—violence in the name of a vision that, however lofty, is forced on the self from without rather than grown from within. True self, when violated, will always resist us, sometimes at great cost, holding our lives in check until we honor its truth.

Vocation does not come from willfulness. It comes from listening. I must listen to my life and try to understand what it is truly about—quite apart from what I would like it to be about—or my life will never represent anything real in the world, no matter how earnest my intentions.

That insight is hidden in the word *vocation* itself, which is rooted in the Latin for "voice." Vocation does not mean a goal that I pursue. It means a calling that I hear. Before I can tell my life what I want to do with it, I must listen to my life telling me who I am. I must listen for the truths and values at the heart of my own identity, not the standards by which I *must* live—but the standards by which I cannot help but live if I am living my own life.

Behind this understanding of vocation is a truth that the ego does not want to hear because it threatens the ego's turf: everyone has a life that is different from the "I" of daily consciousness, a life that is trying to live through the "I" who is its vessel. This is what the poet knows and what every wisdom tradition teaches: there is a great gulf between the way my ego wants to identify me, with its protective masks and self-serving fictions, and my true self.

It takes time and hard experience to sense the difference between the two—to sense that running beneath the surface of the experience I call my life, there is a deeper and truer life waiting to be acknowledged. That fact alone makes "listen to your life" difficult counsel to follow. The difficulty is compounded by the fact that from our first days in school, we are taught to listen to everything and everyone but ourselves, to take all our clues about living from the people and powers around us.

I sometimes lead retreats, and from time to time participants show me the notes they are taking as the retreat unfolds. The pattern is nearly universal: people take copious notes on what the retreat leader says, and they sometimes take notes on the words of certain wise people in the group, but rarely, if ever, do they take notes on what they themselves say. We listen for guidance everywhere except from within.

I urge retreatants to turn their note-taking around, because the words we speak often contain counsel we are trying to give ourselves. We have a strange conceit in our culture that simply because we have said something, we understand what it means! But often we do not—especially when we speak from a deeper place than intellect or ego, speak the kind of words that arise when the inner teacher feels safe enough to tell its truth. At those moments, we need to listen to what our lives are saying *and* take notes on it, lest we forget our own truth or deny that we ever heard it.

Verbalizing is not the only way our lives speak, of course. They speak through our actions and reactions, our intuitions and instincts, our feelings and bodily states of being, perhaps more profoundly than through our words. We are like plants, full of tropisms that draw us toward certain experiences and repel us from others. If we can learn to read our own responses to our own experience—a text we are writing unconsciously every day we spend on earth—we will receive the guidance we need to live more authentic lives.

But, if I am to let my life speak things I want to hear, things I would gladly tell others, I must also let it speak things I do not want to hear and would never tell anyone else! My life is not only about my strengths and virtues; it is also about my liabilities and my limits, my trespasses and my shadow. An inevitable though often ignored dimension of the quest for "wholeness" is that we must embrace what we dislike or find shameful about ourselves as well as what we are confident and proud of. That is why the poet says, "ask me mistakes I have made."

In the chapters to come, I speak often of my own mistakes—of wrong turns I have taken, of misreadings of my own reality—for hidden in these moments are important clues to my own vocation. I do not feel despondent about my mistakes, any more than the poet does, though I grieve the pain they have sometimes caused others. Our lives are "experiments with truth" (to borrow the subtitle of Gandhi's autobiography), and in an experiment negative results are at least as important as successes! I have no idea how I would have learned the truth about myself and my calling without the mistakes I have made, though by that measure I should have written a much longer book!

How we are to listen to our lives is a question worth exploring. In our culture, we tend to gather information in ways that do not work very well when the source is the human soul: the soul is not responsive to subpoenas or cross-examinations. At best it will stand in the dock only long enough to plead the Fifth Amendment. At worst it will jump bail and never be heard from again. The soul speaks its truth only under quiet, inviting, and trustworthy conditions.

The soul is like a wild animal—tough, resilient, savvy, self-sufficient, and yet exceedingly shy. If we want to see a wild animal, the last thing we should do is to go crashing through the woods, shouting for the creature to come out. But if we are willing to walk quietly into the woods and sit silently for an hour or two at the base of a tree, the creature we are waiting for may well emerge, and out of the corner of an eye we will catch a glimpse of the precious wildness we seek.

That is why the poem at the head of this chapter ends in silence—and why I find it a bit embarrassing that as this chapter ends, I am drawing the reader not toward silence but toward speech, page after page of speech! I hope that my speech is faithful to what I have heard, in the silence, from my soul. And I hope that the reader who sits with this book can hear the silence that always surrounds us in the writing and reading of words. It is a silence that forever invites us to fathom the meaning of our lives—and forever reminds us of depths of meaning that words will never touch.

REFLECTIVE WRITING QUESTIONS

1. At one point in the essay, Palmer states that the life he was living was not the life that wanted to live in him. What does he mean by this?
2. Palmer claims that too often we live our lives according to imposed virtues, standards, and expectations. What are the sources of these imposed expectations in your life? Do you agree with Palmer that they are antithetical to your true identity?
3. What does Palmer mean when he says that one must live from the inside out, not from the outside in?
4. What are the more important mistakes you've made in your life? What did you learn from them? How did they help you better understand yourself?
5. What might you do to better understand the life you are being called to lead? How might that help?

DISCUSSION QUESTIONS

1. Why does Palmer open his essay with a poem? How does the poem shape your reading of what follows?
2. If, like Palmer, we tried to let our lives speak, how might that influence how we act?
3. Palmer asserts that true vocation comes from listening. What does he mean by that? Why does he think it is so difficult for people today to accomplish this?
4. Given what you have read, do you believe that Palmer sees vocational pursuit as an individual endeavor, a social matter, or some mix of the two?
5. The tone of Palmer's piece is almost confessional. What is the effect of this tone? How does it influence the way you read the essay or what you think of Palmer?

On Freedom of Expression and Campus Speech Codes

The statement that follows was approved by the Association's Committee A on Academic Freedom and Tenure in June 1992 and adopted by the Association's Council in November 1994.

Freedom of thought and expression is essential to any institution of higher learning. Universities and colleges exist not only to transmit knowledge. Equally, they interpret, explore, and expand that knowledge by testing the old and proposing the new.

This mission guides learning outside the classroom quite as much as in class, and often inspires vigorous debate on those social, economic, and political issues that arouse the strongest passions. In the process, views will be expressed that may seem to many wrong, distasteful, or offensive. Such is the nature of freedom to sift and winnow ideas.

On a campus that is free and open, no idea can be banned or forbidden. No viewpoint or message may be deemed so hateful or disturbing that it may not be expressed.

Universities and colleges are also communities, often of a residential character. Most campuses have recently sought to become more diverse, and more reflective of the larger community, by attracting students, faculty, and staff from groups that were historically excluded or underrepresented. Such gains as they have made are recent, modest, and tenuous. The campus climate can profoundly affect an institution's continued diversity. Hostility or intolerance to persons who differ from the majority (especially if seemingly condoned by the institution) may undermine the confidence of new members of the community. Civility is always fragile and can easily be destroyed.

In response to verbal assaults and use of hateful language, some campuses have felt it necessary to forbid the expression of racist, sexist, homophobic, or ethnically demeaning speech, along with conduct or behavior that harasses.

Several reasons are offered in support of banning such expression. Individuals and groups that have been victims of such expression feel an understandable outrage. They claim that the academic progress of minority and majority alike may suffer if fears, tensions, and conflicts spawned by slurs and insults create an environment inimical to learning.

These arguments, grounded in the need to foster an atmosphere respectful of and welcoming to all persons, strike a deeply responsive chord in the academy. But, while we can acknowledge both the weight of these concerns and the thoughtfulness of those persuaded of the need for regulation, rules that ban or punish speech based upon its content cannot be justified. An institution of higher learning fails to fulfill its mission if it asserts the power to proscribe ideas—and racial or ethnic slurs, sexist epithets, or homophobic insults almost always express ideas, however repugnant. Indeed, by proscribing any ideas, a university sets an example that profoundly disserves its academic mission.

Some may seek to defend a distinction between the regulation of the content of speech and the regulation of the manner (or style) of speech. We find this distinction untenable in practice because offensive style or opprobrious phrases may in fact have been chosen precisely for their expressive power. As the United States Supreme Court has said in the course of rejecting criminal sanctions for offensive words:

> [W]ords are often chosen as much for their emotive as their cognitive force. We cannot sanction the view that the Constitution, while solicitous of the cognitive content of individual speech, has little or no regard for that emotive function which, practically speaking, may often be the more important element of the over-all message sought to be communicated.

The line between substance and style is thus too uncertain to sustain the pressure that will inevitably be brought to bear upon disciplinary rules that attempt to regulate speech.

Proponents of speech codes sometimes reply that the value of emotive language of this type is of such a low order that, on balance, suppression is justified by the harm suffered by those who are directly affected, and by the general damage done to the learning environment. Yet a college or university sets a perilous course if it seeks to differentiate between high-value and low-value speech, or to choose which groups are to be protected by curbing the speech of others. A speech code unavoidably implies an institutional competence to distinguish permissible expression of hateful thought from what is proscribed as thoughtless hate.

Institutions would also have to justify shielding some, but not other, targets of offensive language—proscribing uncomplimentary references to sexual but not to political preference, to religious but not to philosophical creed, or perhaps even to some but not to other religious affiliations. Starting down this path creates an even greater risk that groups not originally protected may later demand similar solicitude—demands the institution that began the process of banning some speech is ill equipped to resist.

Distinctions of this type are neither practicable nor principled; their very fragility underscores why institutions devoted to freedom of thought and expression ought not adopt an institutionalized coercion of silence.

Moreover, banning speech often avoids consideration of means more compatible with the mission of an academic institution by which to deal with incivility, intolerance, offensive speech, and harassing behavior:

1. Institutions should adopt and invoke a range of measures that penalize conduct and behavior, rather than speech—such as rules against defacing property, physical intimidation or harassment, or disruption of campus activities. All members of the campus community should be made aware of such rules, and administrators should be ready to use them in preference to speech-directed sanctions.

2. Colleges and universities should stress the means they use best—to educate—including the development of courses and other curricular and co-curricular experiences designed to increase student understanding and to deter offensive or intolerant speech or conduct. These institutions should, of course, be free (indeed encouraged) to condemn manifestations of intolerance and discrimination, whether physical or verbal.

3. The governing board and the administration have a special duty not only to set an outstanding example of tolerance, but also to challenge boldly and condemn immediately serious breaches of civility.

4. Members of the faculty, too, have a major role; their voices may be critical in condemning intolerance, and their actions may set examples for understanding, making clear to their students that civility and tolerance are hallmarks of educated men and women.

5. Student-personnel administrators have in some ways the most demanding role of all, for hate speech occurs most often in dormitories, locker rooms, cafeterias, and student centers. Persons who guide this part of campus life should set high standards of their own for tolerance and should make unmistakably clear the harm that uncivil or intolerant speech inflicts.

To some persons who support speech codes, measures like these—relying as they do on suasion rather than sanctions—may seem inadequate. But freedom of expression requires toleration of "ideas we hate," as Justice Holmes put it. The underlying principle does not change because the demand is to silence a hateful speaker, or because it comes from within the academy. Free speech is not simply an aspect of the educational enterprise to be weighed against other desirable ends. It is the very precondition of the academic enterprise itself.

May 25, 1994

Hate-Speech Codes That Will Pass Constitutional Muster

Lawrence White

Lawrence White is University Counsel at Georgetown University. This article is adapted from a presentation at the Stetson University College of Law's National Conference on Law and Higher Education.

It has been a trying few years for the drafters of hate-speech codes on college and university campuses. The University of Pennsylvania jettisoned its controversial speech code last fall after President Sheldon Hackney, during his confirmation hearing to be Chairman of the National Endowment for the Humanities, questioned whether such codes were the right approach to achieving civility on campus. This year, Central Michigan University became the latest institution to lose a court fight over its speech code. Continuing an unbroken line of victories by the American Civil Liberties Union, a federal judge held in January that Central Michigan had violated its basketball coach's right to free speech when he was disciplined under its "discriminatory harassment" code after he used a racial epithet during a closed-door team meeting. At Wesleyan University, the University of Michigan, and numerous other institutions, administrators have given up and repealed their codes.

Due largely to the court decisions, we now understand the arguments against campus speech codes. They use inherently vague terminology; they are overbroad, sweeping within their regulatory ambit not only pernicious language, but also language that enjoys constitutional protection. "It is technically impossible to write an anti-speech code that cannot be twisted against speech nobody means to bar," concluded Eleanor Holmes Norton, a former Georgetown University law professor who is now the District of Columbia's Delegate to Congress.

Despite the problems raised by speech codes, however, we must not forget that there are salutary purposes underlying the effort to draft codes banning derogatory and hurtful epithets. Such codes were intended to serve, and still serve, an important educational purpose: They are expressions of an institution's commitment to the victims of a pernicious and destructive form of behavior. Whenever anybody commits an act or utters a remark that is motivated by hatefulness, it causes harm to a real, flesh-and-blood victim. Hate-speech codes designed to protect victims are a noble endeavor. If institutions abandon the effort to draft policies against hateful speech, they are abandoning the victims the policies were meant to protect.

Campus administrators can learn important lessons from the court cases against the first generation of speech codes. In every instance, the codes that provoked court challenges were ambitiously, almost sweepingly, worded. Several of them, including those at the University of Michigan and the University of Wisconsin, were modeled on the Equal Employment Opportunity Commission's guidelines on sexual harassment. They used concepts and terminology—"intimidating environment for education," "express or implied threat to an individual's academic efforts"—awkwardly borrowed from employment law. They treated the university campus as a single, undifferentiated "workplace."

The language they used seemed almost deliberately provocative to civil libertarians—phrases such as "expressive behavior" (University of Wisconsin) and other wording that equated physical behavior with verbal behavior (Central Michigan University)—as though there were no distinction under the First Amendment.

What we have come to refer to as "hate speech" takes many forms on the nation's college campuses. The most prevalent involves remarks by students addressed to other students. For every high-profile case involving a campus speech by Khalid Abdul Muhammad of the Nation of Islam, there are literally dozens, maybe hundreds, of incidents that occur behind the closed doors of dormitory rooms, in dining halls, or in the corridors outside student pubs. We know, regrettably, that a strong correlation exists between hate speech and alcohol abuse.

Colleges and universities must now craft a second generation of codes that will serve the important institutional objective of protecting the victims of hateful acts and utterances without violating constitutional principles. These codes would:

*Differentiate between dormitories and classrooms. In an article that appeared in the *Duke Law Journal* in 1990, Nadine Strossen, president of the ACLU, observed that the right to free speech applies with different force in different parts of a college campus. That right, she wrote, "may not be applicable to—students' dormitory rooms. These rooms constitute the students' homes. Accordingly, under established free-speech tenets, students should have the right to avoid being exposed to others' expression by seeking refuge in their rooms." A policy that disciplined students for the hateful acts or utterances against other students in residence halls would probably bring three-quarters of all hate-speech episodes within the regulatory purview of college administrators without offending traditional free-speech precepts.

*Be tailored to the Supreme Court's decision in *R.A.V. v. St. Paul, Minn.* This 1992 decision suggests that anti-discrimination codes are on shaky ground constitutionally if they proscribe some hateful acts or utterances but not others. Any policy that prohibits categories of speech "because of" or "on the basis of" a specific factor—such as race, gender, or sexual orientation—runs the risk of violating the Court's stricture in *R.A.V.* that laws must not single out particular categories of hateful speech for penalties. As ironic as it sounds, the safest hate-speech code may be one that makes no mention of the very groups it is designed to protect.

*Use words emphasizing action and its effects, instead of speech. First Amendment jurisprudence recognizes an important distinction between speech and action and allows a greater degree of latitude when action is being regulated. The first generation of campus speech codes used vocabulary emphasizing speech, which virtually doomed them in advance—for example, they barred certain "comments" or "expressive behavior." By fostering the impression that these policies regulated pure speech, they made an easy target. The receptiveness of courts to arguments that the codes were overbroad—prohibiting speech that should be constitutionally protected along with utterances that deserve no protection (such as yelling "Fire!" in a crowded theater)—requires campuses to be more careful than they were in the past to draft constitutionally acceptable speech codes.

The second generation of codes should favor "action" vocabulary—prohibiting hostile conduct or behavior that might "incite immediate violence" (the latter being the exact phrasing used in the Supreme Court's half-century-old "fighting words" case, *Chaplinsky v. New Hampshire*). Instead of calling them "hate-speech codes," colleges and universities should refer to the new policies as "anti-hate" or "anti-discrimination" codes.

*Enhance the penalties for alcohol-related hate mongering. Most campus conduct codes allow the imposition of disciplinary sanctions for disorderly conduct or violations of drug and alcohol policies. It would be constitutionally defensible to treat hateful acts or utterances as an additional factor to be taken into account when meting out punishment for code violations. For example, a student found guilty of public drunkenness could be sentenced to attend a program designed to treat alcohol abuse, but the same inebriated student could be suspended or expelled for hurling racial epithets or threats at fellow students.

Drafting a new generation of campus codes to curb hate mongering, codes that zero in on areas of highest risk (dormitories, drunkenness) while avoiding the vagueness and overbreadth that doomed the first generation of codes, is an exercise worth undertaking. Colleges and universities began attempting to regulate hate speech a decade ago for an important reason—to communicate a message of support to the victims of hate. That reason is still compelling today. If institutions abandon the effort to implement constitutionally acceptable codes, they will be sending a message chillingly and accurately expressed by the Stanford Univeristy law professor Charles Lawrence in an article that accompanied Ms. Strossen's in the 1990 *Duke Law Journal:*

"I fear that by framing the debate as we have—as one in which the liberty of free speech is in conflict with the elimination of racism—we have advanced the cause of racial oppression and have placed the bigot on the moral high ground, fanning the rising flames of racism."

We all understand civil libertarians' concerns when universities approach the delicate task of regulating certain forms of expressive conduct. But civil libertarians in turn should appreciate the message that is communicated when the rights of insensitive, viciously motivated members of college and university communities are placed above victims' rights to an education untainted by bigoted animosity. By trimming their drafting sails to incorporate the lessons of the first round of court cases, college administrators can satisfy constitutional concerns and at the same time curb the most egregious forms of hate mongering on campus. Then they can send an appropriate message to perpetrator and victim alike: Hateful utterances and behavior are repugnant forms of conduct that colleges and universities will not tolerate.

Fairness To All: Free Speech and Civility in Conflict

"*The harm of exercising certain constitutional rights in certain contexts is not a new concpt.*"
For Narrowly Tailored Limitations on Gender-Based Discriminatory Speech

Ann Browning Masters
St. John River Community College

Ann Browning Masters *is a counselor on the St. Augustine campus of St. John River Community College.*

A major issue on college campuses across the country is the extent to which institutions of higher learning may impose regulations or speech codes to ban sexually harassive speech that is believed to foster gender-based discrimination. This thorny problem, which sees to balance the competing interests of preserving free speech on campus while maintaining a learning environment that is free from harassive speech, goes to the heart of the nature of an institution of higher learning. Dr. Masters takes the position that narrowly crafted controls are necessary to make colleges and universities inviting to all. Dr. Dagley adopts the opposite perspective. He responds that even though speech codes may, so to speak, have their hearts in the right places by attempting to remove hateful speech from campuses, they are improper because they violate the First Amendment by undermining the purpose of institutions of higher learning as places where people can express their minds freely.

FOR NARROWLY TAILORED LIMITATIONS ON GENDER-BASED DISCRIMINATORY SPEECH

The following discussion is limited to the examination of issues pertaining to hostile environment harassment, where sexually harassive speech has been found actionable. This article illustrates how harm can be, and has been, perpetrated through speech that is sexually harassive and that the origin of certain case law used in prohibiting speech does not recognize the harm inflicted by the verbally or symbolically harassive hostile environment.

Current legal standards for limiting speech applied to slander and "fighting words" do not provide support for restricting the harassive speech of the hostile environment. When dealing with slander, the basis of harm is the loss from injury to "reputation, community standing, office, trade, business, or means of livelihood" (*Black's Law Dictionary*, 1990, p. 1244). This injury is akin to the harm of quid pro quo harassment, where tangible loss is suffered from not acquiescing to sexual demands. In hostile environment sexual harassment, however, noneconomic harm is experienced.

The fighting words standard of *Chaplinsky v. New Hampshire* (1942), which gives no protection for words which tend to incite an immediate breach of the peace, also provides difficulty in recognizing harm from sexually harassing words. This case law is reflective of a society that had evolved from one sanctioning duels as a method for resolving personal insult to viewing fisticuffs as a socially acceptable phenomenon for protesting unwelcome or demeaning words. Then, as now, it can be argued that physical violence as a method of conflict resolution was practiced mostly by men. Moreover, *Chaplinsky* recognized social acceptance of such physical violence by validating it as one natural response to insult, although it was not the most natural reply for women who felt themselves to be degraded by speech.[1] Because a "Thelma and Louise" standard of response to harassment has not entered social mores, it is unlikely that speech realistically could be abridged using this focus of *Chaplinsky.*

Case law that is de facto gender based, such as *Chaplinsky,* provides a standard for determining harm that will not be met by most of the population experiencing verbal hostile environment sexual harassment.[2] Case law of the nature also suggests that risking a charge of assault and battery is a viable method of indicating that sexual harassment is an egregious form of personal insult. Reasoning that ignores the fact that persons who wish to remain employed or in class often do not respond to verbal harassment in a physical manner is similar to reasoning that defines rape as occurring only after both arms and legs of the victim were broken during the commission of the crime.

Does the law that requires a tangible loss or imminent breach of peace in order to limit speech square with discrimination law that recognizes severe and pervasive discriminatory speech, even absent a tangible loss, as a violation of civil rights? An answer may be found in reviewing *Meritor Savings Bank v. Vinson* (1986), where the argument that harm occurs only from the tangible loss incurred by quid pro quo sexual harassment was not upheld. Instead, the Court recognized the Equal Employment Opportunities Commission's (EEOC) reliance on prior "judicial decisions and EEOC precedent holding that Title VII affords employees the right to work in an environment free from discriminatory intimidation, ridicule, and insult" (*Meritor,* p. 65). It reasoned that because this principle had been applied to harassment based on race, religion, and national origin, "a hostile environment based on discriminatory sexual harassment should not likewise be prohibited" (*Meritor,* p. 65) from being actionable. The egregiousness of the non-tangible harm of being forced to endure severe and pervasive discriminatory speech was, in effect, recognized in *Meritor.*

Research indicates that in addition to voluntarily dropping courses, changing majors, and changing graduate programs to avoid harassment, noneconomic harm from sexual harassment is reflected in negative changes in psychological and physical health and well-being.[3] Other categories of harm from a hostile environment include the time and effort costs of coping when considering or pursuing a case of hostile environment sexual harassment, negative differential social learning from the imposition of different gender standards for performance, punishment reflected in not allowing the person bringing a claim of hostile environment sexual harassment to continue in daily or planned routine, and altered or deflected educational or career goals due to coping with harassment (see Masters, Milford, & Curcio, 1993). Clearly, the harm from discriminatory speech has been well documented.

Given this review of harm, the antidote of counterspeech that is often suggested to counter offensive speech may be viewed as incomplete, ineffective, and sometimes inappropriate. Other research cites flaws in the "marketplace of ideas" metaphor concerning discriminatory speech (Strauss, 1990). This metaphor relies upon an opportunity for rational and open discussion, a chance for confrontation, and lack of retaliation that would preclude or inhibit discourse; in other words, a perfect marketplace. Because sexual harassment is an issue of power, it is hard to imagine a work or educational setting where subordinates would feel completely free to engage in confrontational dialogue with superiors who "rationally" find it acceptable to discriminate on the basis of gender.

Absent an opportunity for open and equal discussion and with concern for retaliation, to insist on counterspeech as a remedy for discriminatory speech almost guarantees that employees and students must also consider the consequences of quid pro quo discrimination if their superior chooses to view counterspeech as irrational, unprofessional, or insubordinate. This is an undue burden that superiors or other co-workers not subjected to discriminatory speech are not asked to bear.

Therefore, a narrowly tailored threshold for actionable discriminatory speech may be proposed on the basis of the effect of discriminatory speech and not the suppression of ideas. In *Harris v. Forklift Systems* (1993), the Supreme

Court has provided the framework for this threshold through its review of the intent of Title VII and clarification of actionable harm. Further support may be found in *Robinson v. Jacksonville Shipyards* (1991), where First Amendment concerns were addressed in relation to discriminatory speech.

Based on the above rulings, the following should be considered in determining whether speech is actionable sexual harassment:

1. Did the speech occur in an environment under the constraint of Title VII of the Civil Rights Act of 1964 or Title IX of the Education Amendments of 1972 (i.e., in a work or education setting?)
2. Was the speech unwelcome?
3. Was the speech pervasive or severe?
4. Does the complainant view the speech as discriminatory based on gender?
5. Would a reasonable person view the speech as discriminatory based on gender?
6. Was the complainant exposed to disadvantageous terms or conditions from the speech to which others of another gender were not exposed?
7. In reviewing all of the circumstances, does the environment appear hostile or abusive to a person or persons of one gender and not the other?
8. Does the educational institution or employer intend to express itself in the manner of the alleged discriminatory speech?
9. Is a discriminatory harm produced by the speech through disparate treatment or disparate impact based on gender?
10. Is the opportunity for the speech available in a different time, place, or manner?
11. Is the complainant a captive audience or part of a captive audience?
12. Does the speech have a discernible negative effect upon discipline, order, or morale in the environment?
13. Did the speech seem insulting or degrading based upon gender?
14. Would the speech have likely been addressed to a person of another gender?

With the exception of question 8, affirmative responses to the questions should indicate that the effect of the speech needs further examination. This framework for regulation of speech provides for the governmental interest of prohibiting discrimination by focusing on the differentiation by gender and ensuring content neutrality by focusing on the context and effect of the speech and not the suppression of the idea or its content.

A context—rather than content-based limitation differentiates between speech that discriminates and speech that promotes discrimination by focusing on effect and not message. This restriction has commonsense precedent concerning other constitutional rights. One may own a gun but may not be able to take or use it in certain settings such as a classroom. One may jokingly yell "Fire!" in the street, but not in the theater. The harm of exercising certain constitutional rights in certain contexts is not a new concept.

The difficulty in balancing compelling interests is certainly evident when considering freedom from discrimination and freedom of speech. However, the difficulty of the task does not justify its avoidance. The suggested context and effect-based approach provides a beginning that can be understood in relation to balancing other rights, affirms the right to work or become educated without the undue burden of discrimination, and recognizes the value of maintaining untrammeled avenues for expression.

NOTES

1. See the analysis of 1992 FBI Uniform Crime Reports by Steven Bennett Weisburd and Brian Levin (1994) concerning murder in the United States by sex of victim/offender where reported incidents of murder of female victim/male offender are significantly higher than incidents of male victim/female offender and female victim/female offender. The article also cited research on spousal murder indicating that men who murdered wives from whom they were separated viewed murder as a response to the "offense" of being left, obviously an extreme reaction of physical violence to behavior and speech that did not inflict physical harm and that occurs significantly less by women in the same situation.
2. See Truax (1989), Dozier (1990), and Fitzgerald (1993). Summaries of national reports indicate that 95% of sexual harassment is directed by men toward women and estimate that approximately 50% of women in work and education settings have experienced some form of sexual harassment.
3. These negative changes were found to include anxiety, depression, headaches, sleep disturbance, gastrointestinal disorders, weight loss/gain, nausea, sexual dysfunction, posttraumatic stress disorder, elevated fears of rape, and lowered self-esteem (Fitzgerald, 1993, pp. 1071–1072).

REFERENCES

Black's Law Dictionary. (1990). St. Paul, MN: West.

Chaplinsky v. New Hampshire, 315 U.S. 568, 572 (1942).

Dozier, J. (1990). Sexual harassment: It can happen here. *AGB Reports, 32,* 15–20.

Fitzgerald, L. (1993) Sexual Harassment: Violence against women in the workplace. *American Psychologist, 48,* 1070–1076.

Harris v. Forklift Systems, 106 S. Ct. 367 (1993).

Masters, A. B., Milford, A. C., & Curcio, J.L. (1993, June). *The cost of the hostile environment: An analysis of campus cases 1987–1992.* Paper presented at the annual meeting of the American Association of University Women Symposium on Gender Issues in the Classroom and on the Campus, Minneapolis, MN.

Meritor Savings Bank v. Vinson, 477 U.S. 57 (1986).

Robinson v. Jacksonville Shipyards, 760 F. Supp. 1486 (M.D. Fla. 1991).

Strauss, M. (1990). Sexist speech in the workplace. *Harvard Civil Rights-Civil Liberties Law Review, 25*(1).

Truax, A. (1989). Sexual harassment in higher education: What we've learned. *Thought and Action,* 5, 25–32.

Weisburd, B., & Levin, B. (1994) On the basis of sex: Recognizing gender-based bias crimes. *Stanford Law and Policy Review,* 5(2), 21–47.

December 1, 2006

Only Speech Codes Should Be Censored

Gary Pavela

Gary Pavela serves as director of judicial programs at the University of Maryland at College Park.

I often ask audience members at higher-education conferences how many of them come from campuses with "hate speech" codes. A substantial minority raise their hands, confirming research that about a third of the nation's colleges and universities continue to promulgate student disciplinary rules prohibiting expression that "subordinates" others or is "demeaning, offensive, or hateful."

Such continued adherence to speech codes is by now predictable, but remains puzzling. From a lawyer's perspective, the courts have spoken: Broadly written speech codes adopted by public institutions—and private institutions adhering to First Amendment standards—are unconstitutional. The legal parameters are becoming so well settled that enforcement of those codes may expose public-college administrators to personal liability for violating clearly established constitutional rights.

Understanding the speech-code phenomenon, however, requires looking beyond the law to the realities of campus politics. However sporadically enforced, speech codes serve the administrative purpose of broadcasting an easily identifiable institutional commitment to providing a safe and welcoming environment to a wide array of presumably vulnerable students. What's rarely considered, however, is the likely long-term impact on those very students whom administrators seek to protect.

We live in a disputatious society. Beyond a few narrowly defined exceptions to the First Amendment (such as "true threats," defamation, and "severe or pervasive sexual harassment"), our graduates won't be able to turn to a protective government to silence expression they don't like. How are we preparing them to participate in a contentious marketplace of ideas, other than training them to shout a reflexive "Shut up!"?

Court cases testing the limits of the First Amendment usually involve provocative expression. Provocative expression, in turn, tends to be associated with social, political, or ethnic minorities' striving to make themselves heard. Those minorities will be at greatest risk from speech-code enforcement, since majorities on college campuses and elsewhere are unlikely to censor themselves. A classic example in the higher-education setting is the 1973 U.S. Supreme Court decision in Papish v. Board of Curators of the University of Missouri. The petitioner in that case—a journalism graduate student with a prior history of circulating what the university regarded as "pornographic, indecent and obscene" literature from the Students for a Democratic Society—was expelled for selling an underground newspaper that featured a front-page cartoon depicting policemen raping the Statue of Liberty and the Goddess of Justice, and that contained an article with an expletive as a title.

The Supreme Court reversed the student's expulsion and stated that "the mere dissemination of ideas—no matter how offensive to good taste—on a state university campus may not be shut off in the name alone of 'conventions of decency.'" The court rejected the argument that the expression was "obscene" (i.e., appealed to prurient interests) and concluded that "precedents of this Court make it equally clear that neither the political cartoon nor the headline story involved in this case can be labeled as constitutionally obscene or otherwise unprotected."

There is nothing remarkable about the court's conclusion. It echoes Justice Hugo Black's classic dissenting opinion in Communist Party v. Control Board (1961) that the "freedoms of speech, press, petition and assembly guaranteed by the First Amendment must be accorded to the ideas we hate or sooner or later they will be denied to the ideas we cherish." And it can be found in more-recent decisions, like Rosenberger v. University of Virginia (1995), where the court saw student freedom of expression in a campus "marketplace of ideas" as the foundation of higher education itself:

"In ancient Athens, and, as Europe entered into a new period of intellectual awakening, in places like Bologna, Oxford, and Paris, universities began as voluntary and spontaneous assemblages or concourses for students to speak and to write and to learn. . . . For the University, by regulation, to cast disapproval on particular viewpoints of its students risks the suppression of free speech and creative inquiry in one of the vital centers for the nation's intellectual life, its college and university campuses."

What's striking, then, about the Papish case is not the majority opinion, but the dissents by Chief Justice Warren Burger and Justice William Rehnquist.

Chief Justice Burger summarized a core element of their argument when he wrote, "In theory, at least, a university is not merely an arena for the discussion of ideas by students and faculty; it is also an institution where individuals learn to express themselves in acceptable, civil terms." Burger's perspective—that student freedom of expression on college campuses could be circumscribed by pedagogical concerns both in and outside the classroom—would have provided a legal foundation for campus speech codes, had it ever attracted a majority on the court.

Yet out of many law-review articles promoting the campus speech-code movement in the 1980s, I found none that commended the Burger or Rehnquist dissents in Papish. That's a remarkable omission. Why not highlight a key dissent from the chief justice that advances your position? The only conceivable answer is that supporters of speech codes on the left were reluctant to concede that such codes were also attractive to the ideological right. In those heady, self-righteous days, no one wanted to acknowledge that giving universities broadly defined powers to censor uncivil speech might be used in ways most speech-code advocates wouldn't like.

Unfortunately, the fundamental agreement between the right and left on the need to promote campus civility was primarily a consensus about methodology. Both depended on punishment rather than education, suasion, and peer influence. The end result went beyond a series of failed speech codes at some of the nation's leading universities—all eventually struck down by the courts. It ultimately promoted a culture of silence on issues of race and constituted a lost opportunity to teach students how to confront "bad" expression with expression that was better reasoned and better expressed.

Perhaps the best post-mortem of a failed speech code involved the University of Wisconsin code, struck down by a federal court in 1991. In a 1993 Los Angeles Times Magazine article, the Pulitzer-Prize-winning writer Barry Siegel reported that Roger Howard—the associate dean of students at the Madison campus, an initial supporter of the code, and an administrator charged with its enforcement—eventually concluded that "it's better policy not to have a code. . . . The human instinct—or the American instinct—for censorship is just too strong." Howard was particularly concerned that the code promoted a "McCarthyesque venue. . . . I've heard of students saying 'Shhh—don't say anything about affirmative action, the university will punish you.' . . . I think there was a chilling effect."

Siegel's 1993 article on the demise of the UW code, however, also helps explain why speech codes continue to endure on other campuses more than a decade later: "Beyond the desired diversity of color and gender," he wrote, "surely there was also an enforced orthodoxy of thought and expression. . . . [A] mid all this talk of the code's value as symbol, it was a bit unclear just whom the symbol was meant to protect—minority students from harassment by racists or UW leadership from denunciation by minorities." Speech codes, in other words, may serve the primary purpose of diverting attention from more substantive issues of inclusion and civility, allowing administrators to focus on cosmetic approaches unlikely to produce any lasting change in campus cultures.

In 2003, following a lawsuit by a free-speech advocacy group, a federal judge issued an injunction against Shippensburg University that barred it from enforcing parts of its speech code. The university abandoned its code in 2004, even though the case's plaintiffs had not been punished for violating it. The court observed, "While we recognize that citing students under the suspect provisions has not been a common practice, in the hands of another administration these provisions could certainly be used to truncate debate and free expression by students." Indeed, one of the student plaintiffs in the case asserted that she "was reluctant to advance certain controversial theories or ideas regarding any number of political or social issues because . . . she feared that discussion of such theories might be sanctionable."

The Shippensburg case highlights that even dormant speech codes continue to depend upon explicit or implicit threats of punishment. The only beneficiaries of that approach have been a new cohort of campus conservative activists, who thrive on the excitement and attention of being portrayed as First Amendment martyrs.

College administrators simply haven't given sufficient thought to creative alternatives, even though recurring speech-code controversies have created opportunities to promote the holy grail of undergraduate education: enhanced skills in listening, reasoning, gathering and weighing evidence, considering the aims and feelings of others, and understanding core components of citizenship, like the responsibility to protect and promote constitutional freedoms.

Administrators looking for new approaches have several good examples to emulate, most arising out of an earlier era of speech-code development. The columnist Nat Hentoff described one possibility in a 1991 Washington Post article about the response of four black women at Arizona State University to a racially offensive flyer posted on a residence-hall door. Instead of seeking to invoke ASU's speech code, the women told the occupants why they objected to the flyer (which was promptly taken down). Then, with the support of ASU administrators, they helped organize a series of campus forums and discussions, as well as a residence-hall program on African-American history. Lively correspondence continued in the campus newspaper, culminating in a letter to the editor ("names withheld upon request") that read: "We would like to extend our sincerest and deepest apologies to anyone and everyone who was offended by the tasteless flyer that was displayed on our front door. . . . We did not realize the hurt that would come from this flyer. We now know that we caused great distress among many different people, and we would like again to apologize."

Similar outcomes elsewhere aren't guaranteed. Without proper leadership from college deans and presidents, intensely emotional issues can turn into shouting matches rather than thoughtful dialogue. At a minimum, however, offending students can be challenged to become First Amendment practitioners and active participants in a serious discussion, instead of First Amendment martyrs. And offended students can be encouraged and assisted in employing a broad range of strategies—holding open forums, conducting lawful demonstrations or vigils, or simply issuing invitations to public debates—that will help them acquire skills in challenging rather than censoring expression they don't like. Some schools have endorsed this approachprotecting "the right to think the unthinkable, discuss the unmentionable, and challenge the unchallengeable" in published guidelines, like the Yale University Policy on Freedom of Expression (written by the late C. Vann Woodward, one of America's most distinguished historians).

In his 1929 essay "The Aims of Education," Alfred North Whitehead wrote that: "the very intellectual revolution which has ever stirred humanity into greatness has been a passionate protest against inert ideas. Then, alas, with pathetic ignorance of human psychology, it has proceeded by some educational scheme to bind humanity afresh with inert ideas of its own fashioning." A better summary of the speech-code phenomenon would be hard to find. The ideals that gave life to the civil-rights movement arose out of an intense clash of ideologies and convictions. A whole new vocabulary of justice was created in the process. That vocabulary can't be frozen in amber. Each generation should be encouraged to develop the skills to contribute to it. Doing so requires an atmosphere of freedom—an atmosphere in which fundamental values are questioned, tested, reformulated, and revitalized, not turned into stale dogma.

The Real Impact of Virtual Worlds

By *Thomas A. Workman*

Thomas A. Workman *is an assistant professor of communications studies at the University of Houston-Downtown.*

HOW DIGITAL CULTURE SHAPES STUDENTS' MINDS

Colleges that try to set limits on students' use of the Internet often misread their motivations and the meaning of online life for them. Much of what we fear when we see kids spending hours online is filtered through our own generational lens. What looks like plagiarism, slander, copyright infringement, and embarrassing public behavior is for many students just creative and social entertainment.

Five key norms of the digital culture may explain how students think about technology and how we can help them manage it:

Digital Norm 1: Internet use as play. For the past five years, I've conducted focus groups for several research projects, resulting in conversations with more than 500 students from a wide variety of backgrounds. When I have asked how they used the Internet, their responses have usually suggested that online life is ultimately a recreational activity. YouTube's unbridled popularity among young adults, like many virtual communities, is because of its entertainment value, even in moments of political and social advocacy. A case in point: While Barack Obama and Ron Paul each worked tirelessly over weeks to build a Facebook group with one million members, Comedy Central's Stephen Colbert accomplished that in three days in his comic race for president.

As with the playground equipment in the schoolyard, however, what is intended for fun can still produce bruises and bleeding. It is the insults— along with the stalking, cyberbullying, photographs of illegal activity, and slanderous depictions of anyone who (at the moment) has lost favor with the student—that concern student-affairs professionals and campus lawyers. But being unsafe doesn't make Internet play any less exciting for students; it may actually add to the appeal. College students are particularly vulnerable to the sociological phenomenon of "edgework," where risk-taking increases the pleasure and excitement of recreational activities like cliff diving or parasailing. The notion of edgework explains why students engage in outrageous activities that become YouTube uploads and Facebook group photos, and why such posts and high-risk groups are so popular.

Indeed, thinking about virtual interaction as play helps us understand online student behavior as misdirected recreation rather than purposeful misconduct. That can enable us to develop more-effective learning opportunities and interventions. We can redirect the same creative energy that students use to post an elaborate video chronicle of a bar crawl—including violation of campus policies for pre-crawling in the alcohol-restricted residence hall or the provision of alcohol to underage friends—to an assignment where students work together online to solve a social problem.

Viewing the Internet as a playground also helps us understand the challenge of prohibition. When we attempt to limit students' Internet use, we find those who are most interested in high-risk recreation respond much the same way that they do to our alcohol-prohibition policies: with resistance, hiding, and strategic noncompliance. The result is a loss for student-affairs and other administrators who are trying to understand how students think. Although we may not like what we see, by being more open and accepting of students' online activity, we can gain valuable insights to help us design better learning environments and produce better policies and procedures.

Digital Norm 2: virtual identity as fictionalized personas. One of the more difficult concepts for those who were not raised to think digitally is the notion of virtual identity. The student leader who hosts a weekly Bible study may be a wild party animal online. The freshman wallflower, ignored in the real world, may become an international spy, corporate guru, or porn star.

Much like the suburban family that is deep in debt but still drives a Mercedes-Benz to appear affluent to the neighbors, the identities that students create in virtual worlds don't need to be accurate reflections of their daily lives. Rather, they must possess elements popular in whatever culture students seek membership. High-risk activity, sexuality, spirituality, even anti-authority rhetoric all serve the same purpose in declaring to the virtual world that "I personify these values and interests."

It is common, therefore, to see pictures, videos, and stories borrowed from other Web sites or staged for the digital camera. In studying online how students use alcohol, for example, I found that many students' profiles on Facebook and MySpace displayed photos of people with whom they had no direct relationship; the photos were simply lifted from other sites. Many of those photos appeared staged, with a lot of people simply posing in them.

Meanwhile, most students also think they can just commit "virtual suicide" and put an end to such fantasy identities with the push of the delete button. They often don't understand that, real or staged, the presence of a photo or comment will remain forever connected to them.

Given the fictional nature of many online identities, our response to inappropriate student postings may again need to be less punitive and more educational. Each posting offers an opportunity for a conversation about identity integration, an important aspect of emotional and moral development that doesn't always find its way into the college experience. At the very least, many colleges should take the opportunity to teach students the harsh realities of Internet memory, helping them realize that virtual identities may be harder to eliminate than they imagined—and can come back to haunt a student who has developmentally moved on.

Digital Norm 3: virtual socialization as a complement to live community. Ever since Internet social networks became popular, student-affairs professionals and sociologists have worried that the trend would lead to a population of students who were isolated and unable to develop healthy "offline" relationships. But as Nicole B. Ellison, Charles Steinfield, and Cliff Lampe, communications scholars at Michigan State University, noted in a 2007 study on students' use of Facebook and other online social-networking sites, "Online interactions do not necessarily remove people from their offline world but may indeed be used to support relationships and keep people in contact, even when life changes move them away from each other."

Howard Rheingold has argued in The Virtual Community: Homesteading on the Electronic Frontier (HarperPerennial, 1994) that virtual communities may actually be part of the remedy for the loss of live community. He contends that American community dissipated long before the Internet took hold, leading to a sense of isolation and a longing for connection across all generations—a thesis that Robert D. Putman supports in Bowling Alone (Simon and Schuster, 2000).

Institutions of higher education should begin thinking creatively about ways to use virtual community as an access point for students to have more live social interactions with one another, faculty members, and administrators. Abundant examples already exist: Facebook groups support live rallies and publicize local meetings, and YouTube videos of live events whet the appetite of students for more. Colleges should develop more-creative ways to build relationships with students by connecting Internet activities to well-designed, live social interactions. The University of Nebraska at Lincoln, for example, has used student Facebook groups—posted by student employees—to build interest and momentum for service-learning and other student events, making them feel less institutional.

Digital Norm 4: the global town square. A 2007 study on youth civic engagement by Kent E. Portney and Lisa O'Leary of Tufts University found that the majority of college students belong to at least four online political- or social-advocacy groups. With a global audience in place, millennials are moving from simple hijinks to what Neil Howe and the late William Strauss, authors of Millennials and the Pop Culture (Lifecourse Associates, 2006), have always contended they were capable of: postmodern civic engagement. College administrators are justifiably concerned about copyright infringement and other legal issues, especially given students' ability to simply copy documents about public issues and put them online. But rather than attempt to shut down student efforts, it would make more sense to harness that digital energy, protecting students from legal vulnerability by educating them about copyright law.

Digital Norm 5: online community as a response to barriers to live interactions. Particularly at large institutions, new students can become lost in a sea of faces, unable to build a sense of community despite the structure that surrounds them in residence halls or fraternities. Many institutions have worked hard to rectify that problem by instituting residential-learning communities and first-year-experience programs.

Yet, the heart of community involvement may not be structure, but personal satisfaction. In Communities in Cyberspace (Routledge, 1999), Marc A. Smith and Peter Kollock contend that virtual community provides three essential motivations for participation that may help us understand what's missing on our "offline" campuses:

Anticipated reciprocity: Instant messaging, cell texting, even YouTube uploads result in immediate gratification—a response. Someone will write back. A posting will be followed by comments. Many students feel entitled to some reciprocation and are unhappy when a professor or administrator speaks but won't listen, or demands high-quality work but won't give feedback. If live community is to compete with the virtual one, we'll need to take a lesson from the technology and create reciprocity in our offline interactions with this generation.

Increased recognition: Many millennials were raised to believe they are special, and providing them with the recognition that they crave has become complicated and problematic. Coeds flock to high-risk parties with the hope of being captured on "Girls Gone Wild," and young men seek notorious reputations as a way of not getting lost in the crowd. Even a judicial penalty for offensive or illegal uploads may lead to social recognition. But while colleges shouldn't condone that way to gain recognition, many have done little to replace it. Institutions should develop ways in which students can form healthy social identities in their offline lives.

Sense of efficacy: The Internet's greatest impact has been its ability to provide a voice for the many people who have no formal opportunity to speak in the real world. For students, the need for that empowerment is greater than many of us recognize. Virtual community provides an audience and a host of causes that make a significant difference, if only in the lives of their peers.

Students' virtual response to the Virginia Tech tragedy proves the point. Thus, colleges must find ways to help students meet their needs for self-efficacy offline as well as on.

There is no doubt that as technology continues to change, the generation of students will change alongside it. Our best preparation, then, is to train our own minds to think digitally, just like the students', so that we can best create policies, programs, and interactions that enable a student to connect the two worlds in ways that are productive, satisfying, and meaningful.

Generation Text:
The dark digital ages: 13 to 17

New Media – Mark Bauerlein

MARK BAUERLEIN *is a professor of English at Emory University and author of* The Dumbest Generation: How the Digital Age Stupefies Young Americans and Jeopardizes Our Future *(Tarcher/Penguin).*

Children between the ages of 13 and 17 who have a mobile phone average 1,742 text messages each month, according to a report by the Nielsen Company in September 2008. That comes to nearly 60 per day. They also make 231 voice calls each month, close to eight per day. They play games on the device as well, and browse the Web, take pictures and log hours of social networking.

No wonder so many of them consider the cellphone (for some it is a BlackBerry or an iPhone) an essential part of their lives. Half of all young people between the ages of 8 and 12 own one such device, according to a Harris Interactive poll conducted in July 2008. The rate rises to around four out of five for teenagers; that's a 36 percent increase over the previous three years, which means that these tools have swept into young people's lives with the dispatch and coerciveness of a youth fad (like Pokemon and Harry Potter). The devices are more than just consumer goods. They are signs and instruments of status.

The age-old force of peer pressure bears down hard. Indeed, 45 percent of the teens that sport one agree that "Having a cellphone is the key to my social life"—not just helpful or useful, but "the key." If you don't own a cellphone, if you can't text, game, network and chat, then you are out of the loop. It is like not being picked to play kickball back in the primitive days of neighborhood sandlot gatherings. If a 16-year-old runs up 3,000 text messages in one month (and does not have a flat payment plan), mom and dad take the phone away. It's just a silly, expensive toy, they think. But the 16-year-old thinks, "You have destroyed my life!" And for them, this seems true. Digital tools are the primary means of social contact. When they lose them, kids feel excluded and unpopular, and nothing hits a 16-year-old harder than the disregard of other 16-year-olds. They do not care what 40-year-olds think, and they do not worry about what happened at Thermopylae or what Pope John Paul II said about the "splendor of truth." They care about what other students in biology class think, what happened last week at the party and what so-and-so said about them.

It is an impulse long preceding the advent of the microchip, but digital devices have empowered that impulse as never before. Think about the life stage of adolescence. Teenagers stand at a precarious threshold, no longer children and not yet adults, eager to be independent but lacking the equipment and composure. They have begun to leave the home and shed the influence of parents, but they don't know where they are headed, and most of them find meager materials beyond the home out of which to build their characters. So they look to one another, emulating dress and speech, forming groups of insiders and outsiders, finding comfort in boyfriends and girlfriends, and deflecting more or less tenuously the ever-present risk of embarrassment.

Everyone passes through this phase, but this generation's experience marks a crucial change in the process. In the past, social life proceeded intermittently, all day at school and for a few hours after school. Kids hung out for an afternoon over the weekend and enjoyed a movie or party on Friday or Saturday night. Other than that, social life pretty much ended. They went home for dinner and entered a private space with only a "landline" as a means of contact (which appears to young people today a restricted connection—show them a rotary phone and watch them scowl). Teenage social life and peer-to-peer contact had a limit.

Teenagers did not like it. I certainly didn't want to listen to my parents when I turned 16. But the limit was healthy and effectual. Adolescents needed then and need now a reprieve from the tribal customs and peer fixations of middle school and high school. Wounds from lunchroom gossip and bullying, as well as the blandishments of popularity and various niche-crowd memberships, disable the maturing process. These form a horizon of adolescent triumphs and set the knowledge of history, civics, religion, fine art and foreign affairs beyond the pale of useful and relevant acquisitions. If a sophomore sat down on a bus with the gang and said, "Hey, did you see the editorial on school funding in The Times this morning?" the rest would scrunch up their faces as if an alien being sat among them.

A Digital Defense

Not since 1972, when Richard Nixon ran against George McGovern, have so many 18- to 30-year-old Americans voted in a presidential election as they did last November. Young adults did more than vote in November 2008. Many of them campaigned for Barack Obama, harnessing the power of the Internet to cultivate new online communities and to disseminate the message of change that he espoused and many of the young embraced. Just before delivering his acceptance speech in Chicago's Grant Park, president-elect Obama sent bulk e-mail to his young-adult supporters, a fitting communiqué for this technologically advanced generation. "We just made history," he wrote, not just for helping to elect the first African-American president, but also for capturing the hearts and minds of young adults and mobilizing them for a larger cause.

Eboo Patel, director of the Interfaith Youth Corps and author of *Acts of Faith: The Story of an American Muslim, the Struggle for the Soul of a Generation,* is another person who believes in the potential of young adults and uses new media to reach them. Patel's organization brings together young people from many different faith traditions to do charitable work, build relationships and inspire peaceful dialogue among organized religions. But such programs can work only if the younger generation is open-minded. Modern information technologies help young people learn about the diversity of faith traditions and move away from the natural suspicion of the "other." The I.F.Y.C. Web site, for example, hosts an online community called Bridge Builders, a forum where young adult interfaith leaders can connect and share stories of success.

Technology does not make people smarter, but it can help them to connect and rally around a cause in which they believe. We who are age 35 and older cannot simply blame younger generations if they are not interested in the things we deem important. We need to share the blame for not giving them more of what Barack Obama and Eboo Patel have managed to offer them: a cause that transcends their individual needs and that is worth working, even suffering, for. Yes, video games, YouTube and Wikipedia can provide anesthetic brain candy, distractions and easy answers; but if used for a larger cause, technologies like these become tools that can encourage intellectual growth as well as personal, social and ethical development.

DAVID E. NANTAIS, *director of the Leadership Development Institute at the University of Detroit Mercy, has written for America about young adults.*

Youthful mores screen out such things, which is all the more reason for parents to offer an alternative. A home and leisure life separate from teen stuff exposes youths to heroes and villains that surpass the idols of the senior class, to places beyond the food court and Apple Store, to times well before the glorious day they got their driver's license. It acquaints them with adult duties, distant facts and values and truths they will not fully comprehend until much later. They don't like them and rarely find them meaningful, but in pre-digital times teens had nowhere else to go after they entered the front door. They had to sit at the dining table and listen to parents talk about grocery shopping, vacation plans, Nixon, gas prices and the news.

No longer. In 1980, when an angry parent commanded, "Go to your room—you're grounded!" the next few hours meant isolation for the teen. Today, the bedroom is not a private space. It's a social hub. For many kids, the bedroom at midnight provides a rich social life that makes daytime face-to-face conversations seem tame and slow. Amid the pillows with laptop or BlackBerry, they chat with buddies in 11th grade and in another state. Photos fly back and forth while classmates sleep, revelations spill forth in tweets ("OMG, Billy just called Betty his ——"), and Facebook pages gain flashier graphics.

In this dynamic 24/7 network, teen activity accrues more and more significance. The events of the day carry greater weight as they are recorded and circulated. The temptation for teens to be self-absorbed and self-project, to consider the details of their lives eminently memorable and share-able, grows and grows. As they give in online, teenagers' peer consciousness expands while their historical understanding, civic awareness and taste go dormant before they have even had much chance to develop.

This is the hallmark of what I have called the Dumbest Generation. These kids have just as much intelligence and ambition as any previous cohort, but they exercise them too much on one another. They are building youth culture into a ubiquitous universe, and as ever, youth culture is a drag on maturity. This time it has a whole new arsenal.

Viewpoint: Online Social Networks and Learning

Christine Greenhow

Christine Greenhow is an Assistant Professor of Learning Sciences and Technology in the College of Education and the College of Information Studies (joint appointment) at the University of Maryland, College Park, Maryland, USA. She studies literacies broadly within online social network sites and the design of social networking applications for educational purposes. Christine Greenhow can be contacted at: greenhow@umd.edu

ABSTRACT

Purpose—*This viewpoint essay seeks to argue that young people's online social networking can serve as sites for and supports for student's learning in ways not currently assessed.*

Design/methodology/approach—*The two themes presented are based on a select review of the research literature as well as the author's explorations of young people's online social networking practices within MySpace and Facebook, two naturally occurring, youth-initiated sites, as well as in an online social networking application designed for environmental science education and civic action.*

***Findings**—Two themes are presented: (1) social network sites can serve as direct and indirect supports for learning, such as providing an emotional outlet for school-related stress, validation of creative work, peer-alumni support for school-life transitions, and help with school-related tasks: and (2) online social networking can stimulate social and civic benefits, online and offline, which has implications for education.*

Practical Implications—*Currently, social media are largely blocked in schools due to privacy, security, and copyright concerns. In the USA, the National Educational Technology Plan published in November 2010, and recent educational standards, both assume 24/7 access and use of newer web technologies for learning and advocate appropriation of technologies students already use, and prefer to use, for educational purposes. Consideration of how social media, such as social network sites, currently support informal learning may advance one's ability to construct effective social media-enabled environments for more formal learning purposes.*

Originality/value—*This paper presents concrete examples of how social network sites, typically seen as a distraction, might be re-envisioned as supports for revised student learning outcomes.*

Keywords *Learning, Social networking sites, Literacy, Social interaction*

Paper type *Viewpoint*

CHANGING EDUCATIONAL CONTEXTS

In the last decade, internet access, the nature of the web and contexts for learning have evolved, along with the emergence of desired competencies for learners, instructors, and administrators, and these changes impact constructs for learning, teaching, and paths for future research (Greenhow *et al.*, 2009a, b); young people now have more choices over what, how, and with whom they learn in a wide range of settings: classrooms, after school programs, home-school, formal online learning programs, and web-enabled spaces that dominate popular culture. Some of the most critical problems facing education today, as generally agreed upon by administrators, policy-makers, and researchers, are increasing young people's educational attainment, science and math learning, technological fluencies, communication skills, civic engagement and preparation for the twenty-first century workplace (Black and Lynch, 2003; Bureau of Labor Statistics, 2007; Collins and Halverson, 2009; Dohm and Shniper, 2007; National Center for Education Statistics, 2005; National Research Council, 2000; Putnam, 2000; Warschauer and Matuchniak, 2010).

ONLINE SOCIAL NETWORKING: CRISES OR COGNITIVE SURPLUS?

In this same context, adult educational discourses view with apprehension the internet-using practices and preferences of today's young people (Thurlow, 2006). Recent surveys report that use of social network sites, for instance, is the dominant out-of-school, leisure-time computer using activity among US adolescents of various ages, ethnicities, and income levels (Rideout *et al.*, 2010). A form of social media (Barnes, 2006), social network sites (SNS) are web-enabled services that "allow individuals to (1) construct a public or semi-public *profile* within a bounded system, (2) articulate a list of other *users* with whom they share a connection, and (3) view and traverse their *list of connections* and those made by others within the system" (Boyd and Ellison, 2007, p. 1). They feature prominent personal profiling, highlighting the connections between people and content (Cormode and Krishnamurthy, 2008), and allow people to visualize, interact with, and activate existing personal and professional networks, and to create connections with new ones unbounded by geographic distance. Yet, popular media accounts largely characterize young people's practices with social media like Facebook as deficient or harmful to academic achievement (Hamilton, 2009; Karpinski, 2009) as leading to declining standards of literacy (Bauerlein, 2009; Carr, 2008; Thurlow, 2006), and as a "threat to societal values" (Herring, 2007, p. 4).

On the other hand, outside education, a growing number of scholars and social commentators argue we are witnessing a *cognitive surplus* (Gladwell, 2005; Shirky, 2010) spurred by these very same forms of digital media and their attendant social practices—i.e. people volunteering their time, interest, and ingenuity online to participate in news, politics, business, fashion, government, etc.—and that this cognitive surplus can have societal benefits and can change our very notions of "knowledge" and the means of knowledge production (e.g. Wikipedia) (Giles, 2005).

For instance, observe the upstart teen bloggers, on the scene, in the campaign tent, or at the run-way show, pushing their reviews and images to the public while newspaper and magazine editors are still jockeying to feature those subjects in issues that will be published days or months later (Wilson, 2009). In the news industry, viewer participation in the form of online comments, independently produced videos, blog entries, and media-sharing options are being harnessed to enhance the accuracy, power and spread of centrally produced stories (e.g. CNN's documentary *Black in America*) (Nelson, 2008). In politics, potential voters don't just consume campaign propaganda, but help to shape and distribute it via blogs, home-grown videos, tweets and social network sites (Sheehy, 2008). Despite the economic downturn, businesses seeking to tap their employees "social connections, institutional memories and special skills—knowledge that large, geographically dispersed companies often have a difficult time obtaining" are investing in social networking software to connect the company's employees into a single web forum (Stone, 2007, p. C2). In fashion, once locked-down runway shows are now streamed live over the internet with some companies providing viewers with the option to signal their likes or dislikes via Facebook and immediately purchase items online, potentially disrupting traditional production cycles, magazine editors' influence, and industry definitions of fashion itself (Heyman, 2010). This Fall, within the US government, when the Department of Education (DOE) wanted "to identify and solve U.S. education's most pressing classroom problems" it turned to public educators as "creators of both educational processes and products, and as agents who must organize, manage, and assume risks in solving problems," as stated on its Challenge to Innovate website (see http://challenge.gov/ED/60-challenge-to-innovate-c2i). Using a social media space it accepted hundreds of problem submissions, and then invited public educators to review, vote for, and comment on the problems posted. Some of the problems identified were how can educators:

- Better incorporate students' voices in decision making?
- Facilitate parental involvement?
- Help students develop the literacy skills to succeed?

From the public's rankings of these problems, the US DOE will choose a select few to feature as it again turns to public educators to contribute their solutions.

Publishing in the *Stanford Social Innovation Review,* Scearce *et al,* (2010), in studying trends among non-profits, foundations and socially responsible businesses, argue that this facilitation of human relationships and connections via social media has the potential to garner significant organizational advantages, including:

- weaving community;
- encouraging greater openness and transparency;
- accelerating information-sharing;
- accessing more diverse perspectives;
- mobilizing people;
- stimulating collaborative knowledge-building; and ultimately
- reducing the cost of participation and coordination of resources and actions.

Disadvantages to facilitating relational practices via social media are that "half baked" ideas are made public, and those trying to manage work flows and processes must tackle concerns about brand and message control, privacy concerns, dealing with information overload, learning the range of technology options, and leveraging the right social media for one's purposes (Scearce *et al.,* 2010).

TWO THEMES: SOCIAL NETWORK SITES AND LEARNING

How should we think about these broader trends in relation to thinking about learning, teaching, and the incorporation of social media into education? To advance this conversation, I now synthesize what the educational research currently says about learning and social network sites, the aforementioned dominant form of social media used by US young people. My goal is to inform educational leaders, apprehensive or cautiously optimistic about young people's media-using practices, who are asking:

1. What are youth's purposes and practices with social network sites, and are they doing anything of educational value?
2. How might these understandings help us to design for wider civic participation, increasingly sophisticated interactions and accomplishments, and deal with potential dangers?
3. How can existing social networking technologies and attendant practices be appropriated and/or re-envisioned and re-worked to produce improvements in areas of educational priority such as educational attainment, the development of science, math and technology literacies, communication and twenty-first century skills, and preparation for future work lives?

Below I share two insights related to those questions, generated from a review of the educational literature (Greenhow *et al.*, 2009a), from explorations of young people's (ages 16–24) use of the social network sites MySpace and Facebook *in situ* (Greenhow and Robelia, 2009a, b; Greenhow and Burton, n.d.; Greenhow *et al.*, 2009), and an ongoing investigation of older adolescents' use of an open source social networking application, implemented within Facebook, and designed for informal science learning and civic action (Greenhow, n.d., 2010). Moreover, I suggest how each theme might inform the design of technology-mediated spaces for learning and questions we might ask in studying such spaces that would move us closer to understanding these questions above. The studies on which these insights are based included multiple sources of data gathered over the course of 2.5 years: surveys with high school students (n = 600) and college students (n = 346); content analysis of their MySpace and Facebook accounts; think-aloud protocols as students used their social network site; and focus groups and interviews with purposeful samples of high, medium, and low users.

SOCIAL NETWORK SITES CAN SERVE AS SUPPORTS FOR AND SITES OF LEARNING

Young people use social network sites for a wide-range of purposes; they piggy-back on existing online socializing routines to co-opt SNSs as social learning resources in direct and indirect support of education-related tasks and values.

For example, the students we studied from low-income, urban families in the upper Midwestern part of the USA perceived their MySpace as providing social support, relational maintenance, and an outlet for self-expression and self-presentation (Greenhow and Robelia, 2009a, b). Social support has long been identified as an ecological construct that influences individual wellbeing (Schwarzer and Knoll, 2007) often as a buffer to stress, as moderator of stress's effects, or as direct emotional, psychological, cognitive or practical aid. Students believed their support networks were actually stronger after prolonged MySpace membership, citing various channels for communication and frequent personal profile updating as helping them feel closer to, and maintain an awareness of, their close and extended friends; they felt regular online social networking encouraged openness, sharing, and getting to know more "sides" of a person. The majority of students profiled demonstrated between 50 and 150 MySpace "friends" and possessed a nuanced understanding of "friend" that included both intimate friends and family as well as acquaintances, or new people they had just met.

Moreover, students used their online social network to fulfill social learning functions within and across informal and formal learning spheres of activity. The social learning functions included:

- obtaining validation and appreciation of creative work through feedback on their profile pages;
- peer/alumni support—that is, reaching out to former classmates to give or receive help in managing the ups and downs of high school or college life; and
- help with school-related tasks (Greenhow and Robelia, 2009a).

The latter took several forms: "chatting" online through MySpace to mitigate school-related stress, asking questions about instructions or deadlines, planning study groups, requesting educational resources from the network (e.g. "if they know a site that would help me with my project, they'll post it up and I can go see it"), gathering project materials, brainstorming ideas, sharing written work, and exchanging feedback. Interestingly, participants envisioned using a social network site as part of their college transition strategy and felt their regular use of their social network site was developing their creativity, communication skills, technology skills, and openness to divergent viewpoints (Greenhow and Robelia, 2009b). Additional focused research is needed to determine the accuracy of these perceptions across various groups of students.

Of course, it is not particularly surprising that young people would adapt the spaces they frequent for their educational-related purposes, as school-related activities and concerns dominate much of adolescent life. What is surprising is the presence of these behaviors and beliefs even among he majority of our low income high school students, a group understudied in the educational technology literature and presumably experiencing more barriers to (but potentially more to gain from) participating in social network sites where such social media are typically blocked in schools and public libraries (Greenhow *et al.*, 2009). Furthermore, where such informal sharing, peer validation and feedback, alumni support, and spontaneous help with school-related tasks has typically occurred offline, pre-dating the internet, these social processes, moved online into social network sites, can now be archived and tracked with social graphing software. In theory, we should be able to begin to identify what learning resources exactly are moving through the network, to and from whom, and with what impacts over time (e.g. How is learning contagious?) (Christakis and Fowler, 2009). If educational curricula have typically been consumed with learning *what* (learning science, math, social studies content) and with learning as *becoming* (learning to become a scientist or historian by applying the tools and practices of the discipline), we can now also focus deeper attention to understanding social learning: how people learn *with whom*, or learn to be contributors to local and global society with what degree of influence (Brown, 2008; Brown and Duguid, 2002). Moreover, educational designers might think about how some of the socio-technical features most utilized in naturally occurring, youth-initiated social network sites, like MySpace (e.g. multimedia identity-posting capabilities, frequent updating and sharing of microcontent, social search, linking users with content contributions, annotation, ranking, recommendation systems) could be incorporated into the personalized learning systems touted in the new US National Education Technology Plan (United States Department of Education, 2010).

ONLINE SOCIAL NETWORKING CAN STIMULATE SOCIAL AND CIVIC BENEFITS, ONLINE AND OFFLINE, WHICH CAN HAVE IMPLICATIONS FOR EDUCATION

For instance, "social capital" refers to resources or benefits available to people through their social interactions (Lin, 1999) and is valuable to feelings of trust, reciprocity and social cohesion (Putnam, 2000); it emphasizes the importance of developing a network, in that it comprises:

- resources embedded in the social structure;
- accessibility to such resources; and
- mobilization of such resources by individuals in purposeful actions (Lin, 1999, p. 35).

Thus, investment in social networks may benefit individuals through greater access to and use of information, influence, social credentials, and reinforcement of identity and recognition (Lin, 1999, p. 31). Research in education and human development has typically focused on two broad types of social capital among youth and families (rather than among peer networks):

1. *bridging capital*, derived from weak ties that afford us diverse perspectives and new information; and
2. *bonding capital*, derived from strong ties that come from close friends and family and afford us that shoulder to cry on (Putnam, 2000).

Most importantly, the presence of social capital in one's social networks has been linked to a number of educational outcomes, including educational achievement, educational attainment, and other academic and psychosocial outcomes (Dika and Singh, 2002). In other words, learners tend to do better and persist in educational settings when they feel a strong sense of social belonging and connectedness.

Interestingly, in studying predominantly white, middle-class, college students' use of Facebook ($n = 286$), Ellison *et al.* (2007) found that intensive use of Facebook was associated with higher levels of bridging capital, and to a lesser extent, bonding capital and maintained social capital, a concept the researchers developed to describe the ability to "mobilize resources from a previously inhabited network, such as ones high school" (Ellison *et al.*, 2007, p.; 25). They suggested that networking through these sites may help to crystallize relationships that might otherwise remain ephemeral, encouraging users to strengthen latent ties and maintain connections with former friends, thus allowing people to stay connected as they move from one offline community to another. They also found that college students with lower self-esteem gained more from their use of Facebook in terms of bridging social capital than the higher self-esteem respondents (Steinfield *et al.*, 2008). They concluded that Facebook affordances may help reduce barriers some college students experience in forming the kinds of large, diverse networks that are sources of bridging capital.

Replicating this study with high school students from low income families ($n = 607$), a group most at risk for lower levels of educational attainment, achievement, and dropping out, we have found positive associations between these students' use of the social network site, MySpace, and both bonding and bridging social capital. Moreover, qualitative data help to illuminate our survey findings and pinpoint the opportunities or barriers for forging and sustaining relationships through online social network sites. Interestingly, students we interviewed positively identified MySpace and Facebook as part of their learning and college transition strategy (Greenhow and Burton, n.d.; Greenhow and Robelia, 2009a, b). Although this particular exploration occurred only over the course of a spring semester, more longitudinal analysis and racking of learners as they move through high school and into college settings while continuing participation in their online social networks, may help us better understand these phenomena as supports for learning processes and educational outcomes we value.

Moreover, in our research on young people's use of an social networking application called "Hot Dish"—implemented within Facebook, the world's largest social network site—we found that through the design of the application we were able to tie users' online social activities to offline civic behavior (Greenhow, 2010; Greenhow, n.d.). For instance, Hot Dish is an open-source social networking application that facilitates information-sharing about environmental science issues, commentary and debate, and the completion of challenges designed to engage users in pro-environmental behavior around climate change. Located as a tab within one's existing Facebook profile, key features included the ability to post original story entries; share articles from online sources; browse or read articles deeply; curate, rank and comment on posted entries; craft a personal profile; showcase users' statistics and contributions; and participate in Action Team challenges, or activities both online and offline (e.g. writing a letter to the editor, signing an online petition, volunteering for an environmental organization, recycling, starting a local recycling program, engaging in green consumerism) which were showcased within the Hot Dish environment after members documented their completion of them. Similar to gaming environments, users earned points for completing offline challenges and these accumulating point totals were featured prominently in the online environment so that individuals got recognized for changes in offline behavior (environmental activism) and, as role models, stimulated others in the online environment to make changes. Could similar data-tracking and representational features be built into future educational context to foster preferred learning (and teaching) behaviors, role modeling, civic engagement and spread of practices we value not just in education but as members of a participatory democracy? This is just one interesting avenue for future research.

To further our understanding of the social and civic benefits briefly mentioned above, the field of education and information studies needs an accumulation of research and evaluation concerned with students' personal social networks and the interrelationships between online and offline, which have hitherto be under-explored in the social capital in education literature in its focus on parent-child, parent-teacher, or teacher-child face-to-face networks (Dika and Singh, 2002). Similar to studies of parents' personal social networks (Cochran and Walker, 2005) in family social science, we require additional research into learners' network formation and factors that influence social network membership across the learning ecology young people currently inhabit, not merely within the formal classroom. We also require further understanding of network engagement and the importance of personal initiatives (e.g. a student's personality, interest, a life event, developmental phase) that can operate independently on the degree to which students have helpful, collaborative, and satisfying network relationships (high engagement) (Walker and Greenhow, 2010). Finally, we need to better understand the social processes of network influence and the specific benefits available to learners or accruing in online social networks. For instance, how do offers of practical, just-in-time assistance, information, emotional or psychological aid, modeling, coaching, etc. influence learning over time?

Although popular media accounts have portrayed the internet—and its youth-initiated spaces such as social network sites—as distractions at best, and harmful at worst, these exploratory studies suggest alternative views; students' practices within these spaces, although not without potential negative consequences, may also have positive implications for learning, educational attainment, and youth development, helping young people develop social supports for school, caring and capital-enhancing social connections, and meaningful participation in civic life.

REFERENCES

Barnes, S.B. (2006), "A privacy paradox: social networking in the United States", *First Monday*, Vol. 11 No. 9, available at: http://firstmonday.org/issues/issue11_9/barnes (accessed November 5, 2010).

Bauerlein, M. (2009). *The Dumbest Generation: How the Digital Age Stupefies Young Americans and Jeopardizes Our Future (Or, Don't Trust Anyone under 30)*, Vol. 30, Tarcher, New York, NY.

Black, S.E. and Lynch, L.M. (2003), "What's driving the new economy? The benefits of workplace innovation", Center for Economic Studies, US Census Bureau, Washington, DC.

Boyd, D.M. and Ellison, N.B. (2007), "Social network sites: definition, history, and scholarship", *Journal of Computer-Mediated Communication*, Vol. 13 No. 1, available at: http://jcmc.indiana.edu/vol13/issue1/boyd.ellsion.html (accessed October 9, 2008).

Brown, J.S. (2008), "How to connect technology and content in the service of learning", *Chronicle of Higher Education*, Vol. 55 No. 8, available at: http://chronicle.com/free/v55/i08/08a12001.htm (accessed January 29, 2009).

Brown, J.S. and Duguid, P. (2002), *The Social Life of Information*, Harvard Business School Press, Cambridge, MA.

Bureau of Labor Statistics (2007), "The 30 fastest growing occupations covered in the 2008–2009 *Occupational Outlook Handbook*", available at www.bls.gov/news.release/ooh.t01.htm (accessed October 9, 2010).

Carr, N. (2008), "Is Google making us stupid? What the internet is doing to our brains", *The Atlantic Monthly*, July/August, available at: www.theatlantic.com/magazine/archive/2008/07/is-google-making-us-stupid/6868/ (accessed November 15, 2010).

Christakis, N. and Fowler, J. (2009), *Connected: The Surprising Power of Our Social Networks and How They Shape Our Lives*, Little, Brown & Co., New York, NY.

Cochran, M. and Walker, S. (2005), "Parenting and personal social networks", in Luster, T. and Ogakaki, L. (Eds), *Parenting: An Ecological Approach*, Lawrence Erlbaum Associates, Mahwah, NJ.

Collins, A. and Halverson, B. (2009), *Rethinking Education in the Age of Technology*, Teachers College Press, New York, NY.

Cormode, G. and Krishnamurthy, B. (2008), "Key differences between Web 1.0 and Web 2.0", *First Monday*, Vol. 13 No. 6, available at: www.uic.edu/htbin/cgiwrap/bin/ojs/index.php/fm/article/view/2125/1972 (accessed October 5, 2008).

Dika, S.L. and Singh, K. (2002). "Applications of social capital in educational literature: a critical synthesis", *Review of Educational Research*, Vol. 72 No. 1, pp. 31–60.

Dohm, A. and Shniper, L. (2007), "Occupational employment predictions to 2016", *Monthly Labor Review*, Vol. 86, US Bureau of Labor Statistics, Washington DC, available at www.bls.gov/opub/mlr/2007/11/art5full.pdf (accessed September 10, 2010).

Ellison, N.B., Steinfield, C. and Lampe, C. (2007), "The benefits of Facebook 'friends': social capital and college students' use of online social network sites", *Journal of Computer-mediated Communication,* Vol. 12 No. 4, available at: http://jcmc.indiana.edu/vol12/issue4/ellison.html

Giles, J. (2005). "Internet encyclopedias go head to head", *Nature,* Vol. 438 No. 7070, pp. 900–1.

Gladwell, M. (2005), "Brain candy: is pop culture dumbing us down or smartening us up?", *The New Yorker,* May 16, available at: www.newyorker. com/archive/2005/05/16/050516crbo_books (accessed October 10, 2010).

Greenhow, C. (n.d.), "The role of youth as cultural producers in a niche social network site", *New Directions in Youth Development: Theory, Research & Practice* (forthcoming).

Greenhow, C. (2010), "Literacies in a niche online social networking application", paper presented at the American Educational Research Association Annual Meeting, New Orleans, LA, April 8–11.

Greenhow, C. and Burton, L. (n.d.), "Help from my 'friends': social capital in the social network sites of low-income high school students", *Journal of Educational Computing Research* (forthcoming).

Greenhow, C. and Robelia, E. (2009a), "Old communication, new literacies: social network sites as social learning resources", *Journal of Computer-mediated Communication,* Vol. 14, pp. 1130–61.

Greenhow, C. and Robelia, E. (2009b), "Informal learning and identity formation in online social networks", *Learning, Media and Technology,* Vol. 34 No. 2, pp. 119–40.

Greenhow, C., Robelia, E. and Hughes, J. (2009a). "Web 2.0 and classroom research: what path should we take now?", *Educational Researcher,* Vol. 38 No. 4, pp. 246–59.

Greenhow, C., Robelia, E. and Hughes, J. (2009b). "Research on learning and teaching with Web 2.0: bridging conversations", *Educational Researcher,* Vol. 38 No. 4, pp. 280–3.

Greenhow, C.,Walker, J.D. and Kim, S. (2009). "Millennial learners and net-savvy teens: examining internet use among low-income students", *Journal of Computing in Teacher Education,* Vol. 26 No. 2, pp. 63–9.

Hamilton, A. (2009), "What Facebook users share: lower grades", *Time Magazine,* April 14, available at: www.time.com/time/business/ article/0,8599,1891111,00.html (accessed November 10, 2010).

Herring, S.C. (2007). "Questioning the generational divide: technological exoticism and adult construction of online youth identity", in Buckingham, D. (Ed.), *Youth, Identity, and Digital Media,* MIT Press, Cambridge, MA, pp. 71–94, available at: http://ella.slis.indiana.edu/~herring/ macarthur.pdf (accessed January 30, 2009).

Heyman, S. (2010), "Technology gives everyone a great seat at shows", *The New York Times,* September 8, available at: http://tinyurl.com/2e2rcuc (accessed August 10, 2010).

Karpinski, A.C. (2009), "A description of Facebook use and academic performance among undergraduate and graduate students", paper presented at the Annual Meeting of the American Educational Research Association (AERA), San Diego, CA, May 5–10.

Lin, N. (1999), "Building a network theory of social capital", *Connections*, Vol. 22 No. 1, pp. 28–51.

National Center for Education Statistics (2005), *The Condition of Education in Brief*, NCES 2005095, National Center for Education Statistics, Washington, DC.

National Research Council (2000), *Inquiry and the National Science Education Standard*, National Academy, Washington, DC.

Nelson, M. (Executive Producer) (2008), "CNN presents: Black in America", television broadcast, July 23, Turner Broadcasting Service, New York, NY, available at: www.cnn.com/SPECIALS/2008/black.in.america/ (accessed March 23, 2010).

Putnam, R. (2000), *Bowling Alone: The Collapse and Revival of the American Community*, Simon & Schuster, New York, NY.

Rideout, V.J., Foehr, U.G. and Roberts, D.F. (2010), "Generation M2: media in the lives of 8- to 18-year-olds", Report No. 8010, January 20, Kaiser Family Foundation, Menlo Park, CA.

Scearce, D., Kasper, G. and Grant, H.M. (2010), "Working wikily", *Stanford Social Innovation Review*, available at: www.sdsireview.org/articles/ entry/working_wikily/ (accessed September 9, 2010).

Schwarzer, R. and Knoll, N. (2007), "Functional roles of social support within the stress and coping process: a theoretical and empirical overview", *International Journal of Psychology*, Vol. 42 No. 4, pp. 243–52.

Sheehy, G. (2008), "Campaign Hillary: behind closed doors", *Vanity Fair*, August, pp. 79–86.

Shirky, C. (2010), *Cognitive Surplus: Creativity and Generosity in a Connected Age*, Penguin Press, New York, NY.

Steinfield, C., Ellison, N. and Lampe, C. (2008), "Social capital, self esteem, and use of online social network sites: a longitudinal analysis", *Journal of Applied Developmental Psychology*, Vol. 29, pp. 434–45.

Stone, B. (2007), "Social networking's next phase", *New York Times*, March 3, pp. C1–C2.

Thurlow, C. (2006), "From statistical panic to moral panic: the metadiscursive construction and popular exaggeration of new media language in the print media". *Journal of Computer-Mediated Communication*, Vol. 11 No. 3, available at: http://jcmc.indiana.edu/vol11/issue3/thurlow. html (accessed 15 November 2010).

United States Department of Education (2010), "Transforming American education: learning powered by technology", National Educational Technology Plan 2010, March 5, available at: www.ed.gov/sites/default/ files/NEP-2010-final-report.pdf

Walker, S. and Greenhow, C. (2010), "The internet and human relationships: revisiting the personal social networks of parents", paper presented at the Council on Family Relations Annual Meeting, Minneapolis, MN, November 2–3.

Warschauer, M. and Matuchniak, T. (2010), "New technology and digital worlds: analyzing evidence of equity in access, use, and outcomes", *Review of Research in Education*, Vol. 34, pp. 179–225.

Wilson, E. (2009), "Bloggers crash fashion's front row", *The New York Times*, December 24, available at: www.nytimes.com/2009/12/27/fashion/27BLOGGERS.html# (accessed November 10, 2010).

The Daily Show: The Face of American News in 2005

Steve Gennaro

It was a typical Saturday evening broadcast from the NBC television studios in New York City. The year was 1975, and unbeknownst to the television viewer, a news anchor had just uttered the words that would change American news forever, "I'm Chevy Chase and you're not." What began as a three minute segment on *Saturday Night Live*, the "Weekend Update" skit quickly became *Saturday Night Live's* most popular skit and occupied nine minutes of airtime before the first season was over. Chevy Chase "took the stage when the press and public alike were anxious for a new diversion, not unlike the Beatles when they landed in New York soon after the assassination of John F. Kennedy in 1963. America after Watergate was ready to proclaim a new clown prince, someone whose very freshness and confidence was a relief and renewal. In 1975, Chevy Chase was it. "[1] America had fallen in love with comedy-news.

The Daily Show debuted on the American cable channel *Comedy Central* in July of 1996. Originally, Craig Kilborn was the show's host, but he was replaced by current host Jon Stewart on January 11, 1999. Since Stewart took over as the host, the viewing audience of the show has more than tripled to a peak of over a million viewers a night in 2004.[2] *The Daily Show* has become the most trusted source for political news on television. Since the beginning of 2004, Jon Stewart and his cast of reporters have taken hold of the mainstream media. In the lead up to the 2004 Presidential election Jon Stewart's face could be seen everywhere. He was a guest on every imaginable news program from *The O'Reilly Report* to *Crossfire* as every newsroom asked for his opinion on the upcoming election. Jon Stewart's book, *America (The Book): A Citizen's Guide to Democracy in Action*, has spent months atop the *New York Times Best Sellers List*. In 2004, America loves comedy-news more than ever.

This paper examines the rise of *The Daily Show*'s audience over the last five years. Television critics argue that it is Stewart's easy going personality that has endeared him to comedy-news viewers, however, it would be imprudent to ignore the changes in *The Daily Show's* program content (that is the shift from comedy-news to news) and the changes in the surrounding society (most notably America's involvement in Iraq) that have played a part in the rise of *The Daily Show* audience. Just like with Chevy Chase's rise to stardom in 1975, Jon Stewart's rise to prominence and with him the success of *The Daily Show* has largely been in response to America's need for a new clown prince who can provide relief and renewal to its involvement in Iraq.

Furthermore, examining the growth of *The Daily Show* audience also involves examining the shift in program content on *The Daily Show* as witnessed through its transition from comedy-news to real-news. This transition works much like a two way street; *The Daily Show,* traditionally only of comedic value, is used as a source of news, while traditional hard news is becoming entertainment. In one direction, we see an increase of the political prestige of the guests on *The Daily Show* over the last two years, thus making *The Daily Show* more authentic in its news-character. In the other direction we see the transition in news as a television genre to what James Compton would call a "Debordian spectacle," or what Neil Postman would say is responsible for our "amusing ourselves to death." The merger between entertainment and news on the major news stations further highlights that the difference between hard news and *The Daily Show* is decreasing.

This paper seeks to highlight how *The Daily Show* is trying to straddle both sides of the fence; it wants to be fake news so that it can openly criticize the American political infrastructure, and yet it wants to be real news so that it's critiques have credibility. The paper will be divided into two sections. The first half of the paper will examine comedy, news, and their interconnectedness. The point is that the situation in Iraq has left the American audience searching for a different way to interact with news media. Being that humour, namely satire and irony, have always been ways in which the American people have made sense of their government's politics, comedy-news and thus, *The Daily Show* are the logical outlet for current American anxieties. The second half of the paper will examine how news as a genre continues to shift away from journalism towards entertainment and spectacle. As Americans tune in more and more to comedy-news, and news as a whole moves towards a form of entertainment, perhaps *The Daily Show* and its split personality (of being both real and fake news) will be the face of news as a whole in 2005.

Comedy has always played an important role in the ways that a community identifies itself and the types of stories that it tells. "Tragedy, at least since the classical times has dealt with our highest desires, but comedy has been our way of dealing with life as it happens. The kind of comedy that we choose and enjoy tells us a great deal about the kinds of people we are."[3] For the United States over the course of the twentieth century, political humour in particular has been instrumental in defining the public's attitude towards the President. For example, the first half of the twentieth century, or the pre-television era, was marked by a political humour where the comedian acted as a mediator between the public and the President. The comedian would speak about the President by highlighting his humane qualities and making the President accessible to the common person. However, the comedian, while speaking of the non political aspects of the president's life would comment on anything but the political. A great example of this type of comedian is Bob Hope, always in the spotlight with regard to political events, but never speaking about politics.

In contrast, the last half of the twentieth century saw the attitude of comedians (and thus humour) towards the President change, where humour became an avenue through which to openly question or attack the policies of the President in power. A politically charged attitude questioned the policies on key issues such as race, gender, and war. Comedians such as Lenny Bruce or Richard Prior used this type of political satire for social commentary. Giving further credence to the changes taking place were the technological changes; there was a drastic increase in the amount of televisions in American society. In 1950, only 9 percent of all homes in America contained at least one television and by 1966 that number had risen to 92.8 percent. In comparison, in 1966 only 80 percent of all American households had at least one telephone.[4] "The tissue between politics and popular culture had evaporated . . . Television has enforced this connection, making all politicians media-conscious. That is both good and bad. It is good in that the governor or president must never forget that they serve a democracy."[5]

This shift in the uses of political humour throughout the twentieth century has laid the groundwork for what is the current environment, where the lines between humour and news have become blurred. "An important paradox to emerge from this is that, in a political environment frequently styled as 'postmodern', the comedian, now widely acknowledged, in the age of impression management, as truth-teller and iconoclast, may carry more public credibility than the politician."[6] This is perhaps the case with George W. Bush, Jon Stewart, and the American public.

In examining humour in politics, "the most common weapon, however, is ridicule. The authority figure is exposed for what he really is behind his public mask, and his hypocrisy or social inadequacy is held up for all to see and to laugh at. Here is where humor normally plays it's most important role in the comedy, as a social corrective."[7] *The Daily Show* asks audiences not only to consume the news, but to critically think about it. Not only to hear the report on troops in Fallujah, but to think about whether these actions are justified. Humour does not allow us just to ingest the messages; it forces us to digest them as well. Humour invites the viewer to react, by laughing. The decision to laugh, although in many ways a spontaneous physical reaction, first and foremost requires the viewer to process the comment made by the actor, comedian, news anchor, and either agree or disagree. Without this "critical" moment of reflection, a persons' reaction to humour would not be laughter, but instead an "I don't get it" response.

The use of humour and political satire has been effective in *The Daily Show's* ability to attract an audience interested in political issues. The level of engagement of *The Daily Show* audience is staggering. A recent poll by the Annenberg Public Policy Centre at the University of Pennsylvania highlighted that viewers of *The Daily Show* were better informed than conventional news viewers on the key political issues leading up to the 2004 American federal election. While the survey highlighted that the viewers of all late-night television talk shows were better informed on the 2004 Presidential candidates and their platforms than those who relied solely on conventional forms of televised news, viewers of *The Daily Show* scored best; outperforming viewers of late night greats David Letterman and Jay Leno.[8] *The Daily Show* audience also scored greater than those who regularly read newspapers or watched television news, leading *Rolling Stone Magazine* in October 2004 to conclude that "Stewart can now cite objective data to prove that he, like Walter Cronkite before him, deserves to be known as the most trusted name in TV news.[9]

The Daily Show is becoming more credible than traditional news sources as evidenced by the decision of political candidates to use *The Daily Show* as a forum to gain access to voters instead of traditional news sources. The Democratic Party invited *The Daily Show* to cover its 2004 National Convention, which sparked MSNBC to comment that Stewart's "starting to be taken seriously as a political force. The Democratic National Committee announced this month that it plans to invite Stewart & Co. to cover its convention, amazing since "*The Daily Show*" is actually a fake news program."[10] Ten months later, Democratic Presidential Candidate John Kerry chose to grant an interview to Jon Stewart and appeared on *The Daily Show*. An ensuing article on Reuters. com stated:

> It's ironic that a comedian whose livelihood comes from what he calls his "fake news" forum on Comedy Central is staking his ground on serious journalism. On Stewart's watch, "*The Daily Show*" has taken political satire to a new level, so much so that the satirical descendant of David Frost's "That Was the Week That Was" has the power to make news, as it did when presidential candidate John Kerry agreed to be interviewed by an anchor who undoubtedly has more sway with the average 18- to 34-year-old than Tom Brokaw, Peter Jennings and Dan Rather combined.[11]

According to The Pew Research Center for the People and Press, 21 percent of viewers aged 18-29 learnt most of their 2004 presidential campaign news primarily from *The Daily Show* and Saturday Night Live. *The Daily Show* was the top rated news show for 18-34 year olds and only Fox News Channel had more viewers aged 18-49.[12]

The increase in *The Daily Show* credibility is in large part due to the increase to its audience size and demographic. Although Bill O'Reilly of Fox's highly rated talk show *The O'Reilly Factor* accused *The Daily Show's* audience of being a bunch of "stoned slackers" the statistics do not support this perspective. Viewers of *The Daily Show* are 78 percent more likely than the average adult to have four or more years of college education and 26 percent more likely to have a household income over $100,000. The viewers of *The O'Reilly Factor* did not rate so well. In contrast to *The Daily Show*, viewers of *The O'Reilly Factor* were only 24 percent more likely than the average adult to have four or more years of college education and only 11 percent more likely to have a household income over $100,000. According to CNN, "the guy watching Stewart may not only be smart, but may also be rich."[13] The median age of "*The Daily Show*" audience is 33 years old. The audience of *The Daily Show* is educated, interested, and continually growing in market share as people become more and more disenchanted with traditional forms of news.

It is no coincidence that the most recent jump in ratings of *The Daily Show* parallels America's involvement in Iraq. This suggests that Americans are looking for an alternate source of news when it comes to dealing with difficult subjects as opposed to being exposed to only the CNN or Fox news perspective that seems to suspiciously support the political agendas of those in power. Stewart himself says, "I enjoy watching Fox News and I think every country should have their own Al-Jazeera."[14] Perhaps the popularity of humour in news is partly due to the ways in which the messages of news are conveyed through the medium of television. For example, "television has revolutionized politics not because of the quantity and speed of its information, not because of its practitioners' technological savvy, and not even because of its legion of superficialities…television makes us feel good about feeling bad about politics."[15] *The Daily Show's* critique of the Bush Administration allows Americans to feel good about a bad situation in Iraq. "His cut-the-crap humor hits the target so consistently—you've gotta love a show that calls its segments on Iraq "Mess O'Potamia."[16]

The idea of "comedy-news" is itself a misnomer in that all forms of television content, whether news, comedy, or sports, are focused on entertainment value. Therefore, differentiating between real and fake, comedy and broadcast, or hard and soft types of news only creates false dichotomies. All television news has moved away from reporting journalism to entertainment, spectacle, and selling. Neil Postman discussed this movement towards entertainment, not exclusive to news, twenty years ago when he stated, "[o]ur politics, religion, news, athletics, education, and commerce have been transformed into congenial adjuncts of show business, largely without protest or even much popular notice, the result is that we are a people on the verge of amusing ourselves to death."[17]

A large part of this movement from news to entertainment is due to the phenomenon of convergence. The term convergence refers to a remediation of technologies and also to, "the merging of corporations into ever larger entities and alliances, and the convergence of messages and cultures."[18] Elvis Presley is a great example of early forms media convergence, in that Elvis used his television appearances to sell his music, and his music to sell his movies, and his movies to sell his brand name products. The new media conglomerates of the second half of the twentieth century work in a similar fashion, so that, when a person watches a television show on one particular cable channel, they are at the same time being sold products owned by other companies within that cable channels "im-media-te" family. For example:

> AOL-Time Warner, for instance, owns a whole stable of valuable magazine properties-*Time, People, Sports Illustrates, Fortune, Life, Entertainment Weekly, In Style* and many more. While these magazines are each expected to turn a profit, they are also promotional vehicles used to pump and spin other AOL-Time Warner media products...Warner Brothers Studios which produces blockbuster films...cable holdings such as CNN, Cinemax, HBO...music labels such as Atlantic and Elecktra...Warner Books...America On-line... sport franchises that include the Atlanta Braves in baseball, the NHL's Atlanta thrashers and the Atlanta Hawks in basketball...not to mention stadiums and theme parks...in these circumstances, it's often difficult to know where journalism leaves off and self-promotion begins.[19]

At the turn of the millennium, the power of the culture industries lay in the hands of five multi-national media companies: Disney, News Corp, Viacom, Vivendi Universal, and AOL Time Warner.

More recently than Postmans' discussion on "amusing ourselves to death", James Compton in 2004 examined the effects of the phenomenon of convergence on the news room "The question "Will it entertain?' has replaced 'Will it inform?' and journalism's high calling of public service has been eroded, leaving the media to settle in to the muck of low-brow popular culture, the narcissism of celebrity profiles, and the pornography of violence. What happened?"[20] Compton answers his own question; media convergence and integrated newsrooms happened.

> What is significant about integrated newsrooms is that the dividing line between editorial and promotional interests has been blurred irrevocably. In the past, news media sold mass audiences to advertisers who were given the opportunity to place their advertisements in front of the delivered eyeballs...[i]n integrated news rooms, however, the goal is to use editorial content to steer audiences toward preferred nodes on a company's or group of companies proprietary network of multi media outlets.[21]

In much the same way that Fox News gives the viewer "the soft sell" on other Fox products, *The Daily Show* also participates in the media spin of selling its own. For example, when returning from each and every commercial break an announcer reminds viewers to buy the new book by Jon Stewart and *The Daily Show* titled *America (The Book): A Citizen's Guide to Democracy in Action*. Also, it is not a coincidence that *The Daily Show* hit its media peak, with Jon Stewart's face on each and every magazine, newspaper, and television station, at the exact same time that the new book was released. The integrated news spectacle is just one way in which *The Daily Show* has crept towards the world of real news.

The argument could also be made that *The Daily Show* has continually worked to increase its news-like credibility. At the same time as news agencies are moving more towards entertainment than journalism, *The Daily Show* appears to be moving in the other direction: from entertainment to journalism. *The Daily Show* has noticeably altered the political status of its guests. Since Jon Stewart took over as host, guests have included Vice President Al Gore, former Secretary of State Henry Kissenger, and notable Senators such John Edwards, Hillary Clinton, John McCain, Joseph Lieberman, John Kerry, and Bob Dole to mention a few. *The Daily Show* has also gained public prestige by winning five Emmys over the last two years. In 2004, *The Daily Show* was awarded the Television Critics Association award for best news and information program. *The Daily Show* has become the trusted source of news for young people when it comes to political issues. According to the Nielsen ratings, during the 2004 party convention, *The Daily Show* drew higher ratings in the 11:00 pm to 11:30 pm time slot with the 18-34 demographic than any of the cable news channels, including CNN and Fox.[22]

The Daily Show occupies a privileged position in the news world. At the same time as *The Daily Show* sells itself as news, it is quick to state its lack of connection to professional news. During his appearance on CNN's *Crossfire*, Jon Stewart told co-host Tucker Carlson "You're on CNN. The show that leads into me is puppets making crank phone calls."[23] In the media Jon Stewart continually aims to down play his shows significance by noting that the shows, which precede his timeslot on the Comedy channel are shows such as *Puppets That Kill*, or *Southpark* and therefore his show should not be taken seriously. However, even as he discredits his shows legitimacy as news, he cries out for journalistic credibility. Take for example *The Daily Show*'s coverage of "Mess O'Potamia":

> But we are at war, and we here at *The Daily Show* will do our best to keep you informed of any late-breaking...humor we can find. Of course, our show is obviously at a disadvantage compared to the many news sources that we're competing with... at a disadvantage in several respects. For one thing, we are fake. They are not. So in terms of credibility we are, well, oddly enough, actually about even. We're about even.

Stewart's reasoning for denial of the newsworthiness of his show is an attempt to deflect responsibility away from his program to allow the show to maintain its persona as comedy-news and talk show, which in the past has left its writers empowered to say what other network news broadcasts don't, or cant, and which has been its *raison d'etre* and source of popularity. And yet, like real news, Stewart begs his viewers to "stay tuned for the latest updates" and even tries to validate his own credibility as a news service by discrediting the other news agencies. The fact that *The Daily Show* calls itself fake news but is perceived by the audience as being real, allows it to say things that other news programs could not get away with under the guise of humour and still have real impact.

Not everyone is happy about *The Daily Show*'s change in program content. Many fans feel that the program, which began as a harsh critique of the media and its coverage of American politics, has itself, by aiming to affect the voter turnout and impression in the 2004 Presidential election, altered its own political humour and coverage. When asked if his show was equally as critical of the Democrats as the Republicans during the lead up to the election, Jon Stewart told an interviewer at CBS, "We don't consider ourselves equal opportunity anythings, because that's not—you know, that's the beauty of fake journalism. We don't have to—we travel in fake ethics." [24] However, the defense of being fake journalists has left many fans unhappy and unimpressed. A posting on a fan site perhaps best illustrates this: "somehow, over the years, *The Daily Show* slowly transformed into an actual news show, gradually transforming itself bit-by-bit into the very thing it reviled."[25] Much as the audience is sometimes confused as Stewart straddles the barrier between real and fake news, so too is Stewart sometimes confused. While a guest on CNN's *Crossfire*, co-host Tucker Carlson accused Stewart of being more fun on *The Daily Show* than during his appearance on *Crossfire*, suggesting that Stewart was taking himself (and his opinions) too seriously. Stewart took offence to the idea that his own comments about journalism were not appreciated and told Carlson "You know what's interesting, though? You're as big a dick on your show as you are on any show. [26] At the same time as he uses fake news as his defence, Jon Stewart still wants to have the credibility of a real news anchor.

Another way that *The Daily Show* looks to associate itself with the credibility of mainstream news is through the actors it uses to play the roles of its reporters, correspondents and analysts: Stephen Colbert, Samantha Bee, Ed Helms and Rob Corddry. If, as Graeme Burton tells us, "news as genre becomes the same stories told in the same ways to reinforce the same meanings about social power and social relations," then *The Daily Show* as a news program is not excluded from this group.[27] Even though its correspondents may ask the most ludicrous questions, the discourse on the show is still telling the same stories, which reinforce the same social meanings. The shows humour comes from its play on existing relationships of power in society. Take as an example an interview conducted by Samantha Bee with a delegate from Montana at the 2004 Republican Convention in New York:

Samantha Bee: Have you had your picture taken with a black person yet?

Delegate: I haven't, but I wouldn't mind doing that.

Bee: That's something you'd be willing to try?

Delegate: Why, certainly.

Bee: There's plenty of them [in New York]. Do you have any in Montana?

Delegate: We don't. In fact, I guess our kids were pretty old before they saw one.

The humour in this skit comes from the preconceived ideas that the viewer has about: the Republican Party's ideas on black people, the images of country red-necks associated with states like Montana, and the ridiculous attempt of people to appear politically correct during election campaigns. At the same time as the humour attacks the hegemony of American society that it mimics, it also reinforces it, by acknowledging its existence and using it to garner a laugh. On one level, by performing political satire, *The Daily Show* reinforces the political structure that it criticizes. For example, when *The Daily Show* represents George W. Buish as an idiot for one reason or another, it reinforces that he is in fact the chosen leader of the free world and thus gives him power at the same time that it seeks to discredit him. On a semiotic level, by taking a political event out of its original context and using it as a sound bite to elicit laughter *The Daily Show* is in fact participating in the same practices of media manipulation the show pretends to be criticizing.

In his interview on PBS's *Now with Bill Moyers*, Moyers questioned the journalistic practices of *The Daily Show* by stating: "I do not know whether you are practicing an old form of parody and satire...or a new form of journalism."[28] Stewart's response said it all. "Well then, that either speaks to the sad state of comedy or the sad state of news. I can't figure out which one. I think, honestly, we're practicing a new form of desperation." [29] This new form of desperation is the new face of news in 2005, so that whether it is Fox News or CNN, the focus of television news is what is entertaining and not what is news. At the same time, this new desperation is all about the spectacle, and even more so an integrated news spectacle, so that selling is also a driving force. Whether your view of Jon Stewart's program sees his show as critical of the current state or as the leader of it, either way, *The Daily Show* is the face of news in 2005, or as Moyers said in the prelude to his interview with Jon Stewart "when future historians come to write the political story of our times, they will first have to review hundreds of hours of a cable television program called *The Daily Show*. You simply can't understand American politics in the new millennium without *The Daily Show*." [30]

NOTES

[1] Doug Hill and Jeff Weingrad. *Saturday night : a backstage history of Saturday Night Live* (New York: Beech Tree Books, 1986), 213.

[2] John Colapinto "The Most Trusted Name in News: How Jon Stewart and The Daily Show made 'fake news' a hit" *Rolling Stone,* September 2004.

[3] David Grote. *The end of comedy: the sit-com and the comedic tradition.* (Hamden, CT: Archon Books, 1983), 13.

[4] R. Roberts, "The Wide World of Muhammad Ali" in *Muhammad Ali The Peoples Champ,* ed. Elliot J. Gorn (Urbana: Univeristy of Illinois Press, 1995), 133.

[5] Roderick P. Hart, *Seducing America: How Television Charms the Modern Voter.* (Thousand Oaks : Sage Publications, 1999), 177.

[6] Stephen Wagg, 'They Already Got a Comedian for Governor: Comedians and Politics in the United States and Great Britain" in *Because I tell a joke or two: comedy, politics, and social difference* ed. Stephen Wagg (New York: Routledge, 1998), 271.

[7] Grote. *End of comedy,* 30.

[8] Bryan Long, "Daily Show viewers ace political quiz: Survey reveals late-night TV viewers better informed" *CNN.com* Wednesday, September 29, 2004.

[9] Colapinto "Most Trusted Name" *Rolling Stone.*

[10] Marc Peyser, "Who's Next 2004: Red, White & Funny: The new year will bring a host of intriguing faces front and center. Politicians. Actors. Tycoons. Educators. And one fake news anchor, bravely battling pomposity and misinformation. Jon Stewart prepares for Campaign 2004.", *MSNBC.com,* Dec. 29/Jan. 5 issue.

[11] Paul J. Gough, "Daily Show Host Gives Satire a Serious Look", *Reuters. com* Tuesday October 19, 2004.

[12] Alison Romano, "Record Ratings for Daily Show", *Broadcasting & Cable,* www.broadcastingcable.com, October 1, 2004 5:14:00 PM.

[13] Bryan Long, "Daily Show viewers", *CNN.com.*

[14] Interview with Jon Stewart, *Now With Bill Moyers,* PBS: July 11, 2004.

[15] Hart. *Seducing America,*10.

[16] Marc Peyser "Who's Next 2004", *MSNBC.com.*

[17] Neil Postman, *Amusing ourselves to death* (New York: Penguin, 1985), 4-5.

[18] David Taras "The CBC and Canadian Television in the New Media Age" in *A Passion for Identity: An Introduction to Canadian Studies.* (Scarborough, Ontario: ITP Nelson, 1997), 273.

[19] David Taras, "Swimming Against the Current: American Mass Entertainment and Canadian Identity" in *Canada and the United States: Differences that Count.* Edited by David M. Thomas. (Peterborough, Ontario: Broadview Press, 2000).

[20] James Compton. *The Integrated News Spectacle: A Political Economy of Cultural Performance*. (New York: Peter Lang Publishing, 2004), 2.

[21] Ibid, 113.

[22] Author unnamed. "No Joke: Daily Show Viewers Follow Presidential Race" *The Business Journal*, www.business-journal.com. September 21, 2004 12:20 p.m.

[23] Interview with Jon Stewart Crossfire, *CNN*: October 15, 2004.

[24] Author unnamed. "John Stewart Roasts Real News" *CBS.com*: October 24, 2004.

[25] http://www.rotten.com/library/culture/daily-show/

[26] Interview with Jon Stewart Crossfire, *CNN*: October 15, 2004.

[27] Graeme Burton. *Talking Television: An Introduction to the Study of Television* (New York: Oxford University Press, 2000), 122.

[28] Interview with Jon Stewart, *Now With Bill Moyers*, PBS: July 11, 2004.

[29] Interview with Jon Stewart, *Now With Bill Moyers*, PBS: July 11, 2004.

[30] Interview with Jon Stewart, *Now With Bill Moyers*, PBS: July 11, 2004.

What the Mainstream Media Can Learn From Jon Stewart

No, not to be funny and snarky, but to be bold and to do a better job of cutting through the fog

By Rachel Smolkin

Rachel Smolkin is AJR's managing editor. AJR editorial assistant Emily Groves contributed research to this report.

When Hub Brown's students first told him they loved "The Daily Show with Jon Stewart" and sometimes even relied on it for news, he was, as any responsible journalism professor would be, appalled.

Now he's a "Daily Show" convert.

"There are days when I watch 'The Daily Show,' and I kind of chuckle. There are days when I laugh out loud. There are days when I stand up and point to the TV and say, 'You're damn right!'" says Brown, chair of the communications department at Syracuse University's S.I. Newhouse School of Public Communications and an associate professor of broadcast journalism.

Brown, who had dismissed the faux news show as silly riffing, got hooked during the early days of the war in Iraq, when he felt most of the mainstream media were swallowing the administration's spin rather than challenging it. Not "The Daily Show," which had no qualms about second-guessing the nation's leaders. "The stock-in-trade of 'The Daily Show' is hypocrisy, exposing hypocrisy. And nobody else has the guts to do it," Brown says. "They really know how to crystallize an issue on all sides, see the silliness everywhere."

Whether lampooning President Bush's disastrous Iraq policies or mocking "real" reporters for their credulity, Stewart and his team often seem to steer closer to the truth than traditional journalists. The "Daily Show" satirizes spin, punctures pretense and belittles bombast. When a video clip reveals a politician's backpedaling, verbal contortions or mindless prattle, Stewart can state the obvious—ridiculing such blather as it deserves to be ridiculed—or remain silent but speak volumes merely by arching an eyebrow.

Stewart and his fake correspondents are freed from the media's preoccupation with balance, the fixation with fairness. They have no obligation to deliver the day's most important news, if that news is too depressing, too complicated or too boring. Their sole allegiance is to comedy.

Or, as "The Daily's Show's" Web site puts it: "One anchor, five correspondents, zero credibility. If you're tired of the stodginess of the evening newscasts, if you can't bear to sit through the spinmeisters and shills on the 24-hour cable news networks, don't miss The Daily Show with Jon Stewart, a nightly half-hour series unburdened by objectivity, journalistic integrity or even accuracy."

That's funny. And obvious. But does that simple, facetious statement capture a larger truth—one that may contain some lessons for newspapers and networks struggling to hold on to fleeing readers, viewers and advertisers in a tumultuous era of transition for old media?

Has our slavish devotion to journalism fundamentals—particularly our obsession with "objectivity"—so restricted news organizations that a comedian can tell the public what's going on more effectively than a reporter? Has Stewart, whose mission is to be funny, sliced through the daily obfuscation more effectively than his media counterparts, whose mission is to inform?

This is, perhaps, a strange premise for a journalism review to explore. AJR's mission is to encourage rigorous ethical and professional standards, particularly at a time when fake news of the non Jon Stewart variety has become all too prevalent. Stewart's faux news is parody, a sharp, humorous take on the actual events of the day, not to be confused with fake news of the Jayson Blair, Jack Kelley, National Guard memos or even WMD variety, based only loosely on actual events yet presented as real news.

As I posed my question about lessons of "The Daily Show" to various journalism ethicists and professionals, some carefully explained why mainstream news organizations should refrain from engaging in such whimsy.

Ed Fouhy, who worked for all three broadcast networks in his 22-year career as a producer and network executive before retiring in 2004, is a regular "Daily Show" watcher. "Sometimes conventional journalism makes it difficult for a journalist to say what he or she really thinks about an incident. Sometimes you can cut closer to the bone with another form, another creative form, like a novel or a satire on television," Fouhy says. "I think what we're seeing is just a daily dose of it. You think back to 'Saturday Night Live,' and they've satirized the news for a long time with their 'Weekend Update.' 'That Was the Week That Was' was an early television satire on the news."

But Fouhy cringes at the idea that real journalists should model themselves after such a show. When readers pick up a newspaper or viewers turn on a news broadcast, they're looking for serious information, and they should be able to find it. "When you begin to blur the line..to attract more viewers and younger viewers, I think that's a lousy idea," he says.

Adds Robert Thompson, director of the Bleier Center for Television and Popular Culture at Syracuse University, "Journalists have a really inconvenient thing they've got to go through: a process of trying to get [the story] right... I don't think journalists should try to be more hip. Journalists have to learn the one lesson which is important, which is to try to get it right."

Fouhy and Thompson are correct, of course. But Thompson's colleague Hub Brown and some others interviewed for this piece believe the lesson of "The Daily Show" is not that reporters should try to be funny, but that they should try to be honest.

"Stop being so doggone scared of everything," Brown advises journalists. "I think there is much less courageousness than there needs to be. There are people out there who stick out because of their fearlessness. Somebody like Lara Logan at CBS," the network's chief foreign correspondent who has reported extensively from Iraq and Afghanistan, "is a great example who is fearless about saying the truth."

In the hours and days following Hurricane Katrina, state and federal officials dithered while New Orleanians suffered inside the filth and chaos of the Louisiana Superdome. Many journalists, notably CNN's Anderson Cooper, jettisoned their usual care in handling all sides equally. They were bewildered, appalled and furious, and it showed.

"We saw a lot of that during Hurricane Katrina, but it shouldn't take a Hurricane Katrina to get journalists to say the truth, to call it as they see it," Brown says. "The thing that makes 'The Daily Show' stick out is they sometimes seem to understand that better than the networks do." He adds: "I think it's valuable because when the emperor has no clothes, we get to say the emperor has no clothes. And we have to do that more often here... The truth itself doesn't respect point of view. The truth is never balanced... We have to not give in to an atmosphere that's become so partisan that we're afraid of what we say every single time we say something."

Venise Wagner, associate chair of the journalism department at San Francisco State University, argues with her students over whether "The Daily Show" is real journalism. They think it is; she tells them it isn't, explaining that journalism involves not just conveying information but also following a set of standards that includes verification, accuracy and balance.

But she says "The Daily Show" does manage to make information relevant in a way that traditional news organizations often do not, and freedom from "balance" shapes its success. " 'The Daily Show' doesn't have to worry about balance. They don't have to worry about accuracy, even. They can just sort of get at the essence of something, so it gives them much more latitude to play around with the information, to make it more engaging," Wagner says. "Straight news sometimes places itself in a box where it doesn't allow itself— it doesn't give itself permission to question as much as it probably should question." Instead, the exercise becomes one of: "I'm just going to take the news down and give it to you straight."

But what exactly is straight news, and what is balance? Is balance a process of giving equal weight to both sides, or of giving more weight to the side with more evidence? Does accuracy mean spelling everybody's name right and quoting them correctly, or does it also mean slicing to the heart of an issue? "Nowhere is the comedy show balanced," says Wagner, "but it allows them more balance in showing what is really going on."

As journalists, by contrast, "We've presented a balanced picture to the public. But is it accurate? Is it authentic?" She cites coverage of the global warming debate, which, until recently, often was presented as an equal argument between scientists who said global warming was occurring and scientists who denied it. "That reality was not authentic. There were very few scientists who refuted the body of evidence" supporting global warming, Wagner says, yet the coverage did not always reflect that.

Martin Kaplan, associate dean of the University of Southern California's Annenberg School for Communication, dislikes journalists' modern perception of balance. "Straight news is not what it used to be," he says. "It has fallen into a bizarre notion that substitutes something called 'balance' for what used to be called 'accuracy' or 'truth' or 'objectivity.' That may be because of a general postmodern malaise in society at large in which the notion of a truth doesn't have the same reputation it used to, but, as a consequence, straight journalists both in print and in broadcast can be played like a piccolo by people who know how to exploit that weakness.

"Every issue can be portrayed as a controversy between two opposite sides, and the journalist is fearful of saying that one side has it right, and the other side does not. It leaves the reader or viewer in the position of having to weigh competing truth claims, often without enough information to decide that one side is manifestly right, and the other side is trying to muddy the water with propaganda."

Kaplan directs USC's Norman Lear Center, which studies how journalism and politics have become branches of entertainment, and he has worked in all three worlds: former editor and columnist for the now-defunct Washington Star; chief speechwriter for Vice President Walter Mondale; deputy presidential campaign manager for Mondale; Disney studio executive and motion picture and television producer.

He borrows Eric Alterman's phrase "working the ref" to illustrate his point about balance. Instead of "reading a story and finding out that black is black, you now read a story and it says, 'Some say black is black, and some say black is white.'... So whether it's climate change or evolution or the impact on war policy of various proposals, it's all being framed as 'on the one hand, on the other hand,' as though the two sides had equal claims on accuracy."

Therein lies "The Daily Show's" appeal, he says. "So-called fake news makes fun of that concept of balance. It's not afraid to have a bullshit meter and to call people spinners or liars when they deserve it. I think as a consequence some viewers find that helpful and refreshing and hilarious."

In addition to the user-generated satire on YouTube, Kaplan thinks the Web is bursting with commentators, including Alterman and Salon's Glenn Greenwald, who brilliantly penetrate the fog—sometimes angrily, sometimes amusingly, sometimes a bit of both.

Broadcasters have tackled this least successfully, he says, citing CBS' ill-fated "Free Speech" segment. Launched on and then discarded from "The CBS Evening News with Katie Couric," the segment gave personalities such as Rush Limbaugh uninterrupted airtime to trumpet their views. And "the challenge for the great national papers," Kaplan adds, "is to escape from this straightjacket in which they're unable to say that official A was telling the truth, and official B was not."

Part of "The Daily Show's" charm comes from its dexterity in letting public figures from Bush to House Speaker Nancy Pelosi (D-Calif.) speak for—and contradict—themselves, allowing the truth to emanate from a politician's entanglement over his or her own two feet. It's one way to hold government officials accountable for their words and deeds. Some might even call it fact-checking.

Brooks Jackson directs FactCheck.org, a project of the Annenberg Public Policy Center of the University of Pennsylvania, which monitors the accuracy of prominent politicians' statements in TV ads, debates, speeches, interviews and press releases. Jackson himself is a former reporter for the Associated Press, Wall Street Journal and CNN who pioneered "ad watch" coverage at the cable network during the "92 presidential race.

"I'm totally buying it," he told me after I stumbled through my fake-news-gets-at-the-truth-better premise. "I am in awe of the ability of Stewart and however many people he has working for him to cull through the vast wasteland of cable TV and pick out the political actors at their most absurd. They just have an unerring eye for that moment when people parody themselves. And I guess while the cable news hosts are obliged to take those moments of idiocy seriously, Jon Stewart can give us that Jack Benny stare—Does anybody remember Jack Benny?—give us that Jon Stewart stare and let the hilarity of the moment sink in, often without saying a word."

Does this qualify as fact-checking? Not exactly, Jackson replies, but "one thing he does do that is fact-checking: If somebody says, 'I never said that,' and next thing you know, there's a clip of the same guy three months ago saying exactly that, that's great fact-checking," and a great lesson for journalists. Jackson thinks NBC's Tim Russert is the master of that art in the mainstream media, confronting his subjects as he puts their quotes on-screen and reading them verbatim. "Stewart does it for laughs, and Russert does it for good journalistic reasons, and we all can learn from the two of them."

The form has its limits as a fact-checking technique. Jackson doesn't envision Stewart giving a State of the Union address rigorous ad-watch-type treatment, complete with statistical analysis of the president's proposed budget. Why would he? He'd put his audience to sleep. "Not every misleading statement can be debunked out of the person's own mouth," notes Jackson. "That's a particular kind of debunking that's very effective as comedy... There's plenty that needs debunking that isn't funny."

Asked about Stewart's influence on mainstream reporters, Jackson says: "Jon's been holding up the mirror to them for quite a while without any particular effect. The forces that are making the news more trivial and less relevant are frankly much more powerful than a show like Jon Stewart's can change."

Much of the allure of Stewart's show lies in its brutal satire of the media. He and his correspondents mimic the stylized performance of network anchors and correspondents. He exposes their gullibility. He derides their contrivances.

On March 28, the broadcast media elite partied with their government sources at the annual Radio and Television Correspondents' Association dinner. The disquieting spectacle of White House adviser Karl Rove rapping in front of a howling audience of journalists quickly appeared on YouTube. Quipped Stewart, only too accurately, the next night: "The media gets a chance to, for one night, put aside its cozy relationship with the government for one that is, instead, nauseatingly sycophantic."

His 2004 textbook satire, "America (The Book): A Citizen's Guide to Democracy Inaction," devotes a section to media in the throes of transformation and punctures this transition far more concisely, and probably more memorably, than the millions of words AJR has devoted to the subject:

"Newspapers abound, and though they have endured decades of decline in readership and influence, they can still form impressive piles if no one takes them out to the trash... Television continues to thrive. One fifteen-minute nightly newscast, barely visible through the smoky haze of its cigarette company benefactor, has evolved into a multi-channel, twenty-four hour a day infotastic clusterfuck of factish-like material. The 1990s brought the advent of a dynamic new medium for news, the Internet, a magnificent new technology combining the credibility of anonymous hearsay with the excitement of typing."

Phil Rosenthal, the Chicago Tribune's media columnist, thinks part of the reason "The Daily Show" and its spinoff, "The Colbert Report," resonate is that they parody not only news but also how journalists get news. "It's actually kind of a surefire way to appeal to people because if the news itself isn't entertaining, then the way it's covered, the breathless conventions of TV news, are always bankable," Rosenthal says. "You can always find something amusing there."

He adds that "so much of the news these days involves managing the news, so a show like Stewart's that takes the larger view of not just what's going on, but how it's being manipulated, is really effective. I think there's a general skepticism about the process that this plays into... The wink isn't so much we know what's really going on. The wink is also we know you know what we're doing here. It's down to the way the correspondents stand [in front of] the green screen, offering commentary and intoning even when their commentary may not be important."

Irony-deficient journalists have rewarded Stewart over the last five years by devoting more than 150 newspaper articles alone to his show and to studies about his show. Most have discussed the program's popularity. ("The Daily Show" attracted an average 1.5 million viewers nightly from January 1 through April 19, according to Nielsen Media Research. Couric's beleaguered CBS newscast, by contrast, netted an average 7.2 million viewers nightly during the same period.)

Many stories have pondered whether "The Daily Show" has substance and credibility; mourned young people's alleged propensity to rely on such lighthearted fare for news; brooded over what this reliance says about the state of the news media; and grieved that the show poisons young people's outlook on government, leaving them cynical and jaded. Stewart, who declined to be interviewed for this article, has patiently explained that his show is supposed to be funny.

That hasn't stopped the onslaught of serious discourse and research about "The Daily Show." A 2004 survey by the Pew Research Center for the People and the Press found that 21 percent of people age 18 to 29 cited comedy shows such as "The Daily Show" and "Saturday Night Live" as places where they regularly learned presidential campaign news, nearly equal to the 23 percent who regularly learned something from the nightly network news or from daily newspapers.

Even if they did learn from his show, a more recent study indicates Stewart's viewers are well-informed. An April 15 Pew survey gauging Americans' knowledge of national and international affairs found that 54 percent of regular viewers of "The Daily Show" and "Colbert Report" scored in the high-knowledge category, tying with regular readers of newspaper Web sites and edging regular watchers of "The NewsHour with Jim Lehrer." Overall, 35 percent of people surveyed scored in the high-knowledge category.

In October, Julia R. Fox, who teaches telecommunications at Indiana University, and two graduate students announced the results of the first scholarly attempt to compare Stewart's show with traditional TV news as a political information source. Their study, which will be published this summer by the Journal of Broadcasting & Electronic Media, examined substantive political coverage in 2004 of the first presidential debate and political conventions on "The Daily Show" and the broadcast television networks' nightly newscasts. Fox concluded Stewart's show is just as substantive as network news.

Fox says she wasn't surprised by the study results, but she was surprised by the general lack of surprise. "People have e-mailed me and said, 'I think you're absolutely wrong. I think 'The Daily Show' is more substantive.' "

Beyond the debate over whether Stewart's show is a quality source of information or whether wayward young fans have lost their minds, the media have treated him with admiration bordering on reverence. In early 2005, press reports handicapped his chances of landing on the "CBS Evening News," which, like Comedy Central, was then owned by Viacom. After Dan Rather had announced his abrupt retirement following revelations that alleged memos about President Bush's National Guard Service had not been authenticated, CBS chief Leslie Moonves said he wanted to reinvent the evening news to make it more relevant, "something that younger people can relate to." Asked at a news conference whether he'd rule out a role for Stewart, Moonves took a pass, fueling more speculation.

In 2004, the Television Critics Association bestowed the outstanding achievement in news and information award not on ABC's "Nightline" or PBS' "Frontline," but on "The Daily Show." Stewart, who had won for outstanding achievement in comedy the previous year, seemed bemused by the honor. Instead of accepting in person, he sent a tape of himself sitting at "The Daily Show" anchor desk. "We're fake," he informed the TV critics. "See this desk?.. It folds up at the end of the day, and I take it home in my purse."

But Melanie McFarland, the critic who presented Stewart's award, calls him a "truth teller" who speaks plainly about the news and offers a "spoonful of sugar that helps the medicine, the news, go down."

That sugar is not just delightful; it's provocative. "Any comedian can do sort of a 'Saturday Night Live' presentation and just do the punch line," says McFarland, who writes for the Seattle Post-Intelligencer. "He actually gives you some stuff to consider in addition to the punch line. He and his staff show an awareness of the issues and [are] able to take a longer view than a 24-hour news cycle can, which is funny because it's also a daily show." Other news programs and journalists, including "Frontline" and Bill Moyers, do this also, she says, but not as often. "So much of the news is not digestion but regurgitation. He's sort of looking at the raw material and making a common-sense assessment of what it means."

McFarland says Stewart's mockery of the media should galvanize journalists to perform better. "If there's a guy who's making great headway in giving people information by showing people what you're not doing in giving them information, let's try to do our jobs."

For serious news organizations, change is easier advised than enacted. Take Stewart's imitation of the stylized anchor persona, which—with precious little exaggeration—makes TV personalities look silly and stilted. Altering that persona is no easy task, as Katie Couric discovered when she tried to make the nightly news chattier.

"While Jon Stewart is a guy in a suit pretending to be a newscaster, and he acts like a guy in a suit pretending to be a newscaster, there's a certain formality and rigidity we've come to expect from our news, so much so that when Katie Couric opens the news with 'Hi,' or now I think it's 'Hello,' this is thought of as some kind of breakdown in the proper etiquette of newscasting," says the Chicago Tribune's Rosenthal. He thinks perhaps the time has come to abandon the old formality of newscasting but says such a process will be evolutionary.

In other broadcast formats, incorporating a more sardonic tone can work well. Rosenthal cites MSNBC's "Countdown with Keith Olbermann" as one news program that does a pretty good job incorporating the same sorts of elements that make "The Daily Show" successful. "Keith Olbermann gets a lot of attention for his editorializing, but the meat of that show is this hybrid blend of the news you need to know, the news that's entertaining, with a little bit of perspective [in] taking a step back from what the news is and what the newsmakers want it to be," he says. (See "Is Keith Olbermann the Future of Journalism?" February/March.)

Rosenthal thinks ABC's quirky overnight show, "World News Now," also has achieved a more detached, looser tone, and says it's no accident that the program has been "such a fertile breeding ground for unorthodox newspeople," including Anderson Cooper and Aaron Brown.

Public radio, known for its sober (and sometimes stodgy) programming, is experimenting with a more freewheeling search for truth as well. In January, Public Radio International launched "Fair Game from PRI with Faith Salie," a one-hour satirical news and entertainment show that airs on weeknights. The Sacramento Bee's Sam McManis likened the new show to "the quirky love child of 'The Daily Show With Jon Stewart' and 'All Things Considered.' It's smart enough to slake the traditional public-radio fans' thirst for intellectual programming but satiric enough to catch the attention of the prematurely cynical Gen X and Gen Y sets."

Salie is a comedian and a Rhodes Scholar with a bachelor's degree from Harvard and a master of philosophy from Oxford in modern English literature. "I'm not a journalist, and I don't have to pretend to be one," she says, describing herself as her listeners' proxy. When she interviews newsmakers— topics have included the Taliban, Hillary Clinton and the Dixie Chicks – "I don't feel like I have to mask my incredulousness. I can say, 'For real? Are you kidding me?' That leads to spontaneity."

Sometimes humor results from a certain framing of the news. Each Monday, the show revisits metaphors from the Sunday morning news shows. On "Fox News Sunday" on April 8, Juan Williams first compared Republican presidential hopeful John McCain to a "deflated balloon," then declared the Arizona senator was on the "wrong path" with his Iraq policy and concluded that he shouldn't be "tying his tail" to such an albatross. On NBC's "Meet the Press," Judy Woodruff in January described the administration's Iraq policy as akin to "putting a fist in a sink full of water, leaving it there for a few minutes and taking it out."

Salie says "The Daily Show" has demonstrated that young people are savvier than many elders believe, and the mainstream media should learn from that. Young people "are aware of the news and can recognize the preposterousness of some of it." But don't try too hard to be funny, she cautions. "I don't think real news shows should try the scripted, cutesy, pithy banter. It gives me the heebie-jeebies. It makes me feel sad for them, and it feels pathetic."

For an informal, satirical or even humorous take on the news to work in a mainstream newspaper, the format must be exactly right. Gene Weingarten, the Washington Post humor writer, thinks the media would do their jobs better if they had more fun, and he cringes whenever editors insist on labeling his pieces as satire. "Nothing could be worse for satire than labeling it satire," he laments.

But he concedes his editors may have a point. In August, Paul Farhi, a reporter for the Post's Style section (and an AJR contributor), reviewed the debut of colleague Tony Kornheiser on ESPN's "Monday Night Football." The critique was not flattering, and an apoplectic Kornheiser retaliated by publicly trashing Farhi as "a two-bit weasel slug," whom he would "gladly run over with a Mack truck."

The smackdown drew national attention, and Weingarten decided he wanted a piece of the action. So he skewered Kornheiser's second show with an outrageous, over-the-top rant on the front of Style about the "failed Kornheiser stewardship" taking "yet another bumbling misstep toward its inevitable humiliating collapse."

"It was patently unfair," Weingarten says of his tongue-in-cheek diatribe, which was not labeled as satire. "A child would have understood this piece. No one could have misunderstood this."

And yet they did. Weingarten got hundreds, possibly thousands, of complaints from sports lovers pummeling him for attacking Kornheiser unfairly. (Kornheiser himself called Weingarten, unsure how to interpret the piece.) "The mail I got was just absolutely hilarious," Weingarten says. "There is a problem of applying irony, humorous satire, in a newspaper when readers are not accustomed to seeing it there."

Did he learn from the experience? "No," he replies. "Because my reaction was, 'These people are idiots.'"

Perhaps the hardest lesson to take away from "The Daily Show" is the most important one. How can journalists in today's polarized political climate pierce the truth, Edward R. Murrow-style, without a) being ideological, or b) appearing ideological?

Olbermann's show, cited in several interviews as a serious news program that excels in revealing hypocrisy, is unabashedly liberal, and "The Daily Show" itself is frequently tagged with that label. In February, Fox News Channel debuted "The 1/2 Hour News Hour," billed as the conservative riposte to

Stewart's liberal bent; after two pilot shows, the network has agreed to pick up 13 additional episodes.

"Unfortunately, people are heading for news that sort of re-inforces their own beliefs," says Washington Post reporter Dana Milbank. "That may be Jon Stewart on the left, or that may be Rush Limbaugh on the right... Limbaugh isn't funny, but he's starting with something that has a kernel of truth and distorting it to the point of fakery as well, so I think they are parallel."

Milbank is the author of Washington Sketch, an experiment at slashing through the hazy words and deeds of federal power players. Milbank pitched the idea, based on British newspapers' parliamentary sketches, and argued for a few years before getting the green light in early 2005. "There was a lot of sort of figuring out the place, and first it really floated in the news section," he says. "I think we fixed that problem [by] putting it consistently on page two, and it's labeled more clearly."

Occasionally, Washington Sketch has appeared on page one, as it did March 6 when Milbank tartly contrasted the style of two generals who testified before Congress on the deplorable conditions at Walter Reed Army Medical Center. Then and at other times, Milbank's acerbic take has proved more enlightening than the longer, more traditional accompanying news story.

The column lacks a consistent ideology. Milbank says his goal is a "pox on both their houses sort of thing," and adds, "I'm not trying to be 50-50, particularly. The goal is to pick on all of them... It's observational as opposed to argumentative." Too often, he says, "We seem to make the mistake of thinking that if you're not being ideological, you therefore have to be boring, and all sort of 50-50 down the middle and follow the inverted pyramid."

Jeff Jarvis, the blogger behind BuzzMachine.com, says journalists should engage in more open, honest conversations with readers. "I think what Stewart et al do is remind us of what our mission and voice used to be and should be," says Jarvis, who also is a media consultant and head of the interactive journalism program at the City University of New York Graduate School of Journalism. He notes that Stewart is "very much a part of the conversation. He's joking about things we're talking about. And then the next day, we're talking about him talking about it."

Jarvis wants journalists to unleash their inner Stewart. "After enough drinks, reporters talk like Stewart: 'You won't BELIEVE what the mayor said today!' Why don't we talk to our readers that way?" he asks, and then acknowledges: "OK. There's a lot of arguments: 'The mayor won't talk to us again.' 'It's biased.' 'We don't want to turn everything into blogs.' "

Jarvis doesn't mean that every story should become a first-person diatribe, and obviously the mainstream media can't fall back on Stewart's I'm-just-joking excuse after they've infuriated a thin-skinned politician. But there are instances when a little unorthodoxy may be appropriate, and speaking frankly may enhance credibility.

Eric Deggans, the TV and media critic for the St. Petersburg Times, also wants to see a little more pluck. " 'The Daily Show' is pushing us to be less traditional about how we deliver people information," Deggans says. "Are we going to turn around and turn into the Onion?" (The cult publication parodies news in print and online; its facetious Onion News Network debuted on March 27.) "Of course not. But if you've got a longtime state capitol bureau chief, and they see something go down in the capitol, and they have a great, acerbic take on it, why not let them go at it in a column?"

Or, he suggests, experiment just a bit with the sacred space on page one. "Sometimes editors have really rigid ideas about what can go on the front page," he says. "If somebody has a really good column on [Don] Imus, why wouldn't you put it on the front page, as long as you label it clearly as opinion? There are some editors who would say your first next-day story about Don Imus has to be traditional. Why? Why does it have to be traditional? As long as the reader isn't fooled, why do you let yourself be handcuffed like that?"

Deggans is quick to add some caveats, including the importance of fairness. "You always have to be careful because there's a good reason why we had those rules," Deggans says. "But we have to challenge ourselves to subvert them more often. You have to be subversive in a way that maintains your credibility. When you have smart, capable people who want to write in a different way, let them try it."

The mainstream media can not, should not and never will be "The Daily Show." The major news of our time is grimly serious, and only real news organizations will provide the time, commitment and professionalism necessary to ferret out stories such as the Washington Post's exposé of neglected veterans at Walter Reed or the New York Times' disclosures of secret, warrantless wiretapping by the federal government.

But in the midst of a transition, our industry is flailing. Our credibility suffers mightily. The public thinks we're biased despite our reluctance to speak plainly. Our daily newspapers often seem stale. Perhaps "The Daily Show" can teach us little, but remind us of a lot: Don't underestimate your audience. Be relevant. And be bold.

Says Deggans: "In a lot of news organizations, it's the fourth quarter. It's fourth down, man. It's time to show a little pizzazz. It's time to reinvent what's going on, so people get engaged."

The Most Trusted Man in America?

By Michiko Kakutani

It's been more than eight years since "The Daily Show With Jon Stewart" made its first foray into presidential politics with the presciently named Indecision 2000, and the difference in the show's approach to its coverage then and now provides a tongue-in-cheek measure of the show's striking evolution.

In 1999, the "Daily Show" correspondent Steve Carell struggled to talk his way off Senator John McCain's overflow press bus—"a repository for outcasts, misfits and journalistic bottom-feeders"—and onto the actual Straight Talk Express, while at the 2000 Republican Convention Mr. Stewart self-deprecatingly promised exclusive coverage of "all the day's events—at least the ones we're allowed into." In this year's promotional spot for "The Daily Show's" convention coverage, the news newbies have been transformed into a swaggering A Team—"the best campaign team in the universe ever," working out of " 'The Daily Show' news-scraper: 117 stories, 73 situation rooms, 26 news tickers," and promising to bring "you all the news stories—first ... before it's even true."

Though this spot is the program's mocking sendup of itself and the news media's mania for self-promotion, it inadvertently gets at one very real truth: the emergence of "The Daily Show" as a genuine cultural and political force. When Americans were asked in a 2007 poll by the Pew Research Center for the People and the Press to name the journalist they most admired, Mr. Stewart, the fake news anchor, came in at No. 4, tied with the real news anchors Brian Williams and Tom Brokaw of NBC, Dan Rather of CBS and Anderson Cooper of CNN. And a study this year from the center's Project for Excellence in Journalism concluded that " 'The Daily Show' is clearly impacting American dialogue" and "getting people to think critically about the public square."

While the show scrambled in its early years to book high-profile politicians, it has since become what Newsweek calls "the coolest pit stop on television," with presidential candidates, former presidents, world leaders and administration officials signing on as guests. One of the program's signature techniques—using video montages to show politicians contradicting themselves—has been widely imitated by "real" news shows, while Mr. Stewart's interviews with serious authors like Thomas Ricks, George Packer, Seymour Hersh, Michael Beschloss and Reza Aslan have helped them and their books win a far wider audience than they otherwise might have had.

Most important, at a time when Fox, MSNBC and CNN routinely mix news and entertainment, larding their 24-hour schedules with bloviation fests and marathon coverage of sexual predators and dead celebrities, it's been "The Daily Show" that has tenaciously tracked big, "super depressing" issues like the cherry-picking of prewar intelligence, the politicization of the Department of Justice and the efforts of the Bush White House to augment its executive power.

For that matter, the Comedy Central program—which is not above using silly sight gags and sophomoric sex jokes to get a laugh—has earned a devoted following that regards the broadcast as both the smartest, funniest show on television and a provocative and substantive source of news. "The Daily Show" resonates not only because it is wickedly funny but also because its keen sense of the absurd is perfectly attuned to an era in which cognitive dissonance has become a national epidemic. Indeed, Mr. Stewart's frequent exclamation "Are you insane?!" seems a fitting refrain for a post-M*A*S*H, post-"Catch-22" reality, where the surreal and outrageous have become commonplace—an era kicked off by the wacko 2000 election standoff in Florida, rocked by the terrorist attacks of Sept. 11 and haunted by the fallout of a costly war waged on the premise of weapons of mass destruction that did not exist.

Mr. Stewart describes his job as "throwing spitballs" from the back of the room and points out that "The Daily Show" mandate is to entertain, not inform. Still, he and his writers have energetically tackled the big issues of the day—"the stuff we find most interesting," as he said in an interview at the show's Midtown Manhattan offices, the stuff that gives them the most "agita," the sometimes somber stories he refers to as his "morning cup of sadness." And they've done so in ways that straight news programs cannot: speaking truth to power in blunt, sometimes profane language, while using satire and playful looniness to ensure that their political analysis never becomes solemn or pretentious.

"Hopefully the process is to spot things that would be grist for the funny mill," Mr. Stewart, 45, said. "In some respects, the heavier subjects are the ones that are most loaded with opportunity because they have the most—you know, the difference between potential and kinetic energy?—they have the most potential energy, so to delve into that gives you the largest combustion, the most interest. I don't mean for the audience. I mean for us. Everyone here is working too hard to do stuff we don't care about."

Offices for "The Daily Show" occupy a sprawling loftlike space that combines the energy of a newsroom with the laid-back vibe of an Internet start-up: many staff members wear jeans and flip-flops, and two amiable dogs wander the hallways. The day begins with a morning meeting where material harvested from 15 TiVos and even more newspapers, magazines and Web sites is reviewed. That meeting, Mr. Stewart said, "would be very unpleasant for most people to watch: it's really a gathering of curmudgeons expressing frustration and upset, and the rest of the day is spent trying to mask or repress that through whatever creative devices we can find."

The writers work throughout the morning on deadline pieces spawned by breaking news, as well as longer-term projects, trying to find, as Josh Lieb, a co-executive producer of the show, put it, stories that "make us angry in a whole new way." By lunchtime, Mr. Stewart (who functions as the show's managing editor and says he thinks of hosting as almost an afterthought) has begun reviewing headline jokes. By 3 p.m. a script is in; at 4:15, Mr. Stewart and the crew rehearse that script, along with assembled graphics, sound bites and montages. There is an hour or so for rewrites—which can be intense, newspaper-deadlinelike affairs—before a 6 o'clock taping with a live studio audience.

What the staff is always looking for, Mr. Stewart said, are "those types of stories that can, almost like the guy in 'The Green Mile' "—the Stephen King story and film in which a character has the apparent ability to heal others by drawing out their ailments and pain—"suck in all the toxins and allow you to do something with it that is palatable."

To make the more alarming subject matter digestible, the writers search for ways to frame the story, using an arsenal of techniques ranging from wordplay ("Mess O'Potamia," "BAD vertising") to exercises in pure logic (deconstructing the administration's talking points on the surge) to demented fantasy sequences (imagining Vice President Dick Cheney sending an army of orcs to attack Iran when he assumed the presidency briefly last year during President Bush's colonoscopy).

Gitmo, the Elmo puppet from Guantánamo Bay, became a vehicle for expressing the writers' "most agitated feelings about torture in a way that is—not to be too cute—that is not torture to listen to, and that is not purely strident," Mr. Stewart said. And the cartoon strip "The Decider," featuring Mr. Bush as a superhero who makes decisions "without fear of repercussion, consequence or correctness," became a way to satirize the president's penchant for making gut calls that sidestep the traditional policy-making process.

As the co-executive producer Rory Albanese noted, juxtapositions of video clips and sound bites are one of the show's favorite strategies. It might be the juxtaposition of Senator Barack Obama speaking to a crowd of 200,000 in Berlin while Mr. McCain campaigns in a Pennsylvania grocery store. Or it could be a juxtaposition of a politician taking two sides of the same argument. One famous segment featured Mr. Stewart as the moderator of a debate between then-Governor Bush of Texas in 2000, who warned that the United States would end up "being viewed as the ugly American" if it went around the world "saying we do it this way—so should you," and President Bush of 2003, who extolled the importance of exporting democracy to Iraq.

Often a video clip or news event is so absurd that Mr. Stewart says nothing, simply rubs his eyes, does a Carsonesque double take or crinkles his face into an expression of dismay. "When in doubt, I can stare blankly," he said. "The rubber face. There's only so many ways you can stare incredulously at the camera and tilt an eyebrow, but that's your old standby: What would Buster Keaton do?"

Given a daily reality in which "over-the-top parodies come to fruition," Mr. Stewart said, satire like "Dr. Strangelove" becomes "very difficult to make." "The absurdity of what you imagine to be the dark heart of conspiracy theorists' wet dreams far too frequently turns out to be true," he observed. "You go: I know what I'll do, I'll create a character who, when hiring people to rebuild the nation we invaded, says the only question I'll ask is, 'What do you think of Roe v. Wade?' It'll be hilarious. Then you read that book about the Green Zone in Iraq"—"Imperial Life in the Emerald City" by Rajiv Chandrasekaran—"and you go, 'Oh, they did that.' I mean, how do you take things to the next level?"

Mr. Stewart has said he is looking forward to the end of the Bush administration "as a comedian, as a person, as a citizen, as a mammal." Though he has mocked both Mr. McCain and Mr. Obama for lapses from their high-minded promises of postpartisanship, he said he didn't think their current skirmishes were "being conducted on the scale that Bush conducted things, or even the Clintons; I don't think it has the same true viciousness and contempt."

Soon after Mr. Stewart joined "The Daily Show" in 1999, in the waning years of the Clinton administration, he and his staff began to move the program away from the show-business-heavy agenda it had under his predecessor, Craig Kilborn. New technology providing access to more video material gave them growing control over the show's content; the staff, the co-executive producer Kahane Corn said, also worked to choose targets "who deserved to be targets" instead of random, easy-to-mock subjects.

Following 9/11 and the invasion of Iraq, the show focused more closely not just on politics, but also on the machinery of policy making and the White House's efforts to manage the news media. Mr. Stewart's comedic gifts—his high-frequency radar for hypocrisy, his talent for excavating ur-narratives from mountains of information, his ability, in Ms. Corn's words, "to name things that don't seem to have a name"—proved to be perfect tools for explicating and parsing the foibles of an administration known for its secrecy, ideological certainty and impatience with dissenting viewpoints.

Over time, the show's deconstructions grew increasingly sophisticated. Its fascination with language, for instance, evolved from chuckles over the president's verbal gaffes ("Is our children learning?" "Subliminable") to ferocious exposés of the administration's Orwellian manipulations: from its efforts to redefine the meaning of the word "torture" to its talk about troop withdrawals from Iraq based on "time horizons" (a strategy, Mr. Stewart noted, "named after something that no matter how long you head towards it, you never quite reach it").

For all its eviscerations of the administration, "The Daily Show" is animated not by partisanship but by a deep mistrust of all ideology. A sane voice in a noisy red-blue echo chamber, Mr. Stewart displays an impatience with the platitudes of both the right and the left and a disdain for commentators who, as he made clear in a famous 2004 appearance on CNN's "Crossfire," parrot party-line talking points and engage in knee-jerk shouting matches. He has characterized Democrats as "at best Ewoks," mocked Mr. Obama for acting as though he were posing for "a coin" and hailed MoveOn.org sardonically for "10 years of making even people who agree with you cringe."

To the former NBC anchor Tom Brokaw, Mr. Stewart serves as "the citizens' surrogate," penetrating "the insiders' cult of American presidential politics." He's the Jersey Boy and ardent Mets fan as Mr. Common Sense, pointing to the disconnect between reality and what politicians and the news media describe as reality, channeling the audience's id and articulating its bewilderment and indignation. He's the guy willing to say the emperor has no clothes, to wonder why in Senator Hillary Rodham Clinton's "It's 3 a.m." and no one picks up the phone in the White House before six rings, to ask why a preinvasion meeting in March 2003 between President Bush and his allies took all of an hour—the "time it takes LensCrafters to make you a pair of bifocals" to discuss "a war that could destroy the global order."

"The Daily Show" boasts a deep bench when it comes to its writing, research and production and has provided a showcase for a host of gifted comedians who have gone on to other careers—most notably, Stephen Colbert of "The Colbert Report," as well as Mr. Carell, Rob Corddry and Ed Helms. But while the show is a collaborative effort, as one producer noted, it is "ultimately Jon's vision and voice."

Mr. Stewart described his anchorman character as "a sort of more adolescent version" of himself, and Ms. Corn noted that while things "may be exaggerated on the show, it's grounded in the way Jon really feels."

"He really does care," she added. "He's a guy who says what he means."

Unlike many comics today, Mr. Stewart does not trade in trendy hipsterism or high-decibel narcissism. While he possesses Johnny Carson's talent for listening and George Carlin's gift for observation, his comedy remains rooted in his informed reactions to what Tom Wolfe once called "the irresistibly lurid carnival of American life," the weird happenings in "this wild, bizarre, unpredictable, hog-stomping Baroque" country.

"Jon's ability to consume and process information is invaluable," said Mr. Colbert. He added that Mr. Stewart is "such a clear thinker" that he's able to take "all these data points of spin and transparent falsehoods dished out in the form of political discourse" and "fish from that what is the true meaning, what are red herrings, false leads," even as he performs the ambidextrous feat of "making jokes about it" at the same time.

"We often discuss satire—the sort of thing he does and to a certain extent I do—as distillery," Mr. Colbert continued. "You have an enormous amount of material, and you have to distill it to a syrup by the end of the day. So much of it is a hewing process, chipping away at things that aren't the point or aren't the story or aren't the intention. Really it's that last couple of drops you're distilling that makes all the difference. It isn't that hard to get a ton of corn into a gallon of sour mash, but to get that gallon of sour mash down to that one shot of pure whiskey takes patience" as well as "discipline and focus."

Mr. Stewart can be scathing in his dismantling of politicians' spin—he took apart former Under Secretary of Defense Douglas Feith's rationalizations about the Iraq war with Aesopian logic and fury—but there is nothing sensation-seeking or mean-spirited about his exchanges. Nor does he shy away from heartfelt expressions of sadness and pain. The day after the Virginia Tech massacre in 2007, he spoke somberly of the tragic situation there and asked his guest, Ali Allawi, a former Iraqi minister of defense, how his country handled "that sort of carnage on a daily basis" and if there were "a way to grieve."

Most memorably, on Sept. 20, 2001, the day the show returned after the 9/11 attacks, Mr. Stewart began the program with a raw, emotional address. Choking up, he apologized for subjecting viewers to "an overwrought speech of a shaken host" but said that he and the show's staff needed it "for ourselves, so that we can drain whatever abscess there is in our hearts so we can move on to the business of making you laugh."

He talked about hearing, as a boy of 5, of the assassination of Martin Luther King Jr. He talked about feeling privileged to live where you can "sit in the back of the country and make wisecracks." And he talked about "why I grieve but why I don't despair."

Mr. Stewart now says he does not want to listen to that show again: "The process of the show is to bury those feelings as subtext, and that was a real moment of text. It's laying bare the type of thing that is there hopefully to inform the show, but the show is usually an exercise in hiding that."

In fact, Mr. Stewart regards comedy as a kind of catharsis machine, a therapeutic filter for grappling with upsetting issues. "What's nice to us about the relentlessness of the show," he said, "is you know you're going to get that release no matter what, every night, Monday through Thursday. Like pizza, it may not be the best pizza you've ever had, but it's still pizza, man, and you get to have it every night. It's a wonderful feeling to have this toxin in your body in the morning, that little cup of sadness, and feel by 7 or 7:30 that night, you've released it in sweat equity and can move on to the next day."

Michigan Journal of Community Service Learning Fall 2008, pp.5–17

"A Double-Edged Sword": College Student Perceptions of Required High School Service-Learning

Susan R. Jones, Thomas C. Segar, and Anna L. Gasiorski

SUSAN R. JONES is an associate professor and program director in the College Student Personnel program at the University of Maryland-College Park. Much of her research focuses on service-learning in relation to requirements, resistance, student identity development, faculty motivations, and partnerships. She is a previous Ohio Campus Compact faculty fellow and has served on the boards of an AIDS service organization and after-school tutoring program.

THOMAS C. SEGAR is a doctoral student in the College Student Personnel program at the University of Maryland-College Park. He has held positions as a college administrator in residence life, multicultural student affairs, learning assistance, and disability support services for ten years prior to beginning doctoral studies. Tom earned his master's of science degree in counseling with a specialization in college student personnel from Shippensburg University of Pennsylvania, and his bachelor's of science degree in Psychology, with a certificate in African American studies, from the University of Maryland-College Park.

ANNA GASIORSKI currently works for the Ohio Learning Network as manager of quality data control. She is a doctoral candidate in the College Student Personnel program at the University of Maryland- College Park. She received her master's degree from the University of Michigan and her bachelor's degree from the College of William and Mary. Her research interests include service-learning and adult students, student resistance, and predictors of community service participation among college students.

This article presents the findings from a narrative inquiry exploring the perceived outcomes associated with a high school service-learning graduation requirement from a diverse group of college students. In particular, we were interested in participants' stories related to their experiences meeting the requirement, the meaning they made of the requirement, and the relationship between their high school experiences and college involvement. Results suggest a tenuous connection between the two because students focused primarily on completing their hours for the requirement and engaged in service primarily at their schools. Students perceived the requirement as a burden while in high school, but retrospectively understood the value of the requirement once they were in college, describing it as a "double-edged sword."

With increased national, university, and community attention focused on civic engagement and participation, service-learning is increasingly touted as an efficacious strategy to promote such goals (Eyler & Giles, 1999; Hart, Donnelly, Youniss, & Atkins, 2007; Metz & Youniss, 2003; Raskoff & Sundeen, 1999). Growing numbers of high school and college students are involved in community service and volunteering (Higher Education Research Institute, 2006; Spring, Dietz, & Grimm, 2006). Drawing upon data from the U.S. Census Bureau, the Corporation for National & Community Service (CNS) reports a 20% increase in the number of college students who volunteered from 2002 to 2005, attributing this in part to what they referred to as the "9/11 Generation." However, evidence exists to suggest that college students are involved in more "episodic," short-term volunteer activities which may not be directly related to the cultivation of patterns of participation needed for civic engagement (Dote, Cramer, Dietz, & Grimm, 2006; Marks & Jones, 2004) and that college student volunteer activity is on the decline (HERI, 2006). To promote a "culture of college service," the service-learning "pipeline" (Dote et al., p. 3) from high schools to college must be examined.

Community service and service-learning requirements are increasingly common among high schools and colleges, presumably as one strategy to promote continued community participation. Indeed, many school districts throughout the United States have established community service graduation requirements (Education Commission of the States, 2001). However, only Maryland has a statewide mandatory service-learning high school graduation requirement. Implemented in 1997, this mandate stipulates that all students who attend public high schools complete a minimum of 75 service-learning hours. Existing research on the link between required service and continued participation is mixed at best and does not match the certainty with which requirements are increasingly pursued in an effort to develop patterns of civic engagement and continued service (e.g., Deci & Ryan, 1987; Jennings &

Stoker, 2004; Jones & Hill, 2003; Marks & Jones, 2004; McLellan & Youniss, 2003; Metz & Youniss, 2003; Stukas, Clary, & Snyder, 1999). For example, CNS research reports that the state of Maryland is ranked 34th among all states in college student volunteering, with a 30.2% volunteering rate (Dote et al., 2006). This is surprising given that 46.2% of all Maryland public high school graduates become college students in the state's public and private colleges and universities (Maryland State Department of Education, 2006).

What is clear is that despite growing interest in service-learning in high schools and colleges, and investment of resources in promoting such activities, very little is known about the effectiveness of service-learning requirements in promoting civic engagement and continued community involvement (Niemi, Hepburn, & Chapman, 2000). No studies investigate how a statewide service-learning requirement influences students' future intentions to serve in college or beyond, or other outcomes associated with a requirement.

COMPETING RATIONALES FOR REQUIRED SERVICE

Early conceptual arguments associating education and service as a means of encouraging post secondary community involvement can be traced back over 100 years to educational pioneer John Dewey (Harkavy, 2004). More recent advocates such as Ernest Boyer (1983), former Federal Commissioner of Education, recommended mandatory high school service as a means of preparing students to assume responsibility for living as contributing members of their community and society during and after high school. Barber (1994) documented the historical trend of teaching citizenship through service noting that only in recent history has service been separated from education. This rationale positions service in primary and secondary education as a means of promoting continued service involvement in adulthood. Although these arguments may ring true for some, they are not grounded in or borne out in empirical research.

The number of college students who participated in service while in high school has steadily increased over the past two decades (Chronicle Almanac, 2007). According to the Cooperative Institutional Research Program about one-third of first-year college students graduated from high schools with some type of requirement for service (Vogelgesang, 2005). High school service requirements are more prevalent for students attending private and/ or religious high schools (Raskoff & Sundeen, 1999). However, data on collegiate service involvement suggested the number of high school students continuing with service participation in college may be falling. Vogelgesang and Astin (2005) found that the number of high school seniors engaged in service has increased over the past decade, while participation in service during and after college has declined during the same time period.

Relationship between High School and College Service

A review of empirical evidence suggests that the nature of the relationship between mandatory high school service and continued participation in college service is ambiguous. Although a number of studies (e.g., Astin & Sax, 1998; Berger & Milem, 2002; Eyler & Giles, 1999; Hart et al., 2007; Vogelgesang, 2005) have identified high school service as a predictor of college involvement, when the research has focused on required service the results are less clear. Further, the research that does exist examining the outcomes associated with required community service or service-learning suggests a disconnect between the espoused goals, objectives, and purposes of required service and what students actually experience. However, what is clear is that college students bring with them to higher education a whole range of characteristics, including the vestiges of their high school experiences (Cruce & Moore, 2007; McEwen, 2003).

For example, in two longitudinal studies of multiple student cohorts at one public high school in suburban Boston, Metz and Youniss (2003, 2005) found that the completion of a 40-hour service requirement was related to higher rates of high school volunteerism and also associated with an increase in students' intentions to volunteer in the future. However, consistent with HERI results, this study focused on intentions, rather than actual college service activity. In several studies that explored this relationship between high school and college participation, patterns emerge that suggest requirements do not necessarily result in continued service in college. Great variability exists in factors such as school structures to support the requirement and the nature of activities in which students engage to meet their requirement, which have been found to make a difference in outcomes associated with service (McLellan & Youniss, 2003). Further, Jennings and Stoker (2004), in a longitudinal quantitative study, found the effects of students' high school participation in community service may not immediately translate into college involvement.

Marks and Jones (2004) analyzed data from the National Educational Longitudinal Study (NELS) database which contains measures of several educational outcomes. They found that students who attended Catholic high schools and performed service as a requirement were more likely to discontinue serving in college. This trend held true for students who participated in community service as 10th graders or were mandated to perform community service as seniors. Students who were encouraged, but not required, to volunteer as 12th graders were more likely to continue volunteering in college.

Jones and Hill (2003) discovered that college students who participated in service in high school tended to continue in college if their motivation came from an internal commitment along with family and school encouragement. Those who participated more sporadically because of a requirement or to build up their resume were not likely to continue serving once they entered college.

Interviews with participants revealed two reasons against required service. First, if service is framed as a requirement, then it was no longer considered service. Second, students worked only toward completing the requirement and discontinued service once they met the conditions of the requirement. Service requirements can deter any lasting continued involvement in students as well as civic or social responsibility (Jones & Hill). Therefore, service becomes "just another homework assignment" (p. 524).

Finally, Stukas, Snyder, and Clary (1999), in a study of college students enrolled in a service-learning course, found that if students only perform service when required, they are less likely to freely volunteer in the future. This was affected by how much prior community service students had completed. Students with significant prior experience with service were less likely to be negatively influenced by required community service. However, if they had little to no prior experience, they were more likely to decide not to volunteer in the future. Researchers found that student choice regarding type of volunteering emerged as one way to counteract the negative impact of required service (Stukas, Snyder, & Clary).

The overall results from these studies suggest that students who participated in service in high school tended to continue in college if they made an internal commitment and received strong family and school encouragement. Further, those who participated more sporadically because of a requirement or to bolster their resume were not likely to continue serving once they entered college (Jones & Hill, 2003; Marks & Jones, 2004). To date, no studies provide compelling evidence to support the efficacy of required high school service-learning as an impetus for a sustained commitment to service during and after college. As a result, current evidence leaves few clues as to how college practitioners might counter the mediating deterrents to service that may be rooted in the high school experience.

The purpose of this research was to explore the perceived outcomes associated with a high school service-learning requirement from a diverse group of college students. In particular, we were interested in investigating the nature of the service-learning experiences participants had in meeting the requirement, the meaning they made of those experiences, and how these experiences influenced (or not) their college experiences. Specific research questions guiding the investigation included: (a)What meaning do college students make of their high school service-learning requirement? (b) What influence does a high school requirement have on college involvement, particularly continued community service? (c) What is the congruence between espoused goals of high schools and the actual learning as perceived by graduates? (d) What are student perceptions of the requirement? and (e) How do students understand their own service experiences?

METHOD

This study utilized a constructivist theoretical framework and a narrative methodological approach. Because we were interested in students' constructions of meaning of their high school service-learning experiences, a constructivist framework, which assumes knowledge is mutually constructed between researchers and participants (Denzin & Lincoln, 2000) and emphasizes the role of context (Flyvbjerg, 2001), was appropriate. A constructivist design situates the focus of the investigation on research participants' meaning making of their experiences and perceptions of outcomes related to the service requirement (Jones, Torres, & Arminio, 2006).

To access these experiences and perceptions, narrative inquiry was utilized as an approach that illuminates human experiences as lived and told as stories (Chase, 2005; Clandinin & Connelly, 2000; Creswell, 2007; Lieblich, Tuval-Mashiach, & Zilber, 1998). Chase identified five characteristics of narrative inquiry: (1) narrative researchers treat narrative as retrospective meaning making; (2) narratives represent verbal action in the constructing of an experience; (3) narratives are constrained and augmented by context and particulars of time and place; (4) narratives are shaped by the time and setting of the telling and thus, are variable; and (5) narrative researchers serve as narrators as they interpret the stories told (pp. 656-657). Narrative inquiry was particularly well-suited to research grounded in the nature of experiences, reflection on these experiences, and the stories that emerge (Clandinin & Connelly, 2000), such as uncovering narratives that make up the stories of students' experiences with service in high school.

Research Context

In 1997, Maryland became the first state to implement a mandatory service-learning high school graduation requirement stipulating that all students attending public high schools complete a minimum of 75 service-learning hours. More than 99% of graduating seniors complete the 75 hour service-learning requirement prior to graduating from high school (http://www.marylandpublicschools.org/MSDE/prog rams/service-learning/). Maryland residents make up 75.9% of the total undergraduate population at the University of Maryland; therefore the undergraduate population of the University of Maryland alone contributed more than one million hours of service during their high school career.

Procedures

Sampling. Expert nominators who served as informants and purposeful sampling were used to obtain information-rich cases (Patton, 2002). Twenty-three faculty and administrators whom we knew to have reputations for working closely with undergraduate students were sent letters describing the purpose of the study and asked to nominate Maryland undergraduate students from Maryland public high schools. Nominators represented a variety of functional areas within the university (e.g., residence life, campus programs, student judicial programs, academic honoraries and clubs, living learning programs, programs for underrepresented groups, student employment, faculty in scholars programs).We indicated to nominators that we were seeking a wide range of perspectives and experiences and that we were not only looking for undergraduate students who were involved on Maryland's campus, either in community service or other activities, but those less involved on campus or involved in their home communities. We also indicated that we were seeking participants from around the state of Maryland (e.g., rural, suburban, urban), various school sizes (e.g., small, medium, large), and representing diversity in social group membership (e.g., race, ethnicity, social class).

The invitation to nominate student participants resulted in 209 nominations, with 9 out of the 209 duplicate names. We then sent email invitations to each of these 200 students, letting them know they had been nominated for participation and inviting them to participate. This resulted in 54 affirmative responses. Of these 54, 10 were ineligible because they either attended a private Maryland high school or an out-of-state public high school. We then sent to the 44 eligible participants an interest form to complete which asked questions about their high school, how they met their service-learning requirement, when during high school they completed their hours, where their high school was located, college involvements and affiliations, as well as demographic questions related to racial-ethnic background, class year, religion, and age. Forty-three students returned interest forms and then, based on our sampling criteria (e.g., county of high school, racial-ethnic diversity, variety in college involvement), we selected 28 students to interview. Upon selecting these 28 students, we sent email messages to schedule interviews. Nineteen students responded to these requests to schedule interviews.

Participants. The sample included 9 men and 10 women; racial-ethnic background consisted of 5 Asian American (1 Pakistani, 1 Korean, 1 Vietnamese, 1 Filipino,1 Asian American), 2 Biracial, 4 African American/Black, and 8 white; from 10 different counties in the state; and 4 first-year students, 1 sophomore, 9 juniors, and 5 seniors. High school enrollment ranged from 300 to 3000; three high schools were categorized as rural, four as urban, and 12 as suburban. Students' college involvement covered a wide range, from not involved at all to highly involved. Examples of involvement included student government, community service related living and learning programs, various advisory councils, honor societies, and curricular and co-curricular student organizations. All names used are pseudonyms chosen by each participant.

Data collection. Data were collected through two in-depth interviews with each participant. So as not to overwhelm participants with a team of three interviewers, we divided up participants so that each researcher individually interviewed a subset of participants. Two interviews were conducted with each participant, and each participant had the same interviewer for both interviews so that rapport could be developed and a relationship established. Consistent with narrative inquiry, interviews were semi-structured and open-ended to elicit stories about service-learning experiences and how each participant understood those experiences (Chase, 2005; Lieblich, Tuval-Mashiach, & Zilber, 1998). The protocol for the first interview was pilot tested with three students who met the study sampling criteria and was revised based upon their feedback and our experiences with the protocol. The same protocol was used for each participant. The first interview focused on students' experiences meeting the high school service-learning requirement, their perceptions of the requirement, and the meaning they made of these. Consistent with narrative inquiry, we asked participants questions such as "Tell me about your high school experience;" How did you fulfill your high school requirement?" and "Can you tell me a story that you remember from your high school service-learning experience that you still think about today?" The second interview was utilized as an initial member check with emerging themes and to focus on how the state of Maryland describes the service-learning experience. Each participant was shown a copy of "Maryland's Best Practices" and the statement that "all service-learning experiences should meet *all* [emphasis in original] of the Maryland's Best Practices for Service-Learning" (Maryland State Department of Education, 2005, p. 6) and asked to respond to these practices in light of their own experiences.

   Data analysis. Data were analyzed using the constant comparative method (Charmaz, 2006, Strauss & Corbin, 1998), with attention to the content of the narratives, using a categorical content approach (Lieblich, Tuval-Mashiach, & Zilber, 1998) which enabled us both to study the individual stories of each participant, but also to look across the stories for themes. Each researcher independently read and coded every interview and generated themes. We then came together to compare our codes and themes and to generate the patterns within and across all the narratives. We were careful to maintain the "voices within each narrative" (Chase, 2005, p. 663) as well as to listen for the themes that emerged across the interviews. This process led to a continuous process of returning to the interviews themselves to refine the themes and to assure that the themes generated remained close to the words and meanings of all participants. The themes were further revised as we moved from more descriptive categories to analytical and interpretive themes generated to tell the story of these participants.

Trustworthiness

To assure that our interpretive narrative, or re-storying of participants' narrations, was recognizable to our participants, we conducted member checks (Lincoln & Guba, 1985) as a strategy to assure the trustworthiness of findings. We recognized that interpreting others' stories brings with it an ethical responsibility to stay close to participants' meanings (Abes & Jones, 2004; Jones, 2002). To this end we used the second interview as a member check with each participant, reviewing emerging themes with them. As our data analysis proceeded, we then sent each participant a narrative summary, a four-page interpretive re-telling of their stories, presented as one story, and asked them to review this to assure that it accurately captured their experiences and individual story. Out of the 19 participants, 13 responded to this essay and affirmed what they read by stating "this sounds like me." Trustworthiness was also enhanced by the presence of three researchers and our independent coding and analysis.

FINDINGS

The focus of this study was on the narratives of service associated with meeting a high school service-learning graduation requirement and particularly, the meaning college students made of their experiences. We found participants were very eager to discuss their perceptions of the requirement itself, their experiences meeting it, and their ideas about how their high school activities influenced their college experience. However, we were struck by the absence of a "transformative" (e.g., this changed my life) narrative so often found in the service-learning literature, largely due to the way in which the requirement was structured in the high schools. We found that to illuminate the perceived connection between the high school service-learning requirement and college involvement, the high school story needed to be told. We present here what our participants perceived to be "storyworthy" (Chase, 2005, p. 661) about their experiences in the form of three narratives: perceptions on the connection between high school and college (a (dis) serving narrative), their high school experiences (an acquiescent narrative), and a retrospective look back on the requirement (a tenuous narrative).

A(Dis) Serving Narrative: The Connection Between the High School Service-Learning Requirement and College Involvement

Few students expressed any connection between their high school requirement and their college experience, often because they did not learn much from their high school experience. Many either noted that they had not ever considered the possibility of a connection between their high school service-learning experience and college or they indicated that they needed to "take a break" from service. For example, Frank commented, "I don't think my high school service-learning requirement influenced my experiences in college. I never look at anything and say, 'oh, that's because of those 75 hours I did.'" Even those participants who were involved in college, including community service related activities, did not attribute their college participation to their high school experiences meeting the service-learning requirement. For example, Mackenzie commented that she didn't "think that my high school service-learning requirement has influenced my college experience at all. I didn't learn anything from the requirement." Upon reflection, L-B realized "I guess it would be more accurate to say is what I didn't learn is what's impacted me. It's made me want to learn more because I felt like I got cheated in high school in some ways." Others attributed their disinterest in college involvement, including community service-related activities, to the need to "move on" from high school service and "take a break from service," particularly given what they saw as an absence of available time in college.

The one area that many participants commented on in relation to a connection between high school and college was what they perceived as the development of job-related skills through their service-learning activities. These included learning time management, getting along with others, and dealing with difficult people. Karen noted, "I never really worked before and developed a good work ethic, even though I was not getting paid. It taught me how to be professional...how to deal with difficult people and work with a diverse group of peers." Most acknowledged their interpersonal gains came from working with people in their home town communities and indeed, for several participants, service became one vehicle for staying connected. For example, James described his service as "It kind of gives me a reason to go back home. I got from that [the requirement] the interest in still doing it [coaching middle school basketball] and staying rooted in the community where I'm from."

Whether a result of a mismatch between intended outcomes and the actual experience or not, participants' stories suggested the requirement itself had little to do with promoting continued service, civic engagement, or intrinsically driven community participation. To understand why this disconnect between high school and college exists, we turn to their high school experiences.

An Acquiescent Narrative: High School Experiences with the Requirement

Nearly all of our participants could recall how it is they learned of their high school service-learning requirement and went about meeting it. There was little enthusiasm in their voices as they relayed this information to us. Instead, they approached this requirement reluctantly and with little active protest, focusing on what they needed to do to "get it done." This narrative of acquiescence illuminates how participants became aware of the requirement and their perceptions of its purpose, how they met the requirement, and the high school's role in assisting.

"Look to your left and look to your right:" Becoming aware of the requirement. Participants conveyed a diversity of approaches used by their high schools in making them aware of the service-learning graduation requirement. However, all felt the burden of knowing that they would not graduate without meeting

the requirement. Keith described in great detail his freshmen year assembly, during which a senior administrator introduced the requirement by stating,

> 'Look to your left, look to your right, I guarantee one of you won't graduate because of the community service requirement . . . you can be a 4.0 student and get in to any college you want, but you won't graduate because of the community service requirement,' and I was like 'whoa.'

Perhaps because of the way the requirement was typically presented in the schools, many students perceived it as a burden, that was, as Veronikah noted, something administrators "hang over your head." Kyle lamented, "It's just what I have to do to graduate."

Stephanie recalled being told about the requirement in 9th grade and "that it was best to get it out of the way your freshmen year because you wouldn't get a diploma without it." Similarly, Frank was told in middle school "Get it done or you can't graduate." Whether meeting the requirement in middle school or high school, clearly the focus was on getting the requisite hours—this was a prevailing theme among all participants.

"It is all about the hours." Several participants noted awareness of the requirement as Nick stated:

> I guess when you were in the 9th grade they talked to you about it in English classes and said you had to have this many hours. It was not something that they pushed or that they announced or advertised very much. It was something that I guess you were expected to just do...I think most students could have gone through high school being totally unaware of it.

Amanda indicated that she was aware of the requirement but could not recall any of the details about how it is she came to know.

Despite knowledge of the graduation requirement, considered by some such as Bob as "common knowledge," there was quite a bit of ambiguity about what the requirement entailed (e.g., number of hours) and how to meet the requirement (what kind of service activity "counted"); and virtually no mention about why such a requirement existed in the first place. Instead, the focus of students' attention was on accumulating enough hours to meet the requirement. Although the Maryland State Department of Education Code of Regulations clearly specifies 75 hours of student service to meet the requirement, participants were less clear about what was expected. The range of responses to inquiries about their understanding of the requirement included several (3-5 participants) indicating a 60 hour commitment, several noting 36 hours, and several more only aware that they received 30 hours for graduating from middle school. For example, Eric reported, "It was automatic that whatever activities we took part in middle school, as soon as we graduated from the 8th grade, we would automatically get 30 community service hours. By high school I knew I only had to do 30 more hours." Mackenzie declared that her requirement was for "some random big number of hours." A few participants indicated that they were not sure how many hours they needed because it was unclear where their hours were coming from, but they kept appearing on their report cards. For example, several realized that participation in student honoraries and clubs, like National Honor Society (NHS) and the Gifted and Talented Program, brought automatic hours for them. Amelia, in commenting about her awareness of accruing hours, stated, "It was odd, because I kept on receiving credit, through my classes, and I didn't really know what I was receiving credit for. They kept just giving it for the AP classes, every year it would just keep on increasing and then you're done!"

What is it called?: "You can serve anything." The Maryland State Department of Education (2005) requirement is clearly identified as service-learning and is defined in their guidelines:

> Service-learning is a teaching method that combines meaningful service to the community with curriculum-based learning. Students improve their academic skills by applying what they learn in school to the real world; they then reflect on their experience to reinforce the link between their service and their learning. (p. 3)

Participants had very different definitions of service-learning and clearly, no common understanding. Much of how they defined service-learning was in relation to the requirement itself and for many, in opposition to the requirement. For instance, Karen captured the sentiment reflected in many of the participants stating that "service-learning" was "the official name" and "the way you meet the high school graduation requirement." Community service, however, was what you do when you are involved in the community and helping others.

B-E believed that "community service means you actually go out in to the community itself. Service-learning means to me you don't necessarily have to help the community, but it means that you are learning while you are serving something, but you can be serving anything."

James described the distinction in his view as "The difference is that in community service you can go into something once and pat yourself on the back when you leave the door. Community service is more personal service. Service-learning builds the perception that we are supposed to be learning and getting involved with what we are doing." For L-B, the distinction between service-learning and community service had to do with the bureaucratic steps associated with meeting the service-learning requirement, which were in place presumably to prompt learning. He stated, "I think the difference is that with service-learning there is something attached to it like a paper or an action statement. Community service you can learn nothing, you can just go out there and do something and not even think about it ten minutes later." Similarly to James, L-B reported earning his service-learning hours by participating in a car wash for the Bea Gaddy Foundation and by looking up Web sites related to cancer and writing them down for a teacher. Kelli's requirement was called "student service hours—or something like that. It was service-learning because we had to fill out the form."

Sara's requirement was called community service but she found

> it was more service-learning because I think that community service is interacting with people and bettering the community. Service-learning is like doing community service and learning from it, but we never really did community service. We were just learning about [emphasis added] the people we were supposed to be helping.

Sara's school organized "Homeless Days" for all students in a particular science class to meet the requirement. The focus of their service was to find the best way to insulate a cup for homeless people. Sara's reaction to this was the following:

> It was really weird…It was called community service, and we never really did anything besides make these insulated cups. Then there was this box outside and they were trying to tell us how people lived in boxes. I didn't see how this fulfilled the requirement, but it did… We had no interaction with anyone at all. We just insulated cups, and looked at boxes that they could live in.

Although these varying definitions reflect students trying to make sense of their experiences, all indicate confusion about service-learning and a mismatch between students' perceptions and the clear definition of service-learning provided by the Maryland State Department of Education.

What counts as service: How the requirement was met. Participants met their service-learning requirement in a great variety of ways. We generated a long list of activities through which participants garnered hours for service-learning credit in high school. A sampling of these activities included babysitting at participant's synagogue, teaching dance class at school, tutoring, recycling at the school, adopt-a-highway program, working for teachers, working in the attendance and guidance offices, Teen Court, through a number of student clubs and organizations, pie sales, planning a senior citizen prom, chorus, vacation bible school, working in soup kitchen at participant's church, donating blood, junior member of volunteer fire department, nursing home volunteer, park clean up, horse rescue farm, camp counselor, collecting eye glasses for the blind in Spain, and building houses for a week in Mexico. Although many of the students were quite proud of their involvement in these activities, it was striking how passively they were described to us and what little claim on them personally these activities seemed to make.

Many participants received hours for their participation in school sponsored or school-based activities such as Band, theatre stage crew, working in the guidance or attendance offices, picking up trash around the school, and assisting teachers with filing. In a nuanced interpretation, Crimson explained "there was some talk about service-learning. When I got hours for being in the band it was called community service, but when I got hours for working in the attendance office, it was service-learning. The two titles shifted depending on what you were doing." Both, apparently, qualified for meeting the service-learning requirement. In fact, much of their service was actually conducted in and around their schools and in the service of school improvement. For example, Bob explained, "So with service-learning, I could do things, not just volunteer work out in the community, but other things like being involved with school and doing stuff like that. It was all learning that revolved around service." Many of Bob's hours were accrued by helping the advisor ("typing things up for her") to a student organization at the school. Mackenzie noted "I was under the impression that service-learning was community hours that I had to do and I would have to go into the community and help. But it wasn't really like that." Most of Mackenzie's hours were met in English classes each year and included activities such as making books "for kids in underprivileged schools" or donating cans of food. However, it bothered Mackenzie that "I never found out what happened to the books we made and who they went to."

School as service brokerage: "They made it easy for us." Many participants expressed surprise and a bit of skepticism when describing how they received service hours for tasks that defied categorization. School personnel appeared to stretch the boundaries defining service beyond students' imagination. Participants shared example after example of earning their hours by completing tasks within the school, which they perceived as of primary benefit to the teachers and guidance counselors. Batika commented, "I also worked in the guidance office, helping out and answering the phones—it was fun and yeah, I got credit for that too." She went on to further illustrate "how helpful" the teachers were by sharing, "Some students even went up to teachers and said, 'Hey, I really need hours' and...teachers would just sign even if students didn't do anything." Bob relayed his experience, "There was assistance [for getting service hours], people would help out, a teacher would be like, 'ok well, why don't you stay after school a couple of days a week and like help me do this or that and then you can get some service hours.'" In the examples noted with regard to hours through band, the band director played an active role in facilitating the process for students involved, including waiving the reflection component. Crimson referred to this as "kind of unofficial under the table sort of thing. My band director would award people who were in the band... and just give you all of your hours."

Participants recognized this helpfulness as the schools' interest in assuring that students graduated, more so than necessarily advancing service-learning. As a result, they noted that often "real community service doesn't count" and observed the ways in which their peers "got around" the requirement. Participants were creative in their use of euphemisms to describe how students were able to meet their community service requirement. For example, Veronikah referred to the "things you could swing around to get hours" to describe activities that weren't clearly acceptable by the school's definition of what counted. According to her, students routinely exaggerated their hours because they "hated it and needed to get it done." As a result, Crimson mentioned that "you find a lot of stressed out seniors doing some oddball things just to get their hours." Mackenzie referred to this as "skating by without doing anything" and Frank discussed "fudging a few hours" and getting away with this, as did his peers. Several participants extended this "fudging" to describe what appeared to us as outright cheating to meet the requirement. This took the form of submitting hours for service that was never performed or getting credit for far more hours than the activity actually took. As Mackenzie explained, she received five service hours "for something that took 10 minutes to do."

A Tenuous Narrative of Required Service and Participation: A "Double-Edged Sword"

As college students looking back on their experiences meeting the service-learning graduation requirement, nearly all participants acknowledged the possibilities of such mandated service. They were able to see that benefits could be gained and recognized that they and their peers probably would not have been engaged in "service" through their schools had it not been for the requirement. However, the "forced" nature of service and the way in which they and their peers met the requirement rubbed them the wrong way. Several of them used the exact same phrase to capture this dilemma: "a double edged sword." Amelia conveyed this idea precisely:

> It is kind of like a doubled-edged sword, because it is positive, should help the student and the community as well; but the bad side, it is a requirement and reduces feelings of being altruistic, kind and loving, because it is seen just as a mandate that I'll just get done and it will be over with. This cuts down motivation to want to go out and help others and get excited about a great opportunity to go out and help. These benefits aren't highlighted.

Nearly every participant validated the benefits of serving others and the importance of making a contribution to the community, however, the mandated nature of their high school requirement left them cold. For example, L-B emphasized, "I'm very passionate about service in general. I don't know about it being forced upon you, especially in the way the high school does." Keith went further in suggesting, "It is a sense of duty, you can only give yourself, it can't be forced." They also recognized that the requirement, "lame" as it was and something "I hated along with everyone else because it was forced," brought about good activities, for which they were proud, and that without the requirement they would not have been involved in these ways. As Frank noted, "It [the requirement] may seem like a burden at first, but it is a good thing."

Related to this idea of the "double-edged sword," nearly all the participants had difficulty identifying the outcomes and benefits of the requirement to them as individuals. When prompted, they could articulate the larger goals and ideals they thought service-learning could accomplish, but this was not tied to their own experience. In fact, they were apologetic for this inability to come up with a compelling story related to their service. For example, when trying to identify personal outcomes associated with his service, L-B said, "Nothing overly meaningful, I'm sorry."

Several participants did share that their service experience helped them to feel good about themselves and more interested in "helping others." Others related their service to developing a work ethic, becoming more responsible, and learning to work with others. Karen, for example, noted, "I never really worked before. [You] learn so much about yourself as a worker." Others took pride in what they had accomplished through their service-learning experience and felt special and "more well-rounded" as a result; although this mostly had to do with exceeding the number of hours required and pride in giving back to their own communities (which included their high schools).

Despite their ambivalent impressions of the service-learning requirement based largely on their own experiences meeting it, nearly all participants could see the requirement doing more and communicated an interest in the possibilities. None would argue with the intended objectives of a service-learning requirement, but all thought the implementation could be improved upon greatly. In fact, when presented with the list of "Maryland's Best Practices for Service-Learning," several exclaimed "Wow, where did you get this? This is cool," and suggested that if their high schools had actually followed the guidelines, their experiences would have been much improved.

DISCUSSION AND IMPLICATIONS

We set out in this study to elicit the narratives of service associated with students meeting their high school graduation requirement for service-learning. We were also interested in how their high school experiences influenced their college involvement. In nearly all of our interviews with participants we were struck by what seemed to us an absence of the compelling narrative so often found in the service-learning literature. The rich description of their high school experiences acquiescing to the requirement, the narrow focus on completing their hours, and the diverse array of activities, mostly in-school, in which they engaged and counted to meet the requirement do provide a compelling story of a high school service-learning graduation requirement and what graduates are bringing with them to the college context. The results also suggest, consistent with several other studies, that the question is not simply about required versus voluntary service, but more so, how required service is structured in the school setting and the types of service in which students are involved (Jones & Hill, 2003; McLellan &Youniss, 2003).

Our participants were resisting what they perceived as the forced nature of the requirement, not the idea of service-learning or community service. However, their stories reveal that the resistance may have been less about the requirement per se and more so related to the ways in which it was structured in the schools and their ability to meet the requirement by engaging in activities that made very little claim on them psychologically, cognitively, or civically. Indeed, these activities were not congruent with definitions, including Maryland's own, of service-learning and focused more so on service to the schools and led to a tenuous connection between their high school requirement and continued service in college.

The results of this study contribute to what is often described as "mixed results" regarding the efficacy of required service in relation to both outcomes and promoting continued civic participation. Indeed, the very notion of the "double edged sword," as coined by several of our participants, captures the inability to lay claim to one position or the other. Although the goal of qualitative inquiry is not generalizability, the results of this study hold the potential to influence policy and practice. As both high schools and colleges continue to promote service-learning and students convey their interest in and intent to volunteer as members of the "9/11 generation" and the "Katrina generation," the results of this study provide several suggestions for closing the gap between what schools and colleges intend as outcomes and what students actually experience.

First, the array of activities in which students engaged to meet the requirement was dizzying. The majority of these activities took place in the school and with seemingly very little direction from school personnel. The integration of service into the curriculum as a pedagogical tool, consistent with many definitions of service-learning, was virtually absent. So too, was any mention of reflection. Only when prompted did students talk about reflection and always connected to the forms they needed to complete to get credit for their hours. This finding reinforces the importance of meaningful service and the quality of the placement, emphasized in definitions of service-learning and in the research on outcomes associated with service-learning (e.g., Eyler & Giles, 1999; Jacoby, 1996). Also, noted by McLellan and Youniss (2003), "It should not be surprising that these different types of service might produce variable effects" (p. 48). Further, as queried by Chapman (2002), "Does a student who learns that almost anything counts toward the service requirement—so long as he doesn't get paid—develop a keen sense of civil calling? Or does he hone his skill at gaming the system?" (p. 12). Unfortunately, our data suggest the latter may be the case. A more intentional effort to link intended outcomes and activities designed to produce those outcomes is sorely needed.

Second, and related, our results are consistent with those studies that reinforce the importance of structured service as high quality. Despite the occasional good teacher, or parents and churches, most of the participants in this study reported the need to figure out the service requirement on their own. Although not the focus of this study, we suspect that many schools are under-staffed and -resourced such that responding to this legislative mandate is challenging. Hence, they respond in ways to assure that students satisfy their graduation requirements by "making it easy" for students. Research does suggest however, that well designed service-learning makes a difference in producing desired outcomes (e.g., Eyler & Giles, 1999).

The Youth Volunteering and Engagement survey (Spring, Dietz, & Grimm, 2006) examined the benefits of "high quality" service-learning in K-12 education. High quality was defined by three elements: (1) students assist in the planning of the service activity, (2) students participate in regular service for a semester or longer, and (3) students reflect on their service experiences in class. Results found that 77% of all school-based service experiences had a least one of these elements, but only 10% had all three; and that students who participated in programs with all three elements were more than twice as likely as those with none of the quality elements to report that their service experience had a positive impact on them. In addition, as the research by McLellan and Youniss (2003) suggested, "when left to their own devices for fulfilling credit requirements...students tended to choose functionary work, which probably demanded little physical, cognitive, or emotional investment compared, say, with social service" (p. 56). Had students been engaged in high quality service-learning, the stories we heard may have sounded quite different.

In addition, this phenomenon of leaving the service choice and arrangements to the students led to a very narrow view of service-learning by students as only those activities connected to the requirement. In fact, a number of students were engaged in community service through their churches, families, or community organizations, but none of them talked about these activities as service-learning or in relation to the requirement. Tapping in to these familial, social, and community networks may help schools not only help students meet the service-learning requirement, but also, because service connected with these networks does tend to be more consistent with activities that require cognitive and emotional investment from students (McLellan &Youniss, 2003), to promote social responsibility and continued civic participation.

Finally, the relationship between the high school requirement and related service activities and college involvement was tenuous at best. This is consistent with the research that demonstrates that encouraged and high quality service, rather than required service, is more likely to contribute to continued service in college (Jones & Hill, 2003; Marks & Jones, 2004). Because of their emphasis on the required nature of service, several of our participants came to the university setting ready to "take a break" from service. This, and other experiences meeting the requirement, provides several cautions and implications for college educators interested in promoting service-learning and civic responsibility. First, students were not at all clear about what service-learning is and how it differs, if at all, from community service. College educators may need to help reframe students' misconceptions of service-learning and cannot presume that students will come to them with exposure to social issues through service or a commitment to civic engagement.

Because of these misconceptions, and their perspective that a service requirement is a "double-edged sword," engaging students who attended high schools with a service requirement may take extra effort and new strategies. Traditional recruitment methods (e.g., if I market it, they will come) may not work. These students may need to be approached more directly and by engaging them in meaningful service that draws them in. They also may not have the skills of reflection required for high quality service-learning, as reflection was not often a part of their high school experiences. Although absent from most of their high school experiences, research has shown that the most compelling service-learning, even when required, occurs when identity development is involved (Hart et al., 2007; Jones & Abes, 2004; Jones & Hill, 2003; McLellan & Youniss, 2003; Youniss & Yates, 1997). When service is connected to a student's evolving sense of self, then the motivation to engage in service becomes an internal one and a greater likelihood for continued involvement emerges because service becomes integral to identity construction.

Limitations

The results of this study must be considered in light of a few limitations. Although consistent with narrative inquiry, our sample of 19 is relatively small given that we invited 200 to participate and received 44 affirmative responses from those who met sampling criteria. We also included representation from a number of different counties across the state, but to provide a more comprehensive narrative, we did not analyze the data county by county. Because our focus was on students' stories, we are only able to comment on their perceptions and the nature of the service-learning requirement from their perspectives. We therefore, don't know much about the high school environments, except what the participants recalled. We can only speculate that if we interviewed high school teachers, for example, the story would shift. We also did not formerly assess students' general propensity for involvement in high school. Rounding out the picture is important and provides several areas for future research. Finally, as narrators of this story, we were very aware of our own stories as they intersected with the participants. As we noted, the absence of compelling stories from our participants caught our attention. Did this mean we missed the mark, or that our notion of what was "storyworthy" (Chase, 2005, p. 661) was not theirs? The presence of three researchers helped us to monitor our own subjectivity, but nonetheless we were aware of its presence.

Despite these limitations, this study provides compelling evidence about students' perceptions of and experiences with a high school service-learning graduation requirement. It is clear that the requirement alone does not automatically produce outcomes such as civic responsibility, commitment to one's community or social issues, or continued community service involvement. Students resisted the required nature of their community service; however, this was largely due to the way in which it was implemented in their schools. Had the schools been more actively involved in structuring the requirement and assuring meaningful service, it is reasonable to speculate that the outcomes for students would have looked quite different. None of them resisted service and giving back to the community; indeed, many of them were engaged in this kind of service outside of the requirement. The presence of the "double-edged sword" captures this dynamic and serves as an impetus for service-learning educators to sharpen the educational experience for students to produce intended outcomes. Indeed, as McLellan and Youniss (2003) urged, "service needs to be crafted as assiduously as science laboratories or writing seminars" (p. 56). Such a commitment will increase the likelihood that students experience more efficacious service-learning rather than simply "what I do to meet the requirement."

REFERENCES

Astin, A.W., & Sax, L.J. (1998). How undergraduates are affected by service participation. *Journal of College Student Development, 39,* 251-263.

Barber, B. (1994). *An aristocracy of everyone: The politics of education and the future of America.* New York: Ballantine Books.

Berger, J.B., & Milem, J.F. (2002). The impact of community service involvement on three measures of undergraduate self-concept. *NASPA Journal, 40,* 85-103.

Boyer, E. L. (1983). *High School: A report on secondary education in America.* New York: Harper and Row.

Charmaz, K. (2006). *Constructing grounded theory: A practical guide through qualitative analysis.* Thousand Oaks, CA: Sage.

Chapman, B. (2002). A bad idea whose time is past: The case against universal service. *Brookings Review, 20,* 10-13.

Chase, S.E. (2005). Narrative inquiry: Multiple lenses, approaches, voices. In N. K. Denzin & Y. S. Lincoln (Eds.), *Handbook of qualitative research 3rd ed.* (pp. 651-680). Thousand Oaks, CA: Sage.

Chronicle Almanac. (2007, August 31), 53. Retrieved on January 18, 2008, from: http://chronicle.com/weekly/almanac/2006/nation/nation.htm

Clandinin, D. J., & Connelly, F. M. (2000). *Narrative inquiry: Experience and story in qualitative research.* San Francisco: Jossey-Bass.

Creswell, J.W. (2007). *Qualitative inquiry and research design: Choosing among five traditions* (2nd ed.). Thousand Oaks, CA: Sage.

Cruce, T. M., & Moore, J. V. (2007). First-year students' plans to volunteer: An examination of the predictors of community service participation. *Journal of College Student Development, 48*, p. 655-673.

Deci, E. L., & Ryan, R. M. (1987). The support of autonomy and the control of behavior. *Journal of Personality and Social Psychology, 53*, 1024-1037.

Denzin, N. K., & Lincoln, Y. S. (2000). The discipline and practice of qualitative research. In N. K. Denzin & Y. S. Lincoln (Eds.), *Handbook of qualitative research* (pp. 105-117). Thousand Oaks, CA: Sage.

Dote, L., Cramer, K., Dietz, N., & Grimm, R. Jr. (2006). *College students helping America.* Washington, DC: Corporation for National and Community Service.

Education Commission of the States (2001). Institutionalized service-learning in the 50 states. Denver, CO.

Eyler, J., & Giles, D. E., Jr. (1999). *Where's the learning in service-learning?* San Francisco: Jossey-Bass.

Flyvbjerg, B. (2001) *Making social science matter: Why social inquiry fails and how it can succeed.* Cambridge: Cambridge University Press.

Harkavy, I. (2004). Service-learning and the development of democratic universities, democratic schools, and democratic good societies in the 21st century. In M.Welch & S. Billig (Eds.), *New perspectives on service-learning: Research to advance the field* (pp. 3-22). Greenwich, CT: Information Age Publishing.

Hart, D., Donnelly, T. M., Youniss, J., & Atkins, R. (2007). High school community service as a predictor of adult voting and volunteering. *American Educational Research Journal, 44*(1), 197-219.

Higher Education Research Institute. (2006). *The American freshman: National norms for fall 2006.* Los Angeles: University of California.

Jacoby, B., & Associates (1996). *Service-learning in higher education: Concepts and practices.* San Francisco: Jossey-Bass.

Jennings, K. M., & Stoker, L. (2004). Social trust and civic engagement across time and generations. *Acta Politica, 39*, 342-379.

Jones, S. R. (2002). (Re)Writing the word: Methodological strategies and issues in qualitative research. *Journal of College Student Development, 43*, 461-473.

Jones, S. R., & Abes, E. S. (2004). Enduring influences of service-learning on college students' identity development. *Journal of College Student Development, 45*, 149-166.

Jones, S. R., & Hill, K. E. (2003). Understanding patterns of commitment: Student motivation for community service involvement. *Journal of Higher Education, 74*, 516-539.

Jones, S.R., Torres,V., & Arminio, J. (2006). *Negotiating the complexities of qualitative research in higher education.* New York: Routledge.

Lieblich, A., Tuval-Mashiach, R., & Zilber, T. (1998). *Narrative research: Readings, analysis, interpretation.* Thousand Oaks, CA: Sage.

Lincoln, Y. S., & Guba, E. (1985). *Naturalistic inquiry.* Thousand Oaks, CA: Sage.

Marks, H. M. & Jones, S. R. (2004). Community service in the transition: Shifts and continuities in participation from high school to college. *Journal of Higher Education, 75,* 307-339.

Maryland State Department of Education. (2005). *Maryland student service-learning guidelines.* Baltimore, MD.

Maryland State Department of Education. (2006). *College performance of new Maryland high school graduates: Student outcome and achievement report.* Baltimore, MD: Author.

Maryland Student Service Alliance. (1995). *Maryland's best practices: An improvement guide for school-based service-learning.* Baltimore: Maryland State Department of Education.

McEwen, M. K. (2003) The nature and uses of theory. In S. R. Komives & D. B. Woodard (Eds.), *Student services: A handbook for the profession* (4th ed., (pp. 153-178). San Francisco: Jossey-Bass.

McLellan, J.A., & Youniss, J. (2003). Two systems of youth service: Determinants of voluntary and required youth community service. *Journal of Youth and Adolescence, 32*(1), 47-58.

Metz, E., & Youniss, J. (2003). A demonstration that school-based required service does not deter—but heightens— volunteerism. *PS Online,* 281-286.

Metz, E., & Youniss, J. (2005). Longitudinal gains in civic development through school-based required service. *Political Psychology, 26,* 413-437.

Moely, B. E., McFarland, M., Miron, D., Mercer, S., & Ilustre, V. (2002). Changes in college students' attitudes and intentions for civic involvement as a function of service-learning experience. *Michigan Journal of Community Service Learning, 9*(1), 18-26.

Niemi, R.G., Hepburn, M.A., & Chapman, C. (2000). Community service by high school students: A cure for civic ills? *Political Behavior, 22,* 46-69.

Patton, M. Q. (2002). *Qualitative evaluation and research methods* (3rd ed.). Newbury Park, CA: Sage.

Raskoff, S., & Sundeen, R. (1999). Community service programs in high schools. *Law and Contemporary Problems, 64*(4), 73-111.

Service-learning. (2003). Retrieved September 10, 2006, from http://www.marylandpublicschools.org/msde/programs/service-learning/service_learning.htm

Spring, K., Dietz, N., & Grimm, R. Jr. (2006). *Educating for active citizenship: Service-learning, school based service, and civic engagement.* Washington, DC: Corporation for National and Community Service.

Strauss, A., & Corbin, J. (1998). *Basics of qualitative research* (2nd ed.). Thousand Oaks, CA: Sage Publications.

Stukas, A. A., Snyder, M., & Clary, E. G. (1999). The effects of "mandatory volunteerism" on intentions to volunteer. *Psychological Science, 10*(1), 59-64.

Vogelgesang (2005). *Bridging from high school to college: Findings from the 2004 freshmen CIRP survey.* St. Paul, MN: National Youth Leadership Council.

Vogelgesang, L. J., & Astin, A. W. (2000). Comparing the effects of service-learning and community service. *Michigan Journal of Community Service Learning, 7,* 25-34.

Vogelgesang, L. J., & Astin, A.W. (2005). Post college civic engagement among graduates. *Higher Education Research Institute Research Report, 2,* 1-11.

Youniss, J., & Yates, M. (1997). *Community service and social responsibility in youth.* Chicago: University of Chicago Press.

Authors

Linking University and High School Students: Exploring the Academic Value of Service Learning

By Duncan MacLellan

Dr. Duncan MacLellan, Duncan MacLellan is an Assistant Professor in the Department of Politics and Public Administration at Ryerson University, and his teaching and research interests include educational politics and policy making at the local and provincial levels, state and teacher relations and local and urban governance issues. Duncan published an article on teacher unionism in the journal, Canadian and International Education and he is one of the authors of the book, Teachers' Unions in Canada.

Abstract: While universities and colleges aim to become more inclusive and welcoming to students from a variety of backgrounds, major gaps remain in relation to particular high school students being admitted to postsecondary institutions. Located in Toronto, Canada's most culturally diverse city, Ryerson University is committed to both academic and applied learning. Building on that commitment, this paper focuses on one service learning project involving both university students enrolled in a senior level Ryerson course and high school students enrolled in a Grade 12 course located in downtown Toronto. This particular Toronto high school has not scored well in province-wide standardized tests and so few of its students apply to college or university. Bringing together these high school and university students in different activities over one semester will enable both groups to gain insights from each other. In addition, by using reflective assignments, Ryerson students can use course concepts to help ground their interactions with these high school students. Service learning has the potential to build linkages that help both university and high school students.

Keywords: Service Learning, Urban Education, High School Students, University Students, Experiential Learning

INTRODUCTION

Service learning has been identified as an effective mechanism to engage university students in a variety of learning opportunities (Day, 2008;Webster, 2007). For this study, Ryerson University students, in a senior-level course, were linked with students enrolled in a Grade 12 course at Maple Heights High School.[1] This particular urban high school has not fared well in provincial standardized tests, and few of its students continue to pursue academic studies after high school. A number of scholars have pointed to the troubling fact that many urban high school students may be prone to disconnect from their academic studies, which could limit their future career options (Elson, Johns, and Petrie, 2007; Kenny, Simon, Kiley-Brabeck, and Lerner, 2002; Webster, 2007).[2]

Webster (2007) notes that a significant body of literature related to service learning focuses on white middle-class suburban schools. Only of late, has the focus begun to move toward demystifying university and college programs for youth from under-represented urban communities. Well-designed service learning projects in urban schools have the potential to provide university students with opportunities to link with high school students; therefore, enabling both groups to exchange ideas and views on a range of formal and informal topics (Brown, Heaton, and Wall, 2007; Webster, 2007).

The goal of this paper is to present a practice-based case study, which describes an innovative service learning project involving high school and university students. The research question is: Can service learning be a positive means for linking university and high school students?

REVIEW OF LITERATURE RELATED TO SERVICE LEARNING

Bringle and Hatcher's definition of service learning, referenced in Zlotkowski (2003), offers a useful lens to situate this study:

> We view service learning as a credit-bearing educational experience in which students participate in an organized service activity that meets identified community needs and reflects on the service activity to gain further understanding of the course content, a broader appreciation of the discipline, and an enhanced sense of civic responsibility. . . .(p. 64)

O'Quin (2003) refers to the *National and Community Trust Act,* which defines service learning '[a]s a method whereby students learn and develop through active participation in thoughtfully organized service that is conducted to meet the needs of communities' (2003, p. 3697). Some researchers relate service learning's pedagogy to John Dewey's scholarship, which views education as means for promoting democracy and engaging students in their communities (Ramsdell, 2004). More specifically, having a "good fit" between the course and the service learning experience, enables students, faculty, and community partners to see a project's value (Gupta, 2006; Hollander, Saltmarsh, and Zlotkowski, 2002).

Service learning can help students increase community awareness by applying their academic learning, knowledge, and skills to pre-identified local needs (Campus Contact, 2003; Frazer, Raasch, Pertzborn, and Bradley, 2007; Pearce, 2008). For service learning to be considered a viable pedagogic approach, it has to link with specific academic course content. The following quote fromEyler and Dwight, cited by Pearce (2008), responds to the question: Why service learning?

> I can honestly say that I've learned more in the last year (service learning) than I probably have learned in all four years of college. I have learned so much, maybe because I found something that I'm really passionate about, and it makes you care more to learn about it-and get involved and do more. You're not just studying to take a test and forget about it. You're learning and the experiences we have are staying with us. (p. 116)

In addition, as Pearce notes, "well designed, well-managed service learning can contribute to a student's learning and growth, while also helping to meet real community needs" (2008, p.119). The goal is to integrate service with the academic enterprise, so service reinforces and strengthens learning and learning reinforces and strengthens service. One primary goal of service learning is the use of reflection to help connect the broader context of service experience with course content (O'Quin, 2003).

CONNECTING AN URBAN UNIVERSITY TO SERVICE LEARNING

This project aimed to link university and high school students in a series of informal and formal activities that would help familiarize high school students to university. Given Ryerson's evolution, this current service learning project builds on a strong foundation of applied learning. Ryerson University began as a polytechnic school shortly after World War Two, and its mission remains to link academic studies with practical applications. In the mid-1990s, Ryerson was granted standing as a university but maintained its emphasis on career focused education. The 2008-2009 Ryerson University Calendar notes the following description:

> The special mission of Ryerson University is the advancement of applied knowledge and research to address societal need, and the provision of programs of study that provide a balance between theory and application and that prepare students for careers in professional and quasi-professional fields. As a leading centre of applied education, Ryerson is recognized as Canada's leader in career-focused education.... (Ryerson University, 2008, p. 14)

To help guide the organization of this service learning project, the instructor relied on the following definition provided by the Ryerson University Faculty of Arts Service Learning Office:

> Service Learning is a form of experiential learning that links class-room teaching and course readings with meaningful voluntary experiences and critical reflective practices. Students engage in projects and activities in the community in addition to their course work. Learning is facilitated through individual and collective critical reflection in course lectures and assignments that help students integrate 'real world' experiences with course concepts. Service Learning differs from volunteer work and internships/practica in that it focuses on both community priorities and student learning, rather than just on community need (volunteer work) or just on student learning....(Ryerson University, 2008a)

To provide context for this service learning project, a brief overview of significant demographic and socio-economic figures that relate to Toronto and Ryerson University will be helpful.

- During the past decade, close to 50% of Toronto's population of 2.5 million residents were born outside of Canada (City of Toronto, 2009).
- Approximately 25% of the 1 million immigrants that came to Canada from 2001-2006 settled in Toronto (City of Toronto, 2009).
- The 2006 national survey results indicate that 47% of Toronto's 2.5 million residents report themselves as being part of a visible minority (City of Toronto, 2009).
- The 2006 national survey also notes that Toronto's population is made up of residents who claim identity with one or more of the 200 distinct ethnic groups that reside in Toronto (City of Toronto, 2009).
- On Toronto's socio-economic front, during the past few decades, the proportion of middle-income neighborhoods has fallen from 50% to 32%. Yet the proportion of low and very-low income neighborhoods increased from 19% to 50% (MacLellan, 2008).

Ryerson's student population reflects Toronto's ethno cultural mosaic. In 2007, 42.6% of Ryerson's first-year student population came from the City of Toronto. The four suburban areas surrounding Toronto are referred to as the Greater Toronto Area (GTA), and with a combined population of 2.3 million residents, Ryerson drew another 40% of its first-year student population from the GTA. In 2007, close to 12% of Ryerson's first-year student population came from outside Toronto and the GTA but still within Ontario. Approximately 3.8% of Ryerson's first-year students came from a non-Ontario province or territory within Canada (Ryerson University, 2008b).

Maple Heights High School was selected as the site for this service learning project. To a certain degree, Maple Heights's student population is similar in composition to the City of Toronto and Ryerson University. In spring 2008, Maple Heights reported that close to 32% of its students have resided in Canada for less than five years (Toronto District School Board, 2009). Maple Heights's 2007-2008 school profile is presented in Table One.

Table 1: A Selected Profile of Maple Heights High School 2007-2008

	Province of Ontario	Maple Heights High School
Parentage of students who live in lower-income households	31%	16.5%
Percentage of students whose parents have some university education	21%	36.9%
Percentage of students who receive special education services	24%	12.5%
Percentage of students identified as gifted	0.1%	21.8%
Parentage of students whose first language is not English	56%	21.8%
Percentage of students who are new to Canada from non-English speaking country	21.3%	3.2%
Percentage of students who achieved provincial standard in academic math	19%	75%
Percentage of students who achieved provincial standard in applied math (2007-08)	15%	34%
Percentage of students in grade 10 who passed literacy test on their first attempt (2007-08)	42%	84%
These percentages are based on Ontario province-wide averages (Ontario Ministry of Education, 2008).		

Methodology: Education Politics, Urban Schooling, and Social Capital

This qualitative study was prompted by a desire to utilize service learning as the vehicle to connect high school and senior university students. The instructor was contacted by a Ryerson University Faculty of Arts Service Learning staff member to inquire if there was interest in "twinning" his "Education Politics and Policy" course with a Grade 12 course at Maple Heights High School. The "Education Politics and Policy" course relies on cultural and social capital theories to help students understand the social context within which educational decisions are made. In particular, Pierre Bourdieu's work on cultural capital is utilized to explore the idea that schools draw unevenly on social and cultural resources of members of society. Often cultural experiences at home facilitate children's adjustment to both school and academic achievement. This in turn, converts cultural resources into what Bordieu refers to as cultural capital (Lareau, 1987).

Within this course, we discuss how social capital is utilized to enable certain people to gain access to powerful positions through direct and indirect employment of social connections (Oakes, 2005). Howard (2006) contends that social capital promotes linkages that are both formal (volunteering at your local school for a committee) and informal (inviting your neighbors to a barbeque). The benefits from these opportunities can result in personal as well as academic gains for parents and their children. Howard (2006) then asks the following research question: If schools included service learning programs, would these help to close the achievement gaps among different racial and ethnic groups? In his case study of a Seattle middle school, Howard's results, while limited, found that by engaging students in service learning activities, these students spent less time watching television. While Howard's sample size was small, it did offer the potential for service learning to assist academic learning (2006). In summary, both cultural and social capital theories were used to help structure a significant portion of the "Education Politics and Policy" course.

SERVICE LEARNING AT MAPLE HEIGHTS: RESEARCH DESIGN AND REFLECTIVE ASSIGNMENTS

In the lead up to organizing the research design for this service learning project, the instructor benefited from valuable insights offered by Ryerson's Service Learning Office and educators at Maple Heights. The core of this project relied on Ryerson students submitting three reflective assignments that enabled them to offer their thoughts and knowledge with regard to both informal and formal aspects of their placement at Maple Heights over five weeks. To present the observations that emerged from both the reflective assignments and informal conversations that the instructor had with Ryerson students regarding their placement at Maple Heights, it became important to organize these findings in an organized manner. After reviewing a number of scholarly works, the instructor chose to adopt Sterling's (2007) subheadings of Knowledge, Activities, and Reflections because of the appropriate fit provided for this service learning project.

Knowledge

For this paper, we can consider knowledge as concepts, facts, information, and prior experience in the context of experiential learning (Sterling, 2007;

Terry, 2005).More specifically, two aspects of knowledge can be considered. First, upon agreeing to participate in this service learning project, the instructor wanted to become informed about the principles of service learning. Second, the instructor was eager to gain "on the ground knowledge" related to Maple Heights High School. The course instructor and one of Ryerson's service learning liaison staff members met with Ms. Banks (pseudonym), the teacher responsible for Maple Heights's Grade 12 university-preparatory course, "Challenge and Change in Society" that was to be "twinned" with the "Education Politics and Policy" course. This meeting also offered Ms. Banks an opportunity to become familiar with the "Education Politics and Policy" course, and Ms. Banks provided the instructor with the following description of the "Challenge and Change in Society" course:

> This course examines theories and methodologies used in anthropology, psychology, and sociology to investigate and explain shifts in knowledge, attitudes, beliefs, and behavior, and their impact on society. Students will analyze cultural, social, and biological patterns in human societies, looking at the ways in which these patterns change over time. Students will also explore the ideas of classical and contemporary social theories, and will apply those ideas to the analysis of contemporary trends. (Ontario Ministry of Education, 2002, p. 1)

The instructor also attended a professional development workshop on evaluating reflective assignments. This workshop offered the instructor an opportunity to engage with other faculty in relation to constructive approaches to assessing reflective assignments. To create the three reflective assignments for the "Education Politics and Policy" course, attention was given to O'Quin's (2003) comment that one must consider course goals and objectives when designing reflective assignments that connect service learning with a course's academic content. Furthermore, there does not appear to be one "right" way for students to process and assimilate the learning that takes place through their service learning experiences. For this reason, faculty are best suited to select methods of assessment and reflection that meet course goals and learning objectives (Day, 2008; O'Quin, 2003).

As Young, Shinnar, Ackerman, Carruthers, and Young (2007) note, service learning must be more than community service, service-learning assignments must include two components: continuity and interaction. Continuity refers to connections between course materials and assignments—the application of skills and concepts learned in a course to real life situations. Interactions refer to the link between the objective nature of the assignment and the subjective experience—the impressions and thoughts of the student. The link is achieved through reflection. Reflection can come in the form of class discussions, journal writing, term papers, or other assignments that require students to critically reflect upon their experiences. Ramsdell (2004) contends that for service learning courses to be successful, the academic component must be equally as important as the service. The implications of this are that the volunteer work must be directly tied to the course curriculum.

The service learning component of the "Education Politics and Policy" course was voluntary. Nine of 29 students submitted applications for service learning at Maple Heights High School. Due to the fact that students would be working with young adults, the Toronto District School Board (TDSB) required each student who applied to complete a Police Reference Check (PRC). All nine students were accepted for the service learning project at Maple Heights. Shortly thereafter, Ryerson's Service Learning Office organized a half-day orientation session for Ryerson students involved in service learning at Maple Heights. A few days before the visit, an altercation occurred near Maple Heights School property that led the Principal to initiate a school lockdown. This item generated media attention, and a few Ryerson students emailed the instructor regarding the safety of Maple Heights. Ryerson's Service Learning Office sent an email to its Maple Heights service learning students, assuring them that all precautions would be taken to ensure their safety.

The visit remained as scheduled, and Ryerson university students gained a first-hand look at Maple Heights High School. Ryerson students were able to meet with Maple Heights's Principal and teaching staff involved with service learning. At this meeting, Ryerson students asked questions related to the school, and the Principal responded that many of the students attending Maple Heights are first-generation Canadians and a significant number are from low-income families. In addition, according to the Principal, some Maple Heights students are living on their own due to difficult family situations. The Principal also stated that the size of Maple Heights's English as a Second Language (ESL) Program reflects that many of its students are not fluent in English, in part, because of their recent entry into Canada. Geographically, the Principal noted that Maple Heights is located between two high achieving secondary schools; therefore, it has the stigma of being the school where students who cannot gain entry into the other two schools end up. Next Ryerson students met informally with the students they would be working with, this was followed by lunch in the school cafeteria, and then a student-led school tour.

Two weeks later, Maple Heights's service learning students were given a half-day orientation to Ryerson University. The aim of the visit was for these students to see the campus and to help demystify some aspects of higher education. The visit to Ryerson University involved meeting with Student Services personnel. Then Maple Height students met with a group of first-generation Ryerson students to chat informally about university life. A campus tour was organized and this was followed by a brief lecture from the instructor to enable Maple Height students to "experience" a university class.

Activities

Ryerson University students enrolled in service learning at Maple Heights were required to spend two hours per week over five weeks assisting Ms. Banks in a variety of formal and informal activities related to the "Challenge and Change in Society" course. After the first week of observing, Ryerson students were integrated more formally into "Challenge and Change in Society". To ease their transition into this course, Ryerson students were divided into two groups to coincide with the day of their weekly visits.

A Monday group member contacted the course instructor to inquire about using case studies from our "Education Politics and Policy" course as an activity at Maple Heights. The instructor agreed but on the condition that Ms. Banks approve, which she did after reviewing the four case studies. After dividing the class into four groups, with Ryerson students leading each group, Maple Heights students were asked to comment on the cases in relation to their "Challenge and Change in Society" course. Overall, as will be discussed in the reflections section, this activity was well-presented by the Monday group and well-received by Maple Heights students.

The Tuesday group's activity involved taking a cake, referred to as the "World Cake" to one of the "Challenge and Change in Society" classes. The cake was divided into the following geographic regions: North America, Latin America, Europe, Africa, and Asia-Pacific, and the size of each slice of cake represented the per capita gross income of each region. Students were then divided based on the five regions, and the region with the largest slice of cake was Asia and the smallest was Africa. Students representing "regions with small slices of cake" were encouraged to see if they could "trade" with "regions with large slices of cake", thereby increasing their "share" of cake. Immediately, students representing small-slice regions noticed large-slice regions were unwilling to share. To retaliate against this obstacle, one small-slice region "appropriated" a share of cake from a large-slice region to better balance regional incomes.

Reflections

FIRST REFLECTIVE ASSIGNMENT

This assignment involved Ryerson students describing their thoughts and observations related to their half-day orientation at Maple Heights. In par- ticular, students were to compare their visit to Maple Heights to what they thought would be before them, and then to discuss Maple Heights in rela- tion to their own high school experience. Some students found the Principal's responses to their questions a bit surprising because he was so forthright in describing the serious social and economic challenges before Maple Heights's students. Ryerson students commented that they did not realize the degree of poverty and disconnectedness within Maple Heights High School. In some of the first reflective assignments, Ryerson students were surprised at learning from the Principal, that financial difficulties prevent a number of Maple Heights's academically-eligible students from attending university or college. In addition, some Ryerson students were dismayed to learn, from the Principal, some Maple Heights students would like to attend university but had no one in their family to turn to for support, and also that some students felt pressure from their families to seek employment directly after high school. A Ryerson student, who had attended a neighboring high-achieving school, reflected on the perception that only students not bound for university enroll at Maple Heights.

SECOND REFLECTIVE ASSIGNMENT

Ryerson University students commented on how well their case studies and "world cake" activities were received by students in the "Challenge and Change in Society" course. Interestingly, Monday group members reported being pleased at the level of understanding these Maple Heights students demonstrated regarding the case studies, which focused on complex social issues such as: discrimination, racism, and sexual orientation in school and family settings. Tuesday group members were impressed by the degree of resourcefulness and insight Maple Heights students offered with respect to regional income distribution and social justice issues. Ms. Banks expressed gratitude for both the leadership and team-building skills evident in these Ryerson students and the high level of responsiveness from Maple Heights students. Ms. Banks indicated her interest in using the case studies in future offerings of "Challenge and Change in Society".

THIRD REFLECTIVE ASSIGNMENT

Ryerson service learning students were required to incorporate cultural and/or social capital theories as the foundation through which to examine their experiences at Maple Heights. These Ryerson students offered detailed examples of how they came to realize the importance of schools as places that socialize citizens; furthermore, the degree to which one is socialized is dependent on both family and social circumstances. In discussing financial and family issues relating to attending college or university, some Ryerson students reflected that they too faced the same challenges as the Maple Heights students. The Maple Height students learned that what gave these current Ryerson students the drive to apply to university was family encouragement and financial support. In addition, Ryerson students noted that Maple Heights students found the Ryerson orientation session a rewarding and empowering experience. Furthermore, some Maple Height students commented positively to Ryerson students with regard to Ryerson's diverse student population. Ryerson students relayed to the Maple Heights students that many Ryerson students are also first-generation Canadians. As comfort levels grew, Ryerson students reflected that inquiries from Maple Heights students began to focus on university admission and financial requirements.

Ryerson students, in their third reflective assignment, commented that this service learning experience provided different ways to apply course theories hands on, and it gave them the opportunity to interact, learn, and become more familiar with the public school system. Ryerson students also found that service learning enhanced both their perspective on policy in action along with applying certain theories to practice. Students also offered that there was a connection between course content and service learning because the issues students dealt with at Maple Heights were portrayed in course readings and lectures. Ryerson students hoped that these Maple Heights students gained as much as they did from this service learning experience.

CONCLUSIONS

This service learning project was organized to enable Ryerson University students to volunteer their time at an urban high school, and to provide students in a Grade 12 course with an opportunity to interact with these students to help demystify university. The importance of establishing good rapport with the host organization at all stages of the service learning project is vital (Ramsdell, 2004). The initial site visit by the course instructor to Maple Heights was worthwhile, and the orientation sessions at Maple Heights and Ryerson University helped to strengthen this connection. As Ramsdell (2004) suggests, it is virtually impossible for the instructor to understand the organization's needs, and thus to prepare student volunteers, without being physically present to witness the surroundings in which the students will be working. During the site visit, the instructor was able to ascertain aspects of Maple Heights's student population and the setting within which Ryerson students would volunteer their time.

Ryerson students were required to write three reflective assignments that examined first, their perceptions of Maple Heights High School; second, an activity that their group had led at Maple Heights; and third, analyze their Maple Heights service learning experience, using theories discussed in our "Education Politics and Policy" course. Young et al. (2007) note, the benefits of service learning programs are that they may help to improve academic performance of both high school and university students in terms of boosting their sense of personal and social responsibility. Service-learning may also enhance other skills such as: critical thinking, communication, teamwork, problem solving, and time management. Ryerson students reflected that, in leading the case studies and world cake activities, their teamwork and communication skills were enhanced. A few students commented that they would like to enter the teaching profession, and that the Maple Heights service learning experience "opened their eyes" to the complexities of life in an urban high school. Jagla (2008) refers to this as enhancing the relevance of knowledge from service learning. By actively involving students in the process of constructing their own knowledge, they more readily see how it relates to the real world as opposed to just learning the theoretical concepts in isolation. As Catapano (2006) notes, placing people in real situations helps them to compare what they are learning in the course to what they are experiencing in their service learning project.

Ryerson students viewed their service learning experience as an effective way to connect high school and university students, and some hoped that this would motivate more high school students from underrepresented groups to attend university. In addition, service learning helped to break down some educational barriers because it offered university students a chance to get "real-life" experience in an urban school. Ryerson students were enthusiastic that service learning be incorporated in future offerings of "Education Politics and Policy". The instructor was hoping to include comments from Maple Heights students but was unable to due to tight time constraints related to when this service learning project ended. However, Ryerson students commented to the instructor that the verbal feedback they received from Maple Height students was very positive regarding this service learning project. The use of reflective assignments helped to ground this service learning project, both in relation to course expectations and interactions between Maple Heights and Ryerson students. Service learning has the potential to allow for "relevant and meaningful academic learning..." (Payne-Jackson, 2005, p. 60).

Yet, we must keep in mind that service learning is still in its infancy. Actual research in this field reflects the fact that service learning has been viewed quite broadly, so developing a theoretical body in this field has been challenging. Part of this problem stems from the absence of a clear theoretical base in terms of how service learning is to be considered; therefore, a number of theoretical perspective may apply. Furthermore, service learning would benefit from more robust studies based on qualitative, quantitative, or mixed methods. On a related note, service-learning researchers should be mindful not to overstate or over generalise their findings (Billig and Waterman, 2003).

With the above cautions in mind, some service learning projects have the potential to offer students a glimpse into real-world problems that may build on university or high school courses (Desrochers, 2006: Sterling, 2007). This service learning project enabled Ryerson students to widen their educational learning with practical experience, and it offered Maple Heights students the opportunity to help them demystify university. The instructor also became more aware, from visiting Maple Heights and reading Ryerson students' reflective assignments, of the widening social, cultural, and financial gaps that still disengage significant numbers of marginalize urban students from seeking educational training beyond high school. This study is limited in its ability to generalize results, and it is proposed that further research is needed to substantiate and advance the observations noted here.

REFERENCES

Billig, S., and Waterman, A. (2003). Studying service learning: Challenges and solutions. In S. Billing and A. Waterman, (Eds.), *Studying service-learning: Innovations in education research methodology* (pp. vii-xiv). Mahwah, NJ: Lawrence Erlbaum Associates, Publishers.

Brown, B., Heaton, P., & Wall, A. (2007). A service-learning elective to promote enhanced understanding in civic, cultural, and social issues and health disparitiesin pharmacy. *American Journal of Pharmaceutical Education*, 71(1), 1-7.

Campus Contact (2003). *Introduction to service learning toolkit. Readings and resources for faculty.* Providence, RI: Campus Compact.

Catapano, S. (2006). Teaching in urban schools: Mentoring pre-service teaches to apply advocacy strategies. *Mentoring & Tutoring: Partnership in Learning*, 14(1), 81-96.

City of Toronto (2009). *Toronto's racial diversity.* Retrieved 03 June 2009 from http://www.toronto.ca/toronto_facts/diverstiy.htm.

Day, D. (2008). Connecting student achievement and personal development: Service learning and academic personal development: Service learning and academic credit. *The International Journal of Learning*, 15(11), 41-50.

Desrochers, C. (2006). Educating preservice teaching for diversity: Perspectives on the possibilities and limitations of service learning. *Journal of Educational Thought*, 40(3), 263-280.

Elson, D., Johns, L., & Petrie, J. (2007). Jumpstart's service-learning initiative: Enhanced outcomes for at-risk children. In S. Gelmon & S. Billig, (Eds.), *Service learning: From passion to objectivity: International and cross-disciplinary perspectives on service-learning research* (pp. 65-88). Charlotte, NC: Information Age Publishing, Inc.

Frazer, L., Raasch, M., Pertzborn, D., & Bradley, F., (2007). The impact of community clients on student learning: The case of a university service-learning course *Journal of Experiential Education*, 29(3), 407-412.

Gupta, J. (2006). A model for interdisciplinary service-learning experience for social change. *Journal of Physical Therapy Education*, 20(3), 55-60.

Hollander, E., Saltmarsh, J., & Zlotkowski, E. (2002). Indicators of engagement. In M. Kenny, L. Simon, K. Kiley-Brabeck & R. Lerner (Eds.), *Learning to serve: Promoting civil society through service learning* (pp. 31-49). Norwell, MA: Kluwer Academic Publishers.

Howard, R. (2006). Bending toward justice: Service-learning and social capital as means to the tipping point. *Mentoring & Tutoring: Partnership in Learning*, 14(1), 5-15.

Jagla, V. (2008). Service–learning prepares teachers to meet the needs of diverse learners. *The International Journal of Learning*, 15(6), 1-7.

Kenny, M., Simon, L., Kiley-Brabeck, K., & Lerner, R. (2002). Promoting civil society through service learning: A view of the issues. In M. Kenny, L. Simon, K. Kiley-Brabeck, & R. Lerner, (Eds.), *Learning to serve:*

Promoting civil society through service learning (pp. 1-14). Norwell, MA: Kluwer Academic Publishers.

Lareau, A. (1987). Social class difference in family-school relationships: The importance of cultural capitalism. *Sociology of Education,* 60(2), 73-85.

MacLellan, D. (2008). Diversity and immigrant needs: Examining Toronto through a place-based approach. *Policy Matters.* No. 32, 1-13. Toronto, ON: Centre for Excellence in Research in Immigration and Settlement (CERIS).

Ontario Ministry of Education. (2002). *Course profile: Challenge and change in society. Grade 12 University/College Preparation.* Toronto, ON: Author.

Ontario Ministry of Education (2008). *Secondary school profiles.* Retrieved from http://www.edu.gov.on.ca on 09 June 2009.

Oakes, J. (2005). Keeping track: How schools structure inequality, (2nd ed.). New Haven, CT: Yale University Press.

O'Quin, J. (2003). Serve to learn and learn to serve. *The International Journal of Learning,* 10, 3697- 3704.

Payne-Jackson, A. (2005). A model of service learning. *The International Journal of Learning,* 12(10), 55-63.

Pearce, A. (2008). Finding your place in the world of service learning: Is the journey worth the effort? *The International Journal of Learning,* 15(10), 115-121.

Ramsdell, L. (2004). Reciprocity: The heart of service learning. *The International Journal of Learning,* 11, 523-527.

Ryerson University (2008). Ryerson University full-time undergraduate calendar 2008-2009. Toronto, ON: Author.

Ryerson University (2008a). *A toolkit for service learning course design.* Toronto, ON: Faculty of Arts, Ryerson University.

Ryerson University (2008b). *Progress indicators and related statistics for 2008.* Toronto: ON: Author.

Sterling, M. (2007). Service-learning and interior design: A case study. *Journal of Experiential Education,* 20(3), 331-343.

Terry, A. (2005). A K-12 development service-learning typology. *The International Journal of Learning,* 12(9), 321-330.

Toronto District School Board (2009). *Our school 2009-2010.* Toronto, ON: Author.

Webster, N. (2007). Enriching school connection and learning in African American urban youth: The impact of service-learning feasibility in inner-city Philadelphia. In S. Gelman & S. Billing (Eds.), *Service learning: From passion to objectivity: International and cross-disciplinary perspectives on service learning* (pp.159-176). Charlotte, NC: Information Age Publishing.

Young, C., Shinnar, R., Ackerman, R., Carruthers, C., & Young, D. (2007). Implementing and sustaining service-learning at the institutional level. *Journal of Experiential Education,* 29(3), 344-365.

Zlotkowski, E. (2003). Pedagogy and engagement. In Campus Compact (Ed.), *Introduction to service-learning toolkit: Readings and resources for faculty* (pp. 63-77). Providence, RI: Campus Compact Publishers.

FOOTNOTES

[1] Please note that Maple Heights is a pseudonym.

[2] The author would like to extend appreciation to Ryerson University's Service Learning Office, Ryerson's service learning students, and students and teaching staff at Maple Heights for their cooperation in this project.

Service Learning Promotes Positive Youth Development in High School

Both youths and communities benefit when students
engage in service learning in and out of school.

By Jonathan F. Zaff and
Richard M. Lerner

JONATHAN F. ZAFF is vice president of research and policy development, America's
Promise Alliance, Medford, Massachusetts, and **RICHARD M. LERNER** is director
of the Institute for Applied Research in Youth Development, Tufts University, Medford,
Massachusetts. The preparation of this article was supported in part by grants from the
National 4-H Council, the John Templeton Foundation, the Thrive Foundation for Youth, and
the National Science Foundation.

Nurturing young people's civic actions, motivations, and skills can have lasting
benefits for both youth and society. This dynamic of mutual individual and
societal benefit is a cornerstone of the Positive Youth Development perspective, which emphasizes young people's strengths and the potential for healthy
growth (Lerner 2009). As an emerging theory of civic development and
broader social contribution, Positive Youth Development asserts that internal
assets (such as values and motivations) and the external assets in the lives of
youths (such as civic and prosocial experiences in school and other arenas)
work in concert to promote confidence, competence, connection, character,
and caring—and to encourage young people's contributions to family, community, and civil society. These individual and social variables form the civic
context in which youths develop (Zaff, Malanchuk, and Eccles 2008).

> Both required and voluntary school-based service results in increased rates of voting and volunteering in college and adulthood.

Service learning has become an important strategy for encouraging positive youth development and civic contribution by young people. Through service learning, young people experience valued civic participation in their communities and learn to identify community problems, prioritize solutions, and implement problem-solving strategies (Finn and Checkoway 1998). Service learning can help students develop civic motivation, skills, and commitment to continue contributing to civil society and democracy (Flanagan and Sherrod 1998).

For example, high school students who participated in Madison County Youth in Public Service demonstrated significant increases in civic efficacy, civic knowledge, social capital, and commitment to remain involved in the community (Kahne and Westheimer 2006). These students from a rural East Coast community spent a semester learning about government and then worked in small groups with government agencies to tackle real community issues. Projects included studying the feasibility of curbside recycling and developing a five-year plan for the fire and rescue department. Students who participated expressed strong satisfaction with their accomplishments and the commitment to remain engaged in civic affairs.

Youths Learning About Youth

What do out-of-school youths offer the workplace? If you ask the public or look at research statistics, it's easy to conclude: not much. Young people who don't complete high school are often disengaged not only from employment and education opportunities, but also their communities.

Eagle Rock School in Estes Park, Colorado, is an alternative high school for students who didn't thrive in mainstream settings. Its curriculum emphasizes experiential education and service learning. When the W.K. Kellogg Foundation decided to sponsor a national initiative called New Options for Youth, which explores various credentials as alternatives to high school diplomas, it did something unusual. Among the researchers the foundation engaged to collect data were service learning students from Eagle Rock.

Michael Soguero, a math teacher and director of professional development at Eagle Rock, said, "We were really thought of as partners in the project." Soguero's math class covered the use of statistics, and a research firm based in Atlanta, Georgia, offered the students training in the ethnographic skills of neutrality and objectivity in interviewing, surveying, and documentation. Through their carefully designed protocols, eight Eagle Rock students conducted surveys and qualitative interviews with more than 75 young men, predominantly black and Latino, from Baltimore, Maryland, and

Oakland, California, who hadn't succeeded in traditional school settings.

Because the Eagle Rock students had faced similar hurdles themselves, their base of empathy made the experience powerful. Interview subjects seemed more willing to disclose details about their thoughts and their lives with student-researchers. The project underscored the belief that young people are experts about a substantial number of things that adults are not.

Amanda Hansen, one of the young researchers, talked about what she found empowering about the project: "We were dealing with a real-life situation where we got to develop skills in finding a solution." Students explored aspirations and hurdles by asking their interview subjects such questions as, What do you want in life? What makes it hard for you to get it? "I love how I can relate to a lot of these out-of-school youths," said Hansen.

Over a four-month period, the students collected information from multiple perspectives and aggregated and analyzed their data. Students learned to look for patterns among the responses and correlations between the surveys and interviews. "They learned about navigating the real world," said Soguero.

At the end of their project, they flew to Michigan to present their findings to the Kellogg Foundation. Perhaps least surprising, they found that service learning was among the programs that help out-of-school youths take meaningful steps to employment.

Students also left the project feeling that the experience had a profound effect on their ability to make a difference and be involved in the issues affecting their communities.

— Caryn Pernu and Maddy Wegner

Evidence supports the role of service learning experiences in promoting positive youth development and civic contribution, although there are some important qualifications. Several studies have found that both required and voluntary school-based service results in increased rates of voting and volunteering in college and adulthood (Hart et al. 2007; Metz and Youniss 2005; Smith 1999). For example, Dávila and Mora (2007) found that young men were 29% more likely to graduate from college on time if they engaged in service to fulfill a class requirement during high school.

Many factors can affect young people's civic behavior. Parents, peers, and extracurricular activities that don't involve civic participation also appear to complement school-based civic experiences and those that occur outside school, leading to sustained civic participation (Zaff, Malanchuk, and Eccles 2008). The personal characteristics youths bring to civic experiences and the quality of their civic experiences all influence the effects of service learning programs. For these experiences to be successful, youths need to have a voice in identifying the community problem, planning the solution to the problem, and having time to reflect on their experiences (Morgan and Streb 2001).

In Youth in Public Service, changes in the student's civic context appear driven by the sense of satisfaction participants expressed about their accomplishments. For example, when youths felt community partners and other adults they worked with didn't take their views seriously, they had more frustrating experiences (Kahne and Westheimer 2006). In addition, if the service activity isn't relevant to them, youths' investment in the activity and any benefits for positive youth development may be diminished (Ginwright and James 2002). Because of this, teachers and other service learning practitioners should be aware that activities appealing to low-income, academically struggling youths in urban areas might be different from activities appealing to academically excelling, private school students living in suburbs.

VOLUNTARY VS. MANDATORY

Young people's values and motivations also predict participation in service activities (Zaff and Michelsen 2002), and youths disposed to civic participation before civic experiences might gain the most from the experiences (Zaff, Malanchuk, and Eccles 2008). Alternatively, service learning can motivate young people to engage in civic activity. Metz and Youniss (2005) found that high school students who were more inclined to perform voluntary service were not negatively affected by mandatory service. That is, being required to serve didn't have much effect on those already disposed to volunteer. However, among the group less inclined to service, students required to perform mandatory service showed a greater likelihood of civic interest and understanding, future voting, and conventional civic involvement after their experience.

THE BENEFITS OF SERVICE LEARNING PROGRAMS APPEAR TO OUTWEIGH THE LIABILITIES.

Nevertheless, mandatory service may not always be beneficial. Among 6th through 8th graders, Covitt (2002) found that girls had more positive attitudes about required service than boys, and that white students had more positive attitudes than black students. Interestingly, student attitudes about mandatory service requirements, but not the requirements themselves, had an effect on their intentions, caring, or sense of responsibility. Students who had more negative attitudes were less likely to feel responsible to serve and showed lowered intentions to serve. It may be, then, that mandatory community service would not have the long-term effects of increasing volunteerism that proponents expect, at least for youths who perceive themselves as least likely to volunteer freely.

Evidence shows that across the high school years, service learning experiences tend to help young people become more informed and engaged citizens, which supports the aspirations of families, educators, and policy makers. Service learning is linked to positive youth development and to the growth of positive civic characteristics and behaviors. The benefits of service learning programs appear to outweigh the liabilities.

Given the variation in the influences of these programs, more nuanced practice is needed, and the recent K-12 Service Learning Standards for Quality Practice should provide some guidance. Teachers and other practitioners should give young people opportunities to develop and implement service learning projects and should provide the time and direction to reflect on the learning and the service that students accomplish through their work. This process can have the added benefit of ensuring that youths are pursuing initiatives that interest and engage them. Furthermore, given that parents and the broader community are parts of the civic context and can complement young people's service learning experiences, educators interested in service learning can do more to encourage parents to talk with their children about the projects and to connect the projects to activities outside of school. K

REFERENCES

Covitt, Beth A. *Middle School Students' Attitudes Toward Required Chesapeake Bay Service Learning.* Washington, D.C.: Corporation for National and Community Service, 2002.

Dávila, Alberto, and Marie T. Mora. "Do Gender and Ethnicity Affect Civic Engagement and Academic Progress?" *CIRCLE Working Paper 53.* College Park, Md.: University of Maryland, 2007.

Finn, J.L., and Barry Checkoway. "Young People as Competent Community Builders: A Challenge to Social Work." *Social Work* 43, no. 4 (1998): 335-347.

Flanagan, Constance A., and Lonnie R. Sherrod. "Youth Political Development: An Introduction." *Journal of Social Issues* 54, no. 3 (1998): 447-456.

Ginwright, Shawn, and Taj James. "From Assets to Agents: Social Justice, Organizing, and Youth Development." *New Directions for Youth Development* 96 (2002): 27-46.

Hart, Daniel, Thomas M. Donnelly, James Youniss, and Robert Atkins. "High School Community Service as a Predictor of Adult Voting and Volunteering." *American Educational Research Journal* 44, no. 1 (2007): 197-219.

Kahne, Joe, and Joel Westheimer. "The Limits of Political Efficacy: Educating Citizens for a Democratic Society." *PS: Political Science and Politics* 39, no. 2 (2006): 289-296.

Lerner, Richard M. "The Positive Youth Development Perspective: Theoretical and Empirical Bases of a Strength-Based Approach to Adolescent Development." In *Oxford Handbook of Positive Psychology*, 2nd ed., ed. C.R. Snyder and S.J. Lopez. Oxford, U.K.: Oxford University Press, 2009.

Metz, Edward C., and James Youniss. "Longitudinal Gains in Civic Development Through School-Based Required Service." *Political Psychology* 26, no. 3 (2005): 413-437.

Morgan, William, and Matthew Streb. "Building Citizenship: How Student Voice in Service Learning Develops Civic Values." *Social Science Quarterly* 82, no. 1 (2001): 154-169.

Smith, Elizabeth S. "The Effects of Investment in the Social Capital of Youth on Political and Civic Behavior in Young Adulthood: A Longitudinal Analysis." *Political Psychology* 20, no. 3 (September 1999): 553-580.

Zaff, Jonathan F., and Erik Michelsen. "Encouraging Civic Engagement: How Teens Are (Or Are Not) Becoming Responsible Citizens." *Child Trends Research Brief*. Washington, D.C.: Child Trends, 2002.

Zaff, Jonathan F., Oksana Malanchuk, and Jacquelynne Eccles. "Predicting Positive Citizenship from Adolescence to Young Adulthood: The Effects of a Civic Context." *Applied Developmental Science* 12, no. 1 (2008): 38-53.

Free to Choose Service-Learning

By Michael P. Garber and Justin A. Heet

MICHAEL P. GARBER *is a senior fellow and director of education policy at the Hudson Institute, Indianapolis, where* JUSTIN A. HEET *is a research analyst.*

Service-learning, by its activist nature, can easily become politicized. Thus, in the view of Mr. Garber and Mr. Heet, it should exist only in schools that are freely chosen by the families of students who attend them.

Only Disciples of Ayn Rand could oppose the idea of service-learning. In the best situations, when service is part of a school's program, students are challenged to define themselves through a larger sense of their community and of their responsibility to it. They have the opportunity to apply their skills to problems that require judgment and leadership. Service-learning, if properly understood, can help re-create the functional communities that renowned University of Chicago sociologist James Coleman wrote about as being vital to increasing the amount of "social capital" generated by schools.

The problem is that service-learning, by its activist nature, can easily become politicized. Thus it should exist only in schools that are freely chosen by the families of students who attend them.

As beneficial as service-learning may be, it puts our public schools as they are now configured in an untenable position. The opponents of service-learning have often argued that "mandatory volunteerism" is an oxymoron. They're right. But that does not cover the full extent of the problem. In situations in which families are not free to choose the schools their children attend, the introduction of service-learning invariably leads to needless politicization of schools, in many cases weakens schools' ability to serve their primary mission of academic instruction, and attenuates the idea of service-learning itself.

Considerable political conflict already exists within the country's public schools. At school board meetings across the country, bitter arguments continue over the inclusion of various books in the curriculum, over whether or not evolution should be taught as a science, and even over whether Christopher Columbus was a hero or a villain. When implemented in schools that children are compelled to attend, service-learning adds considerable fuel to these fires.

Critics of the current state of service-learning rightly point out that most of its advocates lean strongly to the left side of the political spectrum. Moreover, most of the programs engaged in by students in the U.S. reflect a social-activist bent. We believe that it is the responsibility of schools (particularly those funded by taxpayers and run by government entities) to engage students in honest inquiry and an honest effort to understand the many perspectives on a given issue. It is not the role of the schools to engage in advocacy.

This criticism is equally valid from a "progressive" vantage point. What if students in the public schools in Greenville, South Carolina, teamed with Bob Jones University students to hold a protest outside an abortion clinic? Or what if students in Colorado participated in a signature-gathering campaign to put a referendum on the ballot banning special legal protection for homosexuals? What if students chose to volunteer their time at a drug-rehabilitation program run by a church, which required those receiving services to be members of the church and to accept religious instruction in order to get help?

A service-learning program in Maine highlights the slippery slope on which schools can find themselves. Seven freshmen at Sumner Memorial High School in Sullivan, Maine, recently lobbied the state legislature to prevent certain types of fishing in Taunton Bay. [1] The activities all took place with the oversight of the civics and service-learning instructor.

Many people may believe that Taunton Bay requires greater environmental protection. However, if increased regulation requires lobbying, it is clear that not everyone agrees with the idea. Perhaps the parents of students at the school make their living from the kind of fishing their children—or their children's classmates—seek to have banned. The issue is not who is right or wrong about fishing in Taunton Bay. The issue is that, like the communities of which they are a part, schools serve diverse constituencies. Some citizens will inevitably object when their tax dollars are used to advance causes with which they disagree.

It seems to us that schools with mandatory attendance areas (and no choice offered to parents) have two ways of dealing with the prospect of politicization, neither of which is desirable. First, in the tradition of Dewey, schools can welcome the fight. Many proponents feel that schools should support the social engineering that service-learning can engender. Joel Westheimer and

Joseph Kahne go so far as to criticize many service-learning programs for not being political *enough*. They claim that, in emphasizing personal responsibility or private charity, schools do not do enough to redefine students' conception of citizenship in terms of government action. They lament that few programs "ask students to assess corporate responsibility or the ways government policies improve or harm society. Few programs ask students to examine the history of social movements as levers for change." [2]

The second response schools might adopt is to attempt to avoid controversy by making service-learning as voluntary as possible. Many schools have already chosen this route. (Indeed, students in Bethlehem, Pennsylvania, and Chapel Hill, North Carolina, have sued their schools over "forced volunteerism.") Rather than ask all students in a class to work on the same project, schools can give students the right to design their own individual or small-group projects, thereby insulating their programs from some of the sting of forced volunteerism. At Harbor City Learning Center in Baltimore, Maryland—a school for at-risk youths that has received widespread attention for its service-learning program—the school's coordinator oversees students who are in "individual service placements." [3]

The problem with this individual-centered approach is that it diminishes the potential value of service-learning for students. Most service-learning advocates maintain that its promise is not simply the direct community benefit of the students' activities—e.g., cleaner streets, fewer children without toys on Christmas—but the indirect benefit of greater student awareness and sense of civic responsibility. Even the most optimistic proponents of service-learning acknowledge that these indirect benefits do not happen organically. They come about as a result of reflection, study, and guidance. The lasting lessons grow from working with one's peers to arrive at group solutions rather than from driving toward purely individual solutions. In other words, good service-learning requires what good learning always requires: interaction with other students and the mentoring of an innovative teacher who can help students bridge the gap between good intentions and good results.

Properly understood, service-learning holds tremendous potential for expanding and enriching a child's education. However, problems inevitably result when such programs are implemented in schools that are not freely chosen by the parents of students who attend them. When introduced in these schools, service-learning programs have enormous potential for polarizing, rather than fortifying, the greater school community. The answer is not to dispense with the educationally sound and commonsensical idea of service-learning. The answer is to allow parents to choose schools that are consistent with their priorities and beliefs.

FOOTNOTES

[1] Shawn O'Leary, "Students Lobby for Bill to Protect Bay," *Bangor Daily News,* 4 February 2000.

[2] Joel Westheimer and Joseph Kahne, "Service-Learning Required: But What Exactly Do Students Learn?," *Education Week,* 26 January 2000, p. 32.

[3] Suzanne Goldsmith, "The Community Is Their Textbook: Maryland's Experiment with Mandatory Service for Schools," *The American Prospect,* Summer 1995, p. 54.

Underage, Overweight: The Federal Government Needs to Halt the Marketing of Unhealthy Foods to Kids

By The Editors

The statistic is hard to swallow: in the U.S., nearly one in three children under the age of 18 is overweight or obese, making being overweight the most common childhood medical condition. These youngsters are likely to become heavy adults, putting them at increased risk of developing cardiovascular disease, type 2 diabetes and other chronic ailments. In February, First Lady Michelle Obama announced a campaign to fight childhood obesity. Helping parents and schools to instill healthier habits in kids is an important strategy in this battle. But the government must take further steps to solve the problem.

In an ideal world, adults would teach children how to eat healthily and would lead by example. But in reality, two thirds of U.S. adults are themselves overweight or obese. Moreover, the food and beverage industry markets sugar- and fat-laden goods to kids directly—through commercials on television, product placement in movies and video games, and other media. Its considerable efforts—nearly $1.7 billion worth in 2007—have met with sickening success: a recent study conducted by researchers at the University of California, Los Angeles, found that children who see more television ads tend to become fatter. You might expect that watching TV, being a sedentary activity, is responsible for obesity, but the study found that obesity is correlated not with television per se but with advertising. The more commercial programming children watched, the fatter they got compared with those who watched a comparable amount of public television or DVDs. The majority of products marketed during children's programming are foods.

As nutritionist Marion Nestle of New York University has written, society needs to "create a food environment that makes it easier for parents and everyone else to make better food choices." Protecting children from junk-food marketing would help create conditions conducive to achieving a healthy weight.

Unfortunately, like the tobacco industry before it, the food industry cannot be trusted to self-regulate in this regard. In a study published in the March *Pediatrics*, investigators looked at the prevalence of food and beverage brands in movies released between 1996 and 2005. They noted, for instance, that although Coca-Cola and PepsiCo have pledged to not advertise during children's television programming, their products routinely appear in movies aimed at kids.

Likewise, in the March *Public Health Nutrition*, researchers reported a 78 percent increase from 2006 to 2008 in the use of cartoon characters, toys and other child-oriented cross promotions on food packaging—much of it for nutritionally bereft foods. A whopping 65 percent of these cross promotions came from food manufacturers that have opted into the Children's Food and Beverage Advertising Initiative, sponsored by the Council of Better Business Bureaus, which promises to limit advertising to kids but allows participants to decide for themselves whether to restrict in-store marketing. Such examples of ineffectual commitments on the part of the food industry abound.

In December a group of U.S. agencies—the Federal Trade Commission, the Centers for Disease Control and Prevention, the Food and Drug Administration, and the Department of Agriculture—proposed standards for foods and beverages that are marketed to children between the ages of two and 17. The agencies sensibly recommended that such foods must provide a meaningful contribution to a healthy diet by meeting specified requirements; that the amounts of saturated fat, trans fat, sugar and salt in these foods must not exceed limits set by the group; and that certain clearly healthy foods—such as those that are 100 percent fruits, vegetables or whole grains—may be marketed to kids without meeting the other two standards.

The interagency working group is due to submit a report containing its final recommendations to Congress by July 15. The standards are worthy but have one problem: as they stand, they would be voluntary. They should be mandatory, not optional, and the FDA should implement and enforce them.

The estimated cost of treating obesity-related ailments in adults was $147 billion for 2009. With the health care system already faltering, allowing companies to decide for themselves whether to peddle junk food to kids is a fox-and-henhouse policy this country simply cannot afford any longer.

The Kids Question

How can commerce and responsibility be balanced when marketing food to children?
We ask a food marketer, a business philosopher and a politician

Martin Glenn, Craig Smith and Debra Shipley

Martin Glenn President, PepsiCo UK

The premise here is that consumer goods companies would have any desire to communicate in an irresponsible way, and for my part, I would disagree with such a suggestion. No smart company would want to communicate irresponsibly to parents or their children, because it goes against their best interests.

A company's biggest assets are its brands, and consumer trust in brands is fundamental to its existence. One-and-a-half million consumers make a decision to buy Walkers crisps every day—if they believed we were misleading them, they would very quickly stop buying our brand.

Let's take a step back and look at the role played by advertising. Advertising helps to raise awareness in a commercially competitive environment and encourages brand choice. But while it may encourage consumers to try something once, if the product or service is not good quality or doesn't deliver a consumer need, consumers will not come back for more. In short, advertising cannot make consumers do things they don't want to do; it needs to work with consumer interest and desire.

Why do we believe companies such as ours advertise responsibly? First, because the majority of us are responsible companies and we want to be considered as such by the consumers we serve. Second, because there are very stringent advertising codes of practice in place—particularly with regard to children—that ensure we advertise our products or services responsibly. In the case of snack products, the code ensures our advertising does not encourage children to over-consume or replace main meals with snacks.

And third, because we seek not only to adhere to the letter of the codes, but to practise the spirit of them too. In the case of Walkers, we provide relevant nutritional information on our packs that allows consumers to make an informed choice about the products they eat. We also carry healthy lunchbox suggestions on the back of our multi-packs that clearly define the role of our products in the diet—in other words, as a treat.

We also know that advertising features way down the ranking of influences on children's habits. Research shows that it lies in ninth position, far behind the more significant influences of family and friends.

So why is advertising to children such a hot topic at the moment? Because it's currently seen by some as a major cause of the rise in obesity. But we know that this is simply not true. Advertising is only a very minor driver, if a driver at all, in the obesity issue.

What we need to do, if we are to move this debate forward, is to focus our efforts on addressing the real causes of obesity; too much energy consumed and not enough being expended through activity and exercise.

The right approach to tackling the obesity issue is a holistic one from all stakeholders—in other words, the food industry, the government, schools and parents—which addresses both sides of the equation: calories in and out.

The food industry must continue to provide ever-greater choice to the consumer, through development of healthier products. There is also an opportunity to provide more consistent information to consumers about the nutritional content of food across all sectors of the industry. At the same time, schools and parents must help to educate their children about the importance of a balanced lifestyle and a balanced diet. The government must provide them with the appropriate resources to enable them to do that.

PepsiCo would welcome the opportunity to play its part in helping address the issue of obesity. Companies such as ours should be included, not excluded from being a key part of the solution—not least because as owners of brands that consumers trust, and champions in consumer communication, we have much to offer.

However, companies such as PepsiCo cannot unilaterally take initiatives in this area without the context being right, and it is up to the government to help set the right tone and clarify the process—for example, which government ministry should lead the way—in order to get constructive engagement.

Craig Smith–Associate Professor of Marketing and Ethics and Associate Dean of the Full-time MBA Programme, London Business School

Let's assume there is clear evidence that the advertising of food to children is a major factor in unhealthy diets and, given insufficient physical activity, that this leads to increased obesity. We might well conclude that the advertising is unethical. Indeed, according to the American Marketing Association, marketers should be guided by 'the basic rule of professional ethics: not knowingly to do harm'.

Moral philosophy might also support a judgment of unethical conduct. Utilitarianism, in its simplest form, requires that we consider the consequences for all affected parties and assess whether the act results in the greatest overall welfare, relative to other acts. So, while we need to consider the effects of food advertising on children's diets, we should also allow for other effects, such as better-quality children's programming—which benefits from ad revenues—the sensory pleasures of food, and the entertainment value of ads.

Our analysis might also extend to the healthcare costs of obesity (£3.6bn by 2010) and reduced revenues for food producers and commercial TV. We may conclude welfare is not maximized by advertising to children. But this analysis is problematic given the difficulty of knowing all consequences and weighing up better health versus sensory pleasures.

Because of the challenges in applying moral theories to marketing ethics, I developed the Consumer Sovereignty Test (CST). It ca be used to evaluate ethical issues within the marketer-consumer relationship. It suggests marketers have an obligation to ensure consumers are capable of informed choice. More specifically, the CST requires an assessment of capability (are consumers vulnerable?), information (is it adequate and available?), and choice (are consumers free to choose?). With food advertising to children, the test suggests consumer sovereignty is compromised because of the subjects' vulnerability. The practice is also ethically problematic if children, rather than parents, are the consumer decision-makers.

According to the CST, advertising unhealthy foods to adults is not ethically problematic. They are free to choose from a variety of food, are considered capable of making dietary decisions, understand the persuasive intent of ads and, arguably, have sufficient access to information about a healthy diet. In contrast, all marketing to children under eight is ethically suspect. Advertisers may claim children are simply young consumers—but children lack the conceptual abilities required to make consumer decisions.

The issue of obesity demands policy intervention. But to what extent should measures be directed against advertising to children? The options under consideration by the Food Standards Agency (FSA) range from industry self-regulation to legislation on TV advertising and labeling. With uncertainty about the contribution of marketing to the unhealthy shift in children's diets relative to other influences—parents, peers, school—it is difficult to assert conclusively that advertising restrictions would reverse the trend.

Restrictions may generally be considered contrary to consumer interest, but arguably not in the context of advertising to children, given the inappropriateness of targeting under-eights. And as a review by the FSA shows, there is a balance of evidence suggesting ads do have some effect on children's diets.

Decisions on such a policy must balance the cost of government intervention against the possible benefit of dietary improvements. Such measures must also be part of a broader programme that includes the promotion of exercise and healthier diets.

From an industry perspective, the responsible approach would be to accept the likely effect of advertising and adopt FSA suggestions. Some have acted already: Coca-Cola announced it would no longer advertise to under-12s. This approach has pragmatic appeal. The evidence suggests regulatory intervention is warranted. It is perhaps inevitable if industry fails to act.

Debra Shipley–MP for Stourbridge and a Member of the Culture, Media and Sport Committee

In November last year, I introduced a Bill into the House of Commons to ban the advertising of food and drink high in sugar, salt and fat from children's TV. The Bill ran out of parliamentary time, but the response from the public, professionals and politicians was overwhelming.

As the scale of the childhood obesity and diabetes problem in the UK has become more widely known, the demand for action has become louder and more determined. Almost 100 national organisations back the campaign, ranging from health charities such as the British Heart Foundation to respected groups such as the Women's Institute. The tide has now turned against those who pretend there is no problem, as more people realise that banning children's TV advertisements for certain foods is moderate, reasonable and worthwhile.

The evidence that childhood obesity is a serious problem is overwhelming. The Chief Medical Officer for England has called it 'a health time bomb' and we are warned that today's youngsters may be the first generation that will live shorter lives than their parents.

At age six, one in five children in England are overweight, and a further one in ten are obese. By age 15, these figures have risen to 31% and 17% respectively. Even worse, the first obesity-related cases of Type Two diabetes in Caucasian adolescents have now been reported in the UK.

Is advertising the only cause? No. More must be done to encourage physical activity and improve labeling and food education. But advertising is a significant contributory factor.

The recent Food Standards Agency review examined 119 pieces of research on the topic and concluded that there was a clear impact at the level of both brand and type of food consumed. The University of Liverpool later found that all children over-consume after exposure to food ads, and obese children are particularly susceptible.

Some—usually those with vested interests within the food, drink and advertising industries—will deny the link, but in one hour of children's viewing on Five, kids may see 11 advertisements for foods high in fat, salt or sugar. I doubt that food manufacturers have so little faith in the advertising profession that they honestly believe this does not have a cumulative impact on children's eating patterns.

Jingles are designed specifically to appeal to children and to be catchy and memorable. They are accompanied by images of happy children being made happier by eating and drinking these products. The underlying message to parents viewing with their children is to make their children happy by providing these products.

The question is, where do we draw the line between commercial freedom and protecting public health? I believe that any government action should ultimately place the health of our children as a higher priority than the budget of children's television programmes or the financial concerns of a multinational, multi-billion-pound food and drink industry.

When culture, media and sport secretary Tessa Jowell comes to make her decision on whether or not to stop the ruthless and cynical targeting of small children with food and drink products high in fat, sugar and salt, she should ignore the rich and powerful industry lobby. Instead, she should do what only she has the power to do; ban food and drink advertising high in fat, sugar and salt from children's television.

Policy Statement—Children, Adolescents, Obesity, and the Media

Keywords: media, obesity, overweight, screen time, junk food, television

ABSTRACT

Obesity has become a worldwide public health problem. Considerable research has shown that the media contribute to the development of child and adolescent obesity, although the exact mechanism remains unclear. Screen time may displace more active pursuits, advertising of junk food and fast food increases children's requests for those particular foods and products, snacking increases while watching TV or movies, and late-night screen time may interfere with getting adequate amounts of sleep, which is a known risk factor for obesity. Sufficient evidence exists to warrant a ban on junk-food or fast-food advertising in children's TV programming. Pediatricians need to ask 2 questions about media use at every well-child or well-adolescent visit: (1) How much screen time is being spent per day? and (2) Is there a TV set or Internet connection in the child's bedroom? *Pediatrics* 2011;128:201–208

INTRODUCTION

Obesity represents a clear and present danger to the health of children and adolescents. Its prevalence among American youth has doubled in the past 3 decades,[1] and there are now more overweight and obese adults in the United States than adults of normal weight.[2] However, obesity is also a worldwide problem; rates are increasing in nearly every country.[3,4] It is increasingly clear that the media, particularly TV, play an important role in the etiology of obesity.[5] As a result, many countries are now establishing new regulations for advertising to children on TV, and many government health agencies are now issuing recommendations for parents regarding the amount of time children spend watching TV.[6] Unfortunately, there are currently no data relating other media to obesity.

MEDIA AND OBESITY

There are a number of ways that watching TV could be contributing to obesity: (1) increased sedentary activity and displacement of more physical pursuits; (2) unhealthy eating practices learned from both the programming and the advertisements for unhealthy foods; (3) increased snacking behavior while viewing; and (4) interference with normal sleep patterns. However, most researchers now agree that the evidence linking excessive TV-viewing and obesity is persuasive.[7-9] There have been dozens of longitudinal and correlational studies documenting a connection.[9] An increasing number of these studies hold ethnicity and socioeconomic status—known to be key factors in obesity— constant and still reveal that TV-viewing is a significant contributor to obesity.[7,10] Results of the longitudinal studies are particularly convincing. For example, a remarkable 30-year study in the United Kingdom found that a higher mean of daily hours of TV viewed on weekends predicted a higher BMI at the age of 30. For each additional hour of TV watched on weekends at age 5, the risk of adult obesity increased by 7%.[11] A group of researchers in Dunedin, New Zealand, followed 1000 subjects from birth to 26 years of age and found that average weeknight TV-viewing between the ages of 5 and 15 years was strongly predictive of adult BMI.[12] In a study of 8000 Scottish children, viewing more than 8 hours of TV per week at age 3 was associated with an increased risk of obesity at age 7.[13] Also, in 8000 Japanese children, more TV-viewing at age 3 resulted in a higher risk of being overweight at age 6.[14] Numerous American studies have had similar findings.[15-23]

The presence of a TV set in a child's bedroom seems to exacerbate the impact of TV-viewing on children's weight status.[24-28] A study of 2343 children aged 9 to 12 years revealed that having a bedroom TV set was a significant risk factor for obesity, independent of physical activity.[24] A cross-sectional study of 2761 parents with young children in New York found that 40% of the 1- to 5-year-olds had a bedroom TV, and those who did were more likely to be overweight or obese.[25] Teenagers with a bedroom TV spent more time watching TV, less time being physically active, ate fewer family meals, had greater consumption of sweetened beverages, and ate fewer vegetables than did teenagers without a bedroom TV.[26]

Recent correlational studies have also found a strong association between time spent watching TV and blood glucose level control in young people with diabetes,[29] type 2 diabetes mellitus,[30] insulin resistance,[31] metabolic syndrome,[32] hypertension,[33,34] and high cholesterol levels.[35-37] Furthermore, when TV time is diminished, so are measures of adiposity.[38,39]

MECHANISMS

How might time spent with media result in obesity? Contrary to popular opinion, overweight and obesity probably result from small, incremental increases in caloric intake (or increases in sedentary activities).[40] An excess intake of 50 kcal/day (eg, an extra pat of butter) produces a weight gain of 5 lb/year. Drinking a can of soda per day produces a weight gain of 15 lb/year.[41] Nearly 40% of children's caloric intake now comes from solid fat and added sugars, and soda or fruit drinks provide nearly 10% of total calories.[42] Because obesity is caused by an imbalance between energy intake and energy expenditure, screen time may contribute in several different ways.

DISPLACEMENT OF MORE ACTIVE PURSUITS

Children spend more time with media than in any other activity except for sleeping—an average of more than 7 hours/day.[43] Many studies have found that physical activity decreases as screen time increases,[44-46] but many other studies have not.[47-49] Children and teenagers who use a lot of media may tend to be more sedentary in general,[7,50] or researchers' measures of physical activity may be too imprecise.[9] Nevertheless, increasing physical activity, decreasing media time, and improving nutritional practices have been shown to prevent the onset of obesity, if not decrease existing obesity as well.[51-55] Some of the newer interactive video games may be useful in this way.[56,57] For example, a study of preteens playing *Dance Revolution* and Nintendo's *Wii Sports* found that energy expenditure was equivalent to moderate-intensity walking.[58]

UNHEALTHY EATING HABITS AND EFFECTS OF ADVERTISING

Children and teenagers who watch more TV tend to consume more calories or eat higher-fat diets,[59-64] drink more sodas,[65] and eat fewer fruits and vegetables.[66] Some researchers have argued that the viewing of TV while eating suppresses cues of satiety, which leads to overeating.[60] Others believe that viewers are primed to choose unhealthy foods as a consequence of viewing advertisements for foods high in fat, salt, and/or sugar and low in nutritional content ("junk food").[61] On any given day, 30% of American youngsters are eating fast food and consuming an additional 187 kcal (equaling 6 lb/year).[67,68] Fast food is big business: Americans spend more than $110 billion annually on it, which is more than that spent on higher education, computers, or cars.[69] A December 2010 study examined 3039 possible meal combinations at a dozen restaurant chains and found only 12 meals that met nutrition criteria for preschoolers. The same study found that 84% of parents had purchased fast food for their children in the previous week.[70] More than 80% of all advertisements in children's programming are for fast foods or snacks,[71-73] and for every hour that children watch TV, they see an estimated 11 food advertisements.[74]

Although exposure to food ads has decreased in the past few years for young children,[73] it has increased for adolescents.[75]

In 2009, the fast-food industry alone spent $4.2 billion on advertising in all media.[70] A study of 50,000 ads from 2003–2004 on 170 top-rated shows found that 98% of food ads seen by children aged 2 to 11 years and nearly 90% of food ads seen by teenagers are for products that are high in fat, sugar, and/or sodium and low in nutritional content (junk food).[76] A newer study of 1638 hours of TV and nearly 9000 food ads found that young people see an average of 12 to 21 food ads per day, for a total of 4400 to 7600 ads per year, yet they see fewer than 165 ads that promote fitness or good nutrition.[77] In 1 study, black children viewed 37% more ads than other youth.[78] New technology is enabling advertisers to reach young children and teenagers with a variety of online interactive techniques.[79-82] A study of the top 5 brands in 8 different food and beverage categories found that all of them had Internet Web sites: 63% had advergames (games used to advertise the product), 50% had cartoon characters, and 58% had a designated children's area.[79] Half of the Web sites urged children to ask their parents to buy the products, yet only 17% contained any nutritional information.[79] Teenagers' cell phones can be targeted by fast-food companies that can offer teenagers a discount on fast food as they walk by a particular restaurant.[81]

Available research results clearly indicate that advertising is effective in getting younger children to request more high-fat/low-nutrition food (junk food) and to attempt to influence their parents.[5,9,83-85] For example, a 2006 study of 827 third-grade children followed for 20 months found that total TV time and total screen media time predicted future requests for advertised foods and drinks.[86] Even brief exposures to TV food ads can influence children as young as preschool age in their food choices.[87] In 1 recent experiment, children consumed 45% more snacks when exposed to food advertising while watching cartoons than advertising for other products.[64] Similarly, children who played an online advergame that marketed healthy foods were more likely to eat healthy snacks than those who played an online advergame that advertised junk food.[82] Perhaps the most convincing study about the impact of advertising involved 63 children who tasted 5 pairs of identical foods (eg, French fries) and beverages (eg, milk) from unbranded packaging versus branded packaging. The results of the experiment revealed that the children strongly preferred the branded food and drinks to the unbranded foods.[88]

To illustrate the power of marketing, compare the commitment of the Robert Wood Johnson Foundation to spend $100 million per year to try to decrease childhood obesity with the fact that the food industry spends more than that every month marketing primarily junk food and fast food to young people.[84,89] Food is also unhealthily portrayed in most TV programming and movies.[9,84,90,91] A study of the 30 highest-rated programs among 2- to 5-year-olds found that an average child would see more than 500 food references per week, half of which were to empty-calorie or high-fat/sugar/salt foods

(D. L. G. Borzekowski, EdD, "Watching What They Eat: A Content Analysis of Televised Food References Reaching Preschool Children," unpublished manuscript, 2001). In an analysis of 100 films from 1991 through 2000, fats and sweets were the most common foods depicted.[91] Hollywood product placements are also being used to influence the food preferences and purchasing patterns of children and adolescents.[92,93] In the 200 movies examined from 1996 to 2005, a total of 1180 brand placements were identified. Candy (26%) and salty snacks (21%) were the most prevalent food brands, sugar-sweetened beverages (76%) were the most prevalent beverage brands, and fast food composed two-thirds of the food retail establishment brand placements.[93]

EFFECT OF MEDIA ON SLEEP HABITS

TV and other media are known to displace or disturb young people's sleep patterns.[5,94,95] A longitudinal study of adolescents in New York found that viewing 3 or more hours/day of TV doubled the risk of difficulty falling asleep compared with adolescents who watch less than 1 hour/day.[96] There is also now evidence that later bedtimes and less sleep may be associated with a greater risk of obesity.[97–101] The mechanism may be that sleep loss leads to increased snacking and consumption of less healthy foods to maintain energy,[102,103] that sleep deprivation leads to fatigue and therefore greater sedentary behavior,[104] or that children who do not get enough sleep have metabolic changes as well.[105]

Stress may also play a role, although there are only a handful of studies that have studied this subject so far. For example, a Scottish study of nearly 1500 4- to 12-year-olds found that heavier TV use produced greater psychological stress in children and that this effect was independent of, but exacerbated by, decreases in exercise.[106]

CONCLUSIONS

Media clearly play an important role in the current epidemic of childhood and adolescent obesity. The sheer number of advertisements that children and adolescents see for junk food and fast food have an effect. So, too, does the shift away from good nutritional practices that increased media screen time seems to create. Any success in dealing with the current epidemic will require a major change in society's recognition of media exposure as a major risk factor for obesity and in young people's media habits and the advertisements to which they are exposed.[107,108]

RECOMMENDATIONS

1. Pediatricians should ask parents and patients 2 key questions about media use: (1) How much time per day does the child or teenager spend with

screen media? and (2) Is there a TV set or unrestricted, unmonitored Internet connection throughout the house, including in the child's bedroom?[109] This recommendation should be incorporated into every well-child visit, as outlined in *Bright Futures*.[110]

2. Pediatricians should encourage parents to discuss food advertising with their children as they monitor children's TV-viewing and teach their children about appropriate nutrition.[111–113]

3. Pediatricians should continue to counsel parents to limit total noneducational screen time to no more than 2 hours/day, to avoid putting TV sets and Internet connections in children's bedrooms, to coview with their children, to limit nighttime screen media use to improve children's sleep, and to try strongly to avoid screen exposure for infants under the age of 2 years. In a recent study of 709 7- to 12-year-olds, children who did not adhere to the American Academy of Pediatrics guidelines of less than 2 hours/day of screen time[114] and 11,000 to 13,000 pedometer steps per day were 3 to 4 times more likely to be overweight.[115] Conversely, preschool-aged children who ate dinner with their parents, got adequate sleep, and had limited screen-time hours had a 40% lower prevalence of obesity than those exposed to none of these routines.[116]

4. Pediatricians should work with community groups and schools to implement media education programs in child care centers, schools, and community-based programs such as the YMCA. Such programs that teach children how to understand and interpret advertisements may have the potential to immunize young people against harmful media effects.[117] In addition, programs that educate parents about limiting media use in general have already been shown to be highly effective.[8,38,39,118,119]

5. Pediatricians should work with their state chapters, the AAP, parent and public health groups, and the White House[120] to do the following:

- Ask Congress, the Federal Trade Commission, and the Federal Communications Commission to implement a ban on junk-food advertising during programming that is viewed predominantly by young children.[84,121,122] Currently, several European countries restrict food advertising aimed at young children.[123] Several food manufacturers have already indicated a willingness to implement such a ban voluntarily,[124,125] but it remains to be seen whether they will follow through.[126–128] For example, children's cereals remain considerably unhealthier than adult cereals; they contain 85% more sugar, 65% less fiber, and 60% more sodium.[129] One-quarter of all food and beverage advertising originates from companies that do not participate in the initiative, and two-thirds of all advertising by companies that do participate is still for food and beverages of low nutritional value.[85] In addition, the food and beverage industry remains steadfastly opposed to any regulation. For example, in 2007, 1 soft drink company spent more than $1.7 million to lobby against marketing restrictions and school nutrition legislation.[130] Two recent studies showed that a ban on fast-food ads would reduce the number of overweight children and adolescents in the United States by an estimated 14% to 18%.[131,132] Just eliminating federal tax deductions for fast-food ads that target children would reduce childhood obesity by 5% to 7%.[131] On the other hand, advertisements and public service announcements for health foods and healthy nutritional practices should be encouraged. One recent experiment showed that children exposed to attractive advertisements for healthy foods develop significantly more positive attitudes than children shown junk-food ads.[133]

- Ask Congress and the Federal Communications Commission to prohibit interactive advertising involving junk food or fast food to children via digital TV, cell phones, and other media[79–81,121] and to ban payments for product placement in movies. Restoring power to the Federal Trade Commission to more tightly regulate children's advertising could be another way of accomplishing this goal.[84,134,135]

- Ask Congress to fund media research (eg, the Children Media Research and Advancement Act [CAMRA]). More research is specifically needed to determine (1) how heavy media use in children reflects or contributes to psychosocial elements of the child's life, such as stress in the home, (2) how new media technologies may be playing a role in exacerbating exposure to ads or encouraging more sedentary behavior, and (3) which of the above-mentioned mechanisms is most responsible for contributing to obesity and how such mechanisms can be ameliorated.[83,134]

- Encourage the production of more counteradvertising and more prosocial video games[136,137] and Web sites that encourage children to choose healthy foods.[82]

6. Pediatricians should be aware that children with high levels of screen time have higher levels of childhood stress, which puts them at risk not only for obesity but also for a number of stress-associated morbidities (eg, mood disorders, substance abuse, diabetes, cardiovascular disease, asthma).[138] Consequently, displacing screen time with more prosocial or resilience-building activities (eg, exercise, imaginative or social play) is an important approach to addressing a wide array of societal ills including obesity.[139]

LEAD AUTHOR

Victor C. Strasburger, MD

COUNCIL ON COMMUNICATIONS AND MEDIA, 2010–2011

Deborah Ann Mulligan, MD, Chairperson
Tanya Remer Altmann, MD
Ari Brown, MD
Dimitri A. Christakis, MD
Kathleen Clarke-Pearson, MD
Holly Lee Falik, MD
David L. Hill, MD
Marjorie J. Hogan, MD
Alanna Estin Levine, MD
Kathleen G. Nelson, MD
Gwenn S. O'Keeffe, MD

FORMER EXECUTIVE COMMITTEE MEMBERS

Gilbert L. Fuld, MD, Immediate Past Chairperson
Benard P. Dreyer, MD
Regina M. Milteer, MD
Donald L. Shifrin, MD
Victor C. Strasburger, MD

CONTRIBUTOR

Amy Jordan, PhD

LIAISONS

Michael Brody, MD—American Academy of Child and Adolescent Psychiatry
Brian Wilcox, PhD—American Psychological Association

STAFF

Gina Ley Steiner
Veronica Laude Noland

REFERENCES

1. Skelton JA, Cook SR, Aunger P, Klein JD, Barlow SE. Prevalence and trends of severe obesity among US children and adolescents. *Acad Pediatr.* 2009;9(5):322–329
2. Ogden CL, Carroll MD, McDowell MA, Flegal KM. Obesity among adults in the United States: no statistically significant chance since 2003–2004. *NCHS Data Brief.* 2007;(1):1–8
3. Preidt R. Overweight now a global problem. Available at: http://abcnews.go.com/ print?id 4509129. Accessed April 29, 2010
4. Guthold R, Cowan MJ, Autenrieth CS, Kahn L, Riley LM. Physical activity and sedentary behavior among schoolchildren: a 34-country comparison. *J Pediatr.* 2010;157(1):43–49
5. Jordan AB, Strasburger VC, Kramer-Golinkoff EK, Strasburger VC. Does adolescent media use cause obesity and eating disorders? *Adolesc Med State Art Rev.* 2008;19(3):431–449
6. Kelly B, Halford JC, Boyland EJ, et al. Television food advertising to children: a global perspective. *Am J Public Health.* 2010;100(9):1730–1736
7. Jordan AB. Heavy television viewing and childhood obesity. *J Child Media.* 2007;1(9):45–54
8. Dennison BA, Edmunds LS. The role of television in childhood obesity. *Progr Pediatr Cardiol.* 2008;25(2):191–197
9. Strasburger VC, Wilson BJ, Jordan AB. *Children, Adolescents, and the Media.* 2nd ed. Thousand Oaks, CA: Sage; 2009
10. Singh GK, Kogan MD, Van Dyck PC, Siahpush M. Racial/ethnic, socioeconomic, and behavioral determinants of childhood and adolescent obesity in the United States: analyzing independent and joint associations. *Ann Epidemiol.* 2008;18(9):682–695
11. Viner RM, Cole TJ. Television viewing in early childhood predicts adult body mass index. *J Pediatr.* 2005;147(4):429–435
12. Hancox RJ, Milne BJ, Poulton R. Association between child and adolescent television viewing and adult health: a longitudinal birth cohort study. *Lancet.* 2004;364(9430):257–262
13. Reilly JJ, Armstrong J, Dorosty AR, et al; Avon Longitudinal Study of Parents and Children Study Team. Early life risk factors for obesity in childhood: cohort study. *BMJ.* 2005;330(7504):1357
14. Sugimori H, Yoshida K, Izuno T, et al. Analysis of factors that influence body mass index from ages 3 to 6 years: a study based on the Toyama cohort study. *Pediatr Int.* 2004;46(3):302–310
15. Proctor MH, Moore LL, Gao D, et al. Television viewing and change in body fat from preschool to early adolescence: the Framingham Children's Study. *Int J Obes Relat Metab Disord.* 2003;27(7):827–833

16. Kaur H, Choi WS, Mayo MS, Harris KJ. Duration of television watching is associated with increased body mass index. *J Pediatr.* 2003;143(4):506–511

17. Lumeng JC, Rahnama S, Appugliese D, Kaciroti N, Bradley RH. Television exposure and overweight risk in preschoolers. *Arch Pediatr Adolesc Med.* 2006;160(4):417–422

18. O'Brien M, Nader PR, Houts RM, et al. The ecology of childhood overweight: a 12-year longitudinal analysis. *Int J Obes (Lond).* 2007;31(9):1469–1478

19. Henderson VR. Longitudinal associations between television viewing and body mass index among white and black girls. *J Adolesc Health.* 2007;41(6):544–550

20. Boone JE, Gordon-Larsen P, Adair LS, Popkin BM. Screen time and physical activity during adolescence: longitudinal effects on obesity in young adulthood. *Int J Behav Nutr Phys Act.* 2007;4:26. Available at: www.ijbnpa.org/content/4/1/26. Accessed June 19, 2009

21. Davison BA, Marshall SJ, Birch LL. Crosssectional and longitudinal associations between TV viewing and girls' body mass index, overweight status, and percentage of body fat. *J Pediatr.* 2006;149(1):32–37

22. Danner FW. A national longitudinal study of the association between hours of TV viewing and the trajectory of BMI growth among US children. *J Pediatr Psychol.* 2008;33(10):1100–1107

23. Meyer AM, Evenson KR, Couper DJ, Stevens J, Pereira MA, Heiss G. Television, physical activity, diet, and body weight status: the ARIC cohort. *Int J Behav Nutr Phys Act.* 2008;5(1):68. Available at: www.ijbnpa.org/content/5/1/68. Accessed June 19, 2009

24. Adachi-Mejia AM, Longacre MR, Gibson JJ, Beach ML, Titus-Ernstoff LT, Dalton MA. Children with a TV set in their bedroom at higher risk for being overweight. *Int J Obes (Lond).* 2007;31(4):644–651

25. Dennison BA, Erb TA, Jenkins PL. Television viewing and television in bedroom associated with overweight risk among low-income preschool children. *Pediatrics.* 2002;109(6):1028–1035

26. Barr-Anderson DJ, van den Berg P, Neumark-Sztainer D, Story M. Characteristics associated with older adolescents who have a television in their bedrooms. *Pediatrics.* 2008;121(4):718–724

27. Delmas C, Platat C, Schweitzer B, Wagner A, Oujaa M, Simon C. Association between television in bedroom and adiposity throughout adolescence. *Obesity.* 2007;15(10):2495–2503

28. Sisson SB, Broyles ST, Newton RL Jr, Baker BL, Chernausek SD. TVs in the bedrooms of children: does it impact health and behavior? *Prev Med.* 2011;52(2):104–108

29. Margeirsdottir HD, Larsen JR, Brunborg C, Sandvik L, Dahl-Jørgensen K; Norwegian Study Group for Childhood Diabetes. Strong association between time watching television and blood glucose control in children

and adolescents with type I diabetes. *Diabetes Care.* 2007;30(6):1567–1570

30. Hu FB, Li TY, Colditz GA, Willett WC, Manson JE. Television watching and other sedentary behaviors in relation to risk of obesity and type 2 diabetes mellitus in women. *JAMA.* 2003;289(14):1785–1791

31. Hardy LL, Denney-Wilson E, Thrift AP, Okely AD, Baur LA. Screen time and metabolic risk factors among adolescents. *Arch Pediatr Adolesc Med.* 2010;164(7):643–649

32. Mark AE, Janssen I. Relationship between screen time and metabolic syndrome in adolescents. *J Public Health (Oxf).* 2008;30(2):153–160

33. Pardee PE, Norman GJ, Lustig RH, Preud'homme D, Schwimmer JB. Television viewing and hypertension in obese children. *Am J Prev Med.* 2007;33(6):439–443

34. Martinez-Gomez D, Tucker J, Heelan KA, Welk GJ, Eisenmann JC. Associations between sedentary behavior and blood pressure in children. *Arch Pediatr Adolesc Med.* 2009;163(8):724–730

35. Fung TT, Rimm EB, Spiegelman D, et al. Association between dietary patterns and plasma biomarkers of obesity and cardiovascular disease risk. *Am J Clin Nutr.* 2001;73(1):61–67

36. Martinez-Gomez D, Rey-López JP, Chillón P, et al; AVENA Study Group. Excessive TV viewing and cardiovascular disease risk factors in adolescents. The AVENA crosssectional study. *BMC Public Health.* 2010;10:274

37. Stamatakis E, Hamer M, Dunstan DW. Screen-based entertainment time, allcause mortality, and cardiovascular events: population-based study with ongoing mortality and hospital events followup. *J Am Coll Cardiol.* 2011;57(3):292–299

38. Robinson TN. Reducing children's television viewing to prevent obesity: a randomized controlled trial. *JAMA.* 1999;282(16):1561–1567

39. Epstein LH, Roemmich JN, Robinson JL, et al. A randomized trial of the effects of reducing television viewing and computer use on body mass index in young children. *Arch Pediatr Adolesc Med.* 2008;162(3):239–245

40. Dietz WH Jr. Television, obesity, and eating disorders. *Adolesc Med.* 1993;4(3):543–549

41. Apovian CM. Sugar-sweetened soft drinks, obesity, and type 2 diabetes. *JAMA.* 2004; 292(8):978–979

42. Reedy J, Krebs-Smith SM. Dietary sources of energy, solid fats, and added sugars among children and adolescents in the United States. *J Am Diet Assoc.* 2010;110(10):1477–1484

43. Rideout V. Generation M2: *Media in the Lives of 8- to 18-Year-Olds.* Menlo Park, CA: Kaiser Family Foundation; 2010

44. Nelson MC, Neumark-Sztainer D, Hannan PJ, Sirard JR, Story M. Longitudinal and secular trends in physical activity and sedentary behavior

during adolescence. Pediatrics. 2006;118(6). Available at: www.pediatrics.org/cgi/content/full/118/6/e1627

45. Hardy LL, Bass SL, Booth ML. Changes in sedentary behavior among adolescent girls: a 2.5-year prospective cohort study. *J Adolesc Health.* 2007;40(2):158–165

46. Sisson SB, Broyles ST, Baker BL, Katzmarzyk PT. Screen time, physical activity, and overweight in U.S. youth: National Survey of Children's Health 2003. *J Adolesc Health.* 2010;47(3):309–311

47. Burdette HL, Whitaker RC. A national study of neighborhood safety, outdoor play, television viewing, and obesity in preschool children. *Pediatrics.* 2005;116(3):657–662

48. Taveras EM, Field AE, Berkey CS, et al. Longitudinal relationship between television viewing and leisure-time physical activity during adolescence. *Pediatrics.* 2007;119(2). Available at: www.pediatrics.org/cgi/content/full/119/2/e314

49. Melkevik O, Torsheim T, Iannotti RJ, Wold B. Is spending time in screen-based sedentary behaviors associated with less physical activity: a cross national investigation. *Int J Behav Nutr Phys Act.* 2010;7:46

50. Vandewater E, Shim M, Caplovitz A. Linking obesity and activity level with children's television and video game use. *J Adolesc.* 2004;27(1):71–85

51. Epstein LH, Paluch RA, Consalvi A, Riordan K, Scholl T. Effects of manipulating sedentary behavior on physical activity and food intake. *J Pediatr.* 2002;140(3):334–339

52. Washington R. One way to decrease an obesogenic environment. *J Pediatr.* 2005;147(4):417–418

53. Dietz WH. What constitutes successful weight management in adolescents? *Ann Intern Med.* 2006;145(2):145–146

54. Goldfield GS, Mallory R, Parker T, et al. Effects of open-loop feedback on physical activity and television viewing in overweight and obese children: a randomized, controlled trial. *Pediatrics.* 2006;118(1). Available at: www.pediatrics.org/cgi/content/full/118/1/e157

55. Haerens L, Deforche B, Maes L, Stevens V, Cardon G, De Bourdeaudhuij. Body mass effects of a physical activity and healthy food intervention in middle schools. *Obesity.* 2006;14(5):847–854

56. Mellecker RR, McManus AM. Energy expenditure and cardiovascular responses to seated and active gaming in children. *Arch Pediatr Adolesc Med.* 2008;162(9):886–891

57. Pate RR. Physically active video gaming: an effective strategy for obesity prevention? *Arch Pediatr Adolesc Med.* 2008;162(9):895–896

58. Graf DL, Pratt LV, Hester CN, Short KR. Playing active video games increases energy expenditure in children. *Pediatrics.* 2009;124(2):534–540

59. Robinson TN, Killen JD. Ethnic and gender differences in the relationships between television viewing and obesity, physical activity and dietary fat intake. *J Health Educ.* 1995;26(2 suppl):S91–S98

60. Blass EM, Anderson DR, Kirkorian HL, Pempek TA, Price I, Koleini MF. On the road to obesity: television viewing increases intake of high-density foods. *Physiol Behav.* 2006;88(4–5):597–604

61. Zimmerman FJ, Bell JF. Associations of television content type and obesity in children. *Am J Public Health.* 2010;100(2):334–340

62. Wiecha JL, Peterson KE, Ludwig DS, Kim J, Sobol A, Gortmaker SL. When children eat what they watch: impact of television viewing on dietary intake in youth. *Arch Pediatr Adolesc Med.* 2006;160(4):436–442

63. Barr-Anderson DJ, Larson NI, Nelson MC, Neumark-Sztainer D, Story M. Does television viewing predict dietary intake five years later in high school students and young adults? *Int J Behav Nutr Phys Activity.* 2009;6:7. Available at: www.ijbnpa.org/content/6/1/7. Accessed March 25, 2011

64. Harris JL, Bargh JA, Brownell KD. Priming effects of television food advertising on eating behavior. *Health Psychol.* 2009;28(4):404–413

65. Giammattei J, Blix G, Marshak HH, Wollitzer AO, Pettitt DJ. Television watching and soft drink consumption: associations with obesity in 11- to 13-year old schoolchildren. *Arch Pediatr Adolesc Med.* 2003;157(9):882–886

66. Krebs-Smith S, Cook A, Subar A, Cleveland L, Friday J, Kahle LL. Fruit and vegetable intakes of children and adolescents in the United States. *Arch Pediatr Adolesc Med.* 1996;150(1):81–86

67. Bowman SA, Gortmaker SL, Ebbeling CB, Pereira MA, Ludwig DS. Effects of fast-food consumption on energy intake and diet quality among children in a national household survey. *Pediatrics.* 2004;113(1 pt 1):112–118

68. Brownell KD. Fast food and obesity in children. *Pediatrics.* 2004;113(1 pt 1):132

69. Schlosser E. *Fast Food Nation.* Boston, MA: Houghton Mifflin; 2001

70. Harris JL, Schwartz MB, Brownell KD, et al. *Evaluating Fast Food Nutrition and Marketing to Youth.* New Haven, CT: Yale Rudd Center for Food Policy & Obesity; 2010

71. Harrison K, Marske AL. Nutritional content of foods advertised during the television programs children watch most. *Am J Public Health.* 2005;95(9):1568–1574

72. Powell LM, Szczypka G, Chaloupka FJ, Braunschweig CL. Nutritional content of television food advertisements seen by children and adolescents in the United States. *Pediatrics.* 2007;120(3):576–583

73. Kunkel D, McKinley C, Stitt C. *Food Advertising During Children's Programming: A Two-Year Comparison.* Tucson, AZ: University of Arizona; 2010

74. Stitt C, Kunkel D. Food advertising during children's television programming on broadcast and cable channels. *Health Commun.* 2008;23(6):573–584

75. Powell LM, Szczypka G, Chaloupka FJ. Trends in exposure to television food advertisements among children and adolescents in the United States. *Arch Pediatr Adolesc Med.* 2010;164(9):794–802

76. Powell LM, Szczypka G, Chaloupka FJ. Exposure to food advertising on television among US children. *Arch Pediatr Adolesc Med.* 2007;161(6):553–560

77. Gantz W, Schwartz N, Angelini JR, Rideout V. *Food for Thought: Television Food Advertising to Children in the United States.* Menlo Park, CA: Kaiser Family Foundation; 2007

78. Harris JL, Weinberg ME, Schwartz MB, Ross C, Ostroff J, Brownell KD. *Trends in Television Food Advertising.* New Haven, CT: Yale Rudd Center for Food Policy & Obesity; 2010

79. Weber K, Story M, Harnack L. Internet food marketing strategies aimed at children and adolescents: a content analysis of food and beverage brand Web sites. *J Am Diet Assoc.* 2006;106(9):1463–1466

80. Moore ES. *It's Child's Play: Advergaming and the Online Marketing of Food to Children.* Menlo Park, CA: Kaiser Family Foundation; 2006

81. Montgomery KC, Chester J. Interactive food and beverage marketing: targeting adolescents in the digital age. *J Adolesc Health.* 2009;45(3 suppl):S18–S29

82. Pempek TA, Calvert SL. Tipping the balance: use of advergames to promote consumption of nutritious foods and beverages by low-income African American children. *Arch Pediatr Adolesc Med.* 2009;163(7):633–637

83. Institute of Medicine. *Preventing Childhood Obesity: Health in the Balance.* Washington, DC: National Academies Press; 2005

84. Harris JL, Pomeranz JL, Lobstein T, Brownell KD. A crisis in the marketplace: how food marketing contributes to childhood obesity and what can be done. *Annu Rev Public Health.* 2009;30:211–225

85. Kunkel D, McKinley C, Wright P. *The Impact of Industry Self-regulation on the Nutritional Quality of Foods Advertised on Television to Children.* Oakland, CA: Children Now; 2009

86. Chamberlain LJ, Wang Y, Robinson TN. Does children's screen time predict requests for advertised products? *Arch Pediatr Adolesc Med.* 2006;160(4):363–368

87. Borzekowski DLG, Robinson TN. The 30-second effect: an experiment revealing the impact of television commercials on food preferences of preschoolers. *J Am Diet Assoc.* 2001;101(1):42–46

88. Robinson TN, Borzekowski DLG, Matheson DM, Kraemer HC. Effects of fast food branding on young children's taste preferences. *Arch Pediatr Adolesc Med.* 2007;161(8):792–292

89. Robert Wood Johnson Foundation. *F as in Fat 2009: How Obesity Policies Are Failing in America.* Princeton, NJ: Robert Wood Johnson Foundation; 2009. Available at: http://healthyamericans.org/reports/obesity2009. Accessed April 29, 2010

90. Greenberg BS, Rosaen SF, Worrell TR, Salmon CT, Volkman JE. A portrait of food and drink in commercial TV series. *Health Commun.* 2009;24(4):295–303

91. Bell R, Berger C, Townsend M. *Portrayals of Nutritional Practices and Exercise Behavior in Popular American Films, 1991–2000.* Davis, CA: Center for Advanced Studies of Nutrition and Social Marketing, University of California-Davis; 2003

92. Eisenberg D. It's an ad, ad, ad world. *Time Magazine.* August 26, 2002:38–42. Available at: www.time.com/time/magazine/article/0,9171,1101020902-344045,00.html. Accessed April 29, 2010

93. Sutherland LS, MacKenzie T, Purvis LA, Dalton M. Prevalence of food and beverage brands in movies, 1996–2005. *Pediatrics.* 2010;125(3):468–474

94. Zimmerman FJ. *Children's Media Use and Sleep Problems: Issues and Unanswered Questions.* Menlo Park, CA: Kaiser Family Foundation; 2008

95. Landhuis CE, Poulton R, Welch D, Hancox RJ. Childhood sleep time and long-term risk for obesity: a 32-year prospective birth cohort study. *Pediatrics.* 2008;122(5):955–960

96. Johnson JG, Cohen P, Kasen S, First MB, Brook JS. Association between television and sleep problems during adolescence and early adulthood. *Arch Pediatr Adolesc Med.* 2004;158(6):562–568

97. Sekine M, Yamagami T, Handa K, et al. A dose-response relationship between short sleeping hours and childhood obesity: results of the Toyama Birth Cohort Study. *Child Care Health Dev.* 2002;28(2):163–170

98. Agras W, Hammer L, McNicholas F, Kraemer H. Risk factors for child overweight: a prospective study from birth to 9.5 years. *J Pediatr.* 2004;145(1):20–25

99. Taheri S. The link between short sleep duration and obesity: we should recommend more sleep to prevent obesity. *Arch Dis Child.* 2006;91(11):881–884

100. Bell JF, Zimmerman FJ. Shortened nighttime sleep duration in early life and subsequent childhood obesity. *Arch Pediatr Adolesc Med.* 2010;164(9):840–845

101. Lytle LA, Pasch K, Farbaksh K. Is sleep related to obesity in young adolescents [abstract]? Presented at: Pediatric Academic Societies meeting; May 4, 2010; Vancouver, British Columbia, Canada

102. Wells TT, Cruess DG. Effects of partial sleep deprivation on food consumption and food choice. *Psychol Health.* 2006;21(1):79–86

103. Oliver G, Wardle J. Perceived effects of stress on food choice. *Physiol Behav.* 1999;66(3):511–515

104. Nelson MC, Gordon-Larsen P. Physical activity and sedentary behavior patterns are associated with selected adolescent health risk behaviors. *Pediatrics.* 2006;117(4):1281–1290

105. Van Cauter E, Holmback U, Knutson K, et al. Impact of sleep and sleep loss on neuroendocrine and metabolic function. *Horm Res.* 2007;67(suppl 1):2–9

106. Hamer M, Stamatakis E, Mishra G. Psychological distress, television viewing and physical activity in children aged 4 to 12 years. *Pediatrics.* 2009;123(5):1263–1268

107. Jordan AB, Robinson TN. Children, television viewing, and weight status: summary and recommendations from an expert panel meeting. *Ann Am Acad Polit Soc Sci.* 2008;615(1):119–132

108. Brownell KD, Schwartz MB, Puhl RM, Henderson KE, Harris JL. The need for bold action to prevent adolescent obesity. *J Adolesc Health.* 2009;45(3 suppl):S8–S17

109. Strasburger VC. First do no harm: why have parents and pediatricians missed the boat on children and media? *J Pediatr.* 2007;151(4):334–336

110. Hagan JF Jr, Shaw JS, Duncan PM, eds. *Bright Futures: Guidelines for Health Supervision of Infants, Children, and Adolescents.* Elk Grove Village, IL: American Academy of Pediatrics; 2008

111. Harris JL, Bargh JA. Television viewing and unhealthy diet: implications for children and media interventions. *Health Commun.* 2009;24(7):660–673

112. He M, Piche L, Beynon C, Harris S. Screen-related sedentary behaviors: children's and parents' attitudes, motivations, and practices. *J Nutr Educ Behav.* 2010;42(1):17–25

113. Carlson SA, Fulton JE, Lee SM, Foley JT, Heitzler C, Huhman M. Influence of limit-setting and participation in physical activity on youth screen time. *Pediatrics.* 2010; 126(1). Available at: www.pediatrics.org/cgi/content/full/126/1/e89

114. American Academy of Pediatrics, Committee on Public Education. Media education. *Pediatrics.* 1999;104(2 pt 1):341–343

115. Laurson KR, Eisenmann JC, Welk G, Wickel EE, Gentile DA, Walsh DA. Combined influence of physical activity and screen time recommendations on childhood overweight. *J Pediatr.* 2008;153(2):209–214

116. Anderson SE, Whitaker RC. Household routines and obesity in US preschool-aged children. *Pediatrics.* 2010;125(3):420–428

117. McCannon R. Media literacy/media education. In: Strasburger VC, Wilson BJ, Jordan AJ, eds. *Children, Adolescents, and the Media.* 2nd ed. Thousand Oaks, CA: Sage; 2009:519–569

118. Gortmaker SL. Innovations to reduce television and computer time and obesity in childhood. *Arch Pediatr Adolesc Med.* 2008;162(3):283–284

119. Escobar-Chaves SL, Markham CM, Addy RC, Greisinger A, Murray NG, Brehm B. The Fun Families Study: intervention to reduce children's TV viewing. *Obesity (Silver Spring).* 2010;18(suppl 1):S99–S101

120. White House Task Force on Childhood Obesity. *Solving the Problem of Childhood Obesity Within a Generation: Report to the President.* Washington, DC: Executive Office of the President of the United States; 2010. Available at: www.letsmove.gov/sites/letsmove.gov/files/TaskForce_on_ Childhood_Obesity_May2010_FullReport.pdf. Accessed January 12, 2011

121. American Academy of Pediatrics, Committee on Communications. Children, adolescents, and advertising [published correction appears in *Pediatrics.* 2007;119(2):424]. *Pediatrics.* 2006;118(6):2563–2569

122. Pomeranz JL. Television food marketing to children revisited: the Federal Trade Commission has the constitutional and statutory authority to regulate. *J Law Med Ethics.* 2010;38(1):98–116

123. Strasburger VC. Adolescents and the media. In: Rosenfeld W, Fisher M, Alderman E, eds. *Textbook of Adolescent Medicine.* Elk Grove Village, IL: American Academy of Pediatrics; 2011;359–373

124. Gold J. Snickers maker will aim higher. *Albuquerque Journal.* February 7, 2007:B4

125. Union of European Beverages Associations. *International Council of Beverages Associations Adopts Groundbreaking Guidelines on Marketing to Children* [press release]. Brussels, Belgium: Union of European Beverages Associations; May 20, 2008

126. Wilde P. Self-regulation and the response to concerns about food and beverage marketing to children in the United States. *Nutr Rev.* 2009;67(3):155–166

127. Schwartz MB, Ross C, Harris JL, et al. Breakfast cereal industry pledges to self-regulate advertising to youth: will they improve the marketing landscape? *J Public Health Policy.* 2010;31(1):59–73

128. Noah T. Toy story: why self-regulation of children's advertising is a joke. *Slate Magazine.* Available at: www.slate.com/id/2278241. Accessed January 12, 2011

129. Harris JL, Schwartz MB, Brownell KD, et al. *Cereal FACTS: Evaluating the Nutrition Quality and Marketing of Children's Cereals.* New Haven, CT: Rudd Center for Food Policy and Obesity; 2009

130. Associated Press. Coca-cola spent more than $1.7M to lobby. February 21, 2007

131. Chou SY, Rashad I, Grossman M. Fast-food restaurant advertising on television and its influence on childhood obesity. *J Law Econ.* 2008;51(4):599–618

132. Veerman JL, Van Beeck EF, Barendregt JJ, Mackenbach JP. By how much would limiting TV food advertising reduce childhood obesity? *Eur J Public Health.* 2009;19(4):365–369

133. Dixon HG, Scully ML, Wakefield MA, White VM, Crawford DA. The effects of television advertisements for junk food versus nutritious food on children's food attitudes and preferences. *Soc Sci Med.* 2007;65(7):1311–1323

134. Larson N, Story M. *Food and Beverage Marketing to Children and Adolescents: What Changes Are Needed to Promote Healthy Eating Habits?* Princeton, NJ: Robert Wood Johnson Foundation; 2008

135. Pertschuk M. The little agency that could. *The Nation.* June 29, 2009:21–22

136. Durant NH. Not just fun and games: harnessing technology to address childhood obesity. *Child Obes.* 2010;6(5):283–284

137. Biddiss E, Irwin J. Active video games to promote physical activity in children and youth: a systematic review. *Arch Pediatr Adolesc Med.* 2010;164(7):664–672

138. Strasburger VC, Jordan AB, Donnerstein E. Health effects of media on children and adolescents. *Pediatrics.* 2010;125(4):756–767

139. Ginsburg KR; American Academy of Pediatrics, Committee on Communications and Committee on Psychosocial Aspects of Child and Family Health. The importance of play in promoting healthy child development and maintaining strong parent-child bonds. *Pediatrics.* 2007;119(1):182–191

www.pediatrics.org/cgi/doi/10.1542/peds.2011–1066

doi:10.1542/peds.2011–1066

Women in America: Indicators of Social and Economic Well-Being

White House Council on Women and Girls

III. EMPLOYMENT

Over the past several decades, women have dramatically reshaped their role in the nation's labor force. They have become much more likely to work or seek work outside the home. They are also employed in more varied occupations and are more likely to work year-round. In addition, women have attained higher levels of education. Reflecting their greater work activity and education, women's earnings as a proportion of men's earnings have grown over time and women are contributing increasingly important shares of family incomes, but the earnings gap between men and women remains. As more women have entered the labor force, interest has risen in how they divide their time between their jobs and other activities.

LABOR FORCE PARTICIPATION

The labor force participation rate for women—the percentage of all adult women who are working or looking for work—rose steadily during the latter half of the 20th century.[1] This rate increased from about 33 percent in 1950 to 61 percent in 1999. During the first decade of this century, it has held steady at around 61 percent. In contrast, men's labor force participation rate has declined steadily since the 1950s.

Despite the trends of recent decades, women remain less active in the labor market than men. The labor force participation rate of adult women (age 20 and older) was still significantly lower than that of adult men, 61 percent versus 75 percent in 2009. Moreover, on average, women at every educational level and at every age spend fewer weeks in the labor force than do men. The differences between men and women in labor force attachment are much smaller among those with a college degree or more education.[2]

As part of the overall growth of women's presence in the labor force, the participation rate of mothers also increased. From 1975 to 2000, the labor force participation rate of mothers with children under age 18 rose from 47 percent to a peak of 73 percent. This rate receded to about 71 percent in 2004, where it has remained through 2009. Unmarried mothers had a higher labor force participation rate than their married counterparts, 76 percent compared to 70 percent in 2009.

OCCUPATIONS

The jobs working women perform also have changed as their market activity has increased. A larger share of women now works in management, professional, and related occupations.[3] In 2009, women accounted for 51 percent of all persons employed in these occupations, somewhat more than their share of total employment (47 percent).

One reason for the shift in occupations is women's greater educational attainment. Among women age 25–64 in the labor force, 36 percent held college degrees in 2009, compared to 11 percent in 1970. Over the same period, the proportion of women workers with less than a high school diploma fell from 34 percent to 7 percent. Individuals with higher levels of education generally have better access to higher paying jobs than do individuals with less education. The earnings of both women and men age 25 and older without a high school diploma were less than half of those with a college degree, respectively.

EARNINGS AND CONTRIBUTIONS

The earnings gap between women and men has narrowed over time, but it remains. Among full-time wage and salary workers, women's weekly earnings as a percent of men's have increased from 62 percent in 1979 to 80 percent in 2009.[4,5] This comparison of earnings is on a broad level and does not control for many factors that can be significant in explaining or further highlighting earnings differences.

As women's earnings have risen, working wives' contributions to their family incomes also have risen. In 2008, working wives contributed 29 percent of their families' incomes, up by 5 percentage points from 1988, when wives' earnings accounted for 24 percent of their families' total incomes. The proportion of wives earning more than their husbands also has grown. In 1988, 18 percent of working wives whose husbands also worked earned more than their spouses; in 2008, the proportion was 27 percent.[6] Dual-earner couples made up 57 percent of all married-couple families in 2008, compared to 46 percent in 1970.[7]

Working women spend their days somewhat differently than do working men. In 2009, on the days that they worked, employed married women age 25–54 spent less time in labor market work and work-related activities than did employed married men in the same age group—7 hours and 40 minutes, compared to about 8 hours and 50 minutes. However, these employed wives spent about 40 minutes more time than did their male counterparts doing household activities such as cooking, housework, and household management.

1. **After decades of significant increases, the labor force participation rate for women has held steady in recent years.**

   - The labor force participation rate for women (age 20 and older) nearly doubled between 1948 (32 percent) and 1997 (61 percent). Since 1997, it has held steady (61 percent in 2009). The labor force participation rate for men (age 20 and older) has fallen from about 89 percent in 1948 to 75 percent in 2009. (See chart.)

   - At all levels of educational attainment, the labor force participation rate of men was higher than that of their female counterparts. In 2009, the participation rate of women with less than a high school diploma was only 34 percent, compared to 59 percent for men. Among those with college degrees or higher, the participation rate of women was 73 percent, compared to 82 percent for men.

   - Between 2005 and 2009, the labor force participation rate increased for White women (59.7 percent to 60.4 percent) and Hispanic women (57.4 percent to 59.2 percent). By comparison, the rate for Black women, who have the highest labor force participation among women, has edged down (64.4 percent to 63.4 percent). For men, labor force participation continued to fall across all racial and ethnic groups.

   - Among mothers age 16 and over, those with older children (age 6 to 17 only) were more likely to be in the labor force (77 percent) in 2009 than those with children age 5 or younger (64 percent).

   - The labor force participation rate of persons age 55 and older began to rise in 1996 for both women and men, but the pace of the increase has slowed in recent years.

Labor Force Participation

(Percent of Persons Age 20 and Older, 1948–2009)

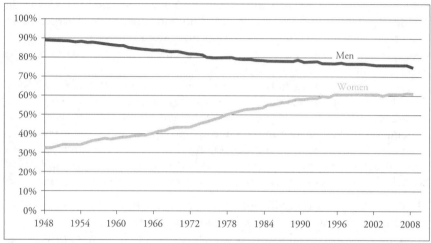

Source: Bureau of Labor Statistics

2. **Unemployment rates for women have risen less than for men in recent recessions.**

   - During the past four recessions, the unemployment rate among women rose less than the rate for men. During the most recent recession, the unemployment rate among women (age 20 and older) rose from 4.4 percent to 7.7 percent; by comparison, the rate for men (age 20 and older) more than doubled, from 4.4 percent to 9.9 percent. (See chart.)

   - Prior to the 1980s, the unemployment rate for women tended to be higher than the rate for men. Since the early 1980s, the jobless rates for both men and women have tracked one another quite closely during economic expansions. (See chart.)

   - During the past four recessions, the relatively large increases in the job-less rates among men can be attributed to their concentration in more cyclically sensitive occupations, such as manufacturing production and construction.

   - In contrast, women are more concentrated in less cyclically sensitive and more rapidly growing occupations, such as health care, which has damp-ened the impact of recent recessions on their unemployment rates.

Unemployment Rates

(Percent of Persons Age 20 and Older in the Labor Force, Seasonally Adjusted,
January 1948– December 2010)

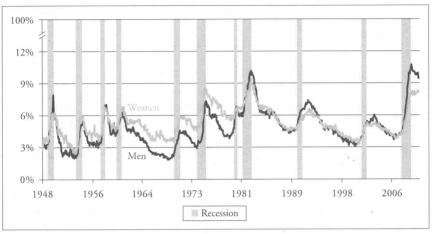

Source: Bureau of Labor Statistics

3. **More women than men work part time, and women and men have roughly equal access to flexible work schedules.**

- Historically, women have been more likely than men to work part time (less than 35 hours per week). In 2009, 24 percent of employed women (age 20 and older) worked part time, compared to 11 percent of men. (See chart.)

- Women are considerably more likely to work year round than they were in past decades. In 2009, 75 percent of women worked year round, up from 51 percent in 1968. The proportion of men who worked year round changed little over this same time period (from 74 percent to 76 percent).

- In May 2004, about 30 percent of wage and salary workers reported having flexible schedules that allowed them to vary their work hours to some degree. Between 1985 and 2004, the proportions of employed men and women able to vary their work hours were about equal; the same was true of both mothers and fathers who work.

Part Time Work

(Percent of Employed Persons Age 20 and Older, Seasonally Adjusted,
January 1968–December 2010)

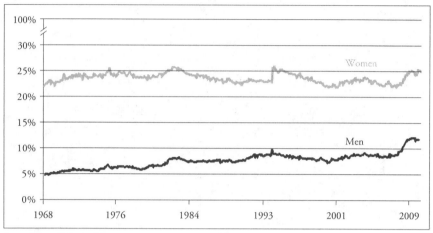

Source: Bureau of Labor Statistics

- Due to the nature of the work required for each particular job, the prevalence of flexible schedules varies by occupation. In May 2004, the proportion of White and Asian workers in occupations in which they could vary their schedules exceeded that of other groups. About 30 percent of employed Whites and Asians could vary their work hours, while the proportion was closer to 21 percent among Black workers and those of Hispanic ethnicity.

4. **Education pays for both women and men, but the pay gap persists.**
   - Earnings for both women and men typically increase with higher levels of education. However, the male-female pay gap persists at all levels of education for full-time workers (35 or more hours per week). (See chart.)
   - Earnings of full-time female workers have risen by 31 percent since 1979, compared to a 2 percent rise in male earnings. In addition, earnings for women with college degrees rose by 33 percent since 1979 while those of their male counterparts rose by 22 percent.
   - At all levels of education, women earned about 75 percent as much as their male counterparts in 2009. Although both women and men with less than a high school diploma have experienced declines in earnings since 1979, the drop for women (9 percent) was significantly less than that for men (28 percent).
   - The earnings gap between women and men narrowed for most age groups from 1979 to 2009. The women's-to-men's earnings ratio

Earnings by Educational Attainment

(Median Weekly Earnings of Full-Time Workers Age 25 and Older, Annual Averages, 2009)

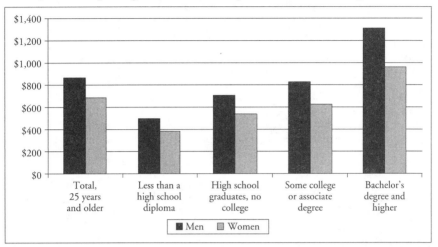

Source: Bureau of Labor Statistics

among 25- to 34-year-olds, rose from 68 percent in 1979 to 89 percent in 2009, and the ratio for 45- to 54-year-olds increased from 57 percent to 74 percent.

- Compared to the earnings of all men (of all race and ethnic groups), Black women earned 71 percent and Hispanic women earned 62 percent as much in 2009. White and Asian women earned 82 percent and 95 percent as much as all men, respectively.

- Compared to their direct male counterparts, however, White women earned 79 percent as much as White men in 2009, while Asian women earned 82 percent as much as Asian men. For Blacks and Hispanics, the figures were 94 percent and 90 percent, respectively.

5. **Women and men continue to work in different occupations.**

- While women are three times more likely to work in administrative support jobs than men, relatively few women have construction, production, or transportation jobs. (See chart.)

- While women are more likely than men to work in professional and related occupations, they are more highly represented in the lower-paying jobs within this category. For example, in 2009, professional women were more likely (nearly 70 percent) to work in the relatively low-paying education (with $887 median weekly earnings) and health care ($970 median weekly earnings) occupations, compared to 32 percent of male professionals.

Employment by Occupation

(Percent of Employed Persons Age 16 and Older in Major Occupation Groups, 2009)

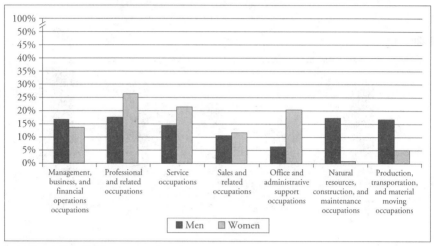

Source: Bureau of Labor Statistics

- In 2009, only 7 percent of female professionals were employed in the relatively high paying computer ($1,253 median weekly earnings) and engineering fields ($1,266 median weekly earnings), compared to 38 percent of male professionals.

- The proportion of women working in management, business, and finance jobs has increased from 9 percent to 14 percent since 1983.

- Women continue to be concentrated in a small number of traditionally female occupations. In 2009, nearly one-fifth of all women were employed in just five occupations: secretaries, registered nurses, elementary school teachers, cashiers, and nursing aides.

6. **Female-headed families have the lowest family earnings among all family types.**

   - Family earnings levels among female-headed families were the lowest among all family types in both 1988 and 2008, despite increasing by 27 percent over this timeframe. (See chart.) A family is a group of two or more people living together and related by birth, marriage, or adoption.

   - In 2008, female-headed families with children earned 30 percent less than their counterparts without children, although their earnings grew faster (43 percent) than the other family types between 1988 and 2008.

   - Over the past two decades, women's earnings have constituted a growing share of family income in all family types.

   - Married couples had the highest family incomes. Incomes for married-couple families with children increased by 28 percent from 1988 to

Family Income by Family Type

(Family Heads Under Age 65, in 2008 Dollars, 1988 and 2008)

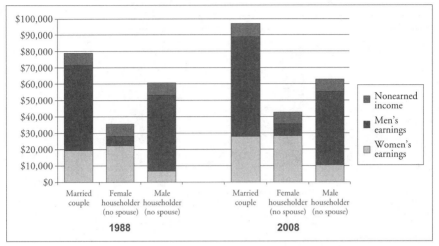

Source: Census Bureau

2008, while incomes for married couple families without children increased by 16 percent over the same period.

• In female-headed families with children, nonearned income as a share of total family income has declined sharply, from 24 percent in 1988 to 16 percent in 2008. About 63 percent of nonearned income for female-headed families with children in poverty is government cash transfer income.

7. **In families where both husband and wife are employed, employed wives spend more time in household activities than do employed husbands.**

• On an average workday in 2009, employed married women spent 1.6 hours in household activities and an additional hour caring for household members. In contrast, employed married men spent nearly one hour in household activities and about 40 minutes caring for household members. (See chart.)

• On average in 2009, employed husbands spent about 3.2 hours engaged in leisure and sports activities on workdays, and employed wives spent about 2.7 hours. (See chart.) For both employed husbands and wives, watching television accounted for just over half of this time (1.8 hours and 1.4 hours, respectively).

• Employed married men spent more time in labor market work and related activities (including commuting) on an average workday in 2009 than did employed married women—8.8 hours and 7.6 hours, respectively. (See chart.)

Time Spent on Workdays

(Average Hours in Selected Activities on a Workday by Employed,
Married Persons Age 25–54, 2009)

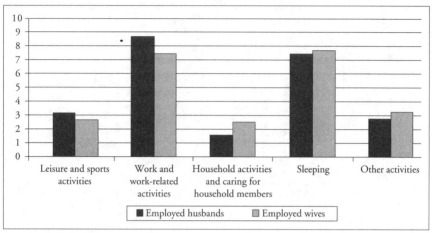

Source: Bureau of Labor Statistics

- On days that they worked, 87 percent of married women also engaged in household activities in 2009, compared to 65 percent of married men. Wives were more likely to do housework and prepare food, while husbands were more likely to care for the lawn and do home maintenance.

- On an average workday in 2009, employed single mothers spent 37 minutes more in labor market work and related activities than did employed married mothers.

8. **Women are more likely than men to do volunteer work.**

- In 2009, 30 percent of women volunteered, compared to 23 percent of men. Women most frequently volunteered with religious organizations (34 percent of all female volunteers), followed by educational or youth service related organizations (28 percent). (See chart.)

- Female volunteers were most likely to fundraise (13 percent); collect, prepare, distribute, or serve food (12 percent); or tutor or teach (11

Volunteer Work

(Percent of Persons Age 16 and Older Doing Unpaid Volunteer Activities Through or for a Main Organization, by Type of Organization, 2009)

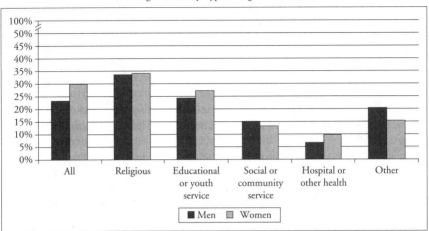

Source: Bureau of Labor Statistics

percent). Male volunteers were most likely to engage in general labor (12 percent); coach, referee, or supervise sports teams (9 percent); provide professional or management assistance (9 percent); or fundraise (9 percent).

Senate Joint Economic Committee Committee Hearing: Equal Pay for Equal Work? New Evidence on the Persistence of the Gender Pay Gap

*Testimony by **Randy Albelda**, Professor of Economics, University of Massachusetts-Boston*

Madam Chairwomen and members of the committee: Thank you for this opportunity to testify about the persistent wage gap between men and women. My name is Randy Albelda and I am a professor of economics and senior research associate at the Center for Social Policy at the University of Massachusetts Boston. I am a labor economist and my expertise is on women's economic status.

While there has been progress in reducing the pay gap between men and women over the last several decades, it is still the case that women, on average, make less than men.

While there are some differences in what men and women "bring" to the workplace that influence levels of pay, these differences account for only a small part of the gender wage gap—the difference in men's and women's pay. Further, the differences in skill levels and experience have been narrowing over the last three decades and doing so at a faster pace than the wage gap is narrowing. There are three enduring and intersecting reasons why women's pay is less than men's: workplace discrimination; occupational sorting; and family responsibilities.

THE WAGE GAP:

In the mid-1970s, the National Organization for Women issued "59" buttons, calling attention to the fact that year-round, full-time women workers earned 59 cents to every man's dollar. Today we could replace those with "78" buttons. [n1]

This graph on the following page comes from the most recent US Census Bureau's Income, Poverty, and Health Insurance Coverage in the United States report. It provides a nice illustration of the median annual earnings of year-round, full-time men and women workers from 1960 through 2007, adjusted for inflation. The most substantial gains were made in the 1980s, with the wage ratio of women's earnings to men's earnings narrowing from .60 in 1980 to .72 in 1990. In the 1990s, there was very little change in this ratio—moving from .72 in 1990 to .74 in 2000. [n2]

Different work, different pay? No. The gender pay gap persists even after taking into account hours worked, skill levels and occupations.

As noted above, looking only at full-time year-round workers, women's annual median earnings are 78 percent of men's. Similarly, the median weekly earnings of full-time wage and salary women workers was 80 percent of men's in 2007. [n3]

Women have somewhat less work time experience than men, which would explain some of the pay gap. However, it explains less and less of that gap over time and several studies have found that each year of men's experience pays off at a higher rate than an additional year of women's work experience.[n4]

Women workers bring higher educational levels to the workplace than do men [n5], which is one reason why "human capital" endowments explain less of the pay gap now than they did in the 1980s.[n6] Still, female college graduates working full-time earned 80 percent less than male college graduates just one year out of school in 2001. [n7]

Women tend to work in different types of jobs than do men. But, even when men and women work in the same fields or even the same occupations, women typically earn less than men.

- The starting salaries for women college graduates were $1,443 less than they were for men in the same fields. [n8]
- Across the occupational landscape, women make less than men. The table below depicts the wage gap (using median usual weekly earnings of full-time wage and salary workers) for some detailed occupations. Of the over 100 detailed occupations with median earnings listed, there are only six in which women's earnings are higher than those of men. [n9]

The Gender Wage Gap in Selected Detailed Occupations, 2006
Managerial Occupations:
Chief executives .72
Human resource specialists .81
Professional Occupations Lawyers .70
Elementary and middle school teachers .90
Service Occupations Security guards .84
Home health care aides .89
Sales and Office Occupations Retail salesperson .68
Secretaries/administrative asst. 1.04
Construction occupations .86
Production and transportation Occupations Electronic assemblers .76
Bus drivers .80
Source: Table 18 of U.S. Department of Labor, U.S. Bureau of Labor Statistics, Women in the Labor Force: A Databook (2008 Edition).

Francine Blau and Lawrence Kahn show that in 2004 after controlling for education, experience, occupation and industry, women earned 83.5 percent of what men did, compared to 81.6 percent without any of those adjustments. That means these factors explain less than 2 percentage points (10 percent) of the entire wage gap between men and women, leaving most of it unexplained by measurable differences between men's and women's attributes. [n10]

Economists have explored the gender pay gap for many decades and produced hundreds (if not 1000s) of articles and reports to explain the reasons for the gender pay gap. No matter how sophisticated and complex their models, they always find that some portion of the wage gap is unexplained by the sets of variables for which they can measure differences between men's and women's education levels, work experiences, ages, occupation or industry in which they work, or region of the country they reside. Because the wage differences cannot be explained by any of the differences in workers' traits, this unexplained portion of the wage gap is attributed to gender discrimination.

- A recent meta-regression analysis that compiled the results of 49 econometric studies of the gender wage gap over the last decade found that on average, there was still a substantial gap—women earned 70 percent of what men did, after adjusting for all the various factors that help explain wage difference. [n11]
- In a forthcoming study of college professors in one specific college of a large public university, researchers controlled for years experience, mobility, teaching and research productivity, and department and found that even in the identical job in the same institution women made three percent less than men. [n12]

Progress toward pay equity has stalled over the last decade.

- The unexplained portion of gender gap (the part attributable to discrimination) got considerably smaller in the 1980s and hardly fell at all in the 1990s. [n13]

There are three intersecting reasons why women's pay is less than men's: workplace discrimination; occupational sorting; and family responsibilities.

- Lilly Ledbetter's experience reminds us that workplace discrimination still exists. Routinely women are not hired at all, hired at lower wages and not promoted over equally qualified men. This shows up in economists' studies as the part of the earnings gaps that can't be attributed to anything else. In addition, using experimental approaches, economists find considerable evidence of hiring discrimination as well. [n14]
- Women are in different occupations than men. Men are much more likely to be in construction and manufacturing jobs which pay more than female dominated jobs with comparable skill levels such as administrative assistants and retail salespersons.[n15] While about one-third of all women are in professional and managerial jobs, these too are often sex segregated, with women predominating in teaching, nursing and social work jobs and men predominating in architecture, engineering and computer occupations. Finally, women predominate in both high and low paying jobs in the "care sector"—the industries which educate our children, provide us with health services, and take care of young children, disabled adults and the elderly. There is a care work wage penalty. Careful research has shown that care workers, in part because they compete with unpaid workers at home, are not rewarded commensurately with their skills and experience.[n16] This sector is large.

About 20 percent of all workers work in the care sector and women comprise 75 percent of all workers.[17]

- Family responsibilities squeeze women's work time and preclude them from taking and keeping jobs that make few or no accommodations for these responsibilities. Jobs that require long hours, often pay well and provide a strong set of employer benefits, but employers also usually assume the workers in those jobs are unencumbered by household and family responsibilities. This "ideal" worker can (and often does) work overtime or just about any time an employer wants.[18] Workers with family responsibilities do not have that flexibility. Regardless of their skill levels, these workers often must work fewer hours or trade off wages for more time flexibility. Research clearly demonstrates a mothers' wage penalty. Mothers earn less than women with the same sets of skills and are rewarded less for experience than are men or women who are not mothers. Some of this is a result of time demands and less job flexibility, but some is attributable to discrimination against workers with family responsibilities.[19]

The recession makes addressing this issue especially important because women's earnings are a vital, if not main component, of family well-being.

- One third of all households are headed by women. Of these households, one-quarter are families with children.[20] Women are almost always the only support of these households.
- One half of households have married couples.[21] In these households, 64 percent of wives are employed, compared to 48 percent in 1970. Further, wives' earnings comprise 35 percent of family income, up from 27 percent in 1970.[22]
- In this recession, more men have lost jobs than women have, since men— so far—are disproportionately found in the hardest hit sectors.[23] As a result, even more households are more dependent on women's earnings. Unequal pay hurts these households.
- The stimulus package will help both men and women, but differently.
- Increased funds for physical infrastructure, improved medical record keeping, and green energy investments will likely create many more jobs for men than women. Assuring access to these jobs and trade apprenticeship programs would be useful for women's employment in these male-dominated and often well-paying jobs.
- Increased funding to the states, especially for health care and education, will help reduce the number of layoffs for more women, since they are more heavily employed in these sectors than are men. However, state budget deficits are deep and even with stimulus funds there will be large cuts to the care sector, which will increase women's unemployment. The cuts will also put more pressure on women's unpaid work time, as their families lose needed care.

REDUCING THE PAY GAP

There are several things that would boost women's wages and reduce the pay gap.

Addressing Workplace Discrimination
- Ensure that our current anti-discrimination laws are enforced.
- Pass the Paycheck Fairness Act. This will strengthen penalties for discrimination and prohibit employer retaliation for workers who inquire about wage practices.
- Pass the Employee Free Choice Act. Unions boost women's wages and improve the likelihood they will have health insurance at work. [n24] Unions also provide workers structured mechanisms to pursue employer discrimination claims.

Addressing Occupational Sorting
- Increase the minimum wage since women predominate in low-wage jobs.
- Support improved wages for care workers. Care work is heavily supported by federal, state and local government funds. This is because care work has many positive spillover effects, making it a vital public good. Government funds for child care and elder care can assure that workers in these fields are compensated appropriately and have opportunities for professional development.
- Target stimulus money to assure that women are included in physical infrastructure projects.

Addressing Family Responsibility Discrimination
- Make sure that current laws that protect workers with caregiving responsibilities, such as the Family and Medical Leave Act, are enforced.
- Extend the Family and Medical Leave Act to cover more workers.
- Support the Family Leave Insurance Act of 2009 which would provide workers with 12 weeks of paid family and medical leave.
- Develop legislation that encourages employers to negotiate with employees over flexible work arrangements.

[n1] In 2007, year-round, full-time women earners made $35,102 while men earned $45,113. Carmen DeNavas-Walt, Bernadette D. Proctor, and Jessica C. Smith, U.S. Census Bureau, Current Population Reports, P60-235, Income, Poverty, and Health Insurance Coverage in the United States: 2007, U.S. Government Printing Office, Washington, DC, 2008; Table 1.

[n2] Ibid, Table A-2.

[n3] U.S. Department of Labor, U.S. Bureau of Labor Statistics, Highlights of Women's Earnings in 2007, Report 1008, October 2008, Chart 1 (accessed 4-23-09 at http://www.bls.gov/cps/cpswom2007.pdf).

[n4] Lalith Munasinghe, Tania Reif and Alice Henriques, "Gender gap in wage returns to job tenure and experience. Labour Economics, 2008: 1296–1916.

This study looked at US men's and women job experience in the early part of their careers with longitudinal data (National Longitudinal Survey of Youth) for the years 1979–1994 (ages 14–22 in 1979 (making the sample between 29–37 years old in 1994). They found men with high school degrees or less worked an average of 6.7 years compared to women's 5.9 years. For those with more than a high school degree, the average amount of work experience was 7.8 years for men and 7.3 years for women. Men worked, on average, about 6 more hours per week than did women. Men accrued 15 percent higher wage growth from an additional year of experience than women. Similar results can be found in Audrey Light and Manuelita Ureta, "Early-Career Work Experience and Gender Wage Differentials" Journal of Labor Economics 1995,13 (1) and Pamela Loprest, "Gender Differences in Wage Growth and Job Mobility" American Economic Review 1992, 82 (5).

[n5] In 2007, 35 percent of all women ages 25–64 in the labor force had a college degree compared to 33 percent of men. Conversely, 42 percent of men ages 25–64 in the labor force had a high school diploma or less education compared to 35 percent of women. Calculated by author from data provided in U.S. Department of Labor, U.S. Bureau of Labor Statistics, Women in the Labor Force: A Databook (2008 Edition) Table 8, (accessed 4-23-09 at http://www.bls.gov/cps/wlf-table8-2008.pdf).

[n6] Francine Blau and Lawrence Kahn, "The US Gender Pay Gap in the 1990s: Slowing Convergence," Industrial and Labor Relations Review, 2006, 60(1):45–66.

[n7] Judy Goldberg Dey and Catherine Hill, Behind the Pay Gap, Washington DC: American Association of University Women Educational Foundation, 2007.

[n8] Judith McDonald and Robert Thornton, "Do New Male and Female College Graduates Receive Unequal Pay?" Journal of Human Resources, 2007, 52(1): 32–48.

[n9] U.S. Department of Labor, U.S. Bureau of Labor Statistics, Women in the Labor Force: A Databook (2008 Edition) Table 18, (accessed 4-23-09 at http://www.bls.gov/cps/wlf-table8-2008.pdf).

[n10] The authors use Current Population Survey data and look at average hourly wages for full-time workers. Francine Blau and Lawrence Kahn, "The Gender Pay Gap" The Economists' Voice, Berkeley Electronic Press, 2007: 1–6.

[n11] Stephen Stanley and T.D. Jarrell, "Declining Bias and Gender Wage Discrimination? A Meta-Regression Analysis. Journal of Human Resources, 2004, 36(3): 828–838.

[n12] Melissa Binder et al. "Gender Pay Differences for the Same Work: Evidence from a United States Public University" forthcoming, Feminist Economics.

[n13] Francine Blau and Lawrence Kahn, "The US Gender Pay Gap in the 1990s: Slowing Convergence," Industrial and Labor Relations Review, 2006, 60(1):45–66.

[n14] David Neumark, using equally experienced male and female "pseudo" applicants, found high-priced restaurants were much more likely to both interview or offer jobs to men ("Sex Discrimination in Restaurant Hiring: An Audit Study," Quarterly Journal of Economics, 1996, 111(3):915–41). Claudia Golden and Cecilia Rouse found that the probability that women would advance and be hired by symphony orchestras was higher when auditions were "blind" (i.e. the gender of the applicant auditioning was unknown) than when they were not ("Orchestrating Impartiality: The Impact of 'Blind' Auditions on Female Musicians," American Economic Review, 2000, 90(4): 715–41).

[n15] In 2007, the median weekly salary of someone in construction occupations was $619 but as a secretary was $583; for a production occupations the week median salary was $559 compared to $494 for a retail salesperson. U.S. Department of Labor, U.S. Bureau of Labor Statistics, Women in the Labor Force: A Databook (2008 Edition) Table 18 (accessed 4-23-09 at http://www.bls.gov/cps/wlf-table8-2008.pdf).

[n16] Paula England, Michelle Budig and Nancy Folbre, "Wages of Virtue: The Relative Pay of Care Work" Social Problems 2002;49(4):455–474; and Nancy Folbre, The Invisible Heart: Economics and Family Values, New York: New Press, 2001.

[n17] Randy Albelda, Mignon Duffy and Nancy Folbre, "Taking Care: The Costs and Contributions of Care Work in Massachusetts" University of Massachusetts, forthcoming.

[n18] See Randy Albelda, Robert Drago and Steven Shulman, Unlevel Playing Fields: Understanding Wage Inequality and Discrimination, Boston, MA: Economics Affairs Bureau 2004, Chapter 7; Joan Williams, Unbending Gender: Why Family and Work Conflict and What to Do About It. New York: Oxford University Press, 2001; Robert Drago, Striking a Balance: Work, Family, Life, Boston, MA: Dollars and Sense, 2007.

[n19] Wendy Single-Rushton and Jane Waldfogel, "Motherhood and Women's Earnings in Anglo-American, Continental European, and Nordic Countries" Feminist Economics 2007,13(2):55–91; Joni Hersh and Leslie Stratton., "Housework and Wages" Journal of Human Resources 2002, 37(1):217–229; and Deboarah Anderson, Melissa Binder and Kate Krause, "Experience, Heterogeneity, Work Effort and Work-Schedule Flexibility" Industrial and Labor Relations Review, 2003, 56(2): 273–294; and Michelle Budig and Paula England, "The Wage Penalty for Motherhood" American Sociological Review, 2001,66(2), 204–225

[n20] U.S. Census Bureau, America's Families and Living Arrangements: 2007, Tables F1 and FM-1, (accessed 2-13-09 from http://www.census.gov/

population/socdemo/hh-fam/cps2007/tabF1-all.xls and http://www.census.gov/population/socdemo/hh-fam/fm1.xls.

[n21] Ibid.

[n22] U.S. Department of Labor, U.S. Bureau of Labor Statistics, Women in the Labor Force: A Databook (2008 Edition),Tables 23 and 24 (accessed 4-23-09 at http://www.bls.gov/cps/wlf-table8-2008.pdf).

[n23] Heather Boushey, Equal Pay for Breadwinners, Washington, DC: Center for American Progress, 2009.

[n24] John Schmitt Unions and Upward Mobility for Women Workers, Washington DC: Center for Economic and Policy Research, 2008.

"Families Can't Afford the Gender Wage Gap"

Heather Boushey,
Jessica Arons, Lauren Smith

Heather Boushey is Senior Economist, **Jessica Arons** is Director of the Women's Health and Rights Program, and **Lauren Smith** is a Research Assistant at the Center for American Progress.

It's no longer breaking news this Equal Pay Day that women are a crucial part of today's workforce. Women edged up to just 50 percent of workers on U.S. payrolls for the first time in October 2009, and two-thirds of American families with children now rely on a woman's earnings for a significant portion of their family's income. *The Shriver Report: A Woman's Nation Changes Everything*, which we released last fall, identified areas where American institutions have and haven't caught up with the realities of today's workforce. Chief among the shortcomings is the fact that a gender pay gap persists almost 50 years after the passage of the Equal Pay Act.

The gender pay gap has taken on added importance as men have been more likely than women to lose jobs during the Great Recession. This loss of a man's paycheck means that millions of families now rely on a woman's job to make ends meet. The persistent gender pay gap is adding insult to injury for families already hit hard by unemployment.

Our newly analyzed state-by-state data demonstrate that mothers in every state and the District of Columbia are financially supporting their families—and many are their family's primary breadwinner. Women's earnings are critical to their families' financial stability. Yet they continue to face a career wage gap that sets them back hundreds of thousands of dollars throughout their lives. Women face this gap regardless of their education, occupation, or where they live.

Congress took an important step in the fight for equal pay last year by passing the Lilly Ledbetter Fair Pay Act, but it has sidelined two pieces of legislation that also directly address the underlying causes of the gender pay gap. The Paycheck Fairness Act would amend portions of the Equal Pay Act to provide stronger enforcement of prohibitions against wage discrimination. The Fair Pay Act would require employers to provide equal pay for jobs that are comparable in skill, effort, responsibility, and working conditions.

It's time for government and businesses to make good on their commitments to American families by taking concrete steps to eliminate the gender wage gap.

FAMILIES RELY ON WOMEN'S EARNINGS

More than 12 million families with children rely primarily on women's earnings. More than a third of mothers in working families in every state but Wyoming and Utah are the family's primary breadwinner—these women provide at least half of a couple's earnings or are single working mothers. The District of Columbia has the highest share of breadwinner mothers, with 63.8 percent of mothers in working families bringing home at least half of their family's earnings.

More than 19 million families with children have a mother that is a breadwinner or co-breadwinner bringing home at least a quarter of the family's earnings. More than half of mothers in almost every state play this role. Utah is the only exception, with 46 percent of mothers as breadwinners or co-breadwinners. But this still means that 4 in 10 working families with children in Utah rely on a mother's earnings.

More than 6 in 10 families with children in 42 states rely on a woman to serve as breadwinner or co-breadwinner. These states are mostly in the eastern half of the country. The District of Columbia again leads the pack with 77.9 percent of mothers acting as their family's breadwinner or co-breadwinner.

A CAREER WAGE GAP

Even though women are significant contributors to their family's economic well-being, they continue to earn less than their male colleagues. Full-time, full-year working women still earn only 77 cents for every dollar that men earn. This wage gap is even larger for women of color. African-American women earn 61 cents and Latinas earn 52 cents for every dollar a white non-Hispanic man earns.

And this inequity accumulates over a lifetime into a shockingly high career wage gap. The career gap lowers women's earnings over a lifetime and reduces their long-term assets and that of their families. The typical woman loses $431,000 in pay over a 40-year career. But the gap is higher in some states than others. The career wage gap is at least $300,000 in 12 states, $400,000 in 23 states, $500,000 in 10 states, and exceeds $600,000 for women living in Wyoming and Alaska.

Education is clearly a route to higher earnings, but getting a degree does not necessarily lead to fair pay over a lifetime of work. The career gap for women with less than a high school education is about $300,000 and more than double that at $723,000 for women with a bachelor's degree or higher. In the 42 states where data is available, the career wage gap for women with at least a bachelor's degree was more than $500,000 in six states, more than $600,000 in 17 states and the District of Columbia, at least $700,000 in 13 states, and exceeds $800,000 in two states. The highest career wage gap for college-educated women is for those who live in Virginia, who lose more than $1 million over a 40-year career.

The career wage gaps are largest for women working in management and finance, sales, and professional occupations. Women working in Connecticut in management and finance jobs face $969,000 in lost earnings throughout their career. And Virginia is home to two of the highest career wage gaps for women in specific job categories—$774,000 for women in sales and $999,000 for women in professional occupations. The smallest career wage gap is for women working as office support staff in California, who lose $134,000 over a career, women in service jobs in Nevada who lose $216,000, and women in production in Tennessee who lose $358,000.

NEXT STEPS FOR EQUAL PAY

The House passed the Paycheck Fairness Act last year, but no action occurred in the Senate until a March 2010 hearing before the Senate Committee on Health, Education, Labor, and Pensions. Nearly all of the committee's senators attended the hearing, which suggests it could become a priority in the months ahead. President Obama was a co-sponsor of the Paycheck Fairness Act when he was in the Senate, and we now need his leadership to push for progress on this vital issue for working families, especially since so many families have been hard hit by the economic downturn.

Congress should move forward with the Paycheck Fairness Act and the Fair Pay Act, and businesses should review their compensation schemes to ensure pay equity for every one of their employees. America's working families cannot afford to wait any longer for a fair day's pay.

DATA AND METHODOLOGY

Wage data in this column comes from the American Community Survey, using the Integrated Public Use Microdata Series from the Minnesota Population Center and analyzed by Jeff Chapman.

The data for analysis of the career wage gap is limited to women and men between the ages of 25 and 64 who worked 50 to 52 weeks during 2008 and typically worked 35 or more hours per week. Workers are divided into 5- and 10-year age groups: 25- to 29-year-olds, 30- to 34-year-olds, and so on. Median wages are calculated separately for women and men within each age group. The wage gap is calculated by subtracting the male median wage from the female median wage. We sum the gap across age groups to illustrate the lifetime wage gap given today's wage difference. Data are not presented where insufficient samples sizes do not allow for meaningful calculation of medians. The wage gap presented here is not necessarily representative of a typical woman's experience, but it is an illustration of the scope of the problem.

Occupational categories follow the Standard Occupation Classification—which the Bureau of Labor Statistics and the Census Bureau use to classify occupations—and are then combined into broad groups. An occupation is classified by the type of work performed and many occupations are found in multiple industries. More information on the classification can be found at http://www.bls.gov/soc/.

Breadwinner mothers include single mothers who work and married mothers who earn as much or more than their husbands. Co-breadwinners include all breadwinners as well as wives who bring home at least 25 percent of the couple's earnings, but less than half. This analysis only includes families with at least one worker and with children under age 18 living in the home.

Interactive Map: The Persistent Career Wage Gap
Interactive Map: Women Provide for Their Families
Download memo with additional data (pdf)

Why The Gender Gap
Won't Go Away. Ever.

Kay S. Hymowitz

Kay S. Hymowitz *is the William E. Simon Fellow at the Manhattan Institute.*

Early this past spring, the White House Council on Women and Girls released a much-anticipated report called *Women in America.* One of its conclusions struck a familiar note: today, as President Obama said in describing the document, "women still earn on average only about 75 cents for every dollar a man earns. That's a huge discrepancy."

It *is* a huge discrepancy. It's also an exquisite example of what journalist Charles Seife has dubbed "proofiness." Proofiness is the use of misleading statistics to confirm what you already believe. Indeed, the 75-cent meme depends on a panoply of apple-to-orange comparisons that support a variety of feminist policy initiatives, from the Paycheck Fairness Act to universal child care, while telling us next to nothing about the well-being of women.

This isn't to say that all is gender-equal in the labor market. It is not. It also isn't to imply that discrimination against women doesn't exist or that employers shouldn't get more creative in adapting to the large number of mothers in the workplace. It does and they should. But by severely overstating and sensationalizing what is a universal predicament (I'm looking at you, Sweden and Iceland!), proofers encourage resentment-fueled demands that no government anywhere has ever fulfilled—and that no government ever will.

Let's begin by unpacking that 75-cent statistic, which actually varies from 75 to about 81, depending on the year and the study. The figure is based on the average earnings of full-time, year-round (FTYR) workers, usually defined as those who work 35 hours a week or more.

But consider the mischief contained in that "or more." It makes the full-time category embrace everyone from a clerk who arrives at her desk at 9 AM and leaves promptly at 4 PM to a trial lawyer who eats dinner four nights a week—and lunch on weekends—at his desk. I assume, in this case, that the clerk is a woman and the lawyer a man for the simple reason that—and here is an average that proofers rarely mention—full-time men work more hours than full-time women do. In 2007, according to the Bureau of Labor Statistics, 27 percent of male full-time workers had workweeks of 41 or more hours, compared with 15 percent of female full-time workers; meanwhile, just 4 percent of full-time men worked 35 to 39 hours a week, while 12 percent of women did. Since FTYR men work more than FTYR women do, it shouldn't be surprising that the men, on average, earn more.

The way proofers finesse "full-time" can be a wonder to behold. Take a recent article in the *Washington Post* by Mariko Chang, author of a forthcoming book on the wealth gap between women and men. Chang cites a wage difference between "full-time" male and female pharmacists to show how "even when they work in the same occupation, men earn more." A moment's Googling led me to a 2001 study in the *Journal of the American Pharmacists Association* concluding that male pharmacists worked 44.1 hours a week, on average, while females worked 37.2 hours. That study is a bit dated, but it's a good guess that things haven't changed much in the last decade. According to a 2009 article in the *American Journal of Pharmaceutical Education*, female pharmacists' preference for reduced work hours is enough to lead to an industry labor shortage.

The other arena of mischief contained in the 75-cent statistic lies in the seemingly harmless term "occupation." Everyone knows that a CEO makes more than a secretary and that a computer scientist makes more than a nurse. And most people wouldn't be shocked to hear that secretaries and nurses are likely to be women, while CEOs and computer scientists are likely to be men. That obviously explains much of the wage gap.

But proofers often make the claim that women earn less than men *doing the exact same job*. They can't possibly know that. The Labor Department's occupational categories can be so large that a woman could drive a truck through them. Among "physicians and surgeons," for example, women make only 64.2 percent of what men make. Outrageous, right? Not if you consider that there are dozens of specialties in medicine: some, like cardiac surgery, require years of extra training, grueling hours, and life-and-death procedures; others, like pediatrics, are less demanding and consequently less highly rewarded. Only 16 percent of surgeons, but a full 50 percent of pediatricians, are women. So the statement that female doctors make only 64.2 percent of what men make is really on the order of a tautology, much like saying that a surgeon working 50 hours a week makes significantly more than a pediatrician working 37.

A good example of how proofers get away with using the rogue term "occupation" is *Behind the Pay Gap*, a widely quoted 2007 study from the American Association of University Women whose executive summary informs us in its second paragraph that "one year out of college, women working full time earn only 80 percent as much as their male colleagues earn." The report divides the labor force into 11 extremely broad occupations determined by the Department of Education. So ten years after graduation, we learn, women who go into "business" earn considerably less than their male counterparts do. But the businessman could be an associate at Morgan Stanley who majored in econ, while the businesswoman could be a human-relations manager at Foot Locker who took a lot of psych courses. You don't read until the end of the summary—a point at which many readers will have already Tweeted their indignation—that when you control for such factors as education and hours worked, there's actually just a 5 percent pay gap. But the AAUW isn't going to begin a report with the statement that women earn 95 percent of what their male counterparts earn, is it?

Now, while a 5 percent gap will never lead to a million-woman march on Washington, it's not peanuts. Over a year, it can add up to real money, and over decades in the labor force, it can mean the difference between retirement in a Boca Raton co-op and a studio apartment in the inner suburbs. Many studies have examined the subject, and a consensus has emerged that when you control for what researchers call "observable" differences—not just hours worked and occupation, but also marital and parental status, experience, college major, and industry—there is still a small unexplained wage gap between men and women. Two Cornell economists, Francine Blau and Lawrence Kahn, place the number at about 9 cents per dollar. In 2009, the CONSAD Research Corporation, under the auspices of the Labor Department, located the gap a little lower, at 4.8 to 7.1 percent.

So what do we make of what, for simplicity's sake, we'll call the 7 percent gap? You can't rule out discrimination, whether deliberate or unconscious. Many women say that male bosses are more comfortable dealing with male workers, especially when the job involves late-night meetings and business conferences in Hawaii. This should become a smaller problem over time, as younger men used to coed dorms and female roommates become managers and, of course, as women themselves move into higher management positions. It's also possible that male managers fear that a female candidate for promotion, however capable, will be more distracted by family matters than a male would be. They might assume that women are less able to handle competition and pressure. It's even possible that female managers think such things, too.

No, you can't rule out discrimination. Neither can you rule out other, equally plausible explanations for the 7 percent gap. The data available to researchers may not be precise; for instance, it's extremely difficult to find accurate measures of work experience. There's also a popular theory that women are less aggressive than men when it comes to negotiating salaries.

The point is that we don't know the reason—or, more likely, reasons—for the 7 percent gap. What we do know is that making discrimination the default explanation for a wage gap, as proofers want us to do, leads us down some weird rabbit holes. Asian men and women earn more than white men and women do, says the Bureau of Labor Statistics. Does that mean that whites are discriminated against in favor of Asians? Female cafeteria attendants earn more than male ones do. Are men discriminated against in that field? Women who work in construction earn almost exactly what men in the field do, while women in education earn considerably less. The logic of default discrimination would lead us to conclude that construction workers are more open to having female colleagues than educators are. With all due respect to the construction workers, that seems unlikely.

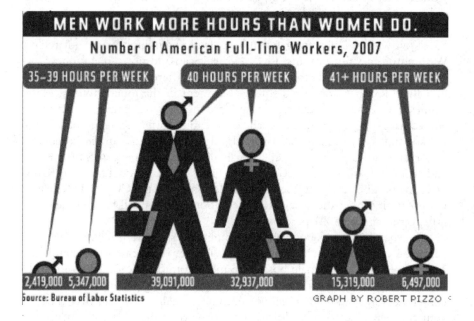

MEN WORK MORE HOURS THAN WOMEN DO.
Number of American Full-Time Workers, 2007

35–39 HOURS PER WEEK | 40 HOURS PER WEEK | 41+ HOURS PER WEEK

2,419,000   5,347,000 | 39,091,000   32,937,000 | 15,319,000   6,497,000

Source: Bureau of Labor Statistics

GRAPH BY ROBERT PIZZO

So why do women work fewer hours, choose less demanding jobs, and then earn less than men do? The answer is obvious: kids. A number of researchers have found that if you consider only childless women, the wage gap disappears. June O'Neill, an economist who has probably studied wage gaps as much as anyone alive, has found that single, childless women make about 8 percent more than single, childless men do (though the advantage vanishes when you factor in education). Using Census Bureau data of pay levels in 147 of the nation's 150 largest cities, the research firm Reach Advisors recently showed that single, childless working women under 30 earned 8 percent more than their male counterparts did.

That's likely to change as soon as the children arrive. Mothers, particularly those with young children, take more time off from work; even when they are working, they're on the job less. *Behind the Pay Gap* found that "among women who graduated from college in 1992–93, more than one-fifth (23 percent) of mothers were out of the work force in 2003, and another 17 percent were working part time," compared with under 2 percent of fathers in each case. Other studies show consistently that the first child significantly reduces a woman's earnings and that the second child cuts them even further.

The most compelling research into the impact of children on women's careers and earnings—one that also casts light on why women are a rarity at the highest levels of the corporate and financial world—comes from a 2010 article in the *American Economic Journal* by Marianne Bertrand of the University of Chicago and Claudia Goldin and Lawrence Katz of Harvard. The authors selected nearly 2,500 MBAs who graduated between 1990 and 2006 from the University of Chicago's Booth School of Business and followed them as they made their way through the early stages of their careers. If there were discrimination to be found here, Goldin would be your woman. She is coauthor of a renowned 2000 study showing that blind auditions significantly increased the likelihood that an orchestra would hire female musicians.

Here's what the authors found: right after graduation, men and women had nearly identical earnings and working hours. Over the next ten years, however, women fell way behind. Survey questions revealed three reasons for this. First and least important, men had taken more finance courses and received better grades in those courses, while women had taken more marketing classes. Second, women had more career interruptions. Third and most important, mothers worked fewer hours. "The careers of MBA mothers slow down substantially within a few years of first birth," the authors wrote. Though 90 percent of women were employed full-time and year-round immediately following graduation, that was the case with only 80 percent five years out, 70 percent nine years out, and 62 percent ten or more years out— and only about half of women with children were working full-time ten years after graduation. By contrast, almost all the male grads were working full-time and year-round. Furthermore, MBA mothers, especially those with higher-earning spouses, "actively chose" family-friendly workplaces that would allow them to avoid long hours, even if it meant lowering their chances to climb the greasy pole.

In other words, these female MBAs bought tickets for what is commonly called the "mommy track." A little over 20 years ago, the *Harvard Business Review* published an article by Felice Schwartz proposing that businesses make room for the many, though not all, women who would want to trade some ambition and earnings for more flexibility and time with their children. Dismissed as the "mommy track," the idea was reviled by those who worried that it gave employers permission to discriminate and that it encouraged women to downsize their aspirations.

But as Virginia Postrel noted in a recent *Wall Street Journal* article, Schwartz had it right. When working mothers can, they tend to spend less time at work. That explains all those female pharmacists looking for reduced hours. It explains why female lawyers are twice as likely as men to go into public-interest law, in which hours are less brutal than in the partner track at Sullivan & Cromwell. Female medical students tell researchers that they're choosing not to become surgeons because of "lifestyle issues," which seems to be a euphemism for wanting more time with the kids. Thirty-three percent of female pediatricians are part-timers—and that's not because they want more time to play golf.

In the literature on the pay gap and in the media more generally, this state of affairs typically leads to cries of injustice. The presumption is that women pursue reduced or flexible hours because men refuse to take equal responsibility for the children and because the United States does not have "family-friendly policies." Child care is frequently described as a burden to women, a patriarchal imposition on their ambitions, and a source of profound inequity. But is this attitude accurate? Do women *want* to be working more, if only the kids—and their useless husbands—would let them? And do we know that more government support would enable them to do so and close the wage gap?

Actually, there is no evidence for either of these propositions. If women work fewer hours than men do, it appears to be because they want it that way. About two-thirds of the part-time workforce in the United States is female. According to a 2007 Pew Research survey, only 21 percent of working mothers with minor children want to be in the office full-time. Sixty percent say that they would prefer to work part-time, and 19 percent would like to give up their jobs altogether. For working fathers, the numbers are reversed: 72 percent want to work full-time and 12 percent part-time.

In fact, women choose fewer hours—despite the resulting gap in earnings—all over the world. That includes countries with generous family leave and child-care policies. Look at Iceland, recently crowned the world's most egalitarian nation by the World Economic Forum. The country boasts a female prime minister, a law requiring that the boards of midsize and larger businesses be at least 40 percent female, excellent public child care, and a family leave policy that would make NOW members swoon. Yet despite successful efforts to get men to take paternity leave, Icelandic women still take considerably more time off than men do. They also are far more likely to work part-time. According to the Organisation for Economic Co-operation and Development (OECD), this queen of women-friendly countries has a bigger wage gap—women make 62 percent of what men do—than the United States does.

Sweden, in many people's minds the world's gender utopia, also has a de facto mommy track. Sweden has one of the highest proportions of working women in the world and a commitment to gender parity that's close to a national religion. In addition to child care, the country offers paid parental leave that includes two months specifically reserved for fathers. Yet moms still take four times as much leave as dads do. (Women are also more likely to be in lower-paid public-sector jobs; according to sociologist Linda Haas, Sweden has "one of the most sex-segregated labor markets in the world.") Far more women than men work part-time; almost *half* of all mothers are on the job 30 hours a week or less. The gender wage gap among full-time workers in Sweden is 15 percent. That's lower than in the United States, at least according to the flawed data we have, but it's hardly the feminist Promised Land.

The list goes on. In the Netherlands, over 70 percent of women work part-time and say that they want it that way. According to the Netherlands Institute for Social Research, surveys found that only 4 percent of female part-timers wish that they had full-time jobs. In the United Kingdom, half of female GPs work part-time, and the National Health Service is scrambling to cope with a dearth of doctor hours. Interestingly enough, countries with higher GDPs tend to have the highest percentage of women in part-time work. In fact, the OECD reports that in many of its richest countries, including Denmark, Sweden, Iceland, Germany, the U.K., and the U.S., the percentage of the female workforce in part-time positions has gone *up* over the last decade.

So it makes no sense to think of either the mommy track or the resulting wage differential as an injustice to women. Less time at work, whether in the form of part-time jobs or fewer full-time hours, is what many women want and what those who can afford it tend to choose. Feminists can object till the Singularity arrives that women are "socialized" to think that they have to be the primary parent. But after decades of feminism and Nordic engineering, the continuing female tropism toward shorter work hours suggests that that view is either false or irrelevant. Even the determined Swedes haven't been able to get women to stick around the office.

That doesn't mean that the mommy track doesn't present a problem, particularly in a culture in which close to half of all marriages break down. A woman can have a baby, decide to reduce her hours and her pay, forgo a pension, and then, ten years later, watch her husband run off with the Pilates instructor. The problem isn't what it used to be when women had fewer degrees and less work experience during their childless years; women today are in better shape to jump-start their careers if need be. The risk remains, however.

It's not at all clear how to solve this problem or even if there is a solution, especially during these fiscally challenged days. But one thing is clear: the wage-gap debate ought to begin with the mommy track, not with proofy statistics.

Getting Inked:
Tattoos And College Students

Lauren Manuel and Eugene P. Sheehan

GETTING INKED: TATTOOS AND COLLEGE STUDENTS: By **Manuel, Laura, Sheehan, Eugene P.**, College Student Journal, 01463934, Dec2007 Part B, Vol. 41, Issue 4

This study explores whether college students with tattoos or piercings demonstrate extreme personalities and behaviors. Participants were 46 men and 164 women (mean=20.0 years). Questions assessed participants' attitudes toward tattooing, presence of a tattoo, and participation in risk taking behaviors. Participants completed the Personality Research Form (PRF) Form E (Jackson, 1984). Those with tattoos scored higher in autonomy (mean=9.96) than those without tattoos (mean=5.55). Women with tattoos scored higher on impulsivity (p=.04). Men with piercings were significantly higher on exhibitionism (p=.02) and sentience (p=.04), and significantly lower on harm avoidance (p=.05). Women with piercings were significantly higher on social recognition (p=.04). Those with and without tattoos reported similar attitudes toward tattoos and levels of risk taking behavior.

Tattooing had a long history even prior to the discovery of a tattooed man embedded in ice, a find that suggested the practice occurred circa 3300 B.C. (Rademackers & Schoenthal, 1992). Prior to that discovery, it was thought that tattooing was primarily an ancient Egyptian practice dating from circa 2000 B.C. (Nadler, 1983). Tattooing was brought to the New World in 1769 by sailors returning from voyages to the South Pacific (Post, 1968; Sanders, 1991). Although the association with sailors has never completely dissipated (Armstrong, Murphy, Sallee & Watson, 2000; Mallon & Russell, 1999; Sanders, 1991; Yamamoto, Seeman, & Boyd, 1963), the practice of tattooing became more widespread and occasionally socially acceptable in the Western world after that time (Sanders, 1991). Tattooing enjoyed a brief period of popularity in the late 19th Century in England, and in the United States in the 1920s (Sanders, 1991). It later began to be relegated to the socially marginal (Armstrong, 1991; Fox, 1976; Post, 1968; Sanders, 1991).

Piercing has almost as long a history as tattooing, having been practiced by Egyptian pharaohs, Mayans, and Roman centurions (Armstrong, 1996). Body piercing is sometimes studied along with tattooing, partly because people with tattoos often have piercings (Buhrich, 1983; Frederick & Bradley, 2000). Piercing, particularly in adolescents, is usually done in tattoo parlors (Armstrong, 1996) or is self-inflicted (Martin, 1997). For women, ear piercing has come to be viewed as a mainstream practice but piercing eyebrows, nose, cheeks, or other areas appears to symbolize one's disaffection from society, much like tattooing (Sanders, 1988). Body piercing other than the earlobe has been associated with the gay subculture (Buhrich, 1983). Researchers in one recent study found that the younger individuals begin piercing the more likely they are to exhibit antisocial tendencies (Frederick & Bradley, 2000). However, piercing is generally regarded as less extreme than tattooing because removing the body jewelry will ordinarily cause the pierced hole to heal (Armstrong, 1996). This may explain why this practice of body alteration has been only briefly mentioned in the literature and rarely studied in its own right.

Tattoos have been empirically associated with a several deviant behaviors (Braithwaite, Stephens, Bowman, Milton, & Braithwaite, 1998; Buhrich, 1983; Ceniceros, 1998; Drews, Allison, & Probst, 2000; Raspa & Cusack, 1990; Verberne, 1969) and criminality (Fox, 1976; Mallon & Russell, 1999; Post, 1968; Taylor, 1970; Yakamoto et al, 1963). Research on tattoos has documented a strong relationship between people with tattoos and antisocial personalities (Post, 1968; Raspa & Cusack, 1990; Taylor, 1968) or actual criminal conduct (Fox, 1976; Measey, 1972; Roc, Howell, & Payne, 1974; Taylor, 1968; Taylor, 1970). For example, studies have documented that more heavily tattooed Naval detainees were more likely to have a previous naval or civilian offense (Measey, 1972). Taylor (1968) found that among delinquent girls incarcerated in juvenile facilities, the more heavily tattooed were more aggressive, uncooperative, and unstable in addition to being more criminal in their attitude and behavior. Female prison inmates with tattoos were more likely to have been in all four types of institutions—juvenile halls, reformatories, jails, and prisons (Fox, 1976).

In a later study, Taylor (1970) attempted to obtain a control group to match his incarcerated girls, 55% of whom were tattooed, but failed because "there was only 1 tattooed woman non-offender available of any age" (p.88). Tattooed women prisoners had more violent and aggressive offenses in addition to more prior convictions (Taylor, 1970). While in prison, women with tattoos were more frequently charged with violation of prison rules, with fighting, and with insubordination (Fox, 1976). In research involving college student respondents, males with tattoos were more likely to report having been arrested and females with tattoos were more likely to report shoplifting (Drews et al., 2000). Tattooed people have been found to be more likely to engage in substance abuse (Braithwaite et al., 1998; Ceniceros, 1998; Drews et al., 2000; Dhossche, Snell, & Larder, 1999; Raspa and Cusack, 1990) and risk taking behaviors (Armstrong, 1991; Ceniceros, 1998; Grief, Hewitt, & Armstrong, 1999). In a study of people who played Russian roulette, there was a strong correlation between this form of risk taking and the kind and quantity of the person's tattoos and body piercings (Ceniceros, 1998). As the severity of the tattoos and piercings increased, all forms of violent behavior increased (Ceniceros, 1998).

Prior studies have reported strong associations between tattoos and homosexual orientation for both males (Buhrich, 1983), and females (Fox, 1976; Taylor, 1970). However, Grief et al. (1999) reported that 87% of their tattooed college student respondents claimed a heterosexual orientation; less than 1% reported a homosexual preference. Grief et al.'s study consisted of college students from 18 universities, 69% of the participants were 18-22 years old. In that study, 24% of the respondents with tattoos reported having 6 to 10 sexual partners and 26% reported having more than 11 partners. In the National Health and Social Life Survey (NHSLS) 15% of the participants 18-24 had 5-10 sex partners and 11% had more than 10 since age 18 (Michael, Gagnon, Laumann, & Kolata, 1994). Although the two studies are obviously not directly comparable, it would appear that tattooed respondents in the Grief study were above national averages for the number of sexual partners.

A less stable heterosexual adjustment has also been found in several studies (Taylor, 1968; Yamamoto et al., 1963). Grief et al. (1999) found that 12% of college respondents reported engaging in bisexual activity. Buhrich (1983) also found a strong association between tattooing and sexual sadomachism, bondage, or fetishism. However, in a recent study of young adults who were mostly college students, only 3% of tattooers or piercers reported engaging in sadomasochistic activities (Frederick & Bradley, 2000).

The association of tattoos with mental illness has been frequently investigated. Tattooing has been empirically associated with personality disorders (Armstrong, 1991; Caplan, Komaroni, & Rhodes, 1996; Ceniceros, 1998; Measey, 1972; Post, 1968) and psychopathic personality (McKerracher & Watson, 1969; Yakamoto, et al., 1963). In Measey's (1972) study of Royal Navy detainees, the correlation with personality disorder increased in significance with the number of tattoos possessed; 48% of those with no tattoos had a personality disorder whereas the percentage increased to 58% for those with 1 to 4 tattoos and up to 82% for those with more than 16 tattoos. Raspa and Cusack (1990) found the association between personality disorders and tattoos so clear that they state "finding a tattoo on physical examination should alert the physician to the possibility of an underlying psychiatric condition" (p. 1481).

One recent study linked the practice of tattooing and suicide (Dhossche, et al., 1999). Suicides and accidental deaths were matched in a 3-year case-control study and it was found that 57% of the young suicides were tattooed compared to 29% of the accidental deaths. The researchers concluded that tattoos may be possible markers for lethality from both suicide and accidental death due to the correlations with substance abuse and personality dysfunction (Dhossche, et al., 1999).

Sanders (1988) has described tattoos as "marks of dissaffliation" with society which become "voluntary stigma" for the bearers, marking their owners as being apart from the mainstream culture. People obtaining tattoos are usually aware of this attribute of tattoos and often state that they obtained the tattoo in order to feel unique (Armstrong, 1991; Sanders, 1988; DeMello, 1995; Phelan & Hunt, 1998), mark their independence (Armstrong, 1991; Sanders, 1991), or as a sign of special affiliation (Armstrong et al., 2000; Measey, 1972; Phelan & Hunt, 1998).

Although tattoos remain negatively regarded by the public (Armstrong, 1991; Armstrong et al., 2000; Hawkins & Popplestone, 1964) and are proscribed by most mainstream religions (Post, 1968; Raspa & Cusack, 1990; Taylor, 1968), it is clear that the popularity of obtaining a tattoo, known as 'getting inked' (Mason, 1991), is rising again (Houghton et al., 1995; Inch & Huws, 1993; Mallon & Russell, 1999; Mason, 1991). The city council of New York was recently persuaded to lift a 37-year ban on tattoo parlors within the city (Kennedy, 1997). Tattoo parlors are the fifth largest growth business in the United States (Armsrong & Fell, 2000; Vail, 1999). It was estimated that there were about 300 tattoo parlors in the United States in the early 1970s compared to about 4,000 in 1991 (Mason, 1991).

The practice remains common among servicemen (Armstrong et al., 2000; Mallon & Russell, 1999), so common, in fact, that the Marine Corp was forced to codify rules on what tattoos recruits may have ("Taboo Tattoos" 1996). Tattooing is also clearly more popular among certain groups, such as the National Basketball Association. Thirty-five percent of the members have tattoos (Ewey, 1998; Mallon & Russell, 1999). Additionally, it is generally agreed that the practice of tattooing is more widespread among prison populations (Fox, 1976, DiFrancesco, 1990; Houghton, Durkin, Parry, Turbett, Odgers, 1996; Mallon & Russell, 1999; Taylor, 1968) and people in mental health institutions (Raspa & Cusak, 1990).

Perhaps the population with the most dramatic increase in tattooing is that of women (Armstrong, 1991; DeMello, 1995; Inch & Huws, 1993; Nadler, 1983; Sanders, 1991). In the past 20 years, the number of women getting tattooed has quadrupled (Nadler, 1983). It is estimated that 40-50% of the clients in tattoo parlors are women (Armstrong, 1991; Sanders, 1991).

Estimates for the prevalence of tattooing itself have varied from a low of 3% in a random national survey conducted in 1990 (Armstrong & Fell, 2000) to 25% of people 15-25 years old (Armstrong et al., 2000). The Alliance of Professional Tattooists estimates that 15-20% of teenagers are tattooed (Braithwaite et al., 1998). Nationwide estimates vary from 7 million people to 20 million people with tattoos (Grief, et al., 1999; Martin et al., 1995).

Some researchers argue that the trend in tattooing and piercing indicates a shift in fashion and a break with body art's exclusive association with lower class people and deviant activities (DeMello, 1995; Ewey, 1998; Martin, 1997). In this argument, the concept that tattoos or piercings are a form of self-mutilation or a way of expressing a negative attitude is rejected (Frederick & Bradley, 2000; Martin, 1997). However, little evidence has been presented to demonstrate that the association between tattooing and various negative behaviors or personality disorders was unjustified in the past or has changed in the current culture.

In this study, we asked two research questions. Research question #1: Are college students who have tattoos more extreme in their personalities and behavior?

Research question #2: Are college students with piercings more extreme in their personalities and behaviors?

METHOD

Participants

Participants in the present study were 210 men and women ranging in age from 17 to 37 with a mean age of 20.0 years. Within the total group, there were 46 men and 164 women participants. Participants were all recruited from psychology classes at a western university.

MEASURES

A set of 12 questions was created to assess the participants' attitudes toward tattooing. An additional 16 questions were asked of those who reported having a tattoo to determine their attitudes toward their own tattoos, the kind of tattoo they had, where it was located on the body, and how old they were when they obtained the tattoo. Participants were also asked to report on body piercings, specifically where they were pierced and how old they were when they modified their body. Seven questions were asked about various behaviors such as driving above the speed limit, smoking marijuana, drinking too much alcohol, engaging in unprotected sex, and shoplifting. Participants were also asked to provide background information about their age, sex, academic major, career plans, race/ethnicity, marital status, and the population size of their hometown.

Participants were then asked to fill in the Personality Research Form (PRF)-Form E (Jackson, 1984). This personality inventory has 352 true-false items. The PRF-E has a reading level of 6th grade (Schinka & Borum, 1994) and was not challenging for any of the student participants. The norms for PRF-E were obtained from college samples and therefore this instrument was considered appropriate for this particular sample (Jackson, 1987). The PRF-E measures the following personality traits: abasement, achievement, affiliation, aggression, autonomy, change, cognitive structure, defendence, dominance, endurance, exhibition, harmavoidance, impulsivity, nurturance, order, play, sentience, social recognition, succorance, understanding, and desirability. The instrument also has a scale for infrequency to detect implausible responses.

PROCEDURE

Surveys were administered to the students in all levels of psychology courses at a Western university. The participants were given course credit for their participation. Participants were given a debriefing sheet when they turned in their completed forms to the primary researcher.

RESULTS

Of the total sample of 210 people, 67 participants had tattoos (32%) and 135 (64%) had piercings. Of the 46 men in the study, 30% reported having obtained a tattoo. Of the 164 women in the study, 53 (32%) reported having tattoos. Most of the women (75%) reported some piercing, primarily ear piercing. Only twelve men reported piercing.

Men and women with tattoos were both higher in autonomy on the PRF-E with a mean score of 6.96 (SD=3.44) compared to their non-tattooed peers' mean score of 5.55 (SD=2.93). When the sexes were viewed separately, the correlation remained for both sexes (men r=.38, p=.008; women r=.17; p=.03). Women with tattoos also scored higher on the PRF-E on impulsivity (r=.16, p=.04).

Men who had pierced their bodies were significantly higher on exhibitionism (r=.34, p=.02) and sentience (r=.31, p=.04). They were significantly lower on harm avoidance (r=-.30, p=.05). Women with piercings, however, were significantly higher on social recognition (r=.16, p=.04).

Both tattooed and non-tattooed students reported similar attitudes toward tattoos, agreeing that they are mainstream and that lots of people have tattoos these days. In addition, there were no differences between the groups on any of the seven behavioral questions (e.g. "I drink too much", "I engage in unprotected sex").

DISCUSSION

A high scorer on autonomy on the PRF-E is defined as a person who "tries to break away from restraints, confinement, or restrictions of any kind...may be rebellious when faced with restraints" (Jackson, 1984, p. 6). The defining trait adjectives also describe the person as "unmanageable, free, self-reliant, independent, autonomous, rebellious, unconstrained, individualistic, ungovernable, self-determined, non-conforming, uncompliant, undominated, resistant, lone-wolf" (Jackson, 1984, p.6). The findings in this study would seem to concur with previous studies that found people with tattoos willing to be regarded as outside mainstream society (e.g., Sanders, 1988, 1991) and therefore are not surprising.

Previous studies have also noted the correlation between impulsivity and tattooing so this finding also supports prior research. Two additional questions related to impulsivity were asked of people who had obtained tattoos: whether they intended to obtain another tattoo and whether they regretted the one(s) they already had. The mean for the former question was 2.5, indicating the midpoint between agreeing and disagreeing. For most people, one tattooing experience may be enough.

In this study, people with tattoos averaged 3.5 on the question about regret (between disagree 3 and strongly disagree 4) indicating they do not yet regret getting a tattoo. Regret is a frequent experience among older people with tattoos (Martin, et al., 1995). It is possible that the reason that these participants do not regret their decision to tattoo is partly due to the fact that people in this study obtained their first tattoo at an average age of 18.2 years and were an average age of 19.8 at the time of the study. It may be a few years yet before any "tattoers' remorse" becomes evident.

Given that there are 21 personality scales on the PRF-E and only two personality variables with significant differences between those with and without tattoos, these results support the recent finding that in some populations, tattooing may be more normal than abnormal (Frederick & Bradley, 2000). There were few differences in the groups.

In addition it seems reasonable that reasons for piercing may be very different by gender. Women may pierce their ears or other body parts in order to be normative, although this may be considered attention-seeking behavior in men. Female participants scored high on social recognition that is described as "approval seeking, proper, and well-behaved" (Jackson, 1984, p. 7). This finding would be in keeping with someone who goes along with normative behavior, which ear piercing clearly is for females. On the other hand, male piercers scored high in exhibitionism, described as being "dramatic, ostentatious, and showy", and sentience, described as being "aesthetic, sensitive, and open to experience" (Jackson, 1984, p. 7). In addition, male piercers scored lower on harmavoidance, described as someone who is not pain avoidant, does not avoid risks, and is not self-protecting.

As with previous studies, this study also found that women tended to place their tattoos on 'private skin'. Fully 48% of the women with tattoos chose the lower back as the first location for a tattoo. In their initial tattooing, only six chose the relatively public area of the upper arm and seven selected the ankle (25%).

Of the 17 women reporting a second tattoo, eight (47%) of them also reported tattoos in relatively private areas (upper or lower back, chest, torso). Only five women reported obtaining a third tattoo (80% on private skin) and only one woman obtained a fourth (on private skin).

For men, upper arms (4) or upper backs (5) were the most popular locations for a first tattoo. Only 5 men reported having second tattoos and these were again located in the upper arm or upper back. Two men had a third tattoo choosing the upper arm and chest for those tattoos. No men reported having a fourth tattoo.

In conclusion, the results of this study concur with most studies in finding that people choosing to tattoo are different on some personality variables. However, in this college population the differences were not as extreme as they have been in previous studies involving less normative people (e.g. incarcerated people, suicides, and mental health facilities).

AUTHOR NOTE

Correspondence concerning this paper should be addressed to the second author: Dr. Eugene P. Sheehan, College of Education, Box 106, University of Northern Colorado, Greeley, CO 80639.

REFERENCES

Armstrong, M. (1991). Career oriented women with tattoos. Image-The Journal of Nursing Scholarship, 23(4), 215-220.

Armstrong, M. (1995). Adolescent tattooing: Educating vs. pontificating. Pediatric Nursing, 21,(6), 561.

Armstrong, M. (1996). You pierced your what? Pediatric Nursing, 22(3), 236-238.

Armstrong, M., & Fell, P. (2000). Body art: Regulatory issues and the NEHA body art model code. Journal Of Environmental Health, 62(19), 25.

Armstrong, M. L., Murphy, K. P., Sallee, A., & Watson, M. (2000). Tattooed army soldiers: Examining the incidence, behavior, risk. Military Medicine, 165(2), pp. 135-141.

Armstrong, M., Murphy, K. P., Sallee, A., & Watson, A. (2000). Tattooed army soliders: examining the incidence, behavior, risk. Military Medicine, 165(2), 135-141.

Braithwaite, R., Stephens, T., Bowman, N., Milton, M., and Braithwaite, K. (1998). Tattooing and body piercing. Corrections Today, 60(2), 120-121, 178.

Buhrich, N. (1983). The association of erotic piercing with homosexuality, sadistic bondage, fetishism, and tattoos. Archives of Sexual Behavior, 12(2), 167-171.

Caplan, R., Komaromi, J., & Rhodes, M. (1996). *Obessive-compulsive disorder and tattooing and bizarre sexual practice.* British Journal of Psychiatry, 168(3), 379-380.

Ceniceros, S. (1998). *Tattooing, body piercing, and Russian roulette.* Journal of Nervous and Mental Disease, 186(8), 503-504.

DeMello, M. (1995). *Not just for bikers anymore: Popular representation of American tattooing.* Journal of Popular Culture, 29(3), 37-52.

Dhossche, D., Snell, K. S., & Larder, S. (2000). *A case-control study of tattoos in young suicide victims as a possible marker of risk.* Journal of Affective Disorders, 59(2), 165-168.

DiFrancesco, C. (1990). *"Dermal body language" among prison inmates: The multiple unprofessional tattoo.* Unpublished Doctoral Dissertation, University of Mississippi.

Drews, D., Allison, C., & Probst, J. (2000). *Behavior and self concept differences in tattooed and nontattooed college students.* Psychological Reports, 86, 475-481.

Ewey, M. (1998, July 1). *Who has a tattoo and where?* Ebony, 76.

Fox, J. (1976). *Self-imposed stigmata: A study among female inmates.* Unpublished Doctoral Dissertation, State University of New York at Albany.

Frederick, C. M., & Bradley, K. A. (2000). *A different kind of normal? Psychological and motivational characteristics of young adult tattooers and body piercers.* North American Journal of Psychology, 2(2), 379-392.

Greif, J., Hewitt, W., & Armstrong, M. (1999). *Tattooing and body piercing.* Clinical Nursing Research, 8(4), 368-385.

Hawkins, R., & Popplestone, J. (1964). *The tattoo as exoskeletal defense.* Perceptual and Motor Skills, 19, 500.

Houghton, S., Durkin, K., & Carroll, A. (1995). *Children's and adolescents awareness of the physical and mental health risks associated with tattooing: A focus group study.* Adolescence, 30(120), 971-988.

Houghton, S., Durkin, K., Parry, E., Turbett, Y., & Odgers, P. (1996). *Amateur tattooing practices and beliefs among high school adolescents.* Journal of Adolescent Health, 19, 420-425.

Inch, H. & Huws, R. (1993). *Tattooed female psychiatric patients.* British Journal of Psychiatry, 162, 128.

Jackson, D. (1984). *Personality Research Form Manual.* Port Huron, Mi. Research Psychologists Press, Inc.

Kennedy, R. (1997, February 26). *City council gives tattooing its mark of approval.* The New York Times, pp. B1, B5.

McKerracher, D. W. & Watson, R. A. (1969). *Tattoo marks and behavior disorder.* British Journal of Criminology, 9, 167-171.

Mallon, W. K. & Russell, M. (1999). *Clinical and forensic significance of tattoos.* Topics in Emergency Medicine, 21, 21-29.

Martin, A. (1997). *On teenagers and tattoos.* Journal of American Academy of Child Psychiatry, 36(6), 860-861.

Martin, R., Dogen, H., Colin, M., Annin, P., Gegax, T. T. (1995, Feb.6). *Turning in the badges of rebellion: Tattooing hits the morning after. Newsweek, 46.*

Mason, M. (1991, Jan. 7). *Every picture tells a story from sailor to sales representative: Tattoos go mainstream. Newsweek, 117.*

Measey, L.G. (1972). *The psychiatric and social relevance of tattoos in Royal Navy detainees. British Journal of Criminology, 19(2), 182186.*

Micheal, R. T., Gagnon, J. H., Laumann, E. O. & Kolata, G. (1994). *Sex in America: A definitive survey. Boston: Little, Brown & Co.*

Nadler, S. (1983). *Why more women are being tattooed. Glamour, 196-198.*

Phelan, M. P. & Hunt, Scott (1998). *Prison gang members' tattoos as identity work: The visual communication of moral careers. Symbolic Interaction, 21(3), 277-298.*

Post, R. S. (1968). *The relationship of tattoos to personality disorders. Journal of Criminal Law, Criminology, and Police Science, 59(4), 516-524.*

Rademaekers, W. & Schoenthal, R. (1992, Oct. 26). *The Iceman's secrets. Time, 140(17), 62-67.*

Raspa, R. F. & Cusack, J. (1990). *Psychiatric implications of tattoos. American Family Physician, 41, 1481-1486.*

Roc, A., Howell, R. & Payne, J. R. (1974). *Comparison of prison inmates with and without juvenile records. Psychological Reports, 34, 1315-1319.*

Sanders, C. (1988). *Becoming and being tattooed. Journal of Contemporary Ethnography, 16(4), 395-432.*

Sanders, C. (1991). *Memorial decoration: Women, tattooing, and the meanings of body alteration. Michigan Quarterly Review, 30, 146-157.*

Schinka, J. & Borum, R. (1994) *Readability of normal personality inventories. Journal of Personnel Assessment, 6(1), 95-101.*

"Taboo Tattoos" (1996, April 8). *Time, 18.*

Taylor, A. J. W. (1968). *A search among Borstal girls for the psychological and social significance of their tattoos. British Journal of Criminology, 8, 171-185.*

Taylor, A. J. W. ((1970). *Tattooing among male and female offenders of different ages in different types of institutions. Genetic Psychology Monographs, 81, 81-119.*

Vail, D. A. (1999). *Tattoos are like potato chips...you can't have just one: The process of becoming and being a collector. Deviant Behavior 20, 253-273.*

Verberne, J. P. (1969). *The personality traits of tattooed adolescent offenders. British Journal of Criminology, 9, 172-175.*

Yamamoto, J., Seeman, W., & Boyd, L. (1963). *The tattooed man. Journal of Nervous and Mental Disease, 136, 365.*

TATTOOING: MIND, BODY AND SPIRIT. THE INNER ESSENCE OF THE ART

Frankie J. Johnson

University of Pittsburgh at Bradford

Editor's Note: **Ms. Johnson** *was the grand prize winner of the undergraduate student paper competition held at the 56th annual conference.*

ABSTRACT

This research began to understand why people choose to get tattoos. The reason was to find out if getting a tattoo was a novelty or if there was more to it than just what we can see inked on their skin. The interest of this research lies in the feeling, emotion, human awareness of expression, and the deeper meaning on the inside that coincides with what is seen only as skin deep on the outside.

Open-ended interviews were conducted, over a period of six months, with four tattoo artists and thirteen people that have tattoos. Time was spent in a local tattoo studio talking with people who were getting a tattoo or who had already been tattooed.

The reasons and the meaning behind getting a tattoo were found to vary as much as the number of people getting tattoos. The similar thread running through the reasons for getting a tattoo, however, was that tattooing is a form of self-expression.

INTRODUCTION

The subject of tattooing has been of interest to this researcher for many years, toying with the idea of getting one on every milestone year that was celebrated. However, enough nerve was never conjured up to go through with it. Then, a few years ago, a talented young artist, who does tattooing for a living, entered the scene. Several of her paintings, done in different media, promoted a certain energy in their presence that was magnetic. It was not known, to the researcher, that she was also a tattoo artist. The researcher's ingrained image of a tattoo artist was extremely the opposite of what was found in her. Her talent, her almost shy, meditative energy, and her knowledge gave a reason to question an unfounded opinion of the art of tattooing. Beginning to relate to it with a new awareness, the desire to acquire a tattoo rose to a new level. One no longer wanted just a cute little ladybug on the foot. The tattoo had to have meaning, to resonate with the spirit within, and portray the intent from which one lives their life.

The research of symbols, sayings, meanings of colors, and different types of tattoos, began while thinking of the places on ones body that one would comfortably wear a tattoo. This led me to wonder why other people got tattooed and what their tattoo meant to them, if anything. How does one arrive at the decision to make a permanent statement on their body? In this paper, the desire is to gain a wider knowledge of the art of tattooing and the people involved in it.

WHO GETS TATTOOS

For purposes of this research, the concentration is on tattooing in Western societies. According to researcher Shannon Bell (1999), there is a differentiation between people who have tattoos and tattooed people. The people who have tattoos only have one or two; usually personal images strategically placed so as not to be seen. Tattooed people have many tattoos, usually larger and more colorful and placed so they can be seen. She states that they have "crossed the point of no return" (Bell 1999: 56) and have chosen to socialize in the subculture of tattooists and others as heavily tattooed as they are. This action allows them to avoid the reactions of the general population and "fully embrace marginalization" (Bell 1999: 56).

Studies over the last ten years show that people from all types of occupations, ages, and social classes are getting tattoos at an increasing rate (Armstrong 1991). According to a study done by Armstrong and Pace-Murphy (1997); 10% of high school adolescents have tattoos. Studies done between 2000 and 2002 found that 16-23% of college students surveyed have tattoos and thirty seven percent of military recruits in basic training have tattoos, with 64% of them entering the military with them, having had them done between the ages of 15 and 21 years old (Armstrong, Pace-Murphy, Sallee, and Watson 2000).

An article in *Newsweek* dated January of 1991 by M. Mason states "from sailor to sales rep: tattoos go mainstream. . . . It's (tattooing) moved up the cultural system. The clients are more and more commonly people in managerial and professional positions." (p. 60)

However, several articles show that those getting tattoos come from all walks of life.

An article in *MacLean's* dated September of 1991 by N. Underwood tells of a 39-year-old mother, who is a bartender, and her 18-year-old daughter getting matching tattoos. One mother, at age 42, decided to get a tattoo after her daughter did, according to the *National Catholic Reporter* (Vineyard 1999). In 2005, *Herizons* magazine had an article by Alexis Keinlen that told of a 46-year-old mother getting a tattoo to memorialize the death of her 20-year-old son.

An article in *Spirituality and Health* dated February of 2006 by Mandi Caruso features a middle age post mastectomy woman who had both breasts removed because of cancer. She has a tattoo across her chest depicting her love of the water and surfing.

Another group that gets tattoos is the convicts. There is a difference between an inmate and a convict. The convict is more covered with tattoos, portraying the acceptance of the lifestyle and marginalization for life (Bell 1999).

Before the 1960s rock stars, popular athletes, and other youth icons were the people that displayed their tattoos. In the late 1980s tattooing was described as "trendy" and "no longer restricted to socially marginal groups" (Forbes 2001: 775). A significant number of well-educated middle-class people began to come on the tattoo scene (Forbes 2001).

The research indicates that there is no one group, no one age or gender, no one personality, and no particular level of social status that get tattoos. Just as diverse as who gets a tattoo are the reasons why people get their tattoos.

WHY PEOPLE GET TATTOOS

According to Bell (1999), American tattooing is unique. Tattoos are images and literal interpretations of things, not surprising because America is a consumer society. Bell states that the meaning of the act of tattooing is "inextricably linked" (p. 54) to the chosen image itself. Any permanent mark on the body signifies a person's separation from the mainstream of culture, and a tattoo can separate someone from society at large. Separation from society is a large factor in her theory about tattoos and why people get them. She states, "tattooing is a struggle for individualization in a society that is increasingly impersonal" (p. 54). They are a sign of resistance to the impermanent and conservative world of today. She quotes Vaclav Havel as saying that being tattooed is synonymous with "living the truth" (p. 54); your own personal truth.

Christensen (2000) found many reasons for getting tattoos including "expressing individuality, communicating rebellion, defining group membership, conveying spiritual meaning, or marking milestones such as life or death" (Christensen 2000: 432, as cited in Armstrong, Owen, Roberts, and Koch 2002). Tattooed career women said that the tattoo "helped them feel good, unique, and special" (Armstrong 1991: 219, as cited in Armstrong, Owen, Roberts, and Koch 2002). Among adolescents and college students, the purpose for their tattoo was "expressing myself" and the reason for doing it with a tattoo was "I just wanted one" (Armstrong and McConnell 1994; Armstrong and Pace-Murphy 1997; Greif et al., 1999: 368, as cited in Armstrong, Owen, Roberts, and Koch 2002). Forbes (2001) found college students "just liked the looks of it" (p. 778) and they offered the tattoo as a form of self-expression. Military recruits' reasons were to "be myself, I don't need to impress people anymore" and because they just wanted one (Armstrong et al. 2000: 137, as cited in Armstrong, Owen, Roberts, and Koch 2002).

Bell also refers to Paul Willis's theory on symbolic creativity, which states that even though the lives of young people are not involved in the arts, they are full of expressions, signs, and symbols to establish the young persons presence, identity and meaning. Being tattooed is an act of this creativity. Forming an identity is important to young and old, and for some, tattoos can be a symbolic part of this identity. Tattoos can honor their family or lover, display their religious beliefs or patriotism, or their association with a certain group (Bell 1999).

Bell writes that women choose softer, more personal images for tattoos and place them where they can be hidden. Men choose macho imagery and place them where they can be seen. Tattoos have long been associated with men because of the stereotype of the tattooed person and the pain associated with it, so when a woman gets tattoos, it is regarded as a resistance to female beauty as society commonly sees it. She writes; "it takes a strong will and sense of self (identity) to withstand the blatant and piercing stares" (p. 56) because of the stigma still attached that differs in every culture and city. As stated earlier, it creates a separation from mainstream society (Bell, 1999).

Prison tattoos are "identity claimers" (p. 55), according to Bell, that are associated with gang or group membership. Prison tattoos are done with single needles and with no color, so they appear very different than tattoos done professionally in a tattoo studio. This difference in imagery and the way it is done creates a class marker between prison and professional tattoos for all of society to see (Bell 1999). Some prison inmates bring their own equipment; a sharpened guitar string for a needle and a melted down checker piece for the ink, according to an article by Ronald Day in *Body Positive* magazine (2005).

An article in *Jet* magazine dated July 2001 writes that athletes get tattoos for several reasons. One athlete has tattoos that portray his attitude in life, such as "Only the Strong Survive" (p. 46), and some that are dedicated to his family and friends. Another uses them to express himself through meaningful symbols. Yet another says his tattoos "revolve around my life. I think tattoos are something that tell who you are and how you feel" (p. 46).

There are myths that people get tattoos for personal advertisement and that every tattoo means something explicit. Some people do get a tattoo with the intention of others seeing and interpreting it, yet others have a tattoo in places that cannot be seen by the general public because it is a symbol for their self and those that they are intimate with. The more tattoos a person has, the less meaning the actual tattoo has. The meaning is in the act of getting the tattoo. It becomes less about it meaning something to them down the road, and more about it being aesthetically pleasing (Bell 1999). "Meanings change, beauty and truth are eternal" (Bell 1999: 57).

Bell writes that tattooing goes beyond the lack of depth of the visually based American consumer society that is superficial in nature. She says that American tattooing is a "product of this surface-oriented society" (Bell 1999: 57) and quotes Marshal Blonsky:

> [Surface] is a characteristic of our fast-flowing time, where everything has to communicate fast and move on. . . . Depth is a category that pretends to penetrate surface. . . . First impressions are decisive [and] surface is individuated by apparel. . . . The search for interiority merely creates more surface. (Blonsky: 17)

There is no other form of adornment or decoration that is permanent. Fashions allow change of mind, tattooing does not. The most common concern about tattoos is their permanence (Bell 1999). This fear of permanence says a lot about society and "its unwillingness to commit to identity and accept the consequences. To do something permanent is to be unable to take it back—it is to live in truth for eternity" (Bell 1999:57).

An article in *Print* dated Jan/Feb 1995 written by Akiko Busch writes of the decoration factor of tattoos. A couple got tattoos together when they decided to get married because they thought it to be more expressive of commitment than jewelry. Another person chose their tattoo because they could imagine being "accompanied through life by such an emblem" (Busch 1995: 112). Tattoos are about intimacy, image and identity (Busch 1995). A young 15-year-old girl got a tattoo, with her mother's permission, as an attempt to reclaim her body with a protective talisman on herself because of being a victim of a crime (Vineyard 1999).

A lot of women get tattoos to reclaim their bodies or to mark incidents in their lives. A mother, father, and several friends of a student that died got tattoos to mark the loss. It is a constant reminder of him and a symbol of the relationship and closeness he had with each one. The pain of getting it done was welcomed as a pain that could be controlled amongst all of the emotional pain that could not be controlled. Another woman got her whole arm tattooed to represent a reclaiming of her childhood. Women tend to get tattoos to mark a change in the way they see themselves, not to change the way society sees them (Keinlen, 2005).

In Cultural Anthropology journal, 1997, Daniel Rosenblatt writes about the "modem primitive", meaning the tattooed person of today in the Western world. Linking modern day tattooing with the ancient world brings in a long history and thus exemplifies it as a human practice. Identifying with tattooing in other cultures allows people to feel like they're connecting with the history of humanity (Rosenblatt 1997). It allows us to see tattooing as a spiritual activity because it is ancient and widespread and "is seen as an expression of a basic human need for rituals that give life meaning" (p. 303) and connects the tattooed person to the rest of humanity (Hardy, as cited in Rosenblatt 1997). The modern tattooed person is seeking other truths and other ways of knowing the world. The tattoo can connect the person wearing it to knowledge of powers in "nature" that the "primitive" people knew in intimacy (Zuluata, as cited in Rosenblatt 1997). The growing popularity of tattooing in the Western world may be interpreted as a sign of a bigger change in society (Rosenblatt 1997). Maybe we are no longer the "monolithic engine of rationality"(p. 304) that we are imagined to be (Rosenblatt 1997).

Judeo-Christian and Jewish tradition look down on tattooing. This is another factor in linking tattoos to identification with non-Western or alternative ways of thought. The outdated social stigma attached to tattooing is melting away. Tattooing is beginning to be seen as more of a meaningful art than a "brand". Tattoos seem to be about representing or expressing an aspect of the self, both in public and privately. It reflects the duality in our notion of the self, and is an attempt to bring these two aspects together (Rosenblatt 1997).

Some people get tattoos to express the aspects of them that go against the stereotyping of society. It can be a process of self-exploration, affirmation of self, and/or a mask. It opens the person up to the world by expressing beliefs or feelings in a visible manner, yet it can create a barrier against the world (Handel, as cited in Rosenblatt 1997).

In Rosenblatt's piece, he quotes Fakir Musafar; "The purpose of the tattoo is to do something for the person, to help them realize the individual magic latent within them [Vale and Juno 1989:11]". The tattoo can be a way to get in touch with the private, intuitive self and can be an act of reclaiming the self. There is a relationship between controlling your body and realizing yourself as an individual. This is why tattoos are popular in prison—no one can take away your skin. They are an expression of freedom (Hardy, as cited in Rosenblatt 1997).

The issue of power and control is also prevalent in the youth who get tattoos according to Georg Simmel in his 1950 essay, "The Metropolis and Mental Life". In this essay he writes of conformity and mistrust in modern life producing an uneasiness that leads people to look for ways to express individuation and find self-fulfillment. He states that deviance is an outlet for this (Koch, Roberts, Cannon, Armstrong, and Owen 2004).

Lyman and Scott (1970) take this idea further by discussing four sites in which the individuation may occur: public territories, home territories, interactional territories, and body territories. Body territories are the most private and sacred of the territories. Even though body territories are sometimes regulated socially, the person can also claim it as a place of self-expression. The body is a viable way to express oneself symbolically, especially if the person has limited access to the other territorial forms. Irwin (2001) and Velliquette and Murray (2002) agree and add that tattoos "represent both a moral passage of sorts and also an attempt to individuate oneself from the larger society" (Koch, Roberts, Cannon, Armstrong, and Owen 2004: p. 83). It is a public display of self-concept and is important in developing the social self for some people (Koch et al. 2004).

For some people, getting a tattoo means that they have done something real about their relationship to the world because of its permanence and its connection to their inner self. The tattoo can express and take away their unhappiness with the roles society offers them, and it can bring them a refuge from societal conditioning. The ancient background of tattoos makes them a human and permanent commitment rather than a fad of society, therefore, tattoos become a culturally recognized way to express self. The body is a way of expressing and altering the relationship between self and society. It uses the skin, sexuality, the body and the "primitive" connection as key symbolic domains to recover and express the self. Primitive cultures encourage development of intuition and magic and allow for more expression of individuality than we do in Western culture. So, a tattoo in Western culture makes the person look different, and also gives their difference a greater meaning. It brings some part of the personal inner self out and makes it part of the social self, and frees the person from society to become human instead of Western. In having control over their body, the person has control over their self, which becomes a powerful emotional experience (Rosenblatt 1997).

Memorial tattoos are popular, especially among the military. Many Marines in Iraq get tattoos as "a way to give ink-and-skin permanence to friends taken young. It's like death—it's forever" (Phillips 2006: A8). "It's also never forget the cost of war, to get people to understand what they're asking for when they support war" (Phillips 2006: A8). For some, the pain of the needle eased the guilt of having survived and the sorrow of the loss. Some said that feeling the pain made it okay that the others got killed and they didn't. It became a way to remember their brothers (Phillips 2006).

Mary Kosut brings another theory of motivation forth in her 2005 article in Deviant Behavior journal where she contributes that some motivations for getting a tattoo are characterized as negative (Kosut 2005). The desire to be tattooed "may be the result of deficiency or because of low levels of cortical arousal and a need for constant stimulation" (Copes and Forsyth 1993; Favazza 1996, as cited in Kosut 2005: 82). Her article also provides that tattoo artists have been associated with "non-normative behavior" (p. 83).

This train of thought has been redefined and reinterpreted throughout the nineteenth and twentieth centuries because of the amount of trained artists in the field of tattooing (Kosut 2005).

METHODS OF RESEARCH

Data were collected through interviews with thirteen people that have tattoos, a sample consisting of seven women and six men ranging in age from 20–65 years old. Four tattoo artists, two men and two women were interviewed. One evening was spent "hanging out" in a tattoo studio observing and interacting with the patrons that visited. Several conversations were had, which did not constitute an interview as such, with students on campus and other people that happened to come in contact with the researcher elsewhere. The researcher designed and had her own tattoo done.

Five of the people were interviewed in person; the other seven were interviewed online by computer. Face-to-face interviews consisting of both closed and open-ended questions were tape recorded and conducted in tattoo studios. The researcher's interest in the subject and her desire to get a tattoo seemed to make for a deep connection with those that she interviewed.

WHO GETS TATTOOS ACCORDING TO THE TATTOO ARTISTS

Tattoo artists claimed that a wide range of people get tattoos. The two male tattoo artists said "everybody" and then went on to elaborate. Mike, a 61-year-old tattoo artist, has been tattooing for 35 or 36 years. He says he has tattooed people from all walks of life; doctors, nurses, lawyers, and surgeons. His clients are mainly a younger crowd ranging from ages 18-40 years, although he said that he gets a considerable amount of people from the 40-70's age group too.

There are also many women in their 60's that he has tattooed. He told a story of five women that all worked in the same office together coming in for tattoos. They all had different reasons, but all got them done.

Rick is a "30-something" tattoo artist that has been tattooing since he graduated from art school. He said that people who get tattoos are anywhere from 18-70 years old, and can range from cops to criminals. He tattooed a 70-year-old funeral director.

The two women tattoo artists that I interviewed went into a little more detail when asked who got tattoos. Lori, who is in her late 30's, is also an art school graduate and started tattooing to support her family when her children were young. She says that people that have been hurt as a child, recovering addicts that don't spend their money on drinking or drugs anymore, bike club members, and just "normal, ordinary" people came in for tattoos. The ages range from 18 years to the oldest at 77 years old.

Janice is 33 years old and no longer does tattooing. She has artistic talent and expressed it through tattooing others. When asked who gets tattoos, she stated:

"The stereotypical 20-year-old guy with a bit of a chip on his shoulder-the James Dean type. Obviously though, women are a larger audience than ever before...and we would see many older men getting touch ups and cover-ups. A lot of college aged people. A sprinkling of retirees . . . she was 77. So, there are all types...but the stats are correct, college age kids, mostly male are the biggest audience. . ."

WHY PEOPLE GET TATTOOS ACCORDING TO THE TATTOO ARTISTS

The reasons and meaning behind the tattoo were as numerous as the people who get them. The artists who do the tattoos were an excellent source of information on this topic. Mike, the tattoo artist, says that people see a lot of it on television and on stars, athletes, and people in public exposure. He did a tattoo on a 78-year-old male who had wanted a tattoo all of his life, but his wife wouldn't let him get one. She passed on, so he got it done. Mike said that younger women wear tattoos like jewelry; it was to beautify. A girl and her brothers got praying hands with a rosary as a memorial to their father when he passed. There was a gentleman that came into his studio undecided about what he wanted. He looked at wolves howling at the moon, bats, and the grim reaper and wanted to work up a scene with them in it. When asked what he did for a living, he said he was a gravedigger. For him, the tattoos were an expression of himself and what he does in life. Mike has also been working on a fellow since 1991 or 1992 who has about 90-98% of his body covered in tattoos. Mike didn't know the reason for it, other than the fellow just likes them. He said, "they have their own reasons and I don't question them". According to Mike, most of it is an expression of themselves. It makes them feel different about themselves, "like a new outfit", it just feels new.

Rick also said it is a form of self-expression. With young kids it is sometimes because a popular person has it. He had a family come in for tattoos when their little girl was hit by a car and killed. He did her portrait on three of the family members. He tattoos the workers at the county jail as well as the inmates. He said that the tattoos are a source of commonality among the prisoners and the workers, something that they can talk about. He found it rare that anyone does it for the pain or because they are addicted to any part of getting a tattoo. He said that "everybody has an instinct to express themselves" whether it be for a rite of passage or for a keepsake.

Lori told of many reasons for people getting a tattoo. Some want to prove their love to a particular person. Some men want their newborn's name and footprint copied from the birth certificate "to attempt to prove their happiness or eternal bond" and comment that the mother will be happy to see it (the tattoo). Some just do it for themselves because they are happy that they just had a baby. People that have been hurt get a tattoo to claim themselves..."it's their skin, this is a decision I'm making...a large number of them say they do not feel any pain at all. Some do it to see if they can feel pain that way". There are people that say, "they love the feel, they really don't care what the image is, and they simply want to feel that sensation". If a "biker" has just purchased a motorcycle, part of the package is to get the bike emblem. They said, "their skin is still soft and supple and hasn't been exposed to the wind yet."

She has had countless people tattoo animal's names and/or portraits, and they would cry from the loss while getting it done. Others get a tattoo to memorialize a loved one. She said, "a family actually believed if they all were together in the shop getting a tattoo for the same person, that person's spirit would be aware of what was happening and they could feel his presence".

She tattoos as many women as she does men. She tattooed a 77-year-old woman that had been in the hospital. The woman thought that she was dying, so when she was released from the hospital, she did the things that she regretted not doing in her lifetime. "A tattoo of a rose was at the top of her list". A 72-year-old man came in to her shop and had two large tattoos of naked women covered. The tattoos had bothered him for years and he was ashamed of them.

Lori did see a lot of influence from television and movies in where people want their tattoos placed on their body. They thought it would make them more like the image on the screen; not physically but through an emotional connection to the character portrayed.

Janice found that most of her clients wanted a tattoo because they are "cool" or they "have always wanted one". She says another reason is for a tribute to someone or some event in his or her life.

Overall, the tattoo artists interviewed could not state a typical reason for getting a tattoo or a typical person that gets a tattoo. They see a very diversified clientele who each have their own unique reason for getting a tattoo. The only commonality, that the artists experienced, is that their clientele do it as a means of self-expression.

WHY GET A TATTOO ACCORDING TO THE CLIENTS

The interviews with those who actually wear tattoos opened up a whole new world to me. The reasons for getting one come from many different levels of themselves. It was thought that one would find a main theme or reason for having ink engraved into your body permanently. Aside from tattoos being some type of an expression, all other reasons are too diversified to compartmentalize into specific categories.

One reason for getting a tattoo is to remember something (whether it was a fleeting moment or a deep happening) such as, a person, an animal, an event, something sad or something happy. A tattoo is a permanent way to remember, an expression of life or a means to assert ones independence or individuality.

There are many other reasons, including women getting tattoos for the beauty, the aesthetic value of having beautiful art on their body. New beginnings, such as adulthood, divorce, marriage, death, birth, etc. warrant a tattoo for some people.

Some people actually appreciate the pain saying that it is temporary pain for a permanent effect. "If it was easy everyone would do it", one interviewee said, so the pain sets them apart from the rest of society.

One of my online interviews said that usually the reason "isn't as emotional or meaningful as many might hope or think". This person got tattoos to remember the city she lived in or to mark happy or sad times in her life. Therefore, many of her tattoos did not have a great meaning.

Another said her tattoos are symbolic of various things, mainly belief structures. She said she gets tattoos "to remind myself of various things, that period of my life, my mind set at the time, or just that I shouldn't take shit from people". Someone else said that they get tattoos to be different from most people, not because they wanted to be noticed, but "because they are a window to your personality". They also remind them of their past, which they thought of as a good thing.

A female interviewed online said that hers is a very personal design. She looked for six years to find the right one, and then altered it to fit her. She is working on designs for three more tattoos that are also very meaningful to her. One will be a ladybug because her mother used to call her "her little ladybug". She is going through some rough times with her family and getting this tattoo will remind her that she and her mom still love each other even through all of this. She thinks of tattoos "as accentuating an already beautiful form—the human body". She felt the "art was already in me; it's a mark on my eternal soul that I wanted to share with those around me. It's not adding or subtracting from me, it's simply bringing an element of myself to the surface". Tattoos are an expression of life for her.

Another online interview of a female found that she got her first tattoo at age 16 as a birthday present for herself. She was "instantly addicted" and got her second one two days later. Her reason was because she loved the way tattoos look. She now has some that memorialize those that she has lost. She finds tattoos "a lot like fashion" and that people get them to feel good about themselves. She is a sailor by trade but had to live on land for a few years, so she got her arm tattoo because she "wanted the ocean with me no matter how far the water was!" and because she worked in male dominant positions and "wanted to be perceived as tougher than your average, high maintenance girl". She stated that she has grown "older and wiser" since then and no longer wants to carry that perception. However, the tattoo still remains as a memory of that time in her life.

Memorial tattoos are quite popular. An online interview with another female was about her memorial tattoo. She had always wanted a tattoo and the passing of her father was her excuse to get one. Her father was an avid gardener so she got a small rose with the stem bending around to "cradle the words 'Daddy's girl'". It is a yellow rose because her power color is yellow. This tattoo also represents a reclaiming of her independence after a divorce from a man who would not let her get a tattoo.

A gentleman wrote online that he "was actually pleased by the adrenaline rush" that made him woozy while sitting seven hours being tattooed.

There were those that compared it to art in other forms. One online interviewee said that she got her tattoo "because I wanted to wear my art, not just hang it on the wall". Another stated:

> For many of us, asking why we like tattoos, or even asking why we like a certain design, is like asking someone why they like a certain Mozart piece, or a certain Van Gogh painting, etc. Tattoos are one of many forms of art—and personally, I think about the coolest medium (i.e. living skin) that I can imagine.

Jolene had always talked about getting a tattoo and just never did until going through a "messy, ugly divorce". At that time she was learning about herself and who she wanted to be, and she was depressed and worried so she began exploring spirituality. She is Native American so tattoos came as a "natural way for me to explore and ultimately express these issues."

Her first tattoo was to cover scars on her stomach. She was ashamed of them, so the tattoo enabled her to cover the scar and to "honor my body and forgive it for being less than perfect." Now, instead of being ashamed of her body, she could be proud of it because of the meaning the tattoo holds for her. She chose to have a tribal sun tattooed encircling her navel.

She states:

> I chose a tribal sun for my stomach piece...it encircles my navel and for me, the sun is the source of life... and my stomach/womb has been a source of life as well, despite its visible imperfections. My next piece was an ankle wrap which is very colorful and has the word "Justice" written in runes. Justice is the Latin meaning of my name, and also a significant source of strength in my life...to me it means karma...it goes around my ankle and has no beginning or end...like karma it keeps coming around. My next two pieces were a ring with my children's birthstones in it, and a crescent moon on my left breast. Moons being the symbol of the goddess, and the left side of our bodies being associated with our feminine energies, and my breasts being the source of food for babies...plus, I was in a car wreck and almost lost that breast...so I honor that breast and thank it for performing miracles, feeding babies despite its flaws and the damage that has been done to it. My fifth piece is a full back mural. It incorporates a stained glass panel of the sun and the phases of the moon, depicts a goddess pouring water (emotion) from a pitcher into a pool of water, a hummingbird (my Native American animal guide and a symbol of the element of air) a tiger lily (which reminds me of creative energies and the element of fire) growing out of a field (element of earth) and the runes which spell out "I am Woman, I am Life." My final piece is my engagement ring from my second marriage.

She has more than one tattoo because she felt she "needed more than one story to help tell about the me who is on the inside". She felt that she had taken back control of her body. She had been taking it for granted and had forgotten that it is connected to her soul. She believes her body should reflect who she is on the inside.

A 21-year-old male college student said that he got his first tattoo at age 18. In the beginning he wanted to get it because his dad did not want him to, but when he got to the tattoo studio and saw the beauty of the artist's work, he had more of an urge to get one. He now has the Chinese symbol for "gates to heaven" in the middle of his back because "if the gates to heaven are behind me then that means I'm already in heaven and the tribal wings I have around that is my wings for when I'm in heaven". He has a tribal shield around his left nipple, over his heart, to protect him from people that may try to hurt him, "mainly females". "TRIP" tattooed on his lower left arm is his nickname for all to see who he is without him having to tell them. The tattoo on his lower back has his zodiac sign incorporated into it. He also admitted to getting more than one tattoo, not only because he liked the way they look, but because of the pain.

During the researcher's evening observing at the tattoo studio she interviewed a gentleman and his wife. He was getting his first tattoos; she already has three. The researcher watched as he got his done and he allowed her to interview him during the process. He is a 28-year-old construction worker and father of two children, one boy and one girl. He was getting a portrait of his daughter on his left forearm and his son on his right forearm. He said he promised his daughter he would have her tattooed on him because then he "always got her on me". His children would be "on me forever". He wants everyone to see them.

His wife is 25 years old and got her first tattoo when she was 18. Her father drew it and she had just had her son, so she put her son's name into what her father drew. She will have it forever to remember her father and her son. Her other tattoos consist of one on her chest that is a butterfly with "Mimi" on it (what her nephews call her), and one around her right wrist that is made up of her niece's, nephew's, and son's initials. She said the bracelet effect is feminine and "no one knows what it really is". She likes that hers can be hidden from others, but that she can see them.

My interview with Tony, a 21-year-old employee of the tattoo studio, is the final entry. He is studying to be a body piercer and also works with the mentally handicapped at the Resource Center in his town. He got his first tattoo just before he turned 21. His friend was leaving for college and they both wanted something that represented their friendship, so they got a broken heart tattooed on both wrists. He said that he has always wanted something on his wrist so he can see it. He also has a lion, his zodiac sign, tattooed on his left forearm. The tattoos make him feel stronger. He stated:

> It is a constant reminder of not only relationships that I have, but also things that people loose in life, things that can mean to me just open and endless possibilities. I put things on my body that reminds me of myself, who I am, where I

came from, plus the things that I want to do in life—learn and the things that I go through. It's almost like an empowerment. The world of body mods is a very beautiful thing. It was around before civilized culture was. You have the tribes in Africa and the Indians here in the Americas that... all their art is very beautiful to me. We as human beings are almost reclaiming that—it's just a more technological society (today).

As for the researcher's own experience of entering into the world of the tattooed, she too has an outward expression of her inner self for all to see. Like most of the people that she read about or interviewed, the meaning of what she has inked on her body is much deeper than the visual image that can be seen. It is not there to be pretty, but is a reminder to her, every time she looks at it, of her beliefs and the intentions she strives to live. Her tattoo is a chameleon to remind her that the only thing in life that is constant is change. The colors that she chose each have a symbolic meaning and representation. The infinity symbol on its back represents that there is no beginning and there is no end, and that life holds endless possibilities. The OM symbol signifies God, Creation and the Oneness of all Creation. It represents the unmanifest and the manifest aspects of God. The eyes of the chameleon are a symbol that means "spirit of all creation" honoring all that is, seen and unseen. The spider has been her animal totem since her vision quest four years ago. Its symbolic meaning is far too lengthy to delve into here. The tattoo is on her foot to remind her of being grounded and staying true to Mother Earth. It also reminds her that life is all about the journey that one walks and not about the destination.

The pain that she experienced getting the tattoo reminded her of what one sometimes needs to go through in life to be true to one's beliefs and oneself It may feel painful for a while, at times almost unbearable, but if one trusts and has faith that all will turn out exactly as it needs to be for the highest and best for all involved, one can live in love without fear.

DISCUSSION

Since ancient times, people worldwide have gotten tattoos. Why would that be? Possibly because of the changes previously discussed, the depressing times, and the crisis that the world is in now. People have the perception that so much is out of their control. Making their mark on the only thing that we have some control of (our body) is a way of easing our anxiety about the world situation, a way of having some control over something. Also, in times of crisis people tend to look for spiritual meaning in life, a meaning that they can hold on to forever, something larger and more powerful than the material world.

According to my data, tattoos are a form of self-expression, a way to touch the depths of one's feelings and bring those feelings out for one's own observation or for the observation of others. Tattoos are a way of expressing thoughts, beliefs, triumphs and trials, and a way of memorializing a loved one, possibly to the extent of feeling control over death by immortalizing their memory forever on one's body to carry with one throughout one's life.

Respondents say tattoos are a way of connecting to that inner self that gets lost in the sea of the material world. Tattoos are a reminder of one's roots, one's ancestors, and the time when everything meant something or had a purpose. There is so much in today's society that is without purpose and without a connection to give meaning to life and the way it is lived. Interviewees said that tattoos can connect the spiritual inner self to the material world that one lives in, or they can separate one from the material world and take one to a place within oneself that longs to be experienced and expressed.

In this fast paced, technological society where everybody is becoming a number, being tattooed is a way of remaining a person, something capable of feeling and expression. It is possibly another coping mechanism that helps an individual get along in the world as it is today. A person's tattoo may look exactly like someone else's, but the feeling and meaning of what it represents to each one of them is entirely different. No one or no thing can take that away from them, not even the worldly powers that control everything else in society.

Tattoos can represent or express anything the person wearing it wants it to without getting "permission" from society to do so. It is a freedom from the many societal restrictions. In the world of crisis today that is commanded by fear, one's body is the only space that is sacred. The only true haven and refuge that one has is one's inner self, one's inner reality, and one's inner essence. Tattooing is a way to bridge the gap between one's inner reality and the outer reality of the world one must live in.

In conclusion, the reasons for getting a tattoo and the meaning behind what is visibly seen are as varied as the people involved. Whether a person gets a tattoo "just because he likes how it looks" or because it symbolizes something for them, the tattoo is a form of self-expression. The purpose of wearing this art on one's body rather than hanging it on a wall signifies a total commitment to what it stands for. It is the most permanent form of self-expression, with no escape from it. It is everywhere they go, they carry it with them, and it is a part of them. It is connected to one's mind and one's body for their time spent here on earth, and connected to their spirit, their inner essence forever.

REFERENCES

Armstrong, Myrna L. 1991 ."Career-oriented women with tattoos." *Image: Journal of Nursing Scholarship* 23 (4): 215-20.

Armstrong, M.L.,Owen, D.C., Roberts, A.E., and Koch, J.R. 2002. "College students and tattoos: The influence of image, identity, friends, and family." *Journal of Psychosocial Nursing* 40(10): 1-8.

Armstrong, M.L., Owen, D.C., Roberts, A.E., and Koch, J.R. 2002. "College tattoos: More than skin deep." *Dermatology Nursing 14*(5): 317-323.

Armstrong, M.L., and Pace-Murphy, K. 1997. "Tattooing: Another risk-behavior in adolescents warranting national health teaching." *Applied Nursing Research* 10(4): 181-189.

Armstrong, M.L., Pace-Murphy, K., Sallee, A.S., and Watson, M.G. 2000. "Tattooed army soldiers: Examining the incidence, behavior, and risk." *Military Medicine* 165, 37-40.

Bell, Shannon. 1999. "Tattooed: A participant observer's exploration of meaning." *Journal of American Culture* 22 (2): 53-58.

Blonsky,Marshall. 1992. *American Mythologies,* New York: Oxford UP.

Busch, Akiko. 1995. "My decorated self." *Print,* January/February 95, 49 (1): 112.

Caruso, Mandi. 2006. "Alive with passion." *Spirituality and Health,* February 06, 9(1): 38-43.

Christensen, M.H. 2000. "Photo essay: Tattoos." *Public Health Reports* 115 (5):430-435.

Copes, J. and C. Forsyth. 1993. "The tattoo: A social psychological explanation." *International Review of Modern Sociology* 23: 83-89.

Day, Ronald F. 2005. "Tattooing in prison: An innocuous practice or a conduit for Hep C?" *Body Positive,* June 05, 18 (1).

Favazza, A. 1996. Bodies under siege: *Self-mutilation and body modification in culture and Psychiatry.* Baltimore and London: Johns Hopkins University Press.

Forbes, G.B. 2001. "College students with tattoos and piercings: Motives, family experiences, personality factors, and perception by others." *Psychological Reports* 89: 774-786.

Greif, J., Hewitt, W., and Armstrong, M.L. 1999. "Tattooing and body piercing: Body art practices among college students." *Clinical Nursing Research* 8 (4): 368-385.

Irwin, Katherine. 2001. "Legitimating the first tattoo: Moral passage through informal interaction." *Symbolic Interaction* 24 (1): 49-73.

Jet Magazine. 2001. "Athletes Tell the Meaning Behind Their Tattoos." July 9, 2001. 100(14):46.

Keinlen, Alexis. 2005. "Skin deep: Tatttoos mark the body's surface. But their inspiration draws from a deeper source." *Herizons,* Fall 2005, 19 (2): 24-28.

Koch, Jerome R., Roberts, Alden E., Cannon, Julie Harms, Armstrong, M.L., and Owen, Donna C. 2004. "College students, tattooing, and the health belief model: Extending social psychological perspectives on youth culture and deviance." *Sociological Spectrum* 25: 79-102.

Kosut, Mary. 2006. "Mad artists and tattooed perverts: Deviant discourse and the social construction of cultural categories." *Deviant Behavior* 27: 73-95.

Lyman, S.M. & Scott, M.B. 1970. *A Sociology of the Absurd*. New York: Meredith.

Mason, M. 1991. "Every picture tells a story." January 7, 1991, *Newsweek* 117 (1):2-4.

Phillips, Michael M. 2006. "Politics & Economics: Tattoos honor marines killed in Iraq and help the survivors." *The Wall Street Journal* February. 15, 2006, pg. A8.

Rosenblatt, Daniel. 1997. "The antisocial skin: Structure, resistance, and "modern primitive" adornment in the United States." *Cultural Anthropology* 12(3): 287-334.

Underwood, N. 1991. "Designs on the body." *Maclean's*, September 9, 1991, 104(36): 42.

Vale, V. & Juno, A. 1989. *Modern primitives. An investigation of contemporary adornment and ritual*. San Francisco: Re/Search Publications.

Velliquette, Ann M., and Jeff B. Murray. 2002. "The New Tattoo Subculture." Pp. 68-80 in *Mapping the Social Landscape: Readings in Sociology*, edited by Susan J. Ferguson. Mountain View, CA: Mayfield Publishing Company.

Vineyard, Mary. 1999. "Tattoo made its mark on this mother." *National Catholic Reporter*, February 19, 1991, 35 (16): 23.

Designer Babies: Eugenics Repackaged or Consumer Options?

By Stephen L. Baird

Stephen L. Baird is a technology education teacher at Bayside Middle School, Virginia Beach, Virginia and adjunct faculty member at Old Dominion University.

The forces pushing humanity towards attempts at self-modification, through biological and technological advances, are powerful, seductive ones that we will be hard-pressed to resist.

Almost three decades ago, on July 25, 1978, Louise Brown, the first "test-tube baby" was born. The world's first "test-tube" baby arrived amid a storm of protest and hand-wringing about science gone amok, human-animal hybrids, and the rebirth of eugenics. But the voices of those opposed to the procedure were silenced when Brown was born. She was a happy, healthy infant, and her parents were thrilled. The doctors who helped to create her, Patrick Steptoe and Robert Edwards, could not have been more pleased. She was the first person ever created outside a woman's body and was as natural a baby as had ever entered the world. Today in vitro *fertilization* (IVF) is often the unremarkable choice of tens of thousands of infertile couples whose only complaint is that the procedure is too difficult, uncertain, and expensive. What was once so deeply disturbing now seems to many people just another part of the modern world. Will the same be said one day of children with genetically enhanced intelligence, endurance, and other traits? Or will such attempts—if they occur at all—lead to extraordinary problems that are looked back upon as the ultimate in twenty-first century hubris? (Stock, 2006.)

Soon we may be altering the genes of our children to engineer key aspects of their character and physiology. The ethical and social consequences will be profound. We are standing at the threshold of an extraordinary, yet troubling, scientific dawn that has the potential to alter the very fabric of our lives, challenging what it means to be human, and perhaps redesigning our very selves. We are fast approaching the most consequential technological threshold in all of human history: the ability to alter the genes we pass to our children. Genetic engineering is already being carried out successfully on nonhuman animals. The gene that makes jellyfish fluorescent has been inserted into mice embryos, resulting in glow-in-the-dark rodents. Other mice have had their muscle mass increased, or have been made to be more faithful to their partners, through the insertion of a gene into their normal genetic make-up. But this method of genetic engineering is thus far inefficient. In order to produce one fluorescent mouse, several go wrong and are born deformed. If human babies are ever to be engineered, the process would have to become far more efficient, as no technique involving the birth of severely defective human beings to create a "genetically enhanced being" will hopefully ever be tolerated by our society (Designing, 2005). Once humans begin genetically engineering their children for desired traits, we will have crossed a threshold of no return. The communities of the world are just beginning to understand the full implications of the new human genetic technologies. There are few civil society institutions, and there are no social or political movements, critically addressing the immense social, cultural, and psychological challenges these technologies pose.

Until recently, the time scale for measuring change in the biological world has been tens of thousands, if not millions of years, but today it is hard to imagine what humans may be like in a few hundred years. The forces pushing humanity toward attempts at self-modification, through biological and technological advances, are powerful, seductive ones that we will be hard-pressed to resist. Some will curse these new technologies, sounding the death knell for humanity, envisioning the social, cultural, and moral collapse of our society and perhaps our civilization. Others see the same technologies as the ability to take charge of our own evolution, to transcend human limitations, and to improve ourselves as a species. As the human species moves out of its childhood, it is time to acknowledge our technological capabilities and to take responsibility for them. We have little choice, as the reweaving of the fabric of our genetic makeup has already begun.

THE BASIC SCIENCE

Biological entities are comprised of millions of cells. Each cell has a nucleus, and inside every nucleus are strings of deoxyribonucleic acid (DNA). DNA carries the complete information regarding the function and structure of organisms ranging from plants and animals to bacterium. Genes, which are sequences of DNA, determine an organism's growth, size, and other charac-teristics. Genes are the vehicle by which species transfer inheritable characteris-tics to successive generations. Genetic engineering is the process of artificially manipulating these inheritable characteristics.

Genetic engineering in its broadest sense has been around for thousands of years, since people first recognized that they could mate animals with specific characteristics to produce offspring with desirable traits and use agricultural seed selectively. In 1863, Mendel, in his study of peas, discovered that traits were transmitted from parents to progeny by discrete, independent units, later called genes. His observations laid the groundwork for the field of genetics (Genetic, 2006).

Modern human genetic engineering entered the scientific realm in the nineteenth century with the introduction of Eugenics. Although not yet technically considered "genetic engineering," it represented society's first attempt to scientifically alter the human evolutionary process. The practice of human genetic engineering is considered by some to have had its beginnings with in vitro fertilization (IVF) in 1978. IVF paved the way for preimplantation genetic diagnosis (PGD), also referred to as preimplantation genetic selection (PGS). PGD is the process by which an embryo is microscopically examined for signs of genetic disorders. Several genetically based diseases can now be identified, such as Downs Syndrome, Tay-Sachs Disease, Sickle Cell Anemia, Cystic Fibrosis, and Huntington's disease. There are many others that can be tested for, and both medical and scientific institutes are constantly searching for and developing new tests. For these tests, no real genetic engineering is taking place; rather, single cells are removed from embryos using the same process as used during in vitro fertilization. These cells are then examined to identify which are carrying the genetic disorder and which are not. The embryos that have the genetic disorder are discarded, those that are free of the disorder are implanted into the woman's uterus in the hope that a baby will be born without the genetic disorder. This procedure is fairly uncontroversial except with those critics who argue that human life starts at conception and therefore the embryo is sacrosanct and should not be tampered with. Another use for this technique is gender selection, which is where the issue becomes slightly more controversial. Some disorders or diseases are gender-specific, so instead of testing for the disease or disorder, the gender of the embryo is determined and whichever gender is "undesirable" is discarded. This brings up ethical issues of gender selection and the consequences for the gender balance of the human species.

A more recent development is the testing of the embryos for tissue matching. The embryos are tested for a tissue match with a sibling that has already developed, or is in danger of developing, a genetic disease or disorder. The purpose is to produce a baby who can be a tissue donor. This type of procedure was successfully used to cure a six-year-old-boy of a rare blood disorder after transplanting cells from his baby brother, who was created to save him. Doctors say the technique could be used to help many other children with blood and metabolic disorders, but critics say creating a baby in order to treat a sick sibling raises ethical questions (Genetic, 2006).

The child, Charlie Whitaker, from Derbyshire, England, was born with Diamond Blackfan Anemia, a condition that prevented him from creating his own red blood cells. He needed transfusions every three weeks and drug infusions nearly every night. His condition was cured by a transplant of cells from the umbilical cord of his baby brother Jamie, who was genetically selected to be a donor after his parents' embryos were screened to find one with a perfect tissue match. Three months after his transplant, Charlie's doctors said that he was cured of Diamond Blackfan Anemia, and the prognosis is that Charlie can now look forward to a normal quality of life (Walsh, 2004). Is this the beginning of a slippery slope toward "designer" or "spare parts" babies, or is the result that there are now two healthy, happy children instead of one very sick child a justification to pursue and continue procedures such as this one? Policymakers and ethicists are just beginning to pay serious attention. A recent working paper by the President's Council on Bioethics noted that "as genomic knowledge increases and more genes are identified that correlate with diseases, the applications for PGD will likely increase greatly," including diagnosing and treating medical conditions such as cancer, mental illness, or asthma, and nonmedical traits such as temperament or height. "While currently a small practice," the Council's working paper declares, "PGD is a momentous development. It represents the first fusion of genomics and assisted reproduction—effectively opening the door to the genetic shaping of offspring" (Rosen, 2003).

In one sense PGD poses no new eugenic dangers. Genetic screening using amniocentesis has allowed parents to test the fitness of potential offspring for years. But PGD is poised to increase this power significantly: It will allow parents to choose the child they want, not simply reject the ones they do not want. It will change the overriding purpose of IVF, from a treatment for fertility to being able to pick and choose embryos like consumer goods—producing many, discarding most, and desiring only the chosen few.

The next step in disease elimination is to attempt to refine a process known as "human germline engineering" or "human germline modification." Whereas preimplantation genetic diagnosis (PGD) affects only the immediate offspring, germline engineering seeks to affect the genes that are carried in the ova and sperm, thus eliminating the disease or disorder from all future generations, making it no longer inheritable. The possibilities for germline engineering go beyond the elimination of disease and open the door for modifications to human longevity, increased intelligence, increased muscle mass, and many other types of genetic enhancements. This application is by far the more consequential, because it opens the door to the alteration of the human species. The modified genes would appear not only in any children that resulted from such procedures, but in all succeeding generations.

The term germline refers to the germ or germinal cells, i.e., the eggs and sperm. Genes are strings of chemicals that help create the proteins that make up the body. They are found in long coiled chains called chromosomes located in the nuclei of the cells of the body. Genetic modification occurs by inserting genes into living cells. The desired gene is attached to a viral vector, which has the ability to carry the gene across the cell membrane. Proposals for inheritable genetic modification in humans combine techniques involving in vitro fertilization, gene transfer, stem cells, and cloning. Germline modification would begin by using IVF to create a single-cell embryo or zygote. This embryo would develop for about five days to the blastocyst stage (very early embryo consisting of approximately 150 cells. It contains the inner cell mass, from which embryonic stem cells are derived, and an outer layer of cells called the trophoblast that forms the placenta. (It is approximately 1/10 the size of the head of a pin.) At this point embryonic stem cells would be removed. These stem cells would be altered by adding genes using viral vectors. Colonies of altered stem cells would be grown and tested for successful incorporation of the new genes. Cloning techniques would be used to transfer a successfully modified stem cell nucleus into an enucleated egg cell. This "constructed embryo" would then be implanted into a woman's uterus and brought to term. The child born would be a genetically modified human (Inheritable, 2003).

Proponents of germline manipulation assume that once a gene implicated in a particular condition is identified, it might be appropriate and relatively easy to replace, change, supplement, or otherwise modify that gene. However, biological characteristics or traits usually depend on interactions among many genes and, more importantly, the activity of genes is affected by various processes that occur both inside the organism and in its surroundings. This means that scientists cannot predict the full effect that any gene modification will have on the traits of people or other organisms.

There is no universally accepted ideal of biological perfection. To make intentional changes in the genes that people will pass on to their descendants would require that we, as a society, agree on how to classify "good" and "bad" genes. We do not have the necessary criteria, nor are there mechanisms for establishing such measures. Any formulation of such criteria would inevitably reflect particular current social biases. The definition of the standards and the technological means for implementing them would largely be determined by economically and socially privileged groups (Human, 2004).

SUMMARY

"Designer babies" is a term used by journalists and commentators—not by scientists—to describe several different reproductive technologies. These technologies have one thing in common: they give parents more control over what their offspring will be like. Designer babies are made possible by progress in three fields:

1. Advanced Reproductive Technologies. In the decades since the first "test tube baby" was born, reproductive medicine has helped countless women conceive and bear children. Today there are hundreds of thousands of humans who were conceived thanks to in vitro fertilization. Other advanced reproductive technologies include frozen embryos, egg and sperm donations, surrogate motherhood, pregnancies by older women, and the direct injection of a sperm cell into an egg.
2. Cell and Chromosome Manipulation. The past decade has seen astonishing breakthroughs in our knowledge of cell structure. Our ability to transfer chromosomes (the long threads of DNA in each cell) has led to major developments in cloning. Our knowledge of stem cells will make many new therapies possible. As we learn more about how reproduction works at the cellular level, we will gain more control over the earliest stages of a baby's development.
3. Genetics and Genomics. With the mapping of the human genome, our understanding of how DNA affects human development is only just beginning. Someday we might be able to switch bits of DNA on or off as we wish, or replace sections of DNA at will; research in that direction is already well underway.

Human reproduction is a complex process. There are many factors involved in the reproduction process: the genetic constitution of the parents, the condition of the parents' egg and sperm, and the health and behavior of the impregnated mother. When you consider the enormous complexity of the human genome, with its billions of DNA pairs, it becomes clear that reproduction will always have an element of unpredictability. To a certain extent we have always controlled our children's characteristics through the selection of mates. New technologies will give us more power to influence our children's "design"—but our control will be far from total (Designer, 2002).

Since the term "designer babies" is so imprecise, it is difficult to untangle its various meanings so as to make judgments about which techniques are acceptable. Several different techniques have been discussed, such as screening embryos for high-risk diseases, selecting the sex of a baby, picking an embryo for specific traits, genetic manipulation for therapeutic reasons, and genetic manipulation for cosmetic reasons. Although, to date, none of these techniques are feasible, recent scientific breakthroughs and continued work by the scientific community will eventually make each a possibility in the selection process for the best possible embryo for implantation.

ARGUMENTS FOR DESIGNER BABIES

1. Using whatever techniques are available to help prevent certain genetic diseases will protect children from suffering debilitating diseases and deformities and reduce the financial and emotional strain on the parents. If we want the best for our children, why shouldn't we use the technology?
2. The majority of techniques available today can only be used by parents who need the help of fertility clinics to have children; since they are investing so much time and money in their effort to have a baby, shouldn't they be entitled to a healthy one?
3. A great many naturally conceived embryos are rejected from the womb for defects; by screening embryos, we are doing what nature would normally do for us.
4. Imagine the reaction nowadays if organ transplantation were to be prohibited because it is "unnatural"—even though that is what some people called for when transplantation was a medical novelty. It is hard to see how the replacement of a defective gene is any less "natural" than the replacement of a defective organ. The major difference is the entirely beneficial one that medical intervention need occur only once around the time of conception, and the benefits would be inherited by the child and its descendants.

ARGUMENTS AGAINST DESIGNER BABIES

1. We could get carried away "correcting" perfectly healthy babies. Once we start down the slippery slope of eliminating embryos because they are diseased, what is to stop us from picking babies for their physical or psychological traits?
2. There is always the looming shadow of eugenics. This was the motivation for some government policies in Europe and the United States in the first half of the twentieth century that included forced sterilizations, selective breeding, and "racial hygiene." Techniques that could be used for designing babies will give us dangerous new powers to express our genetic preferences.
3. There are major social concerns—such as: Will we breed a race of super humans who look down on those without genetic enhancements? Will these new technologies only be available to the wealthy—resulting in a lower class that will still suffer from inherited diseases and disabilities? Will discrimination against people already born with disabilities increase if they are perceived as genetically inferior?
4. Tampering with the human genetic structure might actually have unintended and unpredictable consequences that could damage the gene pool.

5. Many of the procedures related to designing babies involve terminating embryos; many disapprove of this on moral and religious grounds.

As our technical abilities progress, citizens will have to cope with the ethical implications of designer babies, and governments will have to define a regulatory course. We will have to answer some fundamental questions: How much power should parents and doctors have over the design of their children? How much power should governments have over parents and doctors? These decisions should be made based on facts and on our social beliefs.

REFERENCES

Designer Babies. (2002). The Center for the Study of Technology and Society. Retrieved September 14, 2006 from www.tecsoc.org/biotech/focusbabies.htm

Designing Babies: The Future of Genetics. (2005). BBC News. Retrieved September 22, 2006 from http://news.bbc.co.uk/1/hi/health/590919.stm

Genetic Engineering and the Future of Human Evolution. (2006). Future Human Evolution Organization. Retrieved September 19, 2006 from www.human-evolution.org/geneticbasics.php

Human Germline Manipulation. (2004). Council for Responsible Genetics. Retrieved October 18, 2006 from www.gene-watch.org/programs/cloning/germlineposition.html

Inheritable Genetic Modification. (2003). Center for Genetics and Society. Retrieved October 05, 2006 from www.gene-watch.org/programs/cloning/germlineposition.html

Rosen, C. (2003). The New Atlantis. A Journal of Technology and Society. Retrieved October 14, 2006 from www.thenewatlantis.com/archive/2/rosen.htm

Stock, G. (2005). Best Hope, Worst Fear. Human Germline Engineering. Retrieved October 05, 2006 from http://research.arc2.ucla.edu/pmts/germline/bhwf.htm

Walsh, F. (2004). Brother's Tissue "Cures" Sick Boy. BBC News. Retrieved September 27, 2006 from http://news.bbc.co.uk/1/hi/health/3756556.stm

Designer Babies: Choosing Our Children's Genes

Bonnie Steinbock

Bonnie Steinbock teaches philosophy at the State University of New York, Albany

The phrase "designer babies" refers to genetic interventions into pre-implantation embryos in the attempt to influence the traits the resulting children will have. At present, this is not possible, but many people are horrified by the mere thought that parents might want to choose their children's genes, especially for non-disease traits. I want to argue that the objections are usually not well articulated, and that even when they are, it's far from obvious that such interventions would be wrong.

What precisely is the objection? Of course, there are safety objections, especially ones arising from unforeseen and harmful side-effects. For example, in mice, researchers have shown that the addition of a certain gene made them better at running mazes, but also made them hyper-sensitive to pain. Such a possibility would rule out most, if not all, genetic enhancement. However, safety objections are raised by all new technologies, and do not usually instigate calls for blanket prohibition. The interesting question is, assuming genetic enhancement of the embryo is safe and effective, may such techniques ethically be used by parents?

Do the critics base their opposition on a general objection to the attempt to influence children's traits? Surely not. That is exactly what parents are supposed to do. To get our children to be healthy, well mannered, intellectually curious, and well behaved we control what they eat, have them vaccinated, teach them manners, read to them, and discipline them when they misbehave. It would be absurd for a parent to say, "I never attempt to influence my children's development. I just love them for who they are." Thus, it is not influencing our children's traits that is objectionable, but rather the means to accomplish this, that is, choosing their genes. But even this has to be further refined, since just the choice of a partner—surely not morally objectionable in itself—is a way of choosing our children's genes. As Steven Pinker has put it, "Anyone who has been turned down for a date has been a victim of the human drive to exert control over half the genes of one's future children."

Perhaps the objection is not to exerting control over traits, but rather to completely determining in advance what traits one's children will or will not have. Genetic interventions, it may be thought, enable more control over what our children will be like than other modes of shaping children. If this is the objection, it embodies the "fallacy of genetic determinism", the view that our genes determine who we are and what we are like. Of course genes play a role in the traits we have, but what we are actually like is the result of multiple genes interacting with each other, and all of them interacting with the environment. In fact, even if you could choose the entire genome of a child (for example, by cloning), you would not have complete control over the child's traits. As Princeton microbiologist Lee Silver has put it, "all that anyone will ever get from the use of cloning, or any other reproductive technology, is an unpredictable son or daughter, who won't listen to his parents any more than my children will listen to me".

Thus, the very term "designer babies" is a misnomer. No one will ever be able to design a child, that is, determine in advance what talents, skills, abilities, virtues, and vices the child will have. Perhaps the objection is to the fact that the child's genes were chosen for him by his parents, thus forcing the child to have certain talents and not others. For example, it might be thought that if the child's parents picked genes associated with musical ability, their child would be forced to be a musician, when maybe he or she would rather have been an athlete. But this makes no sense. Consider a child of musicians who inherits musical ability naturally. That child may become a musician, but he or she certainly isn't forced to do so because of his genetic inheritance. Far from it; if the child doesn't practice, he won't become a musician, no matter what his genetic make-up.

Admittedly, when parents choose their children's genes, they do so without the child's knowledge and consent. However, this is true of all of us, not just those who are genetically modified. None of us chooses our own genes. What is the moral significance in the fact that our genes were imposed on us due to someone's choice as opposed to just chance? Some people believe that genetically modified people would have personalities, thoughts, and feelings that would be less real, less authentic than the personalities of non-modified people. But this too makes no sense, as an example will reveal. In 2003, Avshalom Caspi and colleagues reported in *Science* that a functional polymorphism in the promoter region of the serotonin transporter (5-HTT) gene may be associated with a predisposition towards depression.

Individuals with one or two copies of the short allele of the 5-HTT promoter polymorphism become depressed more often after stressful events than individuals homozygous for the long allele. So if you're lucky enough to have inherited two long alleles of 5-HTT, you may be more likely to be a cheerful, resilient sort of person than someone who inherited two short alleles. What if it were possible to genetically modify embryos to replace the short alleles with long ones? Would the resulting people not really be as cheerful or resilient as those who naturally inherited the long alleles? Of course not. A more serious objection stems from the idea that people who want to choose, in advance, the traits their child will have, and are willing to spend so much money to get a child with certain traits, demonstrate a kind of desire for perfectionism that seems incompatible with being a good parent. An insistence on having a child of a certain sort, whether a musician or an athlete or a politician, amounts to parental tyranny. As Thomas Murray has put the point, "When parents attempt to shape their children's characteristics to match their preferences and expectations, such an exercise of free choice on the parents' part may constrain their child's prospects for flourishing."

An argument related to parental tyranny has been made by a member of the US President's Council on Bioethics, Michael Sandel. Sandel suggests that genetic engineering threatens what he calls the "ethic of giftedness". He argues that "To appreciate our children as gifts is to accept them as they come, not as objects of our design or products of our will or instruments of our ambition."

This notion of giftedness resonates with many people, because it represents an ideal of parenting that most of us embrace. Sandel contrasts the ethic of giftedness with a style of parenting he calls "hyper-parenting", which ignores the child's own talents and abilities, and instead forces the child to do what will satisfy parental dreams and aspirations. A hyper-parent might insist that a child play sports, when he or she would rather be in the drama club, or that all the child's free time be spent in pursuit of getting into a prestigious university. We can all agree that hyperparents are obnoxious, but is there a necessary connection between hyper-parenting and interest in genetic modification of the embryo? No doubt many hyperparents would be interested in genetically modifying their embryos, but it doesn't follow that everyone who would opt for genetic modification would be hyper-parents. That depends, I think, on the traits chosen, and the reasons for choosing them. If the traits sought were ones that could reasonably be thought to benefit the child, whatever path the child might choose, traits that would help a person flourish, traits that good parents would want to instill in their children anyway, such as kindness, generosity, compassion, or creativity, it is hard to see why choosing such traits, by genetic or conventional means, would be hyper-parenting.

A final objection to "designer children" is that this would exacerbate social differences and the gap between rich and poor. I seriously doubt that genetic interventions would have more of an influence than existing causes of inequality, such as rotten neighbourhoods and lousy schools. In any event, prebirth genetic enhancement could be used to combat social inequality, by giving children from disadvantaged backgrounds a leg up.

Genetic enhancement of embryos is, for the present, science fiction. Its opponents think that we need to ban it now, before it ever becomes a reality. What they have not provided are clear reasons to agree. Their real opposition is not to a particular means of shaping children, but rather to a certain style of parenting. Rather than fetishising the technology, the discussion should focus on which parental attitudes and modes of parenting help children to flourish. It may be that giving children "genetic edges" of certain kinds would not constrain their lives and choices, but actually make them better. That possibility should not be dismissed out of hand.

Designer Babies: What are the Ethical and Moral Issues?

TK McGhie

Correspondence: **Ms TK McGhie,** (Final Year Medical Student, C/o Dean's Office, Faculty of Medical Sciences, The University of the West Indies, Kingston 7, Jamaica, West Indies. E-mail: tkmcghie@yahoo.com This essay won the Medical Protection Society Essay Competition 2001.

The twentieth century can easily be dubbed the biotechnology century, with particularly huge leaps and bounds in the area of reproductive technology. The first milestone and hallmark achievement of this came in 1978 with the birth of Louise Brown, the first test tube baby. From then, *in vitro* fertilization (IVF) has revolutionized medical treatment of infertility, accounting for over 200,000 successful births worldwide (1). The next milestone came with the controversial 1996 birth of the icon for biotechnology, Dolly, the Scottish cloned sheep. Dolly became the first large animal to be cloned from genetic material taken from an adult egg. The potential of human ingenuity in the biological sciences has grown tremendously. Just two years after the birth of Dolly, two research teams from the United States of America (USA) opened another area of biotechnology with the isolation of stem cells. Subsequent to this, there has been the successful completion of the controversial human genome project, an international scientific collaboration that mapped the "blueprint of life", the genetic material of the human deoxyribonucleic acid (DNA) molecule in 2000. Then emerged the advent of genetic manipulation with such feats as mice being engineered to be smarter with greater memory capacity and a genetically modified monkey (2).

With the mapping of the human genome, researchers have access to a wealth of information of thousands of inherited disorders, with the ability to screen for disease even before conception. In fact, even before the completion of the project, there was pre-implantation genetic diagnosis (PGD) in which doctors do limited analysis of an embryo's genes in the laboratory, screening out those that may have defects. The genetic information provided by the human genome may be used by prospective parents to find out a range of traits of an embryo such as eye colour, height and intelligence. That may mean making complex choices about which embryos to implant in the mother. Already doctors can now increase the number of babies born of a particular gender. As the ability to predict traits expands, it will change the very nature of reproduction and it raises perhaps the most topical issue in biotechnology today: the prospect of "designer babies".

The tag, "designer baby", has been bestowed by those with concerns that the reach of reproductive technology could be expanded to eventually facilitate the screening of healthy embryos in advance of implantation for positive subjective characteristics such as physical appearance. Under some debate is a broader ascription of the term "designer baby" to include any circumstance where there is genetic manipulation of the reproductive process such that a desired outcome is attained with respect to the characteristics of the embryo. Thus, a cloned embryo may be considered a "designer baby", having been engineered to have a pre-determined genetic make-up. Also labelled as "designer babies" are those who are selected specifically so that they may have genes that allow them to be disease free and suitable donors of stem cells to matched recipients.

By this definition, "designer babies" are already a reality. On February 14, 2002, the world's second baby to be born with desired genetic characteristics known in advance was born in Britain. This infant was created, in effect, for his five year-old leukaemic sibling who may require a bone marrow transplant if he should relapse in the next few years. The need to create a sibling arose because there was no suitable matched family member or registered donor (3).

The ruling that paved the way for British couples to select an IVF baby to provide a cure for another of their children came from the Human Fertilization and Embryology Authority (HFEA) which said that, in some cases, it might be acceptable for embryos to be checked to see if they were a match for an existing child. This would enable blood from the new baby's umbilical cord to be used in bone marrow transplants. This had enabled the first couple from the USA to give birth to a son who would provide a match for their daughter with Fanconi's anaemia (4). There are similar hopes for a couple in Leeds,

England, whose son has thalassaemia. With no match, either within his family or on international bone marrow registers, this child's only hope is the creation of a matched sibling, a "designer baby". The HFEA, which regulated the use of IVF embryos in the United Kingdom (UK), has given the green light in the case from Leeds, ruling that only those embryos already being tested for genetic flaws (PGD) could be tissue typed. Effectively, the body ruled that where PGD is already being undertaken the use of tissue typing to save the life of a sibling could be justified, but only in those circumstances and under strict controls. Even where the creation of a designer baby is seen to be of life saving importance, the ethical questions still arise.

Gender selection is another possibility in the creation of "designer babies". The technology for doing this has existed for quite some time with a Maryland genetics and *in vitro* fertilization clinic boasting a 92.9% success rate in determining the gender of a child (5). However, it has been used almost exclusively for couples with legitimate fears of having babies with certain genetic diseases. For example, male embryos might be rejected because there is a great likelihood that they may be carriers of haemophilia.

As with all technologies, the danger arises where its application steps beyond the realms for which it was originally designed, especially where the question of exploration comes in; this is the genesis of the concerns in designer babies. Is this indeed the beginning of being able to choose the right colour of the eyes, the right intelligence, athletic prowess or artistic skills? Will it be like buying a new car, where you decide which package of accessories you want?

Unfortunately, ethics and moral development tend to lag behind technological advancements. This is particularly so with human genetic manipulation. With the prospects of designer babies, the ethical and moral issues need to be addressed as a matter of urgency. The ethical issues are mainly related to the context and the process by which they are derived, particularly the creation and ultimate destruction of embryos and the implication on human health. The moral issues are multifocal, ranging from concerns regarding traditional family values, to the question of eugenics and the creation of a master race.

ETHICAL CONSIDERATIONS

Some of the first ethical issues to be considered arose from the use of PGD to select potential donors of stem cells. The ruling by HFEA, though helpful to couples in a very limited and restricted number of cases, has raised many ethical questions about the welfare of the child created for a specific purpose. Whereas the stem cell harvesting is harmless, a bone marrow transplant is not without risk and is an extremely uncomfortable procedure. Where is the line going to be drawn? Even where the approved procedure is not going to put the child through any pain and distress, is it in the best interest of the child to be created as a tissue match for someone else? The child has effectively been brought into the world because it is a medical commodity. There is the concern that the child would be obliged to give other stem cells to a sibling later in life. Being a perfect match for their sibling and having been created essentially as donors, does this child lose the right to choose? If a kidney or any other donation is needed by the sibling, must the designer child be obligated to provide it?

Perhaps the most urgent issue arises in the context and process that may lead to the birth of the early designer babies. As pointed out by scholars, early experiments involving cloning are likely to result in a number of clinical failures and lead to miscarriage, necessitating numerous abortions or births of massively deformed offspring. Early animal experiments, involving cloning, have shown poor outcomes for primates with abnormally high prenatal and antenatal death rates. Since cloning technology itself may be used to create designer babies, examination of the findings in experiments thus far warrants close scrutiny as regards safety. Animal cloning has been shown to be very unsuccessful with an average success rate of 1.4 to 2%. Even the most recent cloning endeavours have been riddled with failure. The first successful cloning of a household pet, a cat called *cc* (copy cat) achieved in December of 2001 and reported to the world in February of 2002, saw the creation of 82 embryos which were implanted into seven surrogate mothers from which only a single fetal clone was derived. This clone which was created by the fusion of harvested cells from the mouth of an adult cat and cat-donor eggs emptied of its genetic material, later died in utero. Researchers then turned to cumulus cells from the ovaries of a female cat creating five cloned embryos that were implanted once again, this time yielding the cloned cat (6). Many critics view *cc* as an ethical dry run for human cloning and they are troubled by how the rehearsal is going. Surely, it cannot be ethical to subject humans to trial and error of this sort, especially, when the psychological trauma of disappointment in failed attempts is considered with respect to hopeful mothers?

Even with successful genetic manipulation, there is the possibility of unforeseen defects manifesting themselves later in life. Recent studies of cloning experiments suggest that a number of defects, often created in the reprogramming of the egg, do not manifest themselves until later in the life of the clones, with some undergoing spectacular unforeseen deaths. Cloning experiments with mice, pigs, sheep and cattle have reported that even apparently normal animals develop disorders at variable times later. Extreme obesity was one such problem in many cloned animals including Dolly who, incidentally, has been reported to also suffer from arthritis. Even in the most recent cloning of cats, some of the animals were being plagued by fatal heart and lung defects in infancy (7). From these results obtained, many scientists theorize that in cloned humans the gene expression flaws could affect personality, intelligence and other human attributes.

Given the limits of our knowledge of important questions about the functioning of genes, there is a general limit to what would be ethically acceptable. Remembering the consequences of using new drugs, like thalidomide, without adequate knowledge of their effects, the risk of unforeseen harm as it relates to modifying germ cells represents a most serious and unacceptable danger in that it may not only harm babies that are the immediate result of the change but could afflict, indefinitely, many subsequent generations. On this basis, human genetic manipulation may be deemed unethical, especially when its reversal is not guaranteed.

Genetic enhancement assumes the right to create and destroy embryos not because of genetic disease, but because of other features not to one's desire. This is an ethical dilemma depending on the status that is accorded an embryo. Defining an embryo ethically has always been surrounded by much debate, giving rise to a spectrum where at one end it is seen as a ball of cells and nothing more, unable to survive outside the womb and devoid of feelings and consciousness. At this end of the spectrum, reproductive and stem cell uses are equally permissible. At the other end of the spectrum, an embryo must be accorded the status of humanity from conception onwards and any technology creating dispensable embryos is forbidden. The present UK act finds middle ground in the spectrum, decreeing that human embryo command a special respect "that is due to human life at all stages of its development" (Code of practice; 1998. Human Fertilization and Embryology Authority). By this, embryos should be used only under certain circumstances and selection of gender or enhanced intelligence is thus deemed a trivial means of throwing away an embryo.

Indeed, the issue of gender selection raises the question of whether parents should be able to select the gender of their child. Would it be ethical for people with fertility problems to choose which fertilized embryos get implanted and have the rest discarded as being the 'wrong' gender? According to the American Society for Reproductive Medicine, a group that establishes ethical guidelines for fertility clinics, the answer is "Yes", reporting in the process that many requests have been made over the years. Despite the fact that this approval of gender selection carries with it situation-specific actions, such as cases where a couple who already have a child of one gender may be allowed to ethically choose the implantation of embryos which would make sure their next child was of the opposite gender, there are still many ethical issues that arise. With this comes the potential for inherent gender discrimination and reinforcement of gender bias in society as a whole, inappropriate control over nonessential characteristics of children, unnecessary medical burdens and costs for parents, and inappropriate and potentially unfair use of limited medical resources. If physicians are using their skills for non-medical reasons, then those resources become less accessible. In 1997, the Parliamentary Assembly of the Council of Europe, comprising members of parliaments (MPs) from 41 countries, passed the European Convention on Human Rights and Biomedicine. It lays down that genetic testing can only be done for health purposes and gender selection must not be permitted except to avoid a serious hereditary sex-linked disease. This draws the line between a serious medical condition and consumer preference. To allow commonplace gender selection is to cross that ethical line. Once crossed, there would be no logical reason not to allow any form of preference in babies—blond hair, intelligence or musical ability.

Arguments for application of the technology in its various forms, as it relates to reproduction, have been put forward mainly on the grounds of procreative autonomy; a couple's right to control their own role in procreation unless the state has a compelling reason for denying them that control. Can this right outweigh the issues raised thus far?

One great supporter of "designer babies", James Watson, who with Francis and Crick shared a Nobel Prize for the discovery of the DNA double helix in 1953, suggests that this right could supersede the concerns that prevail; stating that "the fears over the creation of "designer babies" is misplaced and that the potential benefits of controlling the ultimate engine of human evolution far outweighs the risks" (8). The general consensus, however, seems to be that parents do not 'own' their children and the consequences of their actions will only be suffered by their offspring and not themselves. Thus they should not be entitled to engineer their children solely for their own purposes.

With inventive technologies comes the issue of patenting. Many of the new processes associated with genetic manipulation have been developed in the private sector, and this leads to concerns that proprietary rights to these technologies might mean that many developing countries will be unable to access them should they become safe and socially acceptable. Will there be patenting of genes or transgenic creations? And is the ownership rights of genes and other living matter as intellectual property acceptable? Furthermore, the patenting of gene sequences and biotechnology techniques with broad applications, as is usually the case when a new technology begins, means that developing countries, in particular, may be excluded from affordable access to technologies that they may urgently need. Yet another ethical question is, what would the technology be used for?

Next comes the question of cost. If deemed socially acceptable and safe, will it be available only to a few rich patients, effectively putting profit before human needs? The private company that backed the successful cloning of the cat, "Genetic Savings and Clone", issued a statement forewarning potential cloners that it will cost them "five figures" in $US until the procedure becomes "streamlined" (6). How much will it cost to clone a human being?

MORAL CONSIDERATIONS

Most of the thoughts put forward from a moral perspective stand in opposition to the very notion of "designer babies". With regard to the issue of creating life to save that of another, the moral questions raised are difficult: why should persons die if there is a possibility for them to live? But then, is it right to create a human being for a certain purpose? The creation of a human being exclusively for the benefit of another is a violation of the moral requirement not to use others only as a means. Should wrong be done if good comes of it? All children should be born for their own sake, not as a purpose for someone else's benefit.

There is a great distinction between remedying genetic defects that significantly impact on morbidity, quality and length of life, and pursuing enhancement of human qualities; the first being more acceptable than the latter, which invokes the idea of a division between superior and inferior beings. With the effort to remove genetic defects and the recognition and selection of particular traits through genetic engineering, comes the implied devaluation of persons possessing the defects of lacking the preferred attributes.

Genetic enhancement may represent a new phase of the eugenics movement, that in the early decades of the twentieth century was literally an effort to breed better human beings by encouraging the reproduction of people with "good" genes and discouraging those with "bad" genes in an effort to improve humanity. Eugenicists effectively lobbied for social legislation to keep racial and ethnic groups separate and to sterilize people considered "genetically unfit". Elements of the American eugenics movement were models for the Nazis, whose adaptation of eugenics culminated in the Holocaust. Could the creation of "designer babies" pursue the Nazi ideology of racial purification or worse still, seek to produce a master race that could engineer an underclass of slaves to serve it? This apparent practice of eugenics would be gravely immoral since it fails to show unconditional respect for all human life without exception. Would it amount to a form of human hubris where, in attempting to play God, we find ourselves confronted with an uncontrollable monster of our own making?

Proponents of genetic enhancement may argue that if parents choose to spend their money to give children advantages they should be allowed to, that after all they are already able to do that environmentally by sending their children to private schools or providing better healthcare. However, it is arguable that the advantages of genetic enhancement far surpass those that can be provided by environmental input, such as better education, and as such confer an unfair edge to "designer babies".

Another unfortunate implication is that when parents choose personality traits of their offspring, abortions will become commonplace when they discover, in advance, that the child has traits not desired by them. Should abortions be legitimized for this reason? The lack of subjective traits within a viable offspring should not become an indication for abortions.

With regard to cloning as a potential source of "designer babies", certain questions must be resolved before it can be considered permissible as a remedy for human infertility: Is cloning unnatural self-engineering? Will failures such as deformed offspring be acceptable? Who is socially responsible for cloned humans? Do clones have rights and legal protection? The most formidable challenge is how to define a clone in terms of traditional institutions of family and parenting. Will clones have autonomy? Worse yet, will they be forced to be like their genetic twin? Many legal scholars argue that cloning will violate a child's right to an open future; a child born as the genetic copy of another may feel undue pressure to become like or different from its progenitor.

One opposing perspective put forward, that may not have much weight, comes from some moralists who, having swung from denial that genes have an important effect on behaviour, say that a cloned individual's behaviour will be ultimately determined by the individual's genetic make-up. Indeed, like identical twins, clones will be similar but not the same because of socialization and the influence of the environment on the womb.

To try to reproduce may be a basic human right but as soon as one specifies what sort of child one must have, it becomes a matter of human preference and not human rights. What right has anyone to programme a genetic advantage for their children just because they happen to be rich enough to afford it? Is consumer choice becoming a moral absolute? Moral codes stress that a child is not a right but a gift. We are losing the concept that life is given to us by a higher force and it is not ours to demand or to manipulate.

Whether it is genetic enhancement or cloning, there is a general repugnance for styles of reproduction with such profound potential for vanity that it threatens the freedom of children and the nature of family. This also represents the potential breaching of a natural barrier that is moral in character, taking humans into a realm of self-engineering that truly exceeds any prior experimentation with reproductive technology.

In most areas of science, it matters little to the public whether a particular theory is right or wrong, but in some cases of human genetics, it matters a great deal. The very term 'genetic engineering' conjures up the image of Frankenstein and his maker, Mary Shelley, the unintentional fairy godmother of human genetics. The social obligation that scientists have, as distinct from those responsibilities they share with all citizens, comes from their having access to specialized knowledge of how the world works, not easily accessible to others. Their obligation is both to make public any social implications of their work and its technological applications, and to give some assessment of its reliability and potential harm.

Should the creation of "designer babies" become the new milestone in reproductive biotechnology, all of the processes and the context within which they are applied must be strictly regulated by ethical bodies truly representing the interests of the wider society. Counselling should be mandatory where parents opt for genetic selection. They should be fully informed of all the risks of the procedures and given counselling regarding unrealistic expectations of the outcome that may be largely unpredictable, especially as time passes in the life of the child.

CONCLUSION

Despite the myriad of concerns about "designer babies", the reproductive technology has profound potential benefit for the relief of suffering by eliminating genes encoding disease and for advancing the understanding of human evolution. But without intense review and regard for the ethical and moral issues surrounding it, its potential may be thwarted. Most ethical issues in medicine are best resolved by consideration of the rights of the people involved to determine their own future. Are individuals capable of making the correct decisions in relation to science and its application? Thomas Jefferson's advice is commendable: "I know no safe depository of the ultimate powers of the society but the people themselves, and if we think them not enlightened enough to exercise that control with wholesome discretion, the remedy is not to take it from them but to inform their direction" (9). Unfortunately, the moral issues are not that easily addressed.

REFERENCES

1. The fertility race, twenty years of test-tube babies. *news.mpr.org: 1997*
2. BBC News/SCI/TECH.GM monkey first. *news.bbc.co.uk; 2001.*
3. BBC ON LINE. Baby with selected gene born in Britain. *Bbc.com; 2001*
4. gkt Scientific Editorial. Embryonic selection.
5. BBC ON LINE. Gender selection: the debate. *Bbc.com; 2002.*
6. Kluger J. Here Kitty kitty. Time: February 25, 2002
7. Associated Press. Study raises human cloning doubts. *Wired.com; 2002.*
8. TWJ Headline News. DNA pioneer wants to rid society of genetic defects. *Watchmanjournal.org; 2001.*
9. Wolpert L. Learning to love the grey. *Ring.org.uk; 2000.*

The Literary Mind: Life, Literature, and Politics, From the Inside Out.

by *Ilana Simons, Ph.D.*

Ilana Simons, Ph.D., *is a literature professor at The New School as well as a practicing therapist.*

WHY DO WE DREAM?

Five modern theories for dreams and nightmares.

Published on November 11, 2009 by Ilana Simons, Ph.D. in The Literary Mind

Freud said that whether we intend it or not, we're all poets. That's because on most nights, we dream. And dreams are a lot like poetry, in that in both things, we express our internal life in similar ways. We use images more than words; we combine incongruent elements to evoke emotion in a more efficient way than wordier descriptions can; and we use unconscious and tangential associations rather than logic to tell a story.

Freud essentially called dreams those poems we tell ourselves at night in order to experience our unconscious wishes as real. Dreams allow us to be what we cannot be, and to say what we do not say, in our more repressed daily lives. For instance, if I dream about burning my workplace down, it's probably because I want to dominate the workplace but am too nervous to admit that aggressive drive when I'm awake and trying to be nice to the people who might give me a raise.

Freud certainly had a catchy theory about dreams, but it was also limited. For him, every single dream was the picture of an unconscious wish. But people who have had boring dreams or nightmares might feel something missing from that formulation. In turn, recent theorists have tried to give a more accurate account of why we dream. In the following post, I'll list some of the current theories on why, at night, our brains tell strange stories that feel a lot like literature. I'd like to know if any of these theories resonate with you, or if you have your own belief about why we dream.

(Many great literary minds were obsessed with their dreams. Samuel Coleridge wanted to write a book about dreams—that "night's dismay" which he said "stunned the coming day." Edgar Allan Poe knew dreams fed his literature, and he pushed himself to dream "dreams no mortal ever dared to dream before.")

MODERN THEORIES ON WHY DREAMS EXIST:

Theory #1

The Evolutionary Theory: We Dream to Practice Responses to Threatening Situations

Ever notice that most dreams have a blood-surging urgency to them? In dreams, we often find ourselves naked in public, or being chased, or fighting an enemy, or sinking in quicksand. Antti Revonsuo, a Finnish cognitive scientist, has shown that our amygdala (the fight-or-flight piece of the brain) fires more than normal when we're in REM sleep (the time in sleep when we dream). In REM sleep, the brain fires in similar ways as it does when it's specifically threatened for survival. In addition to that, the part of the brain that practices motor activity (running, punching) fires increasingly during REM sleep, even though the limbs are still. In other words, Revonsuo and other evolutionary theorists argue that in dreams, we are actually rehearsing fight-and-flight responses, even though the legs and arms are not actually moving. They say that dreams are an evolutionary adaptation: We dream in order to rehearse behaviors of self-defense in the safety of nighttime isolation. In turn, we get better at fight-or-flight in the real world.

Theory #2

Dreams Create Wisdom

If we remembered every image of our waking lives, it would clog our brains. So, dreams sort through memories, to determine which ones to retain and which to lose. Matt Wilson, at MIT's Center for Learning and Memory, largely defends this view. He put rats in mazes during the day, and recorded what neurons fired in what patterns as the rats negotiated the maze. When he watched the rats enter REM sleep, he saw that the same neuron patterns fired that had fired at choice turning points in the maze. In other words, he saw that the rats were dreaming of important junctures in their day. He argues that sleep is the process through which we separate the memories worth encoding in long-term memory from those worth losing. Sleep turns a flood of daily information into what we call wisdom: the stuff that makes us smart for when we come across future decisions.

Theory #3

Dreaming is Like Defragmenting Your Hard Drive

Francis Crick (who co-discovered the structure of DNA) and Graeme Mitchison put forth a famously controversial theory about dreams in 1983 when they wrote that "we dream in order to forget." They meant that the brain is like a machine that gets in the groove of connecting its data in certain ways (obsessing or defending or retaining), and that those thinking pathways might not be the most useful for us. But, when we sleep, the brain fires much more randomly. And it is this random scouring for new connections that allows us to loosen certain pathways and create new, potentially useful, ones. Dreaming is a shuffling of old connections that allows us to keep the important connections and erase the inefficient links. A good analogy here is the defragmentation of a computer's hard drive: Dreams are a reordering of connections to streamline the system.

Theory #4

Dreams Are Like Psychotherapy

But what about the emotion in dreams? Aren't dreams principally the place to confront difficult and surprising emotions, and sit with those emotions in a new way? Ernest Hartmann, a doctor at Tufts, focuses on the emotional learning that happens in dreams. He has developed the theory that dreaming puts our difficult emotions into pictures. In dreams, we deal with emotional content in a safe place, making connections that we would not make if left to our more critical or defensive brains. In this sense, dreaming is like therapy on the couch: We think through emotional stuff in a less rational and defensive frame of mind. Through that process, we come to accept truths we might otherwise repress. Dreams are our nightly psychotherapy.

Theory #5

The Absence of Theory

Of course, others argue that dreams have no meaning at all—that they are the random firings of a brain that doesn't happen to be conscious at that time. The mind is still "functioning" insofar as it's producing images, but there's no conscious sense behind the film. Perhaps it's only consciousness itself that wants to see some deep meaning in our brains at all times.

What do you think? We are all authors, in a way, every night. Is there a mind behind what's written in your dreams? Why are your dreams of use?

All in a Night's Sleep

07 July 1990 by Mary Gribbin

For an activity that is so essential to our wellbeing, and that takes up so much of our daily lives, sleep remains something of an enigma

Most People spend a third of their lives asleep. But why? Is it so that our body can repair itself? Is it part of a process in which our brain assimilates the information it has gathered during the day? Or is sleep a mechanism that has evolved to keep us out of harm's way during the hours when we do not need to be out hunting for food, or reproducing? No one knows for sure, though each hypothesis has its supporters.

Scientists are not even certain about the amount of sleep that humans need. Left undisturbed, most people spend around eight hours asleep each night. Some individuals, however, manage with much less—Margaret Thatcher, for one, seems to need little more than four hours sleep a night.

It is easier to say what sleep is than why we sleep. During sleep, our blood pressure falls, the pulse rate drops, respiration slows, body temperature falls, blood vessels in the skin become wider, our gastrointestinal tract sometimes becomes more active, most of our muscles relax, and in general our metabolic rate falls by about 20 percent.

The organ that shows the clearest distinction between the states of sleeping and waking, however, is the brain. As the individual falls asleep, the brain becomes progressively passive, responding less and less to the outside world. Scientists who study sleep, therefore, tend to focus their researches on the brain.

Even in the 19th century, people appreciated the importance of the brain in sleep. Then, rival theories held that tiredness was caused either by a build up of blood "congealing" in the brain during the day, or by blood draining away from the brain and causing "cerebral anaemia", which only sleep could cure.

In the early 20th century, researchers began to suggest that sleep is caused by natural chemicals—sleep substances—that accumulate in the brain. And by the 1930s, scientists were measuring changes in the electrical output of the brain. Their records showed that while the activity of the sleeping brain differs from that of the waking brain, it does not "switch off" during sleep.

Physiologists first measured the brain's electrical activity in 1928. The brain contains billions of individual cells, called neurons (see Inside Science No 19). Neurons communicate with each other using both chemical and electrical signals or "messages". An individual neuron can be excited by chemical messages from its neighbours to produce charged particles (ions) which travel down a nerve fibre, called an axon, to another cell. The pulse of electricity in turn can cause chemicals to be released which trigger a further electrical pulse, and so on.

By attaching electrodes to the scalp of volunteers, physiologists were able to record brain waves, as the electrical activity is known. Over a period of 30 years, the changing pattern of electrical activity during sleep gradually became clear. But scientists have taken much longer to begin to understand the chemical changes involved—their knowledge of these is still incomplete.

BRAIN WAVES

Measuring Sleep

Researchers find that sleep involves five distinct patterns—four stages of successively deeper sleep known as non-rapid eye movement sleep (or NREM sleep), and a fifth stage known as rapid eye movement, or REM, sleep.

During NREM sleep, the brain waves tend to become slow and more regular, and the sleeper lies fairly still and breathes slowly and regularly. Any snoring that takes place will be during NREM sleep. The four levels of NREM sleep are known as stages 1, 2, 3 and 4. It is in stage 4, the deepest level of sleep, that the electrical activity is slowest.

REM sleep is a much lighter sleep. Its distinguishing feature is that the eyes intermittently dart about under closed eyelids; hence the term "rapid eye movement". At the onset of REM sleep, any snoring ceases, breathing becomes irregular, and both the flow of cerebral blood and brain temperature increase. There are also more body movements. The electrical activity of the brain is similar to that in stage 1 sleep.

The sleeper will progress through these five stages in cycles, each cycle lasting about 90 minutes. After falling asleep, a healthy adult will slip into stage 1 sleep, which gives way to 2, to 3 to 4; then the sequence goes into reverse. After the second period of stage 1 sleep, the cycle is completed by between 5 and 15 minutes of REM sleep. The sequence is repeated four or five times, with the portion of REM sleep increasing in each cycle while the NREM portion (especially stages 3 and 4) decreases. A person sleeping for around 8 hours will spend about two hours in REM sleep, and the remainder in NREM sleep.

This pattern of NREM and REM sleep, especially the 90 minute cycle, is remarkably similar from one human to another. Researchers can sometimes gain new insights into sleep problems, and also into the importance of sleep in the development of the brain, from deviations in this pattern.

For example, people with a condition called narcolepsy suffer an uncontrollable urge to fall asleep. No matter where they are or what they are doing, sleepiness will suddenly overtake them. Researchers have recorded the brain activity of sleeping narcoleptics. They found that narcoleptics do not start their night with NREM sleep, but instead go straight into REM sleep.

Young mammals experience a much greater proportion of REM sleep than normal adults. A newborn baby who sleeps around 16 hours a day will spend at least half of that in REM sleep. With premature babies, the percentage of REM sleep is even higher—around 75 percent. A newborn kitten, puppy, rat or hamster experiences only REM sleep. A newborn guinea pig, however, has very little REM sleep.

Some researchers believe that REM sleep is essential for the human brain to mature before and after birth, and that this explains why babies need so much sleep. The small amount of time that the newborn guinea pig spends in REM sleep supports this hypothesis: compared with a helpless kitten or puppy, a guinea pig is "mature" at birth.

HOW MUCH SLEEP?
Cradle to Grave

A team of American physiologists studying sleep patterns found that newborn babies sleep on average 16 hours in every 24. The sleep requirement, however, can be much less. The researchers carried out a detailed study of intellectual development in many babies, including those that stay awake for considerably more than the average 8 hours. They concluded that, provided the babies could sleep as and when they wanted, and for as long as they wanted, the amount of sleep taken during every 24 hour period has no affect on their subsequent development.

The same team found that 16-year-old students liked to sleep between 10 and 11 hours a night; older college students slept on average 8 hours a night. Some of the older students were able to adapt their sleep patterns to the demands of what they had to do the next day.

The need for sleep continues to decline as people age, to about seven hours a night on average for 45–60 year olds, and even less in old age. In particular, stage 4 sleep almost disappears after the age of about 50.

Scientists have never come across a person who can go without sleep. A few individuals, usually in the interests of raising money for charity or seeing their name in The Guinness Book of Records, have attempted to stay awake for as long as possible. The current record holder is Robert McDonald, of

California. In 1988 he held out for 18 days 21 hours 40 minutes during a rocking chair marathon.

Apart from the sheer difficult of staying awake, such record-breakers report side effects such as bizarre hallucinations, paranoia, irritability, blurred vision, slurring of speech, and lapses in concentration and memory. The symptoms disappear after a few nights of normal sleep.

Without close medical supervision, however, it is impossible to tell if those taking part in "wakeathons" are really awake all the time. Not many people realize that humans can not only take cat naps when their eyes are open, but may not even realize that they are doing so.

In the laboratory, researchers have regularly deprived volunteers of sleep for periods of about three or four days. Apart from sleepiness, the main problem is loss of concentration. The volunteers pass any test with flying colours, provided the tasks are very short and interesting. When asked to do long, repetitive tasks—equivalent to monitoring a production line in a factory or driving on a motorway—the sleepy volunteers make lots of mistakes.

People suffering from insomnia have trouble falling asleep and staying asleep throughout the night. The problem is real enough, but it may seem worse; time appears to pass very slowly when you lie awake at night, and insomniacs often think that they have been awake far longer than they really have. Scientists at Stanford University monitored the sleep patterns of some people who complained of very bad insomnia. Only about half of the insomniacs remained awake for more than 30 minutes in the course of the night.

BODY CHEMISTRY

Sleep Substances

It may be that some sleep problems are related to the production—or nonproduction—of sleep substances by the body. Recent research suggests that such chemicals modify and regulate sleep, rather than being its prime cause.

Scientists at Harvard Medical School isolated one substance from human urine in the early 1980s; they called it Factor S. From 3000 litres of urine they extracted just 7 millionths of a gram of Factor S, but this was enough to make 500 doses. When the Harvard scientists gave a dose of Factor S to a rabbit it spent up to six hours in the deeper, NREM stages of sleep—much longer than it normally would.

Factor S is now known to be a muramyl peptide, the remains of bacteria after they have been digested and destroyed by the body's immune system. The brain seems to incorporate this substance into its own biochemistry. Scientists have synthesized a similar chemical, muramyl dipeptide (MDP) and found that this also increases NREM sleep in rats, cats and monkeys, as well as rabbits. No human has yet volunteered to try it.

Another substance discovered within a mammalian brain is "delta sleep-inducing peptide", better known as DSIP. It is found in the blood of sleeping rabbits, and given to other animals it rapidly induces NREM sleep, as well as increasing the amount of REM sleep. Scientists have tested a synthetic form of DSIP on human volunteers, but the effect on them was much less noticeable than in animals. This is probably because the synthetic version is not exactly equivalent to the natural product.

Our bodies produce other chemicals during sleep. In both children and adults, the output of human growth hormone surges during the first 3 hours of sleep. Nobody knows why this occurs, and it does not mean that people grow while they are asleep. Human growth hormone has several roles in the body, including speeding the rate of protein synthesis. However, stimulating cells to grow, which involves protein synthesis, requires a good supply of insulin to be present; and there is no surge of insulin in the early hours of sleep.

MIND GAMES

Why Do We Dream?

When people are woken during REM sleep they often ay that they were dreaming, and have a clear memory of that dream. Sleep research has shown that everyone dreams, even though some people do not remember doing so. But what are dreams?

Clearly, dreaming involves electrical activity in the brain, and so does conscious thought. But is this just the untended machinery of thought ticking over while the owner is effectively not in control? Or is it an automatic process that occurs while nerve connections in the brain are being maintained biochemically, or while the flood of information from the previous day's experiences is being collated, sorted and filed away for use? Nobody knows. But we do know that dreams are not just a filing process, nor are they simply random messages firing off among the brain's neurons.

Dreams can be influenced by things that happen to the sleeper. For example, researchers sprayed a little cold water on to the back of one volunteer while he was in REM sleep and then woke him shortly after. The subject described a dream in which he was acting in a play. He reported that in his dream:

"I was walking behind the leading lady when she suddenly collapsed and water was dripping on her. I ran over to her and water was dripping on my back and head. The roof was leaking."

Problems and ideas as well as physical stimuli can become incorporated in dreams. In one classic experiment a researcher set 500 students a problem: "The letters O,T,T,F,F form the beginning of an infinite sequence. Find a simple rule for determining any or all successive letters. According to your rule what would be the next two letters of the sequence?"

Next day, only nine students had worked out the correct solution. Two had found the answer before they went to sleep; the remaining seven solved the problem in a dream. (The solution, by the way, is that O,T,T,F,F are the first letters of one, two, three, four, five. The next two letters in the sequence would be S,S.)

NATURE'S CINEMA
A Need for Dreams

Amid all the uncertainties of research on sleep—and they are many—one possibility is that REM sleep is what we "need" sleep for, and that NREM sleep is far less important for our wellbeing. Experiments suggest that our brains require a minimum "ration" of fantasy dreams each day. For example, in one study researchers deprived volunteers of REM sleep in the first half of the night. This affected people in very different ways.

Some subjects experienced an increase in REM sleep during the second half of the night. These were people who did not normally fantasise, or daydream, during their waking hours. After several nights deprived of half their REM sleep, they found themselves fantasising, seemingly to make up for the lost REM sleep. Subjects who ordinarily experienced a lot of waking fantasy continued to have their normal quota of REM sleep in the second half of the night, and said they did not notice any change in their daytime fantasising.

It seems that REM sleep, at least, serves a function in keeping us sane, although it is still not clear exactly how dreams serve that purpose. But REM sleep is only a quarter of the total, in adults. Why do we have so much NREM sleep? This is even less clear, and some researchers argue that such sleep may have evolved simply as a handy way to keep our bodies out of mischief in between meals.

This argument gains weight from the observation that prey animals, such as zebra, sleep much less than predators, such as lions. After eating its fill of meat, a lion may sleep for two or three days, more or less continuously. After all, why should the lion waste energy wandering about, or killing things, when its body has absorbed enough food to last for several days?

And maybe that is the answer to the ability some people have to sleep much less than others without suffering harmful effects. As long as they are getting their quota of REM sleep, and a reasonable amount of physical rest during the day, there really may be no reason why they should spend up to a third of their lives in bed.

A Measure of Sleep

Researchers studying sleeping and dreaming monitor and record the electrical activity of a person's brain. They tape or glue one electrode to the scalp and another to the ear. Wires take the signal to a machine called an electroencephalograph, or EEG, which contains an amplifier to boost the signals (only a few millionths of a volt). The EEG also includes pens that move automatically across chart paper in response to the changes in the potential differences created by the electrical activity of the brain. The trace of the brain activity is called an electroencephalogram (also shortened to EEG).

The EEG of REM sleep, though, may look like that of stage 1 sleep. To distinguish between the two, researchers attach electrodes to the face that will pick up the rapid eye movements that are characteristic of this phase of sleep. Because the eye movements are intermittent—researchers also record impulses from the chin muscles. Muscles are extremely relaxed during REM sleep. Physiologists call the trace of eye movements an electrooculogram, or EOG; and that of muscle activity an electromyogram, or EMG.

The traces below show the changes in EEG through the stages of sleep into waking. Stage 2 sleep is deeper than stage 1, and so on. As the sleep deepens, the brain waves become slower and of greater amplitude. The REM stage of sleep is the lightest, but REM and dreaming do not occur at the beginning of the night's sleep. The first period of REM normally begins about 60–70 minutes after the onset of sleep. Overall, REM sleep makes up about 25 percent of the total.

Stage 1 accounts for about 5 percent of sleep, and is really a transition phase from wakefulness to true sleep (stage 2 or deeper). The bulk of sleep, almost 50 percent, is made up of stage 2 sleep. Stage 3 takes up about 7 percent of the night, and mainly acts as a transition between stages 2 and 4 sleep.

The first period of stage 4 sleep is the deepest, and it is very difficult to rouse people from this phase of sleep. If they are awakened, they are likely to feel groggy and be incapable of coherent thought for 10 or 15 minutes. Stage 4 accounts for up to 13 percent of sleep in young adults, but is almost totally absent in that of the elderly. As the night progresses, the depth of the periods of NREM sleep becomes less pronounced, and in the last couple of cycles there may be no stage 3 or stage 4 sleep.

Down to Rhythms

Our bodies are paced by a circadian rhythm that seems to be kept in time by the light and dark cycle. The natural circadian rhythm, however, is longer than 24 hours. When volunteers agreed to live underground for a month with only artificial light available and no external cues, such as clock, radios or television, they developed a circadian rhythm of about 25 hours. The experiment implies that it is external things such as light and the pressures of society that push people into a 24-hour rhythm.

This discovery has helped one group of patients suffering from sleeping difficulties. In "delayed sleep phase syndrome", people have trouble going to sleep in the early part of the night. Only shortly before it is time to wake up do they fall into a sound sleep. Doctors reasoned that, because the natural body clock is set at around 25, not 24 hours, it is easier to go to sleep later than earlier. They therefore advised the patients to go to bed three hours later each day, starting with a bed time of 5 am on the first night. After six days, the patients were going to sleep at 11 pm, and their body clock was reset to the right time. Many were cured permanently of the syndrome.

When people move across time zones, during jet travel, they disrupt their normal circadian rhythms and develop jet lag. The body clock cannot reset enough in one jump to match the time zone it is now in, and needs about five days to get back to normal.

Jet lag is worst when traveling east because you experience sunset much earlier than your body expects, and are trying to persuade your body clock that it is time to go to sleep earlier than usual. Flying west involves trying to sleep later than normal, which is easier. If you have to take a long flight eastbound the best way to minimize jet lag is to get up earlier and earlier on the few days before you fly.

FURTHER READING

The most "user friendly" guide to sleeping and dreaming is Sleep, by J. Allan Hobson (Scientific American Library). An older, but still good, book by Ian Oswald is also called Sleep, and is available in Penguin. At a slightly more technical level, Some Must Watch While Some Must Sleep, by William Dement (W. H. Freeman) is especially good on dreams and on sleep disorders. Ray Meddis presents his views in The Sleep Instinct (Routledge & Kegan Paul). Why we Sleep, by James Horne (Oxford University Press) is strong on biochemistry and "sleep substances".

Dreams: Their Function in Health and Illness

Despite centuries of published theory and research, general agreement on the nature and function of dreaming continues to elude the scientific community. As theory and evidence accumulate and collide, the recounting and analysis of dreams continue as powerful clinical tools for healing self and patients. The article reviews major theories of dreaming, including a description of the basic structure of dreams and mental processes in dream formation; explores the usefulness of dreams in promoting health and dealing with illness through the analyses of three dreams; and identifies basic principles of dream exploration for use in clinical nursing practice.

Key words: *dream theory, dream work, dreams and health, dreams and illness, self-development, self-exploration*

Gloria F. Donnelly, PhD, RN, FAAN
Professor and Dean
School of Nursing
La Salle University
Philadelphia, Pennsylvania

Concetta DeLuca McPeak, MSN, RN
Private Practitioner
Elkins Park, Pennsylvania

Holist Nurs Pract 1996; 10(4):61–68
© 1996 Aspen Publishers, Inc.

THEORIES OF DREAMING

Dreams fascinated Aristotle,[1] who believed that they arose from the sensus communis ("inner sense" or "sixth sense") located in the heart, the seat of intelligence and feeling. Plato[2] made reference to what is now called lucid dreaming, awareness in the dream that one is dreaming. Hippocrates[3] believed in the diagnostic power of dreams to reveal bodily processes too subtle to be perceived during the awake state.

Ellenberger,[4] a historian of the unconscious, illustrated the influence of Romantic philosophy in the late 1700s through the 1800s on the evolution of dream theory. In 1814, von Schubert[5] declared dreams to be the "picture language" of sleep; that is, images produced in dreams are the counterpart of verbal language in the waking state. He elaborated further that this picture language is "hieroglyphic," in that it incorporates many concepts or images into a single symbol or icon. von Schubert also believed in the universal language of dream symbols; that is, dreams transcend culture and time.

After von Schubert, Scherner,[6] Maury,[7] and St Denis,[8] whose works were published in the 1860s, served as precursors to Freud, Jung, and modern theorists and researchers of dreaming. Ellenberger[4] characterized Scherner as the first phenomenologist of dreaming. Scherner identified stages of the dream experience and developed the idea that in dreams there is a language of symbols subject to interpretation and that a system for such interpretation could be devised. He particularly focused on dream symbols that had their roots in bodily sensations. Like Hippocrates, he believed in the relationship between dream symbols and physical illnesses or conditions experienced by the dreamer. For example, the house and its parts, in Scherner's symbol system, represent the human body and a basic dream symbol, dreams about flying are related to an increased functioning of the lungs, and dreams of heavy traffic through streets sometimes represent heart or circulatory conditions.[4] Scherner's symbols of the sex organs (eg, towers, pipes, and pointed weapons as male symbols and narrow courtyards and staircases as female symbols) influence Freud's later explanation of sexual symbols in dreams.

Maury,[7] a contemporary of Scherner, worked with his own dreams in the development of his theory. Upon awakening from a dream, he would immediately write down all the details of the dream itself and any other conditions that might have influenced his sleep (eg, changes in diet, position, or weather). Scherner believed in the primacy of bodily excitations as dream triggers. Maury recognized the importance of bodily excitation in dream production but also discovered the importance of long-forgotten memories in stimulating dreams. Ellenberger[4] credits Maury's theories of dream triggers for prompting research into the experimental stimulation of dreams.

St Denis[5] devised a stage-oriented method of self-training for mastery of one's dreams, that is, to become aware of dreaming during the dream itself, to control points of awakening, and to direct the content of the dream. This method is today called lucid dreaming and is used for developing self-understanding and creativity.[9-11] St Denis confirmed the role of repressed memory in dream activity and also emphasized the role of perception in dream production. He defined the dream processes of abstraction and superimposition, in which a quality from one object is abstracted and comes to stand for or is attributed to another (eg, a house stands for the human body).

FREUD'S THEORY OF DREAMS AND DREAMING

In Freud's[12] scheme, the dream processes described by his predecessors were further defined and developed into a comprehensive theory. Freud advanced three general areas for understanding dreams: the structural components of the dream, dream formation (ie, the mental mechanisms by which dreams are formed), and the process of dreaming by which structure and dream formation disguise and transform meaning for the purpose of protecting sleep.

STRUCTURE OF THE DREAM

According to Freud,[12] a dream is composed of two parts: the manifest dream (dream content) and the latent dream (dream thoughts).

> *The latent dream content (dream thoughts) is unconscious and includes the meanings, impulses, actions, wishes, and conflicts of the dreamer that are disguised as symbols.*

The manifest dream is the narrative that the dreamer remembers, reconstructs, and reports. The dream often appears meaningless or even nonsensical to the dreamer, like a puzzle needing to be unraveled. Dreams include symbols packed with meaning that give disguised expression to unconscious conflict, symptoms, styles of thinking, and ways of feeling. They are often induced by daytime residues, experiences during the waking state that act as triggers to the dream. Contemporary information processing theories advance the notion that dreams exemplify the manner in which individuals process and encode information.[13] The manner of report made by the dreamer is also an important component of the dream. The manifest dream comprises the individual's language, sequence, and emphasis in describing the dream content; attention; interest in the recall; and affect during recounting. For example, one dreamer may remember and recount the visual content of the dream in great detail with little attention to feelings experienced. Another may remember and recount powerful affects experienced in the dream but only sketchy visual detail.

The latent dream content (dream thoughts) is unconscious and includes the meanings, impulses, actions, wishes, and conflicts of the dreamer that are disguised as symbols. Freud's[12] technique of free association, in which individuals let their minds wander over the reported content of the dream, is intended to uncover personal meanings by "unpacking" the dream symbols.

Free association "breaks the dream into parts and follows each line of association separately into latent thoughts and memories that inevitably bear internal connections quite different from the connections in the original dream plot."[14(p7)]

DREAM FORMATION

Freud[12] believed that dreams form through two primary mental processes: condensation and displacement. Condensation is the mental process by which rich meaning and memory are packed into relatively few and often loosely connected dream symbols and images. "If a dream is written out it may fill half a page. The analysis setting out the dream thoughts [latent content] underlying it may occupy six, eight or a dozen times as much space."[12(p313)] The companion process to condensation is displacement. In this process, the mind censors underling issues and translates or distorts them into what is remembered as the manifest dream. "The consequence of the displacement is that the dream-content no longer resembles the core of the dream thoughts and that the dream gives no more than a distortion of the dream-wish that exists in the unconscious."[12(p343)] Freud believed that the processes of condensation and displacement are so powerful that most dreams can never be fully interpreted. Deeper meanings can always be discovered.

DREAMS AND SLEEP

Freud[12] asserted that dreams are the guardian of sleep. Condensation and displacement so disguise meaning that sleep is protected; in the process, so is the self. Contemporary research into rapid eye movement (REM) sleep states is partially confirmatory of the dream as a protector of sleep. Hunt[14] describes REM sleep as compensatory for and protective of lengthy deep sleep periods that large-brained organisms (humans) appear to need. Without the oscillation between cortical arousal in the REM state and the inhibition of deep sleep states, restitution during sleep would be compromised. Thus the dream, produced in the REM state, participates in the restorative function of sleep, except in the case of nightmares and drug-induced dreams.

UTILITY OF DREAMS

HEALTH AND SELF-DEVELOPMENT

Dreams have a long history as tools for self-development. Dreams can be the route to deeper levels of self-understanding,[15] to individuation,[16] to spiritual awareness,[17] and to working effectively in therapeutic relationships.[18] The dream presented below was reported by a middle-age professional woman after approximately 1 year of psychotherapy. This woman, who had successfully juggled family life and a complex, demanding career for 30 years, entered psychotherapy to explore some new directions in her life. It was characteristic of this woman to report intricate visual detail in the dream and to act primarily as observer and evaluator in the dream. There is a pattern of predominance of observational over affective function in the experiencing and reporting of her dream.

I am standing in the living room of my *house* looking at the surroundings. I walk into the adjacent *room* and notice a *door* that I had not seen before. I open the door, walk down three steps, and find myself in a rather large foyer that has doorways at either end. I turn to the left and find the entrance to a *huge ballroom* with a 20-foot ceiling, at least, and a balcony on three sides. The room is made of *rich woods*. As I look up, I notice that the *wooden* molding around the bottom of the balcony is made up of *ornately carved roses and leaves*. I study all the beautifully intricate detail in the carving. On the floor there is a magnificent, huge, oriental aubousson *carpet, also with roses, yellow and red*. There is no one in the ballroom, nor is there furniture or music. I stand in the doorway for some time looking into the room, but *I do not enter*. Instead, I turn back into the foyer and find *four tall men dressed in tuxedos* standing there. They point to the doorway at the other end of the foyer.

I walk *up* two or three steps and find myself in a *narrow hall* with *smaller doorways* to the left and to the right. I remain in the hallway and look into each room. They are beautifully appointed rooms furnished with *antiques*. One has a *gilded mirror* on the wall. I stand in the hallway and look at the rooms, but not with the same intensity with which I examined the ballroom. I turn back to the foyer, and the dream ends.

The italicized words in the dream are those symbols that were deemed important to the dreamer through guided exploration with the therapist. The symbols in a manifest dream are similar to icons on a computer screen. Each icon represents a complex set of functions embedded in the computer's operations. One need only click on the icon to get at what underlies it. The meanings of the symbols in a dream are discerned by the dreamer with the guidance of the therapist through questioning and exploring feelings and memories, both recent and remote, evoked by the symbols.

In a series of therapist-guided explorations, this dreamer discovered the following meanings in her dream. The house had been a recurrent image in her dreams. It clearly represents the self, parts of the self, and aspects of the self. The first sentence of the dream report suggests the action of self-exploration that the woman was consciously pursuing through therapy. The door is a symbol of both the opportunities and the risks inherent in self-exploration. Behind and through every door are symbols of the past, issues of the present, and possibilities for the future.

The huge ballroom is a complex representation of those parts of the self involving passion, pleasure, and affective expression. The fact that the ballroom is only partially furnished and without music indicates that the woman may need to find more time for pleasure and artistic self-expression. The detailed carvings and the rich, colorful carpet suggest what have previously been hidden resources in this aspect of herself. The balcony offers the woman a safe vantage point or a haven from which to observe developments in the event that she decides to enter this aspect of herself. Safety and caution are important to the woman in this new undertaking, as represented by the ballroom's location to the left. The left directional symbol had appeared in previous dreams and had come to represent evil or fear.

The four tall men are representations of the variety of transference relationships simultaneously occurring with the therapist (eg, therapist as father, husband, professional, etc). Their action of pointing to the unexplored rooms is symbolic of the unobtrusive guidance that the woman is able to tolerate. The formality of their dress is indicative of the formal and professional nature of the therapeutic relationship and the authority of the therapist. Conflict inherent in relating to male authority figures also had been a recurrent theme in this woman's dreams. Ongoing exploration of this symbol, its memories, and its meanings eventually resulted in the dreamer's improved functioning, particularly in committee work.

The symbolism in the last paragraph of the dream report, specifically the shrinking passageways and antique furnishings, may refer to the perimenopausal stage of life that the woman was currently experiencing. The gilded mirror is yet another symbol of the opportunity for further self-exploration.

The above analyses barely touch on the richness of this dream as a tool for continuing self-exploration, self-understanding, and self-development for this woman.

EXPLORING ILLNESS ISSUES

The relationship between illness experience and dream content is well documented. Drawing on Hippocrates' and Scherner's views that dreams are medically prognostic, Smith[19] reported that dreams of separation in women and of death in men were most prevalent in subjects who did not recover from their illnesses. The exploration of dreams experienced during illness can help an individual reconnect and deal with affect and conflict surrounding the illness.[20]

The following is a dream of a middle-age woman in her seventh year of psychotherapy, which began shortly after surgery for breast cancer. Because the disease had metastasized to several places in her bones, her physician had recommended that once again she have a course of radiation therapy followed by chemotherapy. During the stressful period in which she was exploring her options, she reported this dream:

It was *nighttime.* I was standing on the steps of a *dark, deserted building* in a deserted area of the city. Only my sisters Mary and Kate were present. They were attempting to attend to my needs in a somewhat stifling fashion. I needed to get away from Mary, because she insisted on doing everything for Kate and me because she persisted in telling me how to take care of myself. Kate thought she knew better than me how to do this. Slowly I lifted myself off the ground and, using what felt like a *fishlike motion,* I began to *fly.* I felt *power* in this action. However, as I began to elevate farther, I saw above me 10 or so *telephone wires* arranged in such a way that to attempt to rise above them might be fatal. I spent time in the space between the ground and the wires trying to figure out how to safely get above them. I lowered myself almost to the ground. Just before my feet would touch down, I rose myself close to the wires. I searched for that safe space for some time until the dream ended.

The darkness of this dream and its nighttime occurrence, as well as the dreamer's depressed affect while reporting the dream, represent the fear that the dreamer was experiencing in dealing with what could be a terminal illness. The presence of the stifling sisters and the dreamer's flight from them represent the oscillation of feelings of dependence and rebellion that this woman had experienced throughout the history of her illness. The dreamer evolves from a fishlike to a birdlike creature in flight attempting to maneuver through the current crisis. She interpreted this evolution as her movement out of the regressed state into which she was propelled each time a new medical crisis occurred. The telephone wires represent the impending radiation treatments that could be both helpful and harmful.

The final part of the dream is representative of those activities in which the dreamer engaged during subsequent weeks while she was searching for a course of treatment that was acceptable to her. Despite the fact that the dreamer was fearful and searching, a strong theme of resilience, determination, and self-control manifests in the dream and was emblematic of the way in which she was dealing with both the illness and the treatment options. Exploring the dream gave the dreamer a clearer sense of the strength of her own personal resources.

After reporting this dream, the patient spent 5 intense weeks gathering information from traditional and alternative health care sources to decide on a treatment approach. She told the following dream to her therapist shortly after she decided to have the radiation and chemotherapy that had been recommended:

It was *bright daytime,* and I was walking on what appeared to be a large deep lake or the ocean. I was able to do this because under each foot, in ski-like fashion, was a *piece of ice* about 6 by 20 inches and about as thick as a piece of heavy window glass. There were *many people* about but none of them interacted with me, nor did they seem to be in danger. As I walked along, I was concerned about what would happen to me if and when these pieces of *ice melted.* The dream ended.

In contrast to the previous dream, this dream occurs in bright daytime. The patient described the early morning as her time to "get things done." The ocean is simultaneously a source of and a threat to life, like the contemplated treatment. Ski-like pieces of ice attached to each foot safely support the woman on the water and allow her to move forward smoothly. Nevertheless, they have the potential to melt and expose her to the dangers of the deep. In contrast to the former dream's intrusive sisters, the presence of the many people who were not in danger is indicative of life going on.

In exploring the progressive themes of these two dreams, the dreamer developed a keener awareness of the challenges presented by this chronic illness and her ability to exercise control over treatments and decisions. For the dreamer, this was a self-validating process.

DREAM EXPLORATION IN CLINICAL PRACTICE

It is natural for patients both at home and in clinical settings to tell their dreams to nurses, particularly in the context of sleep assessment. Responding to and assisting patients in discussing their dreams can be a powerful tool for nurses to get patients to talk about their concerns. Discussing dreams within the context of sleep assessment should not be construed as formal psychotherapy, although such discussions may have great therapeutic value to the patient. Dream work within the context of formal psychotherapy requires specific knowledge and training.

The following guidelines and strategies are useful in discussing dreams with patients and in exploring dreams for self-growth:

- Allow the person to tell the dream as fully as possible without interruption, taking note of what is emphasized by either depth of description or affect.
- Encourage further description of dream symbols for greater clarity (eg, "What was this body of water like? Describe the pieces of ice.").
- Encourage the person to connect dream images to other thoughts that come to mind as he or she is discussing the dream.
- Inquire about feelings experienced during the course of the dream around specific symbols (eg, "What feelings did you experience as you walked on the water with this ice underfoot?").
- Allow the person to make his or her own interpretations even if the meaning of the dream images and symbols appear to be obvious. Remember, the dream belongs to the dreamer. The clinician can only be a guide to the dreamer in his or her search for meaning and self-awareness. The clinician needs to restrain the urge to offer premature and continuing interpretative guesses. The dreamer should be guided to finding his or her own meaning at his or her own pace.
- Assist the person in sensing the trend of the dream and what in the person's life it seeks to change or infuse with new meaning (eg, "Where is this dream taking you? How have you changed in this dream?").
- Validate the richness of the dream for the dreamer (eg, "This is a powerful dream!")

- Encourage the person to write dreams down upon awakening. It is useful to keep a pencil and pad at the bedside for such activity. The construction of the narrative of the dream can be as revealing a process as the dream itself.
- Some books offer fixed meanings for specific dream symbols. The value of these is questionable, and they should be used only as general guides and not permitted to limit the person's search for personal meaning.
- Certain types of dreaming are known side effects of several groups of drug. For example, ophthalmic drugs and naproxen can induce nightmares.[21,22] Fluoxetine can alter the character of dreaming.[23] β Blockers can produce unusually vivid and active dreams.[24] Reports of dreams that are unusual to the dreamer should prompt a medication review.
- The content of disturbing dreams may signal the need for more in-depth exploration over a longer period of time with a psychotherapist. Premature referrals should not be made, however. Instead, the nurse can act as a guide to options available to the patient for self-exploration and healing.

There is a dearth of research-based nursing literature on the significance and utility of dreams in clinical situations. Despite controversy over their nature and function, dreams can be a powerful tool for helping individuals gain insight into psychologic perspectives, patterns of living, and impediments to effective coping and fuller living.

REFERENCES

1. Aristotle; Hett WS, trans. *On the Soul, Parva Naturalia, On Breath,* Cambridge, Mass: Harvard University Press; 1936.
2. Plato; Shorey P, trans. *The Collected Dialogues of Plato.* Princeton, NJ: Bollinger; 1961.
3. Hippocrates; Jones WHS, trans. *Regimen,* Cambridge, Mass: Harvard University Press; 1931.
4. Ellenberger HF. *The Discovery of the Unconscious.* New York, NY: Basic Books; 1970.
5. von Schubert GH. *Symbols of Dreams.* Leipzig, Germany: Wiegel; 1808.
6. Scherner KA. *The Life of the Dream.* Berlin, Germany; Schindler; 1986.
7. Maury A. *Sleep and Dreams,* Paris, France: Didier; 1861.
8. St Denis MH, *Dreams and the Means to Direct Them,* Paris, France: Amyot; 1867.
9. Green CE. *Lucid Dreaming: The Paradox of Consciousness during Sleep.* London, England: Routledge; 1994.
10. Gackenbach J. Frameworks for understanding lucid dreaming. A review. *Dreaming.* 1991; 1:109–128.

11. La Berge S. *Exploring the World of Lucid Dreaming.* New York, NY: Ballentine; 1991.
12. Freud S. *The Interpretation of Dreams.* New York, NY: Avon; 1965.
13. Erdelyi H. *Psychoanalysis: Freud's Cognitive Psychology,* New York, NY: Freeman; 1985.
14. Hunt H. *Multiplicity of Dreams: Memory, Imagination and Consciousness.* New Haven, Conn: Yale University Press; 1989.
15. Langs RL, *The Dream Workbook,* New York, NY: Alliance; 1994.
16. Jung CG, *Memories, Dreams, Reflections.* New York, NY: Vintage; 1961.
17. Dombeck MB, Dream telling: A means of spiritual awareness. *Holist Nurs Pract.* 1995; 9:37–47.
18. Lynch VG, Working with dreams: A collaboration between therapist and patient. *Perspect Psychiatr Care.* 1983; 21:21–25.
19. Smith RC. Evaluating dream function: Emphasizing the study of patients with organic disease. *J Mind Behav.* 1986; 7:397–410.
20. Levitan H. The dream in psychosomatic states. In: Natterson JM, ed. *The Dream in Clinical Practice.* New York, NY: Aronson; 1980.
21. *Nurses Drug Alert.* 1992; 16:89.
22. *Nurses Drug Alert.* 1992; 16:25.
23. *Nurses Drug Alert.* 1992; 16:6.
24. Dennis KE, Froman D, Morrison AS, Holmes KD, Howes DG. β-Blocker therapy; Identification and management of side effects, *Heart Lung.* 1991; 20(5 part 1):459–463.

CLINICAL REVIEW

Sleep, dreaming, and mental health: A review of historical and neurobiological perspectives

Laura Palagini,[a] * *Nicholas Rosenlicht*[b]

[a] Department of Psychiatry, University of Pisa, Pisa, Italy
[b] Department of Psychiatry, School of Medicine, University of California, San Francisco, CA, USA

ARTICLE INFO

Article history:
Received 26 February 2010
Received in revised form 14 July 2010
Accepted 14 July 2010
Available online 19 September 2010

Keywords:
Sleep disorders
Dreams
Depression
Psychiatric disorders

SUMMARY

Theories as to the function of sleep and dreaming and their relationship to emotions have been studied since the beginning of recorded history. Earliest historical records show the predominant view to be that dreams were considered divine in origin and only later did dream theory become linked with the functioning of the brain, perhaps most famously in psychoanalytic theory. The development of sleep laboratory techniques ushered in a new era of the dream study and their relationship to mental health. In this review we outline the history of theories about the genesis and function of dreams and sleep and their relationship to mental illness from ancient mythic and religious views to the first tentative scientific approaches to the ascendency of psychoanalysis and ultimately to the modern era of neuroscience.

INTRODUCTION

Sleep and dreaming have always aroused our curiosity and theories as to their cause and function have been described since the beginning of recorded history.[1-4] This fascination is widely evidenced in the arts and literature.[5,6] In earliest times artists, philosophers, poets, as well as clerics, considered dreams to be divine manifestations.[1,4,7-9] They have also been an important topic of inquiry throughout the history of philosophy.[10] At the end of 19th century the interpretation of dream content and its relationship with human emotions became the focus of psychoanalytic theory.[11,12] In the early decades of this psychoanalytic era dreaming was regarded as the meaningful reflection of unconscious mental functioning. In the 1950s dream research had a central role in the fields of psychiatry and psychology.[13] The development of sleep laboratory techniques ushered in a new era of sleep/dream study and their relation to mental health. The discovery of REM (rapid eye movement) sleep and other advances in sleep research caused a shift in focus. After a half century as the dominant paradigm of dream analysis, psychology was largely eclipsed by neurobiology as dreaming became closely identified with the physiological events of REM sleep[14] as well as NREM (non-rapid eye movement) sleep.[15,16] Studies of dreaming in psychiatric disorders were undertaken from a more neurobiological perspective.[17-22] Beginning in the 1970s, sleep research in mental health shifted its focus towards studying sleep disorders and their relationship to psychiatric disorders.[23-25] Only after 1990 did dream studies in psychiatric disorders experience a resurgence through advances in neuroscience and the development of neuroimaging techniques that allow us to characterize cerebral function throughout the sleep-wake cycle.[26,27] But to date, the definitive functions of dreaming, REM sleep, and even sleep itself and their relation to human emotions continue to elude us and remain the subjects of considerable debate.

In this paper we review the history of the relation between sleep, dreaming, and mental health from the ancient mythic and religious views as they evolved to the first tentative scientific approaches, to the ascendancy of psychoanalysis, and ultimately to the modern era of neuroscientific based research and theory. We conclude with considerations of future approaches to dream, sleep and mental health.

Views of sleep and dreaming from ancient through medieval times

The current assumption that dreaming is a product of the mind was not one generally shared by our ancient forebears. Authors from the earliest recorded civilizations, including the Mesopotamians[7,28] and the Egyptians,[8] firmly held to the belief that dreams were divine in origin, i.e., the product of the gods, and were the means by which they communicated their wishes to mortal men. Dreaming, especially in religious contexts, was thought to be a supernatural manifestation, and considered premonitory or prophetic.[1–4,6]

The significance given to oneiric activity has been documented since 4000 B.C., and the interpretation of dream content dates back to at least the fourth century B.C. as described on clay tablets from that period. The first written record of dream interpretation came from the Egyptians around 1275 B.C. A hieratic papyrus, called the "Dream Book",[29] includes a list of dreams and symbols for interpretation. Considered to be messages from the gods, they were the means by which deities communicated their wishes to mortals who in turn consulted with special temple priests for help in their interpretation. Dream oracles were common; sleep was induced on supplicants in the hopes of producing prophetic dreams that could then be interpreted by a professional diviner or priest. The belief in a divine origin of dreaming was inherited by the ancient Greeks and continued into Roman times.[3,4,9]

The Greeks built temples to Aesculapius, the god of medicine, and utilized dream interpretation as a medical treatment.[9,30] Their belief in the prophetic power of dreams led to the publication of dream interpretation manuals, culminating in the *"Oneirocritica"*.[31] This five-volume text on "oneiromancy", which still survives, was written by Artemidorus Daldianus, a professional "diviner" in the mid-to-late second century A.D., and describes more than 30,000 different types of dreams. For Artemidorus and his contemporaries, dreams were thought to be a pathway to the future and he was committed to producing reliable principles for understanding allegorical dreams. This sentiment is also evident in the epic literature, such as that of Homer and Virgil, in which dreams held prophetic messages.[3,32]

The close relationship between sleep, dreaming and emotional experience is seen widely in Greek mythology. According to their theogony, Oneiros, the god of dreams, helped Hypnos, the god of sleep, to reduce human suffering. Hypnos, the younger twin of Thanatos (Death), was the fruit of the union between Nyx (Night) and Erebus (Darkness) and used his two sons, known together as the Oneiroi, to send sleep and dreams to mortals.[33] These gods of sleep and dreaming, who also included Morpheus (the dream shaper), Ikelos (the god of realistic dreams), Phantasos (the god of strange dreams), and Phobetor (the god of frightening dreams), were the divine system that explained sleep and dreaming to the ancient Greeks.[33]

Greek philosophers debated the meaning of sleep and dreaming, and with advances in philosophy and natural science, we begin to see rationalistic accounts interspersed with divine or supernatural explanations of dreaming. Plato endorsed the possibility of divination through dreams,[34] ascribing the site of dream prophecy to the liver. He also supported the concept of a psychological component to dreams,[35] and that in dream states one expresses the bestial desires that are normally repressed during wakefulness, presaging modern psychological theory.

The first steps towards modern dream interpretation and their relationship to emotions were taken in the 5th century B.C. when the Greek philosopher Heraclitus suggested that a person's dream world was created within hi own mind.[36] Aristotle provides us with the most systematic study of sleep and dreaming in the ancient world, elaborated in three full essays on the subject; *On Sleep and Waking (De Somno et Vigilia)*[37] *On Dreams (De Insomniis)*[38] and *On divination Through Sleep (De Divination per Somnum)*.[38] In the latter studies Aristotle firmly rejects the traditional view of the prophetic power of dreams, and explains away as mere coincidence that dreams could predict future events. In *On Dreams*[38] he posits that dreams are the result of impressions traveling through the bloodstream and thereby activating sensations in the heart. This activity also occurs during wakefulness, but is more apparent in sleep due to the suspension of normal perception and judgment. The variable turbulence of blood in sleep also accounts for why dream "appearances" may at times be coherent and akin to reality, while at other times are incomplete and distorted. He further postulated, in *On Sleep and Waking*[37] that sleep and waking are diametrically opposed phenomena characterized, respectively, by the absence or presence of perception. With Aristotle dreams moved from being viewed as externally driven phenomenon to being the result of residual perceptions.[39]

With the advent of Christianity came a return of the idea that dreams could have prophetic properties. The Old Testament has an abundance of dream stories, and a more modern concept of dream interpretation.[4,40] The most famous interpreter of dreams in the Bible was Joseph, and probably the most famous dream interpreted was that of the king of Egypt in the Book of Genesis.[40]

From medieval times through the 19th century

During medieval times theologians practiced a more careful, and to some extent more scientific, study of sleep and dream phenomena. However, their interpretations were still often constrained by superstition and witchcraft.[2,4]

During the Renaissance, dream interpretation went through a different process. Girolamo Cardano (1501–76),[41] an Italian mathematician and physician wrote *Synesiorum somniorum omnis generis insomnia explicantes libri quatuor* (1562) resurrecting interest in the analysis of dreams, which were seen as complex phenomena strictly related to sleep and emotions. Cardano produced four books about sleep disorders and the relationship between sleep, dreams, and health, with the first 15 chapters describing all possible dreams. He identified four major types of dreams based on causes. The causes he identified, which were "already present in the dreamer," depended on the person's psychic condition. Based on the Hippocratic Theory of Humors in which bodily fluids, called "humors", were responsible for the health and mental stability of individuals. These humors were of four types; "blood", "black bile", "yellow bile", and "phlegm". Cardano believed that each of the humors would correspond to a different dream through "vapours," which then would create the dream. For example, people with black bile usually dreamt of ". . . . darkness, earthquakes, lightning and thunder, jails, mourning. . ." He thus made the first known correlation between pathological emotions, sleep and dream content.

The ancients viewed dreams as passive processes caused by external stimulation such as "vapours." But in many cases dreams were seen as the manifestation of a divinity and therefore were interpreted within a prophetic framework.[9,10,42] Beginning with Leibniz and continuing through modern philosophy dreaming was seen as a product of the mind.[10,42] Leibniz hypothesized that the brain, like other internal organs, was capable of autonomous action, and ideas could be the product of both thought and physiological activity.[43] He permitted his successors to explain dreaming as an endogenous product of the brain in both philosophy[44] and in the first physiologic studies of sleep.[45]

Towards the end of the 1800s dream interpretation centered on the new psychological approach of psychoanalysis in which the content of a dream was analyzed to reveal its underlying or "latent" meaning about the dreamer's psyche. One of the seminal works on the subject is The *Interpretation of Dreams* by Sigmund Freud,[11] probably the best known of relatively modern dream investigators. The first edition was first published in German in November 1899 a *Die Traumdeutung* and describes Freud's process for dream analysis. According to Freud's point of view, dream activity reflects man's emotive side. Dreams were forms of "wish-fulfillment"—attempts by the unconscious to resolve a conflict of some sort, whether recent or from the recesses of the past. With Freud, the study of dream phenomena revived the ancient practice of dream interpretation and established its place in the forefront of human psychological study. Freud also proposed a relationship between psychic functioning and the neurobiology of the brain. In his *"Project for a Scientific Psychology"*,[12] he hypothesized a model of the mind/brain that included consideration of the neurobiological aspects of psychological functions. Meanwhile a group of eager European scientists were systematically studying the phenomenon of dreaming, which became the topic of discussion at scientific meetings. In 1861 Alfred Maury, a French physician, studied over 3000 different dreams.[46] He felt external stimuli were the catalyst of all dreams, and he questioned whether dreams were truly recollections of mental processes occurring during sleep, or were manufactured during the awakening process. In 1886 Goblot[47] also proposed "we dream while we are awakening," and that the dreams we report on awakening may be developed during the waking process. Mary Calkins (1893)[48] was another who undertook a statistical analysis of dream reports.

In the early part of the 20th century, with the advent of electroencephalography, "incidental" observations were made of the occurrence of dream reports by investigators studying brain waves during sleep. Natural observations on the state of the brain during sleep were the seeds of an experimental approach to dreaming which had to wait for more than a century to develop. These researchers reported that "dreams may occur in association with any type of sleep potential pattern," and no specific brain wave activity seemed to be related to dreaming.

The discovery of REM sleep and the era of physiologic-based studies of sleep and dreaming and their relation to mental illness

In 1953 Aserinsky and Kleitman's discovery of REM sleep[14] ushered in an exciting and important epoch of research on this newly identified state of the brain. The resulting explosion in sleep experimentation generated an extensive literature on the nature of REM sleep in humans and much information about the characteristics and content of REM dreams. Many of these studies originally sought to demonstrate a link between REM sleep physiology and specific dream content. After half a century of studying the psychology of dreams based primarily on Freud's theories they had, it seemed, finally found in REM sleep a unique physiologic correlate of dreaming. In 1957 Dement and Kleitman[49] published a report which supported Aserinsky and Kleitman's previous assumptions. In this study the authors reported dream recall rates of about 80% after awakenings from REM sleep and only 7% from awakenings from NREM sleep. They also observed that patterns of eye movements seemed to relate to the dream content. This finding became known as the "scanning hypothesis". A third major observation was that the subjective dream duration seemed consistent with the duration of the REM period preceding the awakening.[50,51]

The discovery of REM sleep also gave impetus to the study of dreaming in psychiatric disorders from a more neurobiological prospective. As a result of the belief in the inseparability of REM sleep and dreaming, studies were pursued looking at dreaming in mental disorders such as schizophrenia,[17] manic episodes[18,21] depression.[19-21] Beginning in the 1970s a number of reports described alterations of REM and NREM sleep correlating with various psychiatric disorders.[23-25] Specific REM sleep alterations were considered for years to be biological markers for depressive disease.[24,25,52-56] Studies in the literature suggest that altered sleep patterns may precede the expression of mood disorders[57,58] and vice versa,[59] thus suggesting a very close relationship with these psychiatric disorders. Refinements in dream research, often based on the assumption of a REM = dreaming isomorphism, and better characterization of dream length, content and recall were employed, and seem to indicate a relationship between dreaming and psychiatric illness. This ushered in a new era of dream studies in mental disorders and suggested that they had diagnostic as well prognostic importance for therapeutic assessment, especially in the mood disorders.

Several studies found that depressed individuals recall fewer or less detailed dreams than healthy controls,[60,61] and in bipolar disorder a shift to depression is associated with a decrease in overall number of dreams reported,[62] and perhaps give an indication on the duration of illness.[61] Overall dream length was also found to be shorter in depressed individuals than healthy controls.[60] Dream content seemed to reflect the prevalent mood state. Barrett et al.,[60] for example, found that depressed mood in the morning may be related to negative dream content. In mania dreams tend to feature bizarre and improbable themes as compared to the negative content of depressed patients, and those with a neutral mood.[62] A change in dream content was found to closely precede an upward shift in mood, especially dreams of death or body injury, which were more frequently reported in developing mania.[62,63] Reductions in the dreamlike quality of REM dreams,[64] or the presence of nightmares and frightening dreams may affect and predict suicidal tendency[64-66] especially if they are repetitive[65] or persistent.[67] Dream characteristics may also predict remission from depression,[68] or reflect response to antidepressant treatment.[69] Dreaming has been further hypothesized to function in mood regulation,[68,70] prevalent mood state and as an indicator of suicidality,[64-67, 71] resistance to treatment,[68] as well as effectiveness of treatment.[69] Naturally, dreaming as a model of psychosis has been proposed and studied.[72,73]

Dream activity in anxiety disorders has also studied, especially in post-traumatic stress disorder where dreaming has both diagnostic and prognostic implications; the occurrence and content of post-traumatic dreams constitute part of the phenomenology of the disorder and may relate to its severity.[74] Recall has been found to be reduced in these patients and may represent a coping mechanism.[74] Specific dream content studied indicates the centrality of dream imagery intensity to the underlying emotional state,[75,76] and its perturbation may serve as a potential guide in clinical care in PTSD[76] as well as a better understanding of the function of dreams.[74]

Diagnostic and clinical implications have also been suggested in studies of dreaming in other psychiatric disorders. Anorexic patients have been found to have less frequent dream recall, fewer pleasurable themes than normal controls and generally saw themselves in their dreams as having a distorted body and experience of food.[77] REM dreams of schizophrenics have also been found to be shorter than those of controls, and dream narratives less bizarre, suggesting these characteristics may reflect an impairment in neurocognitive processes, including emotional processing.[78] As such, data from dream studies in psychiatric disorders suggest important clinical and prognostic implications as dream recall, length and dream content may reflect the psychopathologic evolution of these diseases.

In 1977, Hobson and McCarley[79] suggested that dreaming is fundamentally physiological and not psychologically driven. Their "activation-synthesis hypothesis" proposed that the brain is periodically activated, while sensory input and motor output are blocked—except for the oculomotor pathway. After being "activated" by random stimulation from pontine brain stem structures, the brain compares this input with stored sensorimotor data and "synthesizes" dream content. The authors further postulated that REM sleep is a unique physiological state and that it alone, by providing the requisite conditions to support dreaming, produces bizarre and hallucinoid dreams. According to this theory the relationship between dreams and emotions is not necessarily important to one's psychology, thus ushering in a viewpoint in which dreaming was thought to be more neurophysiological than psychological. This extremely influential hypothesis helped push sleep and dream research away from investigating psychological factors and towards examining physiological and cognitive factors. Hobson and colleagues later proposed an "AIM" model for dreaming and hallucinations. In this model Activation (information processing capacity, i.e., cerebral activation or electroencephalography (EEG) amplitude), Input (gating function, the capacity to exchange information with outside world), and Modulation (aminergic vs. cholinergic balance) interact to produce different types of mental experience. When aminergic modulation is low (more cholinergic), hallucinations and dreaming can occur. As sensory input and motor output is reduced, as in REM sleep, internal sources of stimulation predominate, resulting in more vivid dreaming.[80]

A major complicating factor in much dream research since the discovery of REM, particularly in older studies, was the widespread assumption that REM sleep was equivalent to "dream sleep". More recently, evidence has accumulated that shows the REM = dream isomorphism assumption to be false. Over time, a large body of evidence demonstrated that mental activity persists throughout all stages of sleep[15,16] and one by one the claims defending the integrity of the REM = dreaming equation began to fall. Still, some argued that REM dreams were qualitatively different from NREM reports. It was argued that reports from NREM tended to have less "organismic" involvement, less elaboration, and tended to show a closer relation to walking life—which may explain why they were less likely to be labeled as dreams, while reports elicited from REM sleep were more vivid and bizarre, containing more visual imagery, participation, and affect.

Later findings also disproved the relationship between eye movements and the visual imagery in dreaming.[49,81] By using mechanical rather than electrical measures, the existence of rapid eye movements in congenitally blind subjects was demonstrated[82] and visual imagery was described in the absence of eye movements in both REM[83] and NREM sleep.[15] Also, we were able to show using experimental awakenings, that if one controlled for time of night REM sleep duration did not correlate with length of dream report, as formerly thought.[84] A number of investigators including Antrobus,[85] Foulkes and Schmidt,[16] Fein,[86] Cavellero and Foulkes[87] have also shown that when length of dream report is controlled, there is little or no difference between REM and NREM reports in terms of content or affect. Koulak and Goodenough[88] suggested an arousal-retrieval model, which hypothesized that mental activity persists throughout all stages of sleep, but that the recall and description of this mentation depends on arousal level, which increases as sleep progresses.[84,89] As such, stage differences in dream recall appear more closely related to level of mnemonic activation and to access to memory traces than to any special dream production mechanism unique to one stage of sleep.[90,91] Dream sources, as well as content, appear similar in REM and NREM mentation.[87] In general, these results suggest that the same cognitive systems produce mental activity irrespective of EEG sleep stage, as Foulkes and Schmidt proposed in 1983.[16] Moreover when Cicogna et al.[90] compared memory traces from daydreaming and sleep onset dreaming, they found a similarity, suggesting that "cognitive processes involved in the creation of original narrative sequence may be similar in sleep and waking. Ultimately, since stage REM is neither necessary nor sufficient for dreaming, one must exercise caution in interpreting studies where the two are assumed to be synonymous.

Studies examining sleep architecture and psychiatric illness

Sleep architecture and its relationship to mental illness has also been extensively studied. Beginning around 1970, polysomnographic studies suggested that, in addition to disturbances of sleep continuity, sleep in depression is character-ized by a reduction of slow wave sleep, and a disinhibition of REM sleep—with a shortening of REM latency, a prolongation of the first REM period, and in increase in REM density.[24,25] Shortened REM latency was, in fact, considered by many to be a biological marker for depressive disease.[52–55,92] More recently specific components of sleep, total delta activity, delta ratio, and REM activity, have been considered episode-related bilogical features while other components such as slowest delta activity, have been hypothesized to represent vulnerability factors for recurrence.[56] Polysomnographic studies found not only a 49% incidence psychiatric illness in first-degree relatives of early-onset depressed patients with reduced REM latency, but also a 70% con-cordance rate for shortened REM latency, regardless of psychiatric history.[93]

The relative risk for unipolar depression among relatives with reduced REM latency was almost 2 times[93] and in other studies[94] 3 times greater than for relatives without reduced REM latency. Moreover 1/5 of healthy subjects with a high genetic load for psychiatric disorders showed a conspicuous depressed-like sleep pattern.[95] Short REM latency has been associated with increased risk of major depression beyond the familial risk associated with a depressed proband indicating that polysomnographic abnormalities may precede the clinical expression of depression and may be useful in identifying those at highest risk for the illness.[93] In addition, alterations of REM and NREM sleep have also been associated with schizophrenia,[23] psychosis and schizoaffective disorders.[96] Recent literature suggests that the clinical expression of a sleep disorder may precede the expression of a mood disorder episode and mostly supports the hypothesis that sleep disorders, especially insomnia, may represent a risk factor for the future development of psychiatric illness, especially depression and anxiety disorders.[97–99] Further, sleep disturbance prior to trauma has been found to predict the development of subsequent psychiatric disorders.[100]

Several theoretical models originating from basic research have tried to explain sleep abnormalities in depression. Manipulation of the sleep-wake cycle, using methods such as sleep deprivation have been studied, showing that sleep deprivation appears to have transient antidepressant properties.[101] Thus, the relationship between sleep, dreaming and psychiatric disorders appears to be very complicated and far from fully understood. Further, the relationship appears two-way: psychiatric illness may lead to sleep disturbance, and vice versa.[102]

Recent advances in neurobiology and investigations into the function of sleep

The neurobiology of sleep is undoubtedly important to the development and maintenance of healthy brain function, but its exact role remains elusive. One proposed function of sleep is the maintenance of "synaptic homeostasis." According to this model, several cortical circuits undergo a synaptic potentiation during wakefulness as a product of waking cognitive experience. Sleep, particularly NREM delta sleep, may be important in synaptic remodeling and downscaling, which, in turn, is tied to the beneficial effects of sleep on performance.[103,104] Sleep deprivation or disturbed sleep may compromise synaptic changes and brain plasticity.[105,106] Research over the last few decades has firmly established that new neurons are generated in selected areas of the adult mammalian brain, particularly of the hippocampal formation,[105,107] The function of adult-born neurons is still a matter of debate.[108] In the case of the hippocampus, integration of new cells into existing neuronal circuitry may be involved in memory processes and the regulation of emotionality.[106,109] In recent years, various studies have examined how the production of new cells and their development into neurons is affected by sleep and sleep loss.[105,106,110–115] While disruption of sleep for a period shorter than one day appears to have little effect on the basal rate of cell proliferation,[105,106] restriction or disruption of sleep for 24 h,[110] 48 h,[111] or 72–96 h,[112] reduces cell proliferation in the dentate gyrus and may have cumulative effects leading to a major decrease in hippocampal cell proliferation, cell survival and neurogenesis.[105,106] Importantly, while short sleep derivation may not affect the basal rate of cell proliferation, one study in rats shows that even mild sleep restriction may interfere with the increase in neurogenesis[113] that normally occurs with hippocampus-dependent learning.[113] Since sleep deprivation also disturbs memory formation,[116,117] these data suggest that promoting survival, maturation and integration of new cells may be an unexplored mechanism by which sleep supports learning and memory processes.

The structural integrity and function of the hippocampus appears to depend in part on sleep. Imaging studies in humans have found the importance of sleep to hippocampal function. The formation of memory[118,119] and cognitive performance is disrupted in patients suffering from chronic insomnia,[120] in whom in vivo imaging revealed a significant reduction in hippocampal volume.[121] The functional consequences and cognitive disturbances associated with insomnia, independent of the reduction in volume, may be related to reductions in neurogenesis. These effects of sleep loss may endanger hippocampal integrity, thereby leading to cognitive dysfunction and contributing to the development of mood disorders.[105,106,114,115,122] These findings open new frontiers in the search for sleep's relationship to psychiatric illness, particularly mood disorders.

Advancements in neuroimaging and investigation in sleep and dreaming

Advancements in neuroimaging techniques have made it possible to investigate cerebral function throughout the sleep-wake cycle in normal human subjects. This approach has allowed sleep physiological theories developed from animal data to be confirmed, but has also introduced original concepts about the neurobiological mechanisms of sleep, dreams and memory in humans.[27] NREM sleep, when compared to wakefulness or REM sleep, is characterized by a global decrease in cerebral blood flow, and a decrease in regional cerebral blood flow (rCBF) in the dorsal pons, mesencephalon, thalamus, basal ganglia, basal forebrain and anterior hypothalamus, prefrontal cortex, anterior cingulate cortex and precuneus.[12, 123–125] In contrast to NREM sleep, REM sleep is characterized by high cerebral blood flow[126] and regional activations during REM sleep were found in the pontine tegmentum, thalamus, amygdala, hippocampus, anterior cingulate cortex, temporo-occipital areas, basal forebrain, cerebellum and caudate nucleus; conversely, regional deactivations were located in the dorso-lateral prefrontal cortex, posterior cingulated gyrus, the precuneus and inferior parietal cortex.[127]

Although these changes are usually interpreted in relation to physiological and cellular mechanisms, the specific regional distribution of brain activity during REM sleep has been suggested to relate to specific dream features.[27] For example, the perceptual aspects of dreams could be related to the activation of posterior cortices. Accordingly, patients with occipito-temporal lesions may report a cessation of visual dream imagery.[26] Secondly, emotional features in dreams could similarly be expected to be related to activation of a amygdalar complexes, the orbito-frontal cortex and the anterior cingulated cortex.[26] Thirdly, the relative hypoactivation of the prefrontal cortex could explain the alteration in logical reasoning, working memory, episodic memory and executive functioning that appear in dream reports from REM sleep awakenings[26,27,127] These assumptions are of great theoretical interest to the understanding of dream physiology but remain highly speculative because combined dreaming and functional imaging data are still very sparse and little is known about the physiology of NREM sleep dreaming. We must be cautious not to repeat the earlier mistake of equating REM sleep with dreaming, and examine why many REM and NREM dreams are indistinguishable.[15,16,85–91] As yet, relatively few neuroimaging studies have been dedicated to human sleep disorders, dreaming and their relationship to mental illness. Future studies could attempt to link dreaming experiences with patterns of regional cerebral activity in psychiatric disorders. Thus far, precise neural correlates of dreaming remain elusive and the definitive functions of dreaming and of sleep itself—as well as their relationship to normal and pathological emotion in humans—continue to elude us and remain the subject of considerable debate.

One of the most intriguing similarities of dreams and psychosis is that, in both states, neural activity in an individual's brain is experienced as produced by the external environment. It has been hypothesized that such experiences can be produced when the corollary discharge or feed-forward (CDFF) mechanisms of the mind are disabled. Such mechanisms were first identified in sensorimotor systems where they operate to distinguish sensory experiences produced by self-initiated action (neural commands) from sensory experiences produced by the environment. Feinberg[128] hypothesized that similar systems exist for mental activity, which Hughlings Jackson[129] proposed is simply the highest level of motor activity. In psychoses such as schizophrenia, neural activity produced in the patient's brain is experienced as produced from activity coming from outside, often in the form of "voices". It is true, of course, that in the dreams of normal individuals, the hallucinatory experiences are more often visual than auditory. Nevertheless, in both brain states—dreaming and psychosis—this disorder of "agency" can be understood as a failure of CDFF systems, as Feinberg and Guazzelli[130] pointed out. This field is now ripe for sophisticated experimentation with new imaging techniques.

CONCLUSION

In this review we have traced the evolution of our knowledge and beliefs about sleep and dreaming, their function, and their connection to mental illness. The various theories attempting to explain these phenomena have shifted dramatically through history; for centuries dreams were a means to manage worries about the future, first as messengers from gods, later as a messenger from the unconscious. With new and improved techniques for assessing brain function in vivo, attention has shifted away from studying the subjective characteristics of dreaming to examining specific neurophysiology. Still, the integration of sleep and dream study methodology with recent developments in neuroimaging and functional brain exploration provides an exciting and promising area of inquiry that may one day help answer the many remaining questions about the nature and function of sleep and dreams, and their relationship to psychiatric illness.

RESEARCH AGENDA

1. The integration of sleep and dream study methodology with the study of functional brain exploration in vivo in psychiatric illness is an exciting and promising area of inquiry that may one day help answer the many remaining questions about the nature and function of sleep and dreams in humans, and the pathophysiology of the major psychiatric disorders.
2. Some potentially useful findings from earlier studies on dreaming in patients with mood or anxiety disorders may guide clinical care, as well as help guide future research. Studies on dream content and recall in larger samples of specific psychiatric disorders in future research can increase our knowledge in this field.

PRACTICE POINTS

1. Since earliest times dream content has been studied in relationship with human health and function.
2. The development of sleep laboratory techniques ushered in a new era of the study of dreams and mental health. Over time, this focus has become more neurobiological. Studies on dreaming have focused especially on dreaming mechanisms, functions and relationship with cognitive human functions and sleep research within a more neuroscientific perspective, and shifted from dreaming to the neurobiological activity of sleep and its relationship with mental health.
3. Perturbations of sleep have then been studied as related to pathological emotional states: sleep disorders are thus commonly considered risk factors in the development of psychiatric disorders, particularly mood disorders. Pathological emotional states may lead to sleep disturbance, and vice versa. The neurobiology of sleep may be moreover important in the development and maintenance of brain function and may have a possible role in the maintenance of "synaptic homeostasis." Prolonged restriction or disruption of sleep may have cumulative effects leading to a major decrease in hippocampal cell proliferation, cell survival and neurogenesis.

4. Neuroscience and the development of neuroimaging techniques have made possible the characterization of many aspects of cerebral function throughout the sleep-wake cycle, but to date we do not yet fully understand the significance of sleep and dreaming. The various theories attempting to explain these phenomena have shifted dramatically through history.

ACKNOWLEDGEMENT

Thanks to Aldo Palagini for his important support.

REFERENCES

1. Kurland ML, Oneiromancy: an historic review of dream interpretation. *Am J Psychother* 1972;26(3):408–16.
2. Rupprecht CS. Our unacknowledged ancestors: dream theorists of antiquity, the middle ages, and the renaissance. *Psychiatr J Univ Ott* 1990; 15(2):117–22.
3. Leven KH, History of medicine. "Through the horny or ivory gate"—dream interpretation in the antiquity. I. From Homer to Aristotle. *Praxis* 2004, Apr 14; 93(16):684–8.
4. Hughes JD. Dream interpretation in ancient civilizations. *Dreaming* 2000; 10(1):7–18.
5. Rosselli D. Brief history of dreams. *Rev Neurol* 2000, 16–31; 30(2): 195–8.
6. Stoll RT. Sleep and dreams in pictures. *Praxis* 1995, 11; 84(15);432–9.
7. Oppenheim L. The interpretation of dreams in the ancient Near East, with a translation of an Assyrian dream-book. *Trans Am Phil Soc* 1956; 46(3):179–373. New Series.
8. Szpakowska K. Through the looking glass. Dreams in ancient Egypt. In: Bulkeley K, editor. *Dreams: a reader on the religions, cultural and psychological dimensions of dreaming.* New York: Palgrave; 2001. p. 29–43.
9. Barbera J. Sleep and dreaming in Greek and Roman philosophy. *Sleep Med* 2008; 9:906–10.
10. Dreisbach C. Dreams in the history of philosophy. *Dreaming* 2000; 10:31–41.
11. Freud S. *The Interpretation of dreams.* Modern Library Edition. Toronto: Random House Inc.; 1994.
12. Freud S. Project for a scientific psychology. *Psychoanal Q;* 1950. The Standard Edition of the Complete Psychological Works of Sigmund Freud.
13. Robbins M. Primary mental expression: freud, klein and beyond. *J Am Psychoanal Ass* 2008; 56:177.

14. Aserinsky E, Kleitman N. Regularly occurring periods of eye motility, and concomitant phenomena during sleep. *Science* 1953; **118**:273–4.
15. Foulkes D, Vogel G. Mental activity at sleep onset. *J Abnorm Psychol* 1965; **34**:104–10.
16. Foulkes D., Schmidt M. Temporal sequence and unit composition in dream reports from different stages of sleep. *Sleep* 1983; **6**:265–80.
17. Dement WC. Dream recall and eye movements during sleep in schizophrenics and normals. *Jn Nerv Ment Dis* 1955; **122**(3):263–9.
18. Bastos O, Suerink E. The dreams of manics. *Evol Psychiatr* 1963; **28**:129–38.
19. Bastos O, Dream activity in depressive states. *Evol Psychiatr* 1963; **28**:101–27.
20. Kramer M. Drugs, depression, and dream sequences. *Ohio State Med J* 1966; **62**(12):1277–80.
21. Hartmann, E., Verdone P, Snyder F. Longitudinal studies of sleep and dreaming patterns in psychiatric patients. *J Nerv Ment Dis* 1966; **142**(2):117–26.
22. Miller JB. Dreams during varying stages of depression. *Arch Gen Psychiatry* 1969; **20**(5):560–5.
23. Kupfer DJ, Wyatt RJ, Scott J, Snyder F. Sleep disturbance in acute schizophrenic patients. *Am J. Psychiatry* 1970; **126**(9):1213–23.
24. Kupfer DJ. REM latency: a psychobiologic marker for primary depressive disease. *Biol Psychiatry* 1976; **11**(2):159–74.
25. Kupfer DJ, Foster FG, Coble PA, McPartland RJ. EEG sleep parameters for the classification and treatment of affective disorders. *Psychopharmacol Bull* 1977; **13**(2):57–8.
*26. Schwartz S, Maquet P. Sleep imaging and the neuropsychological assessment of dreams. *Trends Cogn Sci* 2002, 1; **6**(1):23–30.
*27. Dang-Vu TT, Desseilles M, Petit S, Mazza D, Montplaisir J, Maquet P. Neuroimaging in sleep medicine. *Sleep Med* 2007; **8**:349–72.
28. Pangas JC. Dreams, their disorders and their therapeutic function in ancient. *Mesopotamia Vesalius* 2006; **12**(2):94–9.
29. Gardiner AH., *Hieratic papyri*. London: British Museum; 1935.
30. Strunz F. The dream as a tool in diagnosis, healing and life orientation in antiquity. *Fortschr Neurol Psychiatr* 1994; **62**(10):389–98.
31 White R, Artemidorus D. *The interpretation of dreams (Oneirocritica)*. Torrance: Original Books Inc.; 1990.
32. Pratt L. "Odyssey" 19.535–50: on the interpretation of dreams and signs in Homer. *Class Philol* 1994; **89**(2):147–52.
33. Hard R. *Greek mythology*. Routledge; 2003.
34. Plato. Timaeus. In: Jowett B, editor. *The dialogues of Plato (trans.)*. 4th ed, vol. 3. Oxford: Clarendon Press; 1953. p. 631–780.
35. Plato In; Jowett B, editor. *The Republic. The dialogues of Plato (trans.)*, 4th ed, vol. 2. Oxford: Clarendon Press; 1953. p. 1–499.

36. Robinson M. *Heraclitus. Fragments: a text and translation with a commentary.* Toronto: University of Toronto Press; 1987.
37. Gallop D. *Aristotle on sleep and dreams.* Warminster: Aris and Phillips Ltd.; 1996.
38. Gallop D. Aristotle on sleep, dreams and final causes. In: Clearly JJ, Shartin DC, editors. *Proceedings of the Boston area colloquium in ancient philosophy.* Lanham; 1989. p. 257–90.
39. van der Eijk PJ. Aristotle on 'distinguished physicians' and on the medical significance of dreams. *Clia Med* 1995; **28**:447–59.
40. Putscher M. Dreams and dream interpretation in the Bible. *Isr J Psychiatry Relat Sci* 1982; **19**(2):149–55.
41. Cardano G. Synesorium somnorium omnis generis insomnia explicantes libri quatuor 1962. In: Sogni. Montiglio S, Grieco A, Mancia M, Marsilio, Venezia, 1993.
*42. Lavie P, Hobson JA. Origin of dreams: anticipation of modern theories in the philosophy and physiology of the eighteenth and nineteenth centuries. *Psychol Bull* 1986; **2**:229–24043.
43. Loemker LE. *Gottfried Wilhelm Leibnitz: philosophical papers and letters.* 2nd ed. Dordrecht, The Netherlands: Riedel; 1956.
44. Hamilton W. *Lectures on metaphysics and logic.* Edinburgh: William Blackwood; 1860.
45. Carpenter WB. *Mental physiology.* London: Henry S. Kling; 1874.
46. Maury A. *Le sommeil et les rêves. Études psychologiques sur ces phéno`nes et les divers états qui s'y rattachent suivies de recherches sur le dévelopement de l'instinct et de l'intelligencedans leurs rapports avec le phéno`ne du sommeil.* Paris: Didier; 1861.
47. Hall CS. Do we dream during sleep? Evidence for the Goblot Hypothesis. *Percept Mot Skills* 1981; **53**:239–46.
48. Calkins MW. Statistics of dreams. *Am J Psychol* 1893; **5**:311–43.
49. Dement W, Kleitman N. Cyclic variations in EEG during sleep and their relation to eye movements, body motility, and dreaming. *Electraencephalogr Clin Neurophysiol* 1957; **9**(4). 673e90.
50. Dement W, Wolpert EA. Relationships in the manifest content of dreams occurring on the same night. *J Nerv Ment Dis* 1958; **126**(6):568–78.
51. Wolpert EA. Studies in psychophysiology of dreams. II. An electromyographic study of dreaming. *Arch Gen Psychiatry* 1960; **2**:231–41.
52. Kupfer DJ, Foster FG. Interval between onset of sleep and rapid-eye-movement sleep as an indicator of depression. *Lancet* 1972; **30**(2):684–6.
53. Reynolds 3rd CF, Shubin RS, Coble PA, Kupfer DJ. Diagnostic classification of sleep disorders: implications for psychiatric practice. *J Clin Psychiatry* 1981; **42**(8):296–300.
54. Thase ME, Kupfer DJ, Spiker DG. Electroencephalographic sleep in secondary depression: a revisit. *Biol Psychiatry* 1984; **19**(6):805–14.

55. Reynolds 3rd CF, Kupfer DJ. Sleep research in affective illness: state of the art circa 1987. *Sleep* 1987; **10**(3):199–215.
56. Buysse DJ, Frank E, Lowe KK, Cherry CR, Kupfer DJ. Electroencephalographic sleep correlates of episode and vulnerability to recurrence in depression. *Biol Psychiatry* 1997, 15; **41**(4):406–18.
57. Gillin JC. Are sleep disturbances risk factors for anxiety, depressive and addictive disorders? *Acta Psychiatr Scand Suppl* 1998; **98**:39–43.
58. Roberts RE, Shema SJ, Kaplan GA, Strawbridge WJ. Sleep complaints and depression in aging cohort: a prospective perspective. *Am J Psychiatry* 2000; **157**(1):81–8.
*59. Lustberg L, Reynolds CF. Depression and insomnia: questions of cause and effect. *Sleep Med Rev* 2000; **4**(3):253–62.
60. Barrett D, Loeffler M. Comparison of dream content of depressed vs nondepressed dreamers. *Psychol Rep* 1992; **70**(2):403–6.
61. Schredl M. Dream recall in depressed patients. *Psychother Psychosom Med Psychol* 1995; **45**(12):414–7.
62. Beauchemin KM, Hays P. Prevailing mood, mood changes and dreams in bipolar disorder. *J Affect Disord* 1995, 9; **35**(1–2):41–9.
63. Beauchemin KM, Hays P. Dreaming away depression: the role of REM sleep and dreaming in affective disorders. *J Affect Disord* 1996, 25; **41**(12):125–33.
64. Agargun MY, Cartwright R. REM sleep, dream variables and suicidality in depressed patients. *Psychiatry Res* 2003, 15; **119**(1–2):33–9
65. Ağargün MY, Cilli AS, Kara H, Tarhan N. Kincir F, Oz H. Repetitive and frightening dreams and suicidal behavior in patients with major depression. *Compr Psychiatry* 1998; **39**(4):198–202.
66. Ağargün MY, Besiroglu L, Cilli AS, Gulec M, Aydin A, Inci R, et al. Nightmares, suicide attempts, and melancholic features in patients with unipolar major depression. *J Affect Disord* 2007; **98**(3):267–70.
67. Sjöström N, Hetta J, Waern M. Persistent nightmares are associated with repeat suicide attempt: a prospective study. *Psychiatry Res* 2009, 30; **170**(2–3):208–11.
68. Cartwright R, Luten A, Young M, Mercer P, Bears M. Role of REM sleep and dream affect in overnight mood regulation: a study of normal volunteers. *Psychiatry Res* 1998, 19; **81**(1):1–8.
69. Schredl M, Berger M, Riemann D. The effect of trimipramine on dream recall and dream emotions in depressive outpatients. *Psychiatry Res* 2009, 30; **167**(3):279–86.
*70. Kramer M. The selective mood regulatory function of dreaming: an update and revision. In: Moffit A, Kramer M, Hoffmann R, editors. *The function of dreaming*. Albany, NY: State, University of New York Press; 1993. p. 139–95.
71. Maltsberger JT. Dreams and suicide. *Suicide Life Threat Behav* 1993; **23**(1):55–62.

72. Hobson A. A model of madness? *Nature* 2004; **430**:21.
73. Scarone S, Manzone ML, Gambini O, Kantzas I, Limosani I, D'Agostino A, et al. The dream as model for psychosis: an experimental approach using bizarreness as a cognitive marker. *Schiz Bull* 2008; **34**(3):515–22.
74. Wittmann L, Schredl M, Kramer M. Dreaming in posttraumatic stress disorder: a critical review of phenomenology, psychophysiology and treatment. *Psychother Psychosom* 2007; **76**(1):25–39.
75. Hartmann E, Zborowski M, McNamara P, Rosen R, Grace N. Contextualizing images in dreams: more intense after abuse and trauma. *Dreaming* 2001; **11**:115–26.
76. Harmann E, Brezler T. A systematic change in dreams after 9/11/01. *Sleep* 2008, 1; **31**(2):213–8.
77. Frayn DH. The incidence and significance of perceptual qualities in the reported dreams of patients with anorexia nervosa. *Can J Psychiatry* 1991; **36**(7):517–20.
78. Lusignan FA, Zadra A, Dubuc MJ, Daoust AM, Mottard JP, Godbout R. Dream content in chronically-treated persons with schizophrenia. *Schizophr Res* 2009; **112**(1–3):164–73.
79. Hobson JA, McCarley RW. The brain as a dream state generator: an activation synthesis hypothesis of the dream process. *Am J Psychiary* 1977; **134**(12):1335–48.
*80. Hobson JA, Pace-Schott EF, Stickgold R. Dreaming and the brain: toward a cognitive neuroscience of conscious states. *Behav Brain Sci* 2000; **23**(6):793–842.
81. Foulkes D. Stage REM variability and dreaming. *Int Psychiatry Clin* 1970; 7(2):165.
82. Koulack D. Rapid eye movements and visual imagery during sleep. *Psychol Bull* 1972; 78(2):155–8.
83. Antrobus JS, Antrobus JS. Rapid eye movements and rapid eye movement periods. *Psychophysiology* 1969; **6**(1):45–8.
84. Rosenlicht NZ, Maloney T, Feinberg I. Dream report length is more dependent on arousal level than prior REM duration. *Brain Res Bull* 1994; **34**:99–101.
85. Antrobus J. REM and NREM sleep reports: comparison of word frequencies by cognitive classes. *Psychophysiology* 1983; **20**:562–8.
86. Fein G, Feinberg I, Insel TR, Antrobus JS, Price LJ, Floyd TC, et al. Sleep mentation in the elderly. *Psychophysiol* 1983; **22**:218–25.
87. Cavallero C, Foulkes D, Hollifield M. Memory sources of REM and NREM dreams. *Sleep* 1990; **13**:449–55.
88. Koulak D, Goodenough D. Dream recall and dream recall failure: an arousal retrieval model. *Psychol Bull* 1976; **83**:975–84.
89. Palagini L, Gemignani A, Feinberg I, Guazzelli M, Campbell I. Mental activity after early afternoon nap awakenings in healthy subjects. *Brain Res Bull* 2004; **63**:361–8.

90. Cicogna, P, Cavallero C, Bosinelli M. Differential access to memory traces in the production of mental experience. *Int J Psychophysiol* 1986; 4:209–16.
91. Cicogna P, Cavallero C, Bosinelli M. Cognitive aspects of mental activity during sleep. *Am J Psychol* 1991; **104**:413–25.
92. Ansseau M, Kupfer DJ, Reynolds 3rd CF, McEachran AB. REM latency distribution in major depression: clinical characteristics associated with sleep onset REM periods, *Biol Psychiatry* 1984; **19**(12):1651–66.
93. Giles DE, Biggs MM, Rush AJ, Roffwarg HP. Risk factors in families of unipolar depression. I. Psychiatric illness and reduced REM latency. *J Affect Disord* 1988; **14**(1):51–9.
94. Giles DE, Kupfer DJ, Rush AJ, Roffwarg HP. Controlled comparison of electrophysiological sleep in families of probands with unipolar depression. *Am J Psychiatry* 1998; **155**(2):192–9.
95. Lauer CJ, Schreiber W, Holsboer F, Krieg JC. In quest of identifying vulnerability markers for psychiatric disorders by all-night polysomnography. *Arch Gen Psychiatry* 1995; **52**(2):145–53.
96. Kupfer DJ, Broudy D, Spiker DG, Neil JF, Coble PA. EEG sleep and affective psychoses: I. Schizoaffective disorders *Psychiatry Res* 1979; **1**(2):17.
97. Ford D, Kamerow D. Epidemiologic study of sleep disturbances and psychiatric disorders: and opportunity for prevention? *J Am Med Assoc* 1989; **262**(11):1479–84.
98. Ohayon M, Roth T. Place of chronic insomnia in the course of depressive and anxiety disorders. *J Psychiatr Res* 2003; **37**:9–15.
99. Szklo-Coxe M, Young T, Peppard PE, Finn LA, Benca RM. Prospective associations of insomnia markers and symptoms with depression. *Am J Epidemiol* 2010, 15; **171**(6):709–20
100. Bryant R, Creamer M, O'Donnell M, Silove D, McFarlane AC. Sleep disturbance immediately prior to trauma predicts subsequent psychiatric disorder. *Sleep* 2010; **33**(1):69–74.
101. Svestka J. Sleep deprivation therapy. *Neuro Endocrinol Lett* 2008; **29**(1):65–92.
102. Manber R, Chambers AS. Insomnia and depression: a multifaceted interplay. *Curr Psychiatry Rep* 2009; **11**(6):437–42.
103. Tononi G, Cirelli C. Sleep and synaptic homeostasis: a hypothesis. *Brain Res Bull* 2003, 15; **62**(2):143–50.
104. Tononi G. Slow wave homeostasis and synaptic plasticity. *J Clin Sleep Med* 2009; **15**(5):16–9.
105. Cirelli C. Cellular consequences of sleep deprivation in the brain. *Sleep Med Rev* 2006; **10**:307–21.
106. Meerlo P, Mistlbeerger RE, Jacobs BL, Heller HC, McGinty D. New neurons in the adult brain; the role of sleep and consequences of sleep loss. *Sleep Med Rev* 2009; **20**(1):1–17.

*107. Abrous DN, Koehl M, Le Moal M. Adult neurogenesis: from precursors to network and physiology. *Physiol Rev* 2005; **85**:523–69.

*108. Kempermann G, Wiskott L, Gage FH. Functional significance of adult neurogenesis. *Curr Opin Neurobiol* 2004; **14**:186–91.

*109. Phelps EA. Human emotion and memory: interactions of the amygdala and hippocampal complex. *Curr Opin Neurobiol* 2004; **14**:198–202.

110. Roman V, Van der Borght K, Leemburg SA, Van der Zee EA, Meerio P. Sleep restriction by forced activity reduces hippocampal cell proliferation. *Brain Res* 2005; **1065**(1–2):53–9.

111. Tung A, Takase L, Fornal C, Jacobs B. Effects of sleep deprivation and recovery sleep upon cell proliferation in adult rat dentate gyrus. *Neuroscience* 2005; **134**(3):721–3.

112. Guzman-Marin R, Bashir T, Suntsova N, Szymusiak R, McGinty D. Hippocampal neurogenesis is reduced by sleep fragmentation in the adult rat. *Neuroscience* 2007, 10; **148**(1):325–33.

113. Hairston IS, Little MT, Scanlon MD, Barakat MT, Palmer DT, Sapolsky RM, et al. Sleep restriction suppresses neurogenesis induced by hippocampus-dependent learning. *J Neurophysiol* 2005; **94**(6):4224–33.

114. Lucassen PJ, Meerlo P, Naylor AS, van Dam AM, Dayer AG, Fuchs E, et al. Regulation of adult neurogenesis by stress, sleep disruption, exercise and inflammation: implications for depression and antidepressant action. *Neuropsychopharmacology* 2010; **20**(1):1–17.

115. Ad Muller, Pollock MS, Lieblich SE, Epp JR, Galea LA, Mistberger RE. Sleep deprivation can inhibit adult hippocampal neurogenesis independent of adrenal stress hormones. *Am J Physiol Regul Integr Comp Physiol* 2008; **294**(5):1693–703.

116. Stickgold R. Sleep-dependent memory consolidation. *Nature* 2005; **437**:1272–8.

*117. Ruskin DN, Liu C, Dunn KE, Bazan NG, LaHoste GJ. Sleep deprivation impairs hippocampus-mediated contextual learning but not amygdala-mediated cued learning in rats. *Eur J Neurosci* 2004; **19**:3121–4.

118. Peigneux P, Laureys S, Fuchs S, Collette F, Perrin F, Reggers J, et al. Are spatial memories strengthened in the human hippocampus during slow wave sleep? *Neuron* 2004; **44**:535–45.

119. Orban P, Rauchs G, Balteau E, Degueldre C, Luxen A, Maquet P, et al. Sleep after spatial learning promotes covert reorganization of brain activity. *Proc Natl Acad Sci U S A* 2006; **103**:7124–9.

120. Backhaus J, Junghanns K, Born J, Hohaus K, Faasch F, Hohagen F. Impaired declarative memory consolidation during sleep in patients with primary insomnia: influence of sleep architecture and nocturnal cortisol release. *Biol Psychiatry* 2006; **60**:1324–30.

121. Riemann D, Voderholzer U, Spiegelhalder K, Psych D, Hornyak M, Buysse DJ, et al. Chronic insomnia and MRI-measured hippocampal volume; a pilot study. *Sleep* 2007; **30**:955–85.

122. Jacobs BL, Praag H, Gage FH. Adult brain neurogenesis and psychiatry: a novel theory of depression. *Mol Psychiatry* 2000; **5**:262–9.
123. Maquet P, Degueldre C, Delfiore G, Aerts J, Peters JM, Luxen A, et al. Functional neuroanatomy of human slow wave sleep. *J Neurosci* 1997; **17**(8):2807–12.
124. Maquet P. Functional neuroimaging of normal human sleep by positron emission tomography. *J Sleep Res* 2000; **9**(3):207–31.
*125. Andersson JL, Onoe H, Hetta J, Lidstrom K, Valind S, Lilja A, et al. Brain networks affected by synchronized sleep visualized by positron emission tomography. *J Cereb Blood Flow Metab* 1998; **18**(7):701–15.
126. Madsen PL, Holm S, Vorstrup S, Friberg L, Lassen NA, Wildschiodtz G. Human regional cerebral blood flow during rapid-eye-movement sleep. *J Cereb Blood Flow Metab* 1991; **11**(3):502–7.
127. Maquet P, Ruby P, Maudoux A, Albouy G, Sterenich V, Dang-Vu T, et al. Human cognition during REM sleep and the activity profile within frontal and parietal cortices: a reappraisal of functional neuroimaging data. *Prog Brain Res* 2005; **150**:219–27.
128. Feinberg I. Efference copy and corollary discharge: implications for thinking and its disorders. *Schizophr Bull* 1978; **4**(4):636–40.
129. Jackson JH. Selected writings of John Hughlings Jackson. In: Taylor J, editor. New York: Basic Books; 1958.
130. Feinberg I, Guazzelli M. Schizophrenia—a disorder of the corollary discharge systems that integrate the motor systems of thought with the sensory systems of consciousness. *Br J Psychiatry* 1999 Mar; **174**: 196–204.

*The most important references are denoted by an asterisk.

Public Opponents of Vaccination: A Case Study

Julie Leask*, *Peter McIntyre*

*Corresponding author. Tel.: +61-2-9845-0520; fax: +61-2-9845-3082.
E-mail address: juliel3@chw.edu.au (J. Leask).
National Centre for Immunisation Research & Surveillance, Children's Hospital at
Westmead, University of Sydney, Locked Bag 4001, Westmead 2145, Australia*
Received 17 December 2002; accepted 26 June 2003

ABSTRACT

Opposition to mass childhood vaccination is a world-wide phenomenon, particularly in industrialised countries. Unfounded claims about vaccination are perpetuated by parental lobby groups and individual spokespeople, some of whom have a medical or scientific background. This article focuses on one such spokesperson who has achieved particular notoriety. Dr. Viera Scheibner is a retired micropalaeontologist, without any formal training in health-related sciences, who tours the world claiming that vaccines are ineffective and dangerous and lead to a host of ills such as cancer and asthma. Professionals in public health or the clinical arena are from time to time called upon to publicly respond to her, or similar, claims disseminated during tours of Europe, North America or Australasia and in books and articles. Health professionals have expressed at how such spokespersons misrepresent the evidence on vaccine safety, resulting in the potential to undermine public confidence in immunisation. Media coverage, or proposed coverage, particularly of her more extreme claims, often makes health professionals engaged in immunisation feel obliged to respond. This paper describes Viera Scheibner's approach, which follows a repetitious path and is representative of that taken by other public opponents of immunisation. We conclude by suggesting how health professionals might respond in the public arena.

© 2003 Elsevier Ltd. All rights reserved.

Keywords: Vaccine safety; Controversy; Health communication

1. Public opponents of vaccination: a case study

In industrialised countries today, opposition to vaccination occurs through organised lobby groups of mainly parents or individual spokespersons whose medical or scientific background lends credibility to their claims. The most radical opponents of vaccination claim that all vaccines are unsafe and ineffective, tending to attribute all manner of modern ills to vaccination. To support their claims requires highly selective filtering of the findings of scientific and epidemiological studies of vaccine safety and effectiveness. Notwithstanding the need for vigilance regarding vaccine safety, the efforts of these individuals can lead some people to make uninformed decisions about immunisation. For example, evidence suggests that countries with active public opposition to whole cell pertussis vaccination programmes had a higher burden from that disease[1].

One vociferous opponent of vaccination is Dr. Viera Scheibner and she has made considerable efforts over the past decade to publicise her assertions about the dangers of vaccination. This paper describes her efforts as an example of a public opponent of vaccination. It then suggests how health workers might respond to public dissemination of some of her unfounded claims as a model for an appropriate approach to such challenges.

Viera Scheibner is Australia's best known opponent of vaccination. Over the past decade, she has toured the world promoting her message that vaccines are ineffective and unsafe. Typically, her lecture tours are organised by local anti-vaccine lobby groups and advertised via fliers, public notices, and newspaper briefs. In this material, parents, the general public, and health professionals are invited to hear a "scientist and author" speak about vaccination[2]. Journalists from local newspapers can find her theories newsworthy enough to draw press coverage, subsequently sparking a letter writing war between indignant health professionals and people who passionately support her arguments.

Scheibner introduces herself as a retired Principal Research Scientist with the State Government of New South Wales (NSW), Australia, who has a doctorate in natural sciences. She has no formal health sciences training and has co-authored one article in the peer reviewed medical research literature indexed on Medline between 1966 and June 2002[3]. Her doctorate (RNDr) was in micropalaeontology and examined "Jurassic and Cretaceous foraminifera from the Pieniny Klippen Belt in the Western Carpathians". As Viera Scheibnerová, she worked as Assistant Professor in the Department of Geology at Comenius University in Bratislava from 1958 to 1968[4]. She emigrated to Australia in 1968 and worked with the Department of Mineral Resources on the Geological Survey of NSW until 1987[5]. She is now retired from paid employment, devoting much of her time to lecturing about the alleged dangers of vaccination.

By her own account, Dr. Scheibner's interest in vaccines stemmed from 1985 when, testing an infant breathing monitor developed by her late husband, she observed periods of what she called "stressed breathing" in babies in the days following diphtheria, tetanus and whole cell pertussis

(DTP) vaccination. Believing that she had found the cause of sudden infant death syndrome (SIDS), her attempts to alert the scientific community to her findings were met with resistance and disagreement. Thus, began her search for other examples of vaccines causing harm and a heartfelt crusade against the practice. By 1993, she claimed to have studied more than 30,000 pages of medical literature[6].

Other than the SIDS connection, Dr. Scheibner alleges that a host of other diseases and conditions, including AIDS, asthma, cancer, and Legionnaires disease, are caused by vaccines. At one stage "brain eating bugs" drew her attention[7]. She also claims smallpox has not been eliminated but has been re-classified as other pox viruses, thus proving that the vaccine failed to eliminate the disease[6].

A study of 4 years of Australian press coverage about vaccination reveals that her most frequently used arguments against vaccination centre around the experiences of Sweden and Japan[8].

> Sweden stopped whooping cough vaccination in 1979. Not only did they have the second lowest infant mortality in the world, but whooping cough since has become a mild disease. After a spate of 37 cot deaths after DPT vaccinations, Japan moved the minimum vaccination age to 2 years in 1975, which resulted in a virtual disappearance of cot death[9].

It is noteworthy that Dr. Scheibner and other spokespersons focus particularly on conditions where complete control by immunisation has been most difficult to achieve (pertussis and measles), vaccines where allegations of adverse effects have been most strident (whole cell pertussis) and disorders whose causation and pathophysiology are at once frightening and ill-defined or multifactorial such as neurodevelopmental problems and Shaken Baby Syndrome. Her methods in public meetings revolve around the use of overhead transparencies where she highlights fine print in, or reinterprets tables and graphs from, published papers. She makes much of the claim that all her material comes from mainstream medical literature, often implying that medical practitioners have not paid sufficient attention to this information or are actively concealing it. The conceptual and factual details can be refuted but this often requires communication of epidemiological concepts or data interpretation not readily accessible to a lay audience. For instance, the above claims require detailed understanding of the history of pertussis immunisation in Sweden (which is now very well controlled by acellular vaccines)[10] and the epidemiology of SIDS in Japan. In the latter case, Scheibner rests her statement about the "disappearance of cot death" on data showing that no claims were lodged under the compensation scheme when the vaccination age was increased from 3 months to 2 years of age[11]. However, she fails to point out that a SIDS diagnosis is restricted to infants under 12 months[12]. SIDS had merely disappeared as an entity from the vaccination compensation system which was now compensating only for events occurring after 2 years, the new minimum age for vaccination (for a detailed rebuttal of the above claims see http://www.skeptics.com.au/journal/anti-immune.htm[13] and Scheibner's response http://www.vaccination.inoz.com/jsids.html[14]).

More recently, Scheibner has been alleging a link between vaccines and Shaken Baby Syndrome[15]. This has resulted in her corresponding with imprisoned fathers attempting to be cleared of criminal charges of their children's deaths. The following introduces an article she wrote for Nexus, a magazine which declares itself as dedicated to UFOs, suppressed science, government cover-ups, and other conspiracy theories.

> Recently, there has been quite an "epidemic" of the so-called "Shaken Baby Syndrome". Parents, usually the fathers, or other care-givers such as nannies have increasingly been accused of shaking a baby to the point of causing permanent brain damage and death. Why? Is there an unprecedented increase in the number of people who commit infanticide or have an ambition to seriously hurt babies? Or is there something more sinister at play?[15].

The article expands on Scheibner's belief that Shaken Baby Syndrome has been misdiagnosed in many cases. She asserts that vaccine-induced brain swelling and bleeding tendency, with associated haemorrhage is the true culprit. Although her theory is not supported by more detailed consideration of pathophysiology or well-conducted vaccine safety studies, the counter-arguments are again quite complex, requiring sophisticated understanding of the physiology of bleeding tendency and the interpretation of clinical trial data. Scheibner claims to have been asked by lawyers acting for defendants in Shaken Baby cases to provide expert reports[15]. Chadwick and Parrish have called for "irresponsible expert testimony" to be excluded by judges in such cases[16].

In her book, "*Vaccination: 100 years of orthodox research shows that vaccines represent a medical assault on the immune system*," Dr. Scheibner proposes homoeopathy as an alternative to vaccination[6]. Otherwise, her writings tend to maintain a focus on vaccines, with limited discussion of the consequences of vaccine preventable diseases. Measles, for instance, is considered an, "important development milestone in the life and maturing processes in children,"[17] ignoring data that the acute effects of measles leads to death in every 5–10,000 cases[18]. An unwillingness to acknowledge even the slightest benefit from any vaccine may be the Achilles Heel of Scheibner and at least some other public opponents of vaccination. Supporters of vaccination can contrast their uniform acknowledgement that vaccines are neither 100% effective nor 100% safe, while emphasising that very exacting standards of safety and effectiveness are required for licensure and that approaching 100% is a key aim. It is difficult to explain away benefits of vaccines such as the eradication of smallpox, the lack of wards full of paralytic polio patients in iron lungs or the virtual disappearance of *Haemophilus influenzae* type b (Hib) meningitis[19]. The latter is particularly powerful as it has occurred recently and over such a short time period. Attempts to discount these developments as unrelated to vaccination require contortions of logic which can stretch the credulity of even the most devoted follower.

Not all the claims of vaccination opponents are completely erroneous. For example, Dr. Scheibner is critical of doctors for their reluctance to report adverse events after vaccination[20]. There is no doubt that many share a desire for accurate data on adverse events. Indeed, over-arching reference to universal themes of child well-being, concern over scientific arrogance, and natural methods of preventing disease define much of the appeal of public opponents[8].

Although a brief look at the arguments of Dr. Scheibner and others[21] indicates that fanaticism is probably their own worst enemy, such arguments can attract media attention and health workers will often lament these effects. In the case of Dr. Scheibner, the ability to make herself and her claims so widely known probably stems from being an animated speaker, who may appear to those without a very detailed knowledge of the literature (including health professionals) to have an encyclopaedic knowledge of vaccination. Most importantly, a willingness to visit towns, no matter how small, to speak about her beliefs represents an example of strong grass roots activism. This can also stir the resolve of local lobby groups to be more fervent in their public opposition to vaccination. Partly because of the outrageousness of her claims, Scheibner's visits often attract a strong reaction from local health professionals. This can perpetuate publicity and community discussion about them, even seeming to lend her a "whistleblower" status.

2. The response dilemma

Clinicians and public health workers are often perplexed as to how to deal with the perceived threat from, or repercussions following, visits from Dr. Scheibner or similar spokespeople. One concern is that a responding publicly might unwittingly lend credibility to such claims, with some preferring to let fanaticism speak for itself. However, ignoring such lobbyists poses its own risks. In the absence of expert voices refuting the theories advanced, some parents may uncritically accept the information. The local context will often determine whether it is appropriate to respond. For health workers who choose to do so, the following are suggestions based on a broad range of literature about risk perception and communication[22].

3. Suggestions for response

- Become familiar with the most common claims that vaccination opponents put forward. Conduct an Internet search and attend one of the meetings.
- Be available to speak to the media. Inform the journalist about the qualifications and background of your local or invited spokesperson. In the case of Viera Scheibner, her credentials may not be made explicit and the "Dr." title can imply medical training for audiences who may then regard information with the authority they normally ascribe to qualified health professionals.

- Acknowledge vaccines, like other medical interventions, are not 100% safe and effective. Trust is important in maintaining public confidence in vaccine programmes. Over confidence in vaccine safety estimates that are later shown to be incorrect erodes trust[22]. The potential problems arising from over-confident safety reassurances were starkly demonstrated at the height of the UK's Creutzfeld–Jacob Disease (CJD) affair. The then minister for Agriculture attempted to show it was safe to eat beef burgers by feeding one to his daughter. Later, when a possible link between beef consumption and variant CJD was recognised, the photo became inscribed in the public consciousness as symbolising untrustworthy official reassurances.
- Promote the importance of vaccine adverse events reporting and making these data publicly accessible[23].
- Avoid fact-for-fact debates, which tend to get lost in detail, may overwhelm or bore audiences and appear reactive[24].
- Respond to the emotions raised by the claims then reframe the debate to centre on protecting children from diseases. Controversies about vaccine safety tend to draw attention from this ultimate goal.
- Listen to community concerns about vaccination and be open and responsive to them[25,26]. Do not respond to questioning of immunisation in an admonishing way. Such responses tend to play into the medical arrogance frame often set by vaccine opponents.
- Audiences with little familiarity with vaccination issues, for example, new parents, may more readily accept as mainstream, theories which are outlandish in scientific terms. Draw attention to the overwhelming medical and scientific support for vaccination.
- Have prominent community doctors and other credible sources like infant health nurses from the community reinforce the importance of immunisation and give their own accounts of caring for people with vaccine preventable diseases[8].
- Use visual images and stories of those affected to jog the community memory of the effects of diseases like polio. A story or picture can be worth a thousand risk–benefit equations. For example, the following website contains a 1952 photo of a ward of polio sufferers in iron lungs: http://www.immunize.org/images/ca.d/ipcd1861/img0008.htm.
- In order to broaden the coalition of voices supportive of immunisation, obtain the support of other parent organisations like SIDS or autism support groups who do not support claims that these conditions are linked to immunisation[8].

With the rise of the anti-vaccination movement, reduced incidence of vaccine-preventable diseases, increased consumerism and interest in alternative therapies, public health workers will be increasingly compelled to respond to community concerns about vaccination[27]. This point has been highlighted by the attention given to the alleged link between measles–mumps–rubella (MMR) vaccine, inflammatory bowel disease and autism[28]. The above suggestions are based broadly on workshops and conclusions from existing research. However, there is a need to develop and test interventions that help people make considered and balanced decisions about vaccination.

ACKNOWLEDGEMENTS

The authors are grateful to Donna Mitchell, Simon Chapman, Sandy Leask and Mark Ferson for comments on earlier drafts. Competing interests: Julie Leask received funds from CSL Ltd. in 1999 and 2000 to attend two conferences. Peter McIntyre has been Chief Investigator for vaccine trials sponsored by Wyeth and GlaxoSmithKline from 1997 to 2002. Neither receive any salary or direct benefits from any industry group.

REFERENCES

[1] Gangarosa EJ, Galazka AM, Wolfe CR, Phillips LM, Gangarosa RE, Miller E, et al. Impact of anti-vaccine movements on pertussis control: the untold story. Lancet 1998;351:356–61.

[2] Scientist looks at reasons against vaccination. Qld: Sunshine Coast Daily; 2 November 1994.

[3] Tye K, Pollard I, Karlsson L, Scheibner V, Tye G. Caffeine exposure in utero increases the incidence of apnea in adult rats. Reprod Toxicol 1993;7:449–52.

[4] Kovác M, Scheibner V. Personal communication. E-mail to Leask J (JulieL@health.usyd.edu.au) 23 April 2001.

[5] Scheibnerova V. Permian foraminifera of the Sydney basin. Sydney: Department of Mineral Resources; 1982.

[6] Scheibner V. Vaccination: 100 years of orthodox research shows that vaccines represent a medical assault on the immune system. Blackheath (NSW): Viera Scheibner; 1993.

[7] Scheibner V. Brain eating bugs: the vaccines link. Nexus Mag 1996;3(3):43–6, 85.

[8] Leask J-A, Chapman S. An attempt to swindle nature': press anti-immunisation reportage, 1993–1997. Aust N Z J Public Health 1998;22:17–26.

[9] Diseases strike vaccinated kids. Qld: Gold Coast Bulletin; 1994.

[10] Olin P, Hallander HO. Marked decline in pertussis followed reintroduction of pertussis vaccination in Sweden. Eurosurveillance 1999;4:128–9.

[11] Cherry JD, Brunell PA, Golden GS, Karzon DT. Report of the task force on pertussis and pertussis immunization—1988. Pediatrics 1988;81:939–84.

[12] Willinger M, James LS, Catz C. Defining the sudden infant death syndrome (SIDS): deliberations of an expert panel convened by the National Institute of Child Health and Human Development. Pediatr Pathol 1991;11:677–84.

[13] Basser S. Anti-immunisation scare: the inconvenient facts. Aust Skeptic 1998;17(1):18–25.

[14] Scheibner V. Comments on Japanese SIDS rebuttal. http://www.vaccination.inoz.com/jsids.html, accessed 12 June 2002.

[15] Scheibner V. Shaken baby syndrome: the vaccination link, Nexus Mag 1999;5(5):61–3, 79.

[16] Chadwick DL, Parrish R. DTP vaccination or Shaken Baby Syndrome? The role of irresponsible medical expert testimony in creating a false causal connection, 2000. http://www.dontshake.com/sbsfall00dtp.html, accessed 12 February 2001.

[17] Scheibner V. Measles quotes. http://www.whale.to/m/quotes19.html, accessed 8 January 2001.

[18] Hall R, O'Brien E. Immunisation myths and realities: responding to arguments against immunisation. 2nd ed. Canberra: Australian Government Publishing Service; 1998.

[19] McIntyre P, Gidding H, Gilmore R, Lawrence G, Hull B, Horby P, et al. Vaccine preventable diseases and vaccination coverage in Australia, 1999–2000. Commun Dis Intell 2002;26:S1–111.

[20] Treweek A. WA to probe jabs. Perth: The Sunday Times; 1994.

[21] Vaccination: the hidden truth (video). Sydney: Bronwyn Hancock; 1999. Summary available at http://www.vaccination.inoz.com/default.html.

[22] Evans G, Bostrom A, Johnson RB, Fisher BL, Stoto MA, editors. Risk communication and vaccination: summary of a workshop. Washington (DC): National Academy Press; 1997.

[23] Chen RT, Hibbs B. Vaccine safety: current and future challenges. Pediatr Ann 1998;27:445–55.

[24] Leask J-A, Chapman S, Hawe P. Concerns about immunisation. Facts are not enough. Br Med J 2000;321:109.

[25] Bedford H, Elliman D. Concerns about immunisation. Br Med J 2000;320:240–3.

[26] National Research Council. Improving risk communication. Washington: National Academy of Sciences; 1989.

[27] Poland GA, Jacobson RM. Understanding those who do not understand: a brief review of the anti-vaccine movement. Vaccine 2001;19:2440–5.

[28] Elliman D, Bedford H. MMR vaccine: the continuing saga. Br Med J 2001;322:183–4.

VACCINATIONS: Searching for the Middle Ground

By Patrick Hanaway, MD

Each year millions of parents go to doctors' offices wondering if their decisions to vaccinate their children are right. This confusion over the past ten years has been heightened by the increasing polarity of pro-vaccination and anti-vaccination views. It appears that the fear of adverse effects from vaccination is matched only by the fear of infectious diseases from not vaccinating. There appears to be no middle ground.

Fuel has been added to the fire with recent changes in vaccination guidelines that modify the vaccine contents while promoting an ever-expanding number of required and suggested vaccines. While looking at the historical benefit of vaccination, this article will present an approach that seeks to empower parents in their decision-making to find the best answer for their children.

Interestingly, vaccination [from the Latin, *vacca* = cow] began in 1798 when Edward Jenner, an English surgeon, discovered that inoculating humans with material oozing from cows infected with cowpox could prevent smallpox. This is a good example of "like cures like," an early homeopathic treatment principle.

Homeopathic nosodes (substances derived from disease products, tissue samples, mucus, pus from discharges, or pure cultures of microorganisms) have been used to prevent disease since the early 19th century. Anecdotal evidence suggests that homeopathy may be effective on a short-term basis during epidemics. A Brazilian study showed a homeopathic nosode prevented 96% of children from developing meningitis during a 1974 epidemic, though treated children may have been from a healthier sub-group. This form of prevention does not convey long-term protection.

Protocols have been developed for long-term prevention with homeopathic nosodes given repeatedly. Homeopathic preparations have not been shown to raise antibody levels (as vaccinations do), thus the only way to measure the effectiveness of homeopathic prophylaxis is through clinical results. Parents need to understand that there are no studies to show that homeopathic prophylaxis provides lasting immunity from specific diseases.

Vaccination is an effective tool for protecting public health. During the Twentieth Century we eradicated smallpox worldwide and minimized the debilitating effects of polio. But public health data shows that incidence of many diseases such as diphtheria, pertussis (whooping cough), scarlet fever, and measles declined almost completely by 1945 . . . before the implementation of the mass-vaccination programs!

Parents have been raising questions about compulsory vaccination for more than a century. Recently parental concerns have led to increased vigilance by public health officials in reviewing Vaccine Adverse Effect Reactions (VAER). Examples include negative effects of the Diptheria Pertussis Tetanus (DTP) vaccine, the presence of toxic levels of mercury in vaccines, and concerns about the relationship between the Measles/Mumps/Rubella (MMR) vaccine and autism.

Public awareness of side effects, including brain injury, led to a decline in DTP vaccination rates during the 70's, particularly in England and Japan. The exact number of children injured by DTP will never be known. Japan's vaccination rate dropped from 80% to 10%, resulting in an epidemic of whooping cough, with 13,000 cases and 41 deaths. Thus, we see how decreased vaccination can lead to increased disease and death. Conversely, the pressures brought to bear by parents of children injured by DTP led to the creation of an acellular Pertusis vaccine, now conjugated with Diphtheria and Tetanus as DtaP.

More recently, questions have been raised about the presence of the mercury-containing preservative thimerosal in a number of vaccinations. The FDA recently acknowledged that in the first six months of life children get more mercury from vaccines than is considered safe by the EPA. In 1999, based upon parental concern, the US Public Health Service and the American Academy of Pediatrics issued a statement recommending the removal of thimerosal from vaccines. In May 2000, the FDA notified vaccine manufacturers that reducing or eliminating thimerosal from vaccines is merited. As of June 2002, mercury is still present in some vaccines. Mercury toxicity demonstrates symptoms similar to autism. In the last fifteen years, autism rates have risen nearly fifty-fold to 1 in 150 (CDC data). Autism Spectrum Disorders are characterized by delayed neurodevelopment, poor use of language, repetitive behaviors, and social withdrawal. Dr. Andrew Wakefield has found that some children with autism cannot react to the live, modified measles virus present in the MMR vaccine. This data demonstrates a connection, but not necessarily a causal relationship. The Institute of Medicine notes that the MMR vaccine could contribute to autism in a small number of children, but the population data is not precise enough to figure this out. The questions remain.

When I am speaking with parents about the vaccination decision that they are making for their children, I highlight the opportunity for choice. An educated choice requires the following information to help parents take responsibility for their own child's health care:

1. A fair representation of the risks and benefits of each vaccine;
2. A careful review of the birth, family history, and particular genetic risks of the individual child;
3. An evaluation of the environment within which the child lives or travels.

In short, one must consider the vaccine, the child, and the environment.

This unique and holistic perspective can be illustrated by the following example:

Haemophilus influenza B (HiB) is a type of bacteria present in the nose and throat of many children and adults. This common infection can invade through the lining of the throat and into the blood stream and spinal fluid. This form of 'invasive' HiB infection caused meningitis in approximately one in 1000 infants before the dissemination of the HiB vaccines in the early 90s. The rate of HiB meningitis has dropped sharply over the past ten years.

RELIGIOUS EXEMPTION:

All states allow a religious exemption to vaccination except Mississippi and West Virginia.

The religious exemption is intended for people who possess a sincere religious belief against vaccination to the extent that if the state forced vaccination, it would be an infringement on their right to exercise their religious beliefs. Some state laws define religious exemptions broadly to include personal religious beliefs, similar to personal philosophical beliefs. Other states require an individual who claims a religious exemption to be a member of The First Church of Christ, Scientist (Christian Science) or another bonafide religion whose written tenets include prohibition of invasive medical procedures such as vaccination.

Some laws require a signed affidavit from the pastor of the church while others allow the parent to sign a notarized waiver. Prior to registering your child for school, you must check your state law to verify what your health department requires to prove your religious beliefs. The religious exemption is granted based on the First Amendment of the Constitution, which is the right to freely exercise your religion.

Because citizens are protected under the First Amendment of the United States, a state must have a "compelling State interest" before this right can be taken away. One "compelling State interest" is the spread of communicable diseases. In state court cases that have set precedent on this issue the freedom to act according to your own religious belief is subject to reasonable regulation with the justification that it must not threaten the welfare of society as a whole.

In the late 1980's the Yup'ik Eskimo people in Western Alaska had the highest rate of HiB meningitis ever recorded (30 cases in every 1000 infants). The HiB vaccine was introduced in 1989. The vaccine was a tremendous benefit to the Native Alaskan population and produced steady decline in the rate of meningitis. I worked with the Yup'ik people from 1992–1994, during which time there were no cases of HiB meningitis.

The much smaller Caucasian population that lived in Western Alaska did not experience any HiB meningitis, even before the introduction of vaccination. This protection may have been due to genetic protection, better nutrition, or the availability of toilets and running water with the affluent Caucasians.

We see that vaccines are of great benefit for people at risk. Defining the at-risk people (especially children) becomes the critical factor. This raises the question: Should all vaccinations be universally required?

Unfortunately, the data required for us to 'do the right thing' in all cases does not exist. In fact, few studies have ever been done to evaluate the before and after effects of vaccination on the immune system—much less on the child's developing immune system. Has the mass use of multiple vaccines in early childhood, when the brain and immune systems are developing at their most rapid rate, been a co-factor in the brain and immune dysfunctions seen in so many young children today?

Vaccines have driven infectious diseases out of childhood, but over the past quarter century there has been a simultaneous and unprecedented increase in the numbers of children suffering from chronic disease and disability. There are repeated calls for research on the link between vaccines and neurological and immunological disorders in adults and children. The incidence of learning disabilities, attention deficit/hyperactivity disorder, and asthma has doubled, childhood (Type I) diabetes has tripled, and autism soars. The number of children suffering with these chronic disabilities is in the tens of millions in the US, Canada, and Europe.

It would seem intuitively obvious that studies to evaluate these relationships would be required before any new vaccine is put on the market, recommended by the CDC, or mandated by state law. Without proper scientific investigation and proof, we don't know if the increase in childhood chronic diseases is attributable to increases in vaccinations, environmental toxins, exposure to chemicals, antibiotic abuse, or other unknown agents.

The Institute of Medicine, in its 2002 report *Multiple Immunizations and Immune Dysfunction,* discusses biologic mechanisms by which vaccinations influence the risk for allergy and additional infection. It emphasizes the need for research on genetic variability in immune system development and encourages a more flexible schedule for a reduction in the number of vaccines administered at one time.

Study of the developing immune system shows that immunizations during the six months of life require recurrent 'boosting' because the infant's immune system is unable to sustain an immune response. This is why vaccines are required repeatedly during the first year of life.

8 QUESTIONS TO HELP PREVENT VACCINE REACTIONS

1. Is my child sick right now?
2. Has my child had a bad reaction to a vaccination before?
3. Does my child have a personal or family history of vaccine reactions? convulsions or neurological disorders? severe allergies? immune system disorders?
4. Do I know if my child is at high risk of reacting?
5. Do I have full information on the vaccine's side effects?
6. Do I know how to identify a vaccine reaction?
7. Do I know how to report a vaccine reaction?
8. Do I know the vaccine manufacturer's name and lot number?

Source: National Vaccine Information Center website (www.909shot.com).

Given this information it is logical for many patients to ask, "Why do I need to give my child the Polio Vaccine (IPV) three times in the first year of life when there has been no wild-type polio in the U.S. in over twenty years? Do I need to give the Hepatitis B vaccine (now outlawed in France) during the first year of life? Can I delay the MMR to prevent the possible risk of autism?"

Nearly one-quarter of parents in a recent survey believe that children receive more vaccines than are good for them, and that too many vaccinations could overwhelm an infant's immune system. The average child receives fifteen doses of five vaccines in the first six months of life, and a total of 22 shots against eleven diseases by eighteen months of age. It appears that modifying the schedule to allow for flexible scheduling of vaccinations throughout childhood may be of benefit. Studies to assess the risks and benefits of such approaches with parents would allow for 'ground-breaking research' on the differences between partial and/or delayed vaccination versus current vaccination schedules.

Parents who ask more questions and who actively seek to protect the health and well-being of their children want more information, better research, clearer guidelines, and fairer practices in the use of vaccinations. Over the past fifteen years, questions from concerned parents have led in the development of the VAER, legislation to begin the Vaccine Injury & Compensation Program (VICP), changes in the pertussis vaccine, phasing out of the oral polio vaccine, rejection of the rotavirus vaccine, moratorium on the administration of Hepatitis B vaccine at birth, removal of mercury from vaccines and more thorough research on vaccines. Vaccines are safer because of parental questioning and concern. We see that 'when the people lead, the leaders will follow.'

As we listen to parents with heart-breaking stories from adverse reactions to vaccines, we must also remember the countless lives that have been saved from vaccination. The images of friends and family suffering from poliomyelitis have faded from our collective memory. We are fortunate in reaping the societal benefits of vaccination. As fewer cases of vaccine-preventable diseases are present, our focus moves toward the complications from vaccines—for no vaccine is perfectly safe.

When a sufficient percentage of the population is vaccinated for a given disease, non-vaccinated individuals are less likely to catch the disease. This idea of "herd immunity" leads to unvaccinated individuals reaping the benefits without facing the small, but real, risk of vaccination. Data from measles in California shows that unvaccinated individuals are at a 35-fold higher risk of developing infection. They represent a significant source of transmission of disease to those in the general population whose immune systems have not been able to fully integrate the vaccination. The more people choose not to vaccinate, the more all of us are at risk.

An ethical dilemma is created: the rights of the individual versus the needs of society. We have the luxury of having this discussion because of the decline in infectious disease over the past century. Vaccination appears to be helpful, but the current form is problematic at best. We must refine the use of these vaccination tools to apply them with discretion rather than a 'one-size-fits-all' approach.

Every book or paper I have read on this subject has presumed to know the 'right' approach to vaccination. But the truth in medicine is that there is not one right way to treat (or prevent) cancer, heart disease, auto-immune problems, or epidemic infections.

Thus, there is no easy answer to the question, "Are vaccinations safe and effective?" We must recognize that through education and awareness we, as parents, must make individual decisions for which we are willing to take responsibility. We must . . .

Continue to ask questions until we are clear.

Reject doctrine as a sufficient answer.

Develop consensus as parents.

Make choices for the health of our children.

When these guidelines are followed with wisdom and compassion, then we will have found the middle ground.

Patrick Hanaway, MD co-founded FAMILY to FAMILY: Your Home for Whole Family Health in Asheville, NC. He has two children and has struggled with these same questions.

ACTIONS YOU CAN TAKE:

- Contact your Congressman and urge them to support a moratorium on the commercialization of pharmcrops. Contact www.senate.gov and www.house.gov
- Contact Jack Cecil and tell him you do not want WNC to be the next biotech lab: 828-209-2000, jcecil@biltmorefarms.com
- For more information on GE pharmcrops and plans to turn WNC into the next biotech lab, go to www.purefoodpartners.org

REFERENCES

Eat Up Your Vaccines, Seedling Newsletter

Genetically Engineered Pharmcrops, Union of Concerned Scientists

Pharm Crops~A Food Accident Waiting to Happen, Greenpeace

California Biotech Companies Grow Plants with Human Proteins, Agbios

Crop Producing Human Protein Found Growing in Open Field Test, Kim Wilson, Greenpeace activist

How Safe are Genetically Engineered Vaccines? Helen Lawler, M.A.

Amberwaves Calls for a Moratorium on Genetically Engineered Pharmaceutical Rice in California, Press Release, Amberwaves

Growing Pharmaceuticals in Plants, Dow AgroSciences

Debi Athos the director of Pure Food Partners, a non-profit group working to educate the public about the genetic engineering of our food. Contact her at debi@purefoodpartners.org

REFERENCES

Institute of Medicine. "Immunization Safety Review: Measles-Mumps-Robella Vaccine and Autism." 2001. National Academy Press, Washington, DC.

Institute of Medicine. "Immunization Safety Review: Multiple Immunizations and Immune Dysfunction." 2002. National Academy Press, Washington, DC.

McQuillan GM et al. "Serologic Immunity to Diphtheria and Tetanus in the United States." Ann Int Med. 2002:136:60-65.

Regan L. "Show Us the Science: Report on the Second International Public Conference of the National Vaccine Information Center," Mothering. 2001; 105:39-53.

Salmon DA et al. "Health Consequences of Religious and Philosophical Exemptions From Immunization Laws: Individual and Societal Risk of Measles." JAMA. 1999;282:47-53.

Singleton RJ et al. "Decline of Haemophilus influenzae type b disease in a region of high risk; impact of passive and active immunization." Pediatr Infect Dis J. 1994;13:362-67.

FOR FURTHER READING:

MEDLINEplus Health Information http://www.nlm.nih.gov/medlineplus/immunizationvaccination.htm

Understanding Vaccines; Brochure in Adobe Reader http://www.niaid.nih.gov/publications/vaccme/undvacc.htm

A Shot in the Dark by Harris L. Coulter, Ph.D. & Barbara Loe Fisher. Read the book that started it all. Coulter and Fisher didn't intend to write critically of vaccination but the more they researched, the more the reality was revealed. Impeccably documented, meticulously researched, a must read for anyone wishing to understand childhood vaccinations.

Vaccination: The Issue of Our Times. The most comprehensive collection ever printed of articles, research, and references, challenging the conventional viewpoint on vaccinations. Contributors include physicians, public health workers, and parents, Edited by Mothering magazine publisher and editor, Peggy O'Mara. 314 pages

THE VACCINE GUIDE: Making An Informed Choice by Randall Neustaedter, O.M.D. Excellent reference source. Discusses all vaccines, alternative vaccine methods, exemptions, vaccine reactions (short and long-term) and treating vaccine reactions.

WHAT EVERY PARENT SHOULD KNOW ABOUT CHILDHOOD IMMUNIZATION by Jamie Murphy. Do you know what's inside the vaccine your infant is receiving? Murphy explains what vaccines are, how they are made, what little-known toxic chemicals are used and the reactions that may follow the injection.

Autism and Vaccination—The Current Evidence

Lisa Miller, MD, MSPH
and Joni Reynolds, RN, MSN

Lisa Miller, MD, MSPH, is the Disease Control and Environmental Epidemiology Division Director, and **Joni Reynolds, RN, MSN,** is the Immunization Program Director, Colorado Department of Public Health and Environment, Denver, Colorado, USA.

PURPOSE. *The purpose of this article is to review relevant background literature regarding the evidence linking thimerosal-containing vaccine and the measles, mumps, and rubella vaccine to autism.*

CONCLUSIONS. *Rigorous scientific studies have not identified links between autism and either thimerosal-containing vaccine or the measles, mumps, and rubella vaccine.*

PRACTICE IMPLICATIONS. *Nurses are often in the position of providing advice regarding vaccines in their formal practice areas as well as in their daily lives. Families need current and credible evidence to make decisions for their children. Excellent vaccine information resources are available online.*

Search terms: *ASD, autism, immunization, MMR, measles, thimerosal, vaccine*

First Received November 14, 2008; Revision received February 25, 2009; Accepted for publication March 16, 2009.

Autism Spectrum Disorders (ASD) are a group of developmental disabilities characterized by impairments in social interaction and communication and repetitive behaviors. The prevalence of these conditions has increased over the past several decades, but it is unclear whether this is due to a true increase, increasing awareness, or differences in the methods used to assess prevalence. By definition, the onset of ASD occurs prior to age 3 (Volkmar & Pauls, 2003).

No clear etiology has been identified for ASD, although many possible associations have been investigated (Newschaffer et al., 2007). Given the increase in prevalence, there has been interest in "environmental" exposures that may have also increased over the past several decades. One of these exposures, vaccinations, has received widespread interest and attention. An increasing number of vaccinations have become available over the past several decades to protect children against infectious diseases, and many are given at a time period during early childhood that coincides with the onset of developmental concerns related to autism.

This article will explore vaccination history, vaccine safety monitoring systems in the United States, and the two most publicized theoretical vaccine-related exposures that have been associated with autism—the vaccine preservative thimerosal and the measles, mumps, and rubella (MMR) vaccine. Understanding both the history and recent research will assist nurses in providing accurate patient information and in interpreting new findings in an area that continues to generate controversy and research interest.

The art and science of vaccinology is complex and requires significant rigor in educating providers about vaccines and their administration. Vaccines are a cornerstone in public health practice, as "Vaccines are one of the greatest achievements of biomedical science and public health" (Centers for Disease Control and Prevention [CDC], 1999a, p. 247). Yet, the success of vaccines and drastically reduced rates of disease have resulted in parents not experiencing firsthand the significant effects of these diseases. Some parents are now more concerned about the risks, real and theoretical, of recommended childhood vaccines.

HISTORY OF VACCINES

The earliest medical vaccine is considered to be the smallpox vaccination, developed by Dr. Edward Jenner in the eighteenth century. Impressively, Jenner's work preceded the work of Louis Pasteur, who introduced the concept of viruses to the scientific world.

In 1796, Edward Jenner vaccinated James Phipps using material from a cowpox lesion on the hand of a milkmaid, theorizing that vaccination with cowpox would lead to immunity against the dreaded smallpox. A later attempt to give Phipps smallpox demonstrated his immunity, and the vaccination era began. Although Jenner lacked our understanding of viruses, the immune system, or vaccinology, his clinical observations convinced him that milkmaids were protected from smallpox because of their previous exposure to cowpox, and he acted to see if nature could be replicated (Foege, 2006).

Of the many illnesses circulating in the twentieth century, none was as widely feared as polio, which caused crippling illness, particularly in children. There were many pools and beaches closed in the summertime due to concerns of polio epidemic. Parents feared polio and anxiously supported the development of a polio vaccine.

Dr. Salk introduced the first killed polio vaccine in the United States in 1955 through massive clinical trials. There were concerns with the vaccine, however, as several hundred cases of paralytic polio were induced by the vaccine. Dr. Sabin researched and developed a different polio vaccine that was introduced in the early 1960s. This vaccine proved to be safer than and as effective as the prior polio vaccine. An improved Salk Inactivated Polio vaccine is still used routinely for U.S. children today, while the Sabin Oral Polio vaccine is used in some international efforts to eradicate polio worldwide.

These early vaccine pioneers were fortunate to have success. Historically, it was a common trait among scientists to take personal risks for the benefit of science. Jenner, Salk, and Sabin risked their reputations for these early breakthroughs, setting the stage for future vaccine development. Today, the risks and benefits of vaccines are closely calculated and monitored. The early vaccines were developed using a crude approach compared to the laboratory-based vaccine development processes of today.

VACCINES TODAY

Today there are routine vaccines that can protect individuals from measles, mumps, rubella, chickenpox, pertussis, diphtheria, tetanus, invasive *Haemophilus influenzae* type b (Hib) infections, viral hepatitis A, viral hepatitis B, invasive *Streptococcus pneumoniae* infections, influenza, human papillomavirus, rotavirus, invasive meningococcal infections, and polio. In addition, there are vaccines that can protect high-risk individuals from other diseases, including smallpox, yellow fever, rabies, anthrax, Japanese encephalitis, herpes zoster (shingles), and typhoid fever.

The Advisory Committee on Immunization Practices (ACIP) provides recommendations for vaccinations to the CDC. Annually, the CDC, the American Academy of Pediatrics, and the American Academy of Family Physicians jointly publish a schedule of recommended immunizations. Children today are routinely vaccinated against 14 diseases during their infancy and preschool years.

Childhood vaccinations are administered as early as possible to assure that infants are protected against diseases that occur in early childhood. Some have questioned the need to administer vaccines according to the recommended ACIP schedule, essentially indicating it is too many vaccines too early for children (Ball et al., 2001). The timing of vaccines is essential to assure that, if possible, protection precedes the disease exposure. It's key to remember that literally from birth, infants are exposed to environmental organisms that can cause infections. Delaying vaccines can be risky because it extends the time that infants are susceptible to real diseases that can have serious complications, particularly for the youngest children.

The goal of the immune system is to identify "non-self" and destroy it. The basic components of the immune system include antigens (non-self foreign bodies) and antibodies (our defense against the antigens). Immune systems are exposed to hundreds or thousands of antigens daily. Infant immune systems are capable of responding to these routine exposures, which present themselves from the moment of birth. Infants and children build effective antibodies to vaccine antigens and are then able to develop internal defenses against a variety of infectious diseases, many of which took a tremendous toll in the past.

> Infants and children build effective antibodies to vaccine anti-gens and are then able to develop internal defenses against a variety of infectious diseases, many of which took a tremendous toll in the past.

INFORMATION REGARDING SYSTEMS FOR VACCINE SAFETY MONITORING

Parents, nurses, other medical providers, vaccine manufacturers, and the government all play critical roles in monitoring the safety of vaccines. As parents know their children best, it is important to encourage them to trust their instincts related to their children's health. Parents should report any concerns after their children's vaccinations to their primary healthcare provider. Nurses and other healthcare providers are required to record key information (e.g., lot number, product, administration site, and method) for each vaccine administered, which can be used when reporting a possible vaccine adverse event. Vaccine lot numbers can be used to track unusual patterns within a specific vaccine lot. In addition, if necessary, a provider can identify which patients received a dose of recalled vaccine.

The National Childhood Vaccine Injury Act was passed in 1986. The Act created the National Vaccine Injury Compensation Program, which provides compensation for those found to be harmed by specific vaccines. This Act also requires healthcare providers to report any serious adverse events that occur within 30 days after vaccination with any vaccine. The reports must be submitted to the Vaccine Adverse Event Reporting System (VAERS), which was set up in 1990 and is managed by the CDC and the Food and Drug Administration (FDA). Reports can be submitted online at http://vaers.hhs.gov/. This is a passive surveillance system that accepts all submitted reports without validation. The VAERS can identify reporting trends that need further investigation. In 1999, the suspicion of a link between the rotavirus vaccine and intussusception was identified through the VAERS (Department of Health and Human Services, n.d.).

Vaccine manufacturers are required to complete prelicensing vaccine testing through clinical trials for each vaccine. In addition, vaccine manufacturers are required by the National Childhood Vaccine Injury Act to report adverse events to the Department of Health and Human Services (CDC, n.d.). Vaccine manufacturers have a vested interest in assuring vaccines are safe, reinforcing public confidence in vaccines.

The Vaccine Safety Datalink includes data from several health maintenance organizations. This database is used to monitor for any possible adverse event from vaccines. Large, ongoing studies are conducted using these data (CDC, n.d.).

The FDA monitors adverse events reporting rates, using both the VAERS data and manufacturer's data. Among the things the FDA looks for are large numbers of adverse event reports early in the circulation of a lot, clusters of similar cases, syndromes (groups of symptoms), or other patterns; additional information from other sources with knowledge of a particular case; patterns of reported adverse events linked to final lots filled from the same bulk vaccine; and documentation that lots in question have passed all the required tests.

MEASLES, MUMPS, AND RUBELLA (MMR) VACCINE

The MMR vaccine was licensed in the United States in 1971 and includes a live, attenuated measles strain. The vaccine results in an asymptomatic or mild infection that cannot be transmitted to others. Measles vaccination has resulted in a decrease in reported measles cases from about 500,000 cases and 500 deaths per year to a few dozen cases each year in the United States (CDC, 2007). In 2008, however, more than 100 cases were reported, due to importations from other countries. Most of these cases have occurred among unvaccinated persons (CDC, 2008b). The ACIP recommends that MMR be administered between the ages of 12 and 15 months, with a second dose administered between 4 and 6 years of age (Kroger, Atkinson, Marcuse, & Pickering, 2006).

A decade ago, a British researcher and 12 coauthors published a paper describing abnormal gastrointestinal features among 12 children who had been referred to their university pediatric gastroenterology clinic. All children had some type of developmental disorder, and in 9 of the children, a diagnosis of autism had been made. In 6 of these 9 children, either the parent or a physician had linked the onset of developmental regression with the receipt of the MMR vaccine (Wakefield et al., 1998). In 2000, a second paper was published, in which white blood cells in the same 9 autistic children (with what was now referred to as "autistic enterocolitis") were examined for the presence of measles virus. Using polymerase chain reaction, the measles virus RNA fragments were found in 3 out of the 9 children but in none of the

22 controls (Kawashima et al., 2000). In 2004, 10 of the 11 coauthors of Wakefield's original paper asked to "formally retract the interpretation placed upon these findings..." (Murch et al., 2004).

However, these initial reports of a possible relationship between the MMR vaccine and the onset of autism received significant attention, and in England, MMR immunization rates dropped from greater than 90% prior to 1998 (National Statistics, T.I.C., 2005) to a low of 80% in 2003–2004 (National Statistics, T.I.C., 2008).

In response to this concern in the United States, the CDC and the National Institutes of Health convened a panel of experts in the fall of 2000 to examine three vaccine safety issues, the first of which was the hypothesis of a link between the MMR vaccine and autism (Immunization Safety Review Committee, Board on Health Promotion and Disease Prevention, & Institute of Medicine, 2001). The committee, after performing an in-depth review of the relevant scientific and medical literature, rejected a causal relationship between the MMR vaccine and ASD based on the following: (i) a lack of epidemiologic evidence linking autism and MMR vaccine, (ii) case reports of children with autism and bowel disorders that did not address causality, and (iii) a lack of biologic models linking ASD and MMR vaccine. Similarly, the American Academy of Pediatrics and the Medical Research Counsel both published similar conclusions (Halsey & Hyman, 2001; Medical Research Council, 2001) in 2001, based on the research available at that time.

Shortly thereafter, several studies were published refuting the association between MMR vaccine and autism. One of the first examined the California Department of Developmental Services data and the state's MMR immunization rate data. They hypothesized that if there were a link, the pattern of change in the immunization rate should be similar to the pattern of change in the autism rate. Instead, they found that the autism rate had increased by 373% between 1980 and 1994 but the immunization rate had been fairly constant during that period, increasing by only 14% (Dales, Hammer, & Smith, 2001).

In that same year, another pair of British researchers set out to test several theories suggested by the hypothesis of a link between a regressive form of autism and the MMR vaccine. The researchers compared a group of children with autism who had been diagnosed prior to the introduction of the MMR vaccine with two groups of children with Pervasive Developmental Disorder Not Otherwise Specified (PDD-NOS; a condition in which children have some of the features of autism) or autism diagnosed after the introduction of MMR vaccine. Among the theories tested was that the mean age of parental concern should be younger, or closer to the age at vaccination in the vaccinated group. Instead, there was no difference between groups. If MMR vaccine were associated with a regressive form of autism, the authors also theorized that the rate of regression would be higher in the groups of children who had received the vaccine. Such an association was not seen (Fombonne & Chakrabarti, 2001). Later, a group of U.S. researchers tested similar theories with a large group of well-studied children with autism. They also found no support for the hypothesis, though they did find a higher rate of gastrointestinal symptoms in children with autism and regression compared to children with autism but no regression. However, they also documented that for many of the children with regression, communication skills prior to the onset of regression was atypical (Richler et al., 2006).

Kaye, Mar Melero-Montes, and Jick (2001) examined the temporal trends by comparing rates of autism in England between boys born in 1988, when MMR vaccine was introduced, and those born in 1993. They found that while the rate of autism diagnoses increased almost fourfold, the rate of MMR immunization was fairly constant over that time period. The authors also compared the mean age at vaccination among those with an autism diagnosis to the mean age at vaccination among the general population and found no difference.

Madsen et al., in 2002, published findings from a cohort of more than half a million children in Denmark that found no difference in the risk of autism between MMR-vaccinated and unvaccinated children. Further evidence was provided in 2004 from a case control study in which the rate of MMR vaccination among children with PDD-NOS was compared to the rate among those without PDD-NOS. The study concluded that those with PDD-NOS were no more likely to have been vaccinated than those without PDD-NOS (Smeeth et al., 2004).

In 2005, researchers reported on the incidence of autism in an area of Japan where MMR vaccination was withdrawn in 1993. They found that the incidence of autism continued to increase, even after the withdrawal (Honda, Shimizu, & Rutter, 2005). Fombonne, Zakarian, Bennett, Meng, and McLean-Heywood (2006) also examined the relationship of MMR vaccination rates with autism rates in Canada, noting that among children born from 1987 to 1998, PDD-NOS increased in a linear fashion, while MMR immunization rates just slightly increased. In addition, a second MMR was added for children at 18 months beginning with those born in 1996. This additional MMR dose did not affect the rate at which PDD-NOS increased (Fombonne et al.).

In addition to the epidemiologic reports examining the relationship between MMR vaccine and autism, others have tried to replicate the findings of measles virus RNA in children with autism. Three studies (Afzal et al., 2006; D'Souza, 2006; Baird et al., 2008) have found no difference in the prevalence of measles virus in peripheral blood mononuclear cells between children with autism and controls, or failed to find any virus in either group. Martin et al. (2002) did find measles virus RNA more commonly in the bowel tissue of children with autism and regression compared to a group of controls, using a variety of polymerase chain reaction methods. More recently, Hornig et al. (2008) have reported negative findings among 25 children with autism and

13 control children, all with clinically significant gastrointestinal symptoms. No significant difference in the prevalence of measles virus RNA in bowel tissue was found between the cases (4%) and controls (8%).

> **As the preponderance of evidence from around the world has accumulated showing no relationship between MMR vaccine and autism, MMR immunization rates in England have begun to increase.**

As the preponderance of evidence from around the world has accumulated showing no relationship between MMR vaccine and autism, MMR immunization rates in England have begun to increase. In 2007–2008, rates were 85%, up from their low of 80% (National Statistics, T.I.C., 2008). However, measles cases have increased dramatically in England, from only 56 cases in 1998 to 1,370 cases in 2008 (Health Protection Agency, 2008). Interestingly, in the United States, national immunization rates for MMR vaccine have not dipped below 90% since 1995, and they have showed no significant reduction during the controversy (CDC, 2001, 2004, 2008a).

THIMEROSAL

Vaccine manufacturers who produce multidose vaccine vials use thimerosal as a preservative. Thimerosal is approximately 50% mercury by weight, and it has been one of the most widely used preservatives in vaccines. It is metabolized or degraded to ethylmercury and thiosalicylate. Ethylmercury is an organomercurial that should be distinguished from methylmercury, a related substance that has been the focus of considerable study (Thimerosal in Vaccines, n.d.). Methylmercury is bioavailable and can accumulate in the brain and cause neurologic damage. The ethylmercury found in thimerosal is not bioavailable. In studies, ethylmercury does not accumulate in the body or the brain and is metabolized and cleared by the body (Burbacher, Shen, Liberato, Grant, & Cernichiari, 2005).

Thimerosal has antimicrobial qualities that keep vaccines safe from inadvertent contamination through routine multiple punctures in a vial. Thimerosal had been used by vaccine manufacturers for years but came under scrutiny in 1999, as discussed earlier in this article. At that time, the FDA and the CDC published statements that indicated manufacturers should reduce or eliminate the amount of thimerosal used in vaccines. The CDC further recommended the birth dose of hepatitis B vaccine be suspended for infants until thimerosal-free vaccine was available (CDC, 1999b).

The CDC stated:

> ... given the widely acknowledged value of reducing exposure to mercury, vaccine manufacturers, the FDA, and other Public Health Service (PHS) agencies are collaborating to reduce the thimerosal content of vaccines or to replace them with formulations that do

not contain thimerosal as a preservative as soon as possible without causing unnecessary disruptions in the vaccination system. The FDA will expedite review of supplements to manufacturers' product license applications that present formulations for eliminating or reducing the mercury content of vaccines. (CDC, 1999, p. 997)

Vaccine manufacturers then worked to assure removal of thimerosal from vaccines. By 2001, all vaccines routinely recommended for children 6 years of age and under in the United States were produced without thimerosal as a preservative, with the exception of some doses of inactivated influenza vaccine. Today, all vaccines are available without thimerosal, including several influenza vaccine presentations (e.g., single-dose prefilled syringes and the intranasal vaccine).

Many studies have been undertaken to examine the risks associated with thimerosal in vaccines. In 2003, Stehr-Green et al. assessed autism incidence and the use of thimerosal containing vaccines: "Data did not support an association between thimerosal-containing vaccines and autism in Denmark and Sweden where exposure to thimerosal was eliminated in 1992 and where autism rates continued to increase" (Stehr-Green et al., 2003, p. 106).

Another study in 2003 utilized the Vaccine Safety Datalink (VSD) to screen for possible associations between exposure to thimerosal-containing vaccines and a variety of renal, neurologic, and developmental problems: "No consistent significant associations were found between thimerosal-containing vaccines and neurodevelopmental outcomes" (Verstraeten et al., 2003, p. 1,042).

The CDC conducted a follow-up study to the Verstraeten et al. VSD study. This was a large study that also utilized the VSD data to investigate a possible link between thimerosal in vaccines and childhood developmental concerns. An excerpt from the study finding reads:

> ... some people believe increased exposure to thimerosal (from the addition of important new vaccines recommended for children) explains the higher prevalence in recent years. However, evidence from several studies examining trends in vaccine use and changes in autism frequency does not support such an association. Furthermore, a scientific review by the Institute of Medicine (IOM) concluded that "the evidence favors rejection of a causal relationship between thimerosal-containing vaccines and autism." (CDC, 2007, p. 144.)

Thompson et al. (2007) further examined the hypotheses that "increasing exposure to thimerosal is associated with neurodevelopmental disorders. Findings did not support a causal association between early exposure to mercury from thimerosal-containing vaccines and immune globulins and deficits in neuropsychological functioning at the age of 7 to 10 years" (Thompson et al., p. 1,290).

RECENT EVENTS

As a result of public concern about autism and vaccines, thousands of claims have been submitted to the National Vaccine Injury Compensation Program. On February 12, 2009, the U.S. Court of Federal Claims published decisions about these claims, which were considered as a group under the Omnibus Autism Proceeding. The Court found, after reviewing 5,000 pages of transcripts, 939 medical articles, 50 expert reports, and hearing testimony from 28 experts, that the MMR and thimerosal-containing vaccines, independently or together, were not causal factors in the development of autism or ASD (U.S. Court of Federal Claims, n.d.).

HOW DO I APPLY THIS EVIDENCE TO NURSING PRACTICE?

Studies about vaccination and autism are often complex and difficult for consumers to access and review. Yet it is critical that the findings are shared widely to assure all healthcare professionals have this information in order to provide evidence-based information to parents. Providers can guide parents in their review of available vaccine information. A systematic framework can be utilized by parents to assure the available information is reliable. An excellent tool for reviewing information is available on the American Academy of Pediatrics Web site: http://www.cispimmunize.org/fam/facts/FAQ-Internet. pdf. Rigorous scientific studies have not identified concerns with thimerosal in vaccines or the measles, mumps, and rubella vaccine. Vaccines continue to be a vital tool in the prevention of vaccine-preventable disease.

Nurses are often in the unique position of providing advice regarding vaccines in their formal practice areas as well as in their daily lives. Many consider nurses to be experts in all areas of health care, leading neighbors, patients, and others to ask for and value their opinions. Nurses participate in this crucial aspect of the prevention of diseases, and therefore, should have a thorough and complete understanding of the issues, concerns, and facts as related to vaccines. It is imperative that nurses have knowledge of the research and its results, and the information pertaining to the diseases we seek to prevent when discussing vaccines with parents, peers, and medical health professionals.

Nurses should continue to learn about vaccines in order to provide complete and up-to-date information to patients and clients. Excellent vaccine information resources are available online at http://www.immunize.org, http://www.vaccinesafety.edu, and http://www.cdc.gov/vaccines.

Author contact: lisa.miller@state.co.us, joni.reynolds@state.co.us, with a copy to the Editor: roxie.foster@UCDenver.edu

REFERENCES

Afzal, M. A., Ozoemena, L. C., O'Hare, A., Kidger, K. A., Bentley, M. L., & Minor, P. D. (2006). Absence of detectable measles virus genome sequence in blood of autistic children who have had their MMR vaccination during the routine childhood immunization schedule of UK. *Journal of Medical Virology,* 78, 623–630.

Baird, G., Pickles, A., Simonoff, E., Charman, T., Sullivan, P., Chandler, S., et al. (2008). Measles vaccination and antibody response in autism spectrum disorders. *Archives of Disease in Childhood,* 93, 832–837.

Ball, L., Ball, R., Pratt, R. (2001). An assessment of thimerosal use in pediatric vaccines. *Pediatrics,* 107(5), 1147–1154.

Burbacher, T., Shen, D., Liberato, N., Grant, K., & Cernichiari, T. (2005). Comparison of blood and brain mercury levels in infant monkeys exposed to methylmercury or vaccines containing thimerosal. *Environmental Health Perspectives,* 113, 1015–1021.

Centers for Disease Control and Prevention. (1999a). Ten great public health achievements. *Morbidity and Mortality Weekly Report,* 48, 241–264.

Centers for Disease Control and Prevention. (1999b). Recommendations regarding the use of vaccines that contain thimerosal as a perservative. *Morbidity and Mortality Weekly Report,* 48,996–998.

Centers for Disease Control and Prevention. (2001). National, state, and urban area vaccination coverage levels among children aged 19–35 months–United States, 2000. *Morbidity and Mortality Weekly Report,* 50, 637–641.

Centers for Disease Control and Prevention. (2004). National, state, and urban area vaccination coverage among children aged 19–35 months–United States, 2003. *Morbidity and Mortality Weekly Report,* 53, 658–661.

Centers for Disease Control and Prevention. (2007). Measles. In Atkinson, W., Hamborsky, J., McIntyre, L., & Wolfe, S. (Eds.), *Epidemiology and prevention of vaccine-preventable diseases* (10th eds., pp. 129–147). Washington, DC: Public Health Foundation.

Centers for Disease Control and Prevention. (2008a). National, state, and local area vaccination coverage among children aged 19–35 months–United States, 2007. *Morbidity and Mortality Weekly Report,* 57, 961–966.

Centers for Disease Control and Prevention. (2008b). Update: measles–United States, January-July 2008. *Morbidity and Mortality Weekly Report,* 57, 893–896.

Centers for Disease Control and Prevention. (n.d.). Vaccine safety. *Vaccine safety datalink (VSD) project.* Retrieved October 18, 2008, from http://www.cdc.gov/vaccinesafety/vsd

Department of Health and Human Services. (n.d.). *VAERS: Vaccine Adverse Event Reporting System.* Retrieved October 19, 2008, from http://vaers.hhs.gov/

D'Souza, Y., Fombonne, E., & Ward, J. (2006). No evidence of persisting measles virus in peripheral blood mononuclear cells from children with autism spectrum disorder. *Pediatrics,* 118, 1664–1675.

Dales, L., Hammer, S. J., & Smith, N. J. (2001). Time trends in autism and in MMR immunization coverage in California. *Journal of the American Medical Association,* 285, 1183–1185.

Foege, W.H. (2006). Director's perspective. *Morbidity and Mortality Weekly Report,* 55, 1071–1074.

Fombonne, E., & Chakrabarti, S. (2001). No evidence for a new variant of measles-mumps-rubella-induced autism. *Pediatrics,* 108, E58.

Fombonne, E., Zakarian, R., Bennett, A., Meng, L., & McLean-Heywood, D. (2006). Pervasive developmental disorders in Montreal, Quebec, Canada: Prevalence and links with immunizations. *Pediatrics,* 118, e139–e150.

Halsey, N. A., & Hyman, S. L. (2001). Measles-mumps-rubella vaccine and autistic spectrum disorder: Report from the New Challenges in Childhood Immunizations Conference convened in Oak Brook, Illinois, June 12–13, 2000. *Pediatrics,* 107, E84.

Health Protection Agency. (2008). *Confirmed cases of measles, mumps and rubella 1996–2008.* Retrieved March 31, 2009, from http://www.hpa.org.uk/web/HPAweb&HPAwebStandard/HPAweb_C/1195733833790

Honda, H., Shimizu, Y., & Rutter, M. (2005). No effect of MMR withdrawal on the incidence of autism: A total population study. *Journal of Child Psychology and Psychiatry,* 46, 572–579.

Hornig, M., Briese, T., Buie, T., Bauman, M. L., Lauwers, G., Siemetzki, U., et al. (2008). Lack of association between measles virus vaccine and autism with enteropathy: A case-control study. *PloS ONE.,* 3, e3140.

Immunization Safety Review Committee, Board on Health Promotion and Disease Prevention, & Institute of Medicine. (2001). *Immunization safety review: Measles-mumps-rubella vaccine and autism.* Washington, DC: National Academy Press.

Kawashima, H., Mori, T., Kashiwagi, Y., Takekuma, K., Hoshika, A., & Wakefield, A. (2000). Detection and sequencing of measles virus from peripheral mononuclear cells from patients with inflammatory bowel disease and autism. *Digestive Diseases and Sciences,* 45, 723–729.

Kaye, J. A., Mar Melero-Montes, M., & Jick, H. (2001). Mumps, measles, and rubella vaccine and the incidence of autism recorded by general practitioners: A time trend analysis. *British Medical Journal,* 322, 460–463.

Kroger, A. T., Atkinson, W. L., Marcuse, E. K., & Pickering, L. K. (2006). General recommendations on immunization: Recommendations of the Advisory Committee on Immunization Practices (ACIP). *Morbidity and Mortality Weekly Report Recommendations and Reports,* 55, 1–48.

Madsen, K. M., Hviid, A., Vestergaard, M., Schendel, D., Wohlfahrt, J., Thorsen, P., et al. (2002). A population-based study of measles, mumps, and rubella vaccination and autism. *New England Journal of Medicine,* 347, 1477–1482.

Martin, C. M., Uhlmann, V., Killalea, A., Sheils, O., & O'Leary, J. J. (2002). Detection of measles virus in children with ileo-colonic lymphoid nodular hyperplasia, enterocolitis and developmental disorder. *Molecular Psychiatry,* 7, S47–S48.

Medical Research Council. (2001). *MRC review of autism research. Epidemiology and causes.* Retrieved January 15, 2009, from http://www.mrc.ac.uk/Utilities/Documentrecord/index.htm?d=MRC002394

Murch, S. H., Anthony, A., Casson, D. H., Malik, M., Berelowitz, M., Dhillon, A. P., et al. (2004). *Retraction of an interpretation. Lancet,* 363, 750.

National Statistics, T. I. C. (2005). *NHS immunisation statistics: England: 2004–05.* The Information Center for Health and Social Care. Retrieved February 23, 2009, from http://www.ic.nhs.uk/webfiles/publications/immunisaton05/NHSImmunis ationStatistics220905_PDF.pdf

National Statistics, T. I. C. (2008). *NHS immunisation statistics, England: 2007–08.* The Information Center for Health and Social Care. Retrieved February 23–May 25, 2009, from http://www.ic.nhs.uk/webfiles/publications/immunisation2007to2008/Final%202007-08%20Imms%20Bulletin%20%28amended%29.pdf

Newschaffer, C. J., Croen, L. A., Daniels, J., Giarelli, E., Grether, J. K., Levy, S. E., et al. (2007). The epidemiology of autism spectrum disorders. *Annual Review of Public Health,* 28, 235–258.

Richler, J., Luyster, R., Risi, S., Hsu, W. L., Dawson, G., Bernier, R., et al. (2006). Is there a "regressive phenotype" of Autism Spectrum Disorder associated with the measles-mumps-rubella vaccine? A CPEA Study. *Journal of Autism and Developmental Disorders,* 36, 299–316.

Smeeth, L., Cook, C., Fombonne, E., Heavey, L., Rodrigues, L. C., Smith, P. G., & Hall, A. J. (2004). MMR vaccination and pervasive developmental disorders: A case-control study. *Lancet,* 364, 963–969.

Stehr-Green, P., Tull, P., Stellfeld, M., Mortenson, P., & Simpson, D. (2003). Autism and thimerosal-containing vaccines lack of consistent evidence for an association. *American Journal of Preventive Medicine,* 25, 101–106.

Thimerosal in Vaccines. (n.d.). *Thimerosal as a preservative.* Food and Drug Administration. Retrieved October 8, 2008, from http://www.fda.gov/CBER/vaccine/thimerosal.htm#thi

Thompson, W., Price, C., Goodson, B., Shay, D., Benson, P., Hinrichsen, V., et al. (2007). Early thimerosal exposure and neuropsychological outcomes at 7 to 10 years. *New England Journal of Medicine,* 357, 1281–1292.

U.S. Court of Federal Claims. (n.d.). *Autism decisions and background information.* Retrieved February 23, 2009, from http://www.uscfc.uscourts.gov/node/5026

Verstraeten, T., Davis, R., DeStefano, F., Lieu, T., Rhodes, P., Black, S., et al. (2003). Safety of thimerosal-containing vaccines: A two-phased study of computerized health maintenance organizations databases. *Pediatrics,* 112, 1039–1048.

Volkmar, F. R., & Pauls, D. (2003). Autism. *Lancet, 362,* 1133–1141.

Wakefield, A. J., Murch, S. H., Anthony, A., Linnell, J., Casson, D. M., Malik, M., et al. (1998). Ileal-lymphoid-nodular hyperplasia, non-specific colitis, and pervasive developmental disorder in children. *Lancet, 351,* 637–641.

Vaccinations: Myths and Facts

Of all medical miracles, vaccination may be the greatest. At low cost and low risk of adverse effects, vaccination (also known as immunization or inoculation) has saved millions of lives and prevented untold suffering and disability. Smallpox, polio, diphtheria, and measles are only some of the killers and cripplers that can be prevented, even eradicated, by vaccination. This is even more impressive because many diseases we vaccinate against are untreatable—they have to run their course.

Vaccinations call upon the human immune system to defend us from disease. Most vaccines contain components of an infective microbe or toxin weakened so that they can no longer cause disease. When these are injected (or taken orally) the immune system mounts a response, creating special cells that "remember" the microbe and will mount an immune response to it later if need be. The effect may last for many years or for life. Sometimes, as for flu, annual vaccination is needed.

Edward Jenner, an English physician, tried inoculations in the late 1700s. (He was not the first, but he usually gets the credit.) He had observed that when dairy workers contracted a bovine disease called cowpox, they were then safe from smallpox. So he infected a child with cowpox, and then tried to give him smallpox—actions far outside the boundaries of medical ethics today. Fortunately, cowpox had made the boy immune, and a new era in history opened. Smallpox virus now exists only in test tubes (though it could possibly be "weaponized" by terrorists and released).

Nevertheless, people, and especially parents, worry about vaccines—their purity, their potential side effects, the wisdom of just skipping them. Some refuse to immunize their children, others neglect to get themselves vaccinated against flu or tetanus. Failure to immunize endangers not only the individual, but others as well. This article is intended to lay some misinformation to rest, and to list the immunizations children and adults need.

SETTING THE RECORD STRAIGHT

Myths: Childhood immunizations, such as those against measles, mumps, and rubella (MMR), cause autism in children. Polio, diphtheria, tetanus, and pertussis (whooping cough) vaccinations can cause Type I diabetes, brain damage, multiple sclerosis, and other disorders.

Facts: In 1998 a small study in the *Lancet,* a British medical journal, speculated that the MMR vaccine might cause autism. This has been discredited by numerous follow-up studies; the lead researcher's motives have been called into question as well, and several of the researchers have recanted. A new report from the Institute of Medicine (of the National Academy of Sciences) concludes there's no risk of autism from vaccines themselves or from the preservatives they may contain. No evidence links any vaccine to autism, diabetes, or any kind of widespread disease. Very rare side effects have been known to lead to brain damage. But vaccination is not the hidden cause of any epidemic.

Myth: Vaccines contain harmful amounts of mercury and other contaminants.

Fact: Vaccines have long contained an additive called thimerosal, because it is very effective in preventing bacterial contamination. But the amount is very small, and children who have received thimerosal-containing vaccines do not test positive for mercury exposure. Thimerosal does not release mercury in the body. However, it has now been entirely removed from almost all childhood vaccines. Other additives in vaccines, such as aluminum, formaldehyde, and yeast, have never been shown to be harmful in children or adults. But several federal agencies, including the CDC and FDA, continuously monitor vaccines and look into any signs of safety problems with them.

Myth: It's risky to vaccinate infants and small children. You should at least wait until they are older.

Fact: Infants and small children are at greatest risk for diseases such as measles, polio, diphtheria, and pertussis. And they're more likely to suffer lasting harm, or even die, from these diseases. It's taking a big chance to wait until they are older.

Myth: Flu shots cause Alzheimer's disease.

Fact: Since people over 65 most often get flu shots as well as Alzheimer's, it would be easy to draw this conclusion—but it's not supported by evidence. A large study in the *Canadian Medical Association Journal* in 2001 found no connection between Alzheimer's and the flu vaccine, or any vaccine, including diphtheria, tetanus, and polio. *In fact, being vaccinated appeared to help protect against Alzheimer's.* Don't believe what you read on those Internet sites warning against flu shots.

Myths: Diseases like polio were disappearing before vaccines were invented. Nobody has polio in this country now.

Fact: The idea that polio and other diseases were on the wane before vaccination is simply not true. Widespread vaccination put an end to polio in industrialized counties—and without it, polio could make a comeback. Polio should be extinct by 2005, but the goal may not be reached. A major outbreak is underway in Central Africa, originating in northern Nigeria, where some Islamic clerics have until recently opposed vaccination. There have been occasional outbreaks of measles in the U.S. among those who were never vaccinated. Recently an unvaccinated man returned to the U.S. from India with measles. Smallpox, as we've said, is extinct, and thus the U.S. stopped vaccinating for it in the 1970s. But it is too early to stop any other immunizations. Diseases, like humans, travel easily on planes.

A Checklist of Immunizations*

- Diphtheria, pertussis, tetanus: Infants.
- Measles, mumps, rubella (MMR): Infants.
- Polio: Infants.
- Hemophilus influenzae B: Children.
- Tetanus with diphtheria boosters: Everyone, every 10 years for life.
- Pneumonia (pneumococcal): Infants and children; those over 65 or at high risk for complications.
- Chickenpox: Children and anyone who has never had chickenpox.
- Hepatitis A: Travelers to Mexico, Asia, or other areas where hepatitis A is common; children in U.S. likely to be exposed.
- Hepatitis B: Newborns, unvaccinated children and teenagers; sexually active gay men, heterosexuals with multiple partners, health-care workers, drug users who share needles, frequent travelers to high-risk areas, partners of infected people.
- Influenza (every fall). Children 23 months or younger, those over 50 or in ill health; women in second or third trimester of pregnancy; health-care workers and caregivers. Young healthy adults can also benefit from the shot.
- Note: Those traveling in developing countries need special advice about vaccinations—consult www.cdc.gov/travel.

Law, Privacy and Information Technology: A Sleepwalk Through the Surveillance Society?

Mark O'Brien *

School of Law, University of the West of England, Bristol, UK

*Email: mark.o'brien@uwe.ac.uk

The Surveillance Studies Network report of 2006 on the 'surveillance society', highlighting the omnipresence of information technology in British society, once again brought into sharp focus concerns about the types and levels of technological surveillance to which the public are subjected. This article seeks to explore the opportunities for surveillance presented by recent developments, and suggests a number of privacy and civil liberties concerns.

Keywords: privacy; society; surveillance; technology

INTRODUCTION

The continued development of information technology has had a huge impact upon many aspects of our lives in the last quarter century, changing much of what we do in our personal and professional existences, and also how we do it. One of the many consequences of the near-ubiquity of information technology in modern-day society is the potential now afforded for the surveillance of individuals and the storage and dissemination of such information about a huge number of the—often seemingly unremarkable—day-to-day activities that we undertake. Public, academic, governmental and media concern frequently is focused on the impact of the 'information revolution' upon our lives, in particular where this interface impacts upon our ability to lead a *private* life.

The aims of this article are to seek to examine the nature of the technical developments that have resulted in a more 'surveilled' society, exploring how these technical changes have led not only to an ability to allow observation to take place with greater frequency (but not always necessarily accuracy) in a multiplicity of ways, but have also led to the development of new, hitherto unknown modes of surveillance, the development of which would not have been possible without the impact of advancing technology. To illustrate this, this article will focus upon the surveillance of data in the context of combating crime, specifically including the detection and deterrence of the viewing and proliferation of illegal Internet pornography, and the detection and prevention of certain instances of serious public disorder. As will be seen, I will contend that recent developments in this sphere can result, in both predicable and unpredictable ways, in an inappropriate imbalance between the societal need for surveillance and the concomitant individual need for privacy.

CONCEPTS OF PRIVACY

In order to give meaning and context to a discussion on surveillance, and to explore why too much surveillance is regarded as undesirable, it is first necessary to examine the development of, and differing notions within, the privacy debate and the relationship of that debate with surveillance. As many commentators recognise, despite the nebulous nature of the concept, with the literature, according to Wacks, lacking a 'lucid or consistent meaning of privacy' (Wacks 1993: xi; Fenwick 2000: 338), and with debates regarding to what degree rights and privacy have value in different types of societies (Dembour 2001), the links between surveillance and privacy generally are seen as competitive with each other (Bloss 2007: 208) and deep-rooted, particularly in the culture of Western liberal democracies. It is, therefore, useful to begin this analysis with an exposition of the development of privacy, and why we give it value.

Historical Development of Privacy

Meaningful, recorded references to privacy-based ideas stretch back to the work of Aristotle and his bifurcation of the private or the family from the political and the public. This public-private divide concept was developed, post-Enlightenment, by the liberal theorists. John Locke advanced arguments that in nature, all the world's goods are common to all, but that property could be acquired and thus became private by the mixing of the public property with the person's own (private) labour, rendering the end product private property. Similarly, in *On Liberty* (Mill 1994), John Stuart Mill argued for a realm for self-regulation and a separate, narrowly-defined area for government responsibility.

Moreover, the intervening period has seen different emphases being applied to the factors that are considered as constituting privacy 'rights', with some commentators asserting that privacy in relation to information about the individual, or *informational* privacy is of primary concern (Warren & Brandeis 1890; Westin 1967; Fried 1970); that privacy is important for the development of the individual capable of the relationships of love, trust and friendship (the notion of *intimate* privacy) (Fried 1970). There is also a notable body of work that seeks to critique the burgeoning arguments pertaining to privacy rights that emerged during the late 19th and 20th centuries; broadly speaking, the critics of those that elevate privacy rights question whether a set of concerns that can be labeled 'privacy rights' actually exist, alternatively contending that the so-called 'privacy issues' can be 'defended ... in terms of standard moral and legal categories' (Schoman 1984: 5). The proponents of this approach—the reductionists—therefore reconsider 'privacy' issues as part of other interests, such as proprietorial rights (see Thompson 1975; Posner 1981).

There also exist a number of feminist critiques of traditionally-conceived privacy debates, which highlight the perceived dangers accorded by the absence of the public realm from private situations when women may need the assistance of the State to combat harm (MacKinnon 1989).

Reasons for 'Valuing' Privacy

The development of the modern ideas of privacy relevant to the development of this article, however, are those widely ascribed to the body of academic literature that advances what Fenwick (2000: 338) broadly describes as 'informational autonomy'—that is the right to control the information about ourselves—as the central privacy value, for reasons that shortly will be explained. The catalyst for, in particular, United States common law development along these lines, and the more sustained exploration of the concept of privacy generally, including international human rights measures, is often attributed to the 'seminal' (Feldman 2002: 156) 1890 Harvard Law Review article 'The Right to Privacy', written by Samuel Warren and Louis Brandeis (Warren & Brandeis 1890). This essay argued that, due to a combination of 'the right to be let alone' and a range of political, social and economic changes in the late 19th century, which included the advancement of technology, contemporaneous law could be employed to protect individual privacy, of interest in the face of then-new technological developments such as photography (McRobb & Stahl 2007).

Moreover, to justify their privacy argument, Warren and Brandeis advanced the concept of the 'inviolate personality' (Warren & Brandeis 1890: 215), which in essence meant that people required a 'protected field of decision making', for happiness and in order to conduct their own affairs as best as they could (Feldman 2002: 516). This broad view of the role served by privacy is advanced by numerous later academics and theorists (Bloustein 1964; Westin 1967; Fried 1970; Gerstein 1978; Lustgarten & Leigh 1994), with emphasis upon links between the individual's control of information about themselves, but also links on to outcomes that protect the importance of human dignity—

those goals 'which may be seen as essential to human flourishing' (Fenwick 2000: 339).

These essentially instrumentalist arguments for privacy rights can and have been advanced in conjunction with arguments for privacy rights that have an intrinsic base; this is, the right to privacy is advanced for its own sake as a self-evident 'good' or a 'human right', rather than being viewed solely or in part as a tool to facilitate the advancement of other goals that are seen as being of value (McRobb & Stahl 2007: 234). The most significant instance of this, as will be discussed below, being the incorporation of the Art 8 right to privacy enshrined in the European Convention on Human Rights (ECHR) into United Kingdom domestic law by the Human Rights Act 1998.

Concepts of Privacy in Law

Despite some early scepticism, practical developments in jurisprudence followed the initial embrace by the US legal community of Warren and Brandeis's arguments for privacy to be assigned a legal value, with Judge Thomas Cooley arguing for a right to be 'let alone' (Cooley 1888: 29), and the concept being embraced by the United States Supreme Court in *Union Pacific Railway Co v Botsford* (1891) 141 US 250 at 251.

Practical developments regarding privacy in UK law were, for a considerable period however, less significant. Despite the concept of the 'peace' gaining an early importance in the early stages of English law, alongside the principle that a person's home and family life were to be free from intrusion (Feldman 2002: 542), this concept does not appear to have developed in an all-encompassing way, rather attaching itself solely to property rights, leaving the equity system to deal with quasi-'privacy' rights. Nor did this situation improve throughout the late 19th century nor most of the 20th century; in 1972, the Report of the Younger Committee on Privacy highlighted the difficulty associated with the actual definition of a privacy right, and in the case of *Malone v Metropolitan Police Commissioner (No.2)* [1979], *Megarry VC* explicitly ruled out a privacy right based either on US common law or derived from the ECHR—a position in contravention of Art 8 of the at-the-time unincorporated ECHR to which the United Kingdom was a signatory.

The position of privacy in the law of the UK was definitively changed not, as indicated by the above case, by the UK being signatory to the various international instruments pertaining to the protection of human rights, but by the incorporation of the Art 8 privacy provisions of the ECHR into UK domestic law by virtue of the Human Rights Act 1998. There does remain some debate, however, about the impact of the nuances of language between the different conceptions of privacy. Feldman (2002) highlights that the Art 8 right denotes *respect for* 'private and family life, home and correspondence', rather than a right to be *free* from privacy interference, and contends that this could lead to the possibility of an interference—for example, paternalistic— with privacy that would be consistent with the European Convention provision, though he concedes that the right does represent a 'considerable' extension (Feldman 2002: 524).

THE DEVELOPMENT OF SURVEILLANCE

It is against this backdrop of developments in privacy, and their interaction with surveillance, therefore, that this article explores the role that surveillance has played and is continuing to develop in society, particularly as a consequence of developments in information technology.

The concept of surveillance has in itself existed for hundreds of years (Foucault 1977; Bentham 1996; Fenwick 2000), has been widely employed throughout that time by countries and organisations with varying degrees of success, and its periodic use is regularly and relatively uncontroversially characterised as a necessary part of a democratic society. States and their governments usually do retain a right to utilise surveillance techniques in legally ascribed circumstances to protect their legitimate interests—for example, the reaction against persons or groups that seek to overthrow democratic government, or those who seek to indulge in terrorist acts—and in such circumstances an 'approach which succeeds in preserving respect for democracy and for . . . individual privacy, as a hallmark of democracy, while affording respect to state interests' (Fenwick 2000: 339) is one that is valued.

The development of the information society and its attendant technological advances, however, has placed into focus both the development in the extent and nature of the surveillance that can and does take place in society and how traditional understanding of these concepts has changed.

Definitions of Surveillance

Until the information revolution, surveillance predominantly had consisted largely of 'physical surveillance'; that is, the act of physically listening to or watching the actions of a person. In the course of the past three decades, however, society's understanding of surveillance and the extent of its operation significantly have expanded. Several different categorisations of surveillance have resulted from this, including (but not limited to) 'personal surveillance' versus 'mass surveillance' (Clarke 1997) and Alan Westin's early model of characterising surveillance as 'physical surveillance', 'psychological surveillance' (i.e. psychometric testing, interrogation and the triangulation of data), and 'data surveillance' (Westin 1971).

The sphere of data surveillance (or 'dataveillance' (Clarke 1997)) is one area where, due to computerisation and networking, especial change has taken place. By focusing at this stage, by way of example, upon merely non-governmental surveillance (as distinct from State surveillance, which is the main focus of this article), considerable changes in terms of data surveillance and the ready availability of everyday information about the individual (and thus the consequent impact upon the private/public divide in relation to conceptions of privacy) are evident. A shift from payments for goods and services with (anonymous) cash to (identifiable) electronic funds transfer (EFT) transactions, store loyalty cards, electronic withdrawal of funds from bank automatic transaction machines (ATM) (which also note the time and location of withdrawal) rather than traditional over-the-counter transactions are just limited examples of the multiplicity of complex ways that illustrate that citizens automatically are subject to a 'passive' (Lloyd 2003) process of data surveillance. Similarly, the consumer can be rendered the subject of marketing (whether by email, telephone or other means) campaigns on the basis of information held on the databases of companies and traded between companies. Subject to the limitations of the legal protection to privacy and identity afforded by measures such as the Data Protection Act 1998, such as the requirement for an individual to have their information held securely, or the legal right to prevent personal details being utilised for the purposes of marketing or associated activities, this information can easily be bought, sold and utilised in relation to actual and projected customers.

Another example of non-governmental surveillance exists in the workplace, with the potential for computer keystroke speed to be automatically measured, emails to be monitored for personal use or for what an employer deems inappropriate language, telephone conversations, call data and other communications to be recorded, and computer file caches automatically monitored for web-browsing habits, unauthorised behaviour, or any illegal activity (O'Brien 2005).

SURVEILLANCE AND CRIME

Despite the all-pervasive impact both of physical and data surveillance in the contexts of business and e-commerce, with a concomitant impact upon the 'protected field of decision making' identified within the concepts of privacy rights, some of the most significant developments in relation to technological advancement and surveillance have occurred in relation to attempts to utilise the developing technologies to combat crime. Prior to the onset of the information revolution, a panoply of physical surveillance accompanied by some data surveillance techniques were widely employed; these included 'traditional' modes of physical surveillance—such as the interception and opening of letters, scrutinising relevant documents, and once the relevant technologies had sufficiently developed, the application of a range of aural surveillance techniques to private telephone lines to hear what was being said in a particular location.

The considerable developments in technology over the last 30 years, however, have greatly expanded the possibility of an increased level of existing types of surveillance, as well as the instigation of different types of surveillance, including the harnessing of technology to combat crime, employing new methods to augment existing physical surveillance and also adding a portfolio of data surveillance tactics.

At the same time as—and at least partly as a consequence of—the increased prevalence and application of technology, the UK also developed new, so-called 'proactive' models of policing. Prior to the adoption of the 'proactive' policing model in the UK, police forces mainly operated in a way, according to Newburn (2003), which was 'opportunistic and responsive . . . dealing with individual offences reactively and trying to solve them one at a time as evidence happens to be available'.

However, the reputation and effectiveness of this familiar approach to policing was brought into question by inner-city riots in 1981 in Toxteth in Liverpool, Handsworth in Birmingham, St Paul's in Bristol and in Brixton in London, the growth in football hooliganism of the period, the year-long miners' strike and several instances of mass trespass involving counter-cultural groups (O'Brien & Ashford 2002–03), and which all lead to the adoption of the 'proactive' model of policing, focusing upon a prevention of criminality and police intelligence-gathering activities. The rapid development in and increased potential for the application of information technology has meant that technology is now capable of playing a significant role in fulfilling many of the UK's goals in respect of a proactive policing policy. This includes the use of a variety of computer software as part of the Police National Computer for the analysis and the mapping of crime patterns, the use of technology to identify crime patterns across the boundaries between different forces to aid crime detection at regional or national levels, and also (as part of the 'proactive' agenda) to help predict what sort of crime is likely to committed, and where that crime is likely to be committed, in order to police different districts or implement effective crime-prevention strategies.

In relation to 'traditional' manifestations of physical surveillance, electronic developments and improvements in the technical process have resulted in the physical interception of calls becoming easier (Fenwick 2000: 341), with the equipment needed for aural surveillance being compact, easily accessible and cheap (Taylor & Walker 1996). Recording and storage media, and the surveillance devices also, have been improved. In addition, new forms of physical surveillance have become common. The closed-circuit television (CCTV) device, although first employed in a criminal law capacity in 1956 when police in selected forces began to use this 'proto'-red light camera to film drivers ignoring red lights at traffic signals, was increasingly used by the retail sector from the 1970s onwards, and has been extensively employed for surveillance within the public sphere—public spaces, streets, town centres, and places where the possibility of attacks are of concern—for the last 15 years. As a consequence, one estimate is that the UK has five million CCTV cameras, with it being mooted that there is the potential for some citizens to have their movements closed-circuit television recorded up to 300 times in a given day (O'Neill 2006).

Fundamental changes have taken place, however, in the utilisation of data surveillance techniques in the enforcement of the criminal law. A wide range of new or relatively new modes of data surveillance (or tactics that combine physical surveillance with data surveillance to achieve an outcome) have been developed. A non-exhaustive list includes:

(1) *changes relating to road traffic law enforcement*—using automatic number plate recognition systems (ANPR), road-safety cameras, red-light cameras, mobile enforcement cameras, all of which employ an approach that combines physical surveillance (the camera) with data surveillance (comparing the offending photographic evidence with the electronic version of registration document held on the Driver and Vehicle Licensing Agency's database);

(2) *predicting, preventing and quelling serious civil disturbances, possibly linked to public order offences*—utilising closed-circuit television cameras, electronic and physical surveillance; and

(3) *preventing certain serious crimes or terrorist and potential terror-related activities* (a particular preoccupation in relation to surveillance post-2001)—adopting electronic surveillance tactics, DNA sampling and the DNA database, forensic examination of evidence, surveillance of email communications, and obtaining evidence of deleted and undeleted computer material held in computer caches or on computer storage media. Additionally, wider array of tools employed include monitoring so-called email 'chatter'—the prevalence of email communications from sources previously identified as in some way 'suspect'—and the interception of communications and counter-espionage.

The Legal Framework

There is, as has previously been discussed, a legal framework within which both physical surveillance and data surveillance are regulated, whether the surveillance be in the course of e-commerce and associated matters, or in relation to surveillance undertaken with the view of combating some form of crime. The Data Protection Act 1998, in conjunction with European Union measures, provides a statutory framework in relation to the use of personal information, whereas the UK's traditional approach to surveillance relating to state activities, sometimes regarded as limited, fragmentary and devoid of substantive rights for the individual (Feldman 2002; Mirfield 2001), was bolstered by the incorporation of the ECHR into domestic law by virtue of the Human Rights Act 1998 and the passage of the Regulation of Investigatory Powers Act 2000.

This latter measure, introduced as a 'codifying' measure (Feldman 2002) to regulate instances of directed surveillance, intrusive surveillance and covert intelligence, provides for the first time a comprehensive framework for surveillance regulation, but has received a mixed reception from academics.

Whilst it does provide a framework for the regulation of such activities, and the opportunity for review via the Surveillance Commissioners (whose positions were created by the legislation), commentators have expressed concerns about the processes by which the government has extended powers in this sphere (Feldman) and about how some measures, whilst legal, lack moral acceptability (Mirfield 2001).

Data Surveillance Problems

Of particular interest to this article, however, are aspects of the recently developed methods of data surveillance that have become prevalent. Some aspects of these methods, although ostensibly compliant with the relevant legal frameworks, are flawed, with the consequences that personal privacy is invaded to a degree that, in terms of rights protection, can be regarded as excessive, and also that the privacy invasion is not recognised as such, with potentially a consequent subversion of the interests of justice.

A definitive study of all aspects of all flaws, potential and actual, relating to the many aspects of surveillance found in society today clearly is beyond the scope of an article such as this, if indeed all such flaws could easily or exhaustively be identified, so I shall adopt a thematic approach, exploring problems that can be demonstrated to have emerged from technology used for the specific purpose of data surveillance with the goal of combating criminal activity in the UK. The purpose, therefore, is to provide salient examples of particular problems, not to formulate a rigorous critique of the use of data surveillance techniques, but rather to highlight the potential for wider problems and counsel for the need to be more cautious in the employment and interpretation of the relevant methods.

(i) Function Creep

The potential for function creep has long been recognised as an issue in relation to data gathering and data retention generally, and pre-empts the advent of the information revolution. Function creep occurs when data gathered by surveillance methods for a defined, specific purpose, and recognised as being gathered for that specific purpose, is subsequently used to provide information pertaining to different objectives. Notable examples of this, prior to technological advancement, include the use by Artur Seyss-Inquart's World War II administration of Nazi-occupied Holland of the Dutch census records to identify citizens of Jewish origin for deportation to the concentration camps (Lloyd 2003). Another was the US government's use of lists held by an ice-cream company that the company utilised in order to provide promotional ice cream to each American on their 18th birthday; the government used this list to enhance the information that it already held in order to successfully identify so-called Vietnam war 'draft dodgers.'

The reasons for function creep can be argued to include value-for-money considerations—that the considerable money often invested in relevant technologies can or should be recouped by their wider application (Ponder 2007)—and for the protection of the citizen, and one situation where a 'joined-up' approach to existing data was identified as potentially being of use was in relation to information held by various social services agencies on the mistreatment and ultimate death of the eight-year old Victoria Climbie in February 2000, when Lord Laming, the Chairman of the Inquiry into her death, suggested that a National Children's Database be established for the efficient interchange of information (Laming 2003).

Despite some initial reluctance by the courts to allow function creep in relation to data surveillance, with Sir Nicolas Browne-Wilkinson, in *Marcel v Metropolitan Police Commissioner* [1991], expressly forbidding multi-agency access to documentation and describing 'the dossier of private information' as 'the badge of the totalitarian state', there have been a number of moves towards permitting function creep. In July 2007, the Home Secretary Jacqui Smith signed an order allowing an exemption from the provisions of the Data Protection Act 1998 in relation to data held by Transport for London, the body that administers the capital's road-congestion charge. This was to allow the data, collected for administering the fees system in relation to the congestion charge, to be utilised by the Metropolitan Police when investigating threats to national security. Information emerged in the same month regarding police wishes to obtain such congestion charge data for 'all crime fighting purposes' (Travis 2007)—a rather open-ended notion. Further development seems likely. In May 2006, the then UK Constitutional Affairs Minister Harriet Harman told a meeting of the policy group Progress that the National Identity Register (NIR), which was under development in connection with ID cards, could be used for correcting errors in the electoral roll, despite the Identity Cards Act 2006 expressly providing that information on the NIR could only be used in connection with detecting or preventing terrorism, identity fraud, social security fraud and organised crime (Taylor 2006.)

(ii) Complexity and Error

The increased sophistication of the technology employed in order to undertake new forms of data surveillance and the resultant complexity of the evidence-gathering and forensic processes necessary to support such data surveillance introduce into the equation a range of new problems; for example, the increasingly technically complex evidence-gathering processes, and the linked but separate need to introduce more forensic, physical and administrative processes into the *interpretative* processes necessary to give this evidence readily-understandable meaning, both for investigators and for later stages in the criminal justice process such as jury trials, means that the various levels of greater complexity give rise to the potential for greater procedural and interpretive error.

A number of examples of the potential for greater procedural and interpretive error above exist. One such issue manifested itself during the course of Operation Ore, one of the major worldwide inquiries that have taken place in recent years into the distribution of child pornography via the Internet (O'Brien 2005). Here, worldwide investigations were triggered by a raid by US federal authorities on a US company, Landslide, the owners of which were successfully prosecuted for distributing child pornography. What was novel about this case was that the investigation concentrated upon the fact that rather than offering the relevant illegal pornographic material itself, the company provided a portal through which customers could obtain pornographic material from external, independent sites. The situation in terms of the detection and identification of *offending* customers via data surveillance of the company's lists of the names and addresses of subscribers appears to have been further complicated by Landslide also offering a range of legal material via their portal service. Consequently, instead of there being a straightforward, easily provable 'real world' connection between the illegal material and the customer, the evidence consisted of lists of names and addresses, forensically obtained from seized computers, and derived from credit card details that had been used to purchase material from the company. Therefore, in order to identify those that potentially had committed criminal acts: (i) the forensic examination of the seized computers' storage media and subsequent conversion of the data into a meaningful and readable form had to be without technical flaw or human error, especially given the level of trust that would be placed in this evidence by (possibly technically unversed) judges and juries (O'Brien 2005: 159); (ii) those undertaking the extraction of data forensically needed to be suitably qualified and competent to undertake the task; (iii) the data obtained, if accurate, had to be transcribed properly for dissemination to and amongst the investigative authorities worldwide; (iv) in the circumstances, as posited here, of the details of purchasers of legal material being mixed with the purchasers of illegal material, appropriate examination of the data source should take place to prevent infringement of the rights of those demonstrably innocent of the alleged activity; and (v) if this information was derived from credit card details, then due consideration needed to be given to the possibility of credit card fraud, especially given the illegal nature of the activities either by the unauthorised use of a card or by the fraudulent opening of an account in another person's name.

However, in the above instance, the likelihood of flaws in the processes adopted was identified (Bates 2004). Even assuming that all personal details related to those who accessed illegal material (in this scenario highly unlikely), the full list of names and addresses provided to law enforcement agencies in the UK appears not to have been the actual list of 'raw data' as obtained by the Federal Bureau of Investigation (FBI), rather a list prepared by a firm of forensic specialists in the UK (Hamilton 2004); therefore there was the attendant possibility of transcription and other errors, both in the raw and interpreted data.

In relation to the issue of which 'list names' (though at this stage not considering the attendant issue of whether the 'name' and the person were one and the same) had accessed legal material, and which has accessed illegal, the technical arrangements caused further complexity. It was suggested by investigators that the (KEYS) portal (rather than the (AVS) portal) provided access to the illegal, child pornography, material; thus it was assumed that if a 'name' was registered with the KEYS portal, then that was for the purpose of downloading illegal material. However, it has been noted that this was a flawed argument—solicitors acting for accused persons highlighted evidence that the relevant KEYS portal also provided legal, adult pornography, and that, therefore, the *technical* evidence of accessing the relevant portal does not of *itself* necessarily provide evidence of commission of a criminal act (Hamilton 2004.) Moreover, the point regarding credit card fraud appears to have been little considered by the investigative authorities, with warrants for raids being issued by magistrates in the UK on the basis of 'reasonable suspicion' derived the (interpreted) data initially obtained from the FBI.

Similar issues increasingly are being identified in relation to other complex analyses of material obtained by data surveillance. The interpretive processes implicit in the use of DNA evidence, and particularly the matching of DNA samples from scenes of crime with the UK's burgeoning DNA database has raised concerns. These include different and potentially inconsistent procedural processes being adopted by different teams of forensic investigators; in February 2007 it was announced that there would be case reviews where examinations involved a procedure known as Low-Copy Number DNA sampling (utilised where only very small quantity or minimal traces of DNA are present) as it transpired that the Home Office Forensic Science Service analyses of such samples differed from those adopted by external scientists and laboratories, with the obvious potential for differing results (Holden 2007).

(iii) Contextual Issues

A further issue manifests itself in relation to 'cause-and-effect' arguments *per se* in this sphere, both generally and more specifically in relation to the impact of these issues upon the administration of justice.

Wood et al. (2006) argue that the skewed nature of contextual issues is impacting upon how data surveillance policy has evolved and is evolving, with a consequent impact upon privacy. They suggest that a presentation of arguments in this sphere as simple 'cause-and-effect' (for example assertions that 'More CCTV cameras lead to less crime' (Wood 2006) or perhaps 'DNA samples are a foolproof way of accurately identifying the perpetrator of a crime', or even 'People whose name is on our list are paedophiles who will be punished') ignores the complex reality implicit in each area, and potentially impacts upon both development of policy and also public perception and understanding of the issues involved. This demonstrably has a practical impact: a Home Office study led by Professor Martin Gill of Leicester University examined the impact of CCTV systems in 14 areas in the UK and found that a drop in levels of crime could be linked to CCTV in only one of those locations.

However, it is the extremities of these (headline-grabbing) wider debates, rather than the nuances of technical or academic argument, that drive public and media perception (Wood et al. 2006). By way of example, on 26 April 2002, *The Sunday Times* newspaper presented information on the seized lists of names from the Landslide company discussed above, described as ' . . . voyeurs in a cyber-world of depravity', whilst conceding in the same article that some of the names were 'demonstrably false'. Such approaches, when linked to an understandable and entirely justifiable ignorance of obtuse technical detail, have a possible impact in the court room. Recorded instances of 'cause-and-effect'-style arguments employed in cases include evidence of attempts to present a possibly automatically-generated computer username with an attached numerical suffix, e.g. 'JoeBloggs14', as evidence that points to attempts to masquerade as a child (Bates 2003), and one instance where an advocate said that a computer 'contained images of children' (that is, not necessarily *indecent* images of children.)

CONCLUSION

The concept of privacy, and how we undertake the balancing of privacy protections with the other justifiable goals of a society, especially issues such as preventing crime and ensuring national security, has long been a contentious issue, and is rendered more so by current concerns regarding issues such as Internet pornography and 'global terrorism' in the post-9/11 environment, with what has been described as a 'progressive shift between police surveillance authority and individual privacy' (Posner 2003; Chang 2003; Bloss 2007). Pressure from governments can be demonstrated to exist, including the UK government, in relation to the issues explored within this article, for a heightened—or even an overriding—importance to be attached to issues of security. However, the importance of privacy rights in a democratic society demands that the privacy/security tension is fully debated in an open and rational way, devoid insofar as is possible of rhetoric and sensationalism, with an assessment of some of the difficulties.

As a consequence of the above issues, therefore, it can be seen that via a range of technical and contextual means, including the issues of appropriate and inappropriate function creep, the increasingly complex nature of the technical processes and attendant issues associated with forensic examination techniques, and issues regarding the wider arguments in society in relation to data surveillance, its usefulness and how those debates are presented, in combination have an impact upon current debates justifying greater surveillance. This has a consequent direct (and as have been seen, perhaps unnecessary) impact upon our collective ability to lead our individual, private lives. As Lustgarten and Leigh (1994) argue in the wider context of this debate, 'in attempting to protect democracy from threats [...] there is an ever-present risk that ... that which was to be preserved has been lost'.

REFERENCES

Bloustein, C (1964) Privacy as an aspect of human dignity, in Schoman F (ed), *Philosophical Dimensions of Privacy*, New York: Cambridge University Press.

Bloss, W (2007) Escalating U.S. police surveillance after 9/11: an examination of causes and effects, *Surveillance and Society*, 4(3), Part 1, 208.

Dembour, M-B (2001) Following the movement of a pendulum: between universalism and relativism, in J Cowan, M-B Dembour and R Wilson (eds), *Culture and Rights,* Cambridge: Cambridge University Press.

Feldman, D (2002) *Civil Liberties and Human Rights in England and Wales,* Cambridge: Cambridge University Press.

Fenwick, H (2000) *New Labour, Freedom and the Human Rights Act,* Harlow: Longman.

Fried, C (1970) *An Anatomy of Values,* Cambridge: Harvard University Press.

Gerstein, (1978) Intimacy and Privacy, *Ethics 89*(1), 76–89.

Hamilton, A (2004) *Recent Developments in the Law Regulating Child Pornography on the Internet.* Available at: http://www.hamiltons-solicitors.co.uk/archive-docs/operation-ore.htm. Accessed 21 December 2006.

Holden, (2007 December 21) Court cases to be reviewed over DNA concerns, Reuters.

Lustgarten, L and Leigh, I (1994) *In From the Cold: National Security and Parliamentary Democracy,* Oxford: Clarendon.

MacKinnon, C (1989) *Toward a Feminist Theory of the State,* Cambridge: Harvard University Press.

McRobb, S and Stahl, B (2007) Privacy as a shared feature of the e-phenomenon: a comparison of privacy policies in e-government, e-commerce and e-teaching, *International Journal of Information Technology and Management,* Nos 2-4, 232.

Schoman, F (ed) (1984) *Philosophical Dimensions of Privacy: An Anthology,* New York: Cambridge University Press.

Stahl, B (2002) The moral and business value of information technology: what to do in case of a conflict?, in N Shin (ed), *Creating Business Value with Information Technology: Challenges and Solutions,* Hershey, PA: Idea-Group Publishing.

Taylor, (2006) Anger AS Harman electoral role for ID database, *The Guardian,* 11/5/2006.

Wacks, R (ed) (1993) *Privacy,* New York: NYU Press.

Westin, A (1967) *Privacy and Freedom,* Atheneum: New York.

Playing with Fire: The Civil Liberties Implications of September 11th

Jon B. Gould

George Mason University

Jon B. Gould is an assistant professor of public and international affairs and a visiting assistant professor of law at George Mason University, where he is the assistant director of the Administration of Justice Program. Professor Gould has written on the First Amendment, hate speech, racial and sexual discrimination, the Fourth Amendment, and justice administration. Email: jbgould@gmu.edu.

The aftermath of September 11th has seen a worrisome rise in invasive surveillance measures. Both adopted by statute and initiated by agencies, these provisions provide unprecedented powers for government agents to investigate suspects and search individuals, whether they are directly involved in terrorism or not. The prevailing wisdom has been that the American people will accept these restrictions as the natural cost of heightened security, and initial evidence suggests the public has been willing to tolerate greater limits on civil liberties. However, over time such support will erode, leaving in place permanent restrictions on civil liberties that not only will concern Americans, but also may turn them against government officials and civic participation. Thus, contrary to many interpretations of September 11th, this article argues that the policy response has only sown the seeds for greater detachment from and dissatisfaction with government as the public becomes increasingly separated from the workings and operations of public policy.

THE LEGISLATIVE RESPONSE

The horrors of September 11th have been covered extensively by the popular media, both by same-day reporting of the attacks and lengthier analyses of the long-term effects on victims' families. In response to the terrorist threat--one that, interestingly, was interpreted as rising after the initial attacks[1]—Congress passed and President Bush signed the USA PATRIOT Act. Described by Attorney General John Ashcroft as a "package of 'tools' urgently needed to combat terrorism" (McGee 2001), the legislation raises domestic intelligence gathering to an unprecedented level. Among its several provisions, the act stipulates that:

- The standards for wiretapping may be lowered. Whereas previously, the FBI could obtain a court order only if its "primary purpose" was to gather intelligence through wiretapping, the new law permits wiretaps if "a significant purpose" involves intelligence gathering. As a result, people merely suspected of working with terrorists or spies may be wiretapped.
- The FBI may share sensitive grand jury and wiretap information with intelligence agencies without judicial review or any safeguards limiting its future use, so long as the information concerns foreign intelligence or international terrorism.
- Law enforcement may access an individual's internet communications if officials can certify to a court that the information is relevant to an ongoing criminal investigation. This standard is much lower than the showing of probable cause required for most search warrants.
- Financial institutions will be required to closely monitor daily financial transactions and share information with government intelligence services. The law also allows law enforcement agencies secret access to an individual's credit report without judicial review.
- A new crime of domestic terrorism is created, covering conduct that "involves acts dangerous to human life." Presumably, members of Operation Rescue or Greenpeace would be covered under this definition, permitting the FBI to wiretap the homes of individuals who provide lodging or other assistance to activists.
- Non-citizens facing deportation may be held indefinitely on the attorney general's certification that an individual endangers national security.

Even before this act was adopted, the federal government had stepped up security and surveillance, detaining roughly 1,200 people in the weeks following September 11th, proposing military tribunals for captured insurgents, and interviewing nearly 5,000 visa holders. On the home front, security was increased at public buildings and gatherings and, of course, at airports. Most of the public is now aware that a trip through airport security may involve some manner of disrobing.

BALANCING CIVIL LIBERTIES

The first response to these heightened measures has been largely supportive. As Chief Justice William Rehnquist suggests in his book *All the Laws but One: Civil Liberties in Wartime,* national emergencies shift the balance between freedom and order toward order—"in favor of the government's ability to deal with the conditions that threaten the national well-being" (1998,222). Initial public polling bears out that view. In February 2002, 62 percent of respondents in a Greenberg poll agreed that "Americans will have to accept new restrictions on their civil liberties if we are to win the war on terrorism." During the same period, only 12 percent of respondents in a *Newsweek* poll feared the Bush administration's response to terrorism was "going too far in restricting civil liberties," a finding virtually unchanged from a similar poll conducted in November 2001. When asked about specific strategies to root out terrorists, 78 percent of respondents in a September 2001 NBC/*Wall Street Journal* poll said they would be willing to accept surveillance of internet communications, and 63 percent of participants in a similar Harris Poll said they would favor expanded camera surveillance on streets and in public places.

To read these responses as offering the federal government carte blanche to search and pry, however, misreads the public's calculus of civil liberties. At the same time respondents are expressing support for expanded surveillance measures, they also have reservations about the potential creep of government snooping. When asked whether they believed the "U.S. government might go too far in restricting civil liberties," 62 percent of respondents in a March 2002 *Time*/CNN poll expressed concerns, a result that is in line with the 58 percent of respondents who, in a November 2001 *Investor's Daily* poll, said they were concerned about sacrificing "certain civil liberties in light of recently passed anti-terrorism laws."

Still, the issue runs deeper than these potentially conflicting results. Historically, the American public has expressed generic support for civil liberties principles while at the same time backing restrictions against a clearly identified or understood "other"—particularly a group that is reviled. As Chong explains, the public views civil liberties by balancing on one hand "considerations of [legal] principles and rights" and on the other hand "considerations about the people or groups that are involved in the issue, including considerations about how the issue might affect oneself" (Chong 1993, 870; McClosky and Brill 1983). For this reason, vast majorities in the Harris Poll can simultaneously name individual freedom as "a major contributor to making America great," while at the same time recommending the Ku Klux Klan be placed under electronic surveillance. Respondents balance their attachment to civil liberties against the risk of—or their animosity toward—an "out group."

A similar point is true in the area of criminal procedure, where Americans seem willing to countenance surveillance and searches so long as police activity is directed against individuals presumed to be criminals. Over 80 percent of Americans support the "frisking" of individuals who appear "suspicious," and large majorities would allow police officers to search a car for drugs or stolen goods following a stop (Lock 1999). Perhaps the public is balancing the perceived intrusion of the search against the likelihood of uncovering criminal activity, but the more likely answer is that Americans are willing to accept restrictions that do not "directly affect them or the groups to which they belong" (Chong 1993, 887). This is the classic example of the respondent who does not care what the police do to suspected drug dealers—because he is not one—but who opposes home searches because he might have something embarrassing that would be found (ibid.).

There is much in the survey data to support this notion. Americans largely accept dogs sniffing their luggage, but they are resistant to police rummaging through their garbage (Lock 1999). Similarly, they oppose warrantless searches of homes (although there are legal grounds to do so), as well as the government's opening of mail (McClosky and Brill 1983). The common denominator is heightened concern when the search or surveillance hits close to home—that is, when individuals fear they may actually be the target of law enforcement. Among other things, this dynamic explains the curious results found in both Canada and the United Kingdom, where elites, who generally are seen as the "carriers of the democratic creed," were much more supportive than the general public of electronic wiretapping (Fletcher 1989, 227; Sullivan and Barnum 1987). Although researchers speculated that the elites' support may be premised on their understanding of the legal safeguards built into wiretapping (Fletcher 1989), the better explanation is that elites, because they have greater social power, need not fear the exercise of government power. By contrast, the general public worries that elites will authorize the surveillance of *them* (Sullivan and Barnum 1987).

Closer to home, recent surveys identify concerns about the very kinds of surveillance now permitted by Congress. A month before September 11th, over 80 percent of respondents in a Harris Poll said it was extremely important that no one be allowed to watch or listen to them without their permission. Their responses echo previous surveys of internet users, who, by large margins, want to control the information that is collected about them. Although the questions were asked in the context of commercial tracking, the answers paint a consumer—and citizen—base that value its privacy.

Of course, at a time of national emergency, Americans are likely to give government officials increased leeway in surveillance, but in some sense that is the point: Americans' attachment to civil liberties is a balancing test that, if mishandled operationally or politically by government officials, will only backfire. In this respect, I believe there are six factors that help to explain when the public will countenance restrictions—even against themselves—to uncover those individuals who pose a threat. None of these factors is either mutually exclusive or a sufficient condition, but together they provide a checklist of concerns that public administrators ought to consider carefully.

1. When the search or surveillance is not intrusive or the least restrictive method possible.

For several years now, airline personnel have asked travelers whether they packed their bags themselves. Presumably this is a personal question, but it is accepted largely because the method is not intrusive. Were the Federal Aviation Administration to order so, a ticket agent could satisfy himself of the answer by prying open a passenger's suitcase and checking the contents against the passenger's memory, but, quite understandably, government officials recognize both the flying public and the airlines are much more likely to accept a simple question. So, too, courthouses and other public buildings use metal detectors to scan for weapons rather than strip searching each individual who enters. Although there are individuals who approach such machines with dread (consider the example of Congressman Dingell, whose artificial hip set off a detector), most of us tolerate the detectors because we recognize they are the least invasive method available to check for weapons.

2. When the perceived threat is great.

There is a long history in this country of restrictions on liberty during times of war or national emergency. Abraham Lincoln suspended habeas corpus during the Civil War; newspapers were censored during World War I; Japanese Americans were sent to concentration camps during World War II; and the CIA opened mail destined for the USSR during the Cold War. When a national emergency exists, the public is likely to "rally 'round the flag" to support the country or the president and accept such restrictions (Bowen 1989). To reach this point, though, the public must come to see current events as constituting an emergency, a process that relies heavily on news coverage—and with it, the ability of public officials to frame issues as involving national security and not other concerns (Nelson, Clawson, and Oxley 1997). In the post-World War II era, rally effects can be short lived, averaging just under a year (Parker 1995).

3. When those responsible for the search or surveillance are seen as competent.

Interestingly, Attorney General John Ashcroft did not support some of the same measures that are now in the USA PATRIOT Act when he served in the U.S. Senate, in part because he did not trust the Clinton administration to exercise the new powers properly.[2] Similarly, in reforming airport security, Congress and the Department of Transportation worried whether airline passengers would accept heightened security measures if those provisions continued to fall under the control of private, low-cost bidders, some of whom employ minimum-wage employees. In addition to providing better oversight, the federalization of airport security was considered necessary to reassure the flying public that screening is being handled competently.

4. When the method employed is considered effective.

People accept metal detectors at courthouses, not only because the intrusion is relatively minor, but also because they believe the systems are capable of identifying—and then stopping—armed individuals set on harm. We will remain content with such measures until the first suspect brings a plastic explosive into court and detonates himself, at which point there undoubtedly will be calls for more sensitive screening to catch explosive materials. At the same time, the public will reject heightened security if its effectiveness does not overcome the level of intrusiveness involved. For example, drivers may tolerate random sobriety checkpoints so long as drunk drivers do not shift their travels to unchecked roads. To accept stops, searches, or surveillance, the public seeks assurance that the invasive methods will be effective.

5. When limiting the search or surveillance to more relevant suspects might smack of illegal discrimination.

Given the demographics of the September 11th hijackers, some might call for intensive screening of young, Middle Eastern men who seek to board an aircraft. Certainly, past experience suggests this profile is more likely to yield a terrorist than, say, an 88-year-old white grandmother from Iowa. But while some criticize current measures that randomly—and thus, equally—search airline passengers at the gate, even more worry that targeted searches would inevitably lead to ethnic or racial profiling. Indeed, one of the surprising findings following September 11th was that 68 percent of respondents in a *Newsweek* poll said it would be a mistake to "put Arabs and Arab-Americans in this country under special surveillance."

6. When individuals are unaware that the search or surveillance is taking place.

When is a search not intrusive? Potentially when the target is unaware of it. Of course, this is a bit tongue-in-cheek, for liberties are never more at risk than when government agents can intrude without any outside check on their activities. But the public cannot object to surveillance about which it is unaware. This is what makes post-September 11th security so interesting, for the public may object to intrusive searches of which it is aware, but even greater surveillance may take place outside of its purview. On one hand, the USA PATRIOT Act has given the FBI and the intelligence community greater latitude to conduct surveillance without the public's knowledge—searches that, even if more intrusive, will likely persist without objection unless agents trip up and their activities are exposed. On the other hand, the public has begun to experience stepped-up security when entering public buildings, traveling by air, or attending notable public events. Such increasingly intrusive searches are probably the closest that members of the general public have come to the types of intrusions or surveillance that they have approved (at least tacitly) in other areas of

American life, particularly in the criminal justice arena. As "average citizens" begin to taste the invasiveness of pat-down searches, of airport screeners with dirty plastic gloves "unzipping toiletries bag [and] picking through shoes and dirty laundry" (Hilkevitch 2002), of the newly proposed low-level x-ray scan of passengers (Branom 2002), they may very well rebel against the application of heightened security to "innocent individuals"—presumably themselves.

THE AFTERMATH OF SEPTEMBER 11TH—AN INCREASINGLY CIVIL LIBERTARIAN PUBLIC

The challenge for government officials in the wake of September 11th is that the public will become less supportive of extreme security measures as the perception of a terrorist threat drops. Unless the war in Afghanistan is expanded, or until another terrorist attack is leveled on U.S. soil, the immediate memories of September 11th's horrors will fade, to be replaced by an increasing sense of normalcy. News coverage will shift from a frame of warfare to geopolitics, and, in turn, Americans will rebalance the calculus between heightened surveillance and their own civil liberties. To the extent that major airports continue to grind to a halt from false alarms,[3] the flying public—and the rest of the American public who learn about such mistakes from the media—will begin to doubt the competence of federal agents whose new responsibilities extend to airport security. With these doubts will come an unwillingness to submit to heightened security.

Most important, enterprising reporters undoubtedly will uncover cases in which surveillance measures intended for would-be terrorists extend outward and inadvertently ensnare an innocent, sympathetic individual. Maybe it will be the young mother whose credit dries up after her bank mistakenly turns her name over to intelligence authorities for unusual account activity; perhaps it will be the grandmother, whose interest in Islamic history leads federal agents to track her internet usage; or maybe it will be the young father on a green card who faces wiretapping, indefinite detention, and eventual deportation because he attended a meeting to plan protests against the International Monetary Fund. There assuredly will be mistakes in the application of new surveillance powers—there almost always are—and the media will be ready to cover the stories. To the extent that the immediate threat of terrorism has begun to recede, these stories will touch an American people tiring of added restrictions on their behavior.

This is not to say that September 11th will turn this country into a land of civil libertarians: Ultimately, Americans are willing to accept restrictions on "others," particularly if the targets are considered threatening. Nonetheless, as government surveillance moves out of the criminal justice arena and Americans begin to see that they, too, may be targeted or searched, we may well experience a renewed debate about the power of government and the wisdom of narrowing civil liberties protection in the name of generic security.

In essence, government may actually have created its own backlash in its heightened response to September 11th.[4]

WIDENING THE DISTANCE BETWEEN CITIZENS AND GOVERNMENT

That the USA PATRIOT Act may have raised civil libertarian sentiments is only one part of the equation. The stepped-up security following September 11th has widened the distance between citizen and government, potentially dampening citizen participation in government and with it reducing citizens' trust in public institutions and officials. The dynamic here is analogous to the creation of social capital. According to Paxton (1999), social capital is created when individuals share intensive associations and high levels of trust. Given a confluence between interpersonal connections and goodwill, the social capacity for action is increased, in turn facilitating the production of social good. The same is true for political capital. When citizens feel connected to their government or government officials, when they trust these institutions or leaders, citizens are more likely to participate in the governing function, and officials are allowed greater latitude and goodwill to take decisive action to address social problems. By the same token, when citizens feel disconnected from their government, they are far less likely to participate in any type of political activity—including voting—and diminished trust, in turn, strikes a blow at the underlying legitimacy of government institutions and public officials (Lipset and Schneider 1987).

To be sure, the immediate effects of September 11th were to "rally 'round the flag" and the U.S. government. In the first six months following the attack, Americans reflected overwhelming support for national leaders and government policy, a level not seen in more than 30 years (Moore 2002). But it is worth asking whether such approval reflects support for government in general or for the war on terrorism, particularly since pollsters have not always used the correct question design to estimate the public's trust in government (ibid.).[5]

Apart from these issues of measurement, though, there is a larger concern lurking, for the very security measures installed following the September 11th attacks present the grave risk of further separating Americans from government. Whether the barriers are concrete or merely symbolic, government sends an important message to citizens about their role in democratic self-rule when many of the institutions of government are closed to public access, when individuals must undergo intensive screening to enter public facilities or to interact personally with government officials. The message—that the public should be content to delegate government functions to those inside—is only intensified when ever-increasing security measures limit the number of people who have "passed" and thus are privileged to participate in certain government functions while leaving others to sit outside policy deliberations because they are not deemed sufficiently "secure."

Americans may tolerate these distinctions for a while, seeing them as a necessary price to ensure the continued, safe working of American institutions of government. But ultimately, government, and indeed democratic citizenry, accepts a steep risk in accentuating the differences between those on the inside who run government and those on the outside who are subject to it. For years, scholars have noted that political participation turns partly on an individual's belief that his voice can be heard (Verba and Nie 1987). Indeed, trust in government depends on the citizenry's view that public institutions and government officials are accountable and attentive (Weatherford 1992). Yet, when the public is urged to remain silently supportive of an antiterrorism campaign that may extend indefinitely, when citizens are told they will be ministered to, not participate in the ministering of government, when resources are redirected to defense and surveillance and away from direct government services, those on the outside of government may ultimately extend less goodwill to public officials as they feel increasingly more distanced from government's operations.

This change is not likely in the midst of an immediate military campaign, for public institutions and leaders are viewed more positively in times of crisis. But as time passes and war passions wane and as government returns to its more traditional functions, it will face a citizenry that not only retains reservoirs of doubt about government—in particular, the federal government—but also it has added fuel to the fire by adopting security measures that further distance the public. Having enjoyed popular support during a time of national emergency, public officials may face a sinkhole that few would have predicted from the attack, a public that ultimately will be less supportive of government functions from which it has been kept at arms length.

ACKNOWLEDGMENTS

The author thanks Scott Keeter, Ann Springer, and David Rosenbloom for their assistance on this article.

NOTES

1. Presumably the threat was there all along, just inadequately detected. In times of emergency, the presumption seems to be that further attacks must be coming, if only because we could not predict the ones that just hit.
2. In a 1997 op-ed in the *Washington Times,* Ashcroft said, "The Clinton administration's paranoid and prurient interest in [monitoring] international e-mail is a wholly unhealthy precedent especially given this administration's track record on FBI files and IRS snooping. Every medium by which people communicate can be subject to exploitation by those with illegal or immoral intentions. Nevertheless, this is no reason to hand Big

       Brother the keys to unlock our e-mail diaries, open our ATM records or translate our international communications" (A15).

3. The FAA reported that, between February 17 and March 11, 2002, 22 airport terminals had been evacuated nationwide because of "security breaches" (AP 2002). In many of these cases, agents either failed to screen any passengers or were unable to stop an individual whom the x-ray detectors had identified as suspicious.

4. For this reason, Congress may have limited the USA PATRIOT Act to 2005 unless reauthorized. Any backlash, however, would likely start before then.

5. Examining an ABC News poll from January of this year, 69 percent of respondents said they trusted the federal government to handle issues of national security and terrorism at least "most of the time." By contrast, only 39 percent of respondents trusted the federal government to handle social issues. The latter numbers are similar to responses from a 2000 National Public Radio poll testing generic trust in government. Then, 5 percent of respondents "just about always" trusted the "federal government to do what is right," with 24 percent saying they agreed "most of the time."

REFERENCES

Ashcroft, John. 1997. Welcoming Big Brother. *Washington Times,* August 12, A15.

Associated Press. 2002. Logan Has Had Twice the Number of Evacuations as Similar Airports. April 7. Available at *http://www2.bostonherald.com/news/local%5fregional/ap%5flogan04072002.htm.* Accessed June 10, 2002.

Bowen, Gordon L. 1989. Presidential Action and Public Opinion about U.S. Nicaraguan Policy: Limits to the "Rally Round the Flag" Syndrome. *PS: Political Science and Politics* 24(4): 793-800.

Branom, Mike. 2002. New Security Devices at Fla. Airport. Associated Press, March 15. Available at *http://www.kfi640.com/ handel_newstory.html.* Accessed June 10, 2002.

Chong, Dennis. 1993. How People Think, Reason, and Feel about Rights and Liberties. *American Journal of Political Science* 37(3): 867-99.

Fletcher, Joseph F. 1989. Mass and Elite Attitudes about Wiretapping in Canada: Implications for Democratic Theory and Politics. *Public Opinion Quarterly* 53(2): 225-45.

Hilkevitch, Jon. 2002. Where Pawing Dirty Laundry is Part of the Job. Chicago *Tribune* (internet edition), April 1. Available at *http://www.chicagotribune. com/classified/automotive/columnists/chi-0204010230apr01.column.* Accessed June 10, 2002.

Lipset, Seymour Martin, and William Schneider. 1987. *Confidence Gap: Business, Labor and Government in the Public Mind.* Baltimore, MD: Johns Hopkins University Press.

Lock, Shmuel. 1999. *Crime, Public Opinion, and Civil Liberties.* Westport, CT: Praeger.

McClosky, Herbert, and Alida Brill. 1983. *Dimensions of Tolerance: What Americans Believe about Civil Liberties.* New York: Russell Sage.

McGee, Jim. 2001. An Intelligence Giant in the Making: Anti-Terrorism Law Likely to Bring Domestic Apparatus of Unprecedented Scope. *Washington Post,* November 4, A4.

Moore, David W. 2002. Just One Question: The Myth and Mythology of Trust in Government. *Public Perspective* (January/February): 7-11.

Nelson, Thomas E., Rosalee A. Clawson, and Zoe M. Oxley. 1997. Media Framing of a Civil Liberties Conflict and Its Effect on Tolerance. *American Political Science Review* 91(3): 567-83.

Parker, Suzanne L. 1995. Toward an Understanding of "Rally" Effects: Public Opinion in the Persian Gulf War. 1995. *Public Opinion Quarterly* 59(4): 526-46.

Paxton, Pamela. 1999. Is Social Capital Declining in the United States? A Multiple Indicator Assessment. *American Journal of Sociology* 105(1): 88-127.

Rehnquist, William. 1998. *All the Laws But One: Civil Liberties in Wartime.* New York: Knopf.

Sullivan, John, and David Barnum. 1987. Attitudinal Tolerance in the United Kingdom: A Comparison of Members of Parliament with the Mass Public. Paper presented at the annual meeting of the American Political Science Association, September 3-5, Chicago, Illinois.

Verba, Sidney, and Norman H. Nie. 1987. *Participation in America: Political Democracy and Social Equality.* Chicago: University of Chicago Press.

Weatherford, M. Stephen. 1992. Measuring Political Legitimacy. *American Political Science Review* 86(1): 149-66.

Criminal Justice Studies,
Vol. 20, No. 2, June 2007, pp. 149–159

The 'X-Rated X-Ray': Reconciling Fairness, Privacy, and Security

David A. Mackey

Commercial airline flights have been targeted in the events of September 11, later by Richard Reid in December 2001, and more recently in the terrorist plot foiled by British investigators involving an estimated 10 transatlantic flights. Since September 11, 2001, the screening of airline travelers has been redefined in light of its threat to homeland security. Global events have fueled the momentum of policies designed to strengthen homeland security. Some policies, which have the intended goal of protecting individuals and the larger community from harm, may produce unintended negative consequences. A question remains as to what expectation of privacy society is willing to accept as reasonable for travelers on commercial airlines. In particular, X-ray screening using backscatter technology is one technique which has been used to screen airline travelers for weapons and contraband in a number of major US airports. The legal, social, and ethical considerations of airport screening are discussed in the context of homeland security.

Keywords: Global Events; Individual Privacy; Legal Criteria; Ethical Criteria; Scanning Technology

A number of works (Agre & Rotenberg, 1998; Lyon, 2003; Mizell, 1998; Stanley & Steinhardt, 2003; Staples, 2000; Sykes, 1999; Whitaker, 1999) have chronicled a decline in the realization of individual privacy caused by intrusions from the government and other organizations. Among the technologies and policies being debated-are national identification cards using smart-technology (Etzioni, 1999; Hempel, 2001; O'Harrow, 2002; O'Harrow & Krim, 2001), video surveillance (Electronic Privacy Information Center [EPIC], 2005; Lyon, 2003; Stanley & Steinhardt, 2003), data mining frameworks (American Civil Liberties Union [ACLU], 2004; Stanley & Steinhardt, 2003), and scanning equipment (Hawn, 1999; Murphy & Wilds, 2001; Stoughton, 2002). Many of these efforts, as well as the general trend of increasing levels of security in our society, pre-date the attacks of September 11, 2001.

Commercial airline flights have been targeted by Khalid Sheikh Mohammed during 1995, on September 11, later by Richard Reid in December 2001, and more recently in the terrorist plot foiled by British investigators involving an estimated ten transatlantic flights. These events have fueled the momentum of additional policies and procedures designed to strengthen homeland security, yet some of which use technologies that may have a number of unintended negative consequences. For about 40 years, airlines have been the target of terrorist plots including hijackings and bombings (Crank & Gregor, 2005; Fagin, 2006), but recent events have made airline security a central concern of homeland security.

The 9/11 Commission was created to investigate the events leading up to the terrorist attacks, the nation's response to the attacks, as well as to produce recommendations to prevent future attacks. It must be noted that 19 of 19 hijackers on September 11 successfully passed security checkpoints although eight were flagged for additional screening by the CAPPS program (9/11 Commission, 2004). Additional screening requirements at that time called only for screening of checked bags which would then be loaded only after the passenger had boarded the plane. Among the recommendations was the creation of the Transportation Security Administration (TSA) and federal responsibility for passenger screening. Other recommendations by the 9/11 Commission called for screening of passengers for explosives, not just luggage, as well as improving screener performance (2004, p. 562).

Crank and Gregor (2005) note that reoccurring problems plagued airline security prior to the attacks on September 11; the problems concerning passenger screening include: low wages to screeners, inadequate training, and rapid turnover (p. 119). In addition to replacing private security at airports, the TSA has upgraded screening equipment at the nation's largest airports, all walk through metal detectors (WTMD) are now enhanced status (TSA, 2006), which has contributed to a staggering amount of confiscations of prohibited items (see Sweet, 2006, p. 368). Years after the attacks on September 11 and following recommendations from the 9/11 Commission, airline security is very visible but still maintains significant shortcomings (Crank & Gregor, 2005, p. 243) often with reactionary measures such as questioning passengers as to whether they packed their own luggage, prohibiting potential cutting instruments, removing shoes, and prohibitions on gels and liquids in carry-on luggage (Chertoff, 2006). Although several of the 9/11 terrorists were selected for additional screening, the response was to confirm that they had boarded the flight prior to their checked luggage being loaded on board the aircraft (9/11 Commission, 2004). The sensitivity of metal detectors could not detect knives with blades less than four inches in length while written policy did not prohibit the items from carry-on luggage or passenger possession (p. 122). Among the current issues are: the adequacy of no-fly lists, the adequacy of passenger screening, luggage/cargo screening, and the utility of the air marshal program.

While X-rays using backscatter technology have been used for some time to screen employees and visitors as they enter sensitive government facilities (Hawn, 1999), more recently, backscatter X-rays have been used to screen airline travelers in a number of major US airports (Cannon, 1999; EPIC, 2005; Murphy & Wilds, 2001; Stoughton, 2002) as well as other mass transit locations (Webster, 2005). This type of technology would be viewed as a significant upgrade of technological capabilities over traditional metal detectors. As a society, we should avoid evaluating backscatter scanning technology based on a single criterion, even if that criterion is to maximize community safety against a real or perceived threat. The effectiveness of the screening technology and procedures for implementation are a key concern. Legality also should not be the only criterion used to determine whether or not a search using backscatter technology should be allowed. Ethical and social issues associated with the use of this technology should also be considered. Ethical concerns address issues of passenger consent, awareness of the procedure, equality of application, and proportionality of the intrusion of the search compared to the desired government objective. In addition to ethical dimensions, Etzioni's (1999) communitarian perspective provides one model to evaluate the fit between the stated goal of protecting commercial airlines from terrorist attacks and individual privacy.

TECHNOLOGY

X-rays using backscatter technology use low power energy beams to produce a very detailed image of the target. The energy does not penetrate the object or person being scanned as it does with a traditional X-ray (EPIC, 2005; Stoughton, 2002) although clothes are rendered transparent. The purpose of this scanning technology is to provide an efficient and effective means to screen persons for potentially dangerous items concealed under clothing, not visible to the casual observer, without requiring a physical pat-down search. Objects on the outside of the body, yet concealed with clothes, are visible to the operator. Backscatter technology does not suffer from the same limitations as the conventional metal detector, which cannot detect non-metallic objects including bombs, drugs, or non-metallic weapons although backscatter scans cannot detect items smuggled internally (EPIC, 2005). Backscatter scans expose persons to the rays of energy whereas other similar technology uses passive imaging (Mackey, 1997) which relies on energy naturally emitted from the person as well as the composition of the object on the person.

According to Murphy and Wilds (2001, p. 334) backscatter technology is capable of

> pinpointing not only weapons, drugs, and contraband, but also the traveler's breasts, buttocks, and genitalia. In fact, the resolution is so clear that the operator can literally count the hairs on a man's chest or measure the depth of a woman's navel.

Stoughton (2002) presents graphic evidence of the results of backscatter scans by providing a detailed image of a male with concealed weapons but also 'love handles' around his abdomen. One product utilizing this technology is Rapiscan Systems' Secure 1000 Personnel Scanner; the company also produces a model capable of scanning a tractor-trailer, which seems highly suitable for homeland security needs.

LEGAL CRITERIA FOR EVALUATION

One question which emerges from the discussion of backscatter scanning technology is whether its use constitutes an unreasonable search in violation of the Fourth Amendment. It is proposed that backscatter scanning in the context of enhanced airport security does not rise to the level of a Fourth Amendment violation for two reasons. First, as a matter of policy, the scan could be made a condition of purchasing a ticket, converting it into a voluntary search to which a person knowingly and voluntarily submits to as a condition of travel on a commercial aircraft. Secondly, the Fourth Amendment does not create an absolute right to privacy, but one which is qualified to protect individuals against unreasonable searches rather than against all intrusive searches (Etzioni, 1999). The individual may be subject to an intrusive search, such as a body cavity search (*United States v. Montoya De Hernandez*, 1985), which is a lawful and constitutional search so long as the Courts rule it is reasonable considering the context in which it arises. Aronson (2001) notes that judges rather than the community will determine the reasonableness of potential intrusions by the government. Since the Courts will make this determination for backscatter X-rays using logic from previous cases, it is important to identify patterns in previous rulings.

Advances in technology have had a significant impact on law enforcement practices designed to uncover that which was previously hidden. The US Supreme Court continues to recognize the sanctity of the home while recognizing less privacy for the individual in public places and in particular engaging in regulated activities. For instance, in *Kyllo v. United States* (2001), the US Supreme Court ruled that a warrantless search of a home using a thermal imaging device was unreasonable. The Court ruled that such devices would reveal intimate details of lawful activities occurring inside the home in addition to potentially illegal activity. More importantly, the Court marked a firm and bright line for police at the entrance to a home. Fourth Amendment cases involving the home have traditionally been held to higher scrutiny than those involving more public places. The US Supreme Court has taken a more permissive view when looking at searches conducted outside the home.

The US Supreme Court has ruled that warrantless searches conducted without specific suspicion on a particular individual can be reasonable, such as consent searches (*Florida v. Bostick,* 1991), sobriety checkpoints (*Michigan Dept. of State Police v. Sitz,* 1990), border searches (*United States v. Montoya De Hernandez,* 1985), drug dog searches (*Illinois v. Caballes,* 2005; *United States v. Place,* 1983), and drug testing (*Vernonia School District 47J v. Acton,* 1995). Searches of this nature are relevant to the present discussion since the same logic could be applied to backscatter scanning at airports.

In *Florida v. Bostick* (1991), the US Supreme Court reversed a Florida court's ruling that every police encounter with a citizen while on a bus is a seizure. Bostick claimed that a seizure took place and he was not free to leave. He reasoned that he was on a bus about to depart for an interstate trip and if he left the bus he would have been stranded without his luggage away from his departure city and his destination city. The US Supreme Court ruled that Bostick was not seized, was free to terminate the encounter, and voluntarily consented to a search of his luggage. The key concern for the Court was whether the police adequately communicated the right to refuse the search to the suspect so that a reasonable person would know the encounter was voluntary. For instance, in *United States v. Guapi* (1998), a federal circuit court ruled that the police did not effectively communicate the right to refuse the search to the suspect and also created a situation where the average person would not feel free to terminate the encounter.

The police have used other techniques to counter significant threats to society. For instance, in *United States v. Place* (1983) the US Supreme Court noted that the use of a drug dog is not considered a search. In *United States v. Holloman* (1997), a drug dog alerted to the presence of drugs inside a vehicle stopped by police for a minor motor vehicle infraction. The search and seizure was considered reasonable since the driver was not detained longer than was necessary to process the initial traffic stop. The ruling in *United States v. Holloman* has been supported in the US Supreme Court case *Illinois v. Caballes* (2005). The vehicle driven by Caballes was stopped by police for traveling 71 mph on Interstate 80. While the police officer was processing the warning for speeding, another police officer responded to the stop with a drug dog subsequently detecting the presence of marijuana and producing probable cause for the search of the vehicle. The Court ruled that the search was constitutional since the search was conducted during the time necessary to process a lawful traffic stop and the dog detected a substance that the individual had no right to possess.

In *Delaware v. Prouse* (1979), the US Supreme Court ruled that roving police patrols which stop vehicles without individualized suspicion are unreasonable. A police officer stopped a vehicle during a lull in calls and, upon approaching the vehicle, smelled marijuana and saw marijuana in plain view in the vehicle. There was no probable cause or articulable suspicion for an alleged traffic violation as a basis for the stop. The officer wanted to check the driver's license and vehicle registration. The roving patrol is substantially different from the drunk driving roadblock where vehicle stops are more objective. In *Michigan Dept. of State Police v. Sitz* (1990), the US Supreme Court ruled that the use of a sobriety checkpoint was reasonable. The preliminary stop of a vehicle may last about 30 seconds. The duration and level of intrusion of the stop were viewed as reasonable by the Court given the costs of drunken drivers to society. Data may also be produced on alcohol enforcement checkpoints to determine their effectiveness while also documenting the procedures for vehicle stops.

With similar reasoning applied to the use of drug-sniffing dogs to combat the significant social problem of drugs, the US Supreme Court ruled that the government has a substantial interest in keeping the roads safe; but spot checks conducted without probable cause or articulable suspicion are not sufficiently productive to justify their use for safety. In addition, the Court also reasoned that people would be more frightened during a roving patrol stop than in a roadblock-style search. Prohibiting roving patrols was done in an effort to control what Justice White called the unconstrained exercise of discretion by police. It was stated that 'consent to regulatory restrictions is presumptively concurrent with participation in the regulated enterprise' (*Delaware v. Prouse*, 1979). While the concept of regulated enterprise originally referred to driving an automobile, it may also be applied to commercial airline passengers.

While roadblock stops lasting 30 seconds designed to detect and deter drunk drivers may be seen as only a minor intrusion, some searches may be considered very intrusive yet reasonable by the Court. In *United States v. Montoya De Hernandez* (1985) a woman was suspected of being a balloon swallower who was attempting to smuggle drugs into the USA. She was held 16 hours prior to a judicial warrant to conduct a rectal exam and an involuntary X-ray. The Court reasoned that the search initially based on reasonable suspicion was reasonable. The Court based their decision on the sanctity of international borders, the method chosen to smuggle, and De Hernandez's refusal to voluntarily submit to an X-ray. It was noted in the dissenting opinion that only about 15–20% of all body cavity searches conducted by customs revealed drugs.

As these cases indicate, the US Supreme Court tends to view searches in public, or within regulated activities such as driving or border crossings, differently from searches involving the home. The constitutional test of searches is based on reasonableness. The Court recognizes that the state may require a search which is considered intrusive in an effort to achieve a compelling state interest. The degree of intrusiveness would be weighed in light of the government's interests. Would an X-ray scan taking about 30 seconds of an airline traveler which reveals bare breasts and buttocks be considered reasonable? From the cases identified above, different approaches could be used to insure 'reasonableness.' First, backscatter scanning can be performed in a timely, efficient manner with minimal physical intrusion similar to a roadblock stop in the Sitz case. Secondly, backscatter scanning can rely on voluntary informed consent. Passengers would have the right to refuse the search and to seek alternative methods of travel. Third, TSA officials, again using the Sitz case, would need to be collected to demonstrate the effectiveness of backscatter X-ray scanning in detecting potential weapons. Fourth, the procedures used must be implemented in an objective manner with consideration to avoid discriminatory application.

ETHICAL CRITERIA FOR EVALUATION

Marx (1998) provides 29 criteria which can be used to assist in determining the ethical use of technology. Many of the criteria are relevant to the present discussion of backscatter scans. A preliminary application of the criteria to the use of backscatter scans in airports, with some modification to the actual scanning procedures, weighs in favor of using the technology. Among the key criteria identified by Marx are the absence of physical or psychological harm, awareness of the procedures, consent to the procedures, the golden rule, proportionality of the intrusion given the objectives, consequences of inaction, adequate data stewardship, and who benefits from the intervention. Using this framework, if individuals do not consent to the backscatter X-ray they would be denied access to the secure areas of the airport. Travelers have alternatives to travel by air if they choose not to consent to a search. The golden rule is particularly interesting. Are people willing to have other people scanned for weapons, explosives, or other prohibited items using a fairly revealing technology but not willing to undergo the same procedure themselves? Also, given the significance of passenger screening to homeland security interests, it is difficult to justify any exceptions to scanning all passengers, airport staff, and crews.

Several of Marx's (1998) criteria cluster around awareness and consent of the process by the individuals being affected. Marx notes that ethical concerns are raised when the procedures are applied to people without their knowledge and consent. Equality could also be an issue if profiling is used to select only a small percentage of people for scanning. Also, the potential for unequal application of the technology is of concern with regard to private, corporate, and charter flights. Individuals with the economic means could avoid the scanning process associated with commercial flights; private and charter flights pose a threat to homeland security. Also, while passengers and their luggage may be subject to X-ray scanning, cargo from known shippers aboard passenger airlines may not be adequately screened (Sweet, 2006). Marx also warns of the creation of unwanted precedents. For instance, backscatter scanning for all passengers could be seen as reasonable given the risks to society, but this same argument could be used to introduce scanning for sporting events, such as professional football, major league baseball, NASCAR events, or even college football games with large attendance. Likewise, would the nexus of technology and case law allow the application of scanning in gun-crime hotspots which is a similar issue raised by Justice Ginsburg in a dissenting opinion in *Illinois v. Caballes* (2005)? Backscatter technology is already used by 30 federal agencies in a variety of settings (EPIC, 2005).

THEORETICAL CRITERIA FOR EVALUATION

Privacy and autonomy are key values for members of US society. The majority of individuals would question laws which overtly favor the state's interest in homeland security over the individual's right to privacy and autonomy, like the social control exercised in Singapore which includes limitations on magazines, compulsory police/military service, and proscribed hair length for men (Austin, 1987). The nature of individual rights which limit governmental action is the cornerstone of the Bill of Rights. The expectations which arise from the Bill of Rights include, but obviously are not limited to, protections against unreasonable searches and seizures, protections against self-incrimination, and the right to counsel.

The communitarian perspective provides another framework for discussing and evaluating the current technology and the context of its use. Etzioni's communitarian model (1999) provides a standard to determine the correct and just balance to be struck when policies are designed to protect both the public good, in this case homeland security, and the individual's privacy. According to Etzioni (1999, p. 5), 'a good society seeks a carefully crafted balance between individual rights and social responsibility, between liberty and the common good.' From this perspective, the balance between the individual and the community is based on reasonableness of the proposed policy. To pass the test of reasonableness the proposal must consider not only the level of intrusion the individual will experience, but also the substantial public interest or common good that will result.

Etzioni's communitarian model criteria call for the well balanced, communitarian society (1) to take steps to limit privacy only if it faces a *well-documented and macroscopic threat* to the common good, not merely a hypothetical danger (p. 12, italics in original); (2) to act initially to counter a tangible and macroscopic danger by other means rather than *first resorting to measures that might restrict privacy* (p. 12, italics in original); (3) to make privacy-curbing measures that must be introduced as *minimally intrusive* as possible (p. 13, italics in original); (4) to *treat the undesirable side effects* of needed privacy diminishing measures openly rather than ignore them (p. 12, italics in original) and, when given a choice between two or more policies which equally protect the community's interest, to adopt the measure which best limits potential intrusions upon the individual. These criteria will be applied to the current uses of backscatter scans discussed below.

THE CONTEXT OF SCANNING TECHNOLOGY

Murphy and Wilds (2001, p. 339) contend that the

> utilization of X-ray search devices allows unreasonable, subjective searches of an innocent traveler when little or no evidence of criminality is present. The backscatter device effectively reduces the traveler's body to the same legal status as a piece of luggage on a conveyor belt.

Murphy and Wilds contend that backscatter scanning is an unreasonable intrusion into a person's privacy.

The Fourth Amendment states that we are protected against unreasonable searches and seizures. Therefore, reasonable searches are legally justified regardless of how intrusive the search may seem. Contemporary society faces the reality of terrorists using commercial airlines as weapons of mass destruction to cause both mass casualties as well as a severe negative impact on the economy. The reality of the threat calls for responses which effectively screen passengers and luggage on airplanes and requires intrusions into the privacy of passengers. And, according to Etzioni's communitarian model, less intrusive alternatives to widespread implementation of scanning technology at airports for passengers, luggage, and personnel risks compromising the public good.

With a real, documented macroscopic threat to both travelers and the non-flying public posed by unsafe airline travel, the communitarian perspective would focus on making these intrusions as minimally intrusive as possible by treating the undesirable side effects of the intrusion. One concern is the level of detail of the image produced by the scanning technology (EPIC, 2005). Approaches could be devised to address this issue satisfactorily for the vast majority of travelers. For instance, passive imaging technology described elsewhere (Mackey, 1997) utilized technology which did not reveal an image to the operator unless an anomaly indicating the presence of an object was detected by that scan (see also Huguenin, 1994). Without an anomaly present, no detailed image need be revealed to the operator. With knowledge and awareness of the scanning procedures, travelers can avoid carrying any item on their body which may be detected as an anomaly and cause a detailed image output. Another option, described by EPIC (2005), provides for a digital fig leaf imposed on the displayed image. While the recommended security guidelines call for a physical design of security areas which prevents the public from viewing the X-ray screen (TSA, 2006), EPIC has also questioned the long-term storage and retrieval of the images produced by the scans.

As a society, we must determine the reasonable expectation of privacy for individuals in particular contexts. In the aftermath of September 11 when terrorists hijacked four commercial airliners and used them as weapons of mass destruction, do airline travelers have a reasonable expectation of privacy? What level of privacy is society willing to recognize as reasonable for passengers who voluntarily elect to fly on commercial aircrafts? Scanning for all passengers may eliminate the fairness issues associated with profiling practices. As a society, we should be aware of Marx's warning of the creation of unintended precedents. To what extent can entertainment venues, seen as a soft target for homeland security, require either a pat-down, metal detector, or even a backscatter X-ray as a requirement for entrance? Because a person has purchased a ticket to an event, does it guarantee her or him entrance to the event?

DISCUSSION

The right to be left alone, to be an autonomous individual, and to control access to information about oneself is central to a free society. Without a doubt, technology has fueled the intrusion into individual privacy by government and profit-minded organizations and current technology permits these intrusions to be far more intrusive and coordinated, potentially without the individual's knowledge and consent, than in the past. But, as recognized by Etzioni (1999), individual privacy does not trump all other considerations such as public safety and the rights of other individuals to life, liberty, and property. Homeland security, and by implications the public good associated with other's rights, is threatened by unrestricted personal autonomy and right to privacy. Legality should not be the only criterion used to determine whether or not a search should be allowed. Ethical issues associated with the use of the technology should also be considered. Ethical concerns address issues of consent, awareness, equality, and proportionality. The communitarian perspective provides one model to evaluate the fit between the goals of the community and individual privacy.

Aviation security experienced significant changes during the late 1960s and early 1970s when Fagin (2006) notes eight airplanes were hijacked to Cuba within a month in 1969 prompting the installation of metal detector screening for passengers. Airline bombings and hijackings continued in the 1970s, according to Fagin, but were mostly international incidents. According to the 9/11 Commission, onboard explosives were viewed as the most significant threat to domestic aviation. On September 11, the existing metal detectors were designed to detect items with a metal content equivalent to a .22 caliber handgun (9/11 Commission, 2004, p. 4). Contemporary concerns have been expressed regarding the effectiveness of airport screening procedures for passengers and cargo (Sweet, 2006). Department of Homeland

Security (2006) notes there are currently 56,000 screeners deployed in all 429 commercial airports in the USA. Background qualifications and training of screening personnel have still been determined inadequate. Effective screening should be a component of improved airline security which addresses airport security, passenger identification and screening (potentially with biometric identification to screen and validate passengers as recommended by the 9/11 Commission, but certainly with the most comprehensive and coordinated no-fly list), airport proximity security, and in-flight security (Fagin, 2006, p. 157). The use of backscatter technology without substantial improvements to other airport screening efforts may be viewed as unreasonable. For instance, two terrorists on 9/11 triggered alarms at the metal detector station, but follow-up hand wand detection, as indicated by videotape records, failed to identify what triggered the alarm (9/11 Commission, 2004). In addition, steps should be taken to safeguard documents to validate someone's identity such as the USVISIT system and Secureflight. 'For terrorists, travel documents are as important as weapons. Terrorists must travel clandestinely to meet, train, plan, case targets, and gain access to attack' (9/11 Commission, 2004, p. 548). We must recognize the dangers of public safety policies which not only erode personal privacy, liberty, and autonomy, but are also ineffective in their goals of protecting the public from harm.

ACKNOWLEDGEMENT

The author would like to acknowledge Murphy and Wilds (2001) for the term X-rated X-ray.

REFERENCES

Agre, P. E., & Rotenberg, M. (Eds.). (1998). *Technology and privacy: The new landscape*. Cambridge, MA: MIT Press.

American Civil Liberties Union (ACLU). (2004). *Matrix: Myths and realities*. Retrieved March 12, 2005, from http://www.aclu.org/Privacy/Privacy. cfm?ID=14894&c=130

Aronson, B. (2001). *New technologies and the fourth amendment: The trouble with defining a 'reasonable expectation of privacy.'* Findlaw's Legal Commentary. Retrieved January 15, 2002, from http://writ.news. findlaw.com/aronson/20010309.html

Austin, W. T. (1987). Crime and custom in an orderly society: The Singapore prototype. *Criminology, 25*(2), 279–294.

Cannon, S. (1999). X-ray vision. *Latin Trade, 7*(10), 34.

Chertoff, M. (2006, August 10). Remarks by Homeland Security Secretary Michael Chertoff. Press Office, US Department of Homeland Security. Retrieved from http://www.tsa.gov/press/speeches/dhs_press_ conference_08102006.shtm

Crank, J. P., & Gregor, P. E. (2005). *Counter terrorism after 9/11: Justice, security, and ethics reconsidered.* Dayton, OH: Anderson.

Delaware v. Prouse, 440 U.S. 648 (1979). Retrieved from http://laws.findlaw.com/us/440/648.html

Department of Homeland Security. (2006). *Travel and transportation.* Retrieved from http://www.dhs.gov/dhspublic/display?theme=20&content=3096

Electronic Privacy Information Center (EPIC). (2005, June). *Spotlight on surveillance: Transportation agency's plan to x-ray travelers should be stripped of funding.* Retrieved from http://www.epic.org/privacy/surveillance/spotlight/0605/

Etzioni, A. (1999). *The limits of privacy.* New York: Basic Books, Perseus Books Group.

Fagin, J. A. (2006). *When terrorism strikes home: Defending the United States.* Boston, MA: Pearson Education.

Florida v. Bostick, 501 U.S. 429 (1991). Retrieved from http://laws.findlaw.com/us/501/429.html

Hawn, C. (1999, November 29), Yes, we have no illegals. *Forbes, 164*(13), 144.

Hempel, C. (2001, December 31). Whether for business or 'National ID,' smart cards are moving into limelight. *The Union Leader,* C2.

Huguenin, G. R. (1994). *Testimony to the Crime and Criminal Justice Subcommittee of the House Judiciary Committee.* South Deerfield, MA: Millitech Corporation.

Illinois v. Caballes, 543 U.S. __ No. 03-923 (2005). Retrieved from http://laws.findlaw.com/us/000/03-923.html

Kyllo v. United States, 533 U.S. 27 (2001). Retrieved from http://laws.findlaw.com/us/533/27.html

Lyon, D. (2003). *Surveillance after September 11.* Cambridge: Polity Press.

Mackey, D. (1997). The ethics of new surveillance. *Criminal Justice Policy Review, 8*(2/3), 295–307.

Marx, G. T. (1998) An ethics for the new surveillance. *The Information Society, 14*(3). Retrieved from http://web.mit.edu/gtmarx/www/ncolin5.html

Michigan Dept. of State Police v. Sitz, 496 U.S. 444 (1990). Retrieved from http://laws.findlaw.com/us/496/444.html

Mizell, L. R., Jr. (1998). *Invasion of privacy.* New York: The Berkley Publishing Group.

Murphy, M. C., & Wilds, M. R. (2001). X-rated x-ray invades privacy rights. *Criminal Justice Policy Review, 12*(4), 333–343.

9/11 Commission. (2004). *The 9/11 Report: The National Commission on Terrorist Attacks Upon the United States.* New York: St. Martin's Press.

O'Harrow, R., Jr. (2002, January 14). Driver's license as a national ID is pushed. *The Union Leader,* A12.

O'Harrow, R., Jr., & Krim, J. (2001, December 17). National ID card gaining support. *Washington Post Online*. Retrieved January 14, 2002, from   http://www.washingtonpost.com/wp-dyn/articles/A52300-2001Dec16.html

Stanley, J., & Steinhardt, B. (2003). *Bigger monster, weaker chains: The growth of an American surveillance society*. New York: American Civil Liberties Union.

Staples, W. G. (2000). *Everyday surveillance: Vigilance and visibility in post modern life*. New York: Rowman and Littlefield.

Stoughton, S. (2002, January 7). Err-to air combat. *The Boston Globe*, pp. C1, C4.

Sweet, K. M. (2006). *Transportation and cargo security: Threats and solutions*. Upper Saddle River, NJ: Pearson Education.

Sykes, C. J. (1999). *The end of privacy*. New York: St. Martin's Press.

Transportation Security Administration (TSA). (2006). *Recommended security guidelines for airport planning, design and construction*. Washington, DC: US Department of Justice. Retrieved from http://www.tsa.gov/assets/pdf/airport_security_design_guidelines.pdf

United States v. Guapi, 144 F.3d 1393 (1998). Retrieved from http://laws.findlaw.com/11th/976289opn.html

United States v. Holloman, No. 96-2714 (1997). Retrieved from http://laws.findlaw.com/11th 962714opa.html

United States v. Montoya De Hernandez, 473 U.S. 531 (1985). Retrieved from http://laws.findlaw.com/us/473/531.html

United States v. Place, 462 U.S. 696 (1983). Retrieved from http://laws.findlaw.com/us/462/696.html

Vernonia School District 47J v. Acton, 515 U.S. 646 (1995). Retrieved from http://laws.findlaw.com/us/515/646.html

Webster, B. (2005, July 8). Body scan machines to be used on Tube passengers. *Times Online*. Retrieved from http://technology.timesonline.co.uk/article/0_20409-1686151.00.html

Whitaker, R. (1999). *The end of privacy*. New York: The New York Press.